FIRSTHAND AMERICA

FIRSTHAND AMERICA

Brandywine Press · St. James, New York

A History of the United States

THIRD EDITION ★ VOLUME 2

VIRGINIA BERNHARD
DAVID BURNER
ELIZABETH FOX-GENOVESE
JOHN McCLYMER

Library of Congress Cataloguing in Publication Data

Main entry under title:

Firsthand America

Includes bibliographical references and index.
1. United States—History. I. Burner, David, 1937– . II. Burner, David, 1937– . American people.
vol. 1, ISBN 1-881089-17-7, 560 pp., August 1993
vol. 2, ISBN 1-881089-18-5, 608 pp., October 1993
Combined edition, ISBN 1-881089-19-3, 1056 pp., October 1993

PRINTED IN THE UNITED STATES OF AMERICA

First Printing

About the Third Edition . . .

This third edition of *Firsthand America* contains a dialogue between two historians at the conclusion of each chapter. Contributors include Joyce Appleby, Bernard Bailyn, Michael Barnhart, Michael Les Benedict, Ira Berlin, Paul Boyer, Gene M. Brack, David Burner, Hosoya Chihiro, Catherine Clinton, Peter Collier, Paul Conkin, John S. D. Eisenhower, Peter G. Filene, David Hackett Fischer, Elizabeth Fox-Genovese, Paul Fussell, Eugene Genovese, Lawrence Goodwyn, Patricia Guerrin, Oscar Handlin, Louis R. Harlan, David Horowitz, Carol P. Karlsen, Maury Klein, Thomas J. Knock, Alan M. Kraut, Walter LaFeber, Suzanne Lebsock, William Leuchtenburg, Manning Marable, Drew McCoy, Forrest McDonald, James M. McPherson, James Mooney, Gary B. Nash, Stephen Nissenbaum, Shari Osborn, Nell Irvin Painter, Edward Pessen, Thomas Reeves, Robert V. Remini, Martin Ridge, David T. Rodgers, Michael Paul Rogin, Kirkpatrick Sale, Richard H. Sewell, Martin J. Sherwin, Kenneth M. Stampp, Richard B. Stott, Stephan Thernstrom, Hans L. Trefousse, Irwin Unger, Thomas R. West, Sean Wilentz, Joan Hoff Wilson, Gordon S. Wood, and Donald Worster.

Mr. Dooley's Advice (1906)

"I know histhry isn't thrue, Hinnessy, because it ain't like what I see ivry day in Halsted Sthreet. If any wan comes along with a histhry iv Greece or Rome that'll show me th' people fightin', gettin' dhrunk, makin' love, gettin' married, owin' th' grocery man an' bein' without hard-coal, I'll believe they was a Greece or Rome, but not befure. Historyans is like doctors. They . . . tells ye what a counthry died iv. But I'd like to know what it lived iv."

About the Firsthand Materials . . .

All comprehensive United States survey textbooks, including this one, give full coverage to standard political, economic, diplomatic, and legal events. But these elements of history are largely the story of elites. This textbook also provides social history captured in the recognizable lives of ordinary people. Presidents, congressmen, and corporate executives are quoted throughout the book. So are soldiers, slaves, indentured servants, cowboys, working girls and women, and civil rights activists. *Firsthand America,* using more than 2,000 quotations, therefore gives due place both to the traditional leaders and to the myriad Americans never named in formal histories.

American Letter for Gerald Murphy

It is a strange thing—to be an American
Neither an old house it is with the air
Tasting of hung herbs and the sun returning
Year after year to the same door and the churn
Making the same sound in the cool of the kitchen
Mother to son's wife, and the place to sit
Marked in the dusk by the worn stone at the wellhead—
That—nor the eyes like each other's eyes and the skull
Shaped to the same fault and the hands' sameness.
Neither a place it is nor a blood name.
America is West and the wind blowing.
America is a great word and the snow,
A way, a white bird, the rain falling,
A shining thing in the mind and the gulls' call.
America is neither a land nor a people,
A word's shape it is, a wind's sweep—
America is alone: many together,
Many of one mouth, of one breath,
Dressed as one—and none brothers among them:
Only the taught speech and the aped tongue.
America is alone and the gulls calling.

It is a strange thing to be an American.
It is strange to live on the high world in the stare
Of the naked sun and the stars as our bones live.
Men in the old lands housed by their rivers.
They built their towns in the vales in the earth's shelter.
We first inhabit the world. We dwell
On the half earth, on the open curve of a continent.
Sea is divided from sea by the day-fall. The dawn
Rides the low east with us many hours;
First are the capes, then are the shorelands, now
The blue Appalachians faint at the day rise;
The willows shudder with light on the long Ohio:
The lakes scatter the low sun: the prairies
Slide out of dark: in the eddy of clean air
The smoke goes up from the high plains of Wyoming:
The steep Sierras arise: the struck foam
Flames at the wind's heel on the far Pacific.
Already the noon leans to the eastern cliff:
The elms darken the door and the dust-heavy lilacs. . . .

This, this is our land, this is our people,
This that is neither a land nor a race. We must reap
The wind here in the grass for our soul's harvest:
Here we must eat our salt or our bones starve.
Here we must live or live only as shadows.
This is our race, we that have none, that have had
Neither the old walls nor the voices around us,
This is our land, this is our ancient ground—
The raw earth, the mixed bloods and the strangers,
The different eyes, the wind, and the heart's change,
These we will not leave though the old call us.
This is our country-earth, our blood, our kind.
Here we will live our years till the earth blind us—

—ARCHIBALD MACLEISH

About the Points of View . . .

This country, as the poem by Archibald MacLeish reprinted opposite this page of your textbook has it, was born on a naked continent, and it has neither a single race nor a single family nor a single ancient tradition to make it a unity. The ancestors of some of us were here before Columbus, and their descendants have been driven from home after home by European immigrants or their offspring. Other Americans came in the wretched holds of slave ships. Countless others, from Europe, had a somewhat better and yet a miserable journey, packed in the poorer recesses of ships that also provided luxurious quarters for wealthy travelers. Asians among us have Chinese ancestors who worked on the railroads that bound the country in the nineteenth century, or Japanese who labored on California farms amidst vicious discrimination against them. More recently we have added to our numbers Southeast Asians, refugees from a war that we did not begin but enormously escalated, and along with them Koreans whose shops are becoming a visible feature of our cities. And we are also the migrants from south of our borders and from the Caribbean, children of various racial and national strains that have mixed over the centuries since Columbus. What we have to make us a nation besides the physical fact of dwelling here is an idea of what it means to be an American. And that in itself is a ceaseless question for debate.

This country was born of ideas, and innumerable Americans beginning with the Pilgrim and Puritan migrants to New England have thought that the very point of being here was to live one or another of them. A good way of summarizing them is to see in American history a continuing quarrel or partnership between the claims of individualism and the claims of community.

The American economy, for example, has championed the virtues of the self-contained individual: industry, foresight, ambition. It has at the same time been an immensely cooperative venture, stretching across the continent a tight web of roads, factories, electronic communication, and more recently computer networks. It is in contributing skills and effort to this web that personal industry and ambition have found much of their expression. Americans have craved private property. Yet twentieth-century American political conflicts have been over how to extend, limit, tax, or reconstruct institutions of private property for the general good. As popular phenomena, too, these polarities in American culture have varied in specific content. A labor organization is a community of sorts, but so is a lynch mob. A union-breaking financial buccaneer is an individualist of one kind; another sort is a southern small-town newspaper editor, denouncing the bigotry of his subscribers.

As opponents or as partners, individualism and community have in differing ways furnished much of our national political questioning. As an illustration of the breadth of the argument, this text provides a running debate among several dozen prominent American historians. The ability to read controversial argument and gain from the reading is at the heart of a college education. Hence the points of view in *Firsthand America*.

No number of points of view, of course, could cover all the issues over which American historians have quarreled. This is particularly true today, as the tools of scholarly interpretation become increasingly multilayered, while popular argument over the future of the nation grows both angrier and more confused than it has been for some time. It is the hope of the contributors to *Firsthand America* that readers will enjoy following the arguments of scholars as they struggle to give some clarifying order to the endlessly diverse and restless facts of history.

About the Authors . . .

VIRGINIA BERNHARD has published a historical novel, *A Durable Fire,* set in seventeenth-century Virginia and Bermuda, as well as a biography of a Texas governor's daughter. Her scholarly articles have appeared in *New England Quarterly, Virginia Magazine of History and Biography,* and *Journal of Southern History.* She has coedited the forthcoming University of Missouri Press *Southern Women: Histories and Identities* and teaches at the University of St. Thomas in Houston. Professor Bernhard has served on the Advanced Placement test development committee for United States history.

DAVID BURNER has published several books on twentieth-century American politics, most recently *John F. Kennedy and a New Generation* (1988) and, with Thomas West, *Column Right: Conservative Journalists in the Service of Nationalism* (1989). His *Making Peace with the '60s* will be published by Harvard University Press, and he is writing a history of West Point for Knopf. Professor Burner teaches at the State University of New York at Stony Brook.

ELIZABETH FOX-GENOVESE'S highly-praised recent book, *Within the Plantation Household: Black and White Women of the Old South,* was published by the University of North Carolina Press in 1988. Her *Feminism Without Illusions* was published by the same press in 1991. She is Eleanore Raoul Professor of Humanistic Studies at Emory University. Professor Fox-Genovese is currently finishing *Ghosts and Memories: Fictions of Black and White Southern Women.*

JOHN McCLYMER has written *War and Welfare: Social Engineering in America* and has coedited *Images of Women in American Popular Culture* (1985). Professor McClymer, who teaches at Assumption College, has written extensively about pedagogy in *The History Teacher, Teaching History,* and the American Historical Association's newsletter *Perspectives.*

Acknowledgments

We are eager to receive comments on the third edition of this textbook from both teachers and students. We are particularly interested in knowing how you respond to the new Points of View. We welcome corrections, suggestions for fresh firsthand materials, news of omissions, and general criticisms, which may be addressed to any of the authors. Or call our toll-free number 1-800-345-1776.

For various kinds of help and encouragement thanks are gratefully extended to Sandra Burner, Robert Marcus, Mark Buckley, Bonnie Schrack, Alan January, Jim Moore, Roseanne Krzanowski, Robert Burner, Thomas Lavrakas, Jerry Sternstein, James Mooney, Winfrey Purington, Hugh Cleland, Pete Seeger, Francine Medeiros, Ed Krautkremer, Robert London, Terry Cooney, Gus Seligmann, Jr., Everett Kindig, James Olson, Robert McColley, Barbara Posadas, Eric Burner, Michael Barnhart, Wilbur Miller, and David Ellis.

Special thanks for the preparation of the manuscript are due to the tireless perfectionists Rosemary Henault and Renzo Melaragno of Baldwin Printing in Waterbury, Connecticut, and to the firm's helmsman Charles Peach, who is one.

John McClymer wrote the first appendix, "Succeeding in History Courses," as well as most of the Points To Think About that follow each chapter.

The Authors

Dedication

For Thomas R. West

Contents

25 Diplomacy and War 1933–1945 / 779

26 Truman / 819

27 New Frontiers / 851

28 American Society and the Vietnam War / 881

29 New Boundaries / 917

Appendixes / I

Index / XXXIV

Chronology

c. 10,000 B.C. Ice Age ends; glaciation retreats from North America; native Americans begin to spread throughout Western Hemisphere.

c. 5000 B.C. First domesticated plants grown in North America.

A.D. 300-900 Mayan civilization flourishes in present-day Mexico and Guatemala.

c. 600-1600 Rise of the great West African empires.

c. 1000 Vikings led by Leif Ericson reach Labrador and Newfoundland in present-day Canada.

1095 European Christians embark on the Crusades to wrest the Holy Lands from the Muslims.

c. 1100 Inca civilization emerges in modern-day Peru.

1271 Marco Polo begins a twenty-year journey to China.

1347-1352 Plague kills about one-third of European population.

1492-1504 Columbus's four voyages to New World.

1494 Treaty of Tordesillas divides the New World between Portugal and Spain.

1496 Columbus introduces cattle, sugarcane, and wheat to the West Indies.

1497-98 John Cabot explores Newfoundland, Labrador, and Nova Scotia, and establishes English claim to North America.

1501 Spain authorizes the first shipment of African slaves to the Caribbean.

1508-9 Sebastian Cabot explores Hudson Bay.

1509-47 Henry VIII.

1513 Balboa discovers Pacific Ocean after crossing Isthmus of Panama.

1513 Ponce de León discovers mainland of Florida.

1517 Martin Luther's Ninety-Five Theses generally defined as the beginning of the Protestant Reformation.

1519-21 Hernando Cortés and some six hundred Spanish conquistadores begin the conquest of the Aztec empire in present-day Mexico. Soon about ninety percent of the native population will die of measles, chicken pox, smallpox and whooping cough from which they have no immunity.

1523 Verrazano explores coast of North America, establishing French claim.

1528-36 Cabeza de Vaca explores northern Gulf of Mexico, west to Gulf of California.

1532-35 Pizarro conquers Peru.

1534 Cartier's explorations establish French claim to St. Lawrence basin.

1535-39 Spanish conquest of Ecuador, Chile, northern Argentina, and Bolivia.

1539-41 De Soto explores southeastern United States and discovers the Mississippi.

1540-42 Coronado seeks legendary cities of wealth in North American Southwest.

1558-1603 Elizabeth I.

1562-67 Hawkins trades and plunders in Spanish America.

1574 Gilbert leads expedition to Hudson Bay.

1576 About 40,000 slaves brought to Latin America.

1577-80 Drake circumnavigates globe.

1585-87 Raleigh's Roanoke Colony fails.

1603-25 James I.

1603-35 Samuel de Champlain establishes French colonies in Canada.

1607 Virginia Company establishes settlement at Jamestown.

1610 Spanish found Santa Fe, New Mexico.

1616 Chicken pox wipes out most New England Indians.

1619 First Africans arrive in Virginia; First representative assembly meets.

1620 Mayflower Compact signed; Pilgrims establish Plymouth Colony.

1621 Dutch West India Company chartered.

1624 Virginia Company charter annulled; English crown takes control of Virginia; First settlements in New Netherlands by Dutch.

1625-49 Charles I.

1629 Massachusetts Bay founded.

1630 Puritan emigration from England begins.

1632 Cecilius Calvert, Lord Baltimore, receives charter for Maryland colony.

1634 First settlements in Maryland.

1635 Roger Williams banished from Bay Colony.

1636 Harvard College founded; First permanent English settlements in Connecticut and Rhode Island.

1638 Anne Hutchinson convicted of heresy

in Massachusetts; flees to Rhode Island.

1642-48 Civil war in England.

1643 Confederation of New England.

1644 Rhode Island receives patent.

1647 Law requiring towns to maintain schools passed in Massachusetts Bay Colony.

1649 Charles I beheaded; Maryland Toleration Act.

1660 Restoration of Stuart monarchy (Charles II, 1660-85); Navigation Act passed by Parliament (The Enumeration Act).

1663 New navigation act (Staple Act) passed, channeling colonies' importation of European goods through England; Carolina charter granted to eight proprietors; Rhode Island granted charter.

1664 English take over New Netherlands; Grant of New Jersey to two proprietors.

1670 Settlement of Charleston.

1675-76 King Philip's War in New England.

1676 Bacon's Rebellion.

1677 Culpeper's Rebellion in Carolina.

1680 New Hampshire given royal charter.

1681 Pennsylvania charter granted to William Penn; First settlements in 1682.

1686 Dominion of New England.

1688 Glorious Revolution in England drives out James II (1685-88) in favor of William and Mary.

1689-91 Leisler's Rebellion, New York.

1692 Witchcraft hysteria in Salem, Massachusetts; nineteen "witches" hanged, one pressed to death.

1696 English government establishes Board of Trade and Plantations; passage of comprehensive navigation act, extending admiralty courts to America.

1699 Woolen Act.

1732 Georgia established to furnish buffer against Spanish and as philanthropic effort to relocate England's paupers; Hat Act.

1733 Molasses Act restricts colonial importation of sugar goods from French West Indies.

1734-35 Jonathan Edwards's evangelical revival in Northampton, Massachusetts, and Connecticut River valley.

1735 New York jury acquits John Peter Zenger of charge of seditious libel on ground that printing truth can be no libel.

1739-40 George Whitefield tours America and brings major phase of Great Awakening.

1750 Iron Act, limiting production of finished iron goods in colonies, passed by Parliament.

1751 Currency Act, restricting issuance of paper money in New England colonies, passed by Parliament; Publication of Franklin's *Experiments and Observations on Electricity*.

1754 Albany Congress and Plan of Union.

1754-63 French and Indian War (colonial phase of Europe's Seven Years' War, 1756-63).

1759 Quebec falls to British army.

1760-1820 George III.

1763 Treaty of Paris ends Seven Years' War between Great Britain, and France and Spain; Pontiac's rebellion, uprising of Indians in Ohio Valley; Proclamation line drawn along Appalachians by British forbids settlement in West; Paxton uprising by Scotch-Irish settlers in western Pennsylvania.

1764 Sugar Act; Currency Act prohibits issues of legal-tender currency in the colonies.

1765 Stamp Act; Stamp Act Congress meets in New York; Quartering Act.

1766 Stamp Act repealed by Parliament, which adopts Declaratory Act asserting its authority to bind the colonies "in all cases whatsoever."

1767 Townshend Duties passed; American Board of Customs established; John Dickinson's *Letters from a Farmer in Pennsylvania*.

1768 British troops sent to Boston.

1770 Lord North's ministry; Townshend duties repealed, except for duty on tea; Boston Massacre.

1772 British schooner *Gaspée* burned in Rhode Island; Boston Committee of Correspondence formed.

1773 Tea Act imposed; Boston Tea Party.

1774 Coercive or Intolerable Acts; Continental Congress meets in Philadelphia; Galloway's Plan of Union.

1775 Battle of Lexington and Concord; Fort Ticonderoga taken by American forces; Second Continental Congress meets in Philadelphia; George Washington appointed commander in chief of Continental army; Battle of Bunker

Hill; Congress adopts its "Declaration of the Causes and Necessities of Taking Up Arms."

1776 Thomas Paine's *Common Sense;* Declaration of Independence; British troops evacuate Boston; Battle of Long Island, New York; British take New York City; Battle of Trenton.

1777 Battle of Princeton; Battle of Monmouth; Battle of Brandywine, Pennsylvania; British occupy Philadelphia; Battle of Germantown; Burgoyne surrenders at Saratoga; Articles of Confederation adopted by Continental Congress, but not ratified by all states until 1781; Washington retires to Valley Forge for winter.

1778 United States concludes military alliance and commercial treaty with France; British evacuate Philadelphia; Seize Savannah, Georgia.

1779 Spain enters the war against Britain; George Rogers Clark captures Vincennes and ends British rule in Northwest.

1780 Americans surrender 5500 men and the city of Charleston, South Carolina; Battle of Camden, South Carolina; Battle of King's Mountain, South Carolina.

1781 Battle of Cowpens, South Carolina; British under Tarleton defeated by Morgan; Battle of Guilford Courthouse, North Carolina; Cornwallis withdraws to coast; Cornwallis surrenders to Washington at Yorktown, Virginia.

1782 Fall of Lord North's ministry.

1783 Treaty of Paris with Britain signed.

1785 Land Ordinance for Northwest Territory adopted by Congress.

1786 Jay-Gardoqui Treaty rejected by Congress; Virginia Statute for Religious Freedom; Shays's Rebellion in western Massachusetts; Annapolis Convention adopts plan to meet in Philadelphia to revise Articles of Confederation.

1787 Federal Constitutional Convention meets in Philadelphia; Northwest Ordinance enacted by Congress. *The Federalist Papers* by Madison, Hamilton, and Jay.

1788 Ratification of United States Constitution by all states except Rhode Island and North Carolina.

1789 First session of Congress meets; Washington inaugurated as first President; Outbreak of French Revolution.

1790 Hamilton's Report on Public Credit; Father John Carroll made first Roman Catholic bishop of United States.

1791 Bank of the United States established; First ten amendments to Constitution (Bill of Rights) adopted.

1792 Washington reelected.

1793 Citizen Genet Affair; Samuel Slater erects first cotton mill at Pawtucket, Rhode Island; Eli Whitney applies for patent on cotton gin.

1794 Whiskey Rebellion in western Pennsylvania; Battle of Fallen Timbers, Ohio; General Anthony Wayne defeats Indians.

1795 Jay's Treaty with Britain; Pinckney's Treaty with Spain.

1796 Washington's Farewell Address, warning against foreign entanglements and domestic factions; John Adams elected President.

1798 XYZ Affair reported by Adams to Congress; Quasi-war with France on high seas; Alien and Sedition Acts enacted by Federalists in Congress; Virginia and Kentucky resolutions.

1800 Washington, D.C., becomes capital; Thomas Jefferson elected President.

1801 War with Barbary states; John Marshall becomes chief justice.

1803 *Marbury* v. *Madison,* Supreme Court upholds right of judicial review; Louisiana Purchase; Lewis and Clark expedition begun.

1804 Hamilton killed by Vice-President Aaron Burr in duel; Jefferson reelected.

1807 Embargo Act; Robert Fulton's steamboat travels on Hudson River from Albany to New York in 30 hours.

1808 Congress prohibits Americans from participating in African slave trade; James Madison elected President.

1809 Embargo repealed; Nonintercourse Act passed, prohibiting trade with Britain and France.

1810 Macon's Bill No. 2 passed, restoring trade with Britain and France, but providing for trade restrictions to be reimposed on one of the powers if other should abandon its seizure of American ships.

1811 Madison, believing Napoleon has removed restrictions on American commerce, prohibits trade with Britain;

Battle of Tippecanoe, Indiana, in which William Henry Harrison defeats Tecumseh and prevents formation of Indian confederacy.

1812 Congress declares war against Britain; Americans surrender Detroit to British; Madison reelected.

1813 Battle of Lake Erie, Captain Oliver Perry defeats British naval forces; Battle of the Thames; General Harrison defeats British and their Indian allies.

1814 Battle of Horseshoe Bend, Alabama; General Andrew Jackson defeats Creek Indians fighting for British; British burn Washington, D.C.; Commander Thomas Macdonough defeats British fleet on Lake Champlain; invading British turned back at Plattsburgh, New York; Hartford Convention of Federalist delegates from New England; Treaty of Ghent signed between United States and Great Britain.

1815 Battle of New Orleans, Jackson defeats British; *North American Review* founded in Boston.

1816 Second Bank of the United States chartered by Congress; Protective tariff passed; James Monroe elected President.

1818 General Jackson invades Florida to end Seminole War; Rush-Bagot Convention between Britain and United States establishes fishing rights and Canadian boundary.

1819 Depression begins; Adams-Onis Treaty; Spain cedes Florida; *Dartmouth College* Case; *McCulloch* v. *Maryland.*

1820 Missouri Compromise; Reelection of James Monroe without opposition, "Era of Good Feelings."

1822 Denmark Vesey's Conspiracy.

1823 President issues Monroe Doctrine.

1824 John Quincy Adams elected President by House of Representatives after failure of any candidate to win electoral majority.

1828 John C. Calhoun's anonymous *South Carolina Exposition and Protest;* Congress passes "Tariff of Abominations"; Election of Andrew Jackson as President brings victory to new Democratic Party.

1829 Mexico abolishes slavery.

1830 Jackson vetoes Maysville Road Bill; Anti-Masonic Party holds first national party convention.

1831 Nat Turner's slave insurrection in Virginia.

1832 Beginning of Jackson's "war" against Second Bank of the United States (BUS); Special convention in South Carolina nullifies new protective tariff; Jackson relected President.

1833 Congress provides for a gradual lowering of tariffs, but passes Force Bill authorizing Jackson to enforce federal law in South Carolina.

1836 Jackson's "specie circular"; Martin Van Buren elected President.

1838 Aroostook War.

1840 Congress passes Van Buren's Independent Treasury Act; William H. Harrison elected President; Whigs in power; World anti-slavery convention.

1840 American Female Moral Reform Society organized as first national female reform association.

1841 John Tyler becomes President upon Harrison's death.

1842 Webster-Ashburton Treaty settles disputed U.S.-Canada boundary.

1843 First overland caravans to Oregon.

1844 Senate rejects Calhoun's Texas annexation treaty; James K. Polk elected President; Lowell Female Reform Association organized.

1845 Texas enters Union as slave state; John Slidell's unsuccessful mission to Mexico to negotiate purchase of New Mexico and California; Margaret Fuller publishes *Woman in the Nineteenth Century.*

1846 Beginning of Mexican War; General Zachary Taylor invades Mexico from the North; Treaty with Britain divides Oregon Territory along 49th parallel.

1847 General Winfield Scott captures Vera Cruz and Mexico City.

1848 Gold discovered in California; Van Buren, running for President on Free-Soil ticket, receives 10 percent of popular vote; Zachary Taylor elected President; Treaty of Guadalupe Hidalgo ends Mexican War, establishes Rio Grande as border; First Women's Rights Convention at Seneca Falls, New York; Elizabeth Cady

Stanton drafts "Declaration of Sentiments."

1849 California gold rush.

1850 In Congress, sectional debate culminates in Compromise of 1850; Fugitive Slave Law requires federal agents to recover escaped slaves from sanctuaries in the North; Taylor's death makes Millard Fillmore President.

1851 Herman Melville's *Moby Dick.*

1852 Franklin Pierce elected President.

1853 Upsurge of political nativism, the Know-Nothing Party.

1854 Spectacular Know-Nothing election victories; Collapse of Whigs; New Republican Party; Commodore Perry opens Japan to American trade; Kansas-Nebraska Act rekindles sectional controversy over slavery; "Bleeding Kansas."

1856 John Brown's raid at Pottawatomie Creek; James Buchanan elected President.

1857 *Dred Scott* v. *Sanford;* In Kansas, proslavery Lecompton Constitution ratified as free-state men refuse to vote.

1858 Lincoln-Douglas debates.

1859 John Brown's raid on Harpers Ferry.

1860 Democratic Party, deadlocked at Charleston convention, divides along sectional lines at Baltimore; Abraham Lincoln elected President; South Carolina secedes from the Union.

1861 Secession of remaining states of deep South (Texas, Louisiana, Mississippi, Alabama, Georgia, and Florida); Jefferson Davis begins serving as President of the Confederate States of America; Firing on Fort Sumter precipitates war; Secession of Virginia, North Carolina, Tennessee, and Arkansas; Union army routed at first Battle of Bull Run (Manassas); McClellan heads Union Forces; *Trent* affair; Vassar College founded.

1862 Both Union and Confederacy adopt paper money; Union general, U.S. Grant, captures Fort Henry and Fort Donelson; Battle of the ironclads: *Virginia (Merrimack)* vs. *Monitor;* McClellan's Peninsula campaign brings Union army to outskirts of Richmond, the Confederate capital; Robert E. Lee becomes commander of Army of northern Virginia; Confederate victory at second battle of Bull Run; Stalemate between Lee and McClellan at Antietam; Confederate invasion of Kentucky; Lincoln issues preliminary Emancipation Proclamation; Confederate victory at Fredericksburg.

1863 Lincoln issues final Emancipation Proclamation; Confederates defeat Union army under Hooker at Chancellorsville; Lee's invasion of North checked by Union army under Meade at Gettysburg; Grant captures Vicksburg; Draft riots in the North; Confederate army under Bragg defeats Union forces at Chickamauga; Union victory at Chattanooga (Lookout Mountain and Missionary Ridge); Lincoln offers lenient reconstruction program.

1864 Grant named Union general in chief; Grant's direct advance on Richmond checked at the Wilderness, Spotsylvania, and Cold Harbor; Lincoln reelected President; Sherman marches from Atlanta to the sea.

1865 Sherman pushes northward through South Carolina and North Carolina; Lee gives up Petersburg and Richmond; Lee surrenders at Appomattox; Lincoln assassinated; Andrew Johnson becomes President; Johnson moves for speedy, lenient restoration of southern states to Union; Thirteenth Amendment ratified.

1866 Johnson breaks with Republican majority in Congress by vetoing Freedman's Bureau bill and Civil Rights bill (passed over his veto); Congress approves Fourteenth Amendment; Ku Klux Klan formed.

1867 Congress passes Military Reconstruction Act over Johnson's veto; Congress passes Tenure of Office Act and Command of Army Act to reduce Johnson's power.

1868 Former Confederate states hold constitutional conventions, for which former slaves are allowed to vote, and adopt new constitutions guaranteeing universal suffrage; President Johnson impeached; escapes conviction by one vote; Republican Ulysses S. Grant elected President.

1869 Congress passes Fifteenth Amendment; National Women Suffrage Association founded by Elizabeth Cady Stanton and Susan B. Anthony; American Woman Suffrage Association founded by Lucy Stone and Henry Blackwell.

1870 First Ku Klux Klan (or Enforcement) Act gives Grant power to move against white terrorists in South.

1874 Women's Christian Temperance Union organized by Annie Wittenmeyer.

1876 Republicans nominate Rutherford B. Hayes for President; Democrats nominate Samuel J. Tilden. Tilden secures majority of popular vote but electoral vote is in doubt because of disputed returns from three southern states; General Custer's defeat at Little Bighorn; Alexander Graham Bell transmits first telephone message; End of Reconstruction; Declaration of Women's Rights read at Centennial Exposition, Philadelphia.

1877 After political and economic bargaining, Congress creates an electoral commission, which rules that all disputed ballots belong to Hayes, who is inaugurated; *Munn* v. *Illinois*.

1878 Bland-Allison Act; Greenback Labor Movement; "Anthony Amendment" first introduced in Congress.

1879 Frances Willard gains presidency of Women's Christian Temperance Union.

1880 Garfield elected President.

1881 Helen Hunt Jackson, *A Century of Dishonor;* Garfield assassinated; Arthur becomes President.

1882 Pendleton Civil Service Act.

1884 Cleveland elected President.

1885 Josiah Strong, *Our Country*.

1886 AFL Organized; Haymarket Massacre.

1887 Interstate Commerce Act; Dawes Severalty Act; Edward Bellamy, *Looking Backward, 2000-1887*.

1888 Harrison elected President.

1890 Sherman Antitrust Act; Sherman Silver Purchase Act; "Battle" of Wounded Knee; McKinley Tariff; Alfred Thayer Mahan, *The Influence of Sea Power Upon History;* National Woman Suffrage Association and American Woman Suffrage Association merge to form National American Woman Suffrage Association.

1892 Cleveland elected to Presidency again; Homestead Strike; General Federation of Women's Clubs established.

1893-97 Depression.

1894 "Coxey's Army"; Pullman Strike; *Coin's Financial School.*

1895 Venezuelan Boundary Dispute; *United States* v. *E. C. Knight Company*.

1896 McKinley elected President; *Plessy* v. *Ferguson;* National Association of Colored Women founded.

1898 Spanish-American War; Hawaiian Islands annexed.

1899 Thorstein Veblen, *The Theory of the Leisure Class;* National Consumer's League founded.

1899-1900 Open Door Notes.

1900 Gold Standard Act; McKinley reelected.

1901 United States Steel Corporation formed; Platt Amendment; Assassination of McKinley; Theodore Roosevelt becomes President; Hay-Pauncefote Treaty.

1902 Newlands Act.

1903 Departments of Commerce and Labor established; Elkins Anti-rebate Act; Hay-Bunau-Varilla Treaty; Women's Trade Union League founded.

1904 Roosevelt Corollary to Monroe Doctrine; Roosevelt elected President; *Northern Securities Company* v. *United States*.

1905 Portsmouth Peace Conference; *Lochner* v. *New York*.

1906 Hepburn Act; Pure Food and Drug Act; Meat Inspection Act; Algeciras Conference.

1907 Gentlemen's Agreement with Japan.

1908 White House Conservation Conference; *Muller* v. *Oregon;* Taft elected President.

1909 Payne-Aldrich Tariff.

1910 Mann-Elkins Act; Ballinger-Pinchot Controversy.

1911 Triangle Shirtwaist Company Fire.

1912 Socialists nominate Eugene Debs for President; Progressives nominate Theodore Roosevelt on Bull-Moose Ticket; Wilson elected President.

1913 Sixteenth Amendment, the Income Tax; Seventeenth Amendment, Popular Election of United States Senators; Underwood Tariff; Federal

Reserve Act; Charles Beard, *An Economic Interpretation of the Constitution of the United States;* Congressional Union founded by Alice Paul and Lucy Burns.

1914 Federal Trade Commission Act; Clayton Antitrust Act; Margaret Sanger writes *Family Limitation.*

1915 Sinking of the *Lusitania;* National Birth Control League founded by Mary Ware Dennett to include wide middle-class membership.

1916 Adamson Act; Federal Farm Loan Act; Jones Act; Wilson reelected President; Sinking of *Sussex;* National Woman's Party founded as outgrowth of Congressional union and split-off from NAWSA.

1917 United States enters World War I on April 6; Espionage Act; Lever Food and Fuel Control Act; Russian Revolution.

1918 Wilson's Fourteen Points; Sedition Act; War Finance Corporation; Republicans gain control of Congress; Armistice Day, November 11.

1919 League of Women Voters founded.

1919-20 Red Scare.

1920 Palmer Raids, January 2; Harding elected President; Nineteenth Amendment: Women acquire the right to vote; Women's Bureau of the Department of Labor founded; Transportation Act; Sinclair Lewis, *Main Street.*

1921-22 Washington Armament Conference.

1923 President Harding dies, August 2; Calvin Coolidge becomes President; Equal Rights Amendment first introduced by National Women's Party.

1924 Immigration Restriction Act; Dawes Plan; Coolidge elected President.

1925 F. Scott Fitzgerald, *The Great Gatsby;* Scopes Trial.

1927 Charles Lindbergh flies solo across the Atlantic; Sacco and Vanzetti executed.

1928 Hoover elected President.

1929 Black Thursday, October 24 (stock market crash); Young Plan; Ernest Hemingway, *A Farewell to Arms;* Agricultural Marketing Act.

1930 London Naval Conference; Hawley-Smoot Tariff.

1931 Hoover Debt Moratorium; Japanese invasion of Manchuria.

1932 Stimson Doctrine, Reconstruction Finance Corporation; Glass-Steagall Act; Bonus Army; Roosevelt elected President.

1933 "Hundred Days" session of Congress; Agricultural Adjustment Act; Emergency Banking Act; Tennessee Valley Authority; Civilian Conservation Corps; National Industrial Recovery Act; United States Recognizes Soviet Union; Twenty-first Amendment ratified, repealing prohibition.

1934 Gold Reserve Act; Securities and Exchange Act; Platt Amendment abrogated.

1935 National Labor Relations Act; Social Security Act; Works Progress Administration.

1936 Roosevelt reelected; *Butler* v. *United States.*

1937 Administrative Reorganization Act; Congress of Industrial Organizations (CIO).

1938 Munich Agreement.

1939 War breaks out in Europe, September 1.

1940 United States preparedness and defense measures; Battle of Britain; Roosevelt reelected.

1941 Battle of the Atlantic; Lend-Lease Act; Atlantic Charter; Japanese attack Pearl Harbor, December 7.

1942 Battle of Coral Sea; Allied campaign in North Africa.

1943 Casablanca Conference; Allies invade Italy; Teheran Conference.

1944 Invasion of Europe; landing at Normandy, June 6; Roosevelt reelected; Battle of the Bulge.

1945 Yalta Conference; Germany surrenders; Atomic bomb dropped on Hiroshima, August 6; Japan surrenders; United Nations formed; Roosevelt dies; Truman becomes President; Potsdam Conference.

1947 Marshall Plan proposed; Taft-Hartley Act; Truman Doctrine.

1948 Truman elected President; Berlin Blockade; Creation of State of Israel.

1949 North Atlantic Treaty Organization.

1950 Korean War; McCarran Act; Rise of Senator Joseph McCarthy as popular anti-Communist.

1951 General Douglas MacArthur fired by Truman.

1952 Eisenhower elected President.

1953 Stalin dies; Korean ceasefire.

1954 Southeast Asia Treaty Organization; Geneva Conference on Indochina; Senate censure of Joseph F. McCarthy; *Brown* v. *Board of Education of Topeka;* Communist Control Act; Atomic Energy Act.

1955 Geneva Summit Meeting.

1956 Suez Crisis; Eisenhower reelected; Hungarian Revolt.

1957 Eisenhower Doctrine; Sputnik; Eisenhower sends paratroopers to Little Rock.

1958 National Defense Education Act.

1959 Eisenhower and Khrushchev meet at Camp David.

1960 Kennedy elected President.

1961 Bay of Pigs; Berlin Wall; Peace Corps.

1962 Cuban Missile Crisis; President Kennedy appoints Commission on the Status of Women.

1963 Test Ban Treaty; Kennedy is assassinated, November 22; Lyndon B. Johnson becomes President; Betty Friedan publishes *The Feminine Mystique.*

1964 Gulf of Tonkin Resolution passes Senate with two votes against it; Johnson elected President; Civil Rights Act.

1965 Voting Rights Act; Medicare; Elementary and Secondary Education Act.

1966 National Organization for Women (NOW) formed.

1968 Tet Offensive in Vietnam, January-February; Martin Luther King is assassinated, April 4; Nixon elected President.

1969 Moon landing, Apollo 11.

1970 American invasion of Cambodia.

1971 Kissinger's secret trip to Peking.

1972 Nixon reelected; Congress passes the Equal Rights Amendment.

1974 Nixon resigns Presidency; Ford becomes President.

1976 Carter elected President.

1977 Panama Canal Treaties.

1978 Camp David Agreements.

1979 Three Mile Island Nuclear Accident.

1980 Reagan elected President.

1980-81 Iranian hostage crisis.

1982 Equal Rights Amendment fails to gain ratification.

1983 Soviets shoot down Korean Airlines jet over Russian airspace; 241 United States Marines killed in airport compound, Beirut, Lebanon; United States invades Grenada.

1984 Ronald Reagan reelected President.

1986 Tax Reform Act

1988 George Bush elected President.

1990 Air Quality Act.

1991-92 Crisis in the Gulf.

1992 Los Angeles riots; William Clinton elected President.

Points of View

Firsthand America

Louisiana was one of five southern states to have a majority of black voters after the Civil War. A total of 133 black legislators served in the state from 1868 to 1896. *(Courtesy, Louisiana State Museum)*

CHAPTER 15

"Been in the Storm So Long": Emancipation and Reconstruction

THE NEW ORLEANS RACE RIOT OF 1866

Resentment had been building in New Orleans during 1866, the first year after the victory of the Union and four since wartime federal occupation of the city. Sympathizers with the triumphant cause of Union were to hold a political convention on July 30. Blacks would mix with whites at Mechanic's Hall to demand humiliating measures against the proud former Confederacy, now fallen but allowed under President Andrew Johnson's lenient policy to organize white supremacist state governments like that of Louisiana. Three weeks before the convention, an ex-rebel advised his Unionist friend not to attend the gathering, indicating that no one there would be left alive. On the morning of Monday the 30th, business in New Orleans gunshops was brisk.

At noon a parade of blacks marched up Burgundy Street in support of the convention. Shots were fired and fights broke out, but the parade continued until it stopped in front of Mechanic's Hall. There whites fired shots into the crowd of blacks. Some were armed and returned fire. Outnumbered, the marching crowd broke and scattered, many entering the convention building, where delegates and visitors, black and white, sat waiting for others to arrive. The fire alarm bell rang and police descended on the hall. Pistols fired indiscriminately through the windows. Abetted by the mob, police broke open the doors, rushed to the top of the steps leading into the convention room, and fired their weapons into the crowded delegates. The massacre spread over many blocks. Whites assaulted blacks openly on the streets. The riot continued until 3:00 p.m., when federal troops arrived. By the end of the disturbance, an estimated thirty-four black and three white Unionists were dead and 119 blacks and seventeen whites wounded.

The year of the riot was also that of the founding of the first Ku Klux Klan. The New Orleans massacre was preceded by the Memphis riot in May 1866, when forty-six blacks, including three women and two children, were killed. Racism permeated the South. But was the New Orleans riot attributable purely to racial hatred? The North was also steeped in racism. What distinguished the violence in New Orleans was its connection to an ongoing struggle, in Louisiana, in much of the rest of the defeated Confederacy, and in the national government, over what kind of power and society were to prevail in the South. Was the South to pass back into the hands of the former slave-owning aristocracy and its friends among the plain folk; or would southern blacks win racial equality? Even the white South was divided. There were white Unionists, who during the war had stayed loyal to the old United States. And they too were split: some were conservatives capable of joining with the Democrats; others were committed to political equality for the black population, or at least opportunistically allied with the Radicals. In New Orleans, the struggle between Radicals and defenders of the old order was very much a struggle for control of the police.

In 1868 the state, now submissive to a federal Radical plan insuring that ex-secessionists would not dominate politics, elected a Radical governor and was readmitted to the Union. The Radical state government thereupon put the New Orleans police under a state board of commissioners, to which the governor appointed a majority of blacks. The police recruited veterans of both armed forces of the Civil War. In 1870 a white-supremacist organization, the White League, seized control of the city after an essentially military engagement against the police. Once again, intervention by the federal military was necessary. But in 1877, competing parties formed separate state governments. The Democratic gubernatorial claimant used members of the White League to occupy police stations, and organized a police force under his board of commissioners. The Radicals, with the support of the old police and the federal military, now held only the state house. The settlement of the disputed national presidential election of 1876 meant that radical Reconstruction was going to be abandoned.

Emancipation and Reconstruction

"I have vowed," declared a southerner toward the end of the Civil War, "that if I should have children—the first ingredient of the first principle of their education shall be uncompromising hatred & contempt of the Yankee."

Hatred crackled and seared among white southerners in the first postwar days, amidst other emotions: sadness, resignation, relief, doubtless in a few cases a renascent loyalty to the Union. The feelings of the freed slaves are easy to imagine: their joy at the dizzying prospect of freedom has been documented. "I'm free as a frog!" one exultant former slave exclaimed. The southern land, meanwhile, was in a physical disruption to match the broiling emotions of the more irreconciled of its inhabitants.

Wherever travelers went in the months following Appomattox they saw abandoned fields, twisted rails, and burned structures. People in creaking wagons drove their gaunt mules for miles to find fords across bridgeless streams. For decades to come, men hobbling on one leg or dangling an empty sleeve were to be common sights throughout Dixie. In 1866 the state of Mississippi would spend a fifth of its revenues on artificial arms and legs for Confederate veterans. The defeat of the Confederacy had also wiped out millions of dollars of bank capital and made all Confederate money worthless. But most unsettling of all the changes the war had brought was the end of slavery. For generations it had been the foundation on which the entire southern economy rested. Now that it was gone, what would take its place?

Many former slaves remained on farms and plantations, but others had departed. Some had gone to the towns, where life seemed more interesting than in the sleepy countryside. Others took to the road to test their new freedom. Many others went traveling to seek out lost relatives and friends separated years ago by the migration of white masters or by the domestic slave trade. Eventually most would return to the land somewhere in the South.

Lincoln and most other northerners had entered the Civil War determined only to preserve the Union. Southerners, believing they saw larger and more menacing aims on the part of the North, had been as determined to protect their independence. The Emancipation Proclamation gave the Union a moral purpose and confirmed the fears of many white southerners that victory for the Union would mean social revolution. It was the leveling of the southern social and racial hierarchy as much as it was the leveling of Atlanta that caused bitterness among southerners after Appomattox.

Together, the ending of slavery and the social dislocations of defeat prepared the South for the very thing that white southerners had dreaded and most northern Unionists had been careful not to intend. The South was ripe for social revolution. That revolution, in fact, had already come in the sheer numbers of black southerners free and in motion across the countryside. What form that revolution would take, how long it might endure: all this in 1865 was a matter of endless and unpredictable possibility. Would liberty fulfill itself, as black southerners wanted, in the independence that comes of owning a plot of land? Would liberty amount to the freedom defined by northern capital: freedom on the part of workers, black and white, to sell their labor to the highest bidder?

What form would black family life take on: the patriarchy of the white family or the community of affection that had developed in slave quarters? Would blacks achieve social equality and integration with whites? What were white southerners going to think about black freedom, now that they had to think about it? Such questions would have been unimaginable two or three years earlier as immediate practical considerations. Unplanned conditions now made them inescapable. There could be no retreat. Too many memories survived like those of Della Garlic, a field hand on a Louisiana plantation in 1861. Born in Virginia and sold three times, she recalled:

> Dem days was hell. Babies was snatched from dere mother's breas' an' sold to speculators. Chilluns was separated from sisters an' brothers an' never saw each other ag'in. Course dey cry; you think dey not cry when dey was sold lak cattle? . . . Folks a mile away could hear dem awful whippings. Dey was a turrible part of livin'. . . .

In the end, social revolution was not to endure. That failure has defined the character of American social and political life ever since.

The Black Family

The country roads in the early days after Appomattox, crowded with newly freed slaves seeking lost loved ones, speak of the violence the slave system had done to the black family. Protecting their absolute right to their property, slaveholders had refused to give formal and legal recognition to slave marriages. Masters had often found it in their interest, however, to encourage slave unions, for the children they produced and because family responsibility would restrain rebelliousness. Yet when the economics of plantation life demanded it, husbands would be separated from wives, wives sold away from husbands, and children parted from mothers and fathers. Advertisements, angry or pathetic, were placed in newspapers by blacks following the war:

> Information Wanted, of Caroline Dodson, who was sold from Nashville, Nov. 1st, 1862, by James Lumsden to Warwick, (a trader then in human beings), who carried her to Atlanta, Georgia, and she was last heard of in the sale pen of Robert Clarke, (human trader in that place), from which she was sold. Any information of her whereabouts will be thankfully received and rewarded by her mother. Lucinda Lowery, Nashville.

It is logical to suppose that in the absence of socially protected marriage, the mother would assume the primary parental role. Historians have described the slave family as matriarchal. That view is under question. Evidence indicates the presence within the slave community of males who performed the tasks of husband and father: providing their families with game or fish as dietary supplements, fashioning articles of furniture, passing along to a child some memory from an earlier time and a different land, and, when possible, protecting a wife or child against an abusive overseer or master.

But beyond these elements of similarity between black and white fatherhood, little division of responsibilities along gender lines existed within slave quarters. The necessities of plantation agriculture assured, for example, that the great majority of slave men and women worked alongside one another in the fields. Slave parents, faced with the problem of bringing children to maturity safely, rarely observed Victorian distinctions in sex roles. Both parents taught their children survival, the subtle art of accommodation to the plantation system. And even within the unimaginably racist conditions of the slave system, whites might accept from a slave woman a degree of aggressiveness in defense of her children that they would not tolerate from black fathers.

Unable under the conditions of slavery to enjoy a secure and stable nuclear family life, blacks established an enlarged community of relations, stretching from one plantation to the next, of "brothers" and "sisters," "aunts" and "uncles" who took up family responsibilities. When the opportunity presented itself after the war, the freed slaves rejoined their immediate biological families and sought legitimacy and protection in legally recognized marriages. The Freedmen's Bureau, a federal agency set up in 1865 to ease the slave's transition to freedom, presided over many of these unions and made them a matter of public record. Under General O. O. Howard as commissioner, the Bureau attempted to rent abandoned land to blacks who would own it after three years. The Bureau also negotiated labor contracts and set up schools and courts.

For blacks, gaining control of their own families was perhaps the most important immediate consequence of freedom. But emancipation also worked to alter relations within the black family. Slavery had flattened, though not entirely, the differences between men's roles and the roles of women; emancipation made possible a differentiation between roles that the larger society endorsed. Black males most often went to work for whites in various jobs as they had done before the war, but now for hire. They generally preferred, however, that their wives not work for the white man, and many black females wished to create a conventional household and give their energies to raising children. In the years immediately following the war, white southern landowners complained of the scarcity of black women and children available for field work or domestic employment. For black men and women emancipation was supposed to mean at least the freedom whites enjoyed to organize a household.

Freed women when they stepped out from their homes encountered barriers already set up for the rest of their sex. Black women who had to seek employment complained to Freedmen's Bureau officials that they received wages lower than men were getting for the same work. Bureau policy required husbands to sign contracts for the labor of their wives. Though black men acquired more and more political liberty throughout the Reconstruction era, especially the right to vote and hold office, black women like their white sisters remained outside the political system. The experience of sexual equality

---

BLACKS *recalling slavery decades later had a wide spectrum of memories:*

Might as well tell the truth. Had just as good a time when I was a slave as when I was free. Had all the hog meat and milk and everything else to eat.

—HARDY MILLER

De white folks wuz good ter us, an' we loved 'em. But we wanted ter be free 'cause de Lawd done make us all free.

—TOM WILCOX

There was no such thing as being good to slaves. Many white people were better than others, but a slave belonged to his master, and there was no way to get out of it.

—THOMAS LEWIS

I thought slavery wuz right. I felt that this wuz the way things had to go—the way they were fixed to go. I wuz satisfied. The white folks treated me all right. My young missus loved me, and I loved her. She whupped me sometimes—I think, just for fun, sometimes.

—JOE HIGH

Some colored people say slavery was better, because they had no responsibility. It is true, they were fed, clothed, and sheltered, but I'm like the man that said, "Give me freedom or give me death!"

—BELLE CARUTHERS

Store for freedmen, Beaufort, South Carolina. The Freedmen's Bureau coordinated relief efforts and tried to ease the transition from slavery to freedom. *(Courtesy, National Archives)*

that had belonged to slavery was being swallowed in theories of male primacy that came with freedom.

The black family, meanwhile, thrived in freedom. By 1870 a large majority of black children were growing up in households of two parents. Relations between the sexes, while not so nearly equal as under slavery, were not so sharply defined and as hierarchical as conventional morality might have demanded. Blacks, in any event, now had a stable home foundation on which to build wider forms of community and political organization.

Building the Black Community

From the earliest days of Reconstruction, there emerged into full public view an institution that had maintained a powerful place in slave society and among antebellum free blacks. Evangelical Protestantism spoke to the condition of American blacks. Most slave states had made it illegal to educate slaves. But the incomparable vocabulary of the King James Bible was available. Illiterate blacks could learn the cadences by ear; free blacks with schooling could read it, as could slaves who had learned to read despite the prohibitions. A story of ancient Jews whose lot seemed close to that of the slaves; a language of bondage, flight, and deliverance, of suffering endured, rendered into prayer and devotion and in time ended: all was magnificent material for preaching and for hymns. With religion came a ministry of slaves and free blacks. During Reconstruction, blacks pressed for separate churches, nurturing their own congregations already established. The black ministry gained political leadership to supplement its spiritual role, taking a place within the black community that it would still occupy during the civil rights struggles of the 1950s and 1960s.

Side by side with the ministers in a position of leadership stood the teachers, now at liberty openly to instruct other blacks and to enlarge their own education. Ex-slaves and black southerners who had been free even in slavery times now joined with black and white teachers who had come from the North to serve in the new time of emancipation. Schools flourished: vast numbers of tiny schools ran on a shoestring; all received the countenance and aid, however meager, of the Freedmen's Bureau. The teachers might be passing on the fragments of learning they had snatched and hoarded in the days of slavery; pupils, eager for a schooling that Americans in general have traditionally prized as a means of success and a good in itself, might have the ambition to become teachers. The halting eloquence to be found among the papers of newly schooled Reconstruction blacks has its counterpart in the letters of immigrants, trying in their freshly acquired English to explain their place and hopes in their adopted country.

Even before the end of the war, black southerners in regions under control of federal troops were meeting in committees or larger conventions to provide a voice for their community. Enormously impressive to black southerners had been the coming of black soldiers to the South:

> We march through these fine thoroughfares where once the slave was forbid being out after nine P.M., or to puff a 'regalia,' or to walk with a cane, or to ride in a carriage! Negro soldiers!—with banners floating. . . . [walking] fearlessly and boldly through the streets of a southern city . . . without being required to take off his cap at every step, or give all the sidewalks to those lordly princes of the sunny south, the planters' sons!

The main insistence was on political and legal rights. More generally, such meetings appear to have had as their objective the establishment of an organized and articulate presence in American society. Underlying this purpose was a fear that even the more enlightened of white Americans were likely to treat the freed slaves as no more than wards and recipients of white benevolence. That was not going to be to the liking of

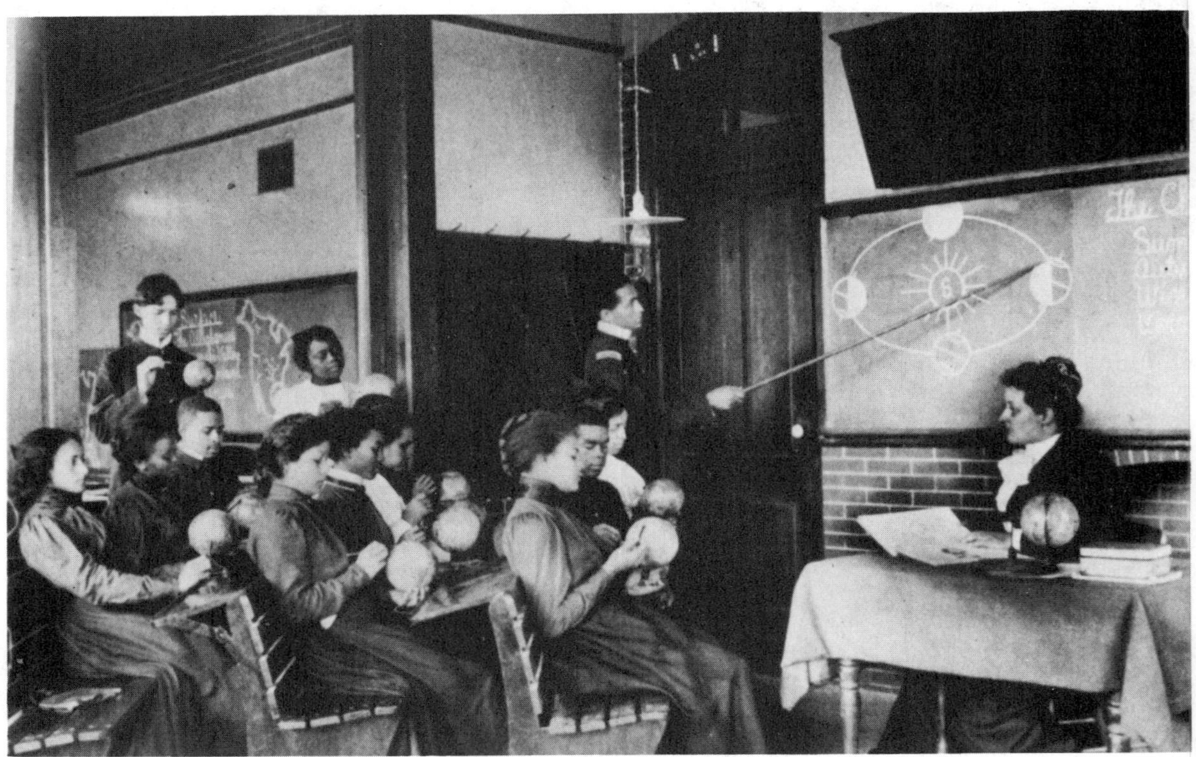

Black students learning geography. *(Courtesy, Hampton Institute)*

blacks who had won for themselves an education, whether pieced together in defiance of laws forbidding literacy schooling for slaves or acquired in the precarious margins of southern society allowed to free blacks before the war. Blacks made more particular demands during the early days of Reconstruction for the right to vote, to serve on juries, to exercise the other freedoms of Americans. These demands too can perhaps best be understood as reflecting the determination to be an active rather than a passive component of the nation. The plan of Reconstruction imposed by Congress later in the decade would succeed, if only for a moment, because there existed among southern blacks a roughly hewn political structure, a stratum of educated leaders, and a political will. These could respond to the congressional program for bringing the freed slaves into the nation's public life.

Emancipation and Reconstruction

Reorganizing the Union The Confederate surrender opened a difficult constitutional question about the status of the defeated states. Did the former rebel states have the right, as members of the Union, to come straight back to Congress and resume their old political life under the Constitution? Would the government have no authority to set conditions that they would have to meet before they resumed their seats in the House and Senate? If so, Congress would lack the power to force on the South whatever reforms might be necessary for the protection of the freed slaves and the prevention of any future disloyalty. Republicans who favored a coercive policy toward the South argued that by the act of secession the Confederate states had forfeited their status of statehood and reverted to the condition of territories. If they were no longer states, they were not entitled to the rights of states and could therefore be directly subject to the will of the federal government.

Some fundamental reform of the South, at any rate, was necessary, especially since the southern states were imposing oppressive codes of conduct on the freed slave. In the absence of reform, the Union victory might actually give the South a stronger presence in the House of Representatives than the region had enjoyed before the war, and with no consequences to the white majority. The Constitution had provided that in counting the population of a state for determining how many members it was to have in the House, three-fifths of the slaves in the state were to be counted in. But if slavery no longer existed and the blacks were legally free, the whole black population rather than three-fifths of it would be counted within the population of the state, and the South would gain about twenty seats in the House of Representatives. And if former Confederate states should succeed in finding methods for denying full freedom for the black populace, the South would be getting extra seats without even having to give up its oppression of the black race.

Overshadowing all these issues was the question of the future status of the black people. By eradicating slavery, the country unwittingly confronted long-delayed questions regarding the civil and political status of blacks. Would the ballot and citizenship be conferred on them?

Such questions had to be worked out amid a legacy of bitterness and frustration created by the war. White southerners found themselves in the unique position of being the only Americans to know defeat in wartime, their region burned and bare, their economy a shambles. The North had not suffered the physical and economic devastation experienced by the South. Even its human losses were proportionally less. But northerners had sacrificed to preserve the Union. They needed to know that their expenditures had gone for something, that their principles had been vindicated. They expected a measure of symbolic satisfaction from the South as well as physical surrender.

Lincoln's Reconstruction Plan In the efforts during the war to settle on some scheme for restoration of the rebel states to the Union, President Lincoln generally favored policies that would make few demands on the South. He had originally hoped for a speedy end to the war and a rapid resumption of antebellum political ties. Although the prolonged struggle on the battlefield made that impossible, the President continued to advocate a moderate postwar Reconstruction. Lincoln had not been an advocate of black equality. He always approached racial issues cautiously. He had hoped that the process of emancipation would be gradual and under the direction of officials of the former slave states. Believing that the colonization of blacks outside the United States was the ideal solution, Lincoln's administration sponsored efforts to resettle blacks in the Caribbean and Central America. And Lincoln was a cagey politician. An ex-Whig himself, he may have had it in mind that moderate policies attractive to southern former Whigs might draw them to the Republican Party.

In December 1863 Lincoln outlined a formal plan for Confederate areas coming under Union control. It clearly contemplated swift restoration, with no penalties for ex-rebels beyond loss of their slaves. It did not anticipate black participation in Reconstruction. Under Lincoln's "ten percent plan," whenever a total of whites equal to one-tenth the number who had voted in 1860 took an oath of future loyalty to the United States and its laws—which included the abolition of slavery—they could form a new state government. Before the war ended Lincoln had recognized "ten percent" governments in Arkansas, Tennessee and Louisiana. But Congress refused to admit representatives from these states, and their votes were not counted in the 1864 presidential election. Lincoln agreed that Congress should take some role in the reconciliation process, but he always sought to keep restoration under presidential leadership.

The national legislators were looking for a plan more firmly insuring that the new southern governments would remain loyal. The Wade-Davis Bill of 1864 required that, before a formerly seceded state could form a government, fifty percent of the adult white males in that state would have to take an oath of loyalty to the Union. The state could then hold a constitutional convention to make a new government for itself. But voting for delegates to that convention would be limited to people who had taken an oath that they had never supported the secession. The state must outlaw slavery. The plan was not to go into effect until the war had ended. Thinking the Wade-Davis Bill too severe and an invasion of presidential responsibility for reconstruction, Lincoln pocket vetoed it.

Neither Lincoln's plan nor that of the Wade-Davis Bill provided for blacks to be given the vote. But some Republicans in Congress wished for a program of reconstruction that would grant a wide range of rights to the freedmen and guarantee protection of these rights. Legislators of this kind wanted the national government to have strong control over former rebel states, so that their legal and social systems could be thoroughly reshaped and white southerners would not get the chance to bring back the old slavery system in a new form.

During the final year of the war President Lincoln appeared to be moving somewhat toward a more active and progressive solution to the race question. In March 1864 he came out in favor of granting the vote to "very intelligent" black people and black Union soldiers. He pressed for the Thirteenth Amendment outlawing slavery. A month before his death Lincoln signed the bill creating a Freedmen's Bureau to aid the ex-slaves in their transition to freedom.

In the end, Reconstruction was to be in hands other than Lincoln's. But in the spring of 1865 the President and the Union public did have a brief period to savor victory.

Lincoln's Last Days

On April 4 Lincoln went to Richmond to view the Confederate capital now evacuated by the government of Jefferson Davis. Accompanied by his son and a military escort, he walked up Main Street to the Confederate executive mansion. Black men and women crowded around the presidential party and sang and shouted. When he entered the Confederate President's house and took a seat in Davis's chair, the Union troops, black and white, cheered. Later the President toured the captured city that for four bloody years had been the supreme goal of Union armies. Like many other large southern towns Richmond was in ruins: it was blackened by a fire set accidentally by the Confederate authorities before they withdrew.

Lincoln returned to Washington on April 9, the day Lee surrendered to Grant at Appomattox Court House. The news reached

Charleston, South Carolina. At the war's end, much of the South lay in ruins. *(Courtesy, Library of Congress)*

Washington the next day and the government declared a holiday for its employees. On the tenth, throngs gathered on the streets of the capital. The crowds eventually converged on the White House, where Lincoln was working at his desk. They interrupted him several times by their shouts for a speech until he finally made an appearance. He would deliver some appropriate remarks the following evening, he said, but for the moment he would just order the bands to play "Dixie." The Confederate anthem, he noted, was now the lawful property of the Union.

The next evening the President came to the upper window of the White House as he had promised and made some graceful remarks. "We meet this evening . . . in gladness of heart" he began, and then went on to deliver a thoughtful address, his last, on the problems to come. If the crowd had wanted a rousing cock-crow of triumph, it was disappointed. At least one man in the audience, however, found himself deeply moved, but to rage and anger. John Wilkes Booth was a Marylander, an actor from a distinguished theatrical family. The defeat of the South had sent him into despair.

On the evening of April 14 the President, accompanied by his wife and several friends, went to see the comedy *Our American Cousin* at Ford's Theater. The President's party arrived late but quickly settled down to enjoy the story of a shrewd comic American visiting his English relatives. During the third act the sounds of a muffled shot and a scuffle came from the President's box. Suddenly a tall figure leaped from the box to the stage and shouted *Sic semper tyrannis*! (thus ever to tyrants), the motto of Virginia. Before he could be stopped Booth escaped into the night.

They carried the unconscious President to a house across the street. While high officials and family members gathered around, the doctors examined him. The bullet had entered the rear of his head and lodged near his eye. Nothing could be done. He died at 7:22 a.m.

Andrew Johnson

Like other Vice Presidents in American history, Andrew Johnson was selected without much consideration that he might become President. A self-educated tailor from east Tennessee and a strong Jacksonian Democrat, Johnson had been in 1861 the only senator from a secessionist state to support the Union. After Tennessee fell to Union troops, Lincoln made him war governor, a task he performed with vigor and courage. In 1864 the Republican Party, seeking to broaden itself into a Union party, turned naturally to Johnson, an ex-Democrat and a southern Unionist, to be Lincoln's running mate. Then suddenly, on April 14, 1865, he was the President.

Johnson, a President without a party, had to deal with a Republican Congress. And Johnson was a southern white supremacist, willing and perhaps happy to accept emancipation and some rights for black Americans but cooperative with southerners who wished to place strict controls over the black population. This brought him into conflict not only with the increasingly strong band of radical Republicans in Congress but with moderates as well. Courageous and stubborn but belligerent and lacking in political tact, Johnson both endured and to an extent brought on himself one of the most troubled presidential administrations in American history.

Johnson wanted an easy restoration of the seceded states. There was not yet any clearly defined program that would instruct a rebel state in how it must go about reorganizing itself so as to be accepted back into the Union, and Johnson did not wait for Congress to reconvene (it was out of session until December) before dealing with the problem. He announced at once a program of restoration similar to Lincoln's. He too offered pardon to ex-rebels pledging future loyalty. He asked only that the reorganized state governments nullify their ordinances of secession, repudiate their Confederate debts, and ratify the Thirteenth Amendment.

Assuming primary responsibility for Reconstruction, Johnson chiseled a policy bound to alienate Republicans in Congress. His leniency toward the South angered Radicals. Southerners, moreover, took a course that aroused northern resentment. They elected to state office and to Congress prominent ex-rebels, including Vice President Alexander Stephens and numerous generals. Some of the reorganized state governments refused to repudiate their Confederate debts or nullify their secession ordinances. A number of them passed "black codes" defining the rights of emancipated slaves in ways that severely restricted their freedom.

A typical black code might bar blacks from jury duty and from testifying in court against whites; it might forbid them to take up any occupation except agriculture or to rent land on their own; some subjected unemployed blacks to arrest and forced labor. The character of the "restored" governments and the "black codes" seemed to indicate that southerners remained rebels at heart. "Nigger life's cheap now," a white Tennesseean soon observed. "When a white man feels aggrieved at anything a nigger's done, he just shoots him and puts an end to it." The Freedmen's Bureau Commissioner in Mississippi and Louisiana wrote:

> I hear the people talk in such a way as to indicate that they are yet unable to conceive of the negro as possessing any rights at all. . . . To kill a negro they do not deem murder; to debauch a negro woman they do not think fornication; to take the property away from a negro they do not consider robbery. The people boast that when they get freedmen affairs in their own hands, to use the classic expression, 'the niggers will catch hell.'

Early Reconstruction

When Congress met in December 1865, it refused to seat newly elected southern representatives, but disagreed on what to do next. Radicals demanded a thoroughgoing political and economic shakeup of the South. Moderate Republicans wanted only minimal guarantees of legal protection for the ex-slaves. "To have refused the Negroes the simplest rights granted to every other inhabitant, native or foreigner, would be outrageous," de-

Andrew Johnson's attempt to assume primary responsibility for Reconstruction after Lincoln's death alienated Congress, while his leniency toward the South increasingly angered northern voters.

clared Senator John Sherman of Ohio, a moderate leader. The emancipated slave, warned another senator, would "be tyrannized over, abused, and virtually reenslaved without some legislation by the nation for his protection."

At this point moderates still dominated Republican policy. But they too wanted to insure the civil rights of black southerners. In 1866 Congress passed a bill giving to a Freedmen's Bureau the power to try by military commission anyone charged with depriving freedmen of their civil rights. It also put through a bill that gave the freedmen citizenship and civil rights. Johnson vetoed both bills as unconstitutional extensions of federal power. Congress thereupon enacted the civil rights measure over his veto, passed a revised bill for a Freedmen's Bureau, and overrode Johnson's veto of it.

Congress's establishment of the Freedmen's Bureau departed from normal government policy by addressing various aspects of people's lives that had normally been left to private initiative. The Bureau was essentially responsible for protecting blacks against reenslavement in the unsettled conditions of the southern states.

The Fourteenth Amendment

The national legislature soon offered Johnson and the South another chance. It framed an elaborate Fourteenth Amendment covering a range of issues and gave each of the state governments favored by Johnson the opportunity to return to Congress if it should ratify.

The Fourteenth Amendment declared that "All persons"—the lawmakers were thinking particularly of black Americans—"born or naturalized in the United States, and subject to the jurisdiction thereof, are citizens of the United States and of the State wherein they reside." The Amendment prohibited the states from violating the "privileges or immunities of citizens of the United States," depriving "any person of life, liberty, or property, without due process of law," or denying "to any person within its jurisdiction the equal protection of the laws." The Amendment did not directly extend the right to vote. It attempted instead to entice the states to give the vote to blacks. It provided that a state would lose seats in the House of Representatives in proportion to the number of its adult males denied the right to vote.

A state ratifying the Amendment could expect to be granted readmission without further reform. Implicit in the offer was a penalty for rejection: restoration would begin anew, with Congress dictating terms. Had it not been for Johnson, the South might have ratified. But Johnson refused to bend. On his advice all the southern states except his Tennessee rejected the Amendment. Tennessee ratified and was readmitted to the Union. The other ten, said James A. Garfield, had "flung back into our teeth the magnanimous offer of a generous nation."

The break between the President and Congress was now complete. In the fall of 1866 Johnson stumped the North encouraging the defeat at the polls of leading Republican congressmen. The tour was a disaster for the President personally and politically. Forgetting that he was no longer a Tennessee stump-speaker, Johnson engaged in undignified arguments with hecklers and even suggested hanging leading Radicals. In November the Republicans swept the elections, winning over a two-thirds majority in both houses of Congress. Reconstruction would begin anew, under the leadership of such Radicals as the Massachusetts Senator Charles Sumner and Representative Thaddeus Stevens of Pennsylvania.

Radical Reconstruction

The situation when Congress met in December 1866 was very different from that a year earlier. Events during 1866 had conspired to bring together moderate and Radical Republicans, at least temporarily. A majority in Congress now agreed on the necessity of creating new southern state governments on the basis of black suffrage and excluding ex-rebels. Arming blacks with the ballot, Republicans hoped, would give them a weapon against white Democratic oppression and build up a strong Republican Party in the South.

The Military Reconstruction Act of 1867 set the terms of the congressional program. It divided the South into five military districts. Military governors in each were to register voters, including blacks but not whites who had held public office before the Civil War and then supported the Confederacy. The governors would thereupon call elections for new constitutional conventions. These conventions had to write black suffrage into the new state constitutions. Once the voters had approved these constitutions and the Fourteenth Amendment, the states might apply to Congress for readmission. If the constitution met approval, the state would be readmitted to the Union and its representatives seated. Three other Reconstruction Acts followed the first.

Reconstruction had something in common with the economic policy of the Republican Party and with the party's defense of the Union during the Civil War. It represented that commitment to strong and active central government toward which Republicans tended. In the enforcement of civil rights, the effort to establish universal male suffrage, and the work of the Freedmen's Bureau, the federal government for the first time in its history was lending its resources, or some of them, to a political and social revolution.

To southern whites haunted by the old antebellum fear of slave insurrection, Radical Reconstruction seemed a nightmare come true. With their traditional leaders barred from office and illiterate ex-slaves enfranchised, they predicted a grim era of black rule.

Changing Interpretations of Reconstruction The earliest critics of Reconstruction condemned it as a rape of southern society. Political opportunism and hatred of the South, so such critics argued, had motivated the Radical Republican policies: military rule, black suffrage, and violation of the spirit, if not the letter, of the Constitution. Accounts sympathetic to the white South stressed the corruption of Reconstruction state regimes, the unruliness—by which some of them may have meant the claims to equality—of former slaves, the greed of northern "carpetbaggers," and the treachery of southern "scalawags." Reconstruction was a "blackout of honest government." In this view, the lifting of Radical rule by the white "redeemers" represented a return to constitutional government and to proper racial relations in the South.

By the 1930s historians were becoming increasingly interested in explaining events by economic causes. That brought a new way of interpreting Reconstruction. Now writers looked back to the days before the Civil War when southerners had opposed such measures favorable to northern business as the protective tariff, which would force the South to buy its manufactured goods from the North rather than at cheaper European prices. Scholars now perceived the Radical Republicans as representatives of northeastern business interests. These interests had feared that a speedily reconstructed South might regain its political power and overturn the control of the national government acquired by northern business during the war years.

More recently, a generation influenced by the civil rights struggles of the 1950s and 1960s has begun describing Reconstruction

Massachusetts Senator Charles Sumner and Pennsylvania Representative Thaddeus Stevens, leaders of Radical Reconstruction. *(Courtesy, Library of Congress)*

as another phase in the black American search for justice. Radical Republicans, this analysis insists, represented the last moment of abolitionist idealism. The Radicals tried to provide national protection for the rights of the freed people and to extend some measure of social and economic assistance. Not particularly vindictive and not the tools of a capitalist conspiracy, congressional Republicans, moderates as well as Radicals, undertook their actions only after they realized the extent of white southern stubbornness and presidential obstructionism. And their measures were not especially severe, particularly when compared to the postwar policies of other victorious nations. The national government committed only a small number of troops to military Reconstruction, and the whole process lasted only a few years. This recent idea of Reconstruction would hold that if any fault is to be found with the policy, it is not for being too severe toward the defeated South but for not being thorough enough to win the black race full and permanent equality and justice. The very word "Radical" has been questioned since most measures passed were compromises unsatisfactory to true radicals.

Blacks in the South

The Road to Freedom In 1870 Congress brought the right to vote under federal control. The Fifteenth Amendment declared that a citizen's right to vote "shall not be denied or abridged . . . on account of race, color, or previous condition of servitude." The Amendment applied to black males in the North—much of the North had not allowed black Americans to vote—as well as to former slaves in the South. Most of the black vote went to Republicans, and some northern supporters of the Amendment may have been mainly concerned with strengthening the Republican Party. But others risked a white backlash to guarantee suffrage to the black man.

The vote that was granted to black males was denied to both black and white females. White women leaders of the movement for women's rights were incensed. Before the war, they had worked within the abolitionist movement and then supported the Republican cause. In 1866, Susan B. Anthony, Elizabeth Cady Stanton, Lucy Stone, and Lucretia Mott organized the American Equal Rights Association (AERA) to support suffrage for both white women and blacks. Some even asserted that white women were better fitted to vote than black men. In the ensuing dispute about priorities, the AERA split into two groups. Lucy Stone and Henry Blackwell formed the American Woman Suffrage Association, which in order not to jeopardize the vote for black men accepted the refusal to grant women the vote. Susan B. Anthony and Elizabeth Cady Stanton organized the more militant National Woman Suffrage Association. Bitter about what they took to be betrayal by male Republican leaders, they warned that women could not trust men, refused to support the freedmen's right to the vote, and even used racist arguments to explain that it was of greater importance to give the vote to white women. Although their racism declined after the passage of the Fifteenth Amendment, it left a disturbing legacy to the women's movement.

In most southern states, Reconstruction lasted for only a few years. In states with large white majorities, conservatives regained political control rather quickly. Virginia was "redeemed" in 1869, Tennessee and North Carolina in 1870. Georgia fell under conservative rule in 1872, Alabama, Texas, and Arkansas in 1874, and Mississippi in 1875. In only three states—Louisiana, Florida and South Carolina—did Radical Republican government last a full decade, and they were all "redeemed" in 1877.

Even in those states where blacks made up a majority of the voters, they did not dominate the reconstructed state governments. They formed a majority in one state constitutional convention, that of South Carolina, exactly one half the membership in the Louisiana convention, and a minority in eight others. After the new governments were formed, blacks never held a majority in both houses of a state legislature. No state had an elected black governor; only two black senators and fourteen black representatives were elected to the national Congress. At the local level, blacks never enjoyed a proportionate share of offices. In the constitutional conventions and in legislatures, blacks rarely pressed for equal access to public facilities.

Nor were the Reconstruction governments particularly incompetent or corrupt. Much of the leadership of Republican regimes fell to native whites or to northerners who had resettled in the South after the war. Local whites who supported or entered Reconstruction governments were known derisively as "scalawags"; most of these were ex-Whigs seeking to reenter politics. The northerners—some nicknamed "carpetbaggers" for the light baggage they were pictured as bringing southward with them—defy easy characterization. Many were former Union soldiers attracted by the South's climate and cheap land. Some undoubtedly were profiteers; others, like Governor Adelbert Ames of Mississippi and Governor Daniel Chamberlain of South Carolina, were idealists. Any discussion of corruption must be measured against the records of previous white southern administrations and against the sorry performance of several northern governments during this era. On the whole, Reconstruction governments made substantial progress toward postwar recovery and social reform. They drafted progressive new constitutions, reapportioned legislatures to give backcountry districts equitable representation, expanded social services, improved roads, encouraged railroad construction, and established the South's first substantial public school system. Much of the so-called extravagance of Reconstruction legislatures merely represented expenditures for public services that previous regimes had neglected.

Humanitarian Efforts

During the Reconstruction years, the national government provided some assistance to the freed people in the South. The Freedmen's Bureau coordinated relief activities and tried to ease the difficult transition from slavery to freedom. The Bureau found employment opportunities, supervised labor contracts, and attempted to safeguard the legal rights of black people. Critics at the time generally indicted the Bureau for doing too much to assist blacks. Later historians have found quite the opposite. Many well-meaning officials were overly paternalistic; others displayed outright prejudice toward black people; some encouraged freedmen to enter into exploitive labor contracts; the agency did too little to enlarge opportunities for the former slaves. Yet the Bureau represented a notable though mild and temporary expansion of the social role of the federal government. One freedman observed:

> Perhaps some *will* get an education in a little while. I *knows* de *next generation will*. But . . . we has been kep down *a hundred years* and *I* think it will take *a hundred years to get us back again*.

Another ex-slave recalled sending his children to school:

> We had no idea that we should see them return home alive in the evening. Big white boys and half-grown men used to pelt them with stones and run them down with open knives, both to and from school. Sometimes they come home bruised, stabbed, beaten half to death, and sometimes quite dead. My own son himself was often thus beaten. He has on his forehead today a scar over his right eye which sadly tells the story of his trying experience in those days in his efforts to get an education. I was wounded in the war, trying to get my freedom, and he over his eye, trying to get an education.

Private philanthropic and religious groups also tried to aid freed people. Various churches, especially the Congregationalists and the Quakers, sent both money and volunteers to the South. Educational institutions related to the churches gave many black children and adults their first opportunity to learn to read and write. Blacks rushed to make use of the new schools, where northern female schoolteachers took an especially important role. Their devotion to the people they were teaching mingled with their commitment to inculcating them with northern, middle-class values. Church groups also helped establish black colleges and industrial schools, and the Freedmen's Bureau extended some financial assistance to missionary schools, including Howard University in Washington, D.C.

Many northern black churchmen and educators journeyed south to spread the gospel and the primer among the ex-slaves. Former slaves themselves put up school houses and paid for teachers, established churches, organized conventions to lobby for equal rights and the ballot, and opened savings banks. A black convention speaker in New Orleans in 1865 explained:

> If we are men—as our friends contend we are—we are able to attend to our own business. There is no man in the world so perfectly identified with our own interest as to understand it better than we do ourselves. . . . We need friends, it is true; but we do not need tutors. The age of guardianship is past forever. We now think for ourselves, and we shall act for ourselves.

The Land Question

The blacks were legally free and had the vote. But they lacked the one essential basis of independence and equality: land or an equivalent property. Both races in the postwar South recognized the importance of the land question. "The way we can best take care of ourselves is to have land and turn it and till it by our labor," contended a delegation of freed people in 1865. This is exactly what former slaveholders feared, and they determined early on to prevent blacks from owning land. Without access to employment except on white-owned land, all the ballots and education in the world would be worthless. "They who own the real estate of a country control its vote," warned one observer. It is this as much as anything else that explains the successful overthrow of Reconstruction in the South.

A few antislavery activists had wanted to provide land for emancipated slaves. As early as 1862 Congress passed legislation confiscating plantations of Confederate sympathizers, and it was proposed to resettle blacks on them. But the Lincoln administration showed little interest. In 1865 General William T. Sherman temporarily allotted to thousands of homeless ex-slaves small tracts of confiscated land along the South Atlantic coast. After the war Representative Thaddeus Stevens of Pennsylvania advocated breaking up the large southern plantations and allocating them in forty acre tracts to freed people. "Forty acres and a mule" became a byword among landless ex-slaves.

This was as close as anyone came to providing a new life for the blacks to move into when they moved out of slavery. Andrew Johnson restored confiscated lands to their previous owners and evicted the black tenants. Few northerners supported Stevens' plan to confiscate private property, even from slaveholders. Congress soundly defeated his watered-down confiscation plan in 1866. It did set aside certain public lands in the South for purchase by freed people. This scheme failed badly, however, because the land available was inferior, and because few ex-slaves had the capital to buy land and farm equipment.

In many areas, the first system to develop in the absence of slavery was that of wage labor. Guided and prodded by agents of the Freedmen's Bureau, blacks signed contracts to work for so much a month and were provided with cabins, often in the former plantation slave quarters, and sometimes with food. Yet work in the fields at the white man's bidding, on the white man's land, under the immediate supervision of a white overseer seemed far too much like old slavery in a new guise. Many blacks would have none of it and sabotaged the arrangement. One way was to collect wages during the planting and cultivating months and then decamp just before the crucial harvest, which left the owner with the problem of gathering in the cotton or tobacco without a work force.

Sharecropping The specific reason for the rejection of the gang labor system was that it suggested the organization of field work under slavery. But in looking for some alternative, the freed slaves were acting in keeping with an American tradition that identified personal independence with the possession of property. One estimate has a fifth of black farm workers owning land by the 1880s. For most, conventional ownership was not an immediate option. Sporadic attempts, soon after the defeat of the rebels, to seize the land of planters met with resistance by the federal government. An alternative, however inadequate, gave the black family an opportunity to work independently on a plot of ground. The black newspaper in New Orleans predicted that

> A kind of general serfdom and humiliation is about to take the place of slavery. . . .

This land and labor system finally devised in the postwar South was sharecropping. In this form of tenancy the black worker contributed labor and perhaps the use of some tools

---

A SHARECROPPING CONTRACT

This contract made and entered into between A. T. Mial of one part and Fenner Powell of the other part both of the County of Wake and State of North Carolina—

Witnesseth—That the Said Fenner Powell hath bargained and agreed with the Said Mial to work as a cropper for the year 1886 on Said Mial's land on the land now occupied by Said Powell on the west Side of Poplar Creek and a point on the east Side of Said Creek and both South and North of the Mial road, leading to Raleigh, That the Said Fenner Powell agrees to work faithfully and dilligently without any unnecessary loss of time, to do all manner of work on Said farm as may be directed by Said Mial, And to be respectful in manners and deportment to Said Mial. And the Said Mial agrees on his part to furnish mule and feed for the same and all plantation tools and Seed to plant the crop free of charge, and to give the Said Powell One half of all crops raised and housed by Said Powell on Said land except the cotton seed. The Said Mial agrees to advance as provision to Said Powell fifty pound of bacon and two sacks of meal pr month and occasionally Some flour to be paid out of his the Said Powell's part of the crop or from any other advance that may be made to Said Powell by Said Mial. As witness our hands and seals this the 16th day of January A.D. 1886

Witness — *A. T. Mial* [signed] [Seal]

his
W. S. Mial [signed] — *Fenner* X *Powell* [Seal]
mark

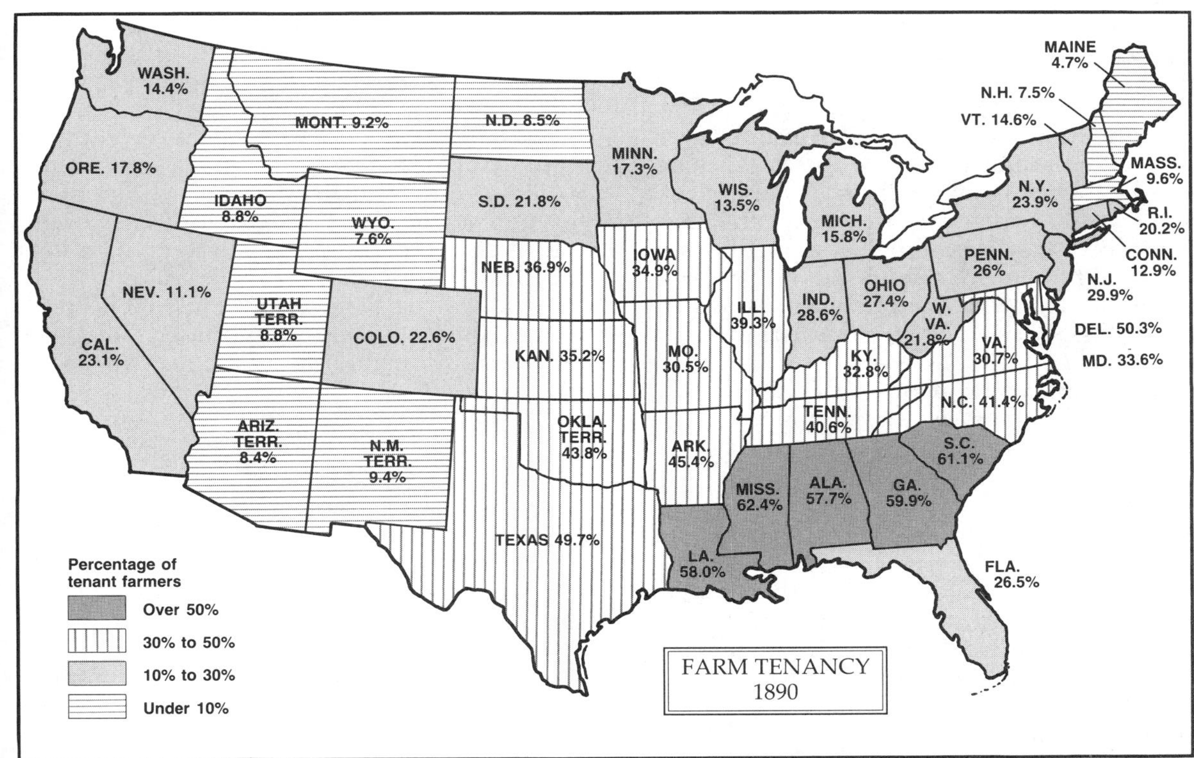

and a mule, and received from the landlord some land to farm. At harvest time the cropper got to keep from one-half to two-thirds of the crop, the remaining portion going to the landowner.

The system had some advantages. Blacks now had some personal freedom; there was no overseer to supervise their work. Instead of living in the old slave quarters, moreover, each black family could reside apart on its own rented piece of land. Some blacks simply raised the slave cabin from the old quarters and removed it to their own farm. Blacks could now decide how to spend their money. And they could arrange their own family division of labor.

The sharecropper system was a poor substitute for landowning. Sharecroppers, like other tenants, had little incentive to improve the land they farmed since they did not own it. The credit system that grew up alongside sharecropping was its worst element. Tenants often could not wait until harvest to buy the things they needed during the year. Storekeepers sold them cloth, tools, knickknacks, and even food on credit, taking out a lien, a kind of mortgage, on the crop as security until harvest time in the fall. Then, when the crop was sold, the storekeeper subtracted the debt from the cropper's share. Those caught in this crop-lien process might not ever see any cash once the storekeeper and the landlord had taken their shares. Goods bought on credit were far more expensive than those bought with cash. The system also allowed many opportunities for fraud. Storekeepers, themselves under considerable economic pressure, kept the accounts and sometimes juggled the books to make sure that the sharecropper remained permanently in debt. Such a tenant remained tied to the storekeeper as a perpetual customer, unable legally to deal with any other storekeeper until the debt was discharged. Some scholars have seen this debt peonage as the virtual reenslavement of the South's black population. It certainly weakened the possibility that sharecropping might become for any sizable number of former slaves a waystation to land ownership.

As pursuers of the nineteenth-century American ideal of small property ownership, the ex-slaves had been from the beginning cousins to the middling and poor whites of the South. In Reconstruction days as before, landowning was common among whites who had possessed no slaves or few. In this respect much better off than the newly freed black population, the white plain folk in this time of uncertainty and open possibility had reason for antagonism to the planters who had led them on a fruitless war for the maintenance of a slaveholding system in which they had largely not shared. But no politics of cooperation materialized between blacks and whites. Racist psychology dominated, and instead of seeing blacks as fellow victims of planter hegemony, poor whites would soon come to view them as upstart competitors for the scraps and tatters of poverty. This gave added cause for the violence that blacks even a century later have suffered from their white neighbors.

As regional impoverishment continued throughout the remainder of the nineteenth century, increasing numbers of whites were ground down into sharecropping. All in all, racial animosity never gave way to a politics of class, but by the late 1880s there were to be some feeble beginnings of just such a politics. Tentative agriculture-based alliances between a few poor blacks and poor whites form a remarkable though faltering episode of late nineteenth-century southern history.

Impeachment of Johnson

Although his policies had clearly been rejected, President Johnson continued to resist Radical Reconstruction by every possible means. Using the authority he possessed as commander-in-chief, he issued orders curtailing the powers of the military commanders in the South. He also removed from office people friendly to radical policies. Congress responded in 1867 and 1868 by trying to trim the President's powers so as to reduce his capacity for harm. In particular it passed the Tenure of Office Act, which forbade him to dismiss federal officials without the consent of the Senate. Another law required him to issue all orders to the army through its commanding general, U. S. Grant.

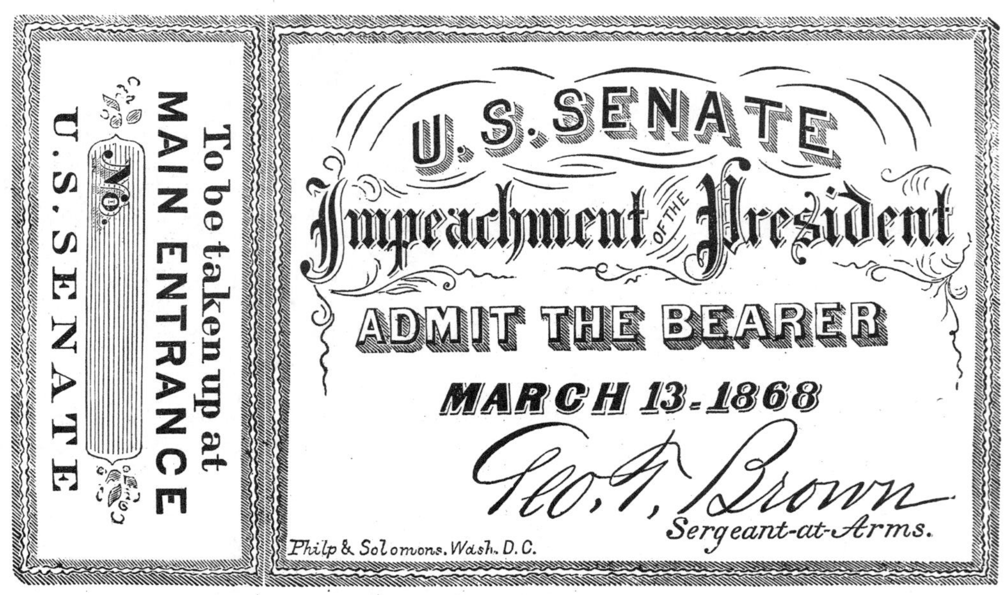

Facsimile of a ticket to Andrew Johnson's impeachment trial. Though Johnson was guilty of no crime other than continued resistance to Radical Reconstruction, a switch of a single Senate vote would have removed him from office. *(Courtesy, Library of Congress)*

There had been talk among Radicals for some time of removing Johnson from office. Under the Constitution a President could be removed for "Treason, Bribery, or other high Crimes and Misdemeanors." Johnson had committed none of these. His only real offense was to refuse to cooperate in legislative policies that Congress and the public had approved. This might indicate bad political judgment. But bad judgment is not a high crime or misdemeanor.

Then Johnson, always his own worst enemy, blundered. In August 1867 he suspended Secretary of War Edwin M. Stanton, a close ally of the Radicals. There followed a comic opera in which Stanton barricaded himself in his office while his successor stood outside begging him to vacate. Outraged at Johnson's defiance, and convinced that he intended to destroy Radical Reconstruction, the House of Representatives in February 1868 impeached the President—that is, charged him with misconduct. Johnson stood accused of a number of doubtful offenses such as delivering "inflammatory and scandalous" speeches, but especially the offense of dismissing Stanton in violation of the Tenure of Office Act. Impeachment meant that Johnson now had to go on trial before the Senate, which would decide whether to remove him from the presidency. For three months the Senate sat as a court, listening to arguments from attorneys for both sides. Johnson's lawyers argued that a President could be removed only for violation of criminal law; counsel for the House contended that Johnson had exceeded his presidential authority and therefore provided adequate grounds for removal. Suspense mounted as it became clear that Republican senators were divided over the question of Johnson's guilt. In the end, seven Republicans broke with their colleagues and voted with Democrats against conviction. As a result the Senate fell one vote short of the required two-thirds needed to remove the President from office.

Johnson's impeachment and trial were the product of nerves stretched to the limit after three years of feuding. So convinced were many northerners that Johnson had joined with unrepentant rebels to undo the results of the war that they sanctioned any means to drive him from office. Johnson's conviction—especially on such flimsy grounds—might have damaged permanently the role of the President in the American political system.

The End of Racial Progress

Reconstruction remained, at least in fragments, into the 1870s. After white organizations, among them the Ku Klux Klan, began threatening and committing violence on black citizens for exercising their newly acquired rights, the national legislature in the early 1870s put through several Force Acts that aimed at restraining the terrorist groups. The administration of Ulysses S. Grant, elected President in 1868 as the candidate of the Republican Party, broke the Klan by the end of 1871. In 1875 Congress passed a Civil Rights Act—which in 1883 the Supreme Court was to find unconstitutional—that required states to provide equality to blacks in public places and prohibited the exclusion of blacks from jury duty. For a while into the 1870s, some southern states had Reconstruction governments that represented black as well as white voters. And in 1876 there were still a few federal soldiers in the South whose object was to defend the rights of the black community. But by that year American politics had been turning away from Reconstruction for some time.

In 1868 Grant, as a war hero, had won a solid victory over Democratic presidential candidate Horatio Seymour of New York. In the next years Democrats made politically effective attacks on Reconstruction policy, winning voters unsure of the wisdom of Radical Reconstruction or unfriendly to the rights black people were gaining. Some Republicans were also challenging the party's southern programs. In 1872 Congress lifted from many former rebels the penalties prescribed in the Fourteenth Amendment and passed an Amnesty Act pardoning most of the remainder. Democrats and a faction of Republicans put up newspaperman Horace Greeley as a presidential candidate. Grant won reelection, but his administration suffered from a number of political scandals that suggested widespread corruption. Crédit Mobilier, a dummy corporation formed by an inner circle of Union Pacific Railroad shareholders, extorted wealth from the company and distributed bribes to prominent congressmen. In the elections of 1874 the Democratic Party won control of the House of Representatives and cut into Republican strength in the Senate. The era of Reconstruction was nearing an end.

The Compromise of 1877

Finally, in the events that followed the presidential contest of 1876 between the Republican candidate Rutherford B. Hayes of Ohio and Democrat Samuel J. Tilden of New York, the Republican Party ended Reconstruction and abandoned black southerners and their rights. After the general election, which chose the presidential electors who were to cast the actual vote for President, charges of irregularities had arisen concerning procedures in three southern states, South Carolina, Florida, and Louisiana. There the election boards that had counted the popular presidential vote, giving it in each case to the Republicans, were under the control of Republican Reconstruction forces; Democrats suggested that the vote in each state had actually gone for the Democrats. Both parties also claimed one disputed electoral vote in Oregon. Unless the Republican claims could stand in each of the four states, the majority in the whole electoral college would be Democratic and Tilden would be the next President. Democrats and Republicans worked out a scheme for a commission that was to decide among the disputed electors; it was supposed to be balanced between Democratic and Republican members, with one other member who would be independent of either party in his decisions. When it came to appear that this member, a justice on the Supreme Court, was going to decide in all cases in favor of the Republicans, Democrats believed that they were about to have the election taken away from them. After the dispute had lasted for months, during which there was talk of renewed civil war, the parties came to a solution. In return for a Democratic agreement not to oppose the selection of Hayes electors, Republicans agreed that a Republican presidential administration would not only remove the remaining federal troops from the South but also give political patronage to white southerners and be friendly to economic legislation beneficial to southern states. Hayes, who had expressed concern for the rights of black southerners, presided over the end of a policy that by 1877 no longer had political support. The Republican effort to protect civil rights in the South in a major way had ceased.

Points To Think About

1. Historians have long speculated over how Lincoln would have approached the problem of postwar reconstruction. And in so doing they are merely following the lead of his contemporaries, most of whom claimed their own proposals reflected Lincoln's plans. The real question may be: did Lincoln have any plans?

It seems probable that he did, but Lincoln confided them to no one. In this matter, as in most others, he kept his own counsel. The result is that, following the assassination, people have tried to infer his postwar plans from his wartime programs. This is a very dubious enterprise. The reason is that Lincoln sought throughout the war to shorten it by enticing the seceding states back into the Union. The generous terms he offered were contingent on their willingness to lay down their arms. And so those terms should be seen as the carrot Lincoln used alongside the military stick. That they should not be seen as likely precedents for his postwar plans is suggested by this logic. Leniency was held out as a reward for voluntarily returning to the Union. None of the Confederate states earned that reward. That means that Lincoln, by his own terms, was free to deal with them as harshly as circumstances might demand. All this is technically true, and indicates Lincoln's essential conservatism. Yet there is a contrary truth to the Emancipation Proclamation. Lincoln knew what it implied, and so did the white South in its angry former public reaction to the Proclamation. It was, by implication and beneath its limited surface, a declaration of war against slavery. We also have Lincoln's reaction to the Wade-Davis Bill to go by. He objected not so much to its rigor as that it would tie his hands in advance. Lincoln wanted to be free to deal with a defeated South as circumstances might suggest.

All in all it seems that we will never know what Lincoln would have proposed. But the disastrous course of Johnson's attempts at reconstruction will always invite speculation on what Lincoln might have done had he lived.

2. Reconstruction has, until recently, been almost universally seen as a failure. And it is certainly true that it left many vital problems unresolved. After more than a century blacks still suffer discrimination. What went wrong? The obvious answer is: plenty.

After the war President Johnson decided not to summon a special session of Congress. This was a disastrous mistake because Congress would be highly critical of plans adopted in its absence, no matter how wise. It was a mistake too because Johnson, as a southerner himself, could not give even the appearance of leniency without creating the suspicion on the part of northerners that they were being cheated of the fruits of victory. And it was a mistake because it gave the South the false impression that if it followed Johnson's lead, all would be well.

By the time Congress met, in December of 1865, northern public opinion was convinced: by issuing wholesale pardons, Johnson had betrayed the nation. The South was trying to reinstitute slavery by passing the notorious black codes; and only the Congress could be trusted to safeguard the rights of the slave and preserve the fruits of victory. Southern opinion, meanwhile, was convinced that the southern states had already met every reasonable demand and should be readmitted as quickly as possible. Under these circumstances, Congressional Reconstruction began. There were two further handicaps. Republicans in Congress were unwilling to break up the plantation system because respect for property rights was basic to their ideology. And northerners, while determined to give the former slaves some protection, were themselves racist. The limits of their sympathies for black people were quickly reached.

All things considered, it is a marvel that Reconstruction accomplished so much. The race question ran too deep to be resolved in so short a time. The South's economy was in a shambles. The task would perhaps have been impossible under the best circumstances. The schools and roads built, the hundreds and thousands fed, the protection given to life and property were not negligible achievements.

Suggested Readings

Recent books on Reconstruction start with Eric Foner's volume of that title (1988). Kenneth Stampp's *The Era of Reconstruction, 1865–1877* (1965) is also thorough on the Reconstruction years. An important study of the consequences of freedom for blacks is Leon F. Litwack's *Been in the Storm So Long: The Aftermath of Slavery* (1979). Michael Les Benedict, *The Impeachment and Trial of Andrew Johnson* (1973) is a superior analysis of the divisions and alignments within the Radical Reconstruction Congress and its relationships with the President, whom the author depicts unfavorably. See also Benedict's *A Compromise of Principle: Congressional Republicans and Reconstruction* (1974), which argues the radical Republicans found the Reconstruction measures mere compromises. C. Vann Woodward's *Reunion and Reaction* (1951) is about the Compromise of 1877. See also John Hope Franklin, *Reconstruction After the Civil War* (1961), William Gillette, *Retreat from Reconstruction* (1980), Eric McKitrick, *Andrew Johnson and Reconstruction* (1965), and Allen W. Trelease, *White Terror: The Ku Klux Klan Conspiracy and Southern Reconstruction* (1971). See also William E. Nelson, *The Fourteenth Amendment* (1988), and Richard Current, *Those Terrible Carpetbaggers* (1988).

On the Freedmen's Bureau see George R. Bentley, *A History of the Freedmen's Bureau* (1955) and William S. McFeely, *Yankee Step-Father: General O. O. Howard and the Freedmen's Bureau* (1968). A good state study is Joe Gray Taylor's *Louisiana Reconstructed, 1863–1877* (1974).

Herbert Gutman in *The Black Family in Slavery and Freedom* (1976) argues that even under slavery there was often a strong nuclear family with the father in charge. See also Hans Treffouse's excellent *Andrew Johnson: A Biography* (1989), William Gillette's *Retreat from Reconstruction, 1869–1879* (1979), and William S. McFeely's *Grant: A Biography* (1981).

☆ ☆ ☆ POINTS OF VIEW: ☆ ☆ ☆

Should Andrew Johnson Have Been Impeached?

Michael Les Benedict

As Americans for the first time seriously discussed the possibility of impeaching a president, they arrived at two opposing concepts of the law of impeachment. . . .

Democrats, Republicans who opposed impeachment, and most lawyers argued that a government officer could be impeached only for an act actually criminal, a violation of a criminal statute. Many historians have accepted this view as embodying the proper law of impeachment, accusing those who insisted on a broader interpretation of using impeachment wrongly in a purely political vendetta. But those who espoused the narrow view had an extremely difficult task in sustaining it, because in fact it was a novel argument, running counter to precedent, the overwhelming weight of American legal authority, and logic. . . .

Since legal authorities had almost unanimously adopted the broad view of impeachment, conservatives proceeded to the lawyerlike task of citing their testimony on questions not quite in point. They argued that the power of impeachment should be determined primarily by the words of the Constitution. The framers had authorized the House of Representatives to impeach government officers for "treason, bribery, or other high crimes and misdemeanors." Arguing that the language raised the presumption that impeachment lay only for actual crimes, despite the number of impeachments that seemed to imply the opposite, conservatives cited the great English constitutional commentators Blackstone, Wooddeson, and Hale to the effect that a crime was a violation of law and that laws must be known to the people. . . .

Radicals argued that the "misdemeanors" the Constitution referred to as grounds for impeachment included misfeasance and malfeasance in office as well as crimes indictable before criminal courts. . . .

The radicals' greatest strength resided in the unanimity with which the great American constitutional commentators had upheld the broad view of the impeachment power. . . .

As a practical matter, American constitutional commentators—[Supreme Court Justice Joseph] Story, [William A.] Duer, [James] Kent, [William] Rawle, and the authors of *The Federalist*—recognized that the maintenance of proper checks and balances in government, which they believed guaranteed liberty, depended upon the good faith and restraint of those entrusted with power. They recognized that the danger to liberty and the efficient workings of government lay not in the possibility that the president or lesser executive officers might act illegally, but rather that they might abuse the powers the Constitution *had* delegated to them. . . . The abuses commentators feared were precisely those "too artful to be anticipated by positive law, and sometimes too subtle and mysterious to be fully detected in the limited period of an ordinary investigation. . . ."

Had Republicans acted upon these doctrines, there can be no doubt that Andrew Johnson could have been impeached, tried, convicted, and removed at any time after December 1865, for his activities fitted precisely into the pattern Pomeroy, Rawle, and others had outlined. . . .

Historians have often interpreted the impeachment movement as part of a drive for congressional supremacy. Had it succeeded, some suggest, the government of the United States might have evolved into a parliamentary system. But in fact it had not been Congress but the President who had been claiming broad new powers. It was Andrew Johnson who had appointed provisional governors of vast territories without the advice and consent of the Senate, who had nullified congressional legislation, who claimed inherent quasi-legislative powers over Reconstruction. In many ways, Johnson was a very modern president, holding a view of presidential authority that has only recently been established. Impeachment was Congress's defensive weapon; it proved a dull blade, and the end result is that the only effective recourse against a president who ignores the will of Congress or exceeds his powers is democratic removal at the polls.

Michael Les Benedict, *The Impeachment and Trial of Andrew Johnson* (New York: W. W. Norton and Co., 1973). Reprinted by permission.

Hans L. Trefousse

So Johnson had won. . . . To find the reasons for his victory, the political situation and the circumstances of the trial must be kept in mind. True, the Republicans enjoyed an overwhelming majority in both houses, the president had forfeited much of his popularity, and the country was anxious to proceed with Reconstruction, but it proved impossible to convict the executive on the charges presented. In the first place, they were dubious. From the very beginning, Thaddeus Stevens himself realized their weakness. "As the Committee are likely to present no articles having any real vigor in them," he wrote [Representative Benjamin F.] Butler on February 28, "I submit to you if it is not worth our while to attempt to add at least two other articles." The result was the addition of the last two charges [one accusing Johnson of having brought Congress into disrepute and the other summarizing the previous charges], which even radical newspapers and editors criticized as a mere afterthought. . . .

The House should have waited a few days before acting, Representative Thomas A. Jenckes heard from his home in Rhode Island. "Johnson would then have been mad enough to commit some further misdemeanor upon which you could have prosecuted him with the certainty of convicting him." The charges added up to a "penny whistle affair," thought Benjamin B. French, and Senator John B. Henderson characterized them as counts of "narrow bounds in offense both in act and intent."

If the case was weak, the managers' conduct did not help. "The managers of the House of Representatives have been poor judges of human nature and poor readers of human motives," wrote the Chicago *Tribune* on May 9. One could hardly call Johnson a "great" criminal as they had done. Butler, who had vowed to try the case as he would a horse case, appeared aggressive and offensive. Because the managers had a poor case, they took refuge in various legal devices, a tactic seen as a confession of weakness.

Constitutional considerations also played a role in Johnson's acquittal. The genius of the American system was widely believed to be founded on the tripartite division of government. The legislative, executive, and judicial branches operated each in its proper sphere, and as the impeachment trial coincided with attacks on the Supreme Court, there was widespread fear of the danger of legislative supremacy. Assessing the case many years later, Edmund Ross came to the conclusion that "the impeachment of the President was an assault upon the principle of coordination that underlies our political system and thus a menace to our established political forms, as, if successful, it would, logically, have been the practical destruction of the Executive Department." And [Senator Lyman] Trumbull, in justifying his vote for acquittal, stated: "Once set the example of impeaching the President for what, when the excitement of the hour shall have subsided, will be regarded as insufficient causes . . . no future President will be safe who happens to differ with a majority of the House and two-thirds of the Senate on any measure deemed by them important, particularly if of political character. . . . what then becomes of the checks and balances of the Constitution, so carefully devised and so vital to its perpetuity? They are all gone."

The short time left of Johnson's term was also a factor. "To convict and depose a Chief Magistrate of a great country while his guilt was not made palpable by the record, and for insufficient cause, would be fraught with greater danger to the future of the country than can arise from leaving Mr. Johnson in office for the remaining months of his term," Trumbull wrote in his opinion. Conviction would not have benefited Grant, and the Republicans were now determined to elect him president. Thus Republicans failed to find Johnson guilty, as he had gambled they would.

And what had the president accomplished by his victory? Above all, he had succeeded in preserving the Constitution that he admired so much. No other president would ever again be impeached for political differences with Congress; the separation of powers was preserved, and the United States retained its presidential form of government, which set it apart from the cabinet systems of European countries.

Hans L. Trefousse, *Andrew Johnson: A Biography* (New York: W. W. Norton and Co., 1989). Reprinted by permission.

Driving the Golden Spike on May 10, 1869, at Promontory Point, Utah, joining the Union Pacific and Central Pacific lines and completing the first transcontinental railroad. *(Courtesy, Union Pacific Railroad Museum Collection, Omaha, Nebraska)*

CHAPTER 16

The American West 1865–1900

THE GOLDEN SPIKE: MAY 10, 1869

"What do we want with . . . this region of savages and wild beasts, of deserts of shifting sands and whirlwinds of dust, of cactus and prairie dogs?" asked Daniel Webster in 1845. "To what use could we ever put those endless mountain ranges, impenetrable and covered to their bases with eternal snow? What could we do with the western coast three thousand miles away, rockbound, cheerless and uninviting?" When Webster made this estimate of the value of California, the four hundred immigrants from the East who lived there knew nothing of the gold beneath their feet. To get there they had traveled for months over waterless plains and forbidding mountains, or sailed completely around the Americas, or made the dangerous crossing of the Panamanian isthmus. In 1855, the U.S. Army Engineers published in twelve detailed volumes *The Pacific Railroad Surveys of 1853–55*, which pointed out that California—its riches by then well known—could be conquered by a foreign power before military assistance would arrive from the East. With the coming of the Civil War, a federally subsidized transcontinental rail connection became a political and military necessity.

On July 1, 1862, Congress granted charters to two companies: the Union Pacific, to build westward from Omaha, and the Central Pacific, to build eastward from San Francisco, across the Sierras and through Nevada. Government aid, in the form of alternate sections of land along the right-of-way and government bonds for each mile of completed track, induced each company to race ahead so as to move the final meeting point as far into its competitor's territory as possible. The race was on.

The Union Pacific rolled steadily across the plains. In this flat country, nature was easy to subdue. Not so the Indians seeing their land about to be permanently split by steel rails. The Union Pacific organized its crews—which after the war swelled with ex-soldiers—in military fashion in order to be ready to fight off any trouble.

Meanwhile, the Central Pacific brutally shouldered its way up the Sierra Nevada, blasting and tunneling, indifferent to expense, winter storms, or workers' lives, hoping to reach the profitable flat plains where the government subsidies would be worth much more. Charles Crocker, relentless boss of the construction crews, had solved by hiring Chinese immigrants the problem of where to find tens of thousands of railroad workers in labor-scarce California. An associate had at first objected because the Chinese workers "were not masons," but Crocker lightly countered that the Chinese had built the greatest piece of masonry in the world—the Great Wall. They quickly proved their worth in breaching the great wall of the Sierra. In 1866–67, under white foremen, Crocker's work gangs crossed the mountain summit at the famous Donner Pass. Working furiously to get tunnel headings constructed before they were locked in snowdrifts, the crews continued throughout the winter, gouging out the insides of hill after hill.

The great "iron horse race" aroused extraordinary feats in 1868–69 as the two roads pushed ever closer. On a single day the Union Pacific crews, after elaborate preparation of men and teams and materials, laid over seven miles of track. Not to be outdone, Crocker boasted that his men would top ten miles in a day. On April 27, 1869, after the Central Pacific had spent days hauling material into place and rehearsing 4,000 men in their duties, an engine ran off the track, ending the day's proceedings. But the next morning at 7:00 a.m., railroad cars, small hand cars, horse teams, and disciplined crews began dropping rails and spikes along the prepared grade and eight Irish rail handlers started moving rails into place. As the rails were bolted by Chinese gangs, fresh rails were hauled along the new track and the process was repeated. Maintaining a frantic pace, this collective John Henry advanced six miles before the foremen called a halt for lunch. Working more slowly through the afternoon, the crews by seven in the evening had added ten miles and fifty-six feet of new track. The rail handlers, heroes of the day, had each lifted 125 tons of iron in that one long march.

The two lines met reluctantly, on May 10, 1869, at Promontory Point, Utah, on the northern shore of the Great Salt Lake. The meeting had in fact been scheduled for May 8, and then delayed by rain. In San Francisco and Sacramento, plans for festivities for the 8th had advanced too far to be canceled, and those two points on the new transcontinental route were forced to celebrate the momentous event for three days. Elaborate national preparations included wiring the final spike, made of pure gold, to the Western Union telegraph system so that the blows of the hammer could register throughout the nation. In several cities, cannon were wired to the telegraph to detonate from the blow thousands of miles away. The man given the honor of striking the blow—Leland Stanford, ex-governor of California and president of the Central Pacific—was not up to the occasion: he missed the spike. The local telegraph operator closed the circuit anyhow, so that the cannons, bells, and whistles blasted across the nation on schedule. Stanford, a practical man even if not adept with a hammer, talked more plainly of transporting "coarse, heavy and cheap products for all distances at living rates to the trade." The golden spike was a fit symbol for a nation that had endured four bloody years to remain indivisible.

Proud Americans who crossed the continent on the silver rails added their descriptions in diaries and letters: "My boyish dreams were realized," one man recorded:

> For hours, at the school desk, have I pondered over the map and wandered, in imagination, with Lewis and Clark, the hunters and trappers and early emigrants, away off to these Rocky Mountains, about which such a mystery seemed to hang,—dreaming, wishing and hoping against hope, that my eyes might, some day, behold their snow-crowned heights. And here lay the first great range in the pureness of white; distant, to be sure, but there it lay, enshrined in beauty.

Rain and snow were exciting events. The train on which Harvey Rice was journeying in 1869 ran through a violent Great Plains thunderstorm:

> The heavens became, suddenly, as black as starless midnight. The lightning flashed in every direction, and electric balls of fire rolled over the plains. It seemed as if the artillery of heaven had made the valley a target and that we were doomed to instant destruction. But happily our fears were soon dissipated. The storm was succeeded by a brilliant rainbow.

Engineer Cy Warman told of bucking an eighteen-foot snow drift with double engines so hard that his locomotive trembled and shook as if it were about to be crushed to pieces:

> Often when we came to a stop only the top of the stack of the front engine would be visible. . . . All this time the snow kept coming down, day and night, until the only signs of a railroad across the range were the tops of the telegraph poles.

Passengers recorded the resounding names: Castle Rock, Hanging Rock, Pulpit Rock, Devil's Gate, Devil's Slide, Horsethief Trail. Along the way lay reminders of the pioneers: solitary grave markers, the bones of long-dead horses or oxen, broken wagon wheels, relics of a time that the railroad was consigning to history.

Filling in the Continent

Between the Civil War and 1900 Americans enormously increased the lands they effectively occupied. In 1865 the continental United States had already reached its present three million square miles, but vast expanses remained virtually empty of people. In the next thirty-five years the population swept across the sparsely settled plains. By the beginning of the twentieth century the United States had not only filled in its continental limits; it had expanded its land area to 3.6 million square miles by acquiring nonadjacent territory, such as Alaska and Hawaii. Besides this, it had extended its influence and economic power far beyond the borders of the parochial nation that had renewed its bonds at Appomattox Courthouse.

The Plains and the Great Basin

The Great Plains are an enormous flat plateau rising gradually from the Mississippi River to about 5,000 feet above sea level, where it reaches the edge of the Rocky Mountains. The Great Basin to the west of the Plains is a vast shallow bowl dotted with a few mountainous regions between the eastern Rockies and the Sierra-Cascade ranges of California, Oregon, and Washington. Both regions are deficient in rainfall; the Basin approaches true desert in places. And both are treeless, except along stream banks or in other especially moist spots. The Plains are covered with short grass; the Basin is sprinkled with sagebrush, cacti, and creosote brushes. The Plains rivers are shallow, especially in the fall. In the Basin, the few streams have water only in the spring, when melt-off from mountain snows fills their banks. None of these has any ocean connection. They simply die in some sink hole where the water gives out.

The weather of the Plains and Great Basin can most charitably be described as interesting. The climate is of the type geographers called "continental." Winters are often fiercely cold, with temperatures plunging to as low as forty degrees below zero. On the Plains, the frost comes with roaring blizzards covering the land with a white layer that sometimes drifts roof-high. Springs are fre-

"Down the Sierra Nevadas," 1865, etching. *(Courtesy, Scribner's Archives)*

quently balmy, with the ground covered by a carpet of wildflowers brought forth by melting snow or brief rains; they are usually short, however, followed by brutally hot summers when temperatures climb into the nineties and the sun beats down remorselessly from cloudless skies. Among the more disturbing characteristics of the region's climate and weather is its inconsistency. In the arid Basin, where rainfall seldom exceeds one or two inches per year, a sudden cloudburst can pour down the average yearly allotment in an hour or two. The Plains do not usually experience such deluges, but rainfall can vary sharply from year to year and decade to decade. Some periods are quite dry and drought-afflicted. These will be followed by extended periods of abundant rainfall, when the grass remains green and copious for much of the year.

The Plains and Basin have sheltered a profusion of animals. Antelope, rabbits, gophers, squirrels, wolves, and coyotes were once found everywhere. Along many streams, especially at the mountain edges, were beaver with thick, soft pelts prized as raw material for felt hats. The most visible and abundant of all the Plains animals were the bison or American buffalo, the "natural cattle" of the North American grasslands.

For the native peoples of the region, the buffalo were an extraordinary asset. Fresh buffalo meat was a staple of their diet. Dried meat, sliced thin, was carried on long trips, along with pemmican—dried meat mixed with berries, fat, and marrow and stuffed into a buffalo-gut bag. Buffalo skins served as clothing and as the walls of tents, or tepees, and were used to make containers of various kinds. Buffalo sinews became rope and bowstrings. Even buffalo droppings, or chips, were valuable: when dried, they made an excellent fuel on the treeless Plains. It was "a rather hard matter," wrote one pioneer woman, "that the Buffalo should furnish the meat and then the fuel to cook it."

Although only thinning herds of buffalo remained near the Union Pacific right-of-way after train travel began, the iron horses of the Kansas Pacific occasionally were surrounded by buffalo and had to slow down or wait until the herd passed. In its early days, the Kansas Pacific engineers willingly stopped trains to permit the passengers to leave the cars and shoot at passing buffalo.

Developing the West

Visions of land had brought the first European colonists to America in the seventeenth century, and that same dream pushed their descendants across the continent in the eighteenth and nineteenth centuries. In pursuit of Manifest Destiny, the United States in the 1840s acquired title to Texas, the Far West, and the Southwest. After the Civil War those

Ada McCall gathering buffalo chips near Lakin, Kansas. *(Courtesy, The Kansas State Historical Society)*

areas began to fill up with settlers. Millions of Americans wanted land out west, and it became the express purpose of federal and state governments to assist and finance them.

Government Policy Because railroad building required enormous capital investment, those governments donated land to help finance construction. The subsidies began in 1830 with the first state land grants, and in 1871 the federal government issued its final grant to the Texas & Pacific Railroad. During those years seventy railroads received title to 130 million acres of public domain land. Providing access to the transportation network, railroad land was prime property, and the railroads sold it as quickly as possible to incoming settlers.

The federal government also made it progressively easier for settlers to acquire land. The Homestead Act of 1862 provided 160 acres of free public domain land to a settler agreeing to live on the claim. Congressional legislation in 1870 permitted the sale of federal mineral lands for $2.50 an acre, and the Desert Land Act of 1877 allowed settlers to acquire up to 640 acres of free land in more arid regions. Many lumber companies used this legislation to acquire land for themselves.

Water Policy The dry climate of the Great Plains, Great Basin, and Southwest posed formidable obstacles to land development, since possession of water rights determined who throve and who perished. Water law became dominated by what has become known as the "Prior Appropriation Doctrine." It allocated water rights on the basis of beneficial use. The individual who first put water to beneficial use retained rights to that water for as long as the use continued. During periods of water shortages, these senior users were allowed to consume all of their appropriation before junior users received any water.

Water development, then, was a priority of public policy. If the arid West was going to fill up with large numbers of small farmers, they had to have water. Without some type of federal legislation, most of the water would end up in the hands of a privileged few. To promote the dry West as an attractive place for settlement, Congress passed the Carey Act of 1894, which ceded millions of acres of public domain lands to the states. With the proceeds from the sale of those lands, the state governments were supposed to embark on ambitious water development projects. When the states failed to establish workable programs, Congress passed the Newlands Act (Reclamation Act) of 1902, which set up the Reclamation Service and charged it with the obligation of seeing to the construction of flood control, irrigation, and river development projects throughout the West.

The results of the land and water development legislation were dramatic. In 1840 only one percent of the non-Indian population of the United States—perhaps 175,000 people—had lived west of the Mississippi River, but forty years later there were more than ten million people there, approximately twenty percent of the population. Between 1862 and 1904, those settlers established titles to more than 755 million acres of land. The pioneers, convinced like other Americans of their right to property, were determined to acquire a chunk of it in the West. They were also relatively indifferent to the possibility that any race or people unlike themselves might have a prior claim to it. Relatively few of them set out for the frontier hoping to injure the Indian or Mexican inhabitants living there. They simply wanted to better themselves—to leave something behind for their children. But the collective impact of millions of well-meaning settlers moving across the landscape with the backing of the government was a political and economic catastrophe for the original inhabitants of the American West.

The Native Peoples

Before the coming of the whites, 250 to 300 thousand Indians had inhabited the region, divided into many major tribes and dozens of bands.

"Digger Indians" The major tribes of the Basin included the Bannock, Shoshoni, Paiute, Ute, and Snake. Theirs was a harsh environment where agriculture was impossible without a highly developed social organization to promote irrigation.

Among these peoples, tribes existed as linguistic entities, but they were not usually joined politically. The only true social unit was the extended family of about twenty-five to thirty individuals. There were no chiefs, only talkers, influential men considered wise and worthy of being consulted. Each winter a group of families might gather together to take shelter in some especially warm spot. During these months they formed loose personal and group connections. But in the spring these villages would break up. The Basin peoples lived almost entirely by food-gathering supplemented by a little hunting. In the spring they would collect edible plants in the valleys. Later they would wander to higher land where they gathered berries, nuts, seeds, and roots. They also ate lizards, mice, birds, and grasshoppers. Their use of sticks to extract roots got them the name "Digger Indians."

The Basin peoples lived in brush huts and even in hollowed-out depressions in the earth. Their clothing was rudimentary. The men wore breechcloths; the women, an apron of milkweed fiber. Often both wore nothing at all. They had baskets, but no pottery. They lacked any sort of domesticated animals.

Plains Indians At the eastern fringes of the region, the Great Basin tribes merged with the more numerous Indians of the Plains. Originally an agricultural people, the Plains Indians by about 1500 had become, except in the more humid eastern parts, overwhelmingly nomadic hunter-gatherers whose chief source of sustenance was the buffalo. About 1700 this nomadic pattern was reinforced by the arrival of horses, strays from the Spanish lands at the northern edges of Mexico. He is "awkward on the ground," a painter wrote of the Plains Indian, but "the moment he lays his hand upon a horse, his face . . . becomes handsome, and he gracefully flies away like a different being."

Canyon de Chelly, New Mexico, walls of the Grand Canyon about 1200 feet in height, 1873. *(Courtesy, Scribner's Archives)*

The Plains Indians are the classic redmen of American legend. Tall, bronzed, well-muscled, hawk-nosed, wearing fringed leather clothing and feathered war bonnets, living in colorfully decorated tepees, magnificent horsemen, renowned as marksmen with the bow and arrow, they have entered our folk history as the worthy opponents of the cavalry or the cowboy. There were many Plains tribes. To the north, spilling over into Canada, were the Blackfeet, a confederation of several tribes. Adjacent were the Crows. In western South Dakota and Nebraska, as well as parts of Montana and Wyoming, were the various bands of the Sioux. South of these were the Cheyenne, while on the southern Plains lived the Comanches, Kiowas, and Kiowa-Apaches. At the opening of the nineteenth century the Plains culture, as white Americans came to know it, had fully emerged. The Plains tribes decorated their leather clothing with beads, quills, eagle feathers, and pictures; they recorded important occurrences and drew calendars with paint on leather. Many of their tepees were large structures with abundant room for a whole family.

Social organization was more complex than that of the Basin peoples. Tribes, many of them large, were guided by chiefs, though ruled by councils of leading men. The typical social unit was the band of a few hundred, rather than the tribe. Within the bands there was often a multitude of male societies that resembled white men's lodges, with regalia, ceremonies, officers, and songs. The societies were also charged with the authority to police behavior.

Unlike the Indians farther west, the Plains people gave scope to the full tribe. Periodically there were gatherings of whole tribal groups where people visited, gambled, played games, raced, met in councils, and shared in religious ceremonies. Many of the Plains tribes performed a ritual called the Sun Dance, usually held in the summer. Sun

Dance performers gathered near a painted pole and danced for days without food and water until they fell down exhausted. The purpose of the dance was to produce a trance and visions. Some tribes sought to produce trances or religious ecstasy by self-torture that included suspension from a sacred tree by skewers inserted through slits in the chest.

White-Indian Relations

The first white intrusion came well before the Civil War. During the war itself, the railroads began to penetrate the region, stimulating wide bands of settlement along their rights-of-way. To protect the railroads and then the settlers, the federal government established numerous army posts that became centers of white culture and points of contact between white and red peoples.

The Indians both feared whites and admired them. Many Indians could see that the future belonged to the whites, and many wanted to acquire some of their ways. The horse, a contribution of European whites, was, of course, a splendid animal for enabling the tribes to travel and bring along heavy loads. Acquiring food became less of a problem. Sometimes Indians took the white man's vices. Ever since the colonial period, rum and brandy had been used in the Indian trade, and by the end of the nineteenth century drinking had become a chronic problem among some tribes.

In general, Anglo-Saxons—unlike the French, Spanish, and other Latins—did not sexually mingle with Indians. In this American Protestants were acting in accord with their general cultural provincialism. More compelling as a reason for antagonism was greed. The Indians had what the whites wanted—land, millions of acres of the finest land on earth. To the western farmer or the land speculator, the presence of the original inhabitants was an obstacle in the way of livelihood and profit. But even many people not directly involved in western development asked whether a few thousand "primitives" should be allowed to retain so much of America's rich resources while each year the nation's white population grew at an explosive rate. Undoubtedly there was a large element of cultural chauvinism in this. Yet by white standards, the retention of so much of the West by a few thousand hunter-gatherer nomads seemed a criminal waste of resources.

Red Armed Panther, Cheyenne Scout. Efforts to force Cheyennes and Arapahos into smaller land areas than promised sparked an Indian war in 1861. *(Courtesy, The Huffman Pictures, Coffrin's Old West Gallery, Miles City, Montana)*

Greed and contempt were not the sole white responses to the Indians. Generally the most aggressive opponents of Indian claims were westerners. Easterners could afford to be more generous and philosophical, and by the mid-nineteenth century many sincerely regretted the way the Indians had been treated. Few of these people actually wanted to leave the great West permanently in the hands of the tribes, but they did wish to guarantee fair treatment. Many also hoped that the Indians could be weaned away from their traditional nomadism, "civilized," and confined to settled compact agricultural communities where they could support themselves as small farmers like other Americans. Yet earlier in the century the Cherokees, who had actually conformed to this prescription, had been swept aside from their Georgia lands anyway.

Mexican Americans In addition to confronting several hundred thousand American Indians on the frontier, the pioneers encountered around 90,000 to 100,000 Mexican Americans living in the Southwest. Beginning in the late seventeenth century, Hispanic pioneers had moved north out of New Spain and then Mexico. When the Treaty of Guadalupe Hidalgo ended the Mexican War in 1848, approximately 50,000 of them lived in and around Santa Fe, New Mexico, while another 30,000 were split evenly between south Texas and the coast of California. The vast majority of Mexican Americans were small farmers, although there were large estates and business communities in cities like San Antonio, Santa Fe, and San Francisco. The Treaty of Guadalupe Hidalgo guaranteed them citizenship in the United States, freedom of religion, and protection of their land titles. But guarantees of citizenship and property were little protection when millions of Anglo pioneers settled in the West after the Civil War.

The Plains Indians Subdued

Indian Policy Before the Civil War, the government's Indian policy had at first been based on the idea of a permanent Indian domain west of the Mississippi into which whites would not intrude. In the late 1840s, after thousands of whites began to cross the Plains on their way to Oregon and California, the policy gave way to a plan of establishing Indian reservations, the land between being made available to settlers. Meanwhile, the migrants to California and Oregon pushed through the tribal territories, altering the environment and economy of the Indians. In the Treaty of Fort Laramie, the

General George Armstrong Custer, whose bravado exceeded his wisdom, did not hesitate to attack a much larger force of Sioux Indians at the Little Big Horn River. It was his last stand. *(Courtesy, Anheuser-Busch, Inc.)*

Plains tribes, in exchange for a promised long-term federal subsidy, agreed to move to reservations. The new arrangement did not preserve peace. Whites encroached on Indian lands; Indians found the reservations too confining after their free roaming life.

During the Civil War General John Pope, the failed commander of the Union Army of Virginia, set about to subdue the Sioux of the northern Plains, an Indian group not yet brought under the reservation policy. After Sioux attacks on several Minnesota towns, Pope ordered his deputy, Colonel Henry Sibley, to make an example of the Sioux. "They are," he ordered, "to be treated as maniacs or wild beasts, and by no means as people with whom treaties or compromises can be made." Sibley attacked the Indians in September 1862 and captured 1,800 warriors, more than 300 of whom he condemned to death. President Lincoln reprieved all but thirty-eight, to the disgust of Minnesota settlers.

War Other troubles soon followed. Efforts to force the Cheyenne and Arapaho into smaller land areas than those promised sparked an Indian war throughout Colorado Territory in 1861. A Sioux chief, Spotted Tail, later remarked:

> We do not like to live like the white man. . . . The Great Spirit gave us hunting grounds, gave us the buffalo, the elk, the deer, and the antelope. Our fathers have taught us to hunt and live on the plains and we are contented.

In late November 1864 the Colorado militia under Colonel John Chivington, a former preacher, surrounded a friendly band of Cheyenne at Sand Creek in eastern Colorado Territory, and attacked them without provocation. The militia fired volleys at the men. Women and children who fled to nearby caves were dragged out to be knifed or shot. An Indian trader at the scene later testified:

> They were scalped, the brains knocked out; the men used their knives, ripped open women, clubbed little children, knocked them in the head with their guns, beat their brains out, mutilated their body in every sense of the word.

Only fifty escaped the bestial Chivington massacre. For the next three years many of the Plains tribes went to war.

In 1867 President Johnson appointed a commission that patched up a peace. During the next thirty years the military commanders at the Plains army posts had to deal frequently with hostile tribesmen who found the reservations confining and longed to return to their old ways. A few of the commanders were insensitive or cruel men; officers like General Oliver O. Howard and George Crook, however, were men of their word whom many Indians respected. But they had the thankless task of defending every renegade white man, however brutal he had been toward the Indians, and of enforcing the basically harsh reservation policy.

In this period, as in preceding centuries, white Americans disgraced themselves in their treatment of the Indians. But lest we romanticize the beleaguered Indian, driven from his ancestral home by greed and bigotry, remember also the tales of Indian cruelty and of sudden violence inexplicable to whites. The history of relations between Indians and settlers in this country reflects badly, not solely on the white race or on the red, but on the human race.

A series of Indian depredations, raids, and pitched battles lasted until the 1890s. Indians inflicted heavy casualties on the United States Army. In 1866 they had wiped out Captain William Fetterman's detachment of eighty men on the Bozeman Trail. In 1876 General George Custer's troop of 265 men set out after Sitting Bull's Sioux warriors, who had left their reservations in protest against the government's allowing gold prospectors to trespass on their reservation in the Black Hills. The megalomaniacal Custer encountered the Sioux at the Little Big Horn River and foolishly attacked the much larger force of Indians. Custer and his band were wiped out to a man. White Bull recounted the engagement:

> The fight lasted only a short time. All of us were crazy. We had killed many soldiers. They had attacked us and meant to wipe us out. We were fighting for our lives and homeland. Cries of victory went up. Our women came through the timber by the river and began to strip the dead soldiers. Some of the sisters and wives and mothers of slain warriors cut the bodies of the soldiers to pieces. They were crazy with sorrow.

Cruelties and brutalities were committed on both sides. One scholar maintains that between 1798 and 1898 whites killed some 4,000 Indians, while the Indians themselves killed some seven thousand soldiers and civilians. These figures, however, do not include the many Indians who died by starvation and disease as a result of federal policy. Nor do they take it into account that the white killers were the advance forces of a culture that perceived itself as advanced and humane.

The Nez Percé One case involved the Nez Percé of the far Northwest, who contradicted almost every stereotype of the Indian. Ensconced in the narrow valleys between the Cascade and Bitterroot mountains (lands now parts of Idaho, Washington, and Oregon), they apparently never attacked settlers before their great war with the whites in 1877. Their forebears had aided Lewis and Clark in 1805. In 1831 the Nez Percé sent a delegation to St. Louis to discover the source of the white man's "medicine." They welcomed outsiders and were quick to learn from them. The tribe even survived a gold rush into its lands in the 1860s, remaining at peace despite numerous outrages by the miners. Nonetheless, friction sharpened in the 1860s as cattle ranchers eyed lands on which Indian horses grazed. In 1863 the federal government negotiated a treaty to delimit Indian land titles, but a group of braves, loosely led by Old Joseph, the father of a more famous Joseph, rejected it. Turning away from the Christianity they had learned from missionaries, they began a peaceful but determined resistance to the white man's designs on their ancestral lands. "My son," Old Joseph whispered as he lay dying,

> you are the chief. . . . You must stop your ears whenever you are asked to sign a treaty selling your home. . . . This country holds your father's body. Never sell the bones of your father and your mother.

Chief Joseph was ever true to this stern injunction. Although he struggled to avoid con-

SITTING BULL'S TRANCE

This secondhand account describes Sitting Bull's preparation for the famous encounter where he wiped out the forces of General George Custer at the Battle of the Little Big Horn (1876).

SITTING BULL WENT OUT one day in the hope of being able to communicate with the "Great Spirit." On the second night he was seized with a strange feeling, and near morning he met the Great Spirit, clad in a beautiful robe. His hair flowed upon his shoulders and reached almost to his feet. When Sitting Bull beheld this wonderful apparition, he fainted and had a strange dream. He related his story of the trance thus:

"The Great Spirit appeared to me with a formidable band of Sioux, who have long since been dead, and they danced, inviting me to join them. Presently I was restored to my senses, and the Great Spirit talked with me. He asked me if the Indians would not be glad to see their dead ancestors and the buffalo restored to them, and to life. I assured him that they would be deeply gratified. Then the Great Spirit told me that he once came to save the white race, but that they had persecuted him; and now he had come to save and rescue the defenseless and long-persecuted Indian race. All day the Great Spirit gave me evidence of his power and instructed me.

"He said that the white men would come to take me, but as they approached the soil would become quicksand, and the men and horses would sink. He showed me how to make medicine to put on war-shirts to turn aside the bullets of the white man. He told me the Indians had suffered long enough, and that he was now coming for their deliverance. We are to occupy the earth again, which has been taken from us. Great herds of buffalo will wander about as they did long ago, and the Indian who now sleeps in death will rise again, and forever wander over the earth. There will be no reservation; no messenger from the government to say to the Indians, come back here, stay here, starve here on this spot of ground.

"The Great Spirit said that the Indians must keep dancing; that the earth was theirs at his command, and for all this privilege, they must dance the dances which are pleasing to him. He said that all the Indians who would not listen to his words, or refuse to join in the ceremonies which are pleasing to him, will be destroyed with the white race."

flict, his people's fate was all too typical: rapacious settlers pressing for land, unfeeling Indian agents, bungling in governmental departments, an unsympathetic general, a forced and hurried evacuation of their lands, and finally young braves driven to fury and terrible violence. Once at war, Joseph and his tribe enacted one of the great feats of military prowess and human endurance (for this army traveled with its women and children, its sick and aged.) A United States Army ROTC instruction manual describes Joseph's achievement: "In 11 weeks, he had moved his tribe 1600 miles, engaged 10 separate U.S. commands in 13 battles and skirmishes, and in nearly every instance had either defeated them or fought them to a stand-still." Joseph and fewer than two hundred braves withstood an army. The effort, of course, was doomed, and with its failure, the Nez Percé would no longer exist as an independent people. Chief Joseph surrendered on October 5, 1877. His memorable speech gave all the reasons:

> I am tired of fighting. Our chiefs are killed. Looking Glass is dead. The old men are all killed. It is the young men who say yes or no. He who led the young men is dead. It is cold and we have no blankets. The little children are freezing to death. My people, some of them, have run away to the hills and have no blankets, no food; no one knows where they are, perhaps freezing to death. I want time to look for my children and see how many of them I can find. Maybe I shall find them among the dead. Hear me, my chiefs, I am tired; my heart is sick and sad. From where the sun now stands. I will fight no more forever.

For all his fame as a guerrilla leader, Chief Joseph was essentially a diplomat. When the United States government immediately reneged on the terms under which he had surrendered, shipping the tribe to Indian Territory (the present state of Oklahoma), Joseph began a careful and patient campaign to return his people to their mountain home. While he never succeeded in regaining his beloved Wallowa Valley—Old Joseph's gravesite—after five years of direct interviews with the President, the secretary of the interior, and numerous congressmen, and by enlisting the editorial support of several eastern journals, he did get his dispirited and rapidly decreasing tribe back to the mountains where they could thrive again. In his new home in western Washington, Joseph became an Indian elder statesman, a national symbol of courage and freedom. He returned to the Wallowa Valley but once, in 1900, an old man. There he found only the consolation that a settler—a man with, as he said, "a spirit too rare among his kind"—had enclosed and cared for his father's grave.

The Decline of the Buffalo

In the end, it was not the army that subdued the Plains Indians. It was the destruction of the buffalo. So long as the tribes could hunt the great shaggy beasts, they could survive off the reservations. Once the buffalo were killed off, the dependence of the Indians on white largesse became almost complete.

During the building of the great western railroads, tens of thousands of buffalo were killed for food and sport. Then in 1871 a Pennsylvania tanner discovered that buffalo skins made good leather. With hides selling at two to three dollars apiece, a hunter could make a fine profit slaughtering the beasts. Soon groups of hunters accompanied by wagons were swarming over the Plains, often killing fifty or more a day, skinning them, and leaving the carcasses to rot. Between 1872 and 1874 alone, some nine million animals were killed. By 1878 the southern herd was no more; by 1883 the northern herd was gone. In 1903, in the place of all the millions that had once thundered across the Plains, there survived a known total of thirty-four bison.

Without the buffalo the Indians were tied down to the reservation. Yet even now they were not completely subjugated. In 1890 the Teton Sioux of South Dakota faced hunger as a result of drought and congressional stinginess. They fell under the spell of a prophet, Wovoka, who told them that if they performed certain dances the dead would be resurrected, white men driven out, and Indian lands restored. The "Ghost Dancers" alarmed the local whites, who called for troops. The soldiers, in turn, frightened the Indians, who came under the influence of aggressive Sioux warriors. "If the soldiers surround you," one warrior promised, "three of you, on whom I have put holy shirts, will sing a song around them, then some of them will drop dead. Then the rest will start to run, but their horses will sink into the earth." The upshot of all this was the massacre at Wounded Knee, when soldiers armed with repeat-firing Gatling guns mowed down at least 146 Indians of both sexes, young and old.

A Sioux educated in New England wrote of

This watercolor, painted in about 1858, shows Indians driving buffalo over a cliff. At a similar site in Montana, archaeologists have counted some one half million buffalo skeletons most of which are from pre-Columbian times. *(Courtesy, Walters Art Gallery, Baltimore)*

what he saw on a bright New Year's Day in 1891:

> On the day following the Wounded Knee massacre, there was a blizzard. On the third day it cleared, and the ground was covered with fresh snow. We had feared that some of the wounded Indians had been left on the field, and a number of us volunteered to go and see.
>
> Fully three miles from the scene of the massacre, we found the body of a woman completely covered with a blanket of snow, and from this point we found them scattered along as they had been hunted down and slaughtered. When we reached the spot where the Indian camp had stood, among the fragments of burned tents and other belongings, we saw the frozen bodies lying close together or piled one upon another. I counted eighty bodies of men, who were almost as helpless as the women and babes when the deadly [gun] fire began, for nearly all their guns had been taken from them.
>
> Although they had been lying in the snow and cold for two days and nights, a number had survived. Among them I found a baby of about a year old, warmly wrapped and entirely unhurt. Under a wagon, I discovered an old woman, totally blind and helpless. . . .

Indian "Reform"

Although Wounded Knee was the last actual Indian battle, the Indian issue did not go away. For nearly three centuries American economic interests—farmers and later railroads and timber and mining companies—worked diligently at seizing land from the Indians. They preferred taking the land peacefully, but if violence was necessary, the settlers and their companies were usually more than willing to resort to it. But many Americans hated the genocidal ravings of the economic interest groups and wanted to end the violence by assimilating Indians into the larger society—converting them to Christianity, awarding them citizenship, and helping them make the transition to the ways of a modern economy. Congress took the first step toward assimilation by passing legislation transferring Indian affairs from the Department of State to the Department of the Interior. No longer would Indian tribes be treated as sovereign nations. Nor would the United States government ever again sign treaties with them. The reformers worked through such organizations as the Indian Rights Association to awaken concern for the Indian. Particularly effective was *A Century of Dishonor* (1881), by the novelist Helen Hunt Jackson.

In the late nineteenth century, the reform panacea was known as "allotment." To bring about assimilation, Congress passed the Dawes Severalty Act of 1887, dividing reservations into smaller allotments—usually 160 acres—which would be awarded to each Indian family. With their allotment of land, Indians would also receive United States citizenship. Reformers hoped the Indians would become small farmers like millions of whites.

The Dawes Severalty Act received widespread support from reformers committed to protecting Indians as well as from economic interest groups out to take their land, primarily because of a provision to distribute "excess" reservation land to whites. In 1887, for example, the Sisseton Sioux of South Dakota owned 918,000 acres of rich virgin farm land on their reservation. But since there were only 2,000 members of the tribe, the Dawes Act left about 600,000 acres available for white families. In short order the Department of the Interior opened the surplus Sisseton land to white farmers, who moved in among the Indians. In 1887, when the federal government launched the allotment program, American Indians controlled more than 138 million acres of land on their reservations. When the allotment program ended in 1934, the Indians had forty-eight million acres left, and most of that in the arid deserts of the Southwest.

Besides setting up the allotment program, Congress appropriated money for establishing special schools where Indian youths could learn the white man's agricultural and mechanical trades. Frequently finding it difficult to lead Indian men out of their customary ways and attitudes, reformers put considerable effort into the education of Indian women. Members of the Bureau of Indian Affairs in Washington insisted that the best way to bring the Indians to the modern world was to transform the women into proper domestic beings who could raise the next generation acting in accord with white society's values. The women were to be trained in the white American way of performing such domestic work as spinning, sewing, housekeeping, and child rearing. This approach essentially embodied the attitude of the social workers who also would try to teach immigrant women to be proper American wives and mothers.

The policy of assimilation, which violated Indian traditions, was eventually abandoned. At the time all it accomplished was the destruction of tribal life and the further demoralization of the Indians. Yet as a policy humane in intent it may have saved the Indian from grosser exploitation.

Hispanics

The Mexican peoples of California, Texas, and New Mexico did not receive much more consideration at the hands of the incoming Anglo settlers. Their inclination and that of the authorities was to see Hispanic inhabitants as being, along with Indians, an inconvenience to be brushed aside as neatly as possible.

Anglo settlers migrated in peak numbers during the first years of the Gold Rush, and the Mexican inhabitants of California, who were known as *californios,* were soon greatly outnumbered. When the gold rush played out, tens of thousands of Anglo immigrants squatted on *californio* land. To resolve the question of title, the state legislature passed the Land Act of 1851, creating a Board of Land Commissioners to mediate conflicting claims. The board was hopelessly biased. The commissioners were all Anglos, the hearings were conducted in English, and the burden of proof rested on the *californio* owners, not the Anglo squatters. By 1860 the board had turned more than four million acres of land over to the Anglo squatters. When the board decided in favor of the *californio* owners, the squatters often resorted to the federal court system, where cases took an average of seventeen years to resolve. During the litigation, the squatters were allowed to remain on the land.

Ethnic relations were even worse in Texas. The state legislature and local townships imposed heavy taxes on Mexican land owned by Mexican Americans, and when they failed to pay and went into default, county sheriffs auctioned their land to Anglo owners. Intimidation was common. During the second half of the nineteenth century theTexas Rangers may have killed nearly 5,000 *tejanos,* as the Mexican in Texas were called. In hundreds of cases the Rangers simply helped Anglos dislodge *tejanos* from the land. Richard King was one of the Texas robber barons who used the Rangers to secure his land claims. The son of poor Irish immigrants, King moved to South Texas and founded the King Ranch. In 1852 he bought the 15,000-acre Santa Gertrudis Grant for two cents an acre, and as president of the Stock Raisers Association of Western Texas he eventually increased his holdings to more than 600,000 acres. Similar events occurred throughout South Texas, and by 1880 only two of the wealthiest 300 landowners in the state were *tejanos.* The transfer of land was nearly complete.

In New Mexico, the Santa Fe Ring seized control of much *nuevo mexicano* land between 1860 and 1890. The ring was a small clique of Anglo bankers, merchants, and lawyers who were closely tied to the wealthiest twenty *nuevo mexicano* landowners and controlled the territorial legislature. Like their Hispanic counterparts in California and Texas, many *nuevo mexicanos* found themselves facing heavy property taxes, high interest rates, tax auctions, and land losses. To deal with the controversy, Congress created the Court of Private Land Claims for New Mexico, Colorado, and Arizona in 1891, but the proceedings were conducted in English and the burden of proof rested on *nuevo mexicano* owners, not the Anglo claimants. Between 1892 and 1905 the court evaluated 301 claims and found for the Anglo 226 times.

The Gold Frontier

The departure of the Indians and the buffalo opened the trans-Mississippi West to white exploitation. First to arrive had been the miners and prospectors who streamed to Colorado when gold was discovered there in 1849 and then moved on to western Nevada, Idaho's Snake River Valley, and western Montana when further deposits were discovered in those areas. Many of these men came to the Great Basin and the Plains from the diggings in California, having failed to find wealth there or having found and lost it. Other adventurers departed from Missouri River towns. Each of these river towns did a land-office business outfitting and supplying the gold-seekers. An observer reported of one: "The streets are full of people buying flour, bacon, groceries, with wagons and out-

***Result of a Miss Deal*, by Frederic Remington.**

fits, and all around the town are little camps preparing to go west."

Mining Towns Few who joined in these rushes and later ones—Leadville in 1870, Black Hills in 1874, Coeur D'Alene in 1883—ever saw many golden flakes in their pans. "The stories you hear frequently," one gold seeker wrote home, "are the most extravagant lies imaginable—the mines are humbug . . . the almost universal feeling is to get home." Another wrote more joyfully:

> It would astonish you to see a town grow up out here. You old fashioned people in the States would go crazy. . . . Some of the most desirable lots [in California] sold at first for $250, now command from $10–$15,000. I saw a hole 20 ft. deep out of which $50,000 has been taken. I am worth now about $10,000.

Some of the unlucky drifted on to the next strike. Those who did strike it rich—and some of those who did not—stayed on and became the founders of Denver, Boise, Helena, and other flourishing cities that grew up around the mining camps.

The most striking feature of the mining towns was the absence of women. At first, generally, there were no women at all, and when one put in an appearance, miners would come to gape at her. Soon, contingents of "fancy women" arrived—dance-hall girls and prostitutes—to help relieve the miners of their newly-gained wealth. Eventually, when and if the mining camp became a permanent community, respectable women arrived: wives, sisters, and mothers, as well as a few schoolteachers, seamstresses, and shopkeepers. The arrival of such women usually marked the end of the initial disorderly and unstructured phase of a mining town's existence.

In their early years the towns were cosmopolitan places where professional men and scholars mingled with roughnecks. The gold-seekers were of every race and nationality. Most were native white Americans from the Midwest and South, but there were many Europeans along with blacks, Indians, and a substantial number of Mexicans. The presence of easily portable wealth in the shape of gold dust or nuggets encouraged theft and gambling. Claim-jumping, the stealing of someone else's strike, was a frequent occurrence in the mining camps and a constant source of violence. And men without families and with money in their pockets often took to heavy drink and general hellraising. At times desperadoes virtually took over whole communities, terrorizing the decent folk and killing and stealing without restraint.

Vigilantes At this point the forces of law and order might rally and organize a vigilance committee. The term "vigilante" is now in bad repute—it has come to suggest the repression of dissent, and we associate it with serious restraints on democratic processes. In mining camps after the Civil War, however, it was sometimes an intelligent and a moderately democratic response to lawlessness. The vigilance committee might draw up a set of rules under which the members agreed to function until order could be restored. Then, confident of their strength, they would make examples of the worst rogues by sudden arrest, quick trial, and at times prompt hanging from the nearest tree. A few of these swift executions were generally enough to end the reign of violence and establish civilization.

Vigilante justice was in part a response to the federal government's slowness in providing government for the mining frontier. It often was many months before Congress took note of the political needs of the mining population and established a territorial government with a governor, courts, and federal law-enforcement officials. In several cases, the people of a region established a provisional regime well before Congress acted, and began to pass laws for dealing with the normal problems of any civilized community. Eventually, the laggard Congress responded, and in a few years had arranged the Great Basin region into organized territories, repeating the process of state-making that had begun farther east back in the 1790s.

The Cattleman's Frontier

The level Plains east of the Rockies followed a different course of development from that of the Great Basin. The vast grasslands of the Plains were ideally suited to grazing and quickly became a stock-raiser's frontier. "Cotton was once crowned king," exulted one westerner, "but grass is now." The process was gradual, a slow spread from south to north.

Texas Cattle The original focus of the Plains cattle industry had been west Texas where, before the Civil War, ranchers raised thousands of cattle. The Texas longhorn was of Spanish ancestry, a hardy beast that could fend for itself on the open range without shelter or fodder. It was not a particularly good beef animal, but that made little difference: in the absence of modern transportation, the markets for beef were too far from Texas. Hides were another matter. In the 1850s thousands of Texas cattle were slaughtered for the tanneries of the Northeast.

During the Civil War, Texas was cut off from its chief customers and the cattle multiplied rapidly. Soon after Appomattox some ranchers conceived the idea of herding the cattle north to Sedalia, Missouri, for shipment east over the Missouri Pacific railroad. The farmers along the way objected to Texas cattle as disease-carriers and as a danger to standing crops, and did not allow the ranchers to pass through. But the idea of the long drive had been born and became practical when the drives were farther west through unsettled country.

In its full development between the end of the 1860s and 1880 the long drive became an annual overland expedition northward from Texas to the nearest east-running railroad. The drives set out when the grass was green so that the cattle could graze along the way. Each group consisted of as many as one thousand cattle driven by cowboys who kept the herd moving and prevented strays from wandering off and stampeding frightened animals. Leading the band was a cook and his chuck wagon, carrying food and supplies, followed by the wrangler with the spare horses, both followed by the herd itself.

The cowboys driving the herds north were a mixed group. Most of them were whites; perhaps forty percent were African-Americans, Mexicans, and mixed-blood Indians. After the Civil War, almost ten thousand black men made their way from the plantations of the South to jobs on ranches and cattle trails in the West. They worked as cooks, wranglers, ordinary hands, and top hands, but they were unable to move all the way to the top of the cowboy hierarchy and become ranch or trail bosses. Pushing a herd across a flooded river was dangerous. Just as railroad construction foremen frequently used Chinese workers to set explosive

---

THE COWBOY'S LAMENT

As I passed by Tom Sherman's bar-room,
  Tom Sherman's bar-room, quite early one morn,
I spied a young cowboy all dressed in his buckskins,
  All dressed in his buckskins, all fit for his grave.

Then bang the drum lowly and play the fife slowly,
  Beat up the death marches as they carry me along;
Take me to the prairie and fire a volley o'er me,
  For I'm a young cowboy and dying alone.

Once in my saddle I used to go dashing,
  Once in saddle I used to ride gay;
But I just took up drinking and then to card-playing,
  Got shot by a gambler, and dying to-day.

Go gather around me a lot of wild cowboys,
  And tell them the story of a comrade's sad fate;
Warn them quite gently to give up wild roving,
  To give up wild roving before it's too late.

Some one write to my gray-headed mother,
  And then to my sister, my sister so dear;
There is another far dearer than mother,
  Who would bitterly weep if she knew I were here.

O bury beside me my knife and my shooter,
  My spurs on my heels, my rifle by my side;
Over my coffin put a bottle of brandy,
  That the cowboys may drink as they carry me along.

charges, cowboy trail bosses often made sure that black, Mexican, or Indian cowboys tested the depth of a river and the strength of its current. A white cowboy remarked that "it was the Negro hand who usually tried out the swimming water when a trailing herd came to a swollen stream."

Cattle Towns Soon the drives were rerouted along the Chisholm Trail, due north to Abilene in central Kansas. There, on the Kansas Pacific railroad, an Illinois cattle dealer, Joseph McCoy, had in 1867 constructed stockyards, cattle pens, loading ramps, and a hotel. McCoy chose the hamlet of Abilene because, as he wrote, "the country was entirely unsettled, well watered, excellent grass, and nearly the entire area of country was adapted to holding cattle." Once arrived in town, the drivers sold their herds to McCoy or some other dealer and departed with money in their pockets. The cattle were loaded on freight cars and sent east.

Abilene was only the first of a number of cattle towns. As the region around this small city became settled farming country, the Texas drives were deflected farther west to Ellsworth, Newton, and Dodge City. Like the mining camps, the cattle towns were at first almost all-male communities. Cowboys with money were just as wild as miners in the same lucky situation. Their average age was only twenty-four. Their job was usually to bring cattle from Texas to wherever a railroad could take them to the slaughterhouses in Chicago. The cattle towns also attracted rogues and outlaws, although never in such numbers as the mining camps. They usually had from the beginning a large stable element of businessmen and families that kept them from ever being as disorderly as the communities farther west. In fact, much of the carousing and hell-raising was tacitly sanctioned, since the city fathers who ran the local banks, hotels, saloons, and clothing and dry-goods stores recognized that they had to cater to the ranchers' and cowboys' tastes or see their business go to competitors.

The Movie Cowboy One woman was to recall an incident from the Lincoln County War during 1881 in New Mexico, which involved bringing law to the raw frontier:

> When Jennie Mae, my second child, was about nine months old, 'The Kid' came to our house and was introduced as Billie Bonney. Could this be the notorious Billy the Kid? I thought, surely not. He looked just like any other seventeen-year-old boy, and not in the least like a desperado. He was very fond of children, and liked Irvin and Jennie Mae at once. He called my little boy 'Pardie' and always wanted to hold the baby. He would take the two of them for a ride on his gray pony.

The writer describes Billy's escape from a burning house under gunfire:

> The Kid ran through the blazing door with a gun in each hand. He jumped from side to side as he ran and made a very elusive target. Not one bullet touched his body, though his clothes were ripped to shreds. His score was one dead and two marked for life—one shot through the jaws and the other lost the lobe of his left ear.

This romantic story of Billy the Kid is as close to reality as are most. What we do know is that Western films have served as America's epics. They distill primal virtues and redeem our national past from a decayed present. Thus Westerns, like *High Noon* (1952) with Gary Cooper, are to a considerable extent about the era when they were made, offering reassurance in hard or worrisome times. Western films particularly reflect Americans' dislike of authority. What they fail to capture is the eighteen-hour days and seven-day weeks driving cattle to market, usually from the Texas plains to a railroad town like Abilene, Kansas, or their cruelty to the animals they tended. Many cowboys suffered unromantic early deaths from exposure and overwork.

Ranching The annual long drive lasted until about 1880. During the years it prospered, about four million cattle were driven north from Texas to Kansas railroads for shipment east. By 1880, the fate that had overtaken Abilene also claimed the other cow towns: an ever-denser farm population increasingly interfered with the drive. In addition, new railroads through the Texas plains made it possible to ship cattle directly from the local ranches of the Texas panhandle. By this time, too, the northern plains—the Dakotas, Wyoming, Montana, and Colorado—were stocked with cattle, hybrids with the hardiness of longhorns and the beef of Angus and Herefords. These animals became the major source of beef for the thriving cities of the East.

For a decade and a half the northern Plains

A COWBOY'S LEXICON

bacon's curled. Cooked. Curled bacon as an image of death persists in cowboy and western song verse.

Badlands. Used to identify areas in the West where erosion has been so violent that little or no vegetation remains in a region of buttes, mesas, and other exotic and forbidding forms, and man and beast find it hard to make their way.

boot hill. A name given the frontier cemetery, because most of its early occupants died with their boots on. The word has had an appeal as part of the romantic side of the West and has become familiar as a picture of the violent end of a reckless life. But, to the westerner, boot hill was just a graveyard where there "wasn't nobody there to let 'em down easy with their hats off." Like the old saying, "There ain't many tears shed at a boot-hill buryin'," and it is "full o'fellers that pulled their triggers before aimin'."

buffalo grass. Great Plains species of grass well adapted to arid steppe conditions; the principal food of bison and other plains ruminants prior to cultivated exploitation of these areas. It grew as high as five feet.

bullwhacker. A man who drove the ox teams in early freighting days.

butte. French; a high detached hill or ridge rising steeply from a plain, especially in the Rocky Mountains and vicinity; a small mesa.

rimrock. The vertical escarpments of southwestern plateaus, buttes, or mesas are known as the rimrocks; seen from the valley floors, they rise like the architectural remains of a cosmic temple.

stage. The horse-drawn stages of the West are one of its favorite stereotyped images. The driver or skinner urges the four-horse team on at a dead run with a flood of vile oaths; the guard beside him, Winchester in hand, scans the countryside for badmen. Among the paying passengers must be found a noble youth, a provocative female, a leering no-good, and a gospel sharp. Before the ride is over there must be an encounter with Indians, or a robbery by Black Bart or some other colorful outlaw.

tumbleweed. Annual weeds that break off at the root at the end of the growing season and, because of spheroid shape, blow across the country, scattering their seeds and piling up on every fence line. They came into the West from Eurasia, where they were eaten as greens and their seeds ground for flour. Some reach a diameter of six feet.

range cattle industry flourished. Young cattle could be bought for a few dollars and put out to pasture on government land. The rancher did not have to invest in barns or other buildings. All he needed was a cabin by a streambank from which he and his hands could ride out occasionally to inspect the stock. The cattle wintered out and gained weight on the nutritious grass. Twice each year—spring and fall—the rancher and his hands conducted a roundup, separating out the mingled herds of neighbors and branding calves with their owner's mark. When shipped to market after four or five years, a calf had increased in value by about ten times.

So long as winters were moderately mild and the range not overstocked, the system worked. But its very success became a pitfall. Attracted by dazzling profits, investors went into the cattle industry by the hundreds. For a while, London investors were in a dither over potential profits in western cattle. "Drawing rooms buzzed with stories of this last of the bonanzas; staid old gentlemen, who scarcely knew the difference between a steer and a heifer, discussed it over their port and nuts." The romance of the open range drew easterners such as the New York aristocrat Theodore Roosevelt, who became a rancher in 1883 in the South Dakota Badlands. In the cattle kingdom itself, the ranchers tried through various livestock associations to limit the number of cattle, but they were unable to prevent overstocking. By the mid-eighties so many cattle were tumbling into the eastern markets that prices began to decline.

Then disaster fell. The hard winter of 1885–86 was followed by a hot, dry summer that withered the grass. Prices of steers dropped from $30 each to $8. The winter of 1886–87 was a catastrophe. By November the snow on the northern Plains was so deep that cattle could not dig down to the grass. In late January the worst blizzard on record roared across the Plains from the Canadian border to Texas. This was followed by a cold snap that sent temperatures plummeting to 68 below zero. On the open plains, cattle froze upright in their tracks. Many thousands crowded into gullies and stream valleys for shelter and were buried in drifts. In the spring, the freshets from melting snow washed thousands of steer carcasses into the tributaries of the Missouri.

Over the next few years, the cattle industry painfully reorganized. Many of the more speculative enterprises, including large cattle corporations representing eastern and European investors, went bankrupt. Thereafter the ranchers turned to smaller and better herds on fenced land and grew hay to provide fodder.

Some cattlemen, especially on the dryer, eastern margins of the plains, turned to raising a hardier species of animal—sheep. Others resisted the sheepmen, and for a while open warfare raged between the ranchers and the herders in parts of the former cattle kingdom. Farmers were also filling in the region. Equipped with barbed wire to fence off the timberless grasslands, with well-digging machinery and windmill pumps to provide drinking water for stock and human beings, and with new techniques of dry farming to offset sparse rainfall, the nesters poured into the more humid portions of the Plains from the East. By the 1890s vast areas of the Dakotas, eastern Montana, and Colorado were covered with wheat fields. In the fall, these bonanza farms were crisscrossed by great harvesters pulled by six horses cutting enormous swaths through the yellow sea of grain.

Simple Farming

Farming a variety of crops was common, but the tendency lay toward specialization. Whether the main crop was corn, which was centered in Iowa, or the riskier crop of wheat in and about the Dakotas and Kansas, these regions welcomed the early families whose hard experiences represent another bit of western lore.

Miriam Peckham, a Kansas homesteader, wrote: "No one can depend on farming for a living in this country. Henry is very industrious and this year had in over thirty acres of small grain, 8 acres of corn and about an acre of potatoes. We have sold our small grain . . . and it come to $100; now deduct $27.00 for cutting, $16.00 for threshing, $19.00 for hired help, say nothing of boarding our help, none of the trouble of drawing 25 miles to market and 25 cts on each head for ferriage over the river and where is your profit. I sometimes think this a God forsaken country, the [grass]-hopper hurt our corn and we have 1/2 a crop and utterly destroyed our garden. If one wants trials, let them come to Kansas."

Still another trial was the notorious dust storm where the wind drove dry topsoil against newly-planted crops. A farmer recalled one such storm in the 1870s:

> The corn I had planted was looking fine, and the potato patch was getting green when on the tenth of May at about 11:30 A.M. we saw a cloud coming across the plain very low, and which sounded like wind. I put the horses under the wagon cover where we kept our grain, and we all rushed for the house. As the cloud approached, the noise increased until we could not hear each other speak, and the light from the sun faded as though night was coming. It was the most awesome and terrifying thing we had ever seen. Then it fell, and for a while we were in almost total darkness. As the light gradually came back, and with it the realization that we were safe in the house, we felt thankful, until we looked outside. There we saw a writhing black blanket that seemed to be crawling toward us from every direction. We each grabbed a child and held it to protect it. Soon the sun came out, but the blanket kept rolling, and the stench was so appalling it left us trembling.
>
> I have no idea how long it lasted, but it seemed eternal. Then as we came to our senses and could think more clearly, we wondered about the Dittons.

Thinking of them seemed to bring us to reality, and we could watch what was going on around us. Gradually the blanket lifted, and we could see the damage. Not a stalk of corn was left, nor a blade of grass; even the leaves on the trees were gone.

"Watch and study the markets and the ways of the marketman . . . learn the art of 'selling well,' " one country editor advised his readers in 1887. Farming particularly depended increasingly on machinery. "It is no longer necessary for the farmer to cut his wheat with sickle or cradle, nor to rake it and bind it by hand; to cut his cornstalks with a knife and shock the stalks by hand; to thresh his grain with a flail," noted one westerner. Farmers had to invest heavily in machinery, such as harvesters and binders. That forced them into heavy mortgages and made them increasingly vulnerable to the wayward shiftings of the market and the will of eastern commercial interests. All this would sharpen the political conciousness of farmers.

Frontier Women Women went west for a variety of reasons. Most of them, of course, were farming women who wanted, like their husbands, to acquire more land and build a better life for their children and grandchildren. Some women migrated for religious reasons. Many Baptists, Methodists, Presbyterians, and Congregationalists went west as missionaries to bring Christianity to Indians and Protestantism to Spanish-speaking Roman Catholics. Other women, converted to Mormonism in the cities of the East or abroad in Great Britain and Scandinavia, went to Salt Lake City and from there to smaller towns and villages throughout the Great Basin to help build Zion in the wilderness. And tens

November Evening, **by Charles E. Hurchfield.** *(Courtesy, The Metropolitan Museum of Art)*

EMMA MITCHELL NEW *remembers her pioneer days, beginning in 1877, on the Kansas prairie. She and her husband were homesteaders, settling public land that became theirs for a small fee after they had lived on it a number of years.*

WE LANDED IN RUSSELL [on the prairie of central Kansas] forepart of December, 1877, with our car-load of goods, consisting of a few household goods, team of horses, a few chickens, a wagon and plow, enough lumber to build a small house, and a fairly good supply of provisions. We boarded at a hotel for two weeks and by that time the house was finished enough that we could move in out on a claim two miles northwest of Russell. Many a homesick day I saw, many a tear was shed. I couldn't bear to go to the window and look out. All I could see everywhere was prairie and not a house to be seen. . . .

I thought I was going to have a good garden, but the rain failed to come and we got nothing. In the meantime we were hunting water and hauling it in barrels. We dug a deep well and got nothing. Many a time I walked a quarter of a mile down into a deep draw with pails and carried water to wash with.

My husband broke prairie as fast as he could with the old team. One time he broke a fire guard around some grass that was quite tall and then set fire to it. The wind carried the sparks across the guards and set the prairie on fire. We worked hard to put it out to save our home and buildings, until we were completely exhausted. And many a time afterward I fought fires until I was all in, for we had so many in those days.

Years came along one after the other and also droughts. Times looked perilous to us. We finally got a cow, which helped us to live. Then there came along the Indian scare. All the people around about flocked to town for safety except me. I was all alone with my two children and knew nothing of it, as my husband was a good many miles from home trying to earn a little something. He worked out many a day for fifty cents and was glad to get it. Grasshoppers were very plentiful in those days. At times, swarms of them would shade the sun.

Our house was very poor, so my husband in a few spare minutes would saw soft rocks into bricks and lay them between the studding to make it firm, as the Kansas wind rocked it so bad. I helped carry all the bricks. We picked up and burned "cow chips" for fuel. . . .

Hardships and trials came along in their turn. Got a young team to deliver our milk to town. A baby girl came to us, making the second that came to us in Kansas without doctor or nurses and practically no help except the two older children.

We got along very well when a terrible storm and cloudburst came upon us and we lost almost everything, except the cows and an old team in the pasture. We had a nice cow barn put up and that day they put up a stack of millet the whole length of the barn. It commenced to rain in the afternoon, but in due time we started the children to town with the milk. It was a general downpour and the creeks were commencing to rise. . . .

The creek was up to the house and still pouring down. My husband investigated and found that the underpinning of the house was going and that we had to get out. We took a lantern and matches and some blankets, and started for the side hills. When we opened the door to get out, the water came up to our necks. We had a struggle to get out and I can't tell to this day how we ever made it, but the Lord must have been with us. My husband carried the baby girl in his arms as high as his head. We soon got out of the deepest water, as there was a turn in the creek. We went by way of the horse stable and found we would be safe in it. Still the water was up and it was pitch dark. The matches were wet, so we couldn't light the lantern.

We stayed there until the storm abated and the water went down. Then we started out to see if we had a home left and to our delight, even in such a mess, we found it still standing. It was still dark and we couldn't see what havoc the storm had made for us. We found some dry matches and lit the lamp. Such a deplorable sight words can't express. There was an inch of mud all over the carpets and floors. . . .

of thousands of seamstresses, laundresses, cooks, waitresses, maids, and teachers tried to make a living on the frontier.

Women making the covered wagon crossing of the plains and deserts and then trying to survive after finding a place to settle might live for years in dugouts or sod houses on the Great Plains or in lean-tos, small shacks, or cabins in the Far West. For the first few years, excess money went into farm equipment and livestock. Women who came from a culture in the East where the cult of domesticity rigidly defined their social and economic roles found living conditions far cruder than they had anticipated. On the frontier, gentility was a luxury. Women fought a constant war against mud and wind and dust. All day long, summer and winter, they kept stoves hot for cooking, bottling, canning, washing clothes and dishes, and heating bathwater. And they often engaged in heavy farm labor alongside their husbands. The rigid divisions of labor so common back east tended to break down on the frontier.

It was a lonely existence. Farms were widely scattered and opportunities to interact with woman friends were rare. Men frequently left home to pan for gold, deliver cattle or sheep to market, engage in business and politics, or work for wages on ranches or in towns in order to buy the goods their farms needed. They could be gone for months at a time. Women stayed behind to watch after the farm and take care of the children. With their men gone, they might worry about bandits. Worst of all, however, was the excruciating, stifling loneliness.

Some historians have argued that the harshness of the frontier and its tendency to blur divisions of labor and social roles helped liberate women. Wyoming gave women the right to vote in 1869, Utah in 1870. But the harshest frontier living conditions only lasted a few years in most areas, and as soon as any semblance of community appeared in the frontier west, traditional sexual roles reasserted themselves. The cult of domesticity, which so narrowly and so powerfully defined women's roles in the nineteenth century, became as strong in the cities, towns, and villages of the West as it had ever been in the East. In Wyoming, the all-male territorial legislature gave women the right to vote because it hoped that feminine virtues would help tame the more lawless elements of the frontier and attract respectable settlers. In Utah, Mormon leaders gave women the right to vote once the completion of the transcontinental railroad threatened to bring large numbers of non-Mormons to the territory. Giving Mormon women the franchise was a way of preserving church control of territorial politics.

THE HISTORIAN FREDERICK JACKSON TURNER ON THE FRONTIER

From "The Significance of the Frontier in American History" (1893)

To the frontier the American intellect owes its striking characteristics. That coarseness and strength combined with acuteness and inquisitiveness; that practical, inventive turn of mind, quick to find expedients; that masterful grasp of material things, lacking in the artistic but powerful to effect great ends; that restless, nervous energy; that dominant individualism, working for good and for evil, and withal that buoyancy and exuberance which comes with freedom—these are traits of the frontier, or traits called out elsewhere because of the existence of the frontier. Since the days when the fleet of Columbus sailed into the waters of the New World, America has been another name for opportunity, and the people of the United States have taken their tone from incessant expansion which has not only been open but has even been forced upon them. He would be a rash prophet who should assert that the expansive character of American life has now entirely ceased. Movement has been its dominant fact, and, unless this training has no effect upon a people, the American energy will continually demand a wider field for its exercise. But never again will such gifts of free land offer themselves.

Frontier Thesis By 1890, the Plains had finally been conquered, and the last continental frontier had ceased to exist. The event was marked symbolically by the words of the Superintendent of the Census in an 1890 bulletin: "Up to and including 1880 the country had a frontier of settlement, but at present the unsettled areas have been so broken into by isolated bodies of settlement that there can hardly be said to be a frontier line. In the discussion of its extent, its westward movement, etc., it can not, therefore, any longer have a place in the census reports." Frederick Jackson Turner, in a paper read before the American Historical Association in 1893, made this bulletin the starting point for the formulation of his famous frontier thesis. He ascribed many of the nation's social and political characteristics, particularly democracy and individualism, to the presence of a western frontier throughout American history. Turner neglected the New England town meetings and various important elements of the European heritage. The thesis also ignored frontiers of New Spain, which had developed along more authoritarian lines. And scholars have since pointed out how premature the census announcement actually was: much land remained to be settled. Yet many Americans thought the frontier experience to be at an end, and with it the expansionist phase of the nation's history. Others believed that only the first chapter had ended. Now the vigorous people who had conquered the North American continent must look outward toward the larger world across the seas. There, expansionists said, lay the country's new destiny.

Points To Think About

1. The United States has, for the most part, avoided seizing foreign territory with the intent of establishing its own rule. Expansion was for the sake not of conquering and controlling foreign people but of occupying what white Americans thought to be largely empty land. The taking of an empire after the war with Spain in 1898 was an exception.

In a broader sense, however, the whole of American history is a story of empire building. Thomas Jefferson called for "an empire for liberty." The rapid territorial expansion of the United States involved the very same process of destroying the cultures and societies of the native peoples as did European conquests in Africa and Asia. If anything, the American subjugation of the Indians was more vicious. The Indians were relatively few, and so instead of having to establish the occasionally cooperative relations with the leadership of conquered peoples that other empires have needed to create, the whites could treat the Indians as disposable. Far from deviating from the general pattern of European imperialism, the history of the United States is a major embodiment of the imperial impulse.

2. Even the best-intentioned white Americans regarded the native American peoples as "primitives" who needed to be taught the white man's ways. Understanding and appreciation of native cultures did not come until the twentieth century.

One of the most incisive and eloquent statements of the Indian viewpoint is *Black Elk Speaks*. The elderly Black Elk, a Sioux medicine man, told his life story in the 1930s shortly before his death. He remembered the destruction of the Plains Indians' way of life, the Wounded Knee Massacre, performances with Buffalo Bill's Wild West Show, and a lengthy and unhappy stay on a reservation in the Black Hills. Black Elk could not fathom the wastefulness of the white man, his willingness to destroy whole herds of buffalo and leave them to rot in the sun. Nor could he make sense of the white man's "rugged individualism," which Black Elk saw as selfishness. While with Buffalo Bill's show, Black Elk had visited New York and other major cities. He was horrified by the hordes of the poor left to fend for themselves. His tribe, he said, would never have allowed the helpless to suffer. The basic difference Black Elk saw was that while his people thought that Nature moved in cycles and so sought to organize their lives in similar fashion—for example, by building circular tepees—the white man thought in straight lines. His housing was square or rectangular. It is not good, said Black Elk, to live in boxes.

3. The Census of 1890 marked the "closing" of the frontier in the sense that there was no longer a continuous unbroken line marking the edge of settlement. In 1893 the young historian Frederick Jackson Turner provided the American people

with a compelling vision of what the frontier had meant. The American national character, Turner believed, had been formed by the centuries-long conquest of the wilderness. Americans owed to the frontier experience their democratic politics, their individualism, and their genius for meeting practical problems with inventive solutions. Less optimistically, Turner wondered whether these qualities would survive once the frontier, which had fostered them, was gone. Although it still has its ardent defenders and still inspires some excellent historians, the Turner thesis no longer dominates American historical thinking. But if most historians no longer look to the frontier for the key to understanding the American experience, they do still ponder the questions Turner raised.

One feature of American history that Turner's thesis illuminated brilliantly is expansionism. Americans, from the earliest colonial days, could seek to outgrow their problems. And they could assume that the way to resolve problems of poverty was not to take from the rich and give to the poor but to increase the total national wealth. Southerners who, in the 1840s and 1850s, believed that the non-slave states were multiplying too rapidly sponsored expeditions to Latin America to conquer new slave territory. And Lincoln's secretary of state, William Seward, hoped overseas expansion could avert the Civil War. Americans, in short, have been conditioned by their historical experience to see in growth, territorial and economic, the sovereign remedy to all problems. Turner's frontier was the most vivid expression of this tendency.

The world's resources have grown scarcer, and international conditions have made the old-style empire building obsolete. The earth is a planet for which the national culture, conditioned by the perpetual opportunity to flee from its troubles by the amassing of more wealth, is ill-fitted.

Suggested Readings

The most recent scholarship on the American West includes William Cronon, George Miles, and Jay Gitlin, *Under an Open Sky: Rethinking America's Western Past* (1992), Terry G. Jordan, *Trails to Texas: Southern Roots of Western Cattle Ranching* (1981), Roger D. McGrath, *Gunfighters, Highwaymen, and Vigilantes: Violence on the Frontier* (1984), Patricia Nelson Limerick, *Desert Passages: Encounters with the American Deserts* (1985), Robert M. Utley, *The Indian Frontier of the American West* (1984), Sandra L. Myres, *Westering Women* (1982), Polly Kaufman, *Women Teachers on the Frontier* (1984), Michael P. Malone, *Historians and the American West* (1983), Harry Drago, *The Great Range Wars* (1985), Joanna L. Stratton, *Pioneer Women: Voices from the Kansas Frontier* (1981), Annette Kolodny, *The Land Before Her* (1984), James S. Olson and Raymond Wilson, *Native Americans in the Twentieth Century* (1984), Julie Roy Jeffrey, *Frontier Women* (1979), Daniel McGood, *Command of the Waters: Iron Triangles, Federal Water Development, and Indian Water* (1987), Patricia Limerick, *The Legacy of Conquest—The Unbroken Past of the American West* (1990), and Robert Hine, *The American West* (2nd ed., 1984).

On that mythic hero see Joe B. Frantz and J. E. Cheate, *The American Cowboy: The Myth and the Reality* (1955), and David Dary, *Cowboy Culture: A Saga of Five Centuries* (1981). Mari Sandoz describes the destruction of the herds in *The Buffalo Hunters* (1945). Henry Nash Smith's masterful study of the impact of the West on the American imagination is *Virgin Land: The American West as Symbol and Myth* (1950). Other fine older books are Bernard DeVoto, *Across the Wide Missouri* (1947) and Walter Prescott Webb, *The Great Plains* (1931). See also V. W. Paul, *Mining Frontiers of the Far West, 1848–1880* (1963), Lewis Atherton, *The Cattle Kings* (1961), and Frederick Merk, *History of the Westward Movement* (1978).

Robert M. Utley details the collapse of Sioux society in *The Last Days of the Sioux Nation* (1963). R. K. Andrist chronicles *The Long Death: The Last Days of the Plains Indians* (1964). See also Wilcomb E. Washburn, *The Indian in America* (1975). Dee Brown's *Bury My Heart at Wounded Knee* (1979) is a moving treatment.

Other good books on the West include Robert F. Berkhofer's *The White Man's Indian: Images of the American Indian from Columbus to the Present* (1978), Duane A. Smith's *Rocky Mountain Mining Camps* (1967), Rodman W. Paul's *The Far West and the Great Plains in Transition, 1859–1908* (1988), Richard W. Slatta's *Cowboys of the Americas* (1990), Francis Paul Prucha's *American Indian Policy in Crisis: Christian Reformers and the Indians* (1976), Paula Petrik's *No Step Backward: Women and Family on the Rocky Mountain Mining Frontier, 1865–1900* (1987), William Cronon, *Nature's Metropolis: Chicago and the Great West* (1991).

☆ ☆ ☆ **POINTS OF VIEW:** ☆ ☆ ☆

The 'Old' vs. the 'New' West

Martin Ridge

Turner's followers studied and wrote about the internal history of the United States in the context of American uniqueness and its causes. Their "West" was an ever advancing frontier of opportunity and revitalization; it was a triumphant national experience that culminated in an individualist democracy that only reached a crisis as the frontier itself—with all the opportunity that it represented—came to a close in the final decades of the nineteenth century. For Turner, the nineteenth century was an era of abundance and success; the twentieth, a century when the institutions formed in the past would be tested in a society of closed space with diminished opportunity.

These views had a profound impact on historical writing. For one thing, they gave new relevance to local and state history. Local historians could now look not only to events in their own communities to show how they demonstrated national trends but also to the lives of persons still remembered to explain their roles in the making of a region.

Although there had been a persistent drumbeat of criticism of the Turnerian thesis beginning in the mid-1920s, it reached a flood tide in the 1930s. During the Great Depression, many American historians suffered a crisis in confidence and doubted the future of their nation, looked askance on a theory that rooted American free institutions in individualism or praised capitalist democracy. The rise of fascism and the onset of the Second World War, however, enforced a renewed respect for American institutions.

[A]n entirely new set of interests among western historians was challenging, broadening, and deepening the Turner paradigm. Although the intellectual and cultural origins of these interests may be debatable, what they are is quite clear. The current historical focus is on race, class, gender, and the environment. Although in itself scarcely new, it has not only reopened old arguments about the significance of the frontier as a liberating economic and political force but also allowed for the examination of previously ignored themes. The polemicists among this new group of historians find it self-gratifying to denounce Turnerians for their male-oriented (Turner did not mention women per se) and triumphalist view of the frontier, which, they insist, praises the economic and political success of white males in the establishment of an individualistic, capitalist democracy at the expense of the frontier's failures, the oppression and exploitation of minorities and women, and a degraded environment.

Turner's critics have their difficulties. In denying the utility of his paradigm, denouncing him for remaining unspoken on issues of class, gender, and the environment, anti-Turnerians are strangely haunted by his silent scholarly ghost, for they deny the usefulness of his historical vision but often unwittingly work within it.

Historians who prefer to continue to analyze the advancing frontier (either as a place or a process) and its consequences are comfortable with the freedom Turner offered. For them, like many artists, novelists, poets, and playwrights, the frontier still beckons. Moreover, there is now the chance to look at race, class, gender, and the environment within the Turnerian context and test its applicability. This strips those issues of the preconceptions of the polemicists who have their own scholarly agenda.

The new western historians, Turner's recent critics, must explain what is new about their work other than their personal assumptions and value judgments, unless they focus on the twentieth century, a period Turner did not treat. They must explain the merit of what they have substituted for the overarching and imaginative work of Turner. They may find that it is exceedingly difficult to bury his ghost.

Excerpted from Martin Ridge, "Frederick Jackson Turner and His Ghost: The Writing of Western History," *Proceedings of the American Antiquarian Society,* 101 (April 1991): 65–76. Reprinted by permission.

Donald Worster

The first historian to undertake serious study of the westward movement, Turner never stopped believing that the old story was literally true. Returning to the wilderness, men could be restored to the innocence of their youth, sloughing off the blemishes of age. He handed on his faith to his disciples, and so western history was born. . . . They would not have to pass foreign language exams, read works from abroad, or keep up with the Paris savants. They were excused from examining radical defects in the West, for there were none to be found. . . .

Around the year 1970 [the] untold side of the western past began to find its tellers. A younger generation, shaken by Vietnam and other national disgraces—poverty, racism, environmental degradation—could not pretend that the only story that mattered in the West was one of stagecoach lines, treasure hunts, cattle brands, and wildcatters, nor for that matter aircraft plants, opera companies, bank deposits, or middle-class whites learning how to ski. What was missing was a frank, hard look at the violent imperialistic process by which the West was wrested from its original owners and the violence by which it had been secured against the continuing claims of minorities, women, and the forces of nature. . . .

[I]t is the younger generation of the 1970s and 1980s who have made this new multicultural perspective their own. They have discovered not only that minorities have not always shared in the rising power and affluence of the West but also that they have in some ways thought differently about the ends of that power and affluence. As part of the reevaluation, we are increasingly asked to reexamine the process by which native peoples were dispossessed in the first place, to remind ourselves of the manner in which whites went about accumulating land and resources for themselves, and to uncover the contradictions in a majority, male-dominated culture that can in the same breath trumpet the idea of its own liberty and deny other peoples the right of self-determination. Further, we have learned to pay more attention to the substantial numbers of nonnative people of color, people from Africa, the Pacific islands, and Asia, who have come into the garden of agrarian myth to live alongside the European settlers, making the West in fact a far more racially diverse place than the myth envisioned—more diverse indeed than either the North or South has been. . . .

The drive for the economic development of the West was often a ruthless assault on nature and has left behind it much death, depletion, and ruin. Astonishing as it now seems, the old agrarian myth of Turner's day suggested that the West offered an opportunity of getting back in touch with nature, of recovering good health and a sense of harmony with the nonhuman far from the shrieking disharmonies of factories, technology, urban slums, and poverty that were making life in Europe and the East a burden to the spirit. . . .

Here again truth is breaking in, driving out myth and self-deception, as we face unblinkingly the fact that from its earliest days the fate of the western region has been one of furnishing raw materials for industrialism's development; consequently, the region was from the beginning in the forefront of America's endless economic revolution. Far from being a child of nature, the West was actually given birth by modern technology and bears all the scars of that fierce gestation, like a baby born of an addict. . . .

Over the past decade or two the neglect of industrial capitalism's impact on the western environment has begun to be repaired, due to the fact that the study of the West, more than of other regions, has come to be allied with the emerging field of environmental history. This alliance has encouraged doubts about the role of capitalism, industrialism, population growth, military expenditures, and aimless economic expansion in the region and has questioned whether they really have blazed a trail to progress. . . .

[W]estern elites have followed the old familiar tendency of those in power, to become corrupt, exploitative, and cynical toward those they dominate. Power can also degrade itself, as it degrades others and the land, yet it commonly tries to conceal that fact by laying claim to the dominant myths and symbols of its time—in the case of the American West, by putting on cowboy boots and snapbutton shirts, waving the American flag, and calling a toxic dump the land of freedom.

Reprinted from Donald Worster, "Beyond the Agrarian Myth," in Patricia Nelson Limerick, Clyde A. Milner, and Charles E. Rankin, eds., *Trails: Toward A New Western History* (Lawrence, KS: University Press of Kansas, 1991).

President Grant starting the Corliss Steam Engine at the opening of the Centennial Exposition, Philadelphia, 1876.

CHAPTER 17

The Ironies of Industrialism 1865–1900

THE CENTENNIAL EXHIBITION

The hundredth anniversary of the signing of the Declaration of Independence, 1876, had as its centerpiece the Centennial Exhibition in Philadelphia. About one in five Americans would visit the dozens of exhibition halls, the restaurants, the galleries, the train ride through the grounds, able to savor the excitement of a great world's fair and the pride of a nation at its hundredth birthday. The Civil War was a recent memory, and the celebrants were mindful both that the Union had barely survived destruction and that its people were just becoming reunited. Nevertheless, "centennial mania" dominated the summer of '76. People wore centennial hats and scarves, attended centennial balls, drank centennial coffee, listened to centennial songs. Some dressed in the fashion of 1776 or contributed artifacts from the nation's history, including a pair of George Washington's false teeth. Temperance organizations at the Exhibition provided visitors with free ice water from a giant fountain they had built in the form of a Greek temple, with twenty-six spigots.

On opening day, May 10, 1876, over 100,000 people came to see the "greatest spectacle ever presented to the vision of the Western World." Banners, flags, and streamers festooned the usually staid city. Before a vast platform filled with dignitaries from all over the world, a 150-piece orchestra played national songs of all the countries represented at the fair. As the maestro called for the Brazilian national hymn, Emperor Dom Pedro of Brazil appeared on the platform, the first reigning monarch ever to appear in the United States. The republican crowd made him the hero of the day, wildly cheering this plainly dressed "true Yankee emperor with go-ahead American traits." Dom Pedro, whose travels the press had closely attended, endeared himself to Americans with his interest in translating the "Star-Spangled Banner" into Portuguese. He had also ordered the abolition of slavery in Brazil. The arrival of President Grant signaled the orchestra to begin the "Centennial March," a piece that the Women's Centennial Committee had purchased from the great German composer Richard Wagner for $5,000.

The exhibit, with its galleries, its statues (the hand and torch of the unfinished Statue of Liberty were a major attraction), its displays of inventions, machinery, furniture, publications (the Newspaper Pavilion had 10,000 up-to-date newspapers, each in its own pigeon-hole, for visitors to read), its commercial displays, was a microcosm of American achievements—gaudy, good-natured, diverse, never accepting the limitations of the present. The chief symbol of the centennial was in the great Machinery Hall. When President Grant and Dom Pedro entered it, silent machines were spread over fourteen acres—machines to saw logs, to spin cotton, to print newspapers—hundreds of different kinds waiting to drive the nation into a glorious commercial future. At the center of the hall stood the giant Corliss engine: forty feet high, 700 tons, capable of generating 2,500 horsepower. The Emperor and the President each turned a lever at the bottom of the vast machine, a hiss of steam escaped, the giant beams of the engine began to rise and fall, and as this power was transmitted over thousands of shafts, belts, pulleys, and gears, all fourteen acres of machinery leaped into life. Foreign visitors recognized that the United States now led the world in machinery and invention.

A few determined women recognized that replacing muscle with steam should open the workplace to women. The Women's Centennial Committee, headed by Mrs. Elizabeth Duane Gillespie, an energetic great-granddaughter of Benjamin Franklin, organized subcommittees in every state that raised money for a Women's Pavilion showing the achievements of women. On May 10 the Empress Teresa, Dom Pedro's wife, opened the Women's Pavilion. She pulled a golden cord that started a six-horsepower steam engine to running spinning frames and looms on which were displayed the work of female artisans, as well as a printing press that turned out a magazine, *The New Century for Women*, written, edited, printed, and published by women. Americans did not consider the operating of machinery to be women's work, and Mrs. Gillespie had scoured the country in search of a woman who knew how to run a steam engine, finally importing from Canada Emma Allison, "an educated and accomplished lady" who became one of the stars of the fair. Operating a steam engine, she assured countless audiences, was far less complicated than caring for a child. The Women's Pavilion was one of the great successes of the Exhibition.

The competition among inventions for Exhibition awards in June produced perhaps the most lasting legacy of the Centennial Exhibition. A reluctant Alexander Graham Bell, thinking that he should stay in Boston where he had examinations to grade and a speech course to finish teaching, took the train to Philadelphia to display his recent "invention in embryo," the "speaking telephone." On a Sunday, June 25, when the exhibits were closed and sounds could therefore be carefully tested, the ubiquitous Dom Pedro and nearly fifty scientists trudged from exhibit to exhibit, while out west at the Little Big Horn River in Montana, Chief Sitting Bull and 5,000 braves were destroying Custer's army. Late in the afternoon, the scientists lingered over the display of one of Bell's competitors in the race to perfect the electronic transmission of sound. They would have ceased their labors for the day, so Bell would later recall, if it had not been for the personal interest of the Emperor, who had met Bell in Boston and was impressed by his work with the deaf. Dom Pedro and the other judges listened to Bell's voice over the wires from across the long gallery asking, "Do you understand what I say?" "I hear, I hear!" shouted the excited Emperor, who then raced across the gallery at a very un-emperor-like gait to congratulate the inventor.

The Great Surge

Economic Growth In 1860 the United States was already among the very richest of nations. Its prosperity largely depended on its bounteous fields, forests, and mines. Many of the manufactured items Americans used came from abroad, paid for by cotton from the South, gold from California, and the shipping that the efficient American merchant marine provided for European commerce. The textile industry of the Northeast, iron manufacturing in Pennsylvania and Ohio, flour mills along the Delaware and on the Chesapeake, and shipbuilding along the New England and Middle Atlantic coast also contributed to American incomes. But as of 1860, the United States was still primarily a producer of food and raw materials for its own people and for consumers elsewhere in the Atlantic world. In the half century that followed, the United States became the world's largest industrial power.

Much of the surge in production of wealth came in agriculture. In 1860 the total value of all farm products had been about $1.5 billion. In 1919 it reached $7.5 billion. American agriculture was meeting the needs of expanding populations at home and abroad. Yet other branches of the economy had grown so much faster that as a proportion of all economic output agriculture had fallen from well over a quarter to about seventeen percent. Manufacturing and mining now dominated the American economy.

In the half century following the Civil War the growth of industry was spectacular. In 1864 the United States had put out 872,000 tons of iron and steel; in 1919, it produced over 24 million tons. From about 20 million tons in 1860 coal production attained 500 million in 1910. Lumber output, at 12.7 billion board feet in 1869, reached over 40 billion by 1910. Petroleum, having yielded half a million barrels in 1860, was at 209 million in 1910.

Americans who lived through the half century of growth did not need to see figures and graphs to understand what had taken place. Everywhere the country displayed change. Lying over the Lehigh Valley of eastern Pennsylvania, the Mahoning Valley of eastern Ohio, the Ohio Valley at Pittsburgh, layers of smog covered steel and glass mills. Everywhere new cities and towns appeared to shelter people at the newly opened mines and mills. During the 1880s, Marcus Daly, head of the Anaconda Copper Company, turned a railroad construction camp into the major mining and copper-refining center of Butte, Montana. In northern Alabama by the 1890s the largest town was Birmingham, a community of 26,000, which twenty years earlier had been an empty cornfield. Outside the most rural and isolated areas, time in communities throughout the country was marked off by the blast of factory whistles summoning employees to work early in the morning and signaling an end to the day.

Economic Infrastructure A necessary basis of industrialization is the development of a modern economic infrastructure, as economists name the network of institutions that makes for the efficient distribution of goods and information. Mass production can occur only if a country has the capacity for the large-scale distribution of manufactured goods.

The most significant improvement by far in the American infrastructure was the construction by 1910 of 240,000 miles of main railroad trackage. Major cities as well as farms and small towns were linked together in a vast transportation system that permitted the efficient mass distribution of raw materials, farm products, and manufactured goods.

In the decades after the Civil War, new technologies made the instantaneous exchange of information a reality. Samuel Morse had earlier invented the telegraph, a mechanism providing for the electromagnetic transmission of coded messages. In 1844 a completed telegraph line connected Washington, D.C., with Baltimore. During the rest of the nineteenth century, contractors built telegraph lines simultaneously with the construction of railroad trackage. By 1900 there were more than 300,000 miles of telegraph lines linking the cities and towns of the nation. Sending a message from St. Louis to San Francisco took only a few seconds. Alexander Graham Bell received a patent on the telephone in 1876, and by 1900 there were nearly 1,500,000 operating telephones in the United States, providing voice transmission among the major towns and cities of the eastern United States. A number of other inventions meanwhile greatly improved the efficiency of producing written documents.

In 1873 the Remington Company began selling large numbers of the recently invented typewriter, and by 1875 the development of the rotary printing press made it possible to print on both sides of a sheet of paper simultaneously. Edmund Barbour invented a calculating machine in 1872 that provided for printed totals and subtotals. By the end of the nineteenth century, businesses had the capacity to produce large volumes of information efficiently and to distribute that information quickly.

While new transportation and information facilities were creating a single national market, that market was thriving on the products of the nation's burgeoning factories, along with the produce of its farm. In 1859 there were 140,000 establishments that had any claim to the label "factory." Most of these were tiny undertakings with one owner and four or five workers. In 1914 there were 268,000 factories, many of them large firms with vast numbers of employees.

The Railroads

Track In 1860 the railroad network was already extensive, measuring over 30,000 miles. But it did not constitute the complete system that would later knit the nation together. Little mileage stretched beyond the Mississippi River, and none beyond the Missouri. The South had a decent amount of track, but it was in short stretches, not tied up with major through routes, and connected at only a few points with northern lines. The country had hundreds of different railroad companies and several distinct rail gauges that required unloading of freight and reloading on different boxcars. In 1860 movement of freight and people was still slow, difficult, and relatively expensive. The railroads were inadequate for the development of national markets. Manufacturers and other producers of commodities could not reach out to customers across the country. Nor could they draw on distant raw materials. The cost and uncertainties of shipment were simply too great. Local firms could count on keeping their business even though they were neither cheap nor efficient. Around each local population center there remained a ring of small producers providing goods for the neighborhood on a small scale, and often at a high price.

Many Americans were conscious of the deficiencies of the country's rail network and sought to overcome them. In the better settled parts of the country it was only a matter of time. There, traffic was potentially heavy and private capital was readily forthcoming. Yet even in the populous Northeast many promoters seeking funds for railroad building resorted to the tactic of promising local communities rail connections if they would lend the promoters money or provide other bonuses. In newer areas the hurdles were greater. Railroads across empty country could be justified on the ground of the needs of society in general, but not on the basis of immediate profit to investors. Eventually, no doubt, the transcontinental railroad would create its own business by opening up the country. But that might take years and meanwhile what would the investors do for dividends? It seemed clear to many Americans that if the country was to have railroads connecting the settled portions of the East with the West Coast it would have to be willing to pay for them in some fashion; private capital alone would not do the job.

The Transcontinentals For a decade or more before 1860, businessmen, journalists, and politicians had debated how to finance a Pacific railroad. Following a practice of land grants that went back as far as the Land Ordinance of 1785, the federal government in 1850 transferred several million acres of the vast public domain to promoters who promised to build a railroad connecting the Great Lakes with the Gulf of Mexico. During the years of sectional conflict preceding 1860 this policy could not be applied to a road that would tie the settled portions of the United States to the Pacific coast. Northerners and southerners agreed on the need for such a road, but they fought furiously over whether the route should be a southern, a central, or a northern one. Not until the South left the Union was the issue settled by the Pacific Railroad bill of 1862.

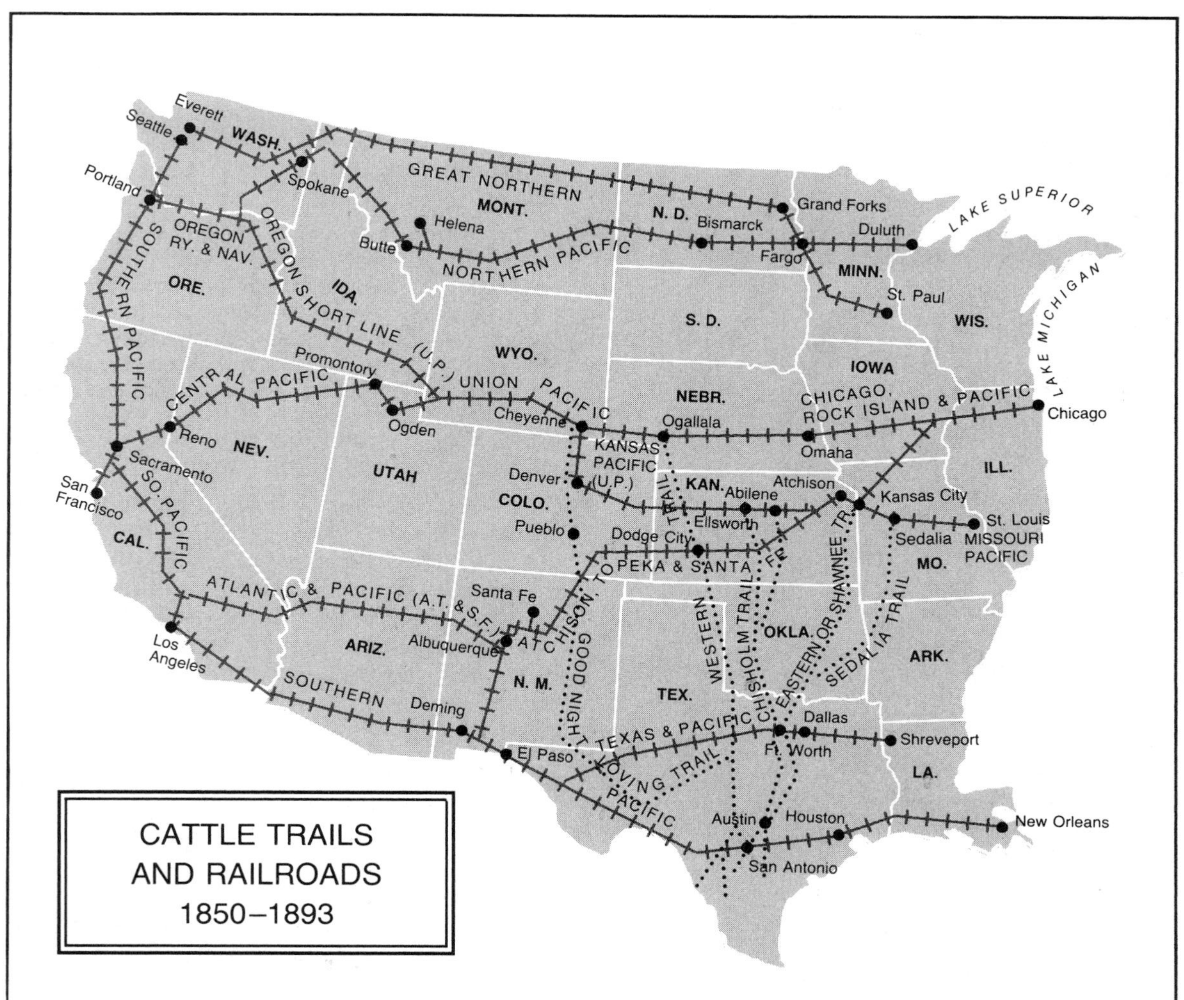

CATTLE TRAILS AND RAILROADS 1850–1893

The Union Pacific-Central Pacific was the first of the transcontinentals subsidized by federal land grants. In 1864 Congress chartered the Northern Pacific Railroad and gave it an even larger land grant but no cash loan. Another road, later to become the Atchison, Topeka, and Santa Fe, also received a land grant, as did a far southern route that eventually came to be called the Southern Pacific. In all, Congress handed out over 131 million acres of federal land to railroad promoters, while the states gave an additional 49 million acres. The total was finally as large an area as the state of Texas.

In later years, many Americans would harshly criticize the railroad land grant policy as a colossal giveaway to powerful interests that benefited only a few. Agrarians were to claim it had deprived American farmers of vast expanses of land that might have helped preserve the family farm. Other critics would charge that the railroad promoters had made vast fortunes by seizing the common heritage of all Americans.

Railroad promoters often bribed legislators who would be instrumental in the granting of government lands. And some promoters made large profits out of the land they had received. But building railroads across wildernesses in advance of settlement meant taking a serious risk. In most cases the federal government was given cheap rates for shipping its own freight over the transcontinentals, and thereby saved itself millions of dollars. The government also gained by the rise in value of federal lands adjacent to the railroad.

Old Mac, the station master at a Chesapeake and Ohio station, ca. 1874, is an interesting face and figure out of the past. Imagine what his various duties were. *(Courtesy, Cook Collection, Valentine Museum)*

It is a mistake to assume that the land that went to the roads was thereby lost to farmers. The railroads were anxious to fill the land with settlers who could provide the commerce the roads needed. Each of the Pacific railroads set up a department that sold land to settlers at from two to eight dollars an acre, often arranging credit and providing free transportation for prospective customers. Each also maintained a bureau of immigration that advertised in Europe and the eastern United States promoting the western lands.

The policy of land grants to railroads has been taken, correctly, to represent the friendliness of the American government to big business. But it also meant that the government was willing to put itself boldly into the economy in a way that went against nineteenth-century doctrines of competitive private enterprise. Between the end of the Civil War and 1910, the country increased its main railroad trackage to 240,000 miles, eight times the mileage of 1865. Railway roadbeds were improved, steel rails substituted for iron, and iron locomotives made larger and more efficient.

A Sioux Indian described his first impression of the locomotive:

> We regarded them as *waken* [mysterious], a race whose power bordered upon the supernatural. I learned that they had made a 'fire-boat.' I could not understand how they could unite two elements which cannot exist together. I thought the water would put out the fire, and the fire would consume the boat if it had the shadow of a chance. This was to me a preposterous thing! But when I was told that the Big Knives had created a 'fire-boat-walks-on-mountains' [a locomotive] it was too much to believe.

In 1886 the last company shifted to the standard gauge of 4′ 8½″. Freight and passengers could be sent long distances over several companies' trackage without interruption. The completion of the railroad network helped to create a national market. Innumerable crossroad hamlets had spurs connecting them to the major commercial trading and manufacturing centers of the nation and the major ports of the world. By 1910 almost every American farm was within convenient wagon distance of some railroad depot and thence connected to the world's markets. Now for the first time manufacturers could locate their plants almost anywhere within broad limits and be assured that they could bring in raw materials cheaply and send their finished products wherever they could find customers. Every region of the country could specialize in crops best suited to its climate and supply consumers with food at lower prices than their own neighborhoods could. Such changes help to explain the rising gross national product of these years.

These powerful machines made for thousands of horrible industrial accidents. A brakeman describes his in 1888:

> It was four or five months before I 'got it.' I was making a coupling one afternoon. . . . Just before the two cars were come together, the one behind me left the track. . . . Hearing the racket, I sprang to one side, but my toe caught the top of the rail. I was pinned between the comers of the cars as they came together. I heard my ribs cave in like an old box smashed with an ax.

Between 1890 and 1917, some 72,000 railroad workers died on the job and nearly two million were injured.

A new railroad bridge goes up in Titusville, Pennsylvania. Between 1865 and 1910 the country's main railroad trackage increased from 30,000 to 240,000 miles, connecting every farm and hamlet to the world's major commercial, manufacturing, and trading centers. *(Courtesy, Drake Well Memorial Park, Titusville, Pennsylvania)*

Agriculture

The Morrill Act

In agriculture as in transportation, the Civil War propelled the government into the economy. In 1862 Congress created the United States Bureau of Agriculture as a separate division within the federal government, below Cabinet rank (not until 1889 did the commissioner of agriculture become a regular member of the Cabinet). Also in 1862, Congress passed the Morrill Land-Grant College Act, donating thirty thousand acres of federal land to every state for each senator and representative it had in Congress. This land was to support at least one agricultural college in the state: ultimately the new schools also taught engineering and a multitude of other subjects. The act mandated that all the colleges established on the basis of its grants be coeducational. It thus represented an important gain for women's education, although decades would pass before the public came to expect women to use their education as a passport into an extensive range of occupations and professions.

Under the Morrill Act some sixty-nine land-grant colleges were established. By the 1890s, a flock of state agricultural and mechanical colleges taught animal husbandry, horticulture, agricultural chemistry, entomology, and other courses designed to train farmers in scientific techniques. Many of these institutions maintained laboratories and experimental farms where their faculties sought to develop new fertilizers, new plant and animal strains, and new ways of dealing with plant and animal diseases.

This agricultural research and development had further encouragement from the Hatch Act of 1887. This law appropriated to each state $15,000 a year from public land sales for the establishment of an experimental station. By 1899 there were fifty-six such stations, in every state and territory, receiving overall more than $1 million a year to try out new crops, new fertilizers, and new plowing, harvesting, and tillage techniques.

Inventions Federal aid was one of a number of contributors to the marvelous growth of American agriculture in the later part of the century. The railroads opened up vast tracts of land. From nineteenth-century inventors and manufacturers farmers received a wealth of farm equipment: the harvester, the product of Cyrus McCormick and the Marsh brothers; James Oliver's chilled-iron plow; James Buchanan's threshing machine; Manly Miles's silo; S.M. Babcock's cream tester. State and regional agricultural journals encouraged farmers to be good businessmen, bold innovators, and careful cultivators. And there was the farmer: eager to produce in quantity for the market, relatively well educated, quick to adopt new methods. American agriculture was very much a branch of modern technology. It was so in its use of new machines and even more in working the land by innovative methods, as the steel or copper industry works raw metal into finished wealth.

Despite new inventions, much of farm work was still drudgery, as this farmer's diary from 1883 attests:

> April 19, 1883 Worked down home all day at the stable.
> 20th Sunday cold.
> 21st Worked on the stable.
> 22nd Worked on the stable.
> 23rd Went to Rushville and . . . worked on the stable.
> 24th Stormed all day and worked on the stable.
> 25th Worked on the stable. . . .
> 26th Worked on the stable.
> May 13, 1884 Finished sowing barley today cleared manure in the forenoon lost one lamb today just one
> 14th Cleared manure all day a nice day all day Cleared 42 loads today
> 15th Cleared manure all day rained part of the day ground very wet and getting wetter some manure spred
> 16th Cleared manure all day and finished clearing manure a better day today but very cold for the time of the year no corn planted yet
> 17th Plowed for corn today for the first [time] and finished the old barn yard and spred manure.

Between 1866 and 1900 the number of American farms increased from 2.6 to 5.4 million, and total farm acreage between 1870 and 1900 rose from 493 million acres to 839. Cattle on American farms increased from 24 million head in 1870 to 52 in 1900. Cotton output, some 2.1 million bales in 1866, reached 11.2 in 1898; wheat, at 152 million bushels in 1866, went to 675 in 1898; corn production shot up from 731 million bushels in 1866 to 2.6 billion bushels in 1900. By the end of the nineteenth century, the United States was an agricultural powerhouse, producing vast amounts of grain, meat, fiber, and other farm products for its own growing population and a large part of the Atlantic world. American economic growth after the Civil War is more visibly and imposingly an industrial event. But without the corresponding boom in agriculture the economic achievements of this period would have been far more modest, for the country could have fed only a small labor force.

Industry

The New South In 1886 Henry Grady, an *Atlanta Constitution* editor, spoke in New York to a group of industrialists. In his talk entitled "The New South" Grady lamented, of a southerner who had been buried amid solid marble in a pine forest, that his marble tombstone was made in Vermont and his pine casket in Ohio. Both should have come from his native South. Grady looked forward to an era of industrial prosperity in "the glorious sunny South" built by the safe investments of northern financiers. Another newspaper predicted that the South would be El Dorado of the next century. Financing did come from the North, particularly for the railroads whose tracks, formerly narrow gauged, were brought into conformity with northern trackage. In the rolling Piedmont growth came particularly in textile mills, which often exploited working children; in Birmingham an iron and steel industry came to thrive; in Richmond 100,000 cigarettes a day issued from the mechanized factories of James Buchanan Duke's American Tobacco Company. But the region was so far behind the North in technical training and general education that it remained largely agricultural and poor throughout the nineteenth century. Northern investors drained the region of its profits, keeping it in economic vassalage. The system of sharecropping and crop liens, begun in Reconstruction, led to a form of peonage for many poor whites as well as for innumerable southern blacks.

Women and children in a food processing plant with foreman watching over them. *(Courtesy, George Eastman House, Inc.)*

Steel

Before the Civil War, steel, an alloy composed primarily of iron and carbon, had been an expensive material, produced in small amounts by hand labor and used largely for knives, razors, swords, and springs. It was far more common not to work iron into steel. Iron itself came in two forms. Cast iron could be poured into molds, but the large amounts of dissolved carbon it contained made it brittle; wrought iron, containing little carbon, was soft and ductile, and used largely for ornamental shapes, nails, and horseshoes. Neither of these forms was very useful in construction, where great strength and the ability to take shock were vital. Americans built their bridges, public buildings, and ships of stone, brick, or wood. Even machinery in these years used much wood.

After the Civil War two new processes appeared—the Bessemer and the open-hearth—that revolutionized the production of steel. Both removed the right amount of dissolved carbon in cast iron to create a form of steel with great strength. Unlike previous steel-making techniques the new methods used little labor for producing large quantities and brought down the price. Suddenly steel became usable in place of wood, brick, or inferior iron, with tremendous gains in strength, durability, and cost. The first great use of the new cheap steel was in rails, where it resulted in increases in safety and load-carrying capacity. Before long, the use of steel spread widely. The first steel bridges came in the 1870s. Steel soon became common for ocean-going vessels, and was the foundation for the giant passenger liners of 20,000 tons or more that plied the Atlantic by the end of the century. Steel made possible the skyscraper, a building constructed around a light but strong metal frame that could soar many stories from the street without the thick, space-wasting walls formerly necessary for tall structures.

The steel industry's expansion was phenomenal. In 1860 the United States produced 13,000 tons of steel. By 1879 American furnaces were turning out over a million tons a year. By 1910 the United States was making over twenty-eight million tons, and was by far the largest producer of steel in the world.

Andrew Carnegie

No one individual can be given credit for this extraordinary transformation, but the most prominent of the steel industrialists was Andrew Carnegie. He was not a typical business leader of this period. Histo-

Andrew Carnegie, self-styled "distributor of wealth for the improvement of mankind," devoted to public causes ninety percent of the fortune he made in the steel industry. *(Courtesy of the Carnegie Corporation)*

rians who have looked into the social origins of late nineteenth-century businessmen have concluded that most of them came from native-born elite backgrounds and had received excellent educations for the day. Carnegie, however, was born of working class parents in Scotland and came to the United States with his family as a thirteen-year-old in 1848. Near Pittsburgh, where the Carnegies settled, Andrew started at the bottom as a $1.20 a week helper in a textile factory, doing piece work. He very quickly moved on to a telegraph office and then, during the Civil War, became a manager with the Pennsylvania Railroad. Wherever he worked the sprightly lad impressed his employers with his energy, intelligence, and enterprise, and they consistently pushed him ahead and let him in on opportunities. Gradually, as he accumulated money, he invested it in various new enterprises including oil refining, Pullman cars, and a company that built iron bridges. In 1872, Carnegie, by now thoroughly familiar with the processes of business and finance, organized the Union Mills to manufacture Bessemer steel.

Neither an inventor nor a gifted financier, Carnegie never really understood the chemistry of iron and steel. Nor did he ever engage in any of those elaborate stock deals that helped enrich speculators such as Jay Gould and James Fisk. Carnegie's chief talents in steel-making were in choosing competent subordinates who knew their jobs well and in ruthlessly cutting costs by the elimination of bottlenecks and by the running of all equipment full blast, even if this meant replacing it early. While others were cutting back on costs during the depression that began in 1873, Carnegie was taking advantage of the cheapness of equipment and improving his plant. His business skill consisted above all of examining every expense to see whether it was needed.

Of course Carnegie was riding the wave of economic expansion that each year created ever greater need for cheap steel. Still, he forged far ahead of all other steel producers. By the beginning of the twentieth century the Carnegie works in the Pittsburgh area were producing 700,000 tons of steel a year, more than all of Great Britain. In 1895 the Carnegie Company earned a profit of $5 million; in 1900 it took in $40 million. Since Carnegie owned by far the largest share of the firm, most of this went into his own pocket—in an era with no graduated income tax.

The production of steel is an example of a good producer's industry—an industry that manufactures a product used by other businessmen rather than by the public directly. Many other fast-growing industries in these years belong in the same category: coal mining, copper smelting, cement manufacture. Other great industries supplied consumers with goods or commodities. An outstanding instance was meatpacking.

Meatpacking Before the railroad age Americans got their meat from their own livestock or from animals slaughtered in the immediate neighborhood. Gustavus Swift saw that the railroads offered an opportunity to center slaughtering operations in one place, preferably close to cheap corn and grass, and distribute meat nationally. Live cattle had been sent to eastern con-

ANDREW CARNEGIE *was once quite an ordinary man. While most business leaders of his and future times came from wealth, Carnegie was free to give this inspirational address, based partially on his own career, to Curry Commercial College in Pittsburgh during 1885:*

THE ROAD TO BUSINESS SUCCESS: A TALK TO YOUNG MEN

It is well that young men should begin at the beginning and occupy the most subordinate positions. Many of the leading business men of Pittsburgh had a serious responsibility thrust upon them at the very threshold of their career. They were introduced to the broom, and spent the first hours of their business lives sweeping out the office. . . . I was one of those sweepers myself, and who do you suppose were my fellow sweepers? David McCargo, now superintendent of the Alleghany Valley Railroad; Robert Pitcairn, Superintendent of the Pennsylvania Railroad, and Mr. Moreland, City Attorney. . . .

Assuming that you have all obtained employment and are fairly started, my advice to you is "aim high." I would not give a fig for the young man who does not already see himself the partner or the head of an important firm. Do not rest content for a moment in your thoughts as head clerk, or foreman, or general manager in any concern, no matter how extensive. Say each to yourself. "My place is at the top." *Be King in your dreams. . . .*

The first and most seductive, and the destroyer of most young men, is the drinking of liquor. I say to you that you are more likely to fail in your career from acquiring the habit of drinking liquor than from any, or all, the other temptations likely to assail you. . . .

Assuming you are safe in regard to these your gravest dangers, the question now is how to rise from the subordinate position we have imagined you in, through the successive grades to the position for which you are, in my opinion, and, I trust, in your own, evidently intended. I can give you the secret. It lies mainly in this. Instead of the question "What must I do for my employer?" substitute "What can I do?" Faithful and conscientious discharge of the duties assigned you is all very well, but the verdict in such cases generally is that you perform your present duties so well that you had better continue performing them. Now, young gentlemen, this will not do. The rising man must do something exceptional, and beyond the range of his special department. *He must attract attention. . . .* Some day, in your own department, you will be directed to do or say something which you know will prove disadvantageous to the interest of the firm. Here is your chance. Stand up like a man and say so. Say it boldly, and give your reasons, and thus prove to your employer that, while his thoughts have been engaged upon other matters, you have been studying during hours when perhaps he thought you asleep, how to advance his interests. You may be right or you may be wrong, but in either case you have gained the first condition of success. You have attracted attention.

Always break orders to save owners. There never was a great character who did not sometimes smash the routine regulations and make new ones for himself. The rule is only suitable for such as have no aspirations, and you have not forgotten that you are destined to be owners and to make orders and break orders. . . .

And here is the prime condition of success, the great secret: concentrate your energy, thought, and capital exclusively upon the business in which you are engaged. Having begun in one line, resolve to fight it out on that line, to lead in it; adopt every improvement, have the best machinery, and know the most about it.

The concerns which fail are those which have scattered their capital, which means that they have scattered their brains also. They have investments in this, or that, or the other, here, there and everywhere. "Don't put all your eggs in one basket" is all wrong. I tell you "put all your eggs in one basket, and then watch that basket." It is trying to carry too many baskets that breaks most eggs in this country. He who carries three baskets must put one on his head, which is apt to tumble and trip him up. One fault of the American business man is lack of concentration.

PHILANTHROPY

Many of the successful industrialists, such as John D. Rockefeller, gave sizable parts of their fortunes to philanthropy. Here Finley Peter Dunne's Mr. Dooley gently satirized Andrew Carnegie's building of public libraries:

"Has Andhrew Carnaygie given ye a libry yet?" asked Mr. Dooley.

"Not that I know iv," said Mr. Hennessy.

"He will," said Mr. Dooley. "Ye'll not escape him. Befure he dies he hopes to crowd a libry on ivry man, woman, an' child in the' counthry. He's given thim to cities, towns, villages, an' whistlin' stations. They're tearin' down gas-houses an' poor-houses to put up libries. Befure another year, ivry house in Pittsburg that ain't a blast-furnace will be a Carnaygie libry. In some places all th' buildin's is libries. If ye write him f'r an autygraft he sinds ye a libry. No beggar is iver turned impty-handed fr'm th' dure. Th' pan-handler knocks an' asts f'r a glass iv milk an' a roll. 'No, sir,' says Andhrew Carnaygie, 'I will not pauperize this onworthy man.' Nawthin is worst f'r a beggar-man thin to make a pauper iv him. Yet it shall not be said iv me that I give nawthin' to th' poor. Saunders, give him a libry, an' if he still insists on a roll tell him to roll th' libry. F'r I'm humorous as well as wise,' he says. . . ."

"Isn't it good f'r lithrachoor, says ye? Sure, I think not, Hinnissy. Libries niver encouraged lithrachoor anny more thin tombstones encourage livin'. No wan iver wrote annythin' because he was tol' that a hundherd years fr'm now his books might be taken down fr'm a shelf in a granite sepulcher an' some wan wud write 'Good' or 'This man is crazy' in th' margin. What lithrachoor needs is fillin' food. If Andhrew wud put a kitchen in th' libries an' build some bunks or even swing a few hammocks where livin' authors cud crawl in at night an' sleep while waitin' f'r this enlightened nation to wake up an' discover th' Shakespeares now on th' turf, he wud be givin' a rale boost to lithrachoor."

sumers from western grasslands and the corn belt for years, but live animals did not travel well. Swift's idea was to slaughter cattle and hogs in Chicago and ship the trimmed carcasses to eastern distributors. Freight costs would be lower, the slaughtering process would be cheapened, and the disposing of vast herds in one spot provided for the convenient gathering of byproducts such as bristle, bone, hides, and fertilizer. For a while the scheme worked only in the winter months, when the cold reduced spoilage. But by 1880 the refrigerator made it possible to ship beef and hog carcasses all year round. By 1890 the Chicago packers were shipping a million trimmed sides of beef a year.

"Vertical" vs. "Horizontal" Integration

American entrepreneurs found two basic ways to transform the small enterprises characteristic of pre-Civil War manufacturing into giant corporations able to dominate national and even international markets. Economists define two structures of consolidation: vertical and horizontal integration.

Of vertical integration Carnegie was the chief exemplar. Carnegie determined to control every stage in the steel-making process from the mining of the iron ore to the manufacture of steel rails and other finished products. So he purchased iron mines on the Mesabi Range, and he took on Henry Clay Frick as a partner because Frick owned the soft coal that Carnegie needed to heat his blast furnaces. He also acquired huge fleets of ships to bring his iron ore to his mills and rail lines to transport his coal. Vertical integration, as Carnegie's example makes plain, involved bringing all the elements in the productive process under the control of a single company. This control allowed Carnegie to produce his steel much more cheaply than his competitors could, and his ability to undersell them enabled him to crush those firms that stood in the way of his ambition to monopolize the manufacture of steel. Most of his competitors, in fact, quickly realized that they could not withstand Carnegie's ability to cut prices below the level at which they could remain in business and so accepted his offers to buy them out.

The great meatpacking giants, like Swift or Armour, provide leading examples of the other organizing method, that of horizontal integration. The packers did not try to buy up huge ranches or raise their own herds. Nor did they seek to acquire their own railroads. Rather than trying to gain control over the entire productive process, as Carnegie was doing, the packers concerned themselves with distribution. The growth of a national rail system, together with the invention of the refrigerator car, made it possible for beef grown in the Southwest and then slaughtered and dressed in Chicago or Omaha to be sold in Worcester, Massachusetts, or Eugene, Oregon, at a lower price than beef grown locally. The secret lay in achieving economies of scale. It was cheaper per cow to raise giant herds in Texas than to support small herds in Massachusetts closer to major cities. The rapidly falling costs of rail transportation meant that the Texas cattle were still cheaper when they reached Chicago. There the enormous slaughterhouses and meatpacking plants butchered, dressed, and packaged the beef much more economically than their small, local competitors could. As a result, even after Swift or Armour paid to transport their meat products via refrigerated railroad cars all the way to the east coast, they could still undersell local butchers and meatpackers. What the giant packers needed to take advantage of these economies of scale was a national network of retail outlets. They needed to control not production but distribution.

Retailing

By late in the nineteenth century, mass production by large corporations for a national market was increasing spectacularly the volume of goods available to consumers and, as this new technique lowered the price of goods, handling the flood of consumer commodities required new methods of retailing them.

The General Store

In the early nineteenth century, when most Americans lived in villages and on farms, they bought either from traveling peddlers or from general stores those goods they did not produce for themselves. The general store, in turn, received agricultural commodities from the surrounding farmers, often in exchange for other goods. A farmer's wife, for example, who wanted a bolt of cloth would pay the merchant with a few dozen eggs or several wheels of cheese if she did not have the cash. Most of the local merchant's goods, especially tropical products and manufactured items, came from the merchants of the big coastal cities, who imported them from the Caribbean or from England and France. To stock their shelves, country merchants trekked annually to the big port towns—New York, Boston, Charleston, Philadelphia, Baltimore, or New Orleans—to visit

The first 5 & 10¢ store in the United States, opened by the F. W. Woolworth Company in Lancaster, Pennsylvania, 1879. *(Courtesy, the F. W. Woolworth Company, New York City)*

the warehouses of the large importers and buy on credit. The general store sold almost everything: silk ribbon, needles, hammers, nails, gunpowder and lead shot, flour, tea and coffee, yarn and cloth, candy, pickled fish, books, and whiskey. These items were seldom packaged; they were placed in barrels or bins and sold by weight or volume. Generally they were carried away in the customer's own container. Prices were not necessarily uniform. Customers bargained with the storekeeper and often received credit.

As manufacturing grew and more and more of the finished goods that consumers bought were produced in the United States, local retailers became less dependent on importers, turning instead to wholesalers who bought up the output of home factories. Located in the larger inland cities as well as on the East Coast, these wholesalers dealt either in a number of items or in some full line such as hardware or dry goods. In the growing cities and towns more and more general merchants began to specialize in selling specific products such as hats, or shoes, or books. General stores continued in smaller communities until the twentieth century.

The Department Store

During the years following the Civil War new kinds of retail outlets—the chain store, the mail-order house, and the department store—revolutionized the merchandizing of goods to consumers. Actually the department store had first made its appearance in the United States in the 1840s, when a few American merchants began to imitate a Paris institution, the Bon Marché, which combined a number of distinct specialty shops under one roof. The first great American department store magnate, A. T. Stewart of New York, was followed soon after by John Wanamaker of Philadelphia. As these stores grew in size it became impossible for owners to bargain with customers over prices. An owner did not care to delegate the responsibility to a clerk, and so the policy of charging one consistent price for an item, first adopted by R.H. Macy's in New York, quickly came to be standard for department stores and then for other retail establishments.

Selling goods on such a large scale, the big stores could exert an enormous amount of market leverage. Rather than deal with wholesalers, they could go directly to the manufacturers and so were able to bypass a whole layer of middlemen. Promising large volume orders, they could also compel manufacturers to give them good prices for their products, which they generally passed on to consumers. Another advantage of the department store was its range of services. It delivered purchases to customers and it guaranteed quality, accepting returns from dissatisfied customers. "Your money back if . . ." became one of the Chicago store's mottos. Another new marketing device was recommended by an Ohio retailer:

> Give store arrangement greater consideration, and create in the mind of the customer a desire for other things she sees, as well as the article she asks for. People used to buy what they needed, now it's what they want; and that want is created by store display or advertisement.

In major cities all over the country department stores soon became prominent landmarks. New York had A. T. Stewart as well as Macy's, the largest store in the world under one roof, and a flock of others. Philadelphia had Wanamaker's and Gimbel's. In Boston there were Jordan Marsh and Filene's. Chicagoans shopped at Marshall Field's and Carson, Price, Scott. In Columbus the big store was Lazarus; in Dallas, Neiman-Marcus; in Los Angeles, Bullock's; in Brooklyn, Abraham and Straus. Many of the department-store owners were either New England Yankees or German-Jewish merchants who had begun as peddlers or small shop-keepers before the Civil War and carried their marketing skills over to the new form when it appeared.

Department stores were especially designed to catch the attention of urban, middle-class women with money to spend and time to shop, and encouraged such women to raise shopping to an important pastime. By the 1880s *The New York Times* deplored the "awful prevalence of the vice of shopping among women," claiming that it was "every bit as bad as male smoking or drinking." The stores made increasing use of decorations, many of them evoking other cultures, exotic countries, and something of a dream world. They provided a protected space in which women could forget their daily cares and imagine themselves transformed by possession of alluringly packaged commodities. Eventually, the department stores provided special corners in which women could enjoy lunch or tea, for middle-class women a novel kind of freedom from domestic confinement.

In the East, entries in many affluent women's diaries might have read like this New Jersey woman's:

> February 26, 1903. To town at 12:30—O'Neill's, Altman's. Lunch at tea rooms on 20th St. . . . Stern's, McCreery's. . . . home 4:35. . . . March 2, 1903. To town on 9:30. . . . to Lax, Macy, Altman's, O'Neill's, Simpson and Arnold's, looking for a grey suit. . . . Home on 5:15 with George.

The department stores also attempted to make those women dependent on buying things that promised to realize their fantasies. The variety of consumer goods and the nurture of a consumer mentality can be seen in this young girl's diary:

> I got three pieces of Dutch silver from Momma and Grandma, a windmill, a mandolin and a little sleigh. A set of little leather box books for odds and ends. Packs of cards in black leather with silver cornered case. Silver gilt needle case from Miss Smith. Two bottles with silver all over them from Momma and Mrs. Yznaga. Pin cushion from Alfred P. Sewing box with initials from Josie, quilt basket filled with candy lined with blue silk and a beautiful black leather book for my photos with G. E. M. in the corner from Poppa, a present from Fraulein and a $5 gold piece from Mom.

The department stores also influenced the lives of the growing numbers of poorer women they employed as clerks. These women rarely could afford to acquire for themselves the goods that they were supposed to supply to other women as a necessity for happiness. Here, for example, is the diary of an apparently contented Brooklyn "working girl" in 1902:

> I made $4 a week by working six days in the week. . . .
>
> I lived at this time with a girl named Ella, who worked in the same factory and made $5 a week. We had the room all to ourselves, paying $1.50 a week for it, and doing light housekeeping. It was in Allen street, and the window looked out of the back, which was good, because there was an elevated railroad in front, and in the summer time a great deal of dust and dirt came in at the front windows. We were on the fourth story and could see all that was going on in the back rooms of the houses behind us, and early in the morning the sun used to come in our window.
>
> We did our cooking on an oil stove . . . the oil for the stove and the lamp cost us 10 cents a week . . . We lived well, as this list of our expenses for one week will show:

ELLA AND SADIE FOR FOOD (ONE WEEK)	
Tea	$0.06
Cocoa	.10
Bread and rolls	.40
Canned vegetables	.20
Potatoes	.10
Milk	.21
Fruit	.20
Butter	.15
Meat	.60
Fish	.15
Laundry	$ .25
Total	$2.42
Add rent	1.50
Grand total	$3.92
Income	$9.00
Expenses	$4.00

Such young women were encouraged to assume a veneer of middle-class respectability or gentility, and to look toward the day when they too could become shoppers.

Chain Stores Along with the department store came the chain store. These establishments flourished especially in the grocery and variety trades, of which the A & P (the Great Atlantic and Pacific Tea Company) and the Woolworth Five and Ten were the prototypes. Each store in a chain was expected to make a profit by itself, but management and accounting tied them together. Still more significant for the consumers was that the chains, like the department stores, could buy cheaply from suppliers. They refused credit, selling for cash only on a one-price basis. The effect was to cut prices to the consumer. This made customers happy but displeased small storekeepers, who charged that the chains engaged in unfair competition. Store owners also protested that the chain outlets were owned by absentees, not the local people who operated the small, familiar store. But by World War I the chain store had become an established feature of the American economy.

So had the mail-order house. Unlike chain stores and department stores, the mail-order or catalog house catered largely to a rural or small-town clientele. But it too sought to replace the middleman, in this case by selling goods ordered from a catalog. Aaron Montgomery Ward's success owed to his shrewd judgment of customers and the hostility of farmers to middlemen. He and his arch-rival, the firm of R. W. Sears and A. C. Roebuck, also benefited from the transportation revolution. By the end of the century a quickening of railroad traffic had improved postal services immensely, and within a few years rural free delivery was bringing letters and packages to the farmer's front door.

Money, Banking, and Finance

All the business of the nation, whether manufacturing, wholesaling, or retailing, rode on a sea of money and credit supplied either by the federal government or by the private banking system. Money and credit aroused controversy not only among businessmen and financial experts, but also among politicians and ordinary citizens. At times it became the focus of fierce and raucous political debate.

Greenbacks Many of the financial issues of the Gilded Age were related to the Civil War. The war had forced the Union government to issue almost a half-billion dollars worth of greenbacks, paper money that the government made legal tender, a currency that creditors must accept in payment of all debts. The government had also sold many hundreds of millions of dollars worth of bonds. Linked to the bonds was a new banking system. Private financial promoters of any bank intended to be designated a national bank had to deposit bonds with the federal Comptroller of the Currency, who would then issue bank notes to the extent of ninety percent of the value of the bonds. These bank notes entered general circulation when the banks lent money to borrowers, and, along with the greenbacks, they became the paper money that Americans used until 1913. The system, though an improvement over the chaotic banking structure prevailing from 1836 to 1863, had many drawbacks.

One of its failings was that the supply of currency did not grow fast enough to meet the needs of the nation's expanding economy. The system also failed to establish a central bank that could come to the rescue of hard-pressed financial institutions in time of panic, when money went into hiding. Agrarians particularly objected to the provision of the national banking acts that forbade the federally chartered banks to accept mortgages as security for loans. There was a parallel state banking system, and during these years it expanded primarily to fill rural needs, but it never could fully meet the farmers' demands for abundant cheap credit on the security of their lands.

The very existence of the bonds and greenbacks made for controversy. It was generally thought that a hard currency—a currency made of metal—would hold more firmly to its value than soft or paper currency: that since the government could easily print more and more paper money, a paper dollar would be distrusted and tend to fall in value. A hard currency would keep prices from becoming inflated, and it benefited creditors, who of course wanted repayment in dollars as valuable as the dollars they had lent. Paper money would benefit debtors, for they would be paying in dollars less valuable than those they had borrowed.

For a time during the Jacksonian period, the advocates of hard metal currency had presented their case as the cause of the plain and poorer classes. By the late nineteenth century, however, debate over currency had reverted to its more normal terms: the prosperous favored hard dollars while spokesmen for debtors demanded paper. Among the advocates of "sound money," as partisans of metallic currency called it, were many bankers and merchants, along with conservatives who believed that paper money cheated creditors and would disrupt the economy. Champions of sound money called for the withdrawal of the greenbacks from circulation, and insisted that the government repay the bonds in gold, as they claimed it had promised. These were the "sound" and "honest" things to do and were essential if the country was to keep up public confidence in the stability of the currency. Soft money partisans—identified immediately after the war with some manufacturers, farmers, and other groups of people whose work was in production rather than finance—feared that the removal of all paper dollars from the currency would drive down prices and therefore lessen profits.

They also argued that it would be an injustice to debtors, forcing them to pay back in hard dollars more valuable than the dollars they had borrowed.

Some partisans of soft currency insisted that even more greenbacks be printed. This scheme, called the "Ohio Idea" and championed by the Ohio Democratic Senator George Pendleton, became a major issue between the parties shortly after 1865. In later years the idea of increasing greenbacks became the basis of a political movement to expand the country's money supply. During the 1870s and 1880s various greenback parties fought for soft money as relief to debtors and advocated general programs of aid to wage earners. In the South blacks formed a significant part of the greenback parties. Observed one letter to the editor:

> Miners, iron workers, farmers and every son of toil, must come to a general understanding. . . . The colored man of the South can be no longer made use of by the political henchmen of Republicans or Democrats, but we who are compelled to work side by side with him must drop our prejudice and bigotry. This is the lever that's keeping labor in bondage to capital.

Silver A second battle between soft and hard currency began in the mid-1870s. Radicals made a sharp distinction between "producers,"—the farmers and workers who actually made some useful commodity—and the financiers who manipulated the market without producing a single steel girder or a single sack of grain. The producers had been victimized when Congress in 1873 stopped issuing the old silver dollar. Because silver is a less precious metal than gold, a silver currency is considered softer, its dollars more likely than gold dollars to shrivel in value. Silver coin, then, was one kind of metal currency that had something of the financial softness of greenbacks. And champions of paper currency found it easy to become champions of silver. Silver advocates insisted that the "Crime of '73," as they called the action of Congress, had been the result of a plot by bankers and other capitalists. Then in 1879 the Treasury redeemed greenbacks in gold, which brought their value to par after an eighteen-year lapse that had begun during the Civil War. This meant that holders of paper money could now have the government give them gold money in exchange for it. Since the supply of gold was limited, the supply of paper money would be limited also. Unless the nation restored silver to the money supply at the ratio of sixteen ounces of silver to one ounce of gold, argued the soft-money people, the country would be at the mercy of the bankers, especially those whose resources were strengthened by connections abroad. Debtors injured by the obligation to repay in dollars dearer than the dollars they had borrowed would have to go to the banks for further loans.

Mining interests in the western states strongly supported the farmers, debtors, and soft-money economists who were calling for the expansion of the money supply by remonetizing silver. The huge discoveries of silver in Nevada, Colorado, and Utah in the 1870s increased silver production but undermined its price. The profits of mine owners declined, as did the wages of miners and the number of jobs in the industry. Congressmen from those states, anxious to raise silver prices and satisfy their constituents, joined hands with the farm and labor groups who wanted soft money. They became a powerful political coalition in Congress.

In 1878 the silverites got Congress to pass the Bland-Allison Silver Purchase Act requiring the treasury to buy monthly not less than $2 million and not more than $4 million of silver on the open market and coin this bullion into dollars. The adding of silver to greenbacks and national banknotes, the advocates of this measure hoped, would not only give the country some needed immediate monetary relief, but make it impossible to uphold the gold standard, since the amount of currency would be too great to be exchangeable for the government's gold. But the treasury had a large enough gold reserve to treat the new silver dollars as just another kind of paper money. Anyone who wished might come to the banks and get a gold dollar for a silver one in the same manner as a bank note was exchangeable for gold. In 1890 came the Sherman Silver Purchase Act ordering the treasury to purchase 4.5 million ounces of silver each month and to issue new paper money against it redeemable in either gold or silver. There the issue rested until the Panic of 1893 produced a great monetary crisis by undermining public confidence in the treasury's reserve and sending thousands to convert their silver and paper into gold coin.

Investment Bankers

The national and state banks had their failings, but they successfully performed business for the nation. In the cities the national banks handled thousands of daily transactions, making business loans, discounting commercial paper for merchants, and transferring funds from place to place. In the small towns and country communities the state banks helped local feed-and-grain merchants and advanced cash to carry farmers over until the time for selling their crops. And farmers could mortgage their property to banks in return for loans with which to buy machinery or to build a barn or house.

Far removed from the farm communities, standing above even the big-city banks, were the investment bankers. These businessmen did not accept deposits and make loans to merchants. Rather, they marketed securities for large private corporations as well as for cities, states, counties, and even the federal government.

J. Pierpont Morgan, banker and financier whose investments in railroads and steel made his company one of the most powerful banking houses in the world. *(Courtesy, Morgan Guaranty Trust Co.)*

Wall Street The investment bankers put much of their funds into the stock market, the institution identified with Wall Street in lower Manhattan, where securities of all sorts—government and private corporation bonds and corporation stocks—were bought and sold. The New York Stock Exchange was a private body of brokers who managed their affairs like a club, but a loosely run club with scant regard for the public.

During the Gilded Age (in 1878 Mark Twain coined this phrase for his times: dazzling on the surface, base metal underneath) buying and selling securities on the Exchange, especially trading in common stock, resembled the operations of a gambling casino. "Bull" speculators bet, as they do today, on a rise in stock prices and "bear" speculators bet on a fall. Few conservative investors cared to buy the common stock traded on Wall Street. The competition of bulls and bears made for wild fluctuation in prices, and ownership seldom brought substantial dividends. Too much of the common stock was "water," issue in excess of the bedrock assets of the companies putting it out, and even the most profitable firm could seldom pay much return on a share. On the other hand, the stock market provided a fair indirect investment to banks and other financial institutions with some excess funds to invest for short periods. Brokers and stock gamblers could use such money and were willing to pay good rates of interest for it. This created a call loan market where money could be lent on a day-to-day basis, subject to instant recall by the lender. The call loan market introduced another element of instability into the country's financial structure. Every fall when money was needed for marketing the country's crops, money left Wall Street to return to the farm areas, and the flight of money from the stock market sometimes turned into a financial panic, as in 1873, 1884, and 1907. Not until the very end of the nineteenth century did Wall Street become a true money market where people with capital to lend on a long-term basis made deals with those who needed capital for long periods.

The enormous expansion of industry after

1865 created a great need for billions in capital. Investors were willing to buy corporate bonds since these represented a debt of the firm and had to be paid, interest and principal, before any other obligation, even if the firm made no profit in a given year. Useful in marketing these securities were special investment bankers who agreed to sell large blocks of bonds, taking a commission for their work. Slowly the public also developed an interest in common stock, especially if it was sold by one of the large investment houses like Kidder, Peabody of Boston, Kuhn, Loeb of New York, and J. P. Morgan and Company. These firms not only stood behind the issues in a general way but also often insisted on putting one of their partners on the corporation's board of directors as insurance to purchasers that the corporation's affairs would be well managed and holders of common stock not be defrauded.

Mergers

Pools, Trusts, and Holding Companies During the last decades of the century firms battled furiously for customers. To keep their share of a business, manufacturers and railroad operators had to cut their prices and costs. This was fine for consumers; in the course of a price war among the trunk railroads connecting New York to Chicago, the rate for a carload of cattle, normally costing the shipper $110, dropped to one dollar. But competition was hard on businessmen, and numbers of them sought in every way possible to reduce it. Often firms in a particular business would arrange informal "gentlemen's agreements" assigning each company a fixed share of the market. This ended any need to cut price in pursuit of a steady business. Pools were similar arrangements but involved an actual written contract among the participants. Both were difficult to enforce. When the agreements fell through, businessmen created other devices for achieving an end to competition. One of these, the trust, required stockholders of several firms to turn over their voting rights to trustees who thereafter ran the businesses as a unit, paying dividends to the original shareholders. John D. Rockefeller, in his effort to reduce the competition in the oil refining business during the early 1880s, was the first to employ the trust scheme. When state and federal courts declared trusts illegal, ingenious businessmen turned to the holding company. Taking advantage of a New Jersey law of 1889 allowing one corporation to hold stock in others, corporation lawyers arranged for a single large firm, a holding company, to acquire stock in companies that had been competing with one another. The holding company executives, of course, could then decide to limit competition in any way they chose among the firms they controlled. Some of their buyouts were generous. But they could ruthlessly drive independent firms out of business. Trusts and their ilk were real enough and led to a concentration of wealth.

At the same time, the existence of mergers awakened suspicions that much of the country was in the hands of conspiratorial, unseen interests. An exaggerated example of this suspicion is to be found in a letter of a dairyman to his senator in 1866:

> Awake, arouse, Senator, to this Butter issue, and act as a STATESMAN. What has so called Politics to do with it? God favors the dairy, as of old he favored Abel, and the devil helps the Oleomargarine tribe. . . . Senator: be a STATESMAN; scan history, sacred and profane, and throughout its pages you will find the dairy and the farm tied for FIRST place in the estimation of all nations.
>
> There is a remarkable connection between Oleomargarine, and Anarchists, Socialists, Dynamitists and Disruptionists. Strikingly significant is it, that law-abiding and order-loving citizens and countrymen do not retail it. Show me a retailer of Oleomargarine, and in him, I'll show you a ready recruit for riot and anarchy—for "Treasons, stratagems and spoils." Does not your patriotism boil now to place a limit upon the encroachments of this foreign plague, sent to strike a death blow to an industry that is the very heart of our nation? Names prominent in the manufacture and sale of the stuff link it to other countries; it is UNAMERICAN in origin and practice. The pulse that quickens at the names of Washington, Jackson, Bunker Hill, Trenton, Yorktown and New Orleans, warms no breast that would harbor a vote to favor Oleomargarine sales at retail.

The blazing steel works in Pittsburgh, Pennsylvania. The 1901 merger of Andrew Carnegie's steel firm with a dozen others formed the United States Steel Company, the largest corporation in the world. *(Courtesy, Scribner's Archives)*

During the 1870s and 1880s consolidations took place on a wide scale in many consumer goods industries: leather products, salt, sugar, biscuits, starch, kerosene, rubber boots, and gloves. During the depression of the early 1890s the movement toward consolidation stopped. After 1897 it resumed with a rush, primarily in the producer or capital goods industries, but also in a few newer consumer goods industries, such as meat and cigarettes, that catered primarily to city people.

In the eight years from 1898 through 1905 more than 3,000 important business mergers occurred in industries that included steel, machinery, tobacco, copper, and cans. In this second wave the role of investment bankers was prominent. The holding company that was to control the formerly competing firms had to raise capital to buy up their stock and this required the services of bankers. The investment bankers were also useful for reassuring stockholders of the individual companies and those with savings to invest that the new firm would be reliable. One of the classic instances of mergers in this era was the formation of the United States Steel Company in 1901.

By the early 1890s, Andrew Carnegie's powerful steel firm was both efficient and profitable. Meanwhile, other steel men were creating parallel firms that unlike the Carnegie Company turned out various finished steel shapes and products. When Carnegie threatened to undertake this kind of work, he frightened his competitors badly. They turned to J. P. Morgan and asked him to organize a merger that would stop this impending war.

At first Carnegie was reluctant to join the merger, but then he yielded. The "star-spangled Scotsman" had long dreamed of withdrawing from business and devoting his time to culture and his money to good causes. Here was his chance, and when Morgan offered him the equivalent of almost half a billion dollars, he agreed to the deal. Most of what he received was in the form of bonds and stock in the United States Steel Company, a firm organized out of the Carnegie firm and a dozen others with a total capitalization of $1.4 billion. United States Steel at its moment of birth controlled sixty percent of the country's steel business as well as vast reserves of ore and coal and over a thousand miles of railroad. It was the largest corporation in the world. Carnegie himself enjoyed his money to the full. But not in the usual way. He founded 3,000 public libraries and provided over 4,000 churches with organs. He founded the Carnegie Institute of Technology, built the Peace Palace at the Hague for the International Court of Arbitration, and constructed Carnegie Hall in New York as a showcase for concerts and cultural events. He set aside $125 million for the Carnegie Foundation. When he died he had given away virtually all his Morgan money.

A Business Civilization

Big businessmen despised trade unionism and believed that they alone were the proper judges of labor's well-being. When John Mitchell, leader of the anthracite coal strike of 1902, asked George Baer of the Philadelphia and Reading Coal Company to submit the dispute to arbitration, Baer allegedly responded: "The rights and interests of the laboring man will be protected and cared for, not by the labor agitators, but by the Christian men to whom God in His infinite wisdom has given control of the property interests of the country, and upon the successful Management on which so much depends." Many businessmen fought to retain control of wages, hours, and working conditions, and refused to share their power with anyone else, whether politicians or labor leaders. The only arrangement they recognized as legitimate was the individual bargain struck with the worker.

The attitude of employers toward unions was at bottom a matter of simple self-interest. It also had to do with a more general notion about economics that much of society, and even workers themselves, shared in some measure.

Laissez-faire and Social Darwinism That notion had as one of its components the principle of laissez-faire that came from the teachings of many British thinkers, among them Adam Smith and David Ricardo. The principle held that the way to get the greatest and cheapest possible productivity was to leave the individual employer and the individual worker to the free market. Any attempt to interfere through unions or through govermental action would distort the market and reduce total production, to the injury of laborers, employers, and consumers. At times laissez-faire thinkers invoked divine sanction for their theories. One economist believed that free markets were governed by "God's laws," and claimed that observing these laws would not only benefit individuals in this life, but prepare them "for the life that is to come."

Ideas such as these had long circulated in the United States. Laissez-faire was the basic economic doctrine of college courses and enjoyed enormous prestige among educated Americans. After about 1870 it had reinforcement from another set of principles, often called Social Darwinism, derived in part from the ideas of Charles Darwin, the English naturalist. Just as Darwin, according to his earliest interpreters, had shown that in the biological world progress from the lowliest creature to man depended on a fierce struggle for survival, so Social Darwinists argued that social progress depended on competition among human beings. To interfere with this struggle in any way would result in the collapse of civilization or, at the very least, in stagnation. When one small businessman was asked what he would do to alleviate the economic evils of the day, he replied:

> Nothing! You and I can do nothing at all. It's all a matter of evolution. We can only wait for evolution. Perhaps in four or five thousand years evolution may have carried man beyond this state of things. But we can do nothing.

The concrete applications of laissez-faire

could be heartless. Sometimes factory owners acknowledged that the wages they paid did not cover workers' basic needs.

Social Darwinism, in fact, had scant approval, if any, from biologists in its use of theories of evolution; it was a mistaken effort to find similarities between biological and economic events. Darwin himself had nothing to do with it. Social Darwinism was promoted most notably in the United States by the Yale sociologist, William Graham Summer. Recent scholarship has indicated that not many businessmen took much serious account of the idea, or perceived of a sound economy as being as brutally competitive as Social Darwinists would seem to insist. But Social Darwinism, along with the free market doctrines that colleges had been teaching for many years, did represent the dominance in American thinking of the principle of laissez-faire. It had further support from a moral and constitutional conviction that individuals should be free to manage their property as they please and to enter into contracts of their own choosing, and that any major interference on the part of the government in relations between labor and management would violate both the employer's property rights and the right of employer and worker to make a contract.

Whatever sense this concept of free contract might make in a small-town or rural economy, it was nonsense in an era of giant corporations and great disparities in property. There was no equality between the bargaining position of a coal miner and that of Baer's coal company over the terms of employment, no free contractual agreement between equals; the individual worker was free only to accept the employer's terms or to accept hunger in place of them. The use that conservatives and businessmen made of doctrines of laissez-faire involved other contradictions as well. Critics pointed out that businessmen actually detested competition when it threatened profits. Cut-throat domestic competition had fueled the merger movement. Afraid to compete with foreign manufacturers, the iron producers, the textile mill owners, the woolen manufacturers, and many others who faced formidable competition from abroad fought for ever higher protective tariffs. In these years Congress gave in to the pressures of American industrialists and raised tariffs far beyond where they had been before the Civil War. Nor were businessmen averse to direct government subsidies when they could be had. Railroad promoters gave no evidence of being troubled that the federal and state policy of making land grants to railroads was contrary to the teaching of laissez-faire.

The Horatio Alger Hero Despite the inconsistencies, it would be a mistake to dismiss the laissez-faire principle as a rationalization and a sham. People are capable of honestly believing two conflicting ideas simultaneously. Ideas, moreover, are not merely rationalizations. They frequently take on a life of their own and become powerful forces. Americans deeply believed in private property and economic freedom. It was assumed that society was open and allowed for movement upward of the hard-working, the sober, and the able, and that no one need settle permanently for a place in the economic cellar.

The story of a boy's odyssey from poverty to riches became an influential genre in the skilled hands of Horatio Alger, a prolific writer who pounded out scores of novels with such titles as *Work and Win, Strive and Succeed, Do and Dare, Sink or Swim, Risen from the Ranks*, and *Facing the World*. Alger's typical hero is a boy of about fifteen, often the age for starting adult life in this period. He possesses all the virtues of honesty, sobriety, willingness to work hard. Tellingly, the Alger hero makes his fortune not by these virtues alone but by a stroke of good fortune such as marrying the boss's daughter or coming to the attention of a rich benefactor. But along the way the young male reader was made aware of the great possibilities open to him in the United States.

This dialogue from Alger's *Ragged Dick* is not untypical:

> 'I wish you'd tell me a little about yourself. Have you got any father or mother?'
>
> 'I aint got no mother. She died when I wasn't but three years old. My father went to sea; but he went off before mother died, and nothin' was ever heard of him. I expect he got wrecked, or died at sea.'
>
> 'And what became of you when your mother died?'
>
> 'The folks she boarded with took care of me, but they was poor, and they couldn't do much. When I was seven the woman died, and her husband went out West, and then I had to scratch for myself.'
>
> 'At seven years old!' exclaimed Frank, in amazement.
>
> 'Yes,' said Dick, 'I was a little feller to take care

of myself, but,' he continued with pardonable pride, 'I did it. . . .'

'I went into the match business,' said Dick; 'but it was small sales and small profits. Most of the people I called on had just laid in a stock, and didn't want to buy. So one cold night, when I hadn't money enough to pay for a lodgin', I burned the last of my matches to keep me from freezin'. But it cost too much to get warm that way, and I couldn't keep it up.'

'There's one thing I never could do,' he added, proudly.

'What's that?'

'I never stole,' said Dick. 'It's mean and I wouldn't do it.'

The myth of success remained exclusively a male myth; women were not encouraged to move upward by their own effort. Among the middle and upper working classes, in fact, one test of a man's success was his ability to support a wife who would devote herself exclusively to providing for the comfort of himself and his children. The scholar Thorstein Veblen perceived and identified an extreme and critical version of this attitude when he described women's fashions as nothing but embodiments of male success. Most women were not fashionable women, but even a woman's reserved domesticity could indicate that a man had made it.

Many ordinary Americans had some reason to believe the success story. A common experience among Americans in the years from 1859 to the early part of the twentieth century was the accumulation of some property over an entire working life. Many did rise occupationally either in level of skill or from manual to white-collar status. Others saw their children move upward.

Another reason the nation gave business a considerable acceptance on its own terms was that so many Americans were themselves businessmen of one sort or another. An enormous number of American family heads in this era were farm owners who

This Currier and Ives print preached that the way to grow rich was through hard work and thrift; in reality, a little shrewdness was also needed.

raised crops for sale. In 1890 there were about 3.3 million of these out of about 13 million families in the country. Add to this another million business concerns, mostly small firms, and the result is a figure that suggests that about a third of all American families of 1890 made their incomes from selling commodities or services. By 1890 many farmers were becoming skeptical of big business, but on two points they certainly agreed with it: private property deserved protection from those who would attack it; and there was nothing intrinsically wrong with the profit system. Agrarian radicals wanted, in fact, a nation of holders of small private property, and they attacked the capitalist classes for depriving the poor of property and robbing the farmers of legitimate profit.

The Supreme Court

The attitudes of the Supreme Court in these years reflected and reinforced values favorable to business. The Court in a number of important decisions resisted governmental regulation of economic life.

State Regulations Upheld and Denied

Such views did not at first prevail. Louisiana had granted to a slaughterhouse company a monopoly of that business. In 1873 the Supreme Court heard arguments that it declare the monopoly invalid. The opponents of the monopoly claimed that in favoring one slaughterhouse company over others Louisiana had violated the provisions of the Fourteenth Amendment that states must offer equal protection of the law. The purpose of the Amendment, the Court declared in upholding the state in the "Slaughterhouse" cases, was to protect black people, not to place the federal government in the position of protecting citizens' property rights against a state legislature. In the case of *Munn v. Illinois* (1877) the Supreme Court upheld a law the Illinois legislature had passed to regulate the price charged by grain elevator companies for storing grain. This was one of a flood of laws passed during the 1870s by midwestern states at the behest of the farmer groups called "Grangers" and designed to regulate railroads and middlemen. An elevator company claimed that it was being deprived of its property in a way that violated the Fourteenth Amendment. Chief Justice Morrison Waite, speaking for the Court, declared that in the case of a business "clothed with a public interest," a business that affected the well-being of the public, it was the right of a legislature to protect that public interest.

Then business had its triumphs. In two cases in the mid-1880s the Court drastically restricted the power of states to regulate business. In *Santa Clara Co. v. Southern Pacific Railroad* (1886) the Court accepted the view that corporations were legal "persons" and so, like black people, protected by the Fourteenth Amendment against being arbitrarily deprived of property. That same year, in *Wabash, St. Louis & Pacific Railroad Company v. Illinois*, it struck down an Illinois law regulating railroads. Here the Court stressed not the Fourteenth Amendment but the section of the Constitution giving the national Congress the authority to regulate interstate commerce. The Illinois law, the Court declared, was an unconstitutional assumption by that state of a power granted only to Congress. The Court also prevented the government from acting in matters of child labor. These conservative Supreme Court decisions, however, by no means ended state efforts to exercise their police powers over corporations. Between 1887 and 1897 the states and territories passed over 1,600 laws dealing with working conditions.

The Supreme Court meanwhile was restricting on constitutional grounds the scope of federal legislation. The Wilson-Gorman Tariff Act of 1894 had established the first income tax in United States history. It imposed a tax on income from personal property and from municipal bonds and raised a storm of protest from business groups and the well-to-do. The Supreme Court heard the case—*Pollock v. Farmers' Loan and Trust Company*—in 1895 and overturned the income tax, arguing that the legislation was unconstitutional because it amounted to a direct tax on personal property. In subsequent years, reformers launched an income tax movement that eventually added the Sixteenth Amendment to the Constitution, permitting the federal government to impose on each income a tax commensurate with its size.

Interstate Commerce Commission Congress, under pressure from farmer and merchant groups who complained about excessive charges for the hauling of their goods, rushed to fill the gap created by the *Wabash* case. Whether the Supreme Court had been correct in denying to states the right to regulate commerce that flowed across state boundaries, there was no doubt that Congress possessed that authority. In 1887 the national legislature passed the Interstate Commerce Act. This measure declared illegal all rebates—portions of rates returned to the payers—that a railroad might make to its more extensive users; all customers must be charged alike for services. The law made it illegal for railroads to engage in the practice, common at the time, of charging higher rates per ton mile for short hauls than for long ones. It outlawed the forming of railroad pools. The Act required that "all charges . . . be reasonable and just." It established a five-member Interstate Commerce Commission (ICC) that could examine complaints or investigate railroad practices on its own initiative. If the Commission found that a railroad had violated the Act, it could bring the violation before the federal courts and compel the railroad to comply with its ruling.

On the face of it the law seemed an effective assertion of federal power to regulate interstate transportation in the public interest. It was not. Thomas M. Cooley, the first chairman of the ICC, was a leading constitutional lawyer who deplored "hostility to railroad management," and believed "antagonism to acquired wealth" to be "dangerous." Under Cooley the ICC favored the railroads and allowed them more or less to charge what the traffic would bear. It even warned against freight and passenger rates that were too low. When the Commission did attempt to limit what the railroads might charge, the Supreme Court in 1897 in the *Maximum Freight Rate* case declared, despite the in-

Coal minors [*sic*] picking slate at a coal chute; their clothes and faces black with coal dust, these boys earned $2.50 for a sixty-hour work week. *(Courtesy, George Eastman House, International Museum of Photography).*

tent of Congress, that the ICC had "no power to prescribe the tariff or rates which shall control in the future."

The Sherman Antitrust Act Trusts were widely seen as squeezing out financially smaller competitors and thereby injuring both small business and the public. In response to widespread anger at trusts, Congress in 1890 passed the Sherman Antitrust Act. The measure declared that "every contract, combination in the form of trust or otherwise, or conspiracy, in restraint of trade or commerce among the several States or with foreign nations, is hereby declared to be illegal." A person who violated the Act would be committing a misdemeanor. An actual person found guilty would be subject to fine or imprisonment. "Person" within the meaning contemplated by the Act referred also, and more importantly, to corporations, which by law are definable for some purposes as persons. A guilty corporation might pay a fine and receive an order for the dissolution of the illegal combination. Federal district attorneys could prosecute suspected violators and those wronged by their actions could sue for triple damages.

In the first important antitrust case brought before it, *United States v. E.C. Knight* (1895), the Supreme Court gutted the Sherman Act. The *Knight* case involved purchases by the American Sugar Refining Company of several refineries in Philadelphia that when added to its existing capacity gave American Sugar control of 98 percent of all American refining. Few monopolies could have been more inclusive. Yet in a decision that dismayed even many lawyers who were partisans of business, the Court declared that sugar refining was manufacturing, not trade or commerce, and was therefore not subject to the Sherman Act. Thereupon, until Theodore Roosevelt and the Progressives invoked it in the new century, the law was made inactive as a regulation of business. Meanwhile it was applied vigorously against labor unions on the grounds that strikes were devices to restrain trade. Under this interpretation the courts issued several injunctions to keep labor unions from interfering with business. In the *Danbury Hatters Case* (1905), the Supreme Court also decided that a labor union could not, under the Sherman Act, initiate a secondary boycott—could not boycott one business to force it to put pressure on another engaged in a labor dispute. "I give you," a New York banker toasted in 1895, "the Supreme Court of the United States—guardian of the dollar, defender of private property, enemy of spoliation, sheet anchor of the republic."

But toward the end of the century an increasing number of state legislatures began to pass laws limiting the working hours of women and children, and of men in unhealthy or dangerous occupations. This represented a new social concern that in the early twentieth century would culminate in a mass of social legislation that contemporaries gave the label "Progressivism." To defenders of laissez-faire, these laws seemed yet another violation of fundamental economic law; and doctrinaire champions of private property thought them an invasion of the rights of employers to control their business. In *Lochner v. New York* (1905) the Supreme Court declared unconstitutional a New York law limiting the hours at which employees in the baking industry could be kept at work. In a famous dissent Associate Justice Oliver Wendell Holmes, Jr., attacked the basis of the majority opinion. The Constitution was "not intended to embody a particular economic theory, whether of paternalism . . . or of *Laissez-faire*."

The Supreme Court drew on the legal doctrine that the act of entering into a contract concerning the conditions of work is a fundamental right—a right that in this case, so the Court believed, the Fourteenth Amendment protected against certain kinds of interference on the part of state governments. Holmes was on strong ground, however, in warning the Court against going beyond its proper role. Often in the real economic world no actual equality of bargaining power exists between employer and employee, and poverty may force people into unhealthy occupations. That reality can make a mockery of such philosophical and constitutional abstractions as the rights of property and the rights of free contract. The Supreme Court had to learn to allow legislatures considerable freedom to look for the real and particular facts of economic life and to make laws accordingly.

In a series of decisions from 1904 onward the Court did allow the Sherman Act to be a weapon against combinations in restraint of trade. And in 1908, in *Muller v. Oregon,* it refused to strike down an Oregon law limiting

Though the Supreme Court did not often look with favor upon laws regulating economic activity, more and more states toward the end of the 1800s began limiting the working hours of children and women. *(Courtesy, International Museum of Photography)*

the working hours of women. Yet despite this moderate change of heart the Supreme Court was to remain skeptical of the constitutionality of laws regulating economic activity. Not until well into the 1930s would it come down with some consistency on the side of the public interest as defined by Congress against the private interest of property holders and business firms.

Points To Think About

1. The growth of the steel industry in the years following the Civil War illustrates the role of the railroad in American economic development. The railroad played an important part in shipping the iron ore and coke to the mills, and the finished steel to the ultimate users. It was also the largest single customer for steel. Rail construction meant steel—for the rails, for the rolling stock, for bridges, trestles, and terminals. Hence the growth of the railroads stimulated the steel industry.

Economists refer to this kind of stimulation as the "multiplier effect."

Fortunately for the steel industry, the automobile and trucking industry that so weakened the railroads was also a huge consumer of steel. That steel is an essential ingredient in so many products is what leads economists to label it a basic industry.

2. There is no doubt that the Supreme Court played a vital role in shoring up a business civilization during the later portion of the nineteenth century. The Court's decision to extend the "due process" clause of the Fourteenth Amendment to corporations had the effect of seriously weakening legislative restraints on corporate behavior. This decision was a revolutionary one, at least in the sense that it reversed several centuries of judicial practice.

Arnold Paul's *The Conservative Crisis and the Rule of Law* is a fascinating study of the Court during this period. Paul points out that Anglo-American jurisprudence is conservative in two senses. It operates on the basis of precedents and so is formally or procedurally conservative, and it has the protection of property as one of its central objectives and so is substantively conservative as well. The Granger Laws and other restrictive legislation of the period caused a "conservative crisis," Paul argues, because while they seemed—to judges steeped in the dogmas of laissez-faire—to threaten property rights, they rested on centuries of legislative practice and judicial approval. Their authority consisted of the state's "police power" to protect the public interest, a power English and American courts had traditionally given wide scope. The Granger Laws, then, pitted two forms of conservatism against each other: a conservatism that exalted private property and another that affirmed the ancient powers of legislatures.

The Court's decision to put property rights above the rights of legislatures acting in the service of the public interest amounted to a revolutionary conservatism. In this context it is worth noting that unrestrained corporations were the primary engines of the economic and social revolutions that transformed American life during this period. And as the late Richard Hofstadter shrewdly observed in his *The American Political Tradition,* American conservatives, from Alexander Hamilton to Andrew Carnegie, have usually been fervent believers in change. It has usually fallen to the liberals, from Thomas Jefferson to Woodrow Wilson, to bemoan the passing of the old order and to seek to legislate its restoration.

Suggested Readings

Recent scholarship on late nineteenth-century industrial America includes Maurey Klein, *The Life and Legend of Jay Gould* (1986), Vincent P. Carosso and Rose C. Carosso, *The Morgans, 1853–1913* (1987), David F. Hawkes, *John D: The Founding Father of the Rockefellers* (1980), Susan P. Benson, *Counter Cultures: Saleswomen, Managers, and Customers in American Department Stores, 1890–1940* (1986), Walter Licht, *Working for the Railroad* (1983), James Ward, *Railroads and the Character of America, 1820–1887* (1986), Alan Trachtenberg, *The Incorporation of America* (1982), and Harold C. Livesay, *Andrew Carnegie and the Rise of Big Business* (1975).

Anthony F. C. Wallace, in *Rockdale: The Growth of an American Village in the Early Industrial Revolution* (1978), analyzes, from the standpoint of a cultural anthropologist, the social and ethnic composition of a nineteenth-century community as it became industrialized. He also considers the religious and moral ideology that the social and business elite fashioned for conditioning the population to the disciplines of industrialism. Alfred D. Chandler, Jr., *The Visible Hand: The Managerial Revolution in American Business* (1977) follows the development of a managerial structure in American business and the reasons for it. The work argues that it was not the "invisible hand" of unregulated economic forces but the conscious decisions of managers that have given shape to the American economy. See also Glenn Porter, *The Rise of Big Business* (1973) and Stuart Bruchey, *Growth of the Modern Economy* (1974). Irwin Unger won a Pulitzer Prize for *The Greenback Era: A Social and Political History of American Finance, 1865–1879* (1964). Albro Martin, *James J. Hill and the Opening of the Northwest* (1976) is superb on development of railroads. Samuel Hays, *The Response to Industrialism* (1957) is a classic study. Robert W. Fogel uses a quantitative approach in *Railroads and American Economic Growth: Essays in Econometric History* (1964). *Andrew Carnegie and the Rise of Big Business* (1975) by Harold C. Livesay supplements Carnegie's *Autobiography* (1920). See Robert C. Bannister, Jr.'s careful *Social Darwinism: Science and Myth in Anglo American Social Thought* (1979).

Other good books on the period include Peter Temin, *Iron and Steel in Nineteenth-Century America* (1964), Sidney Fine, *Laissez Faire and the General-Welfare State* (1956), John Brooks, *Telephone* (1976), W. P. Strassmann, *Risk and Technological Innovation* (1959), H. B. Thorelli, *The Federal Antitrust Policy* (1954), Carl Solberg, *Oil Power* (1976), H. J. Habakkuk, *American and British Technology in the Nineteenth Century* (1962), Leon Wolff, *Lockout* (1965), G. W. Miller, *Railroads and the Granger Laws* (1971), A. D. Chandler, Jr., *Railroads: The Nation's First Big Business* (1965), Almont Lindsey, *The Pullman Strike* (1942), H. C. Passer, *The Electrical Manufacturers* (1953), Julius Grodinsky, *Transcontinental Railway Strategy* (1962), Olive Hoogenboom, *A History of the ICC* (1976), and Gabriel Kolko, *Railroads and Regulation* (1965).

☆ ☆ ☆ POINTS OF VIEW: ☆ ☆ ☆

Jay Gould: Robber Baron or Industrial Statesman?

Maury Klein

[Jay] Gould emerged as the foremost villain of the [Gilded Age] not merely by piling up a fortune; that was acceptable, even desirable, so long as one did it in the proper way with appropriate gestures toward convention. His rise to success followed the classic pattern of the rags-to-riches myth except in the crucial area of method. He did not display the probity and purity of conscience so prominent in Horatio Alger heroes, but neither did the vast majority of businessmen. Elsewhere, however, Gould snubbed convention at every turn. In business he was ruthless and devious, clever and unpredictable, secretive and evasive. Above all he was imaginative, not only brilliant but thoroughly original. In an age that relished flourish, he possessed a stunning economy of motion. . . .

Critics condemned him for his deceit and treachery. Yet the impression lingers that many of them actually loathed Gould because he was too honest for minds used to dealing with reality under wraps. Gould knew what he wanted, went after it, and did not mouth pieties to justify his course. Nor did he ever try to disguise himself in airs of respectability. By keeping his numerous acts of charity behind the scenes he deprived himself of the standard act of atonement expected from men of vast wealth. . . .

There was an intellectuality in his approach to business, the joy of a lawyer handed a juicy brief to write or a Gordian knot to unravel. All these aspects set Gould apart from other men. The role of unsparing realist was not easy in an age that preferred to cushion the harshness of social and economic change with bloated sentimentalism.

Even before Gould's death he had become the symbol for an era tarnished and embarrassing to its children. The writers known loosely as muckrakers and debunkers shrank in horror from the excesses and iniquities of industrial society. Unable to put the larger experience into perspective, tormented by the contradictions and paradoxes of what Twain dubbed the Gilded Age, they seized upon its dominant business personalities as sufficient explanation for its aberrations. They were not the first to cope with a revolution by personalizing the vast forces that impelled it, and their chosen targets were certainly vivid and inviting enough. . . .

"Robber Baron" must surely be the most overused and least useful label in all American history. It is not surprising that the popular notion of the industrial era continues to be shaped by the phrase and portrait made famous by Matthew Josephson half a century ago.

Reprinted from Maury Klein, *The Life and Legend of Jay Gould* (Baltimore: The Johns Hopkins University Press, 1986).

Thomas R. West

The history of American industry in the late nineteenth century is a story of the financial empire building of Jay Gould and his many contemporaries and successors. But it is far more importantly a story of great crude productive endeavors, rails flung across empty stretches of the continent, smokestacks spewing embers over the roofs of factories where immigrant laborers wrestled at clanking machinery. Twisted steel and smashed boxcars meanwhile left their testimony that the country had the worst railroad safety record of any industrialized nation. Accidentally ignited gases in turn-of-the-century mines could send a path of flame through the tunnels, or hurl as far as a mile the massive door at a mine's entrance. Industry did not grow in response to human need or the advice of socially responsible technicians. It grew in ways that serviced the money and power hunger of its financial leaders or their smaller likenesses; and that insured the continuance of the accidents, the machinery run wastefully to ruin.

The beneficiaries of the system of ownership and finance did not for the most part make anything, except money. They did not dig for coal, or pour molten ore, or design a machine, or conduct a laboratory experiment that might advance any of these things. Finance aimed only at profits, and that meant driving the course of industry in whatever direction profits were greatest; and that, in turn, made for the twisted steel along railway lines, the gas flames streaking through mining tunnels. It is true that in the absence of some more sophisticated form of investment, Wall Street and the corporations did bring together the resources under which genuine production took place. But it was not for the purposes of production that they did so. To attribute to the corporation and financial system the preeminent credit for the magnificent productivity of industry is to disgrace industry along with the anonymous workers and technicians who strained it into existence, and wrought ever closer perfection into it.

In short: the system disgraced work itself.

From the time of the American Revolution, citizens had perceived their country, in one form or another, as a republic of workers. But also from that beginning, a corruption had crept into the idea of work: the notion that the aim and the evidence of work are wealth. The belief that wealth can ever be the measure of hard and careful work is nonsense. Good workmanship reveals itself in the conduct of the craftsman and the excellence of the product, and nowhere else. It certainly does not reveal itself in the twists and flips of a market that makes a financial con artist fifty times more affluent than the janitors who do the useful labor of cleaning his floor. The belief that wealth is the prize and ornament of work, elusively present in the American mind from the time of the nation's origins, won wide credence in the age of the financiers. The vision of a republic of honest workers suffered, and has continued to suffer.

Yet there were honest laborers, machinists, and technicians who could take pride in what they did, and know that they were perfecting the nature of work and its instruments. The growing precision and sophistication of machines, the exactitude that modern technology demanded of its skilled operatives and its engineers: all this expressed workmanship of the highest order. The social commentator Thorstein Veblen was soon to note the contrast between the rigor of modern technology and the shoddiness of the financial and business ownership that presided over that technology. A businessman might calculate only the profits of a quick sale; a technician had to calculate to a fraction of an inch the fittings of gear to gear. Industry, even as avarice and competition drove its owners, was also requiring in its actual productive capacity a closer and more widespread cooperation of functions nationwide, and internationally, than any previous form of production had needed. A Minnesota iron miner's yield traveled east to be turned into the steel rails that carried farm machinery to the West, and that region's wheat eastward to the tables of steel workers. But none of this could be adequately recognized and respected so long as the slash-and-burn greediness of the market drew more attention than the quiet skills and the expert knowledge of the age.

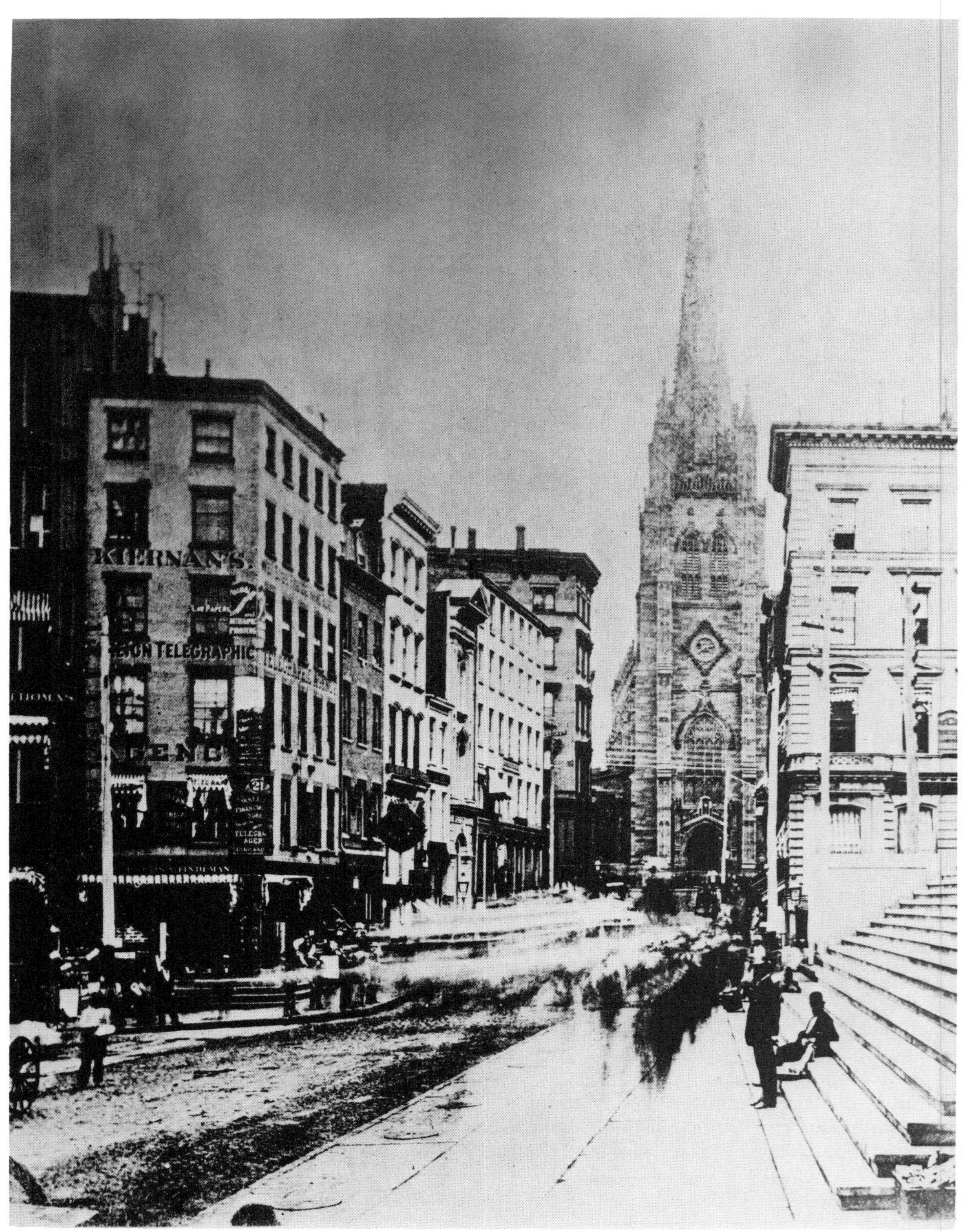

Trinity Church, New York City. *(Courtesy, New York Public Library)*

CHAPTER 18

The American City 1865–1900

TRINITY CHURCH: "GUARDIANS OF A HOLY TRUST"

Trinity Church, Episcopal, located on Broadway facing Wall Street in lower Manhattan, was by the nineteenth century the richest church in the United States. The historian and journalist James Parton described it in 1868 as "a richly furnished, quietly adorned, dimly illuminated, ecclesiastical parlor, in which a few hundred ladies and gentlemen, attired in kindred taste, may sit perfectly at their ease, and see no object not in harmony with the scene around them."

In 1910, when Trinity's vestrymen issued their first public account of church finances, they listed its expenditures for the previous year at $340,870. This included more than $60,000 for music alone. The rector's salary was $15,000, which made him the highest paid clergyman in the country, and the vicars of the nine other churches Trinity operated each received $8,000 a year, or more than what United States senators earned at that time. Yet contributions from churchgoers totaled only $18,210. The bulk of the rest of the money came from the church's real estate holdings, for Trinity owned over $16 million of tenement housing on Manhattan's West Side. This made it the largest slum landlord in the city if not the whole country. As the city's largest landlord Trinity, moreover, was the leading opponent of housing reform in the late nineteenth and early twentieth centuries.

In 1887, for example, New York City passed a tenement ordinance requiring running water on every floor. Trinity's vestry challenged the law and, for the next eight years, until the Federal Court of Appeals upheld the city's power to regulate housing, Trinity's tenants had to continue using a single pump located in the courtyard of each of its buildings. A few years later, in 1901, New York State passed a model tenement house law. This legislation abolished open toilets in back yards and required indoor plumbing on each floor. The law also made it illegal to rent apartments with no windows opening onto the outside, largely because such dark and damp rooms had been linked to the spread of tuberculosis. Trinity delayed compliance through court challenges for three years.

How had a church come to be the foremost enemy of tenement reform? The answer goes back to how Trinity acquired title to all that real estate in the first place. The English crown granted the church a "bonus" in 1705 of the land known as "Queen's farm" along the Hudson River on Manhattan's west side. Originally the grant had been to all "of the inhabitants of our said city of New York" in communion with the Church of England, but in 1814 Trinity's vestrymen successfully petitioned the New York State legislature to limit control over the land to "members of the congregation of Trinity Church or of any of the chapels belonging to Trinity Corporation." The right to decide who among the members would be entitled to vote for vestryman, the most important office, rested with the vestrymen themselves. As a result, control of the church's enormous real estate holdings passed into the hands of the members of what Parton had called an "exclusive ecclesiastical club." Its members sought what they believed would be best for the church, a vision long-time Trinity Rector Morgan Dix defined as "ritual observance," "musical culture," and "ecclesiastical art." Dix dismissed the claims of Protestant reformers associated with the Social Gospel that low wages or dangerous working conditions or substandard housing were matters of pressing concern.

The American City

Besides transforming the incomes and political attitudes of Americans, the rapid growth of industry changed where many of them lived and worked. Between 1860 and 1910 millions of newcomers flocked to the cities. In 1860 over twenty-five million Americans had lived in rural areas and only 6.2 million in what the Bureau of the Census defined as "urban territory": the bureau set the puzzlingly low figure of 2,500 as the base for defining an urban center. Nevertheless, the country was urbanizing. In 1910, forty-two out of ninety-two million Americans resided in communities that were urban by the government's definition. In 1860 there had been no cities of a million, and only two, New York and Philadelphia, with over half a million. By 1910, three American cities had a million people or more, and five additional ones had over half a million each.

Two Pathways to the City Numbers of northern and western Europeans from Britain, Germany, and Scandinavia who came to the United States before the 1880s settled in rural communities. The Irish did not, but they were in some ways exceptional. The newcomers of the last two decades of the nineteenth century and the early part of the twentieth differed from their predecessors. These new immigrants came largely from southern and eastern Europe. Many were from Italy's depressed South or from Sicily. Others were from lands controlled by Austria or Russia. The new immigrants included thousands of Slavic Poles, Croatians, Bohemians, and Serbs, as well as non-Slavic Greeks and Jews.

The United States needed laborers, and for varying motives some organizations were willing to sponsor newcomers. A Polish peasant wrote seeking assistance to emigrate:

> I want to get to America, but I have no means at all because I am poor and have nothing but the ten fingers of my hands, a wife and 9 children. I have no work at all, although I am strong and healthy and only 45 years old. I cannot earn for my family. I have been already in Dombrowa, Sosnowiec, Zawiercie and Lodz, wherever I could go, and nowhere could I earn well. And here they (the children) call for food and clothing and more or less education. I wish to work, not easily only but even hard, but what can I do? I will not go to steal and I have no work.

Besides the crowds that crossed the Atlantic were the tens of thousands who crossed the continental borders from Canada and Mexico. Many of the new arrivals were peasants, who might be expected to settle on the land. But since the 1840s and 1850s, land prices had risen and farm commodity prices fallen, and agriculture was less attractive to newcomers. After 1880, more and more of the immigrants settled in cities to work as wage earners in factories.

Native-born Americans from the nation's farms also were going to the towns and cities. Some Americans in these years sentimentalized farm life, but to young people particularly the farmer's lot seemed a hard one and farm life drab and cramped. When the parents of Hamlin Garland, the novelist, returned from an Iowa village to live again on a farm, their two sons were bitterly disappointed. They despised the "ugly little farmhouse" and the "filthy drudgery of the farmyard" and yearned for the "care-free companionable existence" of town. Writing in *Good Housekeeping* just before World War I, a journalist remarked on how many young women "were pining for neighbors, for domestic help, for pretty clothes, for schools, music, art, and the things tasted when the magazines came in."

These two human streams, one from abroad, one from the rural areas of the nation, converged on the towns, villages, and cities in record numbers in these years. There they were joined by the natural increase of the city population itself. The urban centers swelled.

Conditions in the Cities

By the standards of the great European capitals, the American cities of this period were disappointing. Few places, not even Washington until the twentieth century, could boast the monuments, the boulevards, the imperial buildings of Berlin, Paris, Vienna, St. Petersburg, or London. Too many American cities were dominated by commercial structures. Their streets were jammed with horse-drawn wagons and carriages, and with people pushing carts and wheelbarrows. Overhead the sky was often obscured by a tangle of wires for the city's telephone and telegraph messages. There were few trees or parks. The needs of commerce had won out over beauty and amenities, and almost all public land had been sold off for housing or commercial blocks. A few cities, including New York, Boston, Washington, San Francisco, and New Orleans, had some individuality, but others seemed to be built on a uniform monotonous plan of right-angle streets, with dreary stores and shops and utilitarian hotels.

As for pollution, Pittsburgh, described here in 1868, suffered worse conditions than any other city:

> There is one evening scene in Pittsburg which no visitor should miss. Owing to the abruptness of the hill behind the town, there is a street along the edge of a bluff, from which you can look directly down upon all that part of the city which lies low, near the level of the rivers. On the evening of this dark day, we were conducted to the edge of the abyss, and looked over the iron railing upon the most striking spectacle we ever beheld. The entire space lying between the hills was filled with blackest smoke, from out of which the hidden chimneys sent forth tongues of flame, while from the depths of the abyss came up the noise of hundreds of steam-hammers. There would be moments when no flames were visible; but soon the wind would force the smoky curtains aside, and the whole black expanse would be dimly lighted with dull wreaths of fire. It is an unprofitable business, view-hunting; but if anyone would enjoy a spectacle as striking as Niagara, he may do so by simply walking up a long hill to Cliff Street in Pittsburg, and looking over into—hell with the lid taken off.

Worse still was the level of sanitation and housing that newcomers experienced. By the 1870s a few of the largest American cities had installed underground sewers. But many still used privies and cesspools that periodically had to be cleaned out. In 1877 Philadelphia had 82,000 of these, and Washington, D.C., was not far behind. In some cities, among them Baltimore, New Orleans, and Mobile, sewage was actually allowed to run through open gutters. And even communities with better sewage collection facilities spilled their waste in the surrounding waters. Boston Harbor was "one vast cesspool, a threat to all the towns it washed." Nor were garbage disposal arrangements much better. Port cities usually dumped their garbage at sea, hoping it would not return at the next tide. Inland communities sold local farmers organic garbage for feeding to hogs. The result was a high incidence of trichinosis among swine and also among human beings who ate undercooked pork.

A letter of 1885 to a Little Rock, Arkansas, newspaper described a

> presence—right in the heart of the city—one of the most malignant, pestiferous disease breeders in the land. The town branch, or whatever poetic title you may apply to the muddy, filthy stream that penetrates directly through the city . . . is the root of evil. Open to the rays of the burning sun in the

> summer, great holes dug in its bottom by sand diggers . . . the reeking filth from barnyard, cesspool and worse, lie festering and tainting the atmosphere with diseases, death and odors. . . . Covered in places with boards, right in our business streets, hiding the reeking stench beneath, the death dealing gasses escape and little innocents wither and die, and strong men sicken and gasp. . . . Stop this eternal clamor about paved streets; go to work and convert this great natural artery into a magnificent sewer . . . and then children may thrive; strong men will grow stronger, and our city will be blessed with . . . health.

During the 1860s and 1870s Louis Pasteur in France, Robert Koch in Germany, and Joseph Lister in Britain were learning about the connection between bacteria and disease, and by the next decade the discoveries were influencing the planning of sewage disposal facilities and water supplies. Even before the Civil War, New York, Philadelphia, and a number of other communities had developed decent systems of aqueducts to collect pure water from distant streams or lakes and pipe it into homes. Now, with the new knowledge at hand, the authorities began to clean up the water supply. Some cities depended on the piping of clean water. Others adopted filtration or chlorination. By 1910 over ten million city people drank filtered water; that innovation contributed to the sharp decline in death rates from typhoid fever and cholera. This change was accompanied by the appearance of sanitary bathrooms and running water, improvements that owed much to rising living standards as well as to the growing awareness of infectious organisms.

Tenements All over the world, wherever and whenever cities have grown rapidly, housing for the poor has been wretched. American cities of the late nineteenth century were more successful than Third World cities of the present in solving their housing problems, but not by a great deal. Some of the urban poor crowded into shantytowns at the edges of the cities where they illegally built shacks on land they did not own. In 1870 New York City's West Side north of Fifty-Ninth Street looked like the outskirts of a Third World city today. The castoff houses of the middle class now departing for newer residential sections also became tenements for the poor. These structures were cut up into small apartments that the newcomers could afford. Landlords threw up flimsy buildings for the poor in what had been spacious backyards. Few of the more substantial dwellings put up in response to the growth in the numbers of the poor were adequate in space, comfort, safety, or sanitation.

New York had appalling slums. Many others, like Philadelphia, had more single family homes and so their poor neighborhoods did not look quite so crowded as New York's. But the wooden row houses characteristic of Philadelphia or Cleveland were just as cheaply constructed and even more likely to catch fire than New York's tenements. Sanitary conditions, on the other hand, were somewhat better. New York's "old law" tenements had four or five stories, without hot water and proper bathrooms. After 1879 the city fathers required that all new tenements have at least one window in every room and two water closets to a floor. But the resulting "dumbbell" apartment with narrow air shafts on each side of the building was not appreciably better. In the absence of other means of disposal, air shafts became receptacles for garbage. Inadequacies in construction and in bathing and cooking facilities subjected everyone to noise, disorder, and bad smells. "How is it possible to preserve purity amid such homes, or to bring up children to be moral or decent?" asked one reformer.

The Children The reform writer Jacob Riis took readers on a tour of a tenement: "Be a little careful, please! The hall is dark and you might stumble. You can feel your way, if you cannot see it. Close? Yes! What would you have? All the fresh air that enters these stairs comes from the hall-door that is forever slamming." The tour guide paused at the entrance to a windowless apartment. "Listen! That short, hacking cough, that tiny, helpless wail. . . . The child is dying of measles. With half a chance it might have lived; but it had none. That dark bedroom killed it." Riis was confusing his readers with an overdose of sentiment. He also posed photographs of newsboys sleeping at night outside in alleyways or over steel grates on city streets. But on the substance of what was happening he was right. The nation was neglecting its children.

Thousands of such children were deposited annually at the Children's Aid Society in the late nineteenth century by courts and overcrowded orphan asylums. A group of

Hester and Clinton Streets, New York City, ca. 1896. Immigrant neighborhoods often suffered from overcrowding and poor sanitary conditions. *(Courtesy, The New-York Historical Society, New York City)*

forty orphaned boys and girls was sent from eastern cities to a small midwestern town. In what must have been an unusually successful instance, a protesting fourteen year old named Willie, along with some other children, was taken to the local grange hall, where a group of farmers and their wives waited to look them over. According to the society's annual reports, only one couple wanted Willie. In a heavy German accent the farmer's wife explained: "Because he please my old man." And Willie was carried away, struggling and protesting, in her thick arms. A few months later the agent of the Society returned to check on how his former charges were doing. When the German farmer saw who had come to call, he bridled:

"Mr. Agent," he said, "if you come to dake dot boy away, if you don't got de biggest yob on your hants what you ever had, den I don't know how it is. I wouldn't dake de whole United States for dot boy."

"I haven't come to take him away," the agent hastened to explain. "But how in the world do you manage him?"

"Oh, dot's easy," the farmer's wife said. "You see, we all luff him."

Urban Transportation

Much of the congestion of New York and the nation's other large cities might have disappeared if transportation had been adequate between outlying neighborhoods and the downtowns, where the stores, shops, small factories, and wholesale establishments were located and where working people earned their livings. When men and women had to rely on their own legs or some equally inefficient means of transport, they had no choice but to take nearby housing, no matter how dilapidated or congested.

Before the Civil War a few of the country's largest cities had begun to develop public transportation systems. Horse-drawn omnibuses—essentially elongated carriages—ran over regular routes in New York, Philadelphia, and Boston by 1860. These were slow. The horse-drawn streetcar, pulled on rails, was somewhat better and became almost universal after 1865 in the larger towns and cities. But still the system was inadequate and reformers demanded some means of rapid transit that would help end the congestion on city streets.

A breakthrough came in 1867 when the nation's largest city built the first "el," a steam railroad placed on high pillars above the traffic. New York's elevated system darkened the streets below, scattered ashes on pedestrians, made noise, and constituted an eyesore. But it did move people quickly. It was soon widely imitated. By the opening of the new century, Chicago, Boston, Kansas City, and Brooklyn had all built els. Meanwhile the horsecars had been replaced at street level by electric trolley cars drawing their power from overhead wires. Richmond was the first city to adopt the electric cars. By about 1900 there were 15,000 miles of electric streetcar lines in American cities under the control of some 900 companies.

The final innovation was the subway. Following London and Budapest, Boston in 1895 began construction of an underground railway that would avoid the street level congestion of downtown. New York, with an even greater congestion, embarked on a still more ambitious scheme and in 1904 completed the first leg of what would become the largest subway system in the world.

The new transit systems, especially the electric streetcar, opened up the cities. Now, usually for a fare of five cents, a wage-earner who lived several miles from the job could get to work on time. Builders and developers laid out streets and lots on what had been open fields and put up small houses for city people to buy. Many thousands would put the whole family to work and devote all savings to the single goal of purchasing a home. Before long many cities were surrounded by rings of streetcar suburbs housing families happy to escape the noise, dirt, congestion, and other ills of the city centers.

Immigrants

The New Immigrants

Immigrants gave the late nineteenth-century cities much of their distinctive flavor—and, in the eyes of many native Americans, many of their distinctive problems. From colonial times immigration had nourished American society. Almost all of the white immigrants had come from northern

By the early 1890s New York City teemed with streetcars hauled by cables and elevated trains powered by steam locomotives. *(Courtesy, The H. N. Tiemann Company, New York)*

Europe. Then from about 1880 came another kind of immigrant from eastern and southern Europe.

Many Americans recoiled from the new immigration of the Slavs, Italians, Jews, and Greeks. They held, for example, that a disproportionate number of new immigrants were men who came not to stay, but merely to make money and return home. Trans-Atlantic passage having become cheaper and quicker, some of the newer immigrants were indeed mere sojourners; but many others came to stay and did so. Americans also perceived the newer arrivals as illiterate and unskilled. Again, this was only a partial truth: Jews, northern Italians, and Bohemians were more skilled and literate than most of those who had come before 1860.

The common American estimate of the newcomers, then, made little allowance for individual and group differences. Nevertheless, there are valid distinctions between new and antebellum immigrants. Most of the countries of origin of the newcomers were autocracies, and they had little experience with democratic government. They were poorer than most of the earlier immigrants. A far lower percentage was Protestant. The country they came to, moreover, was notably different from the one their predecessors had entered. In 1850 the United States had still been overwhelmingly agricultural, and many of the new arrivals became farmers. By the 1880s, however, much of the best land was gone, and a giant American industry was pulling into factories former peasants from Poland, Ukraine, Serbia, Greece, Romania, and the south of Italy.

As one observer commented:

> The workers on the hills of Galicia, in the vineyards of Italy, and the factories of Kiev, earn from 25 to 50 cents in a day. When the American immigrant writes home that he earns from $1.50 to $2.00, the ablebodied wage-earner in the fatherland who hears this will not be satisfied until he also stands where the higher wages govern. It is these homegoing letters more than all else which recruit the labor force. They are efficient promoters of immigration. Said Big Sam to me, in his broken English, 'There are no ablebodied men between the ages of sixteen and fifty years left in my native town in Servia; they have all come to America.'

As in the past, most of the Europeans settled in the Northeast or Midwest; few went to the South. The large African-American population in the rural South kept wage levels down, and in the Far West the available land was either too expensive or too dry to attract the immigrants. Instead, they headed for the industrial cities in what historians now call "chain migrations." Once a small contingent of immigrants had settled in a particular area, they tended to attract to their new communities their own relatives and friends from the Old World. Many of the Italian immigrants, most of whom were from southern Italy or Sicily, sought out construction jobs in booming northeastern cities like Boston, New York, or Philadelphia. Most Italian immigrants lived with their relatives in the new country, or, if the immigrant was the first member of the family to come, he would usually seek out companions from his own region of Italy.

Among the "chains" that connected the New World cities with Italian villages, Mott Street in New York City between East Houston and Prince held Neopolitans, as did Mulberry Street. On the opposite side of Mott Street were the Basilicati. Calabrians settled Mott Street between Broome and Grand, Sicilians lived on Prince Street, and the Genoese on Baxter Street. Many Italians even settled along village lines. In Chicago western Sicilians congregated together, with immigrants from Altavilla on Larrabee Street; people from Alimenia and Shiusa Sclafani on Cambridge Street; immigrants from Bagheria on Townsend Street; and people from Sambuca-Zabut on Milton Street.

Jewish immigrants from Austria-Hungary and Russia found jobs in the needle trades and sweat shops of New York City, and like the Italians they tended to settle together in familiar clusters. The Slavic immigrants—Poles, Czechs, Slovaks, Ukrainians, Serbs, and Croatians—did not stop in Boston, New York City, Philadelphia, or Baltimore. They were more likely to move inland to the mills, mines, and stockyards of Pennsylvania, Ohio, Indiana, and Illinois. Cities like Chicago, Detroit, Cleveland, and Buffalo had heavy concentrations of Slavic immigrants.

Wherever they put down roots, the immigrants planted their Old World customs and traditions. Fundamental among these was religion, which for most of these newer groups was a part of daily life. A majority was Catholic. By the 1880s the Catholic Church had been firmly established in the United States. Catholic Italians and Slavs, then, were not deposited in the midst of an alien religion. Yet the American Catholic Church was largely English-speaking and Irish-dominated, and for many years the newcomers would battle with the earlier arrivals over such issues as the language of sermons and the dominance of the Irish among the clergy and hierarchy.

In the Jewish community, too, the newly-arrived clashed with their coreligionists. Many of the German Jews of the antebellum period were by now thoroughly Americanized, and their religious practices had become more closely aligned with prevailing American modes of religious practice. To the great mass of eastern European Jewish newcomers, their German-Jewish predecessors seemed scarcely Jews at all. The German Jews, in turn, found their Polish, Russian, and Romanian brethren outlandish folk, alien to the modern world.

Immigrant Women

The transition from one culture to another weighed especially heavily on immigrant women. Invariably, the different immigrant groups accepted—although for their own reasons—the dominant American belief that women belonged at home. But survival frequently dictated that married women and unmarried daughters contribute to the family income. First-generation immigrant women characteristically worked in the sweat trades, or did piece work at home, or took in boarders. Daughters were more likely to work in factories. Married women had to cope with providing food and clothing for their families under conditions of excruciating poverty in an unfamiliar environment. Anzia Yzierska's

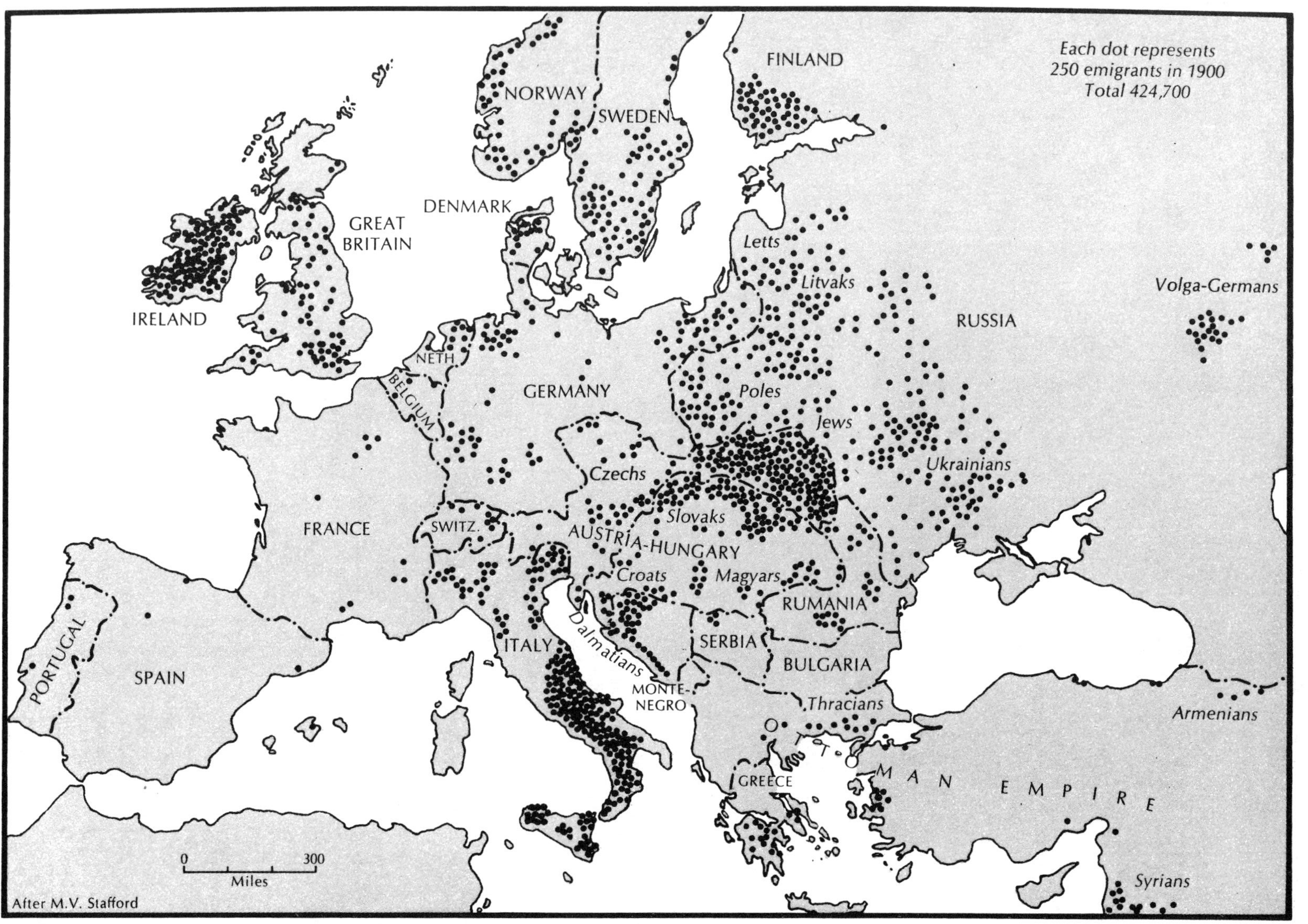

Immigration from Europe to the United States in 1900.

novel *Bread Givers* describes living conditions among Jewish immigrants on New York's lower East Side when a piece of soap or a personal towel was a luxury. In addition, many first-generation immigrant women never learned English properly, if at all. In his novel *Call It Sleep,* Henry Roth poignantly evokes the relation between a mother and her son whom she believes she is losing to a foreign language. Immigrants could frequently resent social workers and especially the school system, which they thought was robbing them of their children by pulling the young into a foreign culture. One mother born in Sicily made a common complaint: "When girls at thirteen and fourteen wasted good time in school, it simply made us regret our coming to America."

The editor of the *Jewish Daily Forward,* a Yiddish-language paper in New York City, gave its new-immigrant readers advice on how to live in the United States. One reader, signing herself "Discontented Wife," wrote this letter:

> Dear Editor,
>
> Since I do not want my conscience to bother me, I ask you to decide whether a married woman has the right to go to school two evenings a week. My husband thinks I have no right to do this.
>
> I admit that I cannot be satisfied to be just a wife and mother. I am still young and I want to learn and enjoy life. My children and my house are not neglected, but I go to evening high school twice a week. My husband is not pleased and when I come home at night and ring the bell, he lets me stand outside a long time intentionally, and doesn't hurry to open the door.
>
> Now he has announced a new decision. Because I send out the laundry to be done, it seems to him that I have too much time for myself, even enough to go to school. So from now on he will count out every penny for anything I have to buy for the house, so I will not be able to send out the laundry any more. And when I have to do the work myself there won't be any time left for such 'foolishness' as going to school. I told him that I'm willing to do my own washing but that I would still be able to find time for study.
>
> When I am alone with my thoughts, I feel I may not be right. Perhaps I should not go to school. I want to say that my husband is an intelligent man and he wanted to marry a woman who was educated. The fact that he is intelligent makes me more annoyed with him. He is in favor of the emancipation of women, yet in real life he acts contrary to his beliefs.
>
> Awaiting your opinion on this. . . .

Answer:

> Since this man is intelligent and an adherent of the women's emancipation movement, he is scolded severely in the answer for wanting to keep his wife so enslaved. Also the opinion is expressed that the wife absolutely has the right to go to school two evenings a week.

Anti-Catholic, Anti-Semitic, and Anti-Chinese Sentiment

In the years of Irish Catholic immigration before the Civil War, there had been a flourishing of nativism, a word applicable to Americans who have feared immigration as threatening to change the country's distinctive character. In the later nineteenth century, when the nation was swelling with immigrants, nativism again became public and vocal. Hostility to immigrants had a basis in feelings of xenophobia, hatred of things foreign. One immigrant group was said to be violent, another given to drink, a third criminally inclined, a fourth dirty, a fifth stupid, a sixth immoral.

Anti-Catholicism ran high within sections of the Protestant population, leading to demands for immigration restrictions and for laws to prevent the Catholic Church from intruding into what the critics conceived of as secular affairs. This movement culminated in the formation of the American Protective Association in 1887; its members were pledged to work to exclude Catholics from political office, to seek to keep Catholic workers from taking jobs of Protestants, and to refuse to join Catholics in strikes. In the 1890s the group allied itself with Republicans in the Midwest in battles over the funding of parochial schools, and some members boycotted Catholic merchants.

Anti-Semitism, an old affliction of the Christian world, flared in these years. In the 1870s Jews had begun to suffer social ostracism and exclusion from resort hotels and clubs. In the 1890s they encountered physical violence at the hands of ruffians and were verbally attacked by both Populists like Ignatius Donnelly and aristocrats like Henry Adams as vulgar, bad-mannered, and mercenary.

The most notorious case of anti-Semitism occurred in Georgia in 1915. Leo Frank was a Jewish businessman living in Atlanta. He managed a pencil factory. In 1914 Mary Phagan, a young female worker, was found murdered in the plant. Frank was arrested, tried,

In *The Steerage*, the photographer Alfred Stieglitz—himself the son of immigrants—captured the poignancy and drama of a new wave of immigrants embarking on the journey to America. *(Courtesy, The Art Institute of Chicago)*

and convicted of the crime, even though the evidence against him was flimsy at best. The case attracted international attention, and in 1915 the governor of Georgia commuted Frank's sentence from the death penalty to life imprisonment. The decision enraged many Georgia whites, and a mob entered the state prison, took Frank from his cell, transported him 175 miles away, and lynched him in the middle of the night.

Violence against Italian immigrants began as early as the 1870s. In 1874 four Italian strikebreakers were killed by union mine workers in Buena Vista, Pennsylvania, and in 1886 a mob in Vicksburg, Mississippi, lynched an Italian-American. The worst incident occurred in 1891. Since the mid-1880s New Orleans newspapers had speculated about the existence of a Black Hand conspiracy, and the Irish police chief of New Orleans, David Hennessey, had built a political reputation investigating Sicilian crime. In 1891 he was murdered, and an outraged public decided the Mafia was responsible. Nine Italians were arrested, but a jury acquitted six of them and declared mistrials for the others. A mob entered the parish jail and lynched eleven Italian inmates, three of whom were Italian nationals. From 1880 to 1910 there were dozens of lynchings of Italians in the United States.

Economic competition also awakened hatred of immigrants, who were willing to work for less and so drove down the wages of native Americans. A Kansas barber complained: "The immigration of foreign laborers has cut down our wages; it should be stopped." In these years unions were often nativist, and in California, with its large Chinese population, white workers in 1877 organized an anti-Chinese Workingmen's Party, led by an Irish-American agitator, Dennis Kearney.

In 1882 Congress responded to strong anti-Chinese sentiment by excluding Chinese laborers from the United States for ten years. Later this was extended. The effects of prejudice on Chinese Americans was devastating. "The schools," one Chinese recalls, "were segregated—Chinese were separated from the Caucasians and so on. . . . The old people could only work maintaining white people's gardens, or picking weeds." Chinese were commonly refused service in West Coast restaurants until the post-World War II era.

Within weeks of passing the restrictive legislation against the Chinese, Congress prohibited the immigration of people with criminal records or signs of mental instability. To keep paupers out of the United States, that same law imposed a fifty cent head tax on each incoming immigrant. Responding to the demands of organized labor, Congress prohibited the importation of contract laborers in 1885. Polygamists and people with communicable diseases were excluded in 1891.

In 1894 a group of upper-class Bostonians organized the Immigration Restriction League, which called for a literacy test that the League thought would exclude Slavic, Italian, and Hispanic immigrants while permitting the continued immigration of people from northern and western Europe. In 1897 Congress responded to the League's pressure by imposing a literacy test on immigrants, but President Grover Cleveland vetoed the bill. The League continued to agitate for restrictive legislation. In 1903 Congress raised the immigrant head tax to $2 (it doubled to $4 in 1907) and prohibited the immigration of prostitutes, anarchists, and epileptics. The mentally retarded were excluded in 1907.

Immigrants themselves fought against measures to exclude their countrymen. Since many urban politicians now relied on their votes, they wielded considerable power. There was also the American tradition of free immigration to reckon with: the nation had always served as a refuge for Europe's impoverished and oppressed millions. Many Americans believed in the endless ability of American society to take the foreigner, strip him of his outlandish clothes, language, and folkways and make him over into a "true" American. According to this way of thinking, the hope for a successful solution of the immigration problem rested with the schools, especially the urban public schools. In these the immigrant child would study American history and traditions, and learn to read and write English. In a few years, it was assumed, he or she would be indistinguishable from the child of the Pilgrim fathers. Such notions were far more friendly to immigrants, of course, than was nativism. But another idea went farther, welcoming immigrants not as potential Anglo Americans with east European names but as people with distinctive cultures who could enrich the British American traditions with new diverse folkways.

Economics could be a force against the restriction of immigration as well as a motive for it. One observer wrote,

> When prosperity is at flood, the men in charge of furnaces, foundries, forges, and mills in the Pittsburgh District cannot get the help they need. The cry everywhere is: 'Give us men.' A foreman, therefore, will assure Pietro and Melukas that if brothers or cousins or friends are sent for, they will get work as soon as they arrive. More than that, the Slav and Italian are no longer dependent upon the English boss in the matter of finding work for their countrymen. The inflow from southeastern Europe has assumed such proportions in the industries of the cities that superintendents have, in some instances, appointed Italian and Polish and Lithuanian foremen; and with these, as with German and Irish, blood is thicker than water. They employ their fellow-countrymen. They know the condition of the labor market and can by suggestion stimulate or retard immigration.

So if some native workers feared the foreigners' "coolie wages," others recognized that they benefited from the cheap labor pool that the immigrant represented. Immigrant workers needed native American foremen and managers, and their arrival in vast numbers thrust up literate old-stock workers into white-collar or managerial ranks. Middle-class people also relied on immigrants as servants. Employers valued the cheap and willing labor of eastern and southern Europeans. Their well-financed campaigns against laws to limit the number of immigrants were probably the most formidable opposition the restrictionists faced.

Immigrant Life

In the communities where they settled, immigrants found a rich life among their countrymen. The neighborhoods eased the adjustment to American life. There the immigrants could attend their own churches and hear their own languages spoken. Their friends, relatives, and countrymen were nearby. The buildings and shops had the flavor of home. Italian immigrants on Mulberry Street in New York saw the cheeses and sausages and pasta in the stores, the opera posters, or the ubiquitous pictures of the Madonna; Greeks, Syrians, and Armenians frequented such coffeehouses as the Acropolis, the Parthenon, or the Beirut House; Jews sat in cafes along Hester Street and talked business or debated religion and politics; Germans in St. Louis or Cincinnati had their beer gardens, bowling alleys, and shooting galleries; Japanese and Chinese could purchase the fish and vegetables they liked in

Not like the brazen giant of Greek fame,
With conquering limbs astride from land to land;
Here at our sea-washed, sunset gates shall stand
A mighty woman with a torch, whose flame
Is the imprisoned lightning, and her name
Mother of Exiles. From her beacon-hand
Glows world-wide welcome; her mild eyes command
The air-bridged harbor that twin cities frame.
"Keep, ancient lands, your storied pomp!" cries she
With silent lips. "Give me your tired, your poor,
Your huddled masses yearning to breathe free,
The wretched refuse of your teeming shore.
Send these, the homeless, tempest-tost to me,
I lift my lamp beside the golden door!"

The New Colossus by Emma Lazarus

A gift from France commemorating America's independence, the Statue of Liberty, unveiled in 1886, came to symbolize a nation of immigrants. *(Courtesy, J. Clarence Davies Collection, Museum of the City of New York)*

the shops of Little Tokyo in Los Angeles or Chinatown in San Francisco; Irish and Slavic immigrants gathered in local taverns. The neighborhoods were rich in ethnic foods, ethnic newspapers, and ethnic holidays, all of which were familiar to the immigrants.

Native-born Americans of a more open turn of mind found the immigrant ghettoes of the big cities to be fascinating places. One reported of New York's Little Italy:

> The sons of Italy . . . are fond of music and outdoor life; and in New York they enjoy both of these luxuries when the band plays in Mulberry Bend Park. Then they pour forth from a hundred tenements . . . and stand listening in rapt delight by the hour to the strains of 'Il Trovatore.' . . . Nearly all the Italian societies give festivals annually, and these have been accompanied . . . by . . . a racket of fireworks. . . . Frequently great wooden and pasteboard shrines are erected on the sidewalk and the streets are arched with lines of Chinese lanterns. In a recent Elizabeth Street fiesta great wire brackets arched the street at intervals of one hundred feet for a quarter of a mile, and huge painted candles, eight to ten feet in height . . . were presented by the wealthier families to the Madonna. . . .

Nor were the immigrants invariably poor and downtrodden. Most no doubt started at or near the bottom. Poles and other Slavic people manned the coal mines and the iron mills. French Canadians replaced the Yankees and Irish in the New England cotton mills. In the Southwest, Mexicans worked on the railroads as laborers. Italians pushed wheelbarrows and wielded picks and shovels in the construction industry. Jews cut and sewed in the garment industry in Chicago, New York, and Rochester. Most groups, however, had their small contingent of professionals and intellectuals who served as doctors, lawyers, priests, teachers, newspaper editors, shopkeepers, and small manufacturers.

More significant was the relative speed of upward movement. Some scholars believe that it was relatively slow for immigrants to advance up the economic ladder; others are impressed by their swiftness. The most convincing formula holds that it varied from place to place and from group to group. Boston's Italians, for example, improved their occupational positions more slowly than the city's Jews and people of British origin. On the other hand, one scholar finds that between 1880 and 1915 many Italians and Jews of New York City moved upward from the wage class into self-employment. Complicating matters further is that occupational mobility was not the only source of striving and satisfaction to immigrants. Some, such as the Poles, marked their success by home ownership. Almost all groups gradually did eventually assimilate into the mainstream, though they retained distinctive national characteristics.

The novelist Edna Ferber, in an affirmation of ethnic identity, wrote that Poles did not covet money. "The Polish farmers," she wrote affectionately:

> spread over the Housatonic River Valley [of New England] and the region bloomed like a garden. . . . Fields thick with tobacco, barns bursting with hay, silos oozing, cattle in the meadows; children and chickens and geese and dogs shouting, cackling, barking, squawking in the yard—that was a Polish farm.

Immigrants did find the United States a land of opportunity, a place where they could improve their lives and those of their children. And this conclusion only stands to reason. Why else would immigrants have continued to come in such enormous numbers over so long a period unless the experience of friends and relatives here demonstrated that in the New World things were indeed better?

Crime

Slums and Crime Cities in this era, as in others, were places where the broken as well as the successful congregated. Crime was by no means exclusively an urban affliction, of course. On the frontier, gangs like the James and the Dalton boys roamed the countryside attacking trains and stagecoaches, and made forays into town to rob banks. Yet it was cities in this era, and others, where the broken and the violent most thickly congregated. Crime increased as cities grew. At the very end of

This unappetizing photograph of a dead horse, taken in New York City, shows the appalling sanitary conditions that persisted into the twentieth century. *(Courtesy, Library of Congress)*

the century, the *Chicago Tribune* estimated that murders and homicides nationally had climbed from 1,266 in 1881 to 7,340 in 1898, or from about 25 per million people to over 107 per million. Statistics on other, lesser crimes are not available, but contemporaries believed that all felonies had skyrocketed, a view seemingly confirmed by the startling increase of fifty percent reported for the national prison population between 1880 and 1890.

Urban crime flourished in the slums. Chicago's crime-ridden West Side in the 1890s was a place of "filthy and rotten tenements, . . . dingy courts, and tumble-down sheds . . . foul stables and dilapidated outhouses . . . broken sewer pipes [and] . . . piles of garbage fairly alive with diseased odors. . . ." In the Five Points area, criminal gangs such as the Whyos, the Dutch Mob, and the Molasses Gang preyed on pedestrians and householders, when they were not fighting one another. San Francisco's Barbary Coast, with streets carrying such labels as Murderers' Corner and Deadman's Alley, was the haunt of hundreds of thieves and murderers. When in New Orleans the French Quarter gangs killed the chief of police, citizens carried out a mass lynching of Italians that had international repercussions.

Prostitution To the mind of the late nineteenth century, crime was closely associated with "vice." The term often meant prostitution. Always a profitable and widespread occupation except in tight-knit, small communities, it achieved in the Gilded Age city a special flamboyance. In New York the trade centered in the Tenderloin area given over to saloons, music halls, and beer parlors. Chicago's "sporting houses" were concentrated in the area between Harrison and Polk and Clark and Dearborn streets. In New Orleans, Storyville in the French Quarter was a semi-official red light district, as well as the birthplace of a music ancestral to present-day jazz. These districts and their denizens were the objects of any number of crusades against vice, usually conducted by middle class, civic-minded women and ministers.

During the last third of the nineteenth century, public attention to prostitution divided into two camps. A group known as the regulationists and led by medical authorities and police officials sought to have all prostitutes registered by the state, closely supervised by the authorities, regularly examined for venereal disease, and subject to compulsory hospitalization if they were infected. On the other hand, women's groups, in alliance with ministers and some social reformers, sought to stamp out vice altogether. This movement has been appropriately called the purity crusade. And, on the whole, it advocated extending to men the standards of purity that custom had imposed on women. It increasingly rejected the notion that prostitution was a necessary evil and condemned it as a social evil—for which men were responsible. The most enlightened women opponents of mere regulation, besides demanding a direct war on prostitution, gradually came to defend the rights and dignity of the women engaged in it. They blamed the practice on social ills—especially economic need—rather than on moral failings. But for the most part the fight against regulation, which was interpreted as a *de facto* endorsement of prostitution, reflected a determination to impose a higher female morality on society.

The crusaders often discovered that the madams enjoyed police protection. The problem persisted because society was ambivalent about it as about so many other violations of social conventions. Middle-class Americans were shocked. Yet many people believed that there was no way of denying men access to sex for sale, and numbers of men, especially bachelors, saw nothing wrong with using the services of prostitutes. The willingness on the part of many men to pay for a service that in numbers of localities was now illegal created a gray area where graft and payoffs could flourish. New legislation that moral reformers had succeeded in winning against Sunday sports, cockfights, boxing, gambling, and drinking beyond certain specified hours opened similar opportunities for entrepreneurs to make money by bribes to police and officials. Reformers might protest and denounce, but they could do little to stop vice or prevent it from becoming a fertile source of political corruption.

City Political Machines

Urban Bosses The beneficiary of much of this corruption was the city machine. Machines were political organizations that ran parallel to the legal government of the city. At their head was a boss. Few were mayors, but bosses came close to running city government. Below the boss were lieutenants, ward captains or, to critics, ward heelers, whose responsibilities and duties were confined to the city wards. Surrounding the ward leaders were crowds of hangers-on and underlings who served the machine at the neighborhood level. The local political clubhouse was the place where the captain and his underlings conducted their business. Most machines were affiliated with the Democrats; in Philadelphia and a few other cities they were Republican.

The successful machine ruled the city. The mayor and members of the city council or Board of Aldermen were members of the machine. Decisions regarding conduct of city affairs and appointments to office were made in the clubhouses or by the boss and merely confirmed by the legal city officials.

Many critics saw the city machines as merely sores on the body politic, instruments for bilking taxpayers, furthering criminal behavior, and lining the pockets of the boss and his followers. And they were these things. In St. Louis, Lincoln Steffens reported:

> franchises worth millions were granted without one cent of cash to the city, and with provision for only the smallest future payment; several companies which refused to pay blackmail had to leave; citizens were robbed more and more boldly; pay-rolls were padded with the names of non-existent persons; work on public improvements was neglected, while money for them went to the boodlers.

"Doc" Ames in Minneapolis was willing to sell exemptions from arrest to any criminal who was willing to pay the price. New York's Tweed Ring collected millions of dollars from builders and contractors who built the municipal court house at wildly inflated costs and then kicked back part of the money to boss William Marcy Tweed and his Tammany Hall henchmen.

The machines, then, were corrupt and ex-

PLUNKITT OF TAMMANY HALL

George Washington Plunkitt's reflections on his political experience were recorded, and perhaps embroidered upon, by the journalist William L. Riordan.

Honest Graft and Dishonest Graft

Everybody is talkin' these days about Tammany men growin' rich on graft, but nobody thinks of drawin' the distinction between honest graft and dishonest graft. There's all the difference in the world between the two. Yes, many of our men have grown rich in politics. I have myself. I've made a big fortune out of the game, and I'm gettin' richer every day, but I've not gone in for dishonest graft—black-mailin' gamblers, saloonkeepers, disorderly people, etc.—and neither had any of the men who have made big fortunes in politics.

There's an honest graft, and I'm an example of how it works. I might sum up the whole thing by sayin': "I seen my opportunities and I took 'em."

Just let me explain by examples. My party's in power in the city, and it's goin' to undertake a lot of public improvements. Well, I'm tipped off, say, that they're going to lay out a new park at a certain place.

I see my opportunity and I take it. I go to that place and I buy up all the land I can in the neighborhood. Then the board of this or that makes its plan public, and there is a rush to get my land, which nobody cared particular for before.

Ain't it perfectly honest to charge a good price and make a profit on my investment and foresight? Of course, it is. Well, that's honest graft. . . .

The Curse of Civil Service Reform

This civil service law is the biggest fraud of the age. It is the curse of the nation. There can't be no real patriotism while it lasts. How are you goin' to interest our young men in their country if you have no offices to give them when they work for their party? Just look at things in this city today. There are ten thousand good offices, but we can't get at more than a few hundred of them. How are we goin' to provide for the thousands of men who worked for the Tammany ticket? It can't be done. These men were full of patriotism a short time ago. They expected to be servin' their city, but when we tell them that we can't place them do you think their patriotism is goin' to last? Not much. They say: "What's the use of workin' for your country anyhow? There's nothin' in the game." And what can they do? I don't know, but I'll tell you what I do know. I know more than one young man in past years who worked for the ticket and was just overflowin' with patriotism, but when he was knocked out by the civil service humbug he got to hate his country and became an Anarchist.

This ain't no exaggeration. I have good reason for sayin' that most of the Anarchists in this city today are men who ran up against civil service examinations. Isn't it enough to make a man sour on his country when he wants to serve it and won't be allowed unless he answers a lot of fool questions about the number of cubic inches of water in the Atlantic and the quality of sand in the Sahara desert? There was once a bright young man in my district who tackled one of these examinations. The next I heard of him he had settled down in Herr Most's saloon smokin' and drinkin' beer and talkin' socialism all day. Before that time he had never drank anything but whisky. I knew what was comin' when a young Irishman drops whisky and takes to beer and long pipes in a German saloon. That young man is today one of the wildest Anarchists in town. And just to think! He might be a patriot but for that cussed civil service. . . . Nothin' doin', unless you can answer a list of questions about Egyptian mummies and how many years it will take for a bird to wear out a mass of iron as big as the earth by steppin' on it once in a century.

pensive for citizens, and direct bribery achieved or swelled some of their victories at the polls. In many American cities, five dollars was the going price for a vote; sometimes it was as little as a shot of whiskey. But city machines conferred more important boons on voters than a few dollars in early November, and it was these favors that explained their success.

The Role of the Machines Late nineteenth-century American cities were difficult places to govern; authority was fragmented. Chicago had eleven different governing bodies in 1890, each with taxing powers and its own set of officials. There were several types of franchises the city did not have the right to grant, and it could not even tax property directly. Anyone wanting to do business with the city had to deal with a multitude of officials, legislative bodies, and agencies. Under the circumstances it often proved impossible to get anything done. Other American cities suffered the same handicaps.

Here the machine could help. The effective boss not only controlled the board of aldermen, but also owned the county board of assessment, along with the local water and police commissioners, and some exerted strong influence in the state legislature, where much city authority was actually lodged. To get something done, businessmen, civic leaders, and ethnic groups usually needed only go to the boss. The boss then was a coordinator for a decentralized system. And he was more.

Newcomers to the city faced poverty, dis-

An early political cartoon by Thomas Nast depicting Tweed and his Tammany Hall ring that had bilked millions of dollars from New York City. *(Courtesy, The New York Public Library, Astor, Lenox and Tilden Foundations)*

ease, congestion, unemployment, and trouble with the law. Cities had their charity societies, counties their poor houses. The Chicagoan, Philadelphian, or New Yorker could turn to the minister, priest, or rabbi. Toward the end of the century, moreover, groups of middle-class philanthropists were establishing settlement houses in city slum neighborhoods to provide the urban poor with educational services, meeting halls, and places where they could get help and advice. But all these were not enough. Too often the middle-class charity and settlement workers had inadequate resources; and some of them patronized the poor or imposed harsh conditions for dispensing aid. Not so the boss and the ward captain. Few were prudes, and they refused to judge the morals or customs of the local people. Many of them were Irish Catholics, yet they were tolerant of ethnic, religious, and racial differences. Gregarious glad-handers, they mixed easily with the city poor and shared their ceremonies, social events, joys, and sorrows.

Among their services was the dispensing of jobs. In the absence of effective municipal civil service procedures, they could hand out jobs at will in the police and sanitation departments, in laboring occupations, even in schoolteaching. Many a poor family owed its regular income to the precinct captain's generosity toward the family breadwinner. There was also the temporary help of a Christmas dinner or some coal to a destitute family in winter. Boss Tweed, as a member of the New York State legislature, got the state to contribute money to Catholic charities, though such action was widely thought to violate the principle of separation of church and state. The machine, through its control of municipal judges and courts, also got minor violations of the law dismissed.

The city's "better element" objected to these favors as expensive, inefficient, or corrupt. The boss did not care. As Martin Lomasney of Boston's Thomas Hendricks Club remarked: "I think there's got to be in every ward a guy that any bloke can go to when he's in trouble and get help—not justice and the law, but help, no matter what he's done."

The Bradley Martin Ball: Conspicuous Consumption

Wealthy urban Americans remembered best the Gay Nineties. The gayest event of all was the Bradley Martin Ball. This unparalleled extravaganza took place at the Waldorf Hotel in New York on the night of February 10, 1897, after weeks of preparation by New York society and of anticipation in newspapers all over the country. Eight hundred socialites spent about $400,000 imitating kings and queens in what newspapers described as "the most splendid private entertainment ever given in this country." The *New York Times* Sunday magazine devoted its first seven pages to photographs of the assembled "royalty." At the ball guests referred to the leaders, Mrs. Cornelia Sherman Bradley Martin and John Jacob Astor, as "Queen" and "King."

Mrs. Bradley Martin, daughter of a New York banker and wife of a wealthy lawyer, conceived this "crowning glory of the social life of New York of this century." One winter morning while reading in the newspapers of how the poor were suffering from the depression, she decided to cheer people up and "give an impetus to trade" with a costume ball. Requiring her guests to dress in accurately rendered court costume from the "most lavish periods of history," Mrs. Bradley Martin quickly precipitated a massive contest in ostentation; her Mary Queen of Scots costume—black velvet and white satin with a jeweled stomacher and a ruby necklace—made its intended impression. Some observers were more struck with Mrs. Astor's uncanny ability to find places on her dark blue velvet gown for $200,000 of diamonds, gold, and silver. The newspapers reported the price of everything. The real losers were the fifty women who dressed as Marie Antoinette: "It was painful to contemplate," reported one society editor, "the future of all these young women who were to lose their heads." But they like everyone else at the ball could lose their sorrows amid the twenty-eight courses—including "Sorbet fin de siècle"—at the midnight champagne supper.

The ball was both a triumph and a disaster. "It may not be surpassed in another hundred years," oozed one society reporter: "It was a gorgeous, superb, and wonderful spectacle."

Yet a prominent Episcopal rector had warned that such an occasion in a time of depression and social tension was "ill-advised." He proved correct. Newspapers condemned the Bradley Martins for their extravagance. Clergymen preached sermons against them. College debating societies resolved their iniquity. The New York assessor wreaked a more practical vengeance by doubling their taxes. The Bradley Martins surrendered their hopes of becoming the royalty of New York society, permanently retreating to England. In a final and characteristic gesture, they gave a farewell dinner for eighty-six intimate friends. The newspapers faithfully reported that it cost $116.28 a plate.

The Bradley Martin Ball ended neither social extravagance nor its fascination for the public. But "society" began to fear the whip of the press, especially when journalists combined reports of such orgies of big spending with muckraking accounts of the business practices that had created these fortunes. Eight years later, the dandy James Hazen Hyde had to flee the country after spending $200,000 on a masked ball. He should have known better: daddy's company, Equitable Life, was under heavy political attack in 1905. Nor did public opinion respond more favorably to Harry Lehr's "dog dinner," at which his friends' dogs dined on expensive pâté. Rich people began to learn that what titilated the public did not necessarily win its approval. Since urban high society learned that lesson, Americans have found it far less interesting.

Lavishly costumed guests at the Bradley Martin Ball aroused much criticism from press, clergy, and reformers outraged at such extravagance during difficult times. *(Courtesy, The Museum of the City of New York)*

Education

The cities that brought slums, smells, bad housing, and political corruption were also places where people learned and enjoyed themselves. In them talent from all over the country congregated in pursuit of training and self-cultivation, audiences and fame. In cities the newest and most interesting ideas got displayed, argued over, and exchanged. There millions of immigrants learned about American life and acquired the skills needed for a living.

Public Schools Those of us used to the failings of big city schools today may be startled to discover that during the late nineteenth century and early twentieth, the city public school systems were at the forefront of American education. Before the Civil War most of the northern and western states had created free public school systems. The South lagged behind. Then in the 1870s the South joined the free school movement while the northern and western states adopted laws requiring attendance at school. In 1878 there were 9.5 million pupils in the country's public schools; by 1898 15 million attended. Growth and improvement, present everywhere, came disproportionately to the city systems.

The typical rural school in 1890 was a small building with a single teacher and students of all ages and levels. These little red school houses were generally not the cozy institutions that a later generation would recall with nostalgia. Some were drafty and cold in winter and stifling and airless in spring. Many of them had only a single class, and underpaid teachers might find it impossible to deal with fifteen-year-olds and children of eight simultaneously. In a crowded room discipline could be bad. Few teachers stayed for more than a year or two. Sessions were usually rather short, seldom lasting more than a hundred days a year. And most students did not stay for even this time. Compulsory attendance laws notwithstanding, parents often kept their children out of school for household or farm chores. In 1870 a former resident of Hancock County, Maine, urged his daughter Mary to learn "to kep school" and not go to the "facters" [factories]. He added from personal experience; "If I had good lerning I wood not be so hard up all the time. I wos oferd the sherff ofes but I dasent take it for I did not know a nof to do the bissness."

City schools were superior. They enforced attendance laws. Each level of pupils had its own classrooms. Teachers were relatively well paid and well trained. The school year sometimes lasted twice as long as in the rural districts. City schools also had money for laboratories, auditoriums, indoor gyms. Many city school systems toward the end of the century adopted kindergartens, borrowing the idea from Germany. Free secondary education first appeared in the cities. Fewer than 100,000 attended public high schools in 1878; in 1898 there were over half a million, most of them located in large or middle-sized urban centers.

City school curricula consisted of reading, writing, and arithmetic, with some history, geography, literature, and civics. Public high schools included Latin and geometry, and had begun to provide science, some commercial courses, and even some modern foreign languages. Nowhere as yet was a public school pupil exposed to the wide range of "practical" courses that, for good or ill, are available to students today. Pedagogy tended to be unimaginative. Much learning was still by memorization from a text and students who were slow might receive punishment by ridicule or paddling.

Assimilation Only a limited number of immigrant parents eagerly attended night schools; those who did, such as this woman, usually gained by the experience:

> For the last two winters I have been going to night school. I have learned reading, writing and arithmetic. I can read quite well in English now and I look at the newspapers every day. I read English books, too, sometimes. . . .
>
> I am going back to night school again this winter. Plenty of my friends go there. Some of the women in my class are more than forty years of age. Like me, they did not have a chance to learn anything in the old country. It is good to have an education; it makes you feel higher.

The greatest task, and triumph, of city school systems in this era was in adapting to American society the foreign-born children or second-generation offspring of recent immigrants. In many big-city neighborhoods these pupils were virtually the entire school population. Almost all of their teachers were

Rural schools such as this red-painted one in turn-of-the-century New England often grouped students of all ages in one class under the care of a solitary teacher. *(Courtesy, The New-York Historical Society, New York City)*

young women either of native stock or of assimilated immigrant backgrounds. Some of these teachers regarded their pupils as strange and difficult to communicate with. Some found distasteful the religion or ethnic backgrounds of those they taught. The pupils often reciprocated those feelings. It is a wonder, then, that the schools did remarkably well. In 1900 the American-born children of European parents were more literate than most children of American-born parents. The schools also tried to imbue their charges with American middle-class values, the work ethic, and knowledge of history and institutions.

In all this the schools also did some injury. Learning to be Americans meant for some children learning to despise their own early culture. Aside from doing emotional damage to the children themselves, the assimilation process often made for conflict between children and their families, and between children deeply affected by their school experience and their peers who failed to accept Americanization as thoroughly. Most immigrants, in fact, attained a dual identity as Americans and as people of their native land. The culture was the richer where that occurred.

Most of the state universities and the land grant colleges that contributed so much to the American achievement in scholarship and learning were located in small communities such as Urbana, Ann Arbor, Madison, Berkeley, or Ithaca. Yet many of the leading institutions in this era were urban. Beginning with Johns Hopkins of Baltimore and joined soon after by the University of Chicago, Columbia, Harvard, Yale, and other city universities, the urban institutions led the movement into graduate education and research that converted the college into the university and brought American higher education to the level of Europe's best.

Starting with Mount Holyoke and Vassar, Smith, Bryn Mawr, and other women's colleges were founded before the end of the century. The movement to provide higher education for women confronted male hostility as well as occasional support. Leading male educators argued that women's physiology in general, and menstrual cycles in particular, made them too weak to support the strains of higher education. Edward Clarke argued that higher education destroyed the health and reproductive capacities of young women. Clarke gave as an example a young Vassar College student:

> Miss D——— went to college in good physical condition. During the four years of her college life, her parents and the college faculty required her to get what is popularly called an education. Nature required her, during the same period, to build and put in working-order a large and complicated reproductive mechanism, a matter that is popularly ignored,—shoved out of sight like a disgrace. She naturally obeyed the requirements of the faculty, which she could see, rather than the requirements of the mechanism within her, that she could not see. Subjected to the college regimen, she worked four years in getting a liberal education. Her way of work was sustained and continuous, and out of harmony with the rhythmical periodicity of the female organization. The stream of vital and constructive force evolved within her was turned steadily to the brain, and away from the ovaries and their accessories. The result of this sort of education was, that these last-mentioned organs, deprived of sufficient opportunity and nutriment, first began to perform their functions with pain, a warning of error that was unheeded; then, to cease to grow; next, to set up once a month a grumbling torture that made life miserable; and, lastly, the brain and the whole nervous system, disturbed, in obedience to the law, that, if one member suffers, all the members suffer, became neuralgic and hysterical. And so Miss D——— spent the few years next succeeding her graduation in conflict with dysmenorrhœa, headache, neuralgia, and hysteria. Her parents marvelled at her ill-health, and she furnished another text for the often-repeated sermon on the delicacy of American girls. . . .

Questions about what education was best suited for women persisted throughout the century. While some women frankly sought to provide women with an education that would permit them to take their place in the public world beside their brothers and enjoy economic independence, other advocates of women's higher education contended that it would make them better companions for middle-class men and better mothers for middle-class children.

Sports

Children have played games wherever they have been. But rural adults, engaged in strenuous physical activities in the open air, had relatively little need for sports. The amusements we associate with them were dances, socials, house-raisings, and "bees" designed to bring isolated people together. But city dwellers, confined to monotonous work in factories or sedentary work in offices and stores, craved recreation in the open air. As one observer noted in 1902, "the disappearance of the backwoods and the growth of large centres of population have created the demand for an artificial outlet, and . . . games are the natural successors of the youthful activities of a pioneer period." Often the facilities did not match the craving. Open space was hard to find. City folk flocked to the parks on weekend afternoons to play baseball, or picnic, or stroll. But until well into the new century there simply were not enough open spaces, and at some risk children played tag, hide-and-seek, and stickball on the city streets.

Bicycling One solution was basketball, invented by James Naismith in 1891, which could be played indoors. Another was the bicycle. Until the 1890s bicycles had enormous front wheels and tiny rear ones, and it was difficult for anyone but trained athletes to use them. Then came the "safety" bicycle with two wheels of equal size. Bicycling soon became a virtual craze. Thousands, including many women, took it up. Frances E. Willard, the prominent temperance advocate, wrote *A Wheel Within a Wheel: How I Learned to Ride the Bicycle* to advertise the pleasures of "wheeling." Another woman wrote in a Minneapolis newspaper: "I can't see but that a wheel is just as good company as most husbands. . . . I would as lief talk to one inanimate object as another. . . . Another great superiority of the bicycle lies in the fact that you can always get rid of it when you wish."

Many American cities and towns had ordinances against Sunday spectacles of any sort, whether games or theatrical performances.

These blue laws sought to keep Sundays as a day of worship and religious contemplation. Largely the work of evangelical Protestants, the Sabbath laws often met resistance from Catholics and others. Toward the end of the century the strict keeping of the Sabbath began to give way. "Where is the city in which the Sabbath is not losing ground?" lamented one rock-ribbed gentleman in 1887. "To the mass of the workingmen Sunday is no more than a holiday . . . it is a day for labor meetings, for excursions, for saloons, beergardens, games and carousels."

Baseball

On those liberated Sundays baseball flourished. Descended from several children's games, baseball in its modern form had appeared during the 1840s in the New York area as a gentleman's game. A decade later it began to attract some artisans and laborers, some of them forced to play at dawn before going to work. Soon people were coming to watch as well as play, and teams charged admission to their fenced fields. During the Civil War, informal soldier teams spread interest in the sport, and that led to a proliferation of teams in the years following. In 1869 the Cincinnati Red Stockings began to hire players for paid admission exhibition games, and soon after William A. Hulbert organized the National League of Professional Baseball Clubs, with teams in New York, Philadelphia, Hartford, Boston, Chicago, Louisville, Cincinnati, and St. Louis. Baseball got still greater attention from the next generation as city crowds reached out for things to keep themselves amused. By the late 1880s annual attendance at the National League games had reached eight million a year. Semi-professional groups and small town clubs drew their own crowds. In 1886 *Harpers Weekly* noted: "the fascination of the game has seized upon the American people, irrespective of age, sex or other condition." The American League was formed in 1899. For a while each league fought to supersede the other. But then they settled their dispute and in 1903 joined in the first world series. Baseball had become the national game.

Boxing and Football

City people were also paying admission to see other sports. Boxing, though many Americans correctly considered it brutal, attracted city crowds. During the 1880s and 1890s some Irish-Americans—Paddy Ryan, Jake Kilrain, Robert Fitzsimmons, and, above all, John L. Sullivan—dominated the heavyweight lists. Like other sports, boxing was a ladder up for the talented of all races, most notably for Germans and blacks. In 1908 Jack Johnson, a black man, won the heavyweight championship.

The first college football game was probably played in New Brunswick, New Jersey, between Rutgers and Princeton in 1869, four years after the Civil War. As James Weeks has written, football was frequently described in the metaphor of war; it was played, one observer wrote, on "the field of battle." A survivor of Richmond's grim Libby prison noted that "the blood of the whole community is stirred by physical contests among the picked youth of the land, as once it was only stirred by tales of battle." During the reform era of the early twentieth century the sport was denounced as brutal. But even death on the gridiron was worthwhile, *The New York Times* said, "if it educated boys in those characteristics that had made the Anglo-Saxon race pre-eminent in history." By the last decade of the twentieth century the yearly tally of deaths had mounted, and at major universities scandals and sleaze marked the continued popularity of the sport.

Sports and Social History

During most of this period sports remained primarily a male interest. Women bicycled, played such genteel games as croquet, and practiced archery. They also became baseball enthusiasts in fair numbers. But girls, though many did heavy farm labor or relentless factory work, were supposed to be fragile, and custom forbade their participation in strenuous body contact sports. It would take another generation before women's interest in sports came to seem perfectly normal, and until almost our own day before professional woman athletes would come into their own.

While both participation in sports and observance of them had ancient precedents, and both could take place in rural as well as in urban cultures, they are strongly expressive of modern urban civilization. Sports as an activity not only serve in the absence of the daily physical routines of agriculture, but also represent in some degree the modern bent for turning the process of living into rational, purposeful projects. Just as for several centuries the Western world, according to some social historians, has made of work

The New York Polo Grounds, ca. 1900, where larger and larger crowds turned out to watch the country's national sport of baseball. *(Courtesy, The New-York Historical Society, New York City)*

something more specific, more conscious and deliberate, more clearly timed than it once was, so in the last century we have pursued exercise and sports as specific activities, instead of merely letting exercise happen in the course of the day. Spectator sports are modern in another way. They are events that engage large numbers of strangers in similar acts of observing and judging, so that people at opposite ends of a city in the late nineteenth century had opinions of the same baseball player on the home team. This bringing together of strangers who observe and think about the same event gives sports something in common with the plays and the musical performances that flourished in late nineteenth-century urban culture. What is happening in all these instances is the shaping of a modern urban public.

Amusements

Until the 1880s most American playwrights produced comic pieces or sentimental melodramas. In the eighties Bronson Howard began to write plays with believable characters and situations. James Herne's *Shore Acres* (1892) was the first prominent American play to embody the artistic style commonly known as realism: a style that in literature and drama presents without sentimental or heroic illusions the facts and troubles of real life. Between 1890 and 1910, David Belasco and Charles Hoyt wrote witty comedies rather than the broad farces of earlier decades.

Music

Many cities established major orchestras. New York's symphony, begun in 1878, the Boston symphony, initiated in 1881, and the Chicago symphony, which dates from 1891, soon rivaled Europe's best. In 1883 a group of wealthy New Yorkers built the Metropolitan Opera House for the first resident American opera company.

Music, to countless Americans of the day, meant the sentimental, catchy products of Tin Pan Alley. New York's music publishing district turned out reams of sheet music to be played on the family piano while mother, father, and the children warbled out the words. Much of this music was saccharine, but some of it entered into the folk heritage of the American people. Tunes such as "After the Ball" (1892), "The Sidewalks of New York" (1894), "On the Banks of the Wabash" (1896), and "O Promise Me" (1889) are sung today.

A considerably zestier brand of popular music had appeared in the "darktowns," the black ghettoes of American cities. Ragtime was syncopated, with the emphasis on the upbeat. Much of it was instrumental, to be played on the piano or on wind instruments. When vocal, it was often fitted with risqué words that offended prim and proper people. Attacked by critics as "vulgar, filthy, and suggestive music," it attracted the young as well as those Americans who had had their fill of sentimental ballads. In the hands of Scott Joplin, a black musician from Texas, it reached a level of sophistication much appreciated today. By 1914 the ragtime craze was over, but it had left its permanent mark. The jazz that became nationally popular in the years after World War I had borrowed from ragtime.

Vaudeville

In the dissemination of popular songs, sheet music took its place beside the vaudeville performance, the stage revue, the minstrel show, and the musical comedy. There were city display cases for popular songs.

In 1907 the impresario Florenz Ziegfeld began to present his reviews, which would feature comedians such as Bert Williams, Eddie Cantor, and Fannie Brice, along with scantily clad showgirls and tuneful songs. More widespread was vaudeville. Composed of comic skits, acrobatic acts, comedy routines, animal performances, dancing, and music both serious and comic, vaudeville achieved immense popularity with city audiences between 1890 and 1920. At one time New York had thirty-seven vaudeville houses, Philadelphia thirty, and Chicago twenty-two. Hundreds of performers made excellent money touring one of the better circuits that took them to scores of American cities. During its heyday, about one in seven Americans attended the vaudeville show at least once a week.

In the working-class neighborhoods and ethnic ghettoes of the great cities lived thousands who could not afford the fifty cents of a vaudeville seat or spoke no English and could not follow the skits and comedy routines. By the opening years of the new century a medium had arrived that would appeal to these people, and attract millions of others as well.

Motion Pictures

Motion pictures had awaited the development of electric or arc lights, photography, flexible celluloid film, and electric motors as well as lenses. The whole complex of inventions came of the fertile brain of Thomas Edison, though not at first as a projected film. Edison's Kinetoscope of 1889 was a black box with a light. The viewer looked through an eye piece at a backlighted moving film strip recording a brief story, or bit of moving scenery, or some action. Edison made these peepshows in a tarpaper shack at his laboratory in New Jersey. He rented these to arcade operators, who quickly learned that the public would pay a penny or two for the novelty of seeing lifelike miniature figures moving before their eyes.

Edison's peepshows could handle only one paying viewer at a time. By 1895, however, the projector that showed a large picture on a screen had appeared. All the operator needed was an empty store where he could place some chairs and his projector. But the new, large audience also called for something more ambitious than a one- or two-minute sketch, and as audiences increased it also became commercially feasible to provide these features. Before long Edison and a dozen other entrepreneurs were producing full-reel films running for twenty minutes or half an hour, with a wide range of stories and themes. These featured chases, comic sketches, dancing, travel scenes, and even early trick photography showing fantastic happenings. Some of the early titles were "Umbrella Dance," "Venice," "A Narrow Escape on the Baltimore and Ohio Railroad," "The Ups and Downs of Army Life," and "The Kiss." Probably the first fully realized film with a story that provided a beginning, development, and denouement was *The Great Train Robbery* (1903).

By the opening years of the twentieth century the "movies" had become a major form of big-city entertainment. Enjoyment of a film did not require literacy or even an understanding of English; since films were silent it was essential for producers to make them understandable by visual means alone. By 1905 three thousand primitive movie theaters were in operation, most charging only a nickel—hence the name "nickelodeon." Soon afterward a few operators began to design halls exclusively for movie viewing and these became ever more elaborate. By the eve of the First World War there were 13,000 movie houses together catering to from five to seven million viewers a day. Audiences belonged to all ranks of society, but much of the popularity was among the poor. As one magazine noted, "in the tenement districts"

The newly invented Ferris wheel, designed by George W. G. Ferris, was a major attraction at the World's Columbian Exposition, Chicago, 1893. *(Courtesy, Chicago Historical Society)*

the movies had "well nigh driven other forms of entertainment from the field."

The building of movie palaces in well-to-do neighborhoods made movie-going respectable for middle-class families and inaugurated an important transformation in the kinds of movies produced. Throughout the early twentieth century, and especially after the advent of talking pictures, more and more attention would be given to middle-class women as the chosen movie audience. Plots accommodated the new clientele, and the whole cult of the movie star grew up around personalities such as Mary Pickford. Stars like her offered one of the few models of female success that corresponded to dominant ideas of women's roles, and girls would begin to dream of becoming stars themselves. But studio publicity departments also forced stars to share details of their own lives and to encourage ordinary middle- and lower-class women to identify with them.

And so, by the second decade of the twentieth century, the lives of millions of Americans had been transformed by the forces of industrialization. In 1860 most adult Americans had worked as farmers or tillers of the soil of some kind, living in isolated farmsteads, cut off from much of the world around them. By 1910 far fewer than half were farmers. For millions in the cities life was congested, noisy, hectic, and often unhealthy. But it was also richer, more colorful, more interesting, and more aware than rural living had been. And many of the city problems, it soon became apparent, were not intractable. By the opening years of the new century there would be those who would call the American city "the hope of democracy."

Points To Think About

1. Before the late nineteenth century, American cities had little in the way of transportation systems, and the overwhelming majority of their residents had to live within walking distance of jobs, stores, churches, and other key points. This meant that all sorts of people had to live close to one another. In Chicago, for example, it was only a two-block walk from the "Gold Coast," one of the richest sections of the city, to one of the worst slums. The streetcar, the commuter railroad, and then the automobile made possible the growth of residential neighborhoods. The affluent moved to the new suburbs, away from the noise and congestion of the central city; away from the unsightly slums, too. The middle class and the best-off segment of the working class also got out of the center of the city. They moved to modest residential neighborhoods within streetcar or subway distance of the business and industrial districts. Sociologists sometimes call their neighborhoods "zones of emergence," since moving to them was usually a family's first step toward respectability.

Hence the new transportation systems not only helped relieve the terrible overcrowding of nineteenth-century American cities, but also made possible the manifold kinds of segregation that currently characterize American society.

2. In the late nineteenth century vice was a code word for prostitution. Since the Victorian era is often presented in the media as the golden age of the bordello, and vice crusaders as narrow-minded hypocrites, students often have a very definite, and highly misleading, impression of what this portion of American social history was like.

David Pivar's *The Purity Chase* is an invaluable corrective. The crusade, one of the largest, most significant, and least studied social movements in American history, throws light on a number of important topics. It helps explain what happened to abolitionists once the Civil War ended slavery; it illuminates some of the ideological underpinnings of feminism; it provides insights into middle-class attitudes toward sexuality; and it is a fascinating case study of how reformers sought to improve society.

The purity crusade enlisted a large number of former abolitionists to whom the evils of "white slavery" seemed only a little less horrible than those of the chattel slavery they had so recently campaigned against. It arose in reaction to the attempt, by physicians and police, to inspect and license prostitutes—a practice already common in Europe. The regulators argued that prostitution could not be eliminated but could be controlled and the diseases associated with it reduced. Anti-regulationists denied the public health benefits of inspection and licensing, a position that argued that there was no reliable diagnostic procedure for detecting venereal infections in their early stages. They also argued that prostitution symbolized the subjugation of women by men. Feminists, in other words, saw the legalization of prostitution as sanctioning the right of men to use women, and then discard them.

The crusade also drew upon religious activists. Many of these—Anthony Comstock is the most notorious—deserve the censure they commonly receive as bigoted and repressed. Others were struggling against practices that were seen as vicious and destructive. Prostitution, after all, was a brutal practice as well as unhygienic; gambling tempted countless people to spend their money unproductively; cockfights were cruel. And these religious idealists made sex education an important part of their program. Hence the crusade sponsored both censorship and sex education. It drew upon abolitionists, feminists, religious idealists, and narrow-minded zealots. It challenged the medical establishment (and won since physicians had to concede their inability to diagnose venereal diseases early) as well as the "sporting set" (and lost since men continued to frequent bordellos).

3. Barbara Welter wrote the pioneering essay on the "cult of domesticity" (reprinted in her *Dimity Convictions*) in which she anatomized the mid-nineteenth-century expectations women were supposed to live up to. The essay explores women's "natural" domesticity, their supposed immunity to sexual temptation, and their consequent higher moral natures. It is worth pointing out that the new professions for women all reflected the continuing influence of the genteel tradition. Women, that is, found their careers outside the home largely limited to those that could be presented as extensions of their domestic or maternal roles.

Hence women became teachers in large measure because of their allegedly instinctive sensitivity to the needs of children (that they could be paid less than male teachers also helped). Similarly nursing became women's work in hospitals as it traditionally had been in homes. And social and settlement work, saturated in the imagery of the family—settlements described themselves as families and social work made the preservation of families and the protection of children its primary goals—could also be made to be seen as proper extensions of the genteel woman's sphere. Not only was progress for women in professional careers limited to a relatively small number of middle-class women; it was also limited by the nineteenth century's conception of women's natures. Women moved out into the world less by rebelling against these stereotypes than by conforming to them.

Suggested Readings

The most recent scholarship on American cities includes Alan M. Kraut, *The Huddled Masses: The Immigrant in American Society, 1880–1921* (1982), Thomas J. Archdeacon, *Becoming American: An Ethnic History* (1983), Alan Trachtenberg, *The Incorporation of America* (1982), Jack Chen, *The Chinese of America* (1980), Gunther Barth, *City People* (1980), John M. Allswang, *Bosses, Machines and Urban Voters* (rev. ed., 1986), Gwendolyn Mink, *Old Labor and New Immigrants in American Political Development* (1986), Cindy Aron, *Ladies and Gentlemen of the Civil Service: Middle Class Workers in Victorian America* (1987), and Zane Miller and Patricia Melvin, *The Urbanization of Modern America* (1987).

Sam B. Warner, Jr., *The Urban Wilderness* (1972) describes the physical development of American cities. Warner has also written a model study of urban spread, *Streetcar Suburbs: The Process of Growth in Boston, 1870–1900* (1971). Stephan Thernstrom's *The Other Bostonions* (1973) and *Poverty and Progress* (1967) test for upward mobility in Boston and Newburyport, Massachusetts. Howard Chudacoff, *The Evolution of American Urban Society* (revised, 1981) is also valuable.

Philip Taylor, *The Distant Magnet: European Immigration to the United States* (1971) is a good introduction to the subject. John Higham, *Strangers in the Land: Patterns of Nativism, 1860–1925* (1955) is standard, and James Olson, *The Ethnic Dimension in American History* (1979) is a fine survey. See also David Ward's *Cities and Immigrants* (1971).

On poverty and the slums see Robert Bremner, *From the Depths* (1956) and Thomas L. Philpott, *The Slum and the Ghetto* (1978). On leisure and entertainment, there is Gunther Barth, *City People* (1980). Family and social structure are considered in Stephan Thernstrom and Richard Sennett, eds., *Nineteenth-Century Cities* (1969) and Thomas Bender, *Community and Social Change in America* (1978). Sheila Rothman's *Women's Proper Place* (1978) discusses that topic from the 1870s to the present.

☆ ☆ ☆ POINTS OF VIEW: ☆ ☆ ☆

Were Immigrants Psychologically Scarred or Dynamically Renewed?

Oscar Handlin

Immigration had transformed the entire economic world within which the [European] peasants had formerly lived. From surface forms to inmost functionings, the change was complete. A new setting, new activities, and new meanings forced the newcomers into radically new roles as producers and consumers of goods. In the process, they became, in their own eyes, less worthy as men. They felt a sense of degradation that raised a most insistent question: Why had this happened?

More troubling, the change was not confined to economic matters. The whole American universe was different. Strangers, the immigrants could not locate themselves; they had lost the polestar that gave them their bearings. They would not regain an awareness of direction until they could visualize themselves in their new context, see a picture of the world as it appeared from this perspective. At home, in the wide frame of the village, their eyes had taken in the whole of life, had brought to their perceptions a clearly defined view of the universe. Here the frame narrowed down, seemed to reveal only fragmentary distorted glimpses that were hardly reminiscent of the old outlines. . . .

This they knew, though, and could not mistake it: they were lonely. In the midst of teeming cities, in the crowded tenements and the factories full of bustling men, they were lonely.

Their loneliness had more than one dimension. It had the breadth of unfamiliarity. Strange people walked about them; strange sounds assailed their inattentive ears. Hard pavements cut them off from nature in all its accustomed manifestations. Look how far they could, at the end of no street was a familiar horizon. Hemmed in by the tall buildings, they were fenced off from the realm of growing things. They had lost the world they knew of beasts and birds, of blades of grass, of sprays of idle flowers. They had acquired instead surroundings of a most outlandish aspect. That unfamiliarity was one aspect of their loneliness.

In the new country, all these were gone; that was hard enough. Harder still was the fact that nothing replaced them. In America, the peasant was a transient without meaningful connections in time and space. He lived now with inanimate objects, cut off from his surroundings. His dwelling and his place of work had no relationship to him as a man. The scores of established routines that went with a life of the soil had disappeared and with them the sense of being one of a company. Therefore the peasant felt isolated and isolation added to his loneliness. . . .

To find a job or not, to hold it or to be fired, in these matters laborers' wills were of slight importance. Inscrutable, distant persons determined matters on the basis of remote, unknown conditions. The most fortunate of immigrants, the farmers, knew well what little power they had to influence the state of the climate, the yield of the earth, or the fluctuations of the market, all the elements that determined their lot. Success or failure, incomprehensible in terms of peasant values, seemed altogether fortuitous. Time and again, the analogy occurred to them: man was helpless like the driven cog in a great machine.

Loneliness, separation from the community of the village, and despair at the insignificance of their own human abilities, these were the elements that, in America, colored the peasants' view of their world. From the depths of a dark pessimism, they looked up at a frustrating universe ruled by haphazard, capricious forces. Without the capacity to control or influence these forces men could but rarely gratify their hopes or wills. Their most passionate desires were doomed to failure; their lives were those of the feeble little birds which hawks attack, which lose strength from want of food, and which, at last surrendering to the savage blasts of the careless elements, flutter unnoticed to the waiting earth.

Alan M. Kraut

The immigrants who came to the United States in such numbers between 1880 and 1921 dramatically affected the shaping of the American population. By their very presence, these newcomers altered the economy, politics, and culture of the country. In turn, the immigrants were changed, in varying degrees, by the society they entered. The history of immigration to America can only be understood in light of "what was done" to a newcomer and native alike by this massive migratory movement. Immigrants were confronted with a series of options not even primarily of their own making, options not entirely to their taste. But it was the immigrants themselves who chose how to react; they were not simply the passive victims of large social forces. To portray the newcomers as hapless wayfarers not only robs them of their dignity, but obscures the part they played in creating a new character for America reflective of values, attitudes, and beliefs imported from around the world. . . .

The contribution of so many varied immigrant cultures to the shape of the American national character is incalculable. Incalculable if only because that contribution is so elusive; often the influence of particular groups did not become apparent for a generation or so after arrival. As the immigrants learned English, they often left the imprint of their native tongue upon local linguistic patterns. In New York, Chicago, and Philadelphia, the English spoken in Polish, Italian, or Jewish enclaves filtered into the speech of nonimmigrant residents and of other ethnic groups. Similarly, the delicacies of Greece, southern Italy, Mexico, and China found their way onto menus throughout the country. More subtly, but even more importantly, the new immigrant groups left a legacy of social, moral, and religious values which their descendants have scattered throughout the population. The fierce loyalty of Italians to family, the yearning of east European Jews for scholarship and intellectual inquiry, the Asian emphasis on family and personal honor—all of these cultural imperatives have been woven into the American consciousness.

At times, cultural differences have promoted the creation of ethnic stereotypes and rivalries damaging to America's social harmony. Ancient antagonisms imported from the Old World have occasionally found their way into national politics, and foreign policy—especially as it relates to the countries of eastern Europe—rouses the slumbering loyalties of second- and third-generation immigrants. Sociologist Orlando Patterson has charged that these loyalties, camouflaged as ethnic pluralism, make a virtue of tribalism and segregation. He and others argue that only a new universalism can counteract the primitive parochialism of those who seek to preserve their old world customs in America at the cost of social cohesiveness and justice for the individual. However, others disagree. Sociologist Richard Gambino uses the term "creative ethnicity" to describe the predominately constructive rather than divisive role that new immigrant values contributed to American culture. According to Gambino, the varied heritages of new immigrants have been and can continue to be the inspiration for creative solutions to social problems which result from life in an affluent, geographically mobile, highly secular society in which individuality, material progress, and change often take precedence over community responsibility, order, and stability. . . .

A standard greeting among Chinese immigrants was, "When are you going back to China?" recalls historian Betty Lee Sung. "As a young child, I remembered the adult conversation invariably revolved around going back to China. I gained a deep impression that China must be some sort of fairyland paradise." Years later, however, the conversation changed, according to Sung. "Nowadays, when I go to visit my mother's good friend, I hear no more talk about going back to China. This woman's children are grown and married, living in their own homes near her. Her life, her roots are deeply imbedded in American soil. . . . She barely speaks a word of English, but her mind is now oriented to the thought that she is going to spend the rest of her days in the United States."

The Huddled Masses: The Immigrant in American Society, 1880–1921, by Alan M. Kraut, from pp. 180, 182, 184, 185, 188. The American History Series,

William C. Wall painted the Homestead Steel Mill in 1884, a year after Andrew Carnegie took it over. By depicting the factory against a pastoral backdrop, Wall was expressing the hope that the new industrial America would harmonize with the country's rural past. *(Courtesy, Scribner's Archives)*

CHAPTER 19

Workers and Farmers 1865–1900

THE HOMESTEAD STRIKE

Homestead, Pennsylvania, in 1892 was a town of about 12,000 inhabitants. Seven miles east of Pittsburgh on the left bank of the Monongahela River, the town was dominated by a Carnegie plant that made steel boiler plates, structural steel, armor plate, and beams. The workforce of the plant—3,800 people—and their families made up the town. Most of this force was unskilled labor working for very low wages and belonging to no union. Many were recent immigrants, predominantly eastern European. But 800 of the skilled workers, many of them earning about $200 per month, belonged to the Amalgamated Association of Iron and Steel Workers. This union, with about 25,000 members, was probably the strongest in the country, just as the Carnegie Corporation, forerunner of the United States Steel Corporation, was among the most powerful and successful corporations in the nation. Since 1889 the union had worked under an agreement by which wages would rise and fall with the market price of steel, but never below a fixed minimum. The agreement was set to expire on June 30, 1892.

In the spring of 1892, Andrew Carnegie, a former proponent of trade unions who no longer actively managed the business, decided along with his chief manager Henry Clay Frick that they would destroy the union at Homestead and henceforth run all their plants on a non-union basis. Frick negotiated with the union in the most cursory way while literally preparing for battle. He turned the steel plant into an armed fortress, with solid board fencing complete with gun holes and topped with barbed wire and high platforms with electric search lights. He arranged with the Pinkerton Detective Agency for 300 armed men to guard the plant so that he could bring in non-union workers, then announced the new terms: no union, and wage reductions that averaged over twenty percent.

The workers were confident they could beat the corporation. They were not a downtrodden desperate proletariat. Rather, the Amalgamated members were part of the local elite. They assumed, correctly, that the unskilled workers would follow their leadership, and that the merchants and professionals of the town would be on their side, extending credit to the men and using their influence to settle the strike to the union's advantage. Most of all, these skilled men, proud to be rollers, or heaters, or shearers, or cutters, did not believe that the plant could be run without them. In the face of national union support, other men with their skills would never become "black sheep" and work for Carnegie as strikebreakers.

The great Homestead strike was technically not a strike but a lockout, since Frick initiated it by shutting the mill hours before the contract was scheduled to expire. The company placed ads for fresh labor in newspapers around the country. The workers, virtually one with the local government anyhow, took over the town, arranging patrols to prevent the influx of strikebreakers, consulting with the saloonkeepers to prevent drunkenness, and generally securing order.

In the early hours of July 6, 1892, the news spread that two barges filled with men were being towed up the river. A huge crowd of workers with their families assembled at the landing. The Pinkertons in the barges attempted to land, a shot rang out—no one knows from where—and Homestead was at war. All that day, the workers besieged the 300 men in the barges. At 5:00 p.m., after nine of the workers and three of the Pinkertons had been killed, the "Pinks" surrendered. The workers marched their captors to a temporary prison in a skating rink and set fire to the barges.

Despite the peace that now appeared to prevail in Homestead, the governor of Pennsylvania called out the National Guard on July 10. The strikers and town government planned a great reception with bands and speeches of welcome, but General Snowden, the Guard commander, had come to put down "revolution, treason, and anarchy." Under the protection of the troops, Frick reopened the plant with non-union men and began legal prosecutions of a number of the leaders. Frick hoped to break the strike by convincing the men that the plant could operate without them and by tying up their leadership in court battles. Frick's plans probably would have succeeded in any case, but the strategy of identifying the strikers with ambitions more sinister than union recognition and the maintenance of their pay scales received unexpected assistance. On July 23, a Russian emigré anarchist, Alexander Berkman, bursting into the corporation's office in Pittsburgh, shot and then stabbed Frick, seriously wounding him. The unions instantly dissociated themselves from this episode, but it robbed the strikers of much public support.

The union fought almost 200 separate charges, exhausting its resources and its leadership. One leader urged the strikers to continue: "The battle is with you; see that you win it. If you lose such conditions as never confronted the slaves in the South will be yours." But with the strike over five months old and the winter approaching, the entire town, not simply the strikers, was at the point of desperation. The union surrendered and the men began trickling back to the plant. Low wages and for many workers a twelve-hour day with a twenty-four-hour stretch every other week when the shifts changed soon became the norm. True to its promise, the Carnegie company, and its successor, the United States Steel Corporation, maintained non-union plants, and led national efforts to retain the open shop until the Congress of Industrial Organizations (CIO) succeeded in organizing steel in the waning years of the Great Depression of the 1930s.

The Outsiders 1865–1900

The United States in the late nineteenth century was for many the land of opportunity it has always been. Yet it had its outsiders, people excluded from enjoyment of the nation's prosperity or excluded by social custom or law from participation in its politics. Most obvious among the oppressed were the southern freedmen and blacks in the North. But other groups, among them women workers and mine and factory workers, and the most recent immigrants, were outsiders as well if their condition is compared with that of the solid, propertied Americans whose images appeared in popular art and literature as representative of American society.

The nation at its founding and then in its defeat of slavery had pledged itself, in rhetoric and in law, to the attainment of equality and justice. Yet it had never been quite clear what that should ultimately mean. Most of the world, of course, had its full share of poor people, or victims of ethnic or racial bigotry, or workers at low wages for wealthy or distant employers. But in the United States such conditions were not only disturbing in themselves but scandalous: they seemed to contradict the country's origins, as only a few years earlier slavery had contradicted it. The nation's commitment to equality provided a continuing and troubling judgment on the condition of the outsiders.

The Wage Earner

In 1870 relatively few Americans worked for wages. Those who did got along relatively well with shop owners. One brass worker recalled that labor and management had worked closely together after the Civil War. Most adults of working age, housewives aside, were still farm owners or, in the case of the South, belonged to the new class of sharecroppers that the breakdown of slavery had created. By 1900, however, a very large proportion consisted of wage earners rather than self-employed persons. Of the twenty-seven million in the labor force in this later year, about nineteen million, or roughly two-thirds, were people who primarily sold their labor or skills to others for a daily or weekly wage. Conditions between workers and owners had deteriorated in the intervening years. The same brass worker who described shop relations as "one happy family" in 1869 wrote in 1883 that "now the boss is superior" and the "average hand" would not think of addressing him. Another laborer observed, "The employer has pretty much the same feeling toward the men that he has toward his machinery."

Few wage earners were the sole support of their families. Many working families had several wage earners beside the male head. Most were sons but, increasingly, daughters and sometimes even the mother of the family worked outside the home for wages. When all went well these earners, even when unskilled, could provide a family with a more than adequate living. But sickness, lack of skill, the needs of young dependents could bring down living standards to a pitiful level. A Joliet, Illinois, railroad brakeman supported his wife and eight children on $360 a year in 1883. All ten people in his family were crammed into a three-room house where they ate chiefly bread and potatoes. The reporting investigator noted: "Clothes ragged, children half-dressed and dirty. . . . They all sleep in one room regardless of sex. The house is devoid of furniture, and the entire concern is as wretched as could be imagined." Many other workers gave honest testimony to their pathetic plight. One testified in 1888, "A coal miner . . . has to work so hard to make wages that he is an old man when he should be in his prime."

Without unions, wage workers for big companies were the creatures of their employers, to be hired or dismissed at will, and when they tried to form unions other Americans looked at them as radicals or hoodlums. The struggle to unionize the mines and the factories was ultimately a struggle to give wage earners a place, a community, a definition within American society.

Shop girls and women at Westinghouse Electric Corporation, 1894. The majority of the 2.6 million women working outside the home in the 1880s and 1890s were young and single. *(Courtesy, Westinghouse Photo)*

Marginal Wage Earners: Blacks, Women, Children

Much of the work of white adult male wage-earners of the Gilded Age was by present standards uncertain and repugnant. But it was enviable beside most of the work of blacks of both genders as well as that of white women and children.

In 1880 women accounted for 2.6 million, or about one-seventh, of the paid labor force of 17.4 million. Although working-class and even many middle-class women worked throughout their adult lives, they did not, like most men, participate in the labor force on a regular basis. Men were expected to work for a wage whenever work was available. Most women who worked outside the home for a wage did so only for a few years during their lives, the majority when they were in their teens, twenties, or early thirties, still single, and still living with their families of origin. Of the 3.7 million women in the publicly defined labor force in 1890, only 500,000 were married. But the labor of a married woman could be necessary to the survival of a family.

Much of that labor escaped the attention of census takers, especially when it was work done in the home, such as piece work, or taking in laundry or boarders. Normally the statisticians and economists did not classify as productive labor the duties of farm women. Since all groups preferred to have married women work for their own families within their own households, we can assume that a married woman's participation in the labor force resulted from need rather than choice, from her husband's inability to support the family by his own efforts. Only after the beginning of the twentieth century did the notion of a "family wage" as a wage large enough to support an entire family, but paid to the male wage earner, become an accepted priority for workers and management. And even then, only the most skilled and successful male wage earners received it.

The preference of both capital and labor for a male work force subjected women to systematic discrimination in the job market. They were virtually excluded from the learned professions. By 1900 a few hundred women were doctors, largely because of the efforts of a few pioneers. Among them was Elizabeth Blackwell, who had, in 1849, become the first American woman to earn an M.D. degree. But there were next to no women in the legal profession. The Supreme Court turned down Myra Colby Bradwell's suit against the Illinois Bar, which had refused to admit her. The Protestant ministry similarly attempted to exclude women, and the natural and social sciences included only a few such as the astronomer Maria Mitchell and the anthropologist Erminnie Smith. Male prejudice and the male monopoly of professionalization explains much of women's exclusion; the opposition of traditionalist women to careers for other females contributed as well.

After the Civil War, women's opportunities for education improved considerably with the founding of the coeducational land-grant colleges and the eastern women's colleges. But the curricula deemed appropriate to women still included a heavy dose of "feminine" subjects, with a minimal offering in the sciences and pre-professional training. And the graduate schools in all fields still largely excluded women. In the 1890s, the new University of Chicago became the first graduate school to train significant numbers of women, especially in sociology and the other social sciences.

Teachers and Nurses

During the last half of the nineteenth century teaching jobs opened for well-educated middle-class women. Earlier in the century many women had taught, but many of them had been at the very lowest levels of informal "dame schools" where young children learned their ABCs. With the advent of the publicly supported common school, women began to replace men in the better elementary school jobs. Upon the arrival of the public high school, largely after the Civil War, they also displaced men in the secondary schools. In 1860 about twenty-five percent of the country's public school teachers were women; by 1880, sixty percent; by 1910, eighty percent. Men usually occupied the supervisory jobs of principals, commissioners, and superintendents at every level of training and grade, and were paid better. Indeed, one reason why school systems hired so many women was that their lower pay placed less of a burden on taxpayers. Yet however imperfect the system, the development of the teaching profession was a great boon to many women.

Nursing, a new profession, was another breakthrough. Before the Civil War, hospitals had employed only male attendants. The work of the attendant was considered dirty, harrowing, and hard, and therefore unsuitable for ladies. During the Civil War, the need for nurses with the armed forces, combined with the earlier example of the Englishwoman Florence Nightingale during the Crimean War of 1853–56, broke down resistance. After 1865 several major hospitals established training schools for female nurses, and gradually these raised their standards of admission and training. By the end of the century the new profession, or semi-profession, of trained or registered nurse had come into being, providing a decent occupation for thousands of ambitious young women.

Social Work

A final professional opportunity for women, appearing at the end of the century, was that of social worker. Until the post-Civil War period, charity of various kinds had been distributed primarily on an informal, emergency basis by churches, benevolent societies, and local governments. Most of those who administered the dispensing of funds were volunteers, predominantly middle-class women, who considered their efforts simply a matter of social responsibility. Toward the end of the century, various reformers, in an attempt to deal more systematically with the brutalities of city life, established city-wide charity organizations to provide welfare on a scientific basis. Along with these agencies grew a professional class of social workers trained in techniques for making charity a means of giving the poor skills and ambitions that would lift them out of poverty. Many of these professionals were women. Much of the growth of social work as a profession would come in the early twentieth century, but by 1900 this new opportunity for educated, middle-class women had already presented itself. Some, however, could not shed their social biases. One wrote of an Italian family that they were not yet Americanized: they were "still eating spaghetti."

Women also took an active role from the beginning in the American Social Science Association, founded in 1865 by an influential group of Boston reformers. It included women, such as Caroline Dall, who were devoted to the rational reform of social problems. During the 1870s and 1880s, the organization spawned affiliates in various cities and such independent organizations as the National Prison Association, the American Public Health Association, the National Association for the Protection of the Insane and the Prevention of Insanity, the National Conference of Boards of Health, and the National Conference of Charities. Many of these groups soon outgrew the parent association, but perfectly captured its spirit of rational, institutional reform with which more and more women were associated. Such participation did not offer women professional careers in the strict sense, but did draw them into reform activities, institutional politics, and advanced currents of thought. Women's interest in social science and rational reform would in many cases merge with their commitment to "social housekeeping" as a particularly female response to the problems of urban society. This doctrine advocated extending to society the standards of purity, such as sexual purity and sobriety, whose enforcement within the family and household was the woman's task.

The openings that came to women in the later nineteenth century expressed those technological and social forces that had swept Welshmen and Irishmen to Pennsylvania coal mines, pulled Americans and Europeans to the western frontiers, and swelled the commercial and industrial cities of the Old and the New World. Social work, nursing, even public education represented, each in its own way, the replacement of traditional skills with scientific technologies. There was to be a technology of social work, a professionalization of caring for the sick, an efficient, regular, and universal education of the young, just as there was a new technology of steel making and a mass production of clothing. Like the factories and the mines, the new professions destroyed slow, customary ways of life. As an Irish peasant, who a century ago would have tended an ancestral plot of ground, now traveled across an ocean and joined the rushing crowds of an industrial city, a woman who might earlier have spent her life at ancient tasks on a farm now entered the ranks of an army of teachers or hospital workers. And the professionalization of teaching, nursing, and charity that was changing the lives of at least a small number of women represented, like the industrialization of the rest of life, a force for social equality of a sort. Once the individual had been defined as a member of a distinct family, or an inhabitant of a particular town, or the practitioner of a family craft. These definitions had put the individual into a structure of social classes: an upper class of landholders, a middling class of merchants, a city class of artisans, a lower class of peasants. Now some women, like very many men, were definable not by the class and community they had been born into but by the skills they had acquired and the work they were ready to do.

Domestics Although these gains were impressive, they were restricted to a relatively small percentage of working women. Most still had to be content with menial, low-paying jobs. One of the largest categories of women workers was that of servants or domestics. Of the five million gainfully employed women workers of 1900, 1.5 million were listed as "private household workers." About a fifth of these were laundresses, the rest "housekeepers" of one sort or another. The conditions under which these women lived and labored varied a good deal. Many, especially among the older women, were married and came into their employers' households to work for the day. They had their own homes, and generally their wages were supplements to their husbands' incomes. Wages for laundresses, maids, cooks, and other domestics were not good—less than a dollar a day—but women had lives of their own after hours. The situation of the "widow-lady" who had to support herself by her wages as a servant, or even herself and young children, was far less tolerable. Equally unhappy was that of the live-in servant girl who was at the beck and call of her middle-class mistress or master for long hours and, living in her employer's household, seldom had much privacy. No doubt some young women found kindly friends and protectors in their employers; no doubt some servant girls became loyal and cherished family retainers within middle-class families. But the circumstances of the live-in maid were inherently unenviable.

Generally speaking, by the late nineteenth century domestic service was not—outside the South—a job that native-born women performed. It seemed far too menial for them. In farm regions, many of the hired girls called in to assist the farmer's wife during the harvest season, when there were many extra hands to feed, were the daughters of a neighbor. They considered their job to be merely helping out, and therefore without stigma. Long-term domestic service was largely confined to Irish and German women in the North and to black women in the South. After 1880 newer immigrants began to take their places. Without skills, these young women had few alternatives.

Another large category of female workers consisted of factory operatives. Like servant girls, most of these were young and unmarried; like their sisters in domestic service, they were underpaid, especially relative to men. The job of the factory girl seldom had anything to recommend it except a modest return that helped to supplement her family's income. The few middle-class women who had any contact with the life found it grim. Factory work was often a harsh and squalid life for young women.

African American Workers

In the half-century following the Civil War, the vast majority of African Americans remained in the South, working the soil for white owners. Al-

Florida strawberry pickers in the 1890s. In spite of emancipation, the majority of blacks remained in the South working the fields. *(Courtesy, New York Public Library Picture Collection)*

though the Civil War and Reconstruction had achieved the abolition of slavery and though the Fourteenth and Fifteenth Amendments to the Constitution were supposed to have guaranteed civil rights for African Americans, the plantation economy was still intact in the South. Continuing in the folkways of the slave past was in part a matter of natural attachment to the familiar and an ignorance of the opportunities available elsewhere. But white landowners had a vested interest in keeping African Americans ignorant of those opportunities. Cotton, sugar, tobacco, rice, and hemp planters still needed a plentiful supply of cheap labor to work their land.

Beginning in the 1880s, only a few years after retaking control of southern state governments, white Democrats created a series of legal institutions designed to keep black workers tied to the plantations. Laws were passed making it difficult for them to relocate outside the county. Southern bankers and lawyers often refused to allow them to purchase land of their own or to finance those purchases. When black people tried, they often encountered severe racism and threats of violence. A typical example occurred in Faulkner County, Arkansas, in 1883 when an African American man attempted to buy fertile land. An armed mob delivered him a message in writing: "Mr. Nigger, just as shore as you locate yourself here—death is your potion." It was difficult for black farmers to secure reasonably long leases on a piece of land. Whites did not want African Americans working a piece of land independently; they wanted them out in the plantation fields. Many southern state practices in effect prohibited them from becoming apprentices in the skilled trades. In the South, the cotton mills that sprang up during the 1880s refused to accept black operatives; the new jobs were reserved for rural whites straight off the farm. By 1900 more than ninety percent of blacks in the South worked as field hands, sharecroppers, maids, or longshoremen.

It was not much better in the North. Northern employers preferred white European immigrants to native American blacks. Black workers seeking jobs in industry met with threats or violence on the part of bigoted white workers. White employers aggravated the hostility, using black strikebreakers when their usual labor force refused to work. Few local unions would admit skilled black workers into their ranks. Among the national unions organized after the Civil War, only the ineffectual Knights of Labor actively sought black members. When it declined in the late 1880s and 1890s, black workers found themselves without protection. The American Federation of Labor (AFL), much of its membership an elite of skilled craftworkers, at first welcomed black members. An 1890 resolution of the AFL declared that the Federation looked "with disfavor upon trade unions having provisions which exclude from membership persons on account of race and color." But then Federation officials began to yield to the prejudices of the workers who made up its constituent unions. Efforts to organize all-black unions proved feeble, and in the end few black workers benefited from the AFL. As the craft unions that made up the Federation increased their control over jobs, their bias reinforced the exclusion of blacks from all but the most menial jobs.

Child Labor The census of 1900 showed that as many as four out of every hundred non-agricultural jobs were still held by youths between the ages of 10 and 15, a total of about 700,000. In the big cities many were messengers and errand boys. Others were newsboys or shoeshine boys. In the Pennsylvania coal fields, hundreds of lads labored for ten hours a day over rushing belts of coal, picking out slate and stones while breathing in dangerous, dust-laden air. Both boys and girls worked in city loft cigar factories, rolling tobacco to make cheap "cheroots." In the southern piedmont, young girls worked from sunup to sundown in the newly established cotton mills.

Children had worked for time out of mind on the farms of the Western world. But there child labor had been part of a family enterprise with mothers and fathers as supervisors and employers. To some extent, it continued to be part of a family enterprise in the early textile mills. In the new Gilded Age, however, it largely ceased to be part of a family system and, once freed of parental supervision, the practice became far more exploitative and cruel.

One southerner described the cotton-mill children of the Tennessee Valley early in the twentieth century:

A federal investigating committee in 1890 examined the superintendent of the Enterprise Manufacturing Company:

Q: How much help do you employ?
A: We have, I think, 485 on our pay-roll.
Q: How many of those are men?
A: I cannot answer that exactly; about one-seventh.
Q: The rest are women and children, I suppose?
A: Yes, sir.
Q: How many of them would you class as women and how many as children?
A: I think about one-third of the remainder would be children and two-thirds women. That is about the proportion.
Q: What is the average wages that you pay?
A: Eighty-two cents a day for the last six months, or in that neighborhood.
Q: What do the women make a day?
A: About $1.
Q: And the men?
A: Do you mean common laborers?
Q: Yes; the average wages of your laborers.
A: About $1 a day.
Q: What do the children make on an average?
A: About from 35 to 75 cents a day.
Q: You employ children of ten years and upward?
A: Yes, sir.
Q: Do you employ any below the age of ten?
A: No.

Eva Lunsky, an employee, testified at a later hearing:

Q: When were you born?
A: I don't know.
Q: Nobody has ever told you?
A: No, sir.
Q: Did you mamma ever tell you when you were born?
A: She told me, but I have forgotten.
Q: You don't know whether you ever had a birthday party or not?
A: Yes, sir; I have had a birthday party.
Q: When?
A: Last year.
Q: How old were you last year?
A: I was 15.
Q: Was it in the winter time?
A: It was in the summer time.
Q: And you don't know the month?
A: No, sir.
Q: Do you know when the Fourth of July is?
A: No, sir.
Q: Do you know when the summer time is when they fire off fire crackers; don't they have any down your way? (The witness gave no answer.)
Q: Did you ever go to school in this country?
A: I went only three months.
Q: When was that, Eva?
A: That was last summer.
Q: What time in the summer was it that you went there; what months, do you know?
A: No.
Q: Do you know the names of the summer months?
A: No, sir.
Q: What month is this; do you know what month this is?
A: No.

They were children only in age . . . little, solemn pygmy people, whom poverty had canned up and compressed into concentrated extracts of humanity . . . the juices of childhood had been pressed out . . . no talking in the mill . . . [no] singing. . . . They were flung into an arena for a long day's fight against a thing of steam and steel. . . . They were more dead than alive when, at seven o'clock, the Steam Beast uttered the last volcanic howl which said they might go home . . . in a speechless, haggard, over-worked procession.

At first, the influence of traditional farm habits stilled the outcry against child labor. But toward the end of the century, as the rural experience receded and as childhood came more to be considered a time for careful nurturing and extended education, protests against the system grew. In the 1890s the National Consumers' League, organized by New York and Chicago women, began to demand the abolition of child labor. Educators too attacked it for interfering with schooling. Yet the practice had its defenders: employers anxious to keep down labor costs and many working-class parents who either saw nothing wrong with supplementing the family income out of child labor or found they had no choice.

The Labor Movement

Average real wages rose, probably by about twenty-five percent, between 1860 and 1900. Many American workers were able to advance in their jobs and in economic standing. Especially in larger communities such as Boston, many Jewish and north European along with native-born workers advanced remarkably. And in middle-sized communities too, those workers who remained in the city for a long time usually could look forward at least to some property or savings at the end of a long working life.

Yet for every male worker who stayed put and advanced in his job or accumulated some property, several failed and departed to seek their fortune in some other place. The geographical mobility of the average working-class family in this era was astonishing. During the six decades from 1830 to 1890, Boston increased its population by about 387,000, while over 3.3 million had at one time or another arrived in the city to live. For the vast majority of new arrivals, then, Boston was a revolving door, and it is to be assumed that most of those who departed had been disappointed in their economic hopes.

The Workplace

Jobs were insecure. Without strong unions to worry about, an employer could let any worker go for union activity or for refusal to accept a speed-up. Corporations worked hard to instill habits of subordination. The International Harvester Corporation gave as its first lesson in a brochure to teach English to its Polish workers:

> I hear the whistle. I must hurry.
> I hear the five minute whistle.
> It is time to go into the shop.
> I take my check from the gate board and hang it on the department board.
> I change my clothes and get ready to work.
> The starting whistle blows.
> I eat my lunch.
> It is forbidden to eat until then.
> The whistle blows at five minutes of starting time.
> I get ready to go to work.
> I work until the whistle blows to quit.
> I leave my place nice and clean.
> I put all my clothes in the locker.
> I must go home.

In the periods 1873–79, 1884–86, and 1893–97, severe business slumps forced many thousands of men and women to lose their jobs. In the last of these, as many as 4.5 million wage earners were out of work—over eighteen percent of the labor force.

Men, women, and children worked amid the smoke, flame, and din of furnaces and exposed machinery. Boiler explosions, mine cave-ins, train wrecks, uncontrollable fires, and other accidents were grim events in the lives of industrial workers. Thousands were maimed or killed, and few workers or bereaved families collected anything in compensation for loss, pain, or suffering. Some workers fell victim to the slower processes of industrial disease. Maladies that we today would recognize as black lung disease or some form of industrial poisoning generally went undetected. The most serious disease of all that working people regularly contracted was the "white plague," tuberculosis, a product in most cases of crowding, overwork, and poor nutrition that afflicted thousands, especially in the big cities.

The workday in American mines, mills, factories, and construction sites was long throughout the half-century following the Civil War. In 1890 factory workers typically labored some sixty hours a week at their machines. Bituminous coal miners had an equally long workweek. Bakers and steelworkers averaged sixty-five hours or more. Only postal employees and other government workers, with their forty-eight-hour week, approached modern standards. A British immigrant observed, "Labour in most occupations is greater, generally speaking, than in any other part of the world. Everything, in fact, connected with trade or business seems to proceed at a sort of railroad pace; all move at the very top speed." An immigrant hatter in Newark complained that Americans "are savagely wild in devouring their work." Whatever its overall achievements, the American industrial economy provided ample cause for unrest among wage earners. In the post-Civil War era discontent would erupt in spasms of violence that shocked middle-class public opinion profoundly and sometimes injured the cause of labor.

Employer-Labor Violence

The murder and intimidation that swept the Pennsylvania anthracite coal regions during the 1860s and 1870s is an early instance of such violence. One coal miner described his working life:

> Day in and day out, from Monday morning to Saturday evening, between the rising and the setting of the sun, I am in the underground workings of the coal mines. From the seams water trickles into the ditches along the gangways; if not water, it is the gas which hurls us to eternity and the props and timbers to a chaos.
>
> Our daily life is not a pleasant one. When we put on our oil soaked suit in the morning we can't guess all the dangers which threaten our lives. We walk sometimes miles to the place—to the man way or traveling way, or to the mouth of the shaft on top of the slope. And then we enter the darkened chambers of the mines. On our right and on our left we see the logs that keep up the top and support the sides which may crush us into shapeless masses, as they have done to many of our comrades.
>
> We get old quickly. Powder, smoke, after-damp, bad air—all combine to bring furrows to our faces and asthma to our lungs.

Out of such conditions sprang a disorderly and long-continuing rebellion that is still legendary.

The Pennsylvania unrest has traditionally been ascribed to a secret society called the Molly Maguires, an outgrowth, supposedly, of an Irish-American benevolent society. The Mollies flourished amid low wages, physical danger, and repression, to which they responded by violence against coal company officials and miners who threatened to reveal their secrets. The Mollies probably did not exist as an organized conspiratorial body, but violence against unfriendly mine operators was common in the east Pennsylvania coal fields, and that intimidation was used to reinforce the more conventional labor weapons of strikes and boycotts.

In 1873 Frank B. Gowen, the tough, anti-union president of the Philadelphia and Reading Railroad, an owner of coal mines, hired an agent of the Pinkerton private detective agency to infiltrate the union supporters. At enormous risk, James McParlan over the next months gained the confidence of the workers by treating liberally at the local saloons and by his happy-go-lucky demeanor.

By this time a major strike had broken out in the coal fields, a dispute marked by violence on both sides as the operators brought in vicious strikebreakers and company police and the miners attacked the scabs. After five months of threats, arson, and murder, the miners surrendered and went back to work. With the strike over, McParlan surfaced with evidence naming union leaders who had been directly involved in the murder of company officials.

During the Molly Maguire trials that followed, McParlan was the state's chief witness. At least one of the accused turned state's evidence and testified against his fellow workers. On dubious evidence twenty-four men were convicted, ten of whom were hanged and fourteen sent to jail. It was many years before the anthracite coal miners were in a position to challenge the mine owners again.

The trials of the Molly Maguires had scarcely concluded before the country experienced an eruption of violence that went far beyond the coal field outburst. In 1873 a sharp stock market panic set off a severe depression. In an economy still marked by fierce business competition, employers found themselves forced to cut back or face bankruptcy. As the economy flattened out, they imposed wage cuts on their men. Their response was widespread.

The 1877 Strikes

Few actions by management are as appalling to workers as wage cuts and when, in 1877, the Baltimore and Ohio Railroad announced the second ten-percent reduction for its workers in eight months, the men became enraged. First at Baltimore and then at Martinsburg to the west, they uncoupled cars from locomotives and stopped passage of trains. Urged on by railroad management, the governor of Maryland called for federal troops and himself sent in state militia to force the men to let the trains through. The militia clashed with the workers and before the week was out, the strike had spread to all parts of the B&O and to other roads coast to coast. By the time it ended it had affected fourteen states and produced a casualty list of over a hundred killed, including strikers, militia, and bystanders. Millions of dollars in railroad property went up in smoke. In this and other strikes in 1877, one

The Haymarket Riot, May 4, 1886. A bomb tossed among policemen trying to disperse a crowd killed or wounded over seventy people. Contemporary line drawing.

observer noted the strong participation of women "boldly urging the men on to acts of outrage and bloodshed."

The 1877 strikes shook the confidence of the middle class in the stability of the economic system. The *Philadelphia Inquirer* charged that the railroad workers, particularly the woman members of mobs, had "practically raised the standard of the Paris commune," while the president of the Pennsylvania Railroad noted that what had begun as a riot had grown into an "insurrection." Allan Pinkerton, the head of the strike-breaking detective agency, claimed that the strikes were "the direct result of the communist spirit spread through the ranks of railroad employees by communistic leaders and their teachings." In the wake of the upheavals, many states passed laws making it a criminal offense to conspire among workers to injure employers.

With the return of good times in 1879, relative quiet descended over labor. But during the next twenty years, workers confronted with wage cuts responded angrily or violently. In 1886, after a political meeting called by Chicago anarchists to protest the labor policies of the McCormick Reaper Company, someone threw a bomb at police in Haymarket Square. The explosion killed seven policemen and injured seventy. The ensuing wave of anti-labor feeling turned otherwise sensible people slightly mad with fear of anarchism and led to the hanging of four anarchists and the imprisoning of four others, although there was no valid proof that any of the convicted men had been directly involved in the crime. In 1892 there was the violence of the Homestead strike. Two years later, President Cleveland sent federal troops to put down disorder in Chicago following a railroad strike in support of the Pullman Palace Car workers in the company town of Pullman, Illinois.

Working people were as often the victims of violence as its perpetrators. Few wage earners ever fired a pistol at a company official, threw a torch through a railroad roundhouse window, or hurled a brick at a strikebreaker hired by Pinkerton. American workingmen were rather conservative, and generally accepted the capitalist institutions of their country. A particularly blatant violation of their rights or a brutal assault on their sense of fair play could arouse them. But normally it was difficult to get them to devote sustained effort to challenging the system of capitalism or even fighting consistently for some sort of cooperative action to advance their common well-being.

Early Labor Unions

For many years after the Civil War American workingmen could not sustain an effective labor movement and did not support radical political action in substantial numbers. Labor organizations had a way of growing in times of prosperity and declining when times were bad, precisely when they were needed most.

During the years immediately following Appomattox, the National Labor Union was formed. It demanded an eight-hour day and wished to establish cooperatives among workers. In 1872 the group turned to politics and supported a labor party. With the panic of 1873 and the depression that followed, the National Labor Union collapsed, along with a number of other unions that had confined their work to particular trades.

Knights of Labor; American Federation of Labor

With the economic revival of the late 1870s, the Knights of Labor, established in 1871, began to gain adherents in large numbers. Headed by Terence V. Powderly from 1878 to 1893, the organization was open to almost every variety of working person. The Knights in 1878 advocated equal pay for women and one year later permitted them to become members. At the height of the Knights' strength, women constituted about ten percent of the membership. It would be a long time before women again did so well in the organized labor movement.

The "true Knight," the order proclaimed, was "sober, respectable, conservative, modest, non-opportunistic, lawful, respectful, educated." During the years of its prosperity the organization seldom supported strikes for the sake of raising wages and improving working conditions. Rather, it concentrated on political agitation for the eight-hour day, a graduated income tax, consumer and producer cooperatives, and, in labor disputes, the use of boycotts and arbitration.

Samuel Gompers, leader of the American Federation of Labor, the first successful federation of trade unions, formed in 1886. *(Courtesy, U. S. Signal Corps, National Archives)*

Despite its professed reluctance to strike, the Knights went out against several railroads in the mid-1880s. Its initial success brought a wave of supporters who pushed the membership list to over 700,000. But thereafter, as a result of specific defeats in strikes as well as the wave of feeling against unions that accompanied the Haymarket incident, the

Knights precipitously declined. During the 1890s the organization survived as a shadow of its earlier self, largely with agrarian support.

Meanwhile, the Knights had been eclipsed by the American Federation of Labor (AFL), a new federated union, founded in 1886 by Peter McGuire, Samuel Gompers, and Adolph Strasser. Gompers and Strasser were cigar makers who in 1879 had organized the skilled cigar workers when, following introduction of the cigar mold, they lost their status of independent self-employed craftsmen. As leaders of the AFL, they elevated the techniques they had earlier learned into a set of principles that enabled the new union to weather depressions and become the first successful national trade union in American labor history.

Under Gompers, the AFL avoided politics. A former socialist, he concluded that capitalism was in America to stay. Whatever benefits wage-earners gained they would have to get within the capitalist system. Taking up with radical movements would only alienate the middle class. Even engaging in middle-of-the-road politics was a mistake. Better to stick to simple trade unionism. As Strasser stated the AFL case in a famous observation:

> Our organization does not consist of idealists. . . . We have no ultimate ends. We are going on from day to day. We are fighting only for immediate objects—objects that can be realized in a few years.

The AFL formula worked. Skilled workers, largely of native background, swelled the ranks of AFL affiliates. Since they could not easily be replaced, their threats to strike were often effective and they were able to maintain a privileged position as an American labor elite. By 1902 over a million wage-earners were in unions, three quarters of them in affiliates of the Federation.

Socialism

In the nineteenth century a number of social critics in Britain, continental Europe, and the United States came to fix their attention on the nature of work in modern society. Part of their concern was in reaction to modern technology itself. Many observers were convinced that modern factories and machines degrade the status of the workers, denying them the creativity that craftsmen once enjoyed. Others perceived a modern economy as offering especially sophisticated forms of work, replacing crude labor with verbal, mechanical, or mathematical forms of thought. But both sets of critics agreed that capitalism debases work by depriving the productive classes of control over the means of production and by reducing economic activities to their commercial values. The object, then, should be to put individuals and small groups of workers in control of the tools, machines, mines, and other instruments of productivity. That meant taking property out of the hands of capitalist and other privileged classes. Such ideas became grouped under the name socialism.

In the nineteenth century the ideas of the German theorist Karl Marx became so prominent that ever since then the terms "socialist" and "Marxist" have often been used synonymously, to the displeasure of a substantial number of non-Marxist socialists. Marx described history as moving in definable stages, in each of which a laboring had been subordinated to an oppressing class. In the most recent stage, according to Marx, workers were under the domination of industrial capitalism. In the end workers, made class-conscious and militant by their experience, were to rise up against the now-rotten system and overthrow it. Thereafter, mankind would be free of economic exploitation and injustice and would finally advance to a new stage of steady progress, equality of wealth and power, and an end to class struggle.

Many socialists have rejected Marxism for describing history as a set of rigidly formal stages rather than as events that can change as a result of human decisions. Anti-Marxist radicals of this kind have wanted socialism to be not a scheme for mapping out history but a flexible and continuing method of criticizing social inequities (including in the twentieth-century inequities of nations that have called themselves socialist.) How the final overthrow of capitalism could be brought about was in contention among Socialists, Marxist and non-Marxist. Some believed that it could be done through peaceful means: a socialist party in a democracy could win a majority and legislate capitalism out of existence. Others believed that only violence could oust the capitalists from the seats of power. Some anarchists have elevated direct violent action to an end in itself; others advocated the "general strike," whereby all workers would simply refuse to work, and thereby would bring down the capitalist system.

Socialist Parties The first Marxist socialists in the United States were Germans who brought their new theories with them, some democratic and peaceful, some violent. During the 1870s the Marxist Workingmen's Party and the Social Democratic Party attracted a few foreign-born workers and a still smaller group of native-born Americans. Daniel DeLeon's Socialist Labor Party, founded in the late 1870s, had fewer than 1,500 members in the early 1880s. At the very end of the century Eugene V. Debs, former leader of the American Railway Union who was sent to jail for defying a federal injunction during the Pullman strike, helped organize the Socialist Party of America. In 1900 the party, with Debs as its presidential candidate, won about 100,000 votes. In the next decade, after the arrival of many thousands of additional eastern European immigrants and an awakening of interest among American workers, the Socialist Party vote and membership rose sharply. In 1912 its growth would peak with the achievement of almost one million votes for Debs in that year's presidential election, about six percent of the total.

Despite the modesty of its political success, socialism made its mark on American life. A number of intellectuals were attracted to it or to other visions of a radical remaking of society. Especially appealing was the pleasant future Edward Bellamy presented in his 1888 utopian novel, *Looking Backward.* During the 1890s writers, artists, editors, and ordinary middle-class men and women joined Nationalist clubs dedicated to the Bellamy "principle of association," that is, to cooperation in place of competition as the basic mode of social and economic conduct. Some Americans found in the socialist call for equality and justice the best articulation of the American democratic credo. In later years, when middle-class reformers confronted the social ills of the nation, the socialist alternative to reformism spurred them on, lest the socialists gain even further support from continuing social ills.

Conservatives saw socialism as an extreme danger and were not averse to discrediting all reform or indeed all attempts to improve the lot of wage earners as being the work of violent revolutionaries. After the Haymarket affair, conservative journalists and opinion-makers were quick to attack all labor union leaders as agitators and dangerous radicals, no better than the anarchists who had thrown the bomb at Haymarket Square. In later years, many who dissented from the social and economic status quo would suffer similar attacks. These assaults would be a heavy burden for both reformers and revolutionaries.

The basic structure of American life doomed the socialists to a peripheral political status. Some intellectual historians argue that to have a truly revolutionary tradition, the United States would have needed an aristocracy or a permanent peasant class, both conspiciously absent here. Even the American Revolution of 1776 was more of a rebellion against British political authority than a genuine revolutionary upheaval against the upper classes. Millions of immigrants came to the new country hoping to better themselves, and they often defined success as the ownership of private property—a farm or a house or a small business of their own. And socialists, many Americans somewhat incorrectly believed, aimed to expropriate all private property.

Black Americans

Among the outsiders were millions of people whose race, national origins, and cultural traditions set them apart from the native white Protestant majority. In various ways, and to varying degrees, these Americans failed to share fully in the economic, social, and political benefits of the richest nation on earth.

The largest single minority consisted of many peoples of African ancestry. By 1880 there were 6.6 million black Americans out of a total population of a little over fifty million, or somewhat over thirteen percent of the whole. Overwhelmingly, these black citizens lived in the South, the deep South of the old Confederacy having the largest proportion. Most were rural, the majority being tenant farmers or sharecroppers living and working on land owned by others and experiencing more than their portion of the general poverty of their region.

Here and there in this period a voice was raised to defend blacks against their detractors and exploiters; a few philanthropists interested themselves in black education or the health of black citizens. But few white Americans cared to involve themselves in the apparently stale battles of the Reconstruction era. Black Americans accordingly were largely thrown back on their own limited resources in their battle for decent treatment and a reasonable chance for economic success.

"Jim Crow" In many ways the lot of black Americans deteriorated in these years. Poverty and economic stagnation had afflicted them as sharecroppers in the post-Civil War South, and they had lost the fight to retain the political rights granted them during Reconstruction. Southern novelists often depicted blacks negatively. To Thomas Nelson Page they were "wild beasts." Joel Chandler Harris, in his Uncle Remus stories written for children, had a black man utter this pronouncement:

> Put a spellin-book in a nigger's han's, en right den en dar' you loozes a plowhand. I kin take a bar'l stave an fling mo' sense inter a nigger in one minnit dan all de schoolhouses betwixt dis en de state er Midgigin.

Southern blacks were economically better off under freedom, or what passed for it, than under slavery but not by much.

By the 1880s they had also begun to be surrounded by rising walls of legal segregation that excluded them from a wide range of public facilities, including good schools, colleges, and universities, and from decent housing in the towns and cities. Black Americans fought back as best they could against this policy of Jim Crow, but with few allies they could accomplish little. In 1883 the Supreme Court, reviewing a suit brought by five black Americans under the 1875 Civil Rights Act, declared that the law limited only the right of states to discriminate, not the right of private individuals. Most of the modest federal protection left was eliminated when, in *Plessy v. Ferguson* (1896), the Court upheld a Louisiana law requiring segregation of blacks on the state's trains. So long as equal facilities were provided, the Court declared, they could be separate without violating the equal-protection clause of the Fourteenth Amendment.

Reinforcing Jim Crow was a growing regime of terror. As a means of keeping blacks in their place, the less reputable elements in southern white society turned more and more to vigilante action. In 1882 forty-nine blacks were lynched in the South. Ten years later there were 161 victims of white mobs. In the new century the number of lynchings declined, but race riots increased in frequency. In 1906 a wave of rioting broke out in Atlanta that left four dead and millions of dollars' worth of property destroyed. Nor were northern communities exempt from

George Washington Carver, the son of a slave, became director of agricultural research at Tuskegee Institute, where his work helped transform the South to a multiple-crop economy. *(Courtesy, Tuskegee Institute, Alabama)*

anti-black violence. A 1908 racial incident in Springfield, Illinois, set off several days of lynching and rioting. Six died and seventy were injured. These riots, like the one that broke out in Atlanta in 1906, involved bands of armed whites invading African American neighborhoods. They set fire to churches, stores, and homes. They attacked bystanders on the street. And they sometimes lynched black males, especially those reputed to be proud or ambitious.

Emancipation and the extension, however limited, of schooling and other opportunities did make it possible for numbers of black Americans to gain property or prominence. Among the most remarkable of these was George Washington Carver, an agricultural chemist born of slave parents. Educated at Iowa State, he became director of agricultural research at Tuskegee Institute in Alabama. His experiments with peanuts, sweet potatoes, and soybeans were a major reason why the southern economy shifted from its single crops, cotton and tobacco, to a healthier, more diversified production.

Even within the South an emerging black middle class was slowly building institutions that would provide coherence and train leaders for blacks. Religion and education drew the principal efforts of black people who were denied access to politics. Blacks founded their own schools and colleges, such as Spelman in Atlanta, to train both men and women to be ministers and teachers for their people. The black Baptist Church developed as an important and many-faceted institution.

Although blacks opposed women's entry into the ministry and their leadership of mixed groups as firmly as did whites, black women developed their own large network within the church that raised money for such church needs as training ministers, and gathered other women much as white women's organizations did in the North. A significant number of black women received higher education and pursued careers in teaching. Members of black women's clubs in cities such as Atlanta sought to improve urban conditions for black families by establishing playgrounds and other services. What these women did to build a cohesive and self-conscious black community laid the groundwork for the progress southern blacks would make during the twentieth century.

As the twentieth century opened, a new group of black leaders emerged. Over the next two generations, these men—Booker T. Washington, W. E. B. DuBois, and Marcus Garvey—would help transform race relations in the United States in fundamental ways.

Agrarian Discontent

Farming, of course, was the oldest of American occupations and countless farmers were of the older European-American stocks. If new immigrants could be made to feel too new, too urban, too distant from American traditions, farmers could feel threatened by newness and by big cities that were the centers of power and finance. There were times when the more restless farmers constituted a force that seemed likely to alter the shape of American political life.

American agriculture was as much a success story as American industry in the Gilded Age. It advanced in every index of productivity, and helped supply the food needed by the nation's growing urban population, besides providing large surpluses for export to other industrial lands. Yet the generation following 1865 was a trying period.

Northeastern farmers, ever since the transportation revolution before the Civil War opened up the fertile Middle West, had been forced to adjust to the stiff competition of the newer region. This competition continued after 1865 and pushed many people off the land in New England and the mid-Atlantic states. Many farms were simply abandoned. Others shifted to the production of fruits, vegetables, dairy products, and other perishables, where closeness to city consumers gave an advantage. By the 1870s farmers of the Midwest were also being forced to make painful adjustments. As the wheat belt moved further west into the Plains, farmers in the Old Northwest found they could no longer compete. And so along the Great Lakes and in Wisconsin they turned to dairying to supply the large midwestern cities. Farther south farmers shifted to corn for feeding hogs and cattle. By the 1880s fields of maize covered the prairie lands of Illinois, Iowa, Indiana, and eastern Kansas and Nebraska. In the barns and pens, hundreds of hogs grew fat from eating the previous year's crop.

Granger Laws And whatever were the tribulations and the successes that came with the transformations of agriculture, farmers in the West, the Midwest, and the East faced the uncertainties of the yearly market. Bad weather and a scanty crop could ruin them; an abundant harvest, driving down prices, could be nearly as bad. Transportation costs or interest rates on loans could upset the delicate balance between expenses and income that some farmers precariously maintained from year to year. Eastern moneylenders were notorious for charging high interest and demanding a great deal of collateral for making loans. One wrote:

> I want property that would sell in hard times for three times the loan and with the small loans—$500; & under want four or more times the value.

Banks, railroads, the merchants who sold agricultural implements to farmers and those who brought their crop for sale to the cities: all these could be the targets of farm protest.

Western and midwestern farmers expressed their discontent through the Patrons of Husbandry, popularly called the Grange. In 1867 Oliver Kelley, an employee of the United States Department of Agriculture, undertook the task of organizing the first national association of farmers. Kelley's objective was primarily social. Farming in the United States, especially on the Great Plains and out West where much of the population was widely scattered, was a lonely existence. Farmers, especially farm women, were desperate for more social contact, and Kelley created the Grange to sponsor lectures, dances, and picnics. The organization became extremely popular, and by 1874 its membership exceeded one million people. Whenever farmers gathered together for their lectures, picnics, and dances, they talked about their problems—falling commodity prices, high interest rates, and exorbitant shipping costs. The Grange was soon a militant political organization.

The Grange analysis of the farmer's plight focused on the middlemen, the various business dealers who stood between the farmers and the consumer and added so much to the price the consumer would pay for food, or charged such a high price for supplying ma-

Harvey Dunn, *Dakota Woman.* *(Courtesy, Friends of the Middle Border Museum)*

chinery and other items the farmer needed. To get around these middlemen, the Grange, which included many small-town merchants, organized cooperative buying schemes for farmers and sought to establish businesses run by farmers that could produce what they needed at moderate expense. Grangers also tried to reduce middlemen's costs by imposing fixed rates on what railroads and grain elevator companies could charge for their shipping and storage services. This effort brought the Grangers into politics, and by the mid-1870s farmers' parties had been organized in eleven states, mostly in the Midwest. In at least four of these—Illinois, Wisconsin, Iowa, and Minnesota—the Grangers gained control of the state legislatures and enacted legislation authorizing the setting of rates for railroad freight and grain elevator storage. The Supreme Court upheld these "Granger Laws" in 1877, before it reversed itself on regulation and embraced laissez-faire.

The Granger era lasted until about 1880. Thereafter, the return of prosperity, together with a successful readjustment to corn-and-hog and other specialty agriculture adjusted to domestic urban markets, pacified the Midwest. In the next two decades it would be from other agricultural regions that political protest came.

The Farmers' Alliances

Wheat and Cotton Farmers To the farm population of the Plains and the South, the 1880s and 1890s brought deep discontent. The wheat of the Plains and the cotton of the South depended on overseas markets far more than did the pork, beef, fruits, vegetables, and dairy products of the Northeast and Midwest. This meant that the chain of middlemen between producer and consumer was even longer for wheat and cotton than for the perishables of those other regions. In addition, the prices of wheat and cotton fell sharply beginning in the 1870s, dropping to about half of their initial level by the early 1890s. It is true that all other prices fell as well in the quarter-century between 1870 and the mid-1890s—interest rates and railroad freight rates declined, as did the price of farm machinery and of many of the manufactured goods that farm families consumed. But the prices of the great staples of the Plains and the deep South fell faster than those of other goods and services.

Meanwhile, bad weather was one of the farmer's worst enemies. The results are best expressed in the words of individual farmers. Sarah Orcutt of Kansas wrote to a friend:

> I take my Pen In hand to let you know that we are Starving to death It is Pretty hard to do without any thing to Eat hear in this God for saken country we would of had Plenty to Eat if the hail hadent cut our rye down and ruined our corn and Potatoes I had the Prettiest Garden that you Ever seen and the hail ruined.

W. M. Taylor of Nebraska wrote to the editor of a farm journal:

> The hot winds burned up the entire crop, leaving thousands of families wholly destitute, many of whom might have been able to run through this crisis had it not been for the galling yoke put on them by the money loaners and sharks—not by charging 7 per cent. per annum, which is the lawful rate of interest, or even 10 per cent., but the unlawful and inhuman country destroying rate of 3 per cent. a month, some going still farther and charging 50 per cent per annum.

And W. R. Christy of Kansas wrote:

> We are worried over what our Poor People of our country are to do for fuel to keep them warm this winter. . . . there are at least ⅔ of the People that have to depend on Cow chips for fuel & as the cattle had to be Sold off verry close that its been difficult to get them. Some have went as far as 13 miles to get them. the thermometer this morning was 16 below zero & .4 or 5 inches of snow on the ground, under those circumstances what are the People to do. at this time our coal dealers have not all told more than 100 bushels of coal on hand & it cant be bought for less than 40¢ per hundred in Less than ton lots.

Grain and cotton farmers could offset the drop of staple prices by cutting costs and getting a larger production with the same investment. This effort to compensate for deflation explains much of the heavy investment of wheat farmers in machinery during these years, and of cotton farmers in fertilizers. Careful attention to the best practices might yield a profit from wheat or cotton. But many farmers lacked the means to achieve that constant vigilance; and in the South and the Plains farm leaders sought other answers to the relentless battle against insolvency, and fastened on middlemen and financiers as scapegoats.

In both the South and the trans-Missouri West, railroad rates were higher than in the Northeast. So were credit costs, a condition that was particularly galling when the dollar was appreciating in value and so making each debt contracted in a given year harder to pay the next. Manufacturers, too, seemed to take advantage of farmers. The farm machinery monopoly appeared to be a particularly effective agency for gouging them. Financiers, farm radicals believed, were conspiring to reduce the money supply of the nation in order to raise interest rates and push up the value of the dollars their debtors would have to pay them. This focus on finance was responsible in the 1870s for the free-silver movement that led to the Bland-Allison Act of 1878 and the Sherman Silver Purchase Act of 1890, and the election of 1896.

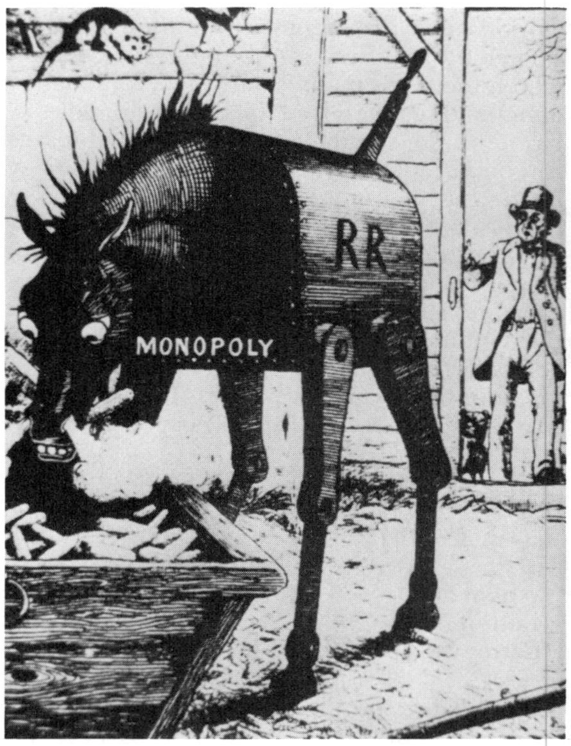

In this political cartoon the railroad, represented here by an iron horse bolted together and breathing steam, is raiding the farmer's corncrib.

The Alliances At the end of the 1870s, various new farmers' groups began to appear. In 1880 Texas farmers organized a Grand State Alliance to keep up prices for their crops, to bring down prices of goods in country stores, and to resist the crop liens by which a creditor could seize part of a crop in payment of a debt. Over the next few years the Texans linked up with various Farmer's Clubs, Agricultural Wheels, and other groups. By 1890 the Southern Alliances, resulting from the merger of these, had a membership of over a million. The Southern Alliances, at least in North Carolina and probably elsewhere, offered a more important role to women than did most of the northern labor organizations. Their programs included demands for education and rights for women and they admitted women as members. The all-white Southern Alliance had its parallel in the Colored Farmers' National Alliance and Cooperative Union, with 1.5 million members in 1890. In the Northwest appeared the National Farmers' Alliance, or Northwestern Alliance. On a platform demanding federal regulation of railroads and free coinage of silver, the Northwest Alliance expanded rapidly in the wheat belt. By 1890 there were 130,000 Northwest Alliance members in Kansas. Nebraska, the Dakotas, and Minnesota were not far behind.

Before long, Alliance leaders moved to merge the two regional groups into one nationwide organization; this, however, proved slow, for each group refused to abandon its own special interests and concerns. By the 1880s the Alliances also began to enter state politics, usually by associating themselves with one or the other of the two major parties. A substantial group of farm leaders from the West and South decided that the mainstream parties were abysmally failing to come to grips with the plight of the rural regions and, beginning in the early 1890s, they came together to organize a new party, the People's Party.

The Mainstream Parties

The two major parties were remarkably well matched during the Gilded Age. From the 1870s onward, control of the national government seesawed back and forth between them. Between the end of the Civil War and the mid-1890s there were more Republican than Democratic Presidents, but Democrats Tilden in 1876 and Cleveland in 1892 received more popular votes than their Republican opponents, though fewer votes in the electoral college. Dominance in Congress shifted from one party to the other. There were very few years between the end of Reconstruction and 1896 when one party simultaneously controlled the presidency and both houses of Congress.

From Grant to Harrison

In 1868 Ulysses S. Grant, the final field commander of the Union forces in the Civil War, defeated his Democratic opponent, former governor Horatio Seymour of New York, on a platform endorsing Radical Reconstruction but also promising sectional peace. Grant's electoral college victory was decisive, but his popular margin was only 300,000 out of almost six million ballots cast. In 1872 Grant badly beat the Democratic candidate, Horace Greeley. In 1876 compromise between the alleged winner, Republican Rutherford B. Hayes, and Democrat Samuel J. Tilden eliminated Republican control of South Carolina, Florida, and Louisiana, and ended Reconstruction. In 1880 the Republican Party pitted Congressman James A. Garfield of Ohio against former Union General Winfield Scott Hancock of Pennsylvania. Garfield won with a solid electoral college majority of 214 to 155, but his popular majority was under 10,000 votes.

In 1884 the Republicans rejected Chester Arthur, who had succeeded to the presidency when Garfield, after only four months in office, was shot by a disappointed federal office-seeker. Though Arthur, who helped pass the civil service reform Pendleton Act (1883), made a surprisingly effective and dignified President, the party regulars turned to the charismatic James G. Blaine of Maine. The Democrats chose the reform governor of New York, Grover Cleveland. The campaign was a dirty one. Blaine was ac-

President James Garfield (left), assassinated four months after taking office in March, 1881, was succeeded by Chester A. Arthur (right). *(Courtesy, The New-York Historical Society, New York City)*

cused, with good reason, of having taken bribes from a southern railroad for his support while he was a United States congressman. Some held it against Cleveland that he had fathered an illegitimate child. The Mugwumps, a group of reformers who favored measures to make government honest and efficient, rallied to the New Yorker. The name Mugwumps, from a northeastern Indian term for a great man, was apparently given them by enemies who saw them as self-importantly moral. Blaine inadvertently offended Catholic voters when he failed to reprove a bigoted Protestant supporter who, in his hearing, declared the Democrats the party of "rum, Romanism, and rebellion." Cleveland won by a hair: the electoral vote, 219 to 182; the popular vote, 4.9 million to 4.8.

Cleveland was the first Democratic President since James Buchanan, and his administration was marked by controversy with Union veterans unused to a man who had not served in the Union Army. They resented deeply his vetoes of pension bills and his effort to have the War Department return to the southern states captured Confederate battle flags. Honest government men, however, admired his principled stands in favor of civil service, a reduction in the protective tariff, and what they called sound money, meaning the gold standard.

In 1888 Cleveland, renominated as the Democratic candidate, emphasized tariff reduction during the campaign. The Republicans nominated the aloof but eloquent Benjamin Harrison of Indiana on a platform supporting pensions and the high tariff. The election turned on the foolish statement of the British minister to the United States that he would like to be able to vote for Cleveland. This "Murchison letter" was published, and many Irish-Americans defected to Harrison to give him the election. But the results again were close. Cleveland actually won 100,000 more popular votes than his rival, but lost the key states of New York and Indiana and received an electoral minority.

As President, Harrison rewarded his business supporters by endorsing the McKinley tariff of 1890, pushing rates to the highest level up to that time. The huge federal revenues that the tariff brought in gave the government large surpluses, with which it awarded generous pensions to Union veterans. So spendthrift was Harrison's first Congress that critics labeled it the "billion dollar Congress." In the 1890 congressional elections the Democrats won a large majority, gaining control of the House of Representatives.

The election of 1892 again pitted Cleveland against Harrison. This time a strong Democratic current was running and Cleveland, emphasizing his support for sound money and a tariff for revenue only, defeated his former opponent by a popular vote of 5.5 million to 5.2 million and an electoral count of 277 to 145.

The Parties in Balance The disputes that informed these elections may not greatly interest a twentieth-century American, accustomed to arguments over poverty, social justice, and war. In considerable measure it was party loyalty itself, a loyalty that by now has much lessened, that drew voters to either of the two stolidly nineteenth-century candidates.

Relatively equal nationally, the two parties differed in strength from region to region. New England tended to be strongly Republican, and areas where people of New England descent lived, in northern New York and the older Midwest, also voted heavily for what had become known as the Grand Old Party. The South, on the other hand, was overwhelmingly Democratic, except in a few areas where, during the Civil War, sentiment for the Union had been strong. In the Midwest, areas settled by southerners before the Civil War—"Copperhead" or peace Democrat country—also voted for the Democracy.

These sectional patterns were an extension of the old antislavery battles of the 1850s: those Americans proud that slavery had been struck down and the Union preserved voted for the party of Lincoln; southerners continued to vote against it. Republican voters remembered the Civil War and, if they did not, Republican politicians quickly reminded them of it. "Every unregenerate rebel . . . calls himself a Democrat," shouted Republican Senator Oliver Morton in one typically fiery speech. "Every bounty jumper, every deserter, every sneak who ran away from the draft. . . . Every man . . . who murdered Union prisoners . . . calls himself a Democrat. . . . In short, the Democratic party may be described as a common sewer . . . into which is emptied every element of treason North and South . . . which has dishonored the age." Republican politicians also went out of their way to cultivate the Union veteran vote and to woo the Union veteran organization, the Grand Army of the Republic (GAR). Former Union soldiers were urged to "vote as you shot."

There were more concrete inducements for veterans to vote Republican. Whenever they could muster majorities in both branches of government, the Republicans appropriated money for Union veterans and their families. The billions paid out as pensions were justified, no doubt, as expressions of a nation's gratitude to those who had served it well. But they also held the veterans more firmly to the Grand Old Party.

Black voters, too, remembered the antislavery battles of the Civil War. In the years following "redemption" in the South, unfriendly southern state governments excluded many blacks from the franchise. In the North, black Americans voted Republican, in gratitude to the party of Lincoln for emancipation and as protest against the party of slavery and rebellion. Not until Franklin D. Roosevelt's New Deal of the 1930s were blacks to enter the Democratic Party in overwhelming numbers.

Citizens also chose their party on the basis of economic philosophy. In contrast to the present-day party, the Democrats were more committed to laissez-faire than the Republicans. Democrats in this period usually supported lower tariffs, for example, and opposed government aid to railroads. Republicans endorsed the protective tariff and federal subsidies to railroads. Democrats were more willing to tolerate paper money and free silver (though Cleveland allied with what was called "sound money"); Republicans were more apt to favor gold. The Democrats, in consequence, had a considerable following among farmers even outside the South, and among exporters and importers whose business would suffer from a protectionist tariff. The Republicans, also drawing on a large farm vote, were notably strong among those classes that identified their fortunes with the prosperity of American industry. In the cities most Irish Catholics and much of the new immigrant population voted Democratic. Economics was a factor here, but not specifically the economic philosophy of the national Democratic Party. The political machines of many cities were Democratic, and these made city politics responsive to the needs, material as well as cultural, of the Irish and newer immigrant communities.

Grover Cleveland campaign badge from the election of 1892, in which Cleveland defeated the incumbent Republican, Benjamin Harrison, and the Populist James B. Weaver to become the only president in American history to serve nonconsecutive terms of office. *(Courtesy, The New-York Historical Society, New York City)*

Few eligible American voters in this era failed to exercise their franchise. Elections were exciting events. A resident of Burnside, Connecticut, in 1876 wrote of "two torchlight processions here one Republican and one

Democrat. . . . We lighted up with candles for the Republican one." Turnouts often reached ninety percent of those eligible, and almost all strongly favored one of the two major parties. At least one group of upper-class, well-educated gentlemen refused to pledge loyalty to either party. The Mugwumps favored civil service reform, efficient and honest government, sound money, and free trade, and were willing to use either party to achieve their goals. But the Mugwumps were not typical of their time. As one observer noted, "What theatre is to the French, or the bull fight . . . to the Spanish, the hustings [electoral campaigning] are to *our* people."

Populism

The People's Party

In 1889 farm Alliance leaders met at St. Louis to forge a political bond with the Knights of Labor. Adopting a national platform endorsing greenbacks, free silver, economy in government, confiscation of excess railroad lands, and public ownership of "the means of communication and transportation," the meeting recommended that all farmers and laboring men support candidates who were willing to pledge themselves to these principles. The following year, the Southern Alliance and the Colored Farmers' Alliance adopted a similar platform. Resistance to a third party collapsed and at St. Louis in 1889, the People's Party—the Populists, they would come to be labeled—was formally established. In July 1890 the first People's Party convention assembled in Omaha to select candidates and a platform for the 1892 election.

The Omaha meeting was a colorful assemblage. Most American males had by now given up the Civil War era practice of wearing beards. Not so the delegates at Omaha. It seemed that there must be some connection between political dissent and abundant facial hair. Also noticeable was the number of women activists. Mary Elizabeth Lease—Mary Ellen to her friends, "Mary Yellin" to her critics—was the most prominent of these. Eloquent, courageous, mother of four, and member of the Kansas bar, she had made hundreds of speeches for the agrarian cause. In one of these, supposedly, she had declared that

> the West and the South are bound and prostrate before the manufacturing East. . . . The parties lie to us. . . . We were told . . . to go to work and raise a big crop . . . and what came of it? Eight-cent corn, ten-cent oats, two-cent beef and no price at all for butter and eggs.

There were four black delegates, one each from Kansas and Virginia, and two from Texas. Amid roars of approval that impressed a reporter as having the "likeness of the enthusiastic Bastille demonstration in France," the convention adopted a platform that summed up the outlook of the agrarian dissenters.

Ignatius Donnelly; James B. Weaver

Written by the romantic and flamboyant Minnesota editor and politician Ignatius Donnelly, the platform preamble sounded the note of emergency that Populists felt. The nation was on "the verge of moral, political, and material ruin." Donnelly, who as a good agrarian prized silver coinage, declared that "silver . . . has been demonetized to add to the purchasing power of gold. . . . A vast conspiracy against mankind [has been] organized on two continents" by the money power, and "if not met and overthrown at once [will produce] terrible social convulsions, the destruction of civilization, or the establishment of an absolute despotism."

After this overwrought invocation, there were specific platform planks: demands for free and unlimited coinage of silver, a graduated income tax, government ownership of the railroads and the telephone and telegraph systems, the secret ballot, direct election of United States senators, and restraints on immigration. The platform called for devices on the state level favoring direct democracy: the initiative, whereby a number of citizens can petition that a particular law be considered; the referendum, submitting a proposed law to a popular vote. Planks designed to attract wage earners attacked the Pinkertons, favored reduced working hours, and endorsed the Knights of Labor in their

THE BIG SQUEEZE *An important part of American history is the story of the entrepreneur. For this businessman, James Kymer, the depression of 1893 was a shock:*

I went to work in Ohio with the rosiest expectations, only to find that there were many things about railroads that I did not know. The financing of such ventures was *terra incognita* to me. The Lancaster and Hamden [Railroad], however, was being built at a time such as I had never before experienced. Without my knowing it, the depression of 1893 was on the way. Some stock in the line had been sold, and a bond issue was to be floated. From these two sources the expense of building was to be met.

I was to do all the work, and things looked bright, but presently I was told that the money that had been raised by the sale of stock had been exhausted, while the bond issue had been delayed. I paid my men and bought my supplies, therefore, out of my own pocket. I could afford to, and thought but little of it. The following month the same thing happened, and the month after that. I was low on funds but had no trouble in borrowing what I needed. . . .

I borrowed more and more, but property values were falling, and my holdings were soon mortgaged to the very hilt. Being told that the bond issue still had not been floated, I myself went to New York to force it through. It was not until then that I realized just what had happened. Bond issues were impossible. Money could not be had.

I returned badly frightened. I pounded tables and argued. I fought and swore and fought again. But it was hopeless. I gathered up my last remaining assets—selling, mortgaging. I raised enough to pay my bills in Ohio. And finally, seeing at last the hopelessness of it all, I took a train for Omaha with barely money enough left in all the world to get me home. I could not even afford a Pullman berth. I did not buy a meal along the way, but existed instead on cheese and crackers that I had bought before I started.

I stepped onto the station platform in Omaha a tired, discouraged man. My wife had preceded me by a month or so, and when I reached home she put her arm about me and I cried.

What a tower of strength she was to me! For a time I could not bring myself to do a thing, thinking that the worst of calamities had befallen me—not knowing that what had happened was a trifle beside what was still to come.

I got about at last, trying to make a little money, but none was to be made. That year of 1893 had come, and with it every opportunity was lost.

I fought with every artifice I knew to keep my home. I traded horses when I could, but a year went past and what few dollars had been left had grown still fewer. At the stockyards in Omaha sheep were offered at fifty cents a head, with few buyers. Farmers were burning their corn because they could not sell it for enough to buy fuel. The whole nation was laboring under an economic collapse of such severity as to seem to us almost unbelievable.

Horses at the stockyards were selling at such ridiculous prices that even I could buy some. I bought a carload and took them east, selling them in Pennsylvania and doubling my money. Still it amounted to nothing, and a letter from my wife telling me that she was ill brought me home as fast as I could come. . . .

She went to the hospital while holders of mortgages were hounding both of us. I fought them off—with nothing. I held them back in every way I could. To Hell with mortgages! How could I pay for the treatment my wife required?

A month passed. My wife grew weaker. The holders of those mortgages were constantly insistent. I fought with all my strength, my back against the wall. On the thirtieth of March, 1895, my wife died. . . .

I was left with two boys—one eighteen and one sixteen years of age. I had nothing. I owed the doctors, owed the undertaker, owed even for the cemetery plot where now my wife was lying.

current battle with Rochester clothing manufacturers. The moment the platform was adopted, "the convention broke over all restraint and went wild" in a demonstration that lasted a full twenty minutes. With the nomination of General James B. Weaver of Iowa for President, the convention adjourned.

In the election that followed, the Populists won a million popular votes out of about seventeen million cast and twenty-two electoral votes. This was the best showing by far of any third party since the Republicans in 1856, and seemed to promise much. Close analysis, however, would have suggested that something was wrong. The Weaver-Field ticket had done very well in three small Rocky Mountain states—Idaho, Nevada, and Colorado; it had also run strongly in the wheat states of Kansas, North Dakota, South Dakota, and Nebraska. Except for Alabama, the South largely rejected the Populists. Worst of all was the showing in the industrial Northeast and older Midwest.

Jacob S. Coxey led his army of unemployed workers into Washington, D.C., where Coxey was arrested and his army dispersed by club-wielding police. *(Courtesy, Library of Congress)*

Coxey's Army Within months of the 1892 election, the nation's economy faltered. In early 1893 a severe panic swept the nation, bringing five full years of depression. Hard times would alter the political perceptions of the American people and intensify the mood of political and social dissent.

The economy sank lower and lower. In the industrial regions, factories closed, and thousands of men were thrown out of work, many to tramp the streets, others to ride the rails from town to town looking for jobs or handouts and clashing with local police. One expression of the general breakdown was a march on Washington organized by Jacob Coxey to demand that Congress appropriate $500 million in greenbacks to finance a public-works program. The program, it was argued, would create jobs, and the greenbacks would inflate the economy, bringing high prices to business and agriculture.

Starting from various parts of the country, including the far West where some followers seized a train, several thousand men in "Coxey's Army" set off for the nation's capital. At first enthusiasm was unrestrained: a Pittsburgh union member wrote:

> The movement is a *glorious* one. Long live *Coxey*. All recruits from here will be provided with rations for two days. One mammoth chicken pie. . . . I am satisfied that this is the turning point in the history of the United States. Indeed I may say the world. The results will be far reaching, and the name of *Coxey* will go thundering down the ages relegating to oblivion that of Washington and Lincoln. Many dropped out of the line of march or were detained by the authorities, who feared that the 'petition in boots' represented a dangerous radicalism. In late April 1894, about four hundred soldiers of the army straggled into Washington led by Coxey's seventeen-year-old daughter dressed as the goddess of peace. Coxey announced 'We're going to camp right on our own property. I claim that the Capitol steps are a part of my property.' But before they could present their petitions, their leaders were arrested for trespassing on the Capitol lawn. Coxey observed to reporters: 'Of course, I appreciate as well as anyone else the fact that the preservation of the grass around the Capitol is of more importance than saving thousands from starvation.'

But once the marchers arrived in Washington many were arrested for trespassing, and the movement petered out.

Silver vs. Gold President Grover Cleveland blamed the economic distress on the Sherman Silver Purchase Act

(1890). Ever since its passage, he believed, business had been jittery. As the amount of silver coming into the Treasury's vaults grew larger and larger, it had become increasingly difficult to uphold the gold standard. Speculators and ordinary citizens, worried about the government's ability to redeem silver coin or paper money in gold on demand as the gold standard required, were coming to the Treasury to demand gold in exchange for their bonds on their silver. With each passing month gold reserves diminished, and speculators and citizens became still more nervous. This uncertainty had knocked the economy off balance. Panic withdrawals of Treasury gold had become a flood, and it looked as if the country would have to go off the gold standard. To "gold bugs" like Cleveland and other Eastern conservatives, such a prospect was terrifying. The fall of gold, some were certain, would bring the collapse of civilization.

One of Cleveland's first responses to the depression was to demand the repeal of the Silver Purchase Act. The Populists in Congress resisted fiercely. So did many southern and western Democrats and a few mountain state Republicans. By this time Populist ideas, especially regarding finance, had deeply penetrated the western and southern Democracy, and Democratic congressmen from these sections were willing to break with the eastern wing of their own party over the issue. Despite the opposition, Cleveland was able to muster enough votes to get the measure repealed; but the administration's position alienated many southern and western Democrats.

The repeal did little to rescue gold. As the depression tightened its grip, imports declined, and with them government gold revenues. At the same time, continued public fears further depleted the Treasury. By December 30, 1893, it had fallen to $80 million. To save the gold standard, Cleveland began to borrow gold from the bankers in exchange for government bonds. But continued public fears promptly drew out of the Treasury the gold that had come into it. By early 1895 the reserve was down to $45 million, and it looked as if the silverites and other inflationists would finally realize their ambition of seeing the nation pulled off the gold standard.

At this point, Cleveland's secretary of the treasury approached the international banking house of J. P. Morgan and Company and August Belmont, a representative of the European Rothschilds. They promised the government 3.5 million ounces of gold on demand in exchange for $62 million in federal bonds. This stemmed the withdrawals temporarily, but led to angry charges by the silverites that the government had sold out the nation to the money power. Finally, after another $100 million gold purchase in 1896 the public became convinced of the Treasury's ability to maintain the gold standard, and the threat to the reserve ended. Cleveland had saved the gold standard, but only at the cost of worsening the split within his party.

Dorothy Gale and the Wicked Witch of the West. In Frank Baum's book *The Wizard of Oz*, written by a Nebraska populist in the 1890's, Dorothy wore silver slippers, symbolic of free silver. The wicked witch of the West is said to represent malign nature. What meanings might be attached to the Tin Woodman or the Imperial Wizard or the yellow brick road? *(Courtesy, MGM)*

The Bryan Campaign of 1896

The circumstances promised that 1896 would be an exciting election year. Both parties had their silver wings, and it appeared that there would be major internal battles in each over both platforms and candidates.

In June 1896, the Republicans met at St. Louis to choose their candidates. Supported by his close friend and financial backer, the industrialist Mark Hanna, former congressman and now Ohio governor William McKinley won the nomination. McKinley's protectionist principles had long identified him with the industrialists, and his choice was a victory for the Northeast: a victory confirmed by the convention's adoption of a high-tariff platform, with only a nod to silver. In reaction, Senator Henry Teller of Colorado and a number of other western Republicans bolted the Convention and soon afterward organized the National Silver Republicans.

The Boy Orator of the Platte

The battle at Chicago, where the Democrats met in July, was far more bitter and divisive. In March 1895, two western Democrats, Congressmen Richard Bland of Missouri and William Jennings Bryan of Nebraska, had thrown the challenge to the eastern leaders by demanding the immediate adoption of free and unlimited coinage of silver. "Silver Dick" Bland was the frontrunner as the delegates gathered, but coming up fast was ex-Congressman Bryan. Young, dynamic, handsome, eloquent, Bryan was in many ways a politician's dream. Born in Illinois in 1860, he had attended a small Protestant college where he had absorbed a moralistic view of society and the oratorical rhythms of the Bible. In 1887 he moved to Lincoln, Nebraska, where he practiced law and joined the Democratic Party. He was elected to Congress in 1890 and served until March 1895.

Bryan was a sincere and simple Christian who accepted the literal truth of the Bible and interpreted human history as a titanic struggle between good and evil. To a Nebraska Democrat at that time, this meant perceiving gold as an agent of the dark forces and silver as an agent of truth and light. Bryan believed that humanity was being oppressed by the money power. In preparation for the struggle in Chicago he honed and polished a memorable address.

Battle was first joined over the platform, the eastern gold bugs insisting on support of the gold standard and the western and southern bloc along with Bryan demanding "the free and unlimited coinage of both gold and silver at the present legal ratio of 16 to 1: sixteen ounces of silver to one of gold." Speakers for the West and South, including Senator Benjamin Tillman of South Carolina and Governor John Peter Altgeld of Illinois, denounced gold and Cleveland. In response, David Hill of New York declared: "I am a Democrat, but I am not a revolutionist. My mission here to-day is to unite, not to divide—to build up, not to destroy." The silver platform, he insisted, would destroy the party in the East.

One of the last speakers was the young Nebraskan, Bryan. The crowd, knowing his reputation for eloquence, was expectant.

Starting with a modest disclaimer of any special insight, Bryan announced that "the humblest citizen in all the land, when clad in the armor of a righteous cause, is stronger than all the hosts of error." Bryan challenged the eastern view that free silver would disrupt the business of the nation. Gold, he said, had already disturbed the business of the West and South. He would not, he declared, "say . . . one word against those who live upon the Atlantic coast, but the hardy pioneers who have braved all the dangers of the wilderness . . . these people . . . are as deserving of the consideration of our party as any people in this country." After reviewing the other planks of the silver group's platform, Bryan moved on to the issue of silver. "The Battle," he proclaimed, was between "the struggling masses" and "the idle holders of idle capital." The Democratic idea is that if you "make the masses prosperous, their prosperity will find its way up through every class which rests upon them." The gold Democrats claimed that the great cities were in favor of the gold standard; the silverites replied that the cities rested on the foundation of the nation's "broad and fertile prairies." "Burn down your cities and leave our farms and your cities will spring up again as if by magic; but destroy our farms and the

BRYAN, BRYAN, BRYAN, BRYAN *by Vachel Lindsay*

The Campaign of Eighteen Ninety-six, as Viewed at the Time by a Sixteen-Year-Old

I brag and chant of Bryan, Bryan, Bryan,
Candidate for president who sketched a silver Zion,
The one American Poet who could sing outdoors,
He brought in tides of wonder, of unprecedented splendor,
Wild roses from the plains, that made hearts tender,
All the funny circus silks
Of politics unfurled,
Bartlett pears of romance that were honey at the cores,
And torchlights down the street, to the end of the world.
There were truths eternal in the gab and tittle-tattle.
There were real heads broken in the fustian and the rattle.
There were real lines drawn:
Not the silver and the gold,
But Nebraska's cry went eastward against the dour and old,
The mean and cold.

It was eighteen ninety-six, and I was just sixteen
And Altgeld ruled in Springfield, Illinois,
When there came from the sunset Nebraska's shout of joy:
In a coat like a deacon, in a black Stetson hat
He scourged the elephant plutocrats
With barbed wire from the Platte.
The scales dropped from their mighty eyes.
They saw that summer's noon
A tribe of wonders coming
To a marching time. . . .

Prairie avenger, mountain lion,
Bryan, Bryan, Bryan, Bryan,
Gigantic troubadour, speaking like a siege gun,
Smashing Plymouth Rock with his boulders from the West. . . .

Election night at midnight:
Boy Bryan's defeat.
Defeat of western silver.
Defeat of the wheat.
Victory of letterfiles
And plutocrats in miles
With dollar signs upon their coats,
Diamond watchchains on their vests
And spats on their feet.
Victory of custodians,
Plymouth Rock,
And all that inbred landlord stock.
Victory of the neat.
Defeat of the aspen groves of Colorado valleys.
The blue bells of the Rockies,
And blue bonnets of old Texas,
By the Pittsburgh alleys.
Defeat of alfalfa and the Mariposa lily.
Defeat of the Pacific and the long Mississippi.
Defeat of the young by the old and silly.
Defeat of tornadoes by the poison vats supreme.
Defeat of my boyhood, defeat of my dream.

grass will grow in the streets of every city in the country." Then came Bryan's electrifying conclusion:

> You shall not press down upon the brow of labor this crown of thorns, you shall not crucify mankind upon a cross of gold.

The Election of 1896 A half-hour of bedlam followed the address, western and southern delegates cheering and parading up and down the aisles of the Chicago coliseum. When brought to a vote, the silver platform passed overwhelmingly. The next day the delegates began to ballot for their presidential candidate. On the fifth roll call, Bryan defeated Bland and became the Democratic candidate.

The Bryan nomination posed a dilemma for the Populists, who met at St. Louis shortly after the Democrats adjourned. Was Bryan, as some argued, a Populist in all but name, and would supporting him give the People's Party its best chance of getting its program enacted? So-called Fusionists favored this course. On the other side were those Populists who opposed reducing their program to the single issue of silver. No doubt Bryan's rhetoric was populistic, but was he a real reformer? No, better to nominate a separate ticket, even at the risk of electing McKinley. The delegates at St. Louis "split the difference," it was said, nominating Bryan for President and choosing their own vice-presidential candidate.

After Chicago, many disgruntled eastern Democrats returned home determined to sit on their hands in the fall. A few, however, were too outraged at their defeat to remain simply inactive. In September these gold Democrats met in convention and nominated a National Democratic Party ticket.

The campaign that now ensued was one of the most exciting in the nation's history. The struggle was largely sectional. If Bryan had won, in all likelihood there would have been a shift of political emphasis toward the needs of the South and West. On the other hand, it is hard to believe that any major change in relations between labor and capital, or any major shifts in wealth and power, would have resulted from victory. It is not even certain that Bryan as President would have succeeded in getting the nation to abandon the gold standard.

Be that as it may, Bryan and his supporters saw the campaign as a crusade for the people, and wherever "the boy orator of the Platte" went, he urged his audiences to support the cause of the "toiling masses." In the West and South, Bryan gathered great crowds who cheered him as an evangelist. But in the East he made little headway. A sober speech before a large audience in New York's Madison Square Garden, designed to quiet eastern fears, was a disappointment and thereafter the Nebraskan entertained little hope of winning the East.

Meanwhile, McKinley conducted a dignified "front porch" campaign. Delegates would come to the McKinley home in Canton, Ohio, with prepared questions and remarks, and the Republican candidate would respond in a neighborly way. The Republicans were gorged with cash raised by Mark Hanna from among fearful industrialists and bankers. This enabled them to send out scores of speakers to follow Bryan to rebut his charges, and to mail out millions of pamphlets and broadsides warning the public that a Bryan victory meant revolution and the collapse of the dollar.

McKinley The Republican campaign had its more positive side. McKinley was depicted as the herald of prosperity. The Republican tariff would restore good times and usher in the era of "the full dinner pail." Republican campaigners also spoke for unity and an end to ethnic and class conflict in the nation.

McKinley's victory in November was fairly decisive. Garnering 7.1 million votes to his opponent's 6.5 million, he carried much of the Midwest, Northeast, and West Coast, leaving Bryan chiefly the southern, plains, and mountain states. And even the South was not solid for the Democratic candidate; for the first time in a generation Delaware, Maryland, West Virginia, and Kentucky went Republican. Even more significant was Bryan's failure to capture the traditionally Democratic cities. Many wage earners, perhaps following the lead of Gompers's AFL, refused to support free silver. The tariff was attractive to workers wishing their industry protected against foreign competition. Bryan's evangelical style, his identification with the rural regions, his homespun character failed to captivate the urban masses. Nor did the Democratic candidate, any more than Popu-

William McKinley (left) decisively defeated "the boy orator from Platte," William Jennings Bryan (right), and the Silver Democrats in 1896 to become the 24th president. *(Left, Courtesy, the New York Public Library Picture Collection; right, Courtesy, Mrs. Ruth Bryan Rohde, Ossining, New York)*

list candidate Weaver in 1892, inspire the more successful farmers of the older Midwest.

McKinley's victory was a turning point in the political history of the era. Thereafter the Republicans forged ahead of their opponents and became the majority party of the nation. Over the next thirty-five years the Democrats would win the presidency only twice, and the first time largely as the result of a severe Republican split. Voting percentages declined; more and more Americans lost interest in the act of voting.

By the time of McKinley's inauguration the country was experiencing a vigorous economic revival. Prices for farm commodities and other products began to rise by 1897, bringing prosperity to farmers and businessmen and providing a lively labor market for wage-earners. During the next decade, except for a brief setback in 1907, the economy advanced rapidly, raising living standards and soothing discontent. In 1900 the silver issue was laid to rest for thirty years by passage of the Gold Standard Act, confirming and reinforcing the American commitment to gold as the backing for the American dollar, and providing some help to farmers in need of loans by authorizing national banks in rural communities.

And there was one other reason why the outsiders ceased to raise their voices in loud protest. Within a year of McKinley's inauguration, the country was at war with Spain over Cuba. Before long, patriotism and the appeal of imperial glory had captured the imaginations of Americans. When new protests appeared, they would come from different people and be couched in a different vocabulary.

Points To Think About

1. Herbert Gutman's "Work, Culture, and Society in Industrializing America" (reprinted in his collection of essays of the same title) talks of the cultural shock of moving from an agrarian society with its seasonal patterns of work and leisure to an industrial society, which aims to organize all activities by the clock. Factory work required new forms of discipline that workers, accustomed to setting their own work pace, resisted. Labor and management confronted each other with mutually exclusive notions of what constituted a fair day's work for a fair day's pay.

All industrializing nations experienced these clashes to some degree, but in the United States the constant immigration of workers with no previous industrial experience prolonged the cultural dislocations. In most other modernizing societies they disappeared with the coming of a second generation of industrial workers, used to the new social patterns of work. Here the constant infusion of inexperienced immigrant workers retarded the growth of an industrial working class. Here the same patterns of dislocation and adjustment repeated themselves until well into the twentieth century.

This unique situation may help explain why unionism was so slow to grow in the United States and why socialism had so little success in attracting American workers.

2. Massachusetts data starting in the 1870s reveal that many working men did not earn enough to support their families. A look at their spending patterns, furthermore, shows that most of the families practiced the most stringent economy. The average working-class family could not achieve the norm the culture held up: a working father supporting a full-time mother while their children attended school. These data refer to families with an able-bodied, employed father present, so they refer to the relatively better off working families.

Another pattern the Massachusetts data make clear is that working-class families nonetheless aspired to the cultural norm. The families that took in boarders, for example, were those in which the father's earnings from his regular job were considerably below the average. The budget data, then, show that families that could manage to get by on just the father's income typically did so. They were willing to live closer to the margin of subsistence in order to achieve the cultural norm of the ideal family.

Over a period of thirty years, average family income increased somewhat, while the cost of food, fuel, housing, and clothing fell sharply, by more than 30 percent between 1872 and 1896. The result was a large increase in the standard of living, almost all of which went to improving the family diet.

3. Andrew Carnegie's change of heart about unionism, signaled by his decision to break the Amalgamated Association of Iron and Steel Workers during the Homestead Strike of 1892, brought him into line with the great majority of large employers of the late nineteenth century. A variety of economic, political, legal, and even demographic factors all played into these employers' hands. The result was that trade unionism developed more slowly in the United States than in any other industrial country. How did willingness of governments to use their powers to break strikes, the attitudes of the courts toward strikes and boycotts, and the increasing number of immigrants come together to weaken unionism? What sorts of differences would a stronger union movement have brought to American history?

Suggested Readings

The most recent scholarship includes Paul Arvich, *The Haymarket Tragedy* (1984), Nick Salvatore, *Eugene V. Debs* (1982), Jack Chen, *The Chinese of America* (1980), Roy Rosenzweig, *Eight Hours for What We Will* (1982), Steven Hahn, *The Roots of Southern Populism* (1983), Mari Jo Buhle, *Women and American Socialism,* (1981), John L. Thomas, *Alternative America: Henry George, Edward Bellamy, Henry Demarest Lloyd and the Adversary Tradition* (1983), Sean Denis Cashman, *America and the Gilded Age* (1984), Barton C. Shaw, *The Wool-Hat Boys: Georgia's Populist Party* (1984), David Montgomery, *The Fall of the House of Labor: The Workplace, the State, and American Labor Activism* (1987), Leon Fink, *Workingmen's Democracy: The Knights of Labor* (1982), Susan Levine, *Labor's True Women: Carpet Weavers, Industrialization, and Labor Reform* (1984), Carlos Schwantes, *Coxey's Army* (1985), Shinshan Henry Tsus, *The Chinese Experience in America* (1986), Daphne Pata, ed., *Looking Backward, 1988–1888: Essays on Edward Bellamy* (1988), and LeRoy Asby, *William Jennings Bryan* (1987).

Irwin Yellowitz in *Industrialization and the American Labor Movement, 1850–1900* (1977) tells of the efforts of labor unionists in the late nineteenth century to halt or modify the mechanization of production that threatened to disrupt older ways of work. Also useful is Herbert Gutman's collection of essays, *Work, Culture, and Society in Industrializing America* (1976). Alice Kessler-Harris has written a history of working women, *Out to Work* (1982).

For an overview of politics in this era, see H. Wayne Morgan's *From Hayes to McKinley: National Party Politics, 1877–1900* (1971). Robert D. Marcus examines the structure of the Republican Party toward the end of the nineteenth-century in *Grand Old Party* (1971). Lawrence Goodwyn, *Democratic Promise: The Populist Movement in America* (1976) presents an interpretation of Populism, emphasizing the place in it of its left wing, the Southern Alliance. After experimenting with cooperative marketing as a solution to the farmers' troubles, Goodwyn observes, the Alliance went on to a radical politics that called for such programs as a subtreasury system to provide farmers with credit.

In *One Kind of Freedom: The Economic Consequences of Emancipation* (1977), Roger L. Ransom and Richard Sutch argue that the credit and landholding systems of the postwar South bore much responsibility for the lack of progress in the region. Having no ownership or secure possession of the land they worked, poor blacks and whites had no incentive to improve it. But blacks suffered more from simple white racism than from an unfair economic system.

☆ ☆ ☆ POINTS OF VIEW: ☆ ☆ ☆

Were the Populists Backward Looking?

Lawrence Goodwyn

Populism in America was not an egalitarian achievement. Rather, it was an egalitarian attempt, a beginning. If it stimulated human generosity, it did not, before the movement itself was destroyed, create a settled culture of generosity. Though Populists attempted to break out of the received heritage of white supremacy, they necessarily, as white Americans, did so within the very ethos of white supremacy. At both a psychological and political level, some Populists were more successful than others in coping with the pervasive impact of the inherited caste system. Many were not successful at all. This reality extended to a number of pivotal social and political questions beside race—sectional and party loyalties, the intricacies of power relationships embedded in the monetary system, and the ways of achieving a politics supportive of popular democracy itself. In their struggle, Populists learned a great truth: cultures are hard to change. Their attempt to do so, however, provides a measure of the seriousness of their movement.

Populism thus cannot be seen as a moment of triumph, but as a moment of democratic promise. It was a spirit of egalitarian hope, expressed in the actions of two million beings—not in the prose of a platform, however creative, and not, ultimately, even in the third party, but in a self-generated culture of collective dignity and individual longing. As a movement of people, it was expansive, passionate, flawed, creative—above all, enhancing in its assertion of human striving. That was Populism in the nineteenth century.

But the agrarian revolt was more than a nineteenth-century experience. It was a demonstration of how people of a society containing a number of democratic forms could labor in pursuit of freedom, of how people could generate their own culture of democratic aspiration in order to challenge the received culture of democratic hierarchy. The agrarian revolt demonstrated how intimidated people could create for themselves the psychological space to dare to aspire grandly—and to dare to be autonomous in the presence of powerful new institutions of economic concentration and cultural regimentation. . . . That idea was a profoundly simple one: the Populists believed they could work together to be free individually. In their institutions of self-help, Populists developed and acted upon a crucial democratic insight: to be encouraged to surmount rigid cultural inheritances and to act with autonomy and self-confidence, individual people need the psychological support of other people. The people need to "see themselves" experimenting in new democratic forms.

In their struggle to build their cooperative commonwealth, in their "joint notes of the brotherhood," in their mass encampments, their rallies, their long wagon trains, their meals for thousands, the people of Populism saw themselves. In their earnest suballiance meetings—those "unsteepled places of worship"—they saw themselves. From these places of their own came "the spirit that permeates this great reform movement." In the world they created, they fulfilled the democratic promise—in the only way it can be fulfilled—by people acting in democratic ways in their daily lives. . . . [T]he substance of American Populism went beyond the political creed embedded in the People's Party, beyond the evocative images of Alliance lecturers and reform editors, beyond even the idea of freedom itself. The Populist essence was less abstract: it was an assertion of how people can *act* in the name of the idea of freedom. At root, American Populism was a demonstration of what authentic political life is in a functioning democracy. The "brotherhood of the Alliance" addressed the question of how to live. That is the Populist legacy to the twentieth century.

Reprinted from Lawrence Goodwyn, *Democratic Promise: The Populist Movement in America* (New York: Oxford University Press, 1976), pp. 541–43.

Irwin Unger

Populists were agrarian men with a limited understanding of the complexities of their era. They proposed solutions to current problems which often reflected their ignorance, their isolation from the best thought of the day, and their profound sense of frustration at the intractability of their social and economic environment. Clearly we today, in a still more complex world, cannot expect inspiration from such a parochial and limited social vision.

When confronted by a more abstruse and complex aspect of the economy, or when faced by the social change which accompanied industrialization, the farmer often embraced naive and simplistic answers.

Take the money and banking systems. The Populists were obsessed with finance. But wasn't this to be expected? Wasn't Populist concern with banks, greenbacks, and silver perfectly plausible given existing conditions? Weren't farmers primarily concerned with the practical matter of reversing the long-term trend of falling commodity prices? Only in part. There were such men: men who were chiefly concerned with high interest rates and the steady decline of staple prices, and who saw inflation as the "producer's" salvation. There was this pragmatic, bread-and-butter side of Populist financial attitudes. But there was another side which was peculiarly abstract and ideological. Many Populists viewed the money question as the key to all that was wrong with American life. Solve the money problem—by abolishing the national banks and by issuing government money—and you solved the problems of poverty and social injustice, as well as the question of who ran the government. To these men, exhortations to destroy the "banks," the "bondholder," and the "money power" were a substitute not only for serious thought about the nation's real financial inadequacies, but often for serious thought about the major social and political issues of the day.

Eliminate the money question from the Populist platform and you have virtually reduced it to its peripheral issues.

Consider next Populism and the contemporary "labor problem." The Populists did seek an alliance with labor, and they did express sympathy for labor's plight. But they could offer little to industrial labor because they were outside it, and could not understand it. Their solution to the labor problem, like their solution to so many others, consisted largely in destroying the money power and manipulating their finances. From the 1860's on, labor had been skeptical of monetary solutions of its problems, and in 1896 McKinley with the tariff, not Bryan with free silver, won the labor vote.

Consider, finally, the Populist response to the city. Perhaps Americans still have not come to terms with the city, but clearly the Populist attitude was peculiarly primitive and retrograde. That the supporters of the People's party did not like the cities is irrefutable. We have all seen the archetypal Populist cartoon of the transcontinental cow grazing on the prairies while being milked in New York. Who does not know those lines from the "Cross of Gold" speech about the grass growing in the streets of the cities if the farms are destroyed? And who is not aware of the disfranchisement, particularly in the South, of the urban areas by Populist dominated legislatures? Is this all circumstantial? Then hear the direct testimony of C. W. McCune's *National Economist:* "It has been shown again and again that the masses of the people in great cities are volatile and unstable, lacking in patriotism and unfit to support a wise and pure government. The city may be the best place to use them; but the finest types of muscle and brain are almost invariably furnished by the country. . . . If the country is drained to populate the cities, decay is sure to set in." Could the message be plainer?

There is no mystery about it. Populism had a dark side as well as a light one, and critics of the agrarian movement have merely detected and described it.

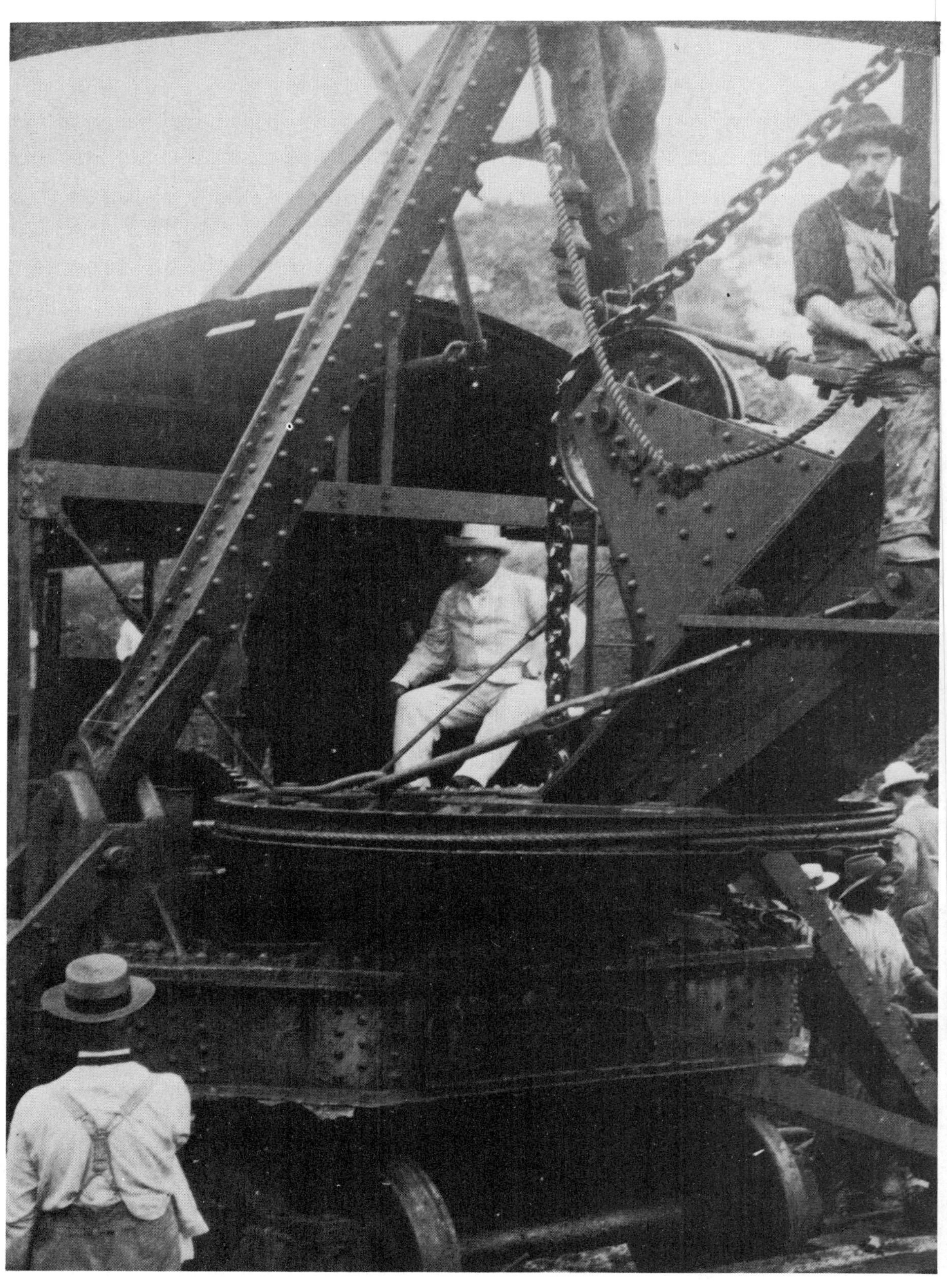

President Theodore Roosevelt operating an American steam shovel at the Panama Canal, 1906.
(Courtesy, Library of Congress)

CHAPTER 20

The Outward Thrust 1865–1914

THE PANAMA CANAL

Since 1513, when the explorers led by Balboa (the poet Shelley mistakenly took him for Cortés), "silent upon a peak in Darien," sighted the Pacific after having traversed the Isthmus of Panama, men and women had dreamed of a linkage between the great oceans. In time that dream envisioned a canal. But formidable jungle, tropical diseases, and differences in elevations between the two oceans had posed enormous engineering barriers. In the 1880s, the great French engineer Ferdinand de Lesseps, who built the Suez Canal, tried and failed to conquer the Panamanian jungle. By 1889 his firm was bankrupt. The New Panama Canal Company was organized in 1894 to assume de Lesseps's assets and, perhaps, to complete the canal. But the financial climate in France during the depression of the 1890s and the reputation of Panama for tropical disease soon moved the company's ambitions to the more modest goal of selling its rights and its rusting machinery to the United States, where public opinion stoutly endorsed ownership of a canal. A dramatic incident in the Spanish-American War, when the U.S.S. *Oregon* was forced to steam around Cape Horn to join the Atlantic fleet off Cuba, convinced most doubters that a canal was imperative.

The new venture pinned its future on two talented adventurers: a swashbuckling French engineer named Philippe Bunau-Varilla and a shrewd New York lawyer, William Nelson Cromwell, who would earn every penny of the $800,000 fee he eventually collected from the company. Their first task was to dissuade Congress and public opinion from choosing a Nicaraguan site for the canal. Only Cromwell's intensive lobbying and a contribution of $60,000 to the Republican National Committee produced the substitution of "Isthmian Canal" for "Nicaragua Canal" in the Republican national party platform for 1900. In May 1902, with Congress about to vote, nature seemed to conspire with Cromwell and Bunau-Varilla. The Frenchman had lobbied mightily, arguing the hazard of Nicaragua's volcanoes; and within days of the final vote, Mt. Monotombo conveniently erupted. The next morning every United States senator found in his mail a copy of an old Nicaraguan stamp showing the mountain in a previous eruption: Bunau-Varilla had scoured the Washington stamp dealers. Panama narrowly won—with the proviso that diplomatic negotiations with Colombia, which was part of Panama, be successful.

President Theodore Roosevelt, by his own report, conducted the negotiations with Colombia "without the aid and advice of anyone." Through his secretary of state John Hay, Roosevelt concluded the Hay-Herran Treaty with Colombia, which offered an indemnity of $10 million and lease payment in perpetuity of $250,000 a year. In addition, there were provisions highly offensive to the sovereignty of Colombia, including the protection of the New Panama Canal Company against any claims by that country. Colombia rejected the treaty, out of pride, but also with a greedy eye to the French company's assets and to negotiating higher lease payments from the United States.

Roosevelt was furious. Negotiating with those "Dagos," he claimed, was like trying to nail currant jelly to a wall. They were "those contemptible little creatures in Bogota," those "jack rabbits," "foolish and homicidal corruptionists," "tricky oppressors" of Panama. Hay translated these racist sentiments into a diplomatic threat of retaliation—perhaps even war. Meanwhile, the President made widely known the pleasure he would take were the Panamanians to revolt against Colombia and form an independent nation agreeable to the treaty provisions that Colombia had rejected. While making plans to seize Panama if necessary, the President was willing to wait—although not so late as the election of 1904—to see whether Cromwell and Bunau-Varilla could bring on a revolution.

They did. At $50 a head, members of the Colombia garrisons in Panama were bought off. Hay gave assurances that warships would be in the area to protect United States life and property if disruption occurred, that is, to prevent Colombian retaliation in the event of revolution. In perfect comic opera fashion, a young woman was delegated to create a national flag, groups of firemen and railroad workers were drilled, shots were fired in the air, and the republic was proclaimed. Someone backed a mule cart up to the subtreasury building, and the Colombia military were paid in gold: $30,000 to the general, who nearly drowned in the gallons of champagne poured over his head; $10,000 to most of the officers.

Washington received news of the revolution two days later and in precisely one hour and sixteen minutes recognized the new government. The Panamanians wasted no time in dispatching two ambassadors to sign the treaty with Washington, but Bunau-Varilla was taking no chances that the new owners of that narrow strip of real estate would become as greedy or as jealous of their sovereignty as had the Colombians; he named himself the Panamanian ambassador. Roosevelt agreed to receive his credentials, and Hay promptly signed the treaty for Panama. The Panamanian republic was all of thirteen days old. Roosevelt airily asserted that the entire process had been carried out "with the highest, finest, and nicest standards of public and governmental ethics." Payment of $25 million to the Colombian government in 1921 expressed a different judgment of the proceedings, agreeing more with another of Roosevelt's statements: "I took the canal zone and let Congress debate, and while the debate goes on the canal does also."

New York World, November 9, 1903.

Roosevelt and the Republican steamship arriving with guns and shovels to build the canal.

The Outward Thrust: Beginnings

American overseas expansion dates from before the Civil War, when American interest in the Pacific resulted in the famous visits of Commodore Matthew Perry's naval squadron to Japan in 1853–54 and the almost simultaneous effort of southerners to compel Spain to sell Cuba to the United States. Neither probe won the United States any territory, and during the Civil War foreign relations, like all other national concerns, were subordinated to the urgent goal of defeating the Confederacy and preserving the Union.

Reasserting the Monroe Doctrine

As secretary of state during the Civil War, William Seward had to pursue defensive policies against European opportunists seeking to take advantage of the Union's preoccupation with the rebellion. During these war years France sent troops to Mexico and established there the regime of a puppet emperor, the Archduke Maximilian of Austria. Meanwhile, Spain tried to regain control of the Dominican Republic and made demands on several South American countries. Seward deplored these violations of the Monroe Doctrine, the policy of excluding further European colonization in the Western Hemisphere, first announced by President James Monroe in 1823. He complained, expostulated, and protested, but he was forced to bide his time.

With the war's victorious conclusion, Seward quickly began to exert pressure on the French and Spanish. He warned the Spanish minister to Washington that if the country persisted in seeking an entrance into the Western Hemisphere, the United States would actively support the Latin American republics feuding with Spain. The Spaniards quickly abandoned their ambitions in the hemisphere. France was a far more powerful nation, yet behind Seward were fifty thousand Union veterans under General Philip Sheridan's Texas command. If these linked up with the forces of Maximilian's Mexican opponent, Benito Juarez, the French puppet empire was done for. Seward demanded that the French set a time limit for ending their occupation of Mexico. By now the French Emperor, Napoleon III, was convinced that the Mexican adventure was becoming too costly and he removed his troops. Juaréz's forces quickly took over, captured Maximilian, and executed him. Having dealt with Europe's version of expansion, Seward was now free to turn to his own. He promised that his countrymen would have "control of the world." Wishing to make the nation's presence felt in the Pacific, Seward favored acquiring the Hawaiian Islands, then an independent kingdom. He also wanted to buy the Virgin Islands from Denmark and to establish a major United States naval base in the Dominican Republic.

The Purchase of Alaska Alaska, that vast northwest corner of North America which provided Seward's one great expansionist success, was then a Russian colony, having been first explored and exploited by the Tsar's agents during the eighteenth century. A beautiful land, it had at most a few thousand inhabitants, almost all either Indian or Eskimo, and few known resources except furs. The fur trade had flourished at first under the Russian-American Company, but by 1865 most fur-bearing animals were gone and the company was in financial trouble. The Tsar made friendly overtures: our "two peoples," he remarked cordially in 1866, "have no injuries to remember." Not only was the region becoming a financial liability to the Tsarist regime, but it was also too far from the Russian heartland to be militarily defensible. Better, then, to sell it to the Americans. Alaska as a United States colony would be a buffer between Russian Siberia and British Canada. Russia made an offer; Seward, with the annexation of all Canada also in mind, quickly accepted. When the Tsar's minister told Seward that the Russians would sell, he eagerly pushed away the evening's card table:

> 'Why wait till tomorrow, Mr. Stoeckl? Let us make the treaty tonight!'
>
> 'But your Department is closed. You have no clerks, and my secretaries are scattered about the town.'
>
> 'Never mind that,' responded Seward. 'If you can muster your legation together, before midnight you will find me awaiting you at the Department, which will be open and ready for business.'

Seward paid Russia $7.2 million for the cession, and in 1867 Russia formally transferred the territory to the United States.

All this had taken place at breakneck speed, before the American public could react. But Congress as a whole, not merely the favorably inclined Senate, had to appropriate the money to pay for the territory. And before the proposed appropriation came to a vote in the House of Representatives, the public had time to respond to the purchase. The response was at best mixed. A few expansionists, like Seward himself, saw the cession as another step toward the nation's eventual dominion over the entire continent. Some Americans hoped that Alaska's purchase would serve to restrain the British. Others favored the treaty to annex Alaska because they felt kindly toward Russia, which had supported the Union during the Civil War. A still larger number of congressmen, apparently, found generous personal gifts from the Russian minister to be a convincing argument.

Yet the opposition was strong and angry. One newspaper editor thought the treaty "a dark deed done in the night." Besides, what was this place for which Americans were paying millions? It was, said a critic, "a barren, worthless, God-forsaken region." It consisted of "walrus-covered icebergs"; it was the land "of short rations and long twilights." In the end, Congress did appropriate the $7.2 million, but it was a near thing. Alaska had cost the United States about two cents an acre.

Seward ceased to be secretary of state in 1869, when Grant succeeded Johnson, and for the next decade or more the United States pursued a rather unaggressive foreign policy. During these years the nation settled disputes with Great Britain left over from the Civil War. The Treaty of Washington in 1871 provided for an international tribunal to assess the degree of British blame for allowing the escape of the Confederate raider *Alabama*, and this tribunal awarded the United States $15.5 million in damages. In 1878 the United States received rights to establish a naval base at Pago Pago in the Samoan Islands in the mid-Pacific. Yet on the whole, few Americans paid attention to international events. American foreign policy of the 1870s has been described as the "nadir of diplomacy." Expansion beyond continental limits seemed a preposterous idea. The *Chicago Tribune* noted soon after the Civil War: "we already have more territory than we can people in fifty years."

Overseas Expansion

Generations of Americans had wanted greatness for their nation, but a greatness that came of the perfection of its own institutions and the example it could set for the Old World. To stride forward beyond its own continental borders, to engage in the international politics that had been the province of aristocratic nations: that ambition a Jefferson or a Jackson or a Lincoln would have hardly dared imagine. By the 1890s, however, a number of influential Americans were restless to have the United States become a power among other world powers, a great presence on the world stage. Some believed that to this end it must acquire an overseas empire.

Arguments For Overseas Expansion One philosophical basis for the change in outlook lay in the doctrines of Social Darwinism. One application of Darwinian ideas had reinforced the economic philosophy of laissez-faire. Another use likened individual countries to distinct species and proposed that in the inevitable competition those that were superior would triumph as superior forms flourish in biological evolution. The racism that attended this kind of thinking held that human characteristics were largely biologically determined. "Scientific" racists at the end of the nineteenth century were proclaiming a doctrine of Nordic supremacy that, they claimed, justified excluding the new immigrants from southern and eastern Europe. American Social Darwinists did not doubt that the United States, along with Britain, and perhaps Germany, was admirably equipped to compete in the race for power, riches, and glory. The "fitness" of the Anglo-Saxon "race," claimed John Fiske, justified its expansion

> until every land on the earth's surface that is not already the seat of an old civilization shall become English in its language, in its political habits and traditions, and to a predominant extent in the blood of its people.

Imperialist Social Darwinism could be optimistic about the nation's future. But there were influential Americans, some of them responding to those same racist doctrines, whose writing breathed not optimism but gloom. Brooks Adams, grandson of one President and great-grandson of another, feared that his country was losing its virility and falling under the sway of plutocrats, rich men without vision or creativity—and hordes of non-Anglo-Saxon immigrants. Other Americans wondered whether a whole generation of peace was rotting the martial virtues. Americans, warned the naval theorist Alfred Thayer Mahan, were ceasing to be "fighting animals" and were "becoming fattened cattle fit only for slaughter."

The End of the Frontier Pessimism had a source beyond Social Darwinist brooding. It fed also on the filling up of the West, the ending of the frontier experience that had been a component of American civilization since the earliest British settlements. The most famous argument that the end of the frontier was a turning point in American history came from the historian Frederick Jackson Turner, not long after the census of 1890, by a necessarily arbitrary definition, announced the frontier's virtual extinction.

The frontier, Turner declared, had encouraged individualism and democracy. With the thickening of population in the West, the United States had to begin a new phase. Turner did not say what this new phase would be like, but other Americans could imagine: in place of democracy, privilege and hierarchy; in place of individualism, conformity; in place of ethnic harmony among Americans of British and northern European stock, a babel of peoples and cultures.

A small group of the brightest men of the

period decided that the only way to save the national character was to revive the martial spirit by an aggressive expansionism. Mahan, in his influential 1890 book *The Influence of Sea Power on History,* argued that a nation could achieve greatness only by sea power. Imperialism, Adams declared, would "grant a reprieve for individualism by continuing the frontier conditions that made it possible." Franklin Giddings, a sociology professor at Columbia, argued that unless it could turn to overseas expansion, the enormous energy of the American people might "discharge itself in anarchistic, socialistic, and other destructive modes that are likely to work incalculable mischief."

Adams, Mahan, and Giddings were all essentially intellectuals, but learning from them was a group of young politicians who in the next few years would have a great impact on the country's political life. The most prominent of these was Theodore Roosevelt. Ever since his childhood Roosevelt had made a fetish of the "strenuous life." During the 1880s he had been attracted by the cattle frontier, becoming a rancher in the Black Hills. Roosevelt had no doubt that the long peace since 1865 had made Americans fat and complacent. At every chance for the country to get into a fight, he became enthusiastic. Then there was the young Indianan Albert Beveridge, who first came to the attention of the American public for his blatant advocacy of imperialism. In 1898, when he ran for the Senate, Beveridge brought his audiences cheering to their feet recounting how the "march of the flag" had taken the American people from the original boundaries of 1789 to the Pacific. It was now inevitable, he intoned, that the flag would wave over "an Isthmian canal . . . over Hawaii . . . over Cuba and the southern seas. . . ."

Economic Reasons for Expansion

The fear of cultural and political stagnation had its counterpart, especially in the economically depressed 1890s, in the worry that the end of the frontier meant an end to expanding domestic markets for the enormous output of the American economy. During these years, businessmen and business spokesmen constantly urged the government to help industry find new markets abroad. "We must have more customers," explained a cotton manufacturer, to absorb "the excessive production of our mills." Francis Thurber, President of the United States Export Association, proclaimed that the expansion of American markets

> is absolutely necessary in view of our increasing productive capacity. . . . We must have a place to dump our surplus, which otherwise will constantly depress prices and compel the shutting down of our mills . . . changing our profits to losses.

Some scholars have concluded that these demands for overseas markets were in fact the primary motive behind the drive for empire at the century's end. Actually, very few of the business or farm groups advocated the grabbing of colonies. Yet these trade expansionists held much common ground with the outright imperialists. Both wanted the country to come out of its isolationism; both favored more use of American muscle in foreign relations.

The "Redeemer Nation"

Among the attitudes and ideas that prepared the way for the nation's outward thrust was a sincerely felt element of altruism, however misplaced. Every nation makes some claim to nobility; the American self-image has been that of a redeemer nation, meant to be an example of freedom and opportunity for all the world. At home, this implied a growth in freedom and prosperity; abroad, it involved championing the world's oppressed. All through the nineteenth century the United States government often depicted itself as a moral force in the world: in 1848, for example, when it protested the Austrian suppression of a liberal and national revolution in Hungary. The abolition of slavery removed that embarrassing contradiction to the country's view of itself as a champion of freedom, and the economic and technological forces pushing and drawing the United States outward toward the end of the century quickly allied themselves with the idea of the nation as a vehicle of civilization to the world.

In the era of expansionism, this notion of the redeemer nation cut both ways. It set a limit to American appetites: Americans could not easily condone outright conquest, nor could they readily swallow the role of a *Herrenvolk,* a super race that had the right to enslave others. Some Americans—the Nordic supremacists, for example—came close to accepting this idea, but they were never more

The White Squadron—battleships of steel painted white—built in response to Congress's call for a modernized navy in 1882. *(Courtesy, Navy Department, Washington, D.C.)*

than a small minority. And even the conviction of racial superiority often produced arguments against imperialism rather than for it. Peoples of alien race, tradition, and language could never be assimilated, so went the reasoning; therefore, let them alone. The redeemer nation self-image nonetheless did also serve to encourage a form of expansionism, especially when clothed in the vestments of religion. Even when they deplored physical conquest, Americans were often willing to condone cultural and religious conquest. The assumption was common that their combination of Protestant Christianity and material progressiveness was a boon to the world.

As far back as the 1820s, societies dedicated to bringing the Protestant word to the "heathens" of Asia and Africa had been sending missionaries east and west to foreign parts. The missionaries had achieved a particularly strong effect in the Pacific region. In Hawaii they transformed Polynesian culture utterly and for good or ill brought the islands headlong into the modern age. A far broader field for evangelization was the Celestial Kingdom of China, a vast society with an ancient, sophisticated, non-Christian civilization. American missionaries first arrived in China in the 1830s. By 1851, out of a total of about 150 Protestant missionaries in China, eighty-eight were American.

The primary purpose of the missionaries, of course, was religious: to gather souls for the Lord by converting the "heathen Chinese" to the true faith. But their work had effects far beyond this. For the missionaries brought not only the Bible but also Western ideas of democracy, the scientific method, material progress. The mission compounds took in Chinese orphans and taught them, along with the word of the Lord, Western concepts of sanitation and practical Western mechanical skills.

No mass conversions occurred, and by the late nineteenth century there were only a few thousand Christians out of China's vast millions. But the missionaries did succeed in creating a small elite imbued with Western ideas and skills. In response, there also appeared antibodies in the form of a deep hostility to the West.

At home the missionary societies had an important role in directing the attention of Americans overseas. Women played especially active parts in the societies for Foreign Missions, for which they raised funds. Some women became missionaries themselves, or traveled overseas with male relatives who were missionaries. On Sundays, in thousands of Protestant churches across the United States, worshippers listened to pleas for contributions for benighted China, or Samoa, or some other exotic land. One of the bestsellers of the 1880s was the Reverend Josiah Strong's *Our Country,* a volume that advocated a Christianized world under American auspices. Strong's message was not only religious. He also pleaded for Western "civilization" and Western material progress, and he promised that "commerce follows the missionary. . . ."

These were the ideas and forces that during the 1880s began to erode the isolationism that had followed Secretary of State Seward's departure. One manifestation of the new mood was the building of an ocean-going navy of steel vessels to replace the decrepit wooden fleet left over from the Civil War. In 1883 Congress authorized a number of modern steel ships. The real turnabout came in the early nineties, with the building of two hundred additional warships that would give the nation the wide reach that befitted a major world power. Although at first Congress indignantly rejected this ambitious program, in the next few years it appropriated funds for constructing the first American battleships with large guns and wide cruising ranges. In 1880, the United States Navy ranked twelfth in the world; by 1900, the nation's fleet made it the third largest naval power. Also in the 1880s began a spirited diplomacy under the auspices of Secretary of State James G. Blaine.

James G. Blaine Previously a powerful Republican senator from Maine, Blaine had been a major figure in American political life for two decades when he became President Garfield's secretary of state in 1881. Garfield's death at the hands of an assassin within months after his inauguration ended Blaine's effort to enhance his own political standing at home by calling a conference of all the independent Western Hemisphere nations to discuss economic cooperation. But Blaine got a second chance when Benjamin Harrison succeeded Cleveland in 1889, and he once again became secretary of state.

Blaine's "Pan-Americanism" was in some ways a refurbishing of the Monroe Doctrine. Blaine himself was a jingoist, meaning a strident nationalist, after a British tune "We don't want to fight/But by jingo if we do/ We've got the ships, We've got the men/ We've got the money, too." But he recognized that the United States could not be arrogant in its relationship with Latin America. This nation should, he believed, involve the Latin republics in their own defense in some sort of loose association with the United States. Blaine's more immediate goal was the improvement of trade relations. Although Latin America sent vast amounts of coffee, sugar, fruits, and other tropical and semitropical products to the United States, it bought most of its manufactured goods from Europe. When in 1889 Blaine once more found himself heading the state department, he worked hard to pull the Latin Americans away from Europe and toward the United States as their source of manufactures. As luck would have it, his Democratic predecessor had already called a second Pan-American conference, although he had not stayed long enough to preside over it; now Blaine was in charge.

Before the conference got fairly down to business, Blaine sent the Latin American delegates on a 6,000-mile railroad journey across the country, to impress them with the might and efficiency of the nation's industry. All this trip probably accomplished was to wear out the delegates. When the conference reconvened, Blaine proposed a customs union among all the American nations so that the goods of each could pass freely among all the rest without the payment of tariffs. He also suggested the establishment of arbitration machinery to settle disputes among the states of the hemisphere. Neither proposal was adopted, and the significance of the 1889 conference consists largely in the precedent it set for the later Pan-American movement and in its marking another beginning of the nation's emergence from isolationism.

American foreign policy toward Latin America during the Blaine years was not uniformly peaceful. Civil war erupted in Chile in 1891, and the United States took exception to the rise to power of the rebel Congressionalist Party. The State Department tried to halt the shipment of weapons and munitions to the new Chilean government, and the policy precipitated a series of demonstrations against the United States in Santiago and Valparaiso. In October 1891, the U.S.S. *Baltimore,* a naval cruiser, docked in Valparaiso on routine maneuvers and let several dozen sailors go on shore leave. They got drunk and precipitated a riot outside of a saloon. When the melee was over, two sailors were dead and seventeen wounded. The other sailors were arrested for disorderly conduct. President Benjamin Harrison denounced the Chilean government for allowing the event to happen and then demanded an apoplogy. Chile refused until Harrison formally threatened to sever diplomatic relations and informally talked of going to war. In January 1892 the Chilean government apologized and paid an indemnity of $75,000. The incident was over.

But the crisis in Chile was the exception. Blaine's policy toward Latin America emphasized the economic issue of free trade among the American nations.

Critics of the United States have accused this country, not inaccurately, of pursuing in the twentieth century a "dollar diplomacy" that would subordinate the well-being of the other American republics to the needs of business in the United States. What Blaine earlier had in mind, apparently, was something milder, a peaceable flow of trade that should go to the benefit of the whole continent. And if an appetite for trade had been an occasion for imperialism and war, the ideal of peaceful trade offered itself as an alternative to strident nationalism. At its best it conceived of the world not as broken into competitive nations but as a single cooperative workplace. Some of the most brutal acts on the part of the United States toward Latin republics, in fact, have come not of trade hunger but of an ideological commitment to stamping out reformist or leftist movements.

Hawaii

At the time of Blaine's energetic management of the nation's foreign policy, American businessmen were beginning to look for new markets in Asia. But exploiting these markets required the acquisition of several strategically placed islands in the Pacific where ships could refuel.

The first opportunity to establish a base of operations came in the Samoan Islands, even though they were located south of what would become the major Pacific trade routes. Germany and Great Britain, however, were also interested in Samoa, and in March 1889 naval vessels from all three countries confronted one another in Apia harbor. Only the arrival of a severe hurricane prevented a naval battle. A conference held in Berlin a few months later led to an agreement in which Samoa was declared independent but supervised by a cooperative protectorate of all three powers. During the next ten years, Germany, the United States, and Great Britain argued constantly over Samoan affairs, and in 1898, after a native rebellion against the local king, United States and British ships bombarded Apia harbor. The instability finally ended in 1899 when the British agreed to surrender their claims to Samoa, and the United States and Germany divided up the islands between them.

The beautiful mid-Pacific chain of Hawaiian Islands, which Blaine also wished to annex, was located on a much more direct trade route to Japan and China. It had long attracted Americans—traders, whalers, and missionaries. The missionaries brought the Bible and a long shapeless gown designed to cover Hawaiian women. Sons of the missionaries stayed and became businessmen and sugar planters. In 1875 the kingdom of Hawaii negotiated a treaty with the United States by which, in exchange for the free admission of its sugar to the American market, it agreed not to allow territorial concessions to other foreign nations.

In the next decade, Hawaii prospered as a supplier of sugar to the United States. It was also pulled into the American political orbit,

Queen Liliuokalani of Hawaii, deposed in 1893 by what she regarded as a conspiracy of American interests. *(Courtesy, New York Public Library, New York City)*

a process welcomed by the many Americans living in the islands. In 1887 Hawaii, in exchange for granting the United States the exclusive right to use Pearl Harbor as a naval station, secured an extension of the sugar agreement. By this time the American contingent had come to control about two-thirds of the islands' taxable real estate and to exert a strong influence on the policies of the Hawaiian government.

In 1890 the United States Congress removed the tariff on all imported sugar, ending Hawaii's advantage in the American market, and causing the Hawaiian economy to collapse. Meanwhile, the Hawaiian government was becoming, at least from the standpoint of the resident Americans, increasingly capricious, arbitrary, and tyrannical. When Queen Liliuokalani in 1891 succeeded her brother on the Hawaiian throne, matters became still worse. The physically formidable Queen despised the liberal constitution that the American residents had recently imposed on her brother, and early in January 1893 she issued a royal edict abolishing it in favor of one far more autocratic. The Americans and other whites in the islands feared that their expulsion, or at least the confiscation of their property, would soon follow. To forestall any such possibility they arranged a coup. Calling on the American minister, John L. Stevens, for support, they set up a provisional government and proclaimed it the legitimate authority in Hawaii. The presence of American servicemen called in by Stevens from a vessel in Honolulu harbor kept the Queen from acting. Stevens then extended United States recognition to the revolutionary government. Soon afterward Liliuokalani abdicated, and Stevens declared Hawaii an American protectorate. He advised the State Department: "The Hawaiian pear is now fully ripe, and this is the golden hour for the United States to pluck it."

By this time a delegation of white Hawaiian residents had arrived in Washington to arrange for the islands to become part of the United States. Blaine was no longer secretary of state, but his successor was equally enamored of expansion and submitted a treaty of annexation to the Senate.

Then the headlong process of transferring Hawaii to the United States hit a snag. Many Americans were still not ready for the acquisition of an overseas empire. The case of Samoa was ambiguous, but Hawaiian annexation would be undisguised colonialism. One writer caught the public doubts in racial overtones:

> 'Shall we take Hawaii in, sirs?'
> that's the question of the day.
> Would the speedy annexation of that
> dusky country pay?
> Would the revenues from sugar and
> from smuggled opium
> Counteract the heavy burdens that
> with them are sure to come?

Fortunately for the anti-annexationists, the Senate was at the moment a lame-duck body with little time to act. Before it could approve the treaty, the Harrison Administration gave way to that of Grover Cleveland, now about to begin his second term.

Cleveland was skeptical of expansion of any kind, and particularly suspicious of the course of events by which white Hawaiians were pushing the island into American hands. In 1893 he abruptly withdrew the treaty from the Senate and appointed a special commissioner, James Blount, to go to Hawaii on a fact-finding mission. Blount's report confirmed Cleveland's doubts. The Hawaiian revolution, the commissioner declared, had been fomented not by the native Hawaiians but by the whites, and would not have succeeded without improper American intervention. These findings convinced Cleveland, and over the next few months he tried to return the Queen to her throne. But Liliuokalani insisted that if and when she resumed power she would cut off the heads of the revolutionaries, a project Cleveland found entirely distasteful. Nor would the provisional government surrender power. In the face of this impasse, Cleveland chose to do nothing. For the moment Hawaii remained an independent republic, governed by its white residents.

Venezuela

For years Venezuela and Great Britain had disputed the proper location of the boundary between Venezuela and British Guiana. To the British the disagreement seemed at first a minor matter; the Venezuelans, concerned with control of the mouth of the mighty Orinoco River and the possibility of finding gold in the disputed area, took it more seriously. In 1887 they suspended relations with Britain and turned to the United States for support, invoking the name of the "immortal Monroe." Early in the following decade they hired a publicist from the United States to write a pamphlet called "British Aggressions in Venezuela, or the Monroe Doctrine on Trial." This publication they circulated widely, paying particular care to get it into the hands of congressmen. During this period, the United States government suggested several times that the dispute be submitted to arbitration, but the British consistently refused.

There matters stood when Cleveland returned to office. The Democratic President was not a jingoist, but he and indeed many of his countrymen considered Great Britain arrogant and overbearing. Irish-Americans, a constituency the Democrats had to court, in particular were hostile to England for its harsh rule over their ancestral homeland over many generations, and it had become a popular practice for politicians to "twist the lion's tail" with rhetorical denunciations of Britain. This bias alone would have been sufficient to make the administration favor Venezuela, but the Cleveland Administration was under pressure for other reasons to deal sternly with Britain. Republicans and other Americans believed that Cleveland's secretary of state, Walter Gresham, had responded weakly to Britain's seizure of the customs house at Corinto, Nicaragua, in 1894, on the pretext that the Nicaraguans had insulted the British consul. They were accusing the Democratic administration of cowardice.

In mid-1895 Gresham, preeminently a man of peace, died and was replaced by Richard Olney, a man of different temper. Soon after taking office he submitted to the British government a dispatch that caused an international furor. Asserting that the Monroe Doctrine was an integral part of American law, he demanded to know whether Britain intended to submit the Venezuela boundary dispute to arbitration. If it did not, the United States would consider it to be in violation of the Monroe Doctrine. This semi-ultimatum to Great Britain was aggressive enough in itself, but its effect was intensified by Olney's arrogant tone. "To-day the United States is practically sovereign on this continent," Olney lectured Lord Salisbury, "and its fiat is law upon the subjects to which it confines its interposition."

The Olney note deeply offended the British, and Salisbury lectured the Americans back: the United States was mistaken in believing that the Venezuela boundary was a Monroe Doctrine issue; Olney had his history all wrong. As for arbitration, the answer was "No."

The British response made Cleveland "mad clear through," and late in 1895 he sent a warlike message to Congress, asking for funds to appoint an investigating commission to determine where the boundary should be drawn. The line so determined should then be forced on Britain, come what may. "I am fully alive to the responsibility incurred, and keenly realize all the consequences that may follow," the President ominously concluded. Congress unanimously appropriated $100,000 for the boundary commission. Meanwhile, the war spirit soared, with Civil War veterans volunteering their services and one Irish-American group pledging 100,000 men to fight the England that dominated their ancestral island.

Clearer heads finally prevailed. In England, too, leading politicians and molders of public opinion moved to calm things down. British policymakers had been startled by the fury of the American reaction. A war with the United States would expose Canada to dangerous attack, and Britain was already deeply embroiled in South Africa, in a dispute that would soon lead to the Boer War. At the same time, imperial Germany was beginning to challenge Britain internationally. To get into a war with the United States over a few thousand square miles of malarial jungle was pointless.

Before many weeks had passed, the worst of the crisis was over. When the boundary commission from the United States began its work, it found the British cooperative. Britain signed a treaty with Venezuela in early 1897 providing for an arbitration commission, as the United States had proposed. By the time the commission handed down its decision, few Americans cared very much. The confrontation had been resolved without war.

Cuba and War

In the Venezuelan boundary crisis, an American public opinion that since the nation's founding had been preoccupied with its own internal affairs was looking eagerly, belligerently outward for some assertion of power in world politics. Cuba was an incitement.

The Cuban Civil War For decades the "Pearl of the Antilles," one of Spain's few remaining possessions in the New World, had attracted the interest of people in the United States. Southerners had hoped to acquire Cuba as a slave state. Then after the Civil War a ten-year Cuban revolt against Spain drew the sympathy of people in the United States, who identified the Cuban struggle for independence with their own nation's revolution a century earlier. In 1878 the revolt was put down, and peace returned, temporarily, to the island. During the years of civil war, however, many sugar planters had suffered serious losses. Eager to get out, they sold their lands to citizens of the United States, who acquired valuable property in Cuba.

Civil war erupted once again in 1895. The rebels, anxious to involve the United States, attacked property owned by its citizens. Sometimes they spared property in exchange for ransoms that were then used for the revolution. Both sides resorted to brutal methods. The *insurrectos* dynamited passenger trains and took civilian hostages. The Spaniards, in turn, under General Valeriano Weyler, rounded up thousands of civilians and put them in "reconcentration" camps where they could not give aid and support to the rebels. Scarcity of food and medical supplies, combined with bad sanitation, soon killed hundreds.

The New York *Journal* wrote of

> Weyler the brute, the devastator of haciendas, the destroyer of families, and the outrager of women. . . . Pitiless, cold, an exterminator of men. . . . There is nothing to prevent his carnal, animal brain from running riot with itself in inventing tortures and infamies of bloody debauchery.

Not to be outdone, a correspondent for Pulitzer's *World* reported:

> Blood on the roadsides, blood in the fields, blood on the doorsteps, blood, blood, blood! The old, the young, the weak, the crippled—all are butchered without mercy. . . . Is there no nation wise enough, brave enough, and strong enough to restore peace in this bloodsmitten land?

Americans were horrified at the mounting barbarism in Cuba. Some of the businessmen with investments on the island favored direct United States intervention, but their views were not typical within the business community. Since 1893, times had been bad, but by 1897 they were beginning to improve. United States involvement in a war with Spain over Cuba would threaten the recovery. In October 1897, the *Commercial and Financial Chronicle* noted that war would destroy "the trade prosperity we are all enjoying." But the business community's attitudes were not decisive. Sympathies were overwhelmingly in favor of *Cuba libre,* free Cuba. General Weyler's actions in Cuba seemed only the latest chapter in a centuries-long Spanish record of cruelty in the New World. "Butcher Weyler" recalled for one journalist Hernando Cortés and the other early *conquistadores,* whose brutality toward the Aztecs and Incas had decimated those native peoples.

Rebels were a match for Spaniards in atrocities, but people in the United States heard little of the *insurrectos'* misdeeds and much of Spain's. The United States daily press functioned as the revolutionaries' propaganda department. Particularly effective were the *New York World,* edited by Joseph Pulitzer, and the *New York Journal,* having as its editor William Randolph Hearst. In the later nineties these two papers engaged in a great circulation war. Every heavyhanded Spanish act produced headlines in one paper or the other, inciting its rival to find, or to invent, something even more brutal and sensational.

It would be a mistake to see United States intervention in Cuba primarily as a propaganda victory for the "yellow press." Without the deeply embedded hostility to the Spanish Empire, and without a growing concern over the end of the nation's open spaces combined with a growing sense of the nation's destiny and superiority, the Hearst-Pulitzer press war would have meant little. The period from 1865 to 1898 was the longest stretch of peace in the nation's history. A new generation of young men had reached maturity without having experienced directly the horrors of death and mutilation that their forebears had known in 1861–65. By the late 1890s, many of these were almost eager for a good fight, especially in such a worthy cause as Cuban independence.

McKinley's Efforts to Avoid War

Neither Cleveland nor his Republican successor, William McKinley, was an interventionist. At one point Cleveland told a group of belligerent Congressmen that if Congress declared war against Spain he would "not mobilize the army." McKinley's reluctance to take action provoked Roosevelt to exclaim that the President had the backbone of a chocolate eclair. McKinley deplored Spanish policy and hoped to end Weyler's brutal repression. He did not see how if it continued the United States could fail to intervene directly. But he did not insist on Cuban independence, nor did he want to force Spain to move faster than it was politically possible for its leaders to do.

McKinley had his own political problems. The Republican Party, like the country at large, was torn between factions who favored caution and those who preferred war. McKinley knew that the best way to satisfy both was to end the conflict quickly. To this end, in June 1897 he sent Stewart Woodford, a level-headed New Yorker, to Madrid as American diplomatic representative. Woodford arrived in September and transmitted McKinley's wishes to the Spanish government. The United States must have assurances that repression would stop. This country would volunteer its good offices to settle the conflict between Spain and the Cubans, but if Spain refused, the United States would feel free to take action directly. The Spanish government promised to recall Weyler, whose harsh steps were popular with frustrated and politically powerful Barcelona shippers, and agreed that reforms in Spanish administration would be necessary, including some degree of Cuban autonomy. But Spain was slow to act. The American militants, hot for war, bombarded the President with demands that he brook no delay in ousting the Spaniards from Cuba.

By the beginning of 1898, McKinley, under intense pressure to intervene, ordered the battleship *Maine* to Havana, ostensibly as a friendly courtesy, but actually to protect the lives and property of United States citizens. The Spanish government was not pleased, but when the vessel arrived, Spanish officials received the *Maine* correctly and wined and dined the officers and crew. It looked as if the visit might help the cause of peace.

While the *Maine* lay at anchor at Havana, Spanish-American relations took an abrupt turn for the worse. The Spanish representative to Washington, Enrique Dupuy de Lôme, was a proud and narrow aristocrat who despised the give-and-take of American politics. He was also indiscreet. In December

1897 he had written a Spanish friend in Havana calling McKinley "weak and a bidder for the admiration of the crowd, besides being a would-be politician." The letter was intercepted by a Cuban rebel and sent to Hearst's *Journal*, where on February 9, 1898, a copy was printed below the headline "Worst Insult to the United States in Its History." Although the Spanish government quickly recalled de Lôme and apologized for his mistake, the harm had been done.

The Sinking of the *Maine*

Worse followed. On February 15 a massive explosion sank the *Maine* at its berth in Havana harbor, with a loss of 260 sailors, almost its entire crew. During the next few frantic days, the President cautioned against too hasty a judgment. "I have been through one war," the former Union major remarked, "and I do not want to see another." The jingo press observed no such restraint. Certain that the explosion had come from outside the ship and had been set by Spanish agents, it demanded action. Hearst's *Journal* thundered "THE WARSHIP MAINE WAS SPLIT IN TWO BY AN ENEMY'S SECRET INFERNAL MACHINE. THE WHOLE COUNTRY THRILLS WITH WAR FEVER."

Mass meetings across the nation demanded that McKinley declare war, while around the country college students began to drill in preparation for a retaliatory attack. Congress, already bellicose, on March 9 appropriated an additional $50 million for the army and navy. Soon after, Senator Redfield Proctor of Vermont, just back from a tour of Cuba, further inflamed public opinion by confirming charges of Spanish brutality in the reconcentration camps. A United States commission reported that the explosion had

The wreck of the *Maine* in Havana Harbor, February 15, 1898, sunk in a still-unexplained explosion. Its destruction was used as a pretext to declare war on Spain. *(Courtesy, Scribner's Archives)*

been caused by a land mine, and could not have been internal.

To this day, no one knows who or what sank the *Maine*. It is hard to believe that the Spanish government, which feared intervention, was in any way responsible. Perhaps it was a lighted cigarette tossed into the ammunition hold. Current scholars have suggested that coal used on the ship gave off dust that was highly explosive; the coal bins were next to the ammunition hold. But the public had made up its mind.

A reluctant McKinley recognized that he had to act. A few days after receiving the *Maine* commission report, he instructed Woodford in Madrid to demand an immediate armistice in Cuba and to insist on an end of the reconcentration camp policy. If peace terms were not achieved by October, Spain would have to accept McKinley's arbitration of the Cuban problem. As the President awaited the Spanish reply, congressmen and the public stormed for immediate action.

The Spanish reply was unsatisfactory. Madrid promised to investigate the *Maine* incident and to abolish the reconcentration camps in some areas, but it refused to suspend hostilities or allow arbitration by the United States. McKinley now knew that he had no choice and turned reluctantly to composing a war message. Still, he moved slowly, allowing the public to get angry and Spain to have second thoughts. On April 10, while Americans awaited war, the Spanish government agreed to suspend hostilities in Cuba. A few days earlier the President might have used this concession as an excuse to avoid a declaration. But now it was too late. On April 11, McKinley asked Congress to be allowed to use the army and navy to end the conflict in Cuba. Congress responded on April 19 with a four-part statement declaring that Cuba was free, that Spain must withdraw, that armed forces would be used to achieve these ends, and that the United States had no intention of annexing Cuba. That last section of this war document was the so-called Teller Amendment.

The Spanish-American War

The war that followed was one of the briefest in American history. Fighting began May 1, 1898, and on July 26 of the same year the Spanish government requested peace terms. Only 379 of the 274,000 officers and men who served in the armed forces died as a result of enemy action. The financial cost was small: about $250 million.

The Navy Takes the Philippines

A Spanish nation only a shadow of the great power that had once ruled half the world faced a young continental giant, by now the world's leading industrial power. The American navy had been thoroughly modernized, its morale was high, and it had vigorous leadership. The army was weak and decrepit. Yet even on land, American numbers and industrial potential would have to tell, and did.

The navy bore most of the burden of the war. Years of rebuilding since the early 1880s now showed their value. With four first-class battleships and many other vessels, the fleet outgunned the Spanish navy by a large margin. In Washington, Assistant Secretary of the Navy Theodore Roosevelt was a whirlwind of energy and intelligence who had been looking for this fight for many years. Though technically the subordinate of the secretary, Roosevelt was by far the more forceful man and, in the frequent absence of his Washington-hating chief, John D. Long, often served as acting secretary.

About two months before the outbreak of official hostilities, Roosevelt telegraphed Admiral George Dewey, in charge of the American Asiatic squadron, that he was to proceed to Hong Kong and keep his vessels fully coaled for an attack on the Spanish-owned Philippine Islands. On May 1, 1898, following the official declaration of war, Dewey steamed into Manila Bay, the harbor of the Philippine capital. Five times the American ships sailed past the inferior Spanish vessels stationed there, hurtling salvos with each pass. In a few hours the entire Spanish fleet consisted of smoking hulks. Then Dewey quickly smashed the land-based Spanish batteries. An English writer called the battle of Manila Bay "a military execution rather than a real contest."

In the Battle of Manila Bay, May, 1898, Commodore Dewey's Pacific squadron destroyed the Spanish fleet in the Philippines. *(Courtesy, New York Public Library Picture Collection)*

Roosevelt along with Dewey wanted to prevent Spain from reinforcing its Atlantic fleet from the Pacific, but he had other purposes in mind as well. A disciple of Alfred Thayer Mahan, the naval historian and theoretician who believed that sea power was the basis of national greatness, Roosevelt wanted to strengthen his nation's ability to project its power in Asia. The Philippines, especially the harbor at Manila on the island of Luzon, would give the United States access to the eastern Pacific, the China Sea, and Indochina. So Dewey, in carrying out Roosevelt's orders, put the United States in the position to claim a Pacific empire. Responding to arguments that the new lands were geographically distant, Senator Albert Beveridge thundered:

> The ocean does not separate us from the lands of our duty and desire—the ocean joins us, a river never to be dredged, a canal never to be repaired. [Applause]. Steam joins us, electricity joins us—the very elements are in league with our destiny. [Continued applause and cheers.] Cuba not contiguous? Porto Rico not contiguous? The Philippines not contiguous? Our navy will make them contiguous!

The War in Cuba

In the main Caribbean theater of operations, matters moved more slowly. Volunteers flocked to the colors at McKinley's call; 223,000 men enlisted. The South's enthusiasm for the fight put an end, many contemporaries said, to the hostility that had prevailed between South and North ever since 1860. Volunteers came from every social stratum. Many black Americans by enlisting expressed their patriotism and temporarily escaped from southern poverty. William Jennings Bryan, McKinley's 1896 Democratic rival, enlisted as colonel of Nebraska volunteers. Unable to stand by while others dashed about firing rifles, Roosevelt quit his post to lead the Rough Riders, a cavalry regiment of western cowboys and eastern swells that he had assembled himself.

Despite the enthusiasm, the army—small, lethargic, poorly led—was not ready. Its civilian chief was Secretary of War Russell A. Alger, a Civil War veteran. Alger would serve as a convenient scapegoat for the nation's neglect of its army, and the inevitable military sloth of a great continental democracy.

Alger had promised the President that he

could get 40,000 men to Cuba in ten days after the outbreak of war. It actually took seven weeks to get 17,000 men to the island. Thousands of volunteers poured into Tampa, Florida, without guns, uniforms, or other equipment, and were forced to wait in the hot spring weather to see action. Whole trainloads of equipment were backed up on sidings. The men soon got bored and restless; many contracted disease. Several weeks elapsed before the giant tangle could be unsnarled and troops put aboard transports for Cuba.

On June 22, the first United States troops finally landed at Daiquiri, near Santiago, amid near total confusion. At Las Guasimas there was a brief but bloody skirmish. The war's major battles took place on July 1–3. The terrain was hilly and wooded and the Spaniards, equipped with accurate Mauser rifles, were well entrenched. At San Juan Hill Roosevelt found himself at the head of his dismounted Rough Riders and a contingent of black troops. Always impetuous, he led them on a charge that swept the Spanish troops off the hill and opened the road to Santiago.

Meanwhile, the Atlantic fleet destroyed the Spanish fleet. The Spanish admiral, Pascual y Topete Cervera, had sailed from the Cape Verde Islands in late April headed for the Caribbean. For a while news of his departure created a panic along the east coast. He evaded capture and slipped into Santiago harbor on May 19, short on coal and unable to go any farther. With the United States troops on the verge of capturing the town, he was faced with the choice of trying to escape or surrendering without a battle. Under pressure from the provincial governor, he reluctantly steamed out of Santiago into the waiting arms of the powerful flotilla. In a few hours the Spanish squadron was destroyed, with 300 of its sailors dead. The United States had not lost a ship and suffered only two casualties. The grossly uneven match attested to the effectiveness of the new navy. Two weeks later, Spanish officials surrendered Santiago. The fighting was over. One Spaniard reported to his commander that the Americans had

> fired grapeshot and all kinds of projectiles on the Playa del Este and Cayo Toro until they set fire to the fort on Playa del Este, burning the house of the pilots . . . The American squadron in possession of the outer bay [of Santiago] has taken it as if for a harbor of rest, they being anchored as if in one of their own ports.

The Peace Treaty

When a peace treaty came before the Senate for ratification, there was unexpected opposition. Despite the opinion shift of the previous months, some Americans were still strongly opposed to colonies. Hitherto United States expansion had been into empty territory, some critics held, where people of the European race and Anglo-Saxon institutions could form self-governing states like the original thirteen. Was it conceivable that these Filipinos, long governed by tyrannical Spain and unused to self-government, could ever become Americans? Implicit in this attitude was a fair amount of racial and cultural xenophobia, a conviction that the "little brown brothers," as McKinley called them, could not assimilate the institutions of northern Europeans. But there was a more generous aspect to anti-imperialism. The philosopher William James argued that Filipinos did not need any uplifting from the Americans. To suppose that they did was "sniveling, loathsome" cant. Acquiring the islands would be a "shameless betrayal of American principles." "What could be a plainer symptom of greed, ambition, corruption and imperialism?" James asked.

Outside Congress the anti-imperialists, many of them Mugwumps who had fought against political corruption during the 1870s and 1880s, organized the Anti-Imperialist League in November 1898. The league sent out thousands of broadsides and pamphlets to influential clergymen, politicians, businessmen, and farm leaders. These bore titles like "The Hell of War and Its Penalties" and "The Cost of a National Crime" and condemned the impending treaty. In Congress League officials fought such arch-imperialists as Henry Cabot Lodge and Albert Beveridge, who believed in the nation's Far Eastern destiny and its mission to uplift and relished the commercial and strategic advantages of possessing the Philippines. One argument for annexing the islands was the likelihood that if the United States did not take them, the Germans would.

A key figure in the Senate debate was William Jennings Bryan. Though skeptical of empire, the former Democratic standard-bearer believed that it was important to end the war officially. The impending presidential election, he claimed, could serve as a referendum on the annexation and if the vote went against the supporters of colonies, the decision to annex could be reversed. That made little sense: reversing an annexation would have been unlikely. Bryan's argument, however, probably changed the minds of a few Democratic senators and on February 6, 1899, the Senate ratified the peace treaty by a vote of 57 to 27, one vote more than the necessary two-thirds.

On the Fighting Line Near Psasy, Philippine Islands, 1899. **Photographer: James Ricalton for Underwood and Underwood.** *(Courtesy, California Museum of Photography, University of California, Riverside)*

An American Empire

And so, as the old century ended, Americans found themselves with an empire; their country had now joined the great powers as a colonial nation ruling over millions of non-Europeans. The new status brought satisfaction to many citizens who gloried in their nation's added prestige. The European powers now clearly saw the United States in a new light, and the nation was dealing with them on new diplomatic terms. For much of its history the United States had exchanged with foreign nations no diplomatic representatives above the rank of minister, believing perhaps that the aristocratic rank of ambassador was not compatible with republican simplicity and virtue. But during the 1890s it had begun exchanging ambassadors. To that subtle change in self-image the United States could now add a very large one: it had stretched its reach across the great Pacific Ocean.

Revolt in the Philippines The final decision about whether to annex the Philippines rested with President William McKinley, who by his own admission had initially been unable even to locate the islands on a map of the world. As he recounted his thinking for a group of visiting clergymen, the President recalled that he had been unable to sleep, so tormented was he by the question. Kneeling next to his bed, he prayed for divine guidance and, after several nights, received the inspiration he sought. We could not give the islands back to Spain. That "would be cowardly and dishonorable." We could not give them to France or Germany since "that would be bad business and discreditable." Nor could we leave the Filipinos to themselves. They "were unfit for self-government" and "they would soon have anarchy and misrule over there worse than Spain's was." This left the United States with only one honorable course of action: "there was nothing left for us to do but to take them all, and to educate the Filipinos, and uplift and civilize and Christianize them, and by God's grace do the very best we could by them, as our fellow men for whom Christ also died." That most Filipinos were already Christians did not sidetrack McKinley's train of thought. And, when he reached his decision, he "went to bed, and went to sleep, and slept soundly."

McKinley had decided, in the words of Rudyard Kipling's 1899 poem urging just such a course, to "take up the White Man's Burden," to rule the Filipinos for their own good. The Filipinos, however, did not share his view that they "were unfit for self-government," and the guerrilla fighters there felt betrayed by the American decision to replace Spain as a colonial power. McKinley in fact was rationalizing what he saw as public opinion. According to one politician, he "keeps his ear to the ground so close that he gets it full of grasshoppers much of the time."

Even as the Senate was considering the treaty with Spain, the Filipinos were rising in anger against the Yankees. Welcomed at first as liberators, they now seemed merely new conquerors no better than their predecessors. By the spring of 1899 a full-scale war, the Philippine insurrection, was raging over the archipelago. Under the leadership of Emilio Aguinaldo, the Filipino rebels attacked American troops, at first in conventional, pitched-battle fashion, and later, when these tactics proved disastrous against the better-armed Americans, in hit-and-run maneuvers. Some American troops responded by committing atrocities—acts that the Filipino insurgents were not above either.

A young soldier from Kingston, New York, wrote home:

> Last night one of our boys was found shot and his stomach cut open. Immediately orders were received from General Wheaton to burn the town and kill every native in sight; which was done to a finish. About 1,000 men, women and children were reported killed. I am probably growing hard-hearted, for I am in my glory when I can sight my gun on some dark skin and pull the trigger.

Before long, reports were reaching the United States that American soldiers were butchering prisoners, while at least one American field commander had ordered his men "to kill and burn and make a howling wilderness of Samar," one of the rebel strongholds. Before the insurrection was put down and Aguinaldo wounded in mid-1902, some seventy thousand American troops, four times the number sent to Cuba, had been engaged in fighting the Filipinos. The antiwar financier Andrew Carnegie, on reading that 8,000 Filipinos had been killed during the first year of the war, wrote McKinley

THE WAR IN THE PHILIPPINES *was the first of four the United States fought in Asia during the twentieth century. In* Spoon River Anthology *(1915) Edgar Lee Masters writes a tombstone inscription for a fictional town; the words exhibit the antiwar sentiment that has long vied in the United States with its martial opposite:*

HARRY WILMANS

I was just turned twenty-one,
And Henry Phipps, the Sunday-school superintendent,
Made a speech in Bindle's Opera House.
"The honor of the flag must be upheld," he said,
"Whether it be assailed by a barbarous tribe of Tagalogs
Or the greatest power in Europe."
And we cheered and cheered the speech and the flag he waved
As he spoke.
And I went to the war in spite of my father,
And followed the flag till I saw it raised
By our camp in a rice field near Manila,
And all of us cheered and cheered it.
But there were flies and poisonous things;
And there was the deadly water,
And the cruel heat,
And the sickening, putrid food;
And the smell of the trench just back of the tents
Where the soldiers went to empty themselves;
And there were the whores who followed us, full of syphilis;
And beastly acts between ourselves or alone,
With bullying, hatred, degradation among us,
And days of loathing and nights of fear
To the hour of the charge through the steaming swamp,
Following the flag,
Till I fell with a scream, shot through the guts.
Now there's a flag over me in Spoon River!
A flag! A flag!

offering congratulations for "civilizing the Filipinos. . . . About 8,000 of them have been completely civilized and sent to heaven." Soldiers sang "Damn, damn, damn the Filipinos":

> In that land of dopy dreams, happy peaceful Philippines,
> Where the bolo-man is hiking night and day;
> Where the Tagalos steal and lie, where Americanos die,
> There you hear the soldiers sing this evening lay;
> Damn, damn, damn the Filipinos, cross-eyed kakiack ladrones,
> Underneath our starry flag, civilize 'em with a Krag,
> And return us to our own beloved homes.

Congress in 1902 passed the Philippine Government Act, setting up a Philippine legislature elected by popular vote. The Jones Act of 1916 announced the intention of the United States to withdraw from the islands as soon as a stable government was established, and conferred on the Filipinos self-government in domestic matters. The act also provided for free trade with the United States, which brought a degree of prosperity but also subordinated the Filipino economy to American interests. Finally, in 1934, Congress made provisions for Philippine independence in the Tydings-McDuffie Act. Passed at the behest of anti-imperialists, beet-sugar producers who disliked the competition of Philippine sugar, and trade union leaders who wanted to end the influx of Filipino workers, the measure provided for eventual Filipino independence. In a "commonwealth" period the islands would be governed by their own legislature and elected governor. This was the islands' status when the Japanese invaded in early 1942. The Philippines received their independence in 1946 as provided by the act, though as recently as 1992 America was still basing its main Pacific naval and air forces there.

Guam, Puerto Rico, and Cuba

Cuba was under a temporary occupation. The occupiers in 1900 helped set Cuban finances in order, and doctors and public health authorities from the United States succeeded in wiping out the yellow fever that had afflicted the island for generations. This was the more be-

Emilio Aguinaldo led a Filipino insurrection against the American invaders; he was defeated only after the United States sent 70,000 troops to the area. *(Courtesy, The New York Public Library Picture Collection)*

nign side of the nation's Cuba policy. There would soon be another side.

In possessions such as Guam and Puerto Rico, the question of self-government was less pressing than it was in the Philippines. Guam was a small island with a small population and eventually became little more than an American naval base. Puerto Rico was large and more densely populated. At first, Puerto Rican nationalism was quite weak, and most islanders seemed content to remain in the orbit. But what should be their status within that orbit of the United States?

In the *Insular Cases* (1901) the Supreme Court declared that while inhabitants of American possessions were entitled to enjoy some fundamental constitutional guarantees, they did not possess all the rights of citizenship. The Court noted, though, that Congress could choose to confer such rights if it wished, and in the next few years Congress did. The Foraker Act of 1900 had already provided for a partially elective legislature in Cuba with an appointive governor. A treaty of 1903 between the United States and Cuba, however, included promises that the Cubans would not enter into any treaty with a foreign power that would impair Cuban independence, would not unilaterally contract any public debt beyond their ability to repay, would allow the United States to establish a naval base on Cuban soil, and ultimately would permit the United States to intervene to preserve Cuban independence. The Platt Amendment to the treaty established for the United States a virtual protectorate over the island: a right, in effect, to control Cuba's affairs, ostensibly to protect the island's safety and interests. The arrangement made a mockery of *Cuba libre,* the professed reason for the war with Spain. In 1917 Congress granted Puerto Ricans United States citizenship and gave them the right to elect both houses of the legislature. Puerto Rico was also to be part of the nation's free trade area; its products were to enter the mainland duty-free. A new treaty with Cuba in 1934 abrogated most of the offensive provisions of the older relationship between the two countries, but it did not remove our privilege of having a naval base in Cuba.

China's "Open Door" The United States had long exploited Chinese labor. Foreign-born laborers were responsible for the massacre of twenty-eight Chinese coal miners in Wyoming in 1885. An obituary of Wan Lee expressed the meaning of a "chinaman's chance" on the west coast:

> Dead, my reverend friends, dead. Stoned to death in the streets of San Francisco, in the year of grace 1869 by a mob of half-grown boys and Christian school children.

American policy toward the Far East was based largely on commercial self-interest. The Open Door policy, which held that no nation trading with China should try to exclude other nations from commerce, sensibly aimed at maintaining peace among the powers interested in trading there. It was even mildly benign toward China itself, seeking to insure that China would enjoy what the Western powers believed to be the benefits of uninterrupted trade with them and that it would not be subject to military intervention on the part of any one country that wished to exclude others. Yet the Open Door policy also assumed that China would be for a long time a field for Western exploitation—peaceable and friendly exploitation, but not an equal relationship between a sovereign China and its sovereign trading partners. In fact, that policy in China had been as much English as American in origin, although it was Secretary of State John Hay who in 1899 sent notes to the major powers calling for it. After some Chinese staged the Boxer Rebellion in 1900 to drive foreign "devils" into the sea, Hay sent another round of notes insisting on China's "territorial integrity," an act partly reflecting traditional friendship between that country and the United States.

In 1903 the United States acquired, under discreditable circumstances, what was perhaps the most lucrative imperial prize of all, the Panama Canal. The last territorial acquisition was the Virgin Islands. Ever since the late eighteenth century those islands, which are located in the Caribbean, had been a Danish possession. By the early 1900s, her own imperial dreams long since shattered, Denmark decided to sell the islands, and Germany became the most interested buyer. But Germany was fast becoming a world power, and the United States did not want the Germans establishing a foothold in the Western Hemisphere. When World War I broke out in Europe in 1914, Woodrow Wilson's administration decided to make an offer to Denmark. The two countries signed a treaty giving the United States sovereignty over the islands in return for a payment of $25 million. The Senate ratified the treaty in January 1917.

By that time the United States had lost interest in the rush to acquire more overseas territories. Colonies were disappointing. After the first flush there appeared little glory in empire; American destiny, it seemed, did not rest on colonial possessions after all. Nor was there any need, it seemed, for a social safety valve. Prosperity returned with the advent of the new century, and so did American confidence. Americans would invest millions of dollars abroad in the years before 1914. Some went to the Philippines, Cuba, and Puerto Rico, but even more flowed to Canada, Mexico, and other nations that were not colonies. Nor did the China market work out. It eventually proved an illusion, and direct government action was necessary to induce American businessmen to risk money in that decaying empire.

Theodore Roosevelt's World Vistas

Despite his reputation for bombast, Theodore Roosevelt was a sophisticated diplomat with a sure grasp of the facts of politics, the uses and limits of power, and what the nation's worldwide interests were. He pursued these interests overseas with a combination of guile and deft skill that he encapsulated in his motto, "Speak softly and carry a big stick." Only one nation, Great Britain, could impress American leaders with its power, and Roosevelt neither provoked the British nor took advantage of their growing preoccupation with Germany. Friendship with England freed Roosevelt for adventures in areas where strategic security and local weakness promised large gains with little risk. Gradually Roosevelt and the country, though little interested in colonization, took on a global role. American influence ranged from the Far East to the Balkans; the American fleet sailed all seven seas; American merchants roamed the planet.

The Russo-Japanese War

Japan, aiming at dominion over East Asia, was consolidating its grip over nearby Korea. Russian activities there, and growing Russian influence in nearby Manchuria, which the weakened Chinese were barely able to hold onto, triggered a war between these two emerging imperial powers. In 1904 Japanese sailors destroyed Russia's far eastern squadron with a surprise attack, a technique they would employ with equal success thirty-seven years later at Pearl Harbor; six months later a skilled Japanese attack pushed Russian troops out of Manchuria. Then Russia's Baltic Fleet, hastily sent into the war by a desperate government in St. Petersburg, was annihilated by Admiral Togo in the Tsushima Strait. The Japanese, everywhere victorious, kept secret the near-bankruptcy to which war had brought their fragile economy. In Washington, meanwhile, President Roosevelt worried that a jubilant Japan, unchecked by Russia, might close the Open Door in China and threaten the tenuous American colonial empire in the western Pacific. Eager to maintain a balance of power between the two antagonists once the fighting was over, he offered to mediate. Both belligerents accepted, hoping to gain more by talk than by renewed struggle.

Roosevelt cajoled the two enemies into a peace. According to the terms of the Treaty of Portsmouth, signed in that New Hampshire town on September 5, 1905, the Tsar granted Japan a "paramount interest" in southern Manchuria and Korea. Russia avoided the humiliation of an indemnity and ceded only half of Sakhalin Island, not all of it as leaders in Tokyo had wanted. Still, Japan's new protectorates did upset the balance of power in East Asia. Three times Roosevelt's intermediaries reached executive understandings with the Japanese. The Taft-Katsura Agreement of 1905 recognized Japan's power in Korea; in return, Japan foreswore "all aggressive designs whatever" on American colonies in the Pacific. Japan, meanwhile, had reason to be angry at the United States. In California, Japanese immigrants were subjected to a prejudice and hostility that went beyond the usual bigotry with which Americans have confronted newcomers. Roosevelt, for all his bluster, had a peculiar ability to get along with the proud Japanese nation. In the so-called Gentlemen's Agreement of 1907–08, Japan voluntarily limited the emigration of her laborers to the American West Coast. But California continued its hostile policies against the Japanese by limiting their right to own or lease farm land. In 1908 the Root-Takahira Agreement pledged both countries to respect the Open Door in China. Roosevelt realized that words could not always restrain the obstreperous Japanese, now a first-class world power, but he did keep on an even keel the relations between Japan and the United States.

The Algeciras Conference

A sense of the fragility of world peace prompted Roosevelt to intercede in Europe's affairs. Arguments over colonies had brought Europe's major powers to the edge of war, but never as dangerously as during the Moroccan crisis of 1904–05. French and British leaders had already worked out an entente that eventually ripened into alliance. They settled disputes over African territory by awarding protectorates to each other. The British gained a protectorate over Egypt. The French received a similar arrangement over Morocco. These colonial pretensions and the budding alliance angered Germany. That nation, like the other European powers, was hungry for a slice of the world that was now getting quickly divided, and the Germans resented any arrangement that seemed to be squeezing their country out of the competition. Kaiser Wilhelm flamboyantly called for an open door in Morocco, while his government demanded that France oust its foreign minister, Theophile Delcasse, the author of the alliance with Britain. Leaders in Paris bridled over such heavy-handed intervention in domestic affairs; the Germans hinted that any delay might bring war. Roosevelt skillfully maneuvered the angry parties into a conference at Algeciras, a resort city in southern Spain. American delegates urged their British and French counterparts "to stand up to the Germans." Roosevelt meanwhile played to the Kaiser with long telegrams praising his "mas-

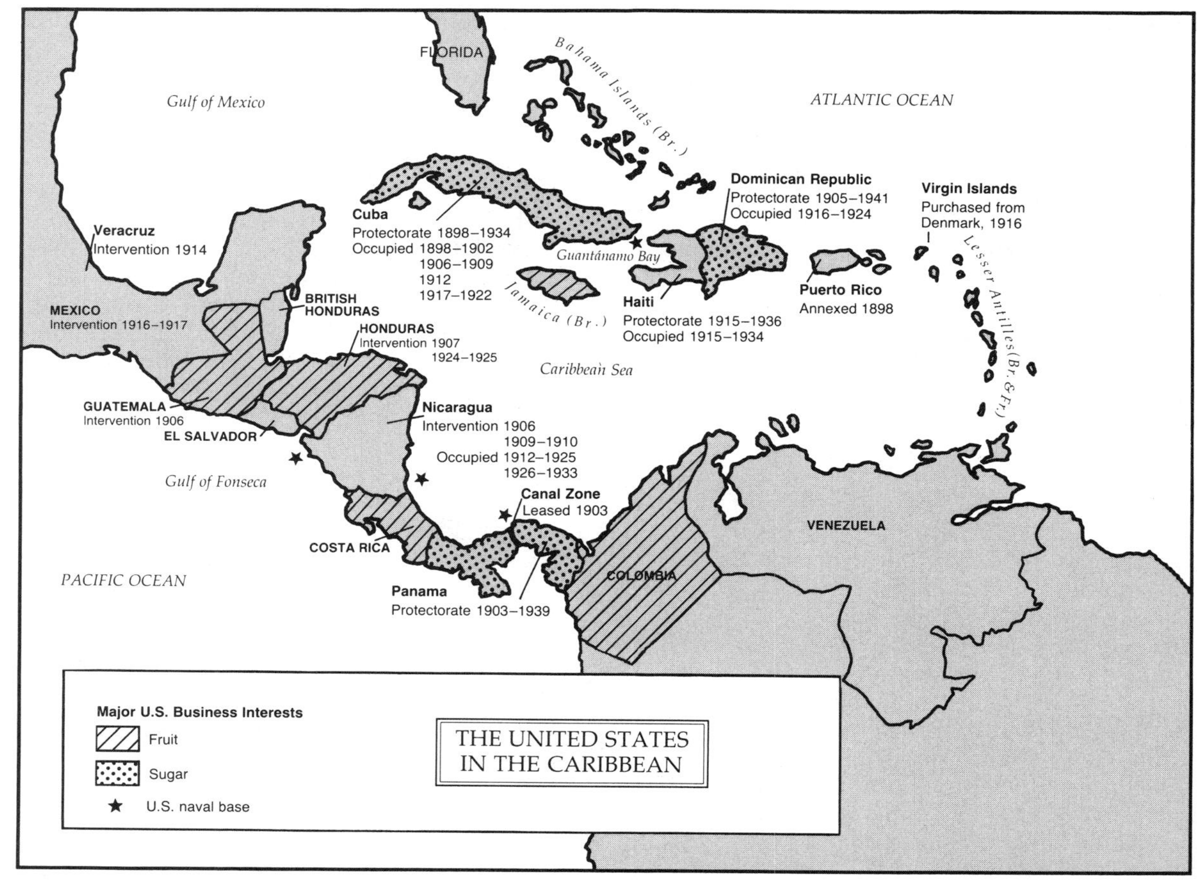

terly politics." Once the conference formally opened, Wilhelm followed Roosevelt's lead. The President brought about an agreement that assured French control in Morocco, but managed still to convince the Germans that they had achieved "epochmaking success."

Most Americans probably did not realize the closeness of war or the extent of their President's involvement in the Algeciras meeting. Roosevelt had contributed in a major way to European peace, which, he privately wrote, "was essential to American security and prosperity." For his peacemaking efforts in both Europe and Asia, the Nobel Committee awarded Roosevelt its Peace Prize for 1906.

Roosevelt's Corollary to the Monroe Doctrine

A delicate problem in international finance roused Roosevelt to further assertiveness. Some unscrupulous bond-brokers had persuaded many governments in Latin America to issue bonds whose proceeds too often financed lavish living for politicians rather than economic development for their countries. Gullible buyers in Europe snapped up the dubious issues because they promised a high rate of return. When the inevitable defaults occurred, European governments supported bondholders who clamored for restitution. More than once, Roosevelt acted to restrain European nations from military enterprises in the Western Hemisphere.

During the Venezuela affair of 1902–03, France, Britain, and Germany blockaded the country, demanding immediate, full payment for a defunct bond issue. Worried that the next step might be occupation, Roosevelt spoke strongly to Germany, whose leaders had talked of a "temporary possession" of territory. The President forced an arbitrated settlement. The tribunal appointed to hear the case ordered Venezuela to pay all its debtors, beginning with those from countries that had manned the blockade.

Soon afterward, Roosevelt defined a specific role for his nation. "The United States can not see any European power occupy the territory of the Latin American republic," he told Congress, "not even if that is the only way to collect its debts." The United States would act in place of European nations on behalf of their legitimate interests, taking to itself an "international police power" to discipline "flagrant wrongdoing in the Western Hemisphere." The policy is known as the Roosevelt Corollary to the Monroe Doctrine. That famous Doctrine had warned Europe against expansion into the Western Hemisphere; Roosevelt was now indicating that the United States, by protecting the just claims of European countries, would make up for excluding them from a military presence in the hemisphere.

Roosevelt's announcement was specifically in reference to a dangerous situation in the Dominican Republic. Some Americans and Englishmen had seized local customs houses there after the government negotiated a repayment scheme favoring French, Belgian, and Italian bondholders. Roosevelt ordered the marines into the capital of Santo Domingo, where they imposed a peace of sorts upon the feuding business community. The United States then negotiated a treaty with the local regime that handed control over customs to a retired United States colonel who divided up tariff receipts among the little nation's creditors. Anger among Dominican patriots prompted Roosevelt to use the United States navy "to keep the island in the status quo." Although financial solvency slowly returned under military occupation, nationalists in the Dominican Republic plotted against the intruders. One such attempt would bring another occupation of the island, from 1916 to 1924. The Roosevelt Corollary, designed to prevent European encroachment, had led the United States to meddle instead.

The Lodge Corollary to the Monroe Doctrine Another twist on the Monroe Doctrine emerged in 1911 when the United States first learned that a Japanese banking syndicate was negotiating with the government of Mexico to purchase a piece of territory there. The Japanese planned to build a major port facility at the strategically significant Magdalena Bay. The State Department immediately lodged a protest, and the United States Senate passed a resolution sponsored by Senator Henry Cabot Lodge expressing grave concern about any foreign corporation's constructing in the Western Hemisphere a facility that had a military potential. The protests brought the negotiations to an end. The Senate resolution, which became known as the Lodge Corollary, extended the Monroe Doctrine prohibitions to non-European powers as well as to foreign companies.

The Era of Dollar Diplomacy, 1909–1917

The expulsion of Spain from Cuba and Puerto Rico in 1898, as well as the acquisition of the Panama Canal in 1903, gave the United States unprecedented power in the Caribbean, while the Open Door notes of 1899 and the Root-Takahira Agreement of 1908 seemed to guarantee the United States access to China. The administrations of William Howard Taft and then Woodrow Wilson decided to use the power of the United States government to promote the nation's business interests abroad, particularly in the Far East and in Latin America. Officials in the departments of state and commerce were charged with the responsibility of expanding opportunities and increasing profits for private businesses. Historians have dubbed the policy "dollar diplomacy."

Despite the intense efforts of Secretary of State Philander C. Knox, dollar diplomacy did not get very far in China. In 1909 a consortium of European bankers began plans to finance construction of large railways in southern and central China. American bankers, excluded from the consortium, complained to the federal government, and President Taft worked personally to get them included in the project. Knox also tried to get the Chinese government to accept a huge loan from American bankers to inaugurate a program of currency reform. The proposals of President Taft and Secretary Knox aroused the suspicions of Russia and Japan, both concluding that the United States was trying to carve out its own sphere of influence in China. The Russian and Japanese protests between 1910 and 1913 frightened off American banking interests, who did not want to invest money in politically unstable areas.

But dollar diplomacy, stillborn in Asia, thrived in Central America and the Caribbean. President Taft and Wilson presided over a foreign policy that treated the Caribbean virtually as an American lake. The economic influence of the United States pervaded the region. The United Fruit Company, for example, was a corporation, based in the United States, that owned dozens of huge banana plantations in Central America, as well as railroads to transport the crop to Pacific and Atlantic ports. It wielded more power than most of the governments in Central America. The American Sugar Refining Company was equally powerful in Cuba. Those companies, and others like them, wanted governments in place throughout the region that would guarantee their assets, and they expected the United States to support and protect them. Eventually, United States marines marched through Nicaragua, Haiti, the Dominican Republic, and Mexico. Woodrow Wilson saw nothing wrong with such conduct: "I'll teach them to elect good men," he bragged. Humanitarians hoped to reform corrupt, poor countries, while strategists became convinced that stability in the region was vital to the security of the United States.

The dictator of Nicaragua threatened during 1909 to cancel a valuable mining lease held by a company based in the United States and to permit the Japanese to build a canal across his country. The threat was bluster. But the dictator's aims to create trouble in neighboring countries and the existence of an insurgence movement inside Nicaragua persuaded Taft to move to overthrow the regime. When two United States citizens caught dynamiting ships in the San Juan River during a street revolution were executed, Taft broke diplomatic relations and financed a makeshift government dominated by the United States. New York City bankers regulated the country's finances. A mining company employee asked Taft in 1912 to send a "legation guard" of 2,700 marines to "keep order." The troops stayed for more than two decades. A treaty signed in 1916 granted the United States an exclusive right both to build any canal and to lease naval bases on Nicaragua's Atlantic and Pacific coasts.

Woodrow Wilson carried the game just short of annexation in Haiti. Perennial misgovernment there had declined into near chaos by 1915. In less than four years, seven Presidents—some of them eventually either blown up or poisoned—had looted the public treasury. Revolution became almost permanent. President Vilbrum Sam, who defaulted in early 1915 on some $24 million in debts owed to western Europeans and United States citizens, launched a vendetta against his opponents, killing 167 of them. Outraged townspeople in Port-au-Prince killed and dismembered Sam. Wilson ordered in the marines. Several thousand of them occupied the capital. New York City bankers, now familiar with the techniques of financial control, once again traveled to the Caribbean. A hastily elected local government signed a treaty that gave control of foreign policy to the United States. Some Haitians revolted; marines crushed them. Haiti remained a virtual protectorate for almost twenty years.

A dictator, Porfirio Diaz, had ruled Mexico since 1876. Roosevelt's secretary of state, Elihu Root, rhapsodized that Diaz was a "great man to be held up for the hero worship of mankind," but Mexicans rejected the advice. Nationalists objected to economic concessions that had given away oil and mining rights to British and American companies. A collection of middle-class reformers, socialists, Indians, adventurers, and radical Catholics called for land reform, national ownership of raw materials, and racial equality. Diaz retired and confusion followed. Power drifted into the hands of Francisco I. Madero, a gentle, indecisive, eccentric man unable to give direction to an emerging revolution. Demanding immediate redistribution of land, regional leaders like Emiliano Zapata and Pancho Villa assembled armies south and north of the capital. Worried by this growing threat to their economic interests, foreign companies and the domestic Catholic hierarchy appealed for help to the United States ambassador. He hinted of Madero's ineptness, and the country's ambitious military chief, Victoriano Huerta, understood. He organized a palace revolt, took control of the regional armies, and installed himself as lifetime President of Mexico. His agents murdered Madero and imposed a military dictatorship over most of the country.

Huerta's brutal rise occurred just before Woodrow Wilson took office on March 4,

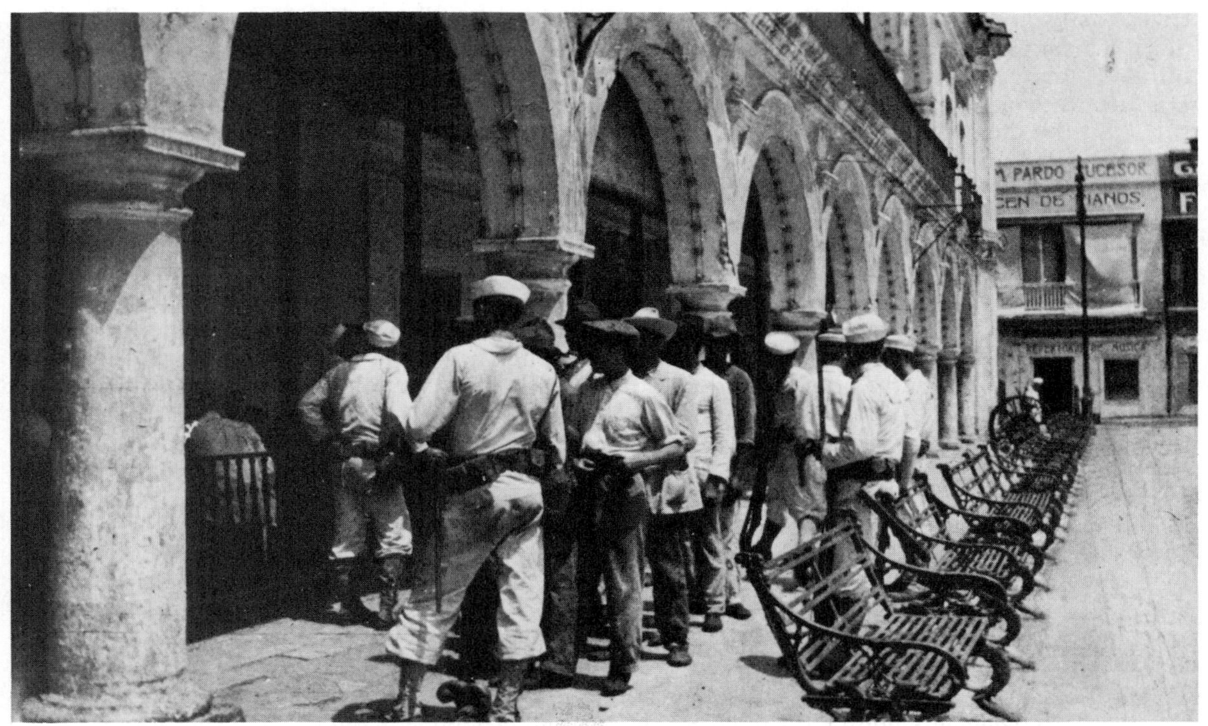

Sailors of the United States in Veracruz after the taking of the city in April 1914 on President Wilson's orders. *(Courtesy, Scribner's Archives)*

1913. "I will not," the new chief executive said, "recognize a government of butchers." Relying on sources prone to exaggeration, Wilson wrote:

> Entire villages have been burned, their inhabitants—men, women, and children—slaughtered and mutilated indiscriminately; plantations have been ravaged and burned, trains have been blown up and derailed, and passengers slaughtered like cattle; women have been ravished and men mutilated with accompaniments of horror and barbarity which find no place in the chronicles of Christian warfare.

The President refused to talk with Huerta's diplomats, arguing that from now on the United States would deal only with "republican governments based upon law, not irregular force." This novel policy, which judged a nation's morality, departed from past recognition procedures, which required only that a regime be in control of its territory. Wilson hoped to isolate Huerta, and persuaded the British to follow his lead. Instead, a diplomatic standoff ensued. Words could scarcely hurt Huerta, who used Yankeephobia to prop up his faltering regime.

Barely a month after Wilson assumed office, Mexican authorities arrested a group of United States sailors in Tampico. The arrests were legitimate, for the men had drifted into a restricted area by mistake. But their commander, Admiral Henry T. Mayo, demanded an apology and a twenty-one gun salute to the Stars and Stripes. Nine days later, Wilson delivered an ultimatum: salute the flag or face the consequences. Huerta's government was now sustained on feeling against the Yankees and he refused. So the President ordered marines to occupy Mexico's chief Gulf port, Veracruz. Street fighting produced a large number of casualties, sixty of the invading troops and over 500 Mexican. Many people in the United States, unaware that relations with their neighbor had so deteriorated, were stunned. The marines remained in Veracruz for six months.

The Tampico incident and occupation of Veracruz humiliated Huerta, disgracing him in the eyes of most nationalists and preventing any foreign help for his regime. His power disintegrated. Venustiano Carranza, who had gathered an army outside Mexico

City, easily occupied the capital. Like Madero, Carranza was a middle-class reformer buffeted by the winds of revolution; like Huerta, he was a vigilante, not a legitimate ruler. So the chaos in Mexico and the deadlock with President Wilson continued. Then Pancho Villa, a restless adventurer from the far north, raised a rebellion against Carranza. The *villistas* added an anti-clerical seasoning to the revolutionary brew of economic reform and extended the violence. On January 11, 1916, Villa attacked a train at Santa Ysabel and slaughtered sixteen citizens of the United States; two months later he raided the New Mexico town of Columbus, burning it to the ground and killing seventeen people. He calculated that an armed intervention by the United States would destroy Carranza just as it had Huerta. Reacting as Villa had hoped, Wilson ordered General John J. Pershing across the border with 6,600 men in pursuit of the guerrilla bandit. The *villistas* eluded the army, so Wilson next called out 150,000 national guard troops to seal off the entire southwestern border. Time passed. Pershing rushed fruitlessly around Mexico's northern provinces; Carranza held on in Mexico City. Early in 1917, at the approach of war with Germany, Wilson quietly withdrew federal forces from Mexico, granted Carranza full recognition, and abandoned his efforts to instruct a nation in democracy. Preoccupied with their revolution, Mexicans withdrew into a sullen hostility toward the United States. So ended that interlude of imperialist good intentions. The cloak of empire fitted awkwardly upon the shoulders of the United States.

Points To Think About

1. That the colonial empire the United States seized as a result of that "splendid little war" with Spain was a "temporary aberration" is perfectly correct, provided the reference is to the formal acquisition of colonies. The United States has, for the most part, avoided seizing foreign territory with the intent of establishing its own rule.

In a broader sense the whole of our history is a story of empire building. Thomas Jefferson called for "an empire for liberty" and the rapid territorial expansion characteristic of the United States after the Revolution shows that Jefferson spoke for his countrymen as well as for himself. And this spectacular empire involved the very same process of destroying the cultures and societies of the native peoples that European conquests in Africa and Asia did. If anything, the subjugation of the Indians was more vicious (and more thorough). With Australia and New Zealand, the Americas stand as a permanent conquest, by Europeans, of indigenous non-white peoples. White citizens of the United States are remarkably oblivious to this fact, and thus remarkably unable to understand why so-called Third World nations view so skeptically those acts of intervention that Washington proclaims to be in defense of freedom and national self-determination.

2. When the Spanish tried to crush the Cuban insurgents they adopted a policy of moving the Cuban population into "reconcentration" camps. Public opinion in the United States was outraged. The reconcentration policy was a response to a basic fact about guerrilla warfare—the insurgents are always able to melt back into the general population. So the Spanish determined to establish certain secure areas and then forcibly remove the people into them. This would keep the guerrillas outside.

The United States adopted a similar approach during the Vietnam War. The reconcentration camps in Vietnam were called "safe hamlets." The parallel should not be surprising. The United States faced the same problem and came up with the same solution. It did not work the second time either.

3. Alfred Thayer Mahan's *The Influence of Sea Power on History* contributed significantly to the rise of an imperialist ideology in the late nineteenth century. In *From Know-How to Nowhere*, his fascinating study of American technology, Elting Morison analyzes the impact of Mahan's book on the modernization of the American navy. It is a story, as Morison points out, with implications well beyond military history.

The Civil War era attended the development of a number of new technologies that called for a revolution in naval strategy. These included the use of steam power on sea-going ships, the new production of cheap and highly durable steel, and chemical breakthroughs in the use of explosives.

The old wooden, sail-driven fleet was clearly obsolete. But what was to take its place? The navy appointed hundreds of commissions to investigate these new developments and built a strange array of ships. Some were made of both wood and steel. Others had both steam and sails. All featured distinctive armaments. The navy had little idea of what to do with these ships. Those that combined steam and sail power were required by naval regulations to travel under sail a certain number of hours each day. The navy, in short, suffered from an embarrassment of technical riches which it had yet to figure out how to use.

Then, says Morison, Mahan wrote his book. In it he ignored these technical questions, and yet solved them all. For *The Influence of Sea Power* provided a clear and convincing rationale for what the navy was for. Once, that is, it became clear what the navy needed to be ready to do, all of the technical problems became relatively easy to resolve and a modern navy became possible. Morison uses the story to point a moral about the role of technology in modern life. We need, he argues, a coherent vision of a good society that will tell us clearly what a particular technological development is good for. In its absence, he writes, we have only progressed from Know-how to Nowhere.

4. The Open Door called upon European powers to stop seeking spheres of influence in China. Instead it proposed that all states freely and fairly compete for Chinese trade while joining together to guarantee China's "territorial integrity."

In a formal sense the policy was anti-imperialist although the timing—McKinley Administration issued the notes at the very time it was consolidating its grip on the Philippines—gives rise to questions about how seriously that aspect of the policy should be taken. As a practical matter too, the United States was in a poor position to carve out its own sphere of influence in China. Britain, Germany, Russia, and Japan had already staked out their claims and not much was left. So the United States had little to lose by calling for the Open Door. And it had much to gain. The United States was seeking the peaceful entrance into new markets, markets it wished open to all comers on an equal basis. This position recalls that taken by England during the mid-nineteenth century when it was the world's dominant industrial nation. Free and open competition always appeals to the country holding the strongest economic cards.

It is possible to argue from here, as William A. Williams does in his *Tragedy of American Diplomacy*, that the Open Door became the cornerstone of American foreign policy in this century. The United States would turn away from formal empire-building, and rely instead on economic penetration to extend its influence.

Suggested Readings

Two studies of Social Darwinism are Michael Ruse, *The Darwinian Revolution: Science Red in Tooth and Claw* (1979) and Cynthia Eagle Russett, *Darwin in America: The Intellectual Response, 1865–1912* (1976). On expansion into Asia see Stanley Karnow, *In Our Image: America's Empire in the Philippines* (1989). Milton Plesur's *America's Outward Thrust, 1865–1890* (1971), sampling newspapers, commercial journals, and other sources of public opinion, concludes that it was not merely economic interests but ideology that took the United States into the expansionism of the period. Other major books on foreign affairs in the late nineteenth century include Walter LaFeber, *The New Empire: An Interpretation of American Expansion, 1865–1898* (1963), David Healy, *United States Expansionism: The Imperialist Urge in the 1890s* (1970), and Charles S. Campbell, *The Transformation of American Foreign Relations, 1865–1900* (1976). Ernest May has written the original *American Imperialism: A Speculative Essay* (1968). Two works on the Spanish-American War are David F. Trask, *The War With Spain* (1981) and Frank Friedel, *The Splendid Little War* (1958). David McCollough is standard on *The Path Between the Seas: The Creation of the Panama Canal 1870–1914* (1977). William Appleman Williams argues, in *The Roots of Modern American Empire* (1969), that behind the American imperialist push at the turn of the century was the American farmer, who wanted his country to open markets abroad. Williams shows how American ideals of self-determination blended with self-interest: keeping peoples free from domination by European powers would insure the availability of their markets to American commerce; but the idea of the virtuousness of open markets made its own appeal. Roger Daniels has written *Asian Americans: Chinese and Japanese in the United States Since 1850* (1988).

☆ ☆ ☆ POINTS OF VIEW: ☆ ☆ ☆

American Imperialism: Economic Self-Interest or Patriotic Mission?

Walter LaFeber

In less than a century and a quarter the United States had developed from thirteen states strung along a narrow Atlantic coastline into a great world power with possessions in the far Pacific.

Until the middle of the nineteenth century this had been, for the most part, a form of landed expansion which had moved over a large area of the North American continent. The Louisiana Purchase in 1803 had been followed by further important acquisitions in 1819, 1848, 1853, and 1867. But when William H. Seward entered the State Department in 1861, the nature of American expansion had begun to change. Under the impact of the industrial revolution Americans began to search for markets, not land. Sometimes the State Department seized the initiative in making the search, as in the Harrison administration. Frequently the business community pioneered in extending the interests of the United States into foreign areas, as in Mexico in the 1870's and in China in the 1890's. Regardless of which body led the expansionist movement, the result was the same: the growth of economic interests led to political entanglements and to increased military responsibilities.

Americans attempted to build a new empire, an empire which differed fundamentally from the colonial holdings of European powers. Until 1898 the United States believed that its political institutions were suitable only for the North American continent. . . .

In 1898, however, the United States annexed Hawaii and demanded the Philippines from Spain. These acquisitions were not unheralded. Seward had pushed his nation's claims far out into the Pacific with the purchase of Alaska and the Midway islands. . . .

One striking characteristic tied these acquisitions to the new territory brought under American control in 1898 and 1899, immediately after the war with Spain. The United States obtained these areas not to fulfill a colonial policy, but to use these holdings as a means to acquire markets for the glut of goods pouring out of highly mechanized factories and farms.

Hawaii had become an integral part of the American economy long before Harrison attempted to annex it in 1893. Missionaries had forged strong religious and secular links between the islands and the mainland, but of much more importance were the commercial ties. American capital, especially attracted by the islands' fertility during the depression years that plagued the mainland in the 1870's and 1880's, developed sugar plantations whose prosperity depended upon the American consumer. . . .

The Philippines marked the next step westward. In 1899 the Secretary of the American Asiatic Association analyzed the reason for the annexation of these islands in a single sentence: "Had we no interests in China, the possession of the Philippines would be meaningless." Mark Hanna, a somewhat more objective observer of the Far East than the gentleman just quoted, also desired "a strong foothold in the Philippine Islands," for then "we can and will take a large slice of the commerce of Asia. That is what we want. We are bound to share in the commerce of the Far East, and it is better to strike for it while the iron is hot."

Throughout the 1890's, debate had raged around the desirability of annexing yet another outlying possession. The growing desire for an American-controlled Isthmian canal partially explains the interest Hawaii held for some Americans. But it should be emphasized that in the 1890's, at least, Americans did not define their interests in a future canal as military; they termed these interests as economic. Policy makers viewed the control of strategic areas such as Hawaii or Guantánamo Bay in the same light as they viewed the Philippines, that is, as strategic means to obtaining and protecting objectives which they defined as economic.

Reprinted from Walter LaFeber, *The New Empire: An Interpretation of American Expansion,* 1860–1898 (Ithaca, New York: Cornell University Press, 1963).

Nell Irvin Painter

A few [critics] denigrated American imperialism as senseless aping of Europeans. But for the most part an overseas empire seemed to admit the United States to an elite club of powerful, advanced, and civilized nations. Preening Americans proclaimed themselves an imperial power and fondly traced the extent of their far-flung—if not massive—new empire. They also located their new-found genius for imperial exploits in their Anglo-Saxon ancestry.

As the British acquired the largest and richest shares of imperial bounty in Africa and Asia through wars of conquest and pacification that they called "our little wars," many white Americans—with the glaring exception of Irish-Americans—renounced their tradition [of] anglophobia (a legacy of the American Revolution and, especially, the War of 1812) to proclaim the kindredness of the English-speaking people and the natural superiority of Anglo-Saxons. The American nation became the expression of a single "race," the Anglo-Saxon, in a view that swept under the rug the Native American Indians, Irish, blacks, and Jews who had been Americans since colonial times and the Asians, Slavs, and Italians just now disembarking in increasing numbers.

Anglo-Saxon chauvinism was no novelty in the 1890s. Versions had flared up from time to time during the nineteenth century, and it was once again on the increase; the American Protective Association, a nativist, anti-Catholic organization, had been founded in Iowa in 1887. More recently Josiah Strong, a Congregational minister, had written an influential report on missions in 1885, *Our Country*, extolling the special gifts of Anglo-Saxons: they possessed a sense of fair play, the ability to gain wealth honestly, the enjoyment of broad civil liberties in democracies in which every man had an equal vote, the genius for self-government and for governing others fairly, and the evolution of the highest civilization the world had ever known and could ever know because the sun of empire moved from east to west, starting in China and ending, once and for all, in the United States. . . .

These American–Anglo-Saxon attributes, he said, were "peculiarly aggressive traits calculated to impress [their] institutions upon mankind." For Josiah Strong, Anglo-Saxon superiority obligated Congregationalists to convert the remainder of the world to American Protestantism. The seizure of territory was not one of his main concerns. But his rhetoric stressed aggression, thereby sounding other chords of Anglo-Saxonism that prevailed in the writing of Theodore Roosevelt. As early as 1895 Roosevelt had remarked that "this country needs a war," not to conquer territory but to restore manliness and military virtues. Pretending that the true Anglo-Saxon (or Nordic) spirit was that of the warrior, Roosevelt and novelists working in the enormously popular medieval genre, such as Charles Major (*When Knighthood Was in Flower* [2d ed., 1898]), and F. Marion Crawford (*Via Crucis: A Romance of the Second Crusade* [1898]), extolled the grandeur of combat. Crawford's knight characterizes Anglo-Saxons as "men who had the strength to take the world and to be its masters and make it obey whatsoever laws they saw fit to impose." Values like these proved exceedingly convenient during the era of seizing other people's lands.

In justifications of empire, Anglo-Saxonism combined variously with arguments for Anglo-American identity of interest, the white man's burden, manifest and ordinary destiny, and duty. In imperialist reasoning, opposition to expansion was utterly futile. For Alfred Thayer Mahan, expansion was "natural, necessary, irrepressible," and for Henry Cabot Lodge, there existed an "irresistible pressure of events." President McKinley spoke of the peculiarly American destiny that decreed Hawaiian annexation in 1898: "We need Hawaii just as much and a great deal more than we did California. It is manifest destiny." William Allen White recalled that "we were the chosen people . . . imperialism was the in the stars." Americans must accept colonies and begin the regeneration of the world or see the world relapse into barbarism.

Nell Irvin Painter, *Standing at Armageddon: The United States, 1877–1919* (New York: W. W. Norton & Company, 1987). Reprinted by permission.

Women trapped in the Triangle Shirtwaist Factory fire on March 25, 1911, had to choose between being burned alive or jumping to near-certain death from windows eight stories high. The disaster took 146 lives. *(Courtesy, Brown Brothers)*

CHAPTER 21

The Progressive Spirit 1900–1917

THE TRIANGLE SHIRTWAIST FACTORY FIRE

In 1900, when Joseph J. Asch began construction of his modern "fireproof" loft building at the corner of Greene Street and Washington Place in lower Manhattan, the shirtwaist had just become the vogue among American women. The ideal American woman now had to look like the Gibson Girl, as drawn by the artist Charles Dana Gibson: stately and aloof, with tousled pompadour, heavy-lidded eyes, sensuous mouth, strong chin, full bosom, and wasp waist. She wore a sheer "shirtwaist," vaguely masculine in its high collar but billowing out to accentuate the bosom, then gathered in a mass of tucks, darts, and pleats to the narrow waist above a tailored skirt. The resulting look seemed peculiarly suited to an age in which women were going to work in increasing numbers: in a shirtwaist and skirt a woman looked tall, tailored, free. It became that generation's uniform, shared by poor working girls, such as those who made shirtwaists in Mr. Asch's building, with the women of elite families.

The Asch Building was 135 feet high on a 100 by 100 foot plot. Construction was of steel frame and stone, but because the building was less than 150 feet tall its window frames, trim, and floors were all made—quite legally—of wood. It had no sprinkler system. The building had several elevators, but only two staircases, and a fire escape ending about 20 feet above a courtyard that, soon after the building's construction, became fully enclosed by other buildings. It had never been the scene of a fire drill. Except for some doubt over whether the fire escape constituted a third staircase, the structure met all legal requirements. It passed fire inspection in October 1910.

At about 4:30 on Saturday afternoon, March 25, 1911, the workday was just ending for 500 employees—most of them young Italian or Jewish immigrant women—of the Triangle Shirtwaist Company, which occupied the top three floors of the building. Just as the cutters were hanging their patterns on the wires above the long worktables on the eighth floor, a flash fire broke out in a bin stuffed with rags beneath one of the tables. It quickly spread to the patterns and the freshly cut pieces of thin cotton and almost instantly passed out of control. Within minutes floors, tables, and partitions were aflame, windows were popping from the pressure, and smoke and fire spread relentlessly through the building. Attempts at an orderly exit turned to panic. Frightened workers discovered doors locked to keep control over employees: a stairwell with no exit to the roof, clawing crowds struggling to gain entrance to the elevators, masses of humanity pressed against metal doors that opened inward to the loft. Flames trapped scores of women and forced them to the windows. There they made a grim choice. A passerby below saw something that looked "like a bale of dark dress goods" falling from one window. "Someone's in there all right. He's trying to save the best cloth," remarked another observer. Then came the next bundle, and halfway down it seemed to open and reveal that it was no bolt of cloth, but a young girl. "Don't jump! Here they come!" men shouted on the sidewalks gesturing toward the arriving fire engines. Firemen spread life nets; the falling bodies tore them from their hands, smashing holes in the pavement. "Raise the ladders!" screamed the crowd assembling on the sidewalks. The ladders reached six floors. Then the firemen turned on the new high-pressure hose system. It reached eighty-five feet—only to the seventh floor. "Thud—dead! Thud—dead! Thud—dead!" so began the eyewitness story by United Press reporter William Gunn Shepherd. On Greene Street he saw people "jammed into the windows. They were burning to death in the windows. One by one the window jambs broke. Down came the bodies in a shower, burning, smoking, flaming bodies, with disheveled hair trailing upward." And watching this holocaust, reporter Shepherd remembered something:

> I looked upon the heap of dead bodies and I remembered these girls were the shirtwaist makers. I remembered their great strike of last year in which these same girls had demanded more sanitary conditions and more safety precautions in the shops. These dead bodies were the answer.

By a little before five o'clock the bodies had stopped falling. One hundred and forty-six people had died.

No one went to jail for the Triangle fire. The company's owners were tried for manslaughter, but the state could not prove that they knew the loft exits were kept locked. The fire and building departments blamed each other. The International Ladies' Garment Workers Union (ILGWU) and some of New York's wealthiest families combined to raise an enormous relief fund for the stricken families. Almost the entire East Side gathered on April 5 for a memorial parade. Amid constant rainfall, about 120,000 people marched through the arch at Washington Square and up Fifth Avenue with neither bands nor banners save a single streamer reading "We Demand Fire Protection."

As a result of the disaster, New York City created the Bureau of Fire Prevention, ending much of the divided responsibility that had made the inspection of factory buildings so ineffectual. The state created a Factory Investigation Commission and placed it under the direction of two rising young urban politicians, Robert F. Wagner, Sr., and Alfred E. Smith. In four years of legislative work, the Commission made New York the most advanced state in the protection of factory workers. It is an ancient story, reform that follows catastrophe instead of preventing it.

The Progressive Era

Much of what came to be known and celebrated as the "American Standard of Living," a critical tenet of the modern democratic credo, emerged from the economy of the first three decades of the twentieth century. New products and new means of transportation and marketing transformed the lives of millions of people—especially the middle class—in their homes, their leisure, and their work.

Consumer Goods

A vast array of goods now presented itself to consumers of sufficient means. Refrigerator cars, innovations in canning, and the proliferation of home iceboxes enriched the previously dull American diet by putting a wide variety of foods on the table regardless of the season: a steady supply of fresh fruit, vegetables, and meat. Modern pasteurizing plants gradually made milk safe to drink, even in cities. Chains like the Great Atlantic and Pacific Tea Company, with over a thousand stores by 1915, offered lower prices through large-scale purchasing, high volume, and the elimination of credit and the middleman—incidentally helping to standardize the quality of products available on the shelves. More and more Americans bought their household goods in the new 5&10¢ stores pioneered by F. W. Woolworth, or in the large department stores, aptly described as "palaces of consumption." Millions of others, especially rural Americans, met their clothing and household needs through the great catalogues distributed by Sears, Roebuck and Montgomery Ward, which helped to lessen the traditional isolation and monotony of farm life. Ready-to-wear clothing, an industry that thrived in this era, made fashionable styles and good fabrics available to all but the poorest Americans. In fact, foreign observers complained that in the United States it was impossible to tell a person's class from his clothing.

Standards of cleanliness and comfort also rose as the inventions and appliances of the late nineteenth century, at first the luxuries of the well-to-do, became the necessities of the middle class. The introduction of the porcelain bathtub and flush toilet, along with the development of the septic tank, made the private indoor bathroom increasingly common in middle-class households. Home electrification, born in the 1880s with the development of the central power station, had spread rapidly by the turn of the century, and made possible a wide variety of new appliances. The first electric household appliance, the flatiron, had its introduction at the Chicago World's Fair in 1893. Washing machines made laundering easier, although housewives now had higher standards of cleanliness, so that probably at least as much time continued to be spent in this traditional activity. Gas stoves facilitated cooking, and mechanical refrigerators began to supplant the widely used icebox by about 1912. Central heating, which spread rapidly after the large-scale production of the cast-iron radiator in the 1890s, brought the luxurious comfort of hotels both to individual houses and to new

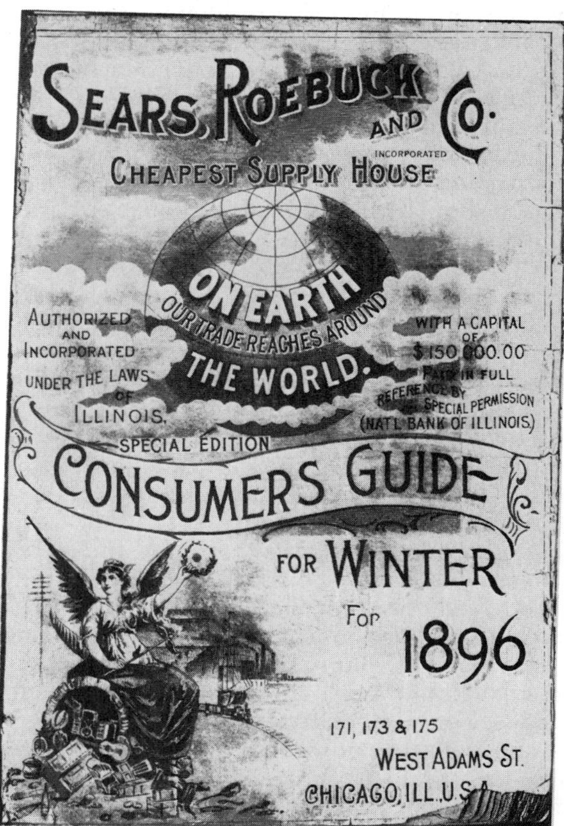

Winter 1896 catalog of Sears, Roebuck, famous as the "world's greatest silent salesman." *(Courtesy, Sears, Roebuck and Co., Chicago, Ill.)*

sky-scraper apartments and office buildings in the cities.

Leisure Americans spent their increased leisure time in new ways. George Eastman developed the Kodak camera, first marketed in 1888 under the slogan "You press the button, we do the rest." Its almost immediate popularity turned photography from the skill of a few to an activity available to everyone for capturing everyday experience. The phonograph, with the new flat-disk record, first marketed in the 1890s for $25, was by 1914 being produced at a rate of some 500,000 per year. With the development of the motion picture in the 1890s Americans also began attending the new nickelodeons where, for a nickel, the audience enjoyed short silent films. By 1908 there were 8,000 nickelodeons in the country. By 1920, the movies had become the most popular form of commercial amusement, and 17,000 theaters around the nation showed them to millions of viewers each week.

Economic Growth

Accelerating Growth This rising standard of living fed and was rooted in a growing economy rapidly eclipsing that of any other industrial nation. After the depression of the 1890s, economic growth accelerated at about six percent per year. Total physical production increased about seventy-five percent in the first decade of the twentieth century. Per capita income increased in real dollars from $496 to $608 in this same period. The burgeoning domestic economy was buttressed by the nation's increasingly favorable position in world markets. After 1892 the United States continuously enjoyed favorable trade balances, investment abroad quadrupling from about $635 million in 1897 to $2.7 billion in 1914.

By 1900 industry had assumed the leading role in the economy. And the value of manufactures almost doubled, from about $13 billion in 1900 to $24.3 billion in 1914. Even more startling was the unprecedented prosperity enjoyed by farmers. Although agriculture's share of the national product was declining relative to that of industry, the long era of depression that had spurred the agrarian protest movements of the 1880s and 1890s was now over. Between 1900 and 1920 the value of farmland and crops increased almost fourfold, and the price of farm products nearly tripled. Later, the New Deal of the 1930s would officially establish the farmer's real purchasing power for the period 1909 to 1914 as the ideal standard. The government would attempt always to bring the farmer's buying power into "parity" or equality with it.

Public investment also contributed to increased economic growth. Between 1903 and 1913, the combined expenditures of federal, state, and local governments in such fields as education, roads, playgrounds, public health, and the civil service almost doubled, from $1.7 to $3.1 billion.

The Cities These tangible signs of prosperity and progress attracted to urban areas both rural Americans and European immigrants. In 1900 only thirty-eight cities had more than 100,000 people; in 1920 there were sixty-eight; in 1930 over a hundred. About seventy percent of the new urban population consisted of rural migrants and of immigrants largely from southern and eastern Europe. In the first decade of the twentieth century alone, 8.8 million immigrants entered the country.

Declining death rates accounted for more than half of the population increase. Improvements in nutrition, sanitation, and public health facilities, along with a wave of immigration that included relatively few children, brought up the average age of the population from 22.9 in 1900 to 25.3 in 1920.

Yet for all the prosperity of these years Americans were experiencing a puzzling inflation. In the years between 1897 and 1917 the cost of living doubled. Popular magazines like the *Ladies Home Journal* and the *Independent* ran articles by women talking about the social consequences of high prices for rent, food, and fuel. Few understood the phenomenon, but urban middle-class Americans, perhaps the hardest hit, indicted the trusts. As Woodrow Wilson put it: "The high cost of living is arranged by private understanding." Others believed that the wages won by organized labor were pushing up prices. Recent economic historians have argued that such inflation is normal and that the long nineteenth-century years of deflation had been an aberration. Then large-scale investment in such industries as railroads, iron, and steel brought an increase in production of goods and services and a consequent lowering in prices. During the Progressive period new forms of long-term investment in both old and new industries deferred immediate production and pushed up prices. Whatever the cause, inflation convinced many Americans that there were important components of their lives over which they had no control.

ONE AMERICAN CITY *found something other than inflation beyond its control. Of the San Francisco earthquake of 1906 one survivor recalled his house being shaken like a rat seized by a terrier. Another, Chester Lincoln, left this graphic account:*

On Wednesday morning, the 18th day of April, 1906, when I woke up at about 5:15 the things in my room were jumping up and down, and the house was rocking back and forth like a baby's cradle. [The earthquake struck at 5:12 a.m., lasted 65 to 75 seconds, and had an estimated magnitude on the Richter scale of between 7.8 and 8.6.] At first I thought it was the wind but soon realized that no wind could make the house rock so much. Then I knew it was an earthquake. I jumped out of bed as soon as I could and put my clothes on. The gas jets in my room would not light. I suppose the pipes had been broken. I had no sooner got dressed when I heard someone call "Chester!" and turn the knob of the door at the same time. It would not give an inch, so Mr. Hart, the man in whose house I was staying, knocked it in for me and told me to come out of there. About the first thing I did when I got out of the room was to go down to the sidewalk and look around me. The house we were living in was built on artificial ground and had settled down. Someone told me that the police station, which was one block from us [at Fourth and Clara], was down with several men under it. I ran down there and saw that the police station and the Phelan branch of the public library, which was adjoining, were both shaken down to a heap of bricks; but someone told me that all the men had been gotten out and I went back. When I was coming back along Clara Street I took a look at the buildings around me. Most of them were out of plumb somewhere. Some were knocked in and some out. People were running and shouting in every direction and were dressed in all kinds of clothes. Some had nothing more than a blanket wrapped around them.

I looked around for the nearest fire and saw one at Sixth and Howard streets. I ran over there and saw that two buildings were burning and the fire was gaining headway rapidly. Several fire companies were trying their best to get control of it, but they could not get much water and did but little good. [The earthquake had broken most of the water mains.] We heard that a man and a woman were in one of the burning buildings which had been shaken in by the earthquake. We ran up to it and tore a few of the boards away. We could see the woman a way back under there, pinned down under one of the scantlings [framing lumber] and calling for help. We could not see the man, but soon the firemen who had the hose saw that all hopes were gone for putting out the fire. They kept the hose in front of them and rushed into the flames. I thought it would be the last of them, but they soon appeared bearing the man they had risked their own lives to save. He was conscious and pointed back into the building, crying for us to save his wife. Then he fainted and was taken into a saloon nearby. We pulled scantling after scantling out of the way in order to get to the helpless woman, but it was no use. The fire got there, the building fell over towards us, and we had to run to get out from under it.

I went down onto Fifth Street where a five-story hotel was afire. While I was there a man appeared in a window of the top story, gave a yell, and jumped out onto the sidewalk. I suppose he had seen the fire and had lost his head. When he struck the sidewalk he was mashed to a jelly. . . .

Getting Around

New forms of transportation and communication sped Americans to work, took them on their vacations, and lessened their isolation from one another. Alexander Graham Bell invented the telephone in 1876, soon bringing people within talking distance of one another. In cities and towns after 1890, electric street railways, or trolleys, replaced horse-drawn cars. These enabled the middle class to move to the newer suburbs of Boston, Chicago, and elsewhere beyond the traditional walking city. Thus began the segregation of work from living places so characteristic of American cities today. The period also encompassed the invention of the airplane and the first successful flight by the Wright brothers at Kitty Hawk, North Carolina, in 1903, although there was no significant development of commercial aviation until well after World War I.

Trains The Progressive Era was preeminently the age of the railroad. Business travel accounted for most passenger service, but the railroads were also successful in promoting pleasure excursions. Millions of Americans took to their vacation spots trains romantically named the *Adirondack Express* or the *Seashore*. Mythical personalities like Phoebe Snow, who extolled the cleanliness of the Lackawanna ("my dress stays white though I ride all night, when I take the road of anthracite"), advertised the ease and comfort of passenger travel. Freight mileage grew rapidly as well, doubling and then doubling again in the two decades after 1900. Innovation and new investment, particularly in the period from 1898 to 1906, allowed the railroads to overhaul their antiquated stock and track, improve the safety of rail travel, and build architecturally significant monuments like New York's Grand Central Station to handle the increased volume of traffic.

The glossy *National Geographic*, especially its frequent colorful articles on the West, helped lure American families into traveling long distances for pleasure. But perhaps the most important spur to increased long-distance passenger travel was the accelerated production of the ornate and luxurious Pullman sleeping, dining, and parlor cars. Pullman journeys rose from 5 million in 1900 to 25 million in 1914. In 1902 luxury rail travel arrived with the inauguration of nonstop all-Pullman trains, among them the *Twentieth Century Limited*, which traveled on a twenty-four-hour schedule between New York and Chicago.

Even comfortable accommodations might not have lured the millions of rail passengers without improvements in safety and efficiency. The introduction of the Westinghouse air brake made it possible to brake simultaneously, from inside the locomotive, all the cars of increasingly long and heavy trains. New types of more powerful steam locomotives and larger all-steel cars carried more passengers and freight at greater speed; new refrigerator and tank cars also added to the volume of freight. Accompanying the improvement in stock was the rebuilding of miles of dilapidated track and the addition of second, third, and even fourth mainline tracks and heavier rails. Hundreds of wooden trestles and bridges were replaced with ones that could support the newer, heavier locomotives. The automatic coupler, making it unnecessary to have workmen standing between cars, enabled railroads to exchange cars on a national basis and slightly reduced the incredibly high accident rate as well. Electrification of some lines in urban high-traffic areas and automatic block signals on some main lines also helped reduce the number of railroad accidents.

Automobiles Adapting earlier German and English "horseless carriages," American bicycle-builders, mechanics, and repairmen like Henry Ford, R. E. Olds, Elwood Haynes and Charles E. Duryea were constructing and selling by the mid-1890s workable motor-driven vehicles that would put the railroads into decline. By 1895 there were some 300 automobiles on the roads, perhaps one-third of them electric, then favored for their relatively quiet and clean ride and their maneuverability. By 1905—within a single decade—the number of registered vehicles had reached 77,988. Nonetheless, the automobile remained an object of popular suspicion, the toy of the mechanically inclined and a luxury of the rich. Autos, argued Woodrow Wilson in 1906, "are a picture of arrogance of wealth [that] spreads socialistic feeling." American capital continued to shun them, and manufacturers

In 1884 Frank L. Sprague started making electric motors. By 1888, a new Sprague electric trolley rode the streets of Boston, Massachusetts. *(Courtesy, General Electric Company, Schenectady, New York)*

resorted to staging races to encourage their use. This somewhat inauspicious start did not deter a new magazine, *The Horseless Age*, from prophecies of a great future for automobiles.

Within a few years improvements in technology and production advances had put the automobile within financial reach of the average citizen. Even before World War I the mechanically simple and more powerful gasoline engine largely displaced steam and electric cars. Engines of four, six, or eight cylinders, along with cord tires, steering wheels instead of tillers, and front radiators improved the appearance and performance of automobiles. With the introduction of the Model T in 1908, the Ford Motor Company offered at $950 an awkward-looking but sturdy vehicle with simple standardized mechanical parts that almost anyone could repair. Before many years assembly-line production was giving the Ford Motor Company a daily production capacity of 1,000 and an annual figure of almost 250,000. The base price eventually dropped to $290 and the popularity of the horseless carriage was assured.

Ford and his Model T became an enduring part of American folklore. For several years beginning around 1914, the nation was overwhelmed with Ford jokes spreading like a respiratory infection from mouth to mouth, then hawked in paper-bound books: "two hundred good jokes for only fifteen cents." Many stressed the car's tinniness. A farmer who stripped the tin off his barn's roof and sent it to Ford received word that "While your car was an exceptionally bad wreck, we shall be able to complete repairs and return it by the first of the week." There were even Ford jokes about Ford jokes: a man in a theater refused to believe that a show was over, saying "That can't be—I haven't heard a Ford joke yet."

THIS DELIGHTFUL VIGNETTE, *set chiefly in Cooperstown, New York, traces the eager enthusiasm of an extraordinarily indulgent father and his son impatiently awaiting delivery of their first automobile in 1909–1910:*

Wednesday, Oct. 13, 1909.

My dearest Boy,

Alea Jacta Est, which meant when I was a boy, The Die is Cast. In other words, The Auto is OURS. Monday morning I went to the Cadillac Office, and paid $250. down, the remainder to be paid on delivery of auto, and thus secured the auto for next May 1st. I was afraid that they might have such a rush of orders that they could not fill them, and I might get left. I send you a copy of the contract. You will see there are quite a lot of extras. But they are necessary. . . .

Your loving father,
Charles F

[New York City]
Wednesday, Jan. 12, 1910.

My dearest Boy,

We received your telegram Sunday afternoon, telling that you had reached Millerton safely, and we felt much relieved. Your postal came yesterday, and the letter to-day. I shall send by express your comb and watch in a box with some fruit. To-day if possible.

Yesterday I went to the Auto show. The Cadillac looked fine, and I got some books with specifications describing it. I send you one, with some other pamphlets that are of interest. The Goodyear detachable-demountable tire was a wonder. You merely pushed the whole thing on the rim, gave it a kick, and it was all right. Some springs held it in position. Nothing could be simpler and easier. I send you a little comic book about autos and Goodyear tires, which I think you will enjoy. I bought still another gauge for tires, quite an original thing, so now I have three, enough to test all the tires in the country. . . .

Sunday, January 16, 1910

Dearest Boy,

. . . . Thursday night Anita and I went to a Bridge Party, and on coming out found it snowing hard. It continued until Yesterday morning, making a pile over a foot high. The worst storm in years. But the sun yesterday and to-day shone with unusual brightness. I suppose you had some of this storm, probably more than we did. How deep was your snow? And now you must be enjoying coasting. We still enjoy seeing autos get stuck in the piles opposite our windows, and they have an awful time getting out. Just now horses have the best of it. . . .

May 24, 1910

My dearest Boy:

Last Friday I got very impatient, and finally wired to New York, asking how soon I might expect the AUTO. Soon after, I received the following answer:—"Received nothing but demis expect touring next week will wire." We all puzzled over the word demis and could make nothing out of it, until I pronounced the word differently from the way it looked, and then solved the mystery. Demis is the plural of Demi, which means "half," like a demi-tasse of coffee after dinner, meaning a small or half cup, and this demi meant a half tonneau or in other words a small car. According to this message I should expect a touring car this week. Well! perhaps! I have been disappointed so often that I am learning to expect nothing. . . .

Wednesday, June 1, 1910.

My dearest Boy.

Hurrah! Hurrah!—No! The auto has not yet arrived, but the Company has just written to me that they hope to ship it to me this week, and I feel much encouraged.

Saturday, June 11, 1910

My dearest Boy,

Just a last word. The Auto has come at last and is now in the Garage. I shall bring the car . . . Tuesday . . . and *you* can take it home. . . .

Your loving father

The Duryea horseless carriage advertised in this circus poster won the Chicago *Times-Herald* road race in 1895, the first such contest held in the United States. *(Courtesy, General Motors Corporation, New York City)*

The increasing popularity of the automobile encouraged a movement for improvement of roads. Until the turn of the century, state and local governments were the prime builders and custodians of the country's approximately two million miles of mainly unpaved rural roads. The bicycle craze of the 1890s and the general desire for rural improvement spurred farm, business, and citizens groups to agitate for better roads. Fuel taxes and automobile registration fees, state aid, and highway supervision would not develop fully until after World War I, but their beginnings occurred during the Progressive period. The American romance with the automobile had begun.

Making Things

American industry grew in these years in the sheer quantity of factories, shops, and human labor; but it grew more spectacularly in techniques and sources of energy. The improvement of engineering, the harnessing of electricity, the study of chemistry, the physical rearranging of factories, the rethinking of the very functions by which a hand and eye complete a job: these give some idea of the character of industry in its years of spectacular twentieth-century growth.

Frederick Winslow Taylor, an engineering and efficiency expert, was the apostle of what became known as the scientific management movement. He pioneered in time and motion studies of specific tasks with the aim of improving worker performance and increasing production. Breaking jobs down into their smallest components, Taylor looked for the best way of completing work with the perfect tool for the given task. He also labored incessantly at reducing unnecessary worker movements on the job. By redesigning floor plans, assembly line flow charts, and the shipping and handling process, Taylor eliminated excess movement. At the Midvale Steel Company in Pennsylvania during the 1880s, Taylor increased production by 300 percent and earnings for workers by more than twenty-five percent. Taylor soon established a very successful consulting business, and the Bethlehem Steel Company hired his firm to bring scientific management to the company. Through ground-breaking work on shoveling, Taylor made it possible for Bethlehem to cut its work force of pig-iron shovelers from 600 to 140 and cut in half the cost of handling the material. Despite considerable opposition from fledgling labor unions suspicious of a system that clamped so tight a discipline on workers, this new discipline of scientific management spread rapidly in American factories and shops.

The Assembly Line Assembly-line production—perhaps the central element in the later phases of the consumer society—awaited an expanded population, technological progress, prosperous times with available capital, and the imperative demands of wartime. Henry Ford preached "a standardized, low cost car for every adult person in America." Improving upon the production of interchangeable parts pioneered by Eli Whitney near the end of the eighteenth century, Ford developed the machinery for standardized quantity production of automobile components. The manufacture of cars was essentially a problem of assembly. Ford began with stationary assembly, and one hundred such assembly stations were set up. Within a few years, a conveyor belt speeded the process further, bringing the Ford chassis to the worker and moving it along at a constant rate. Each arrived at the

Electric power and assembly line production tripled horsepower and greatly increased output per worker. *(Courtesy, General Electric Company, Schenectady, New York)*

appropriate moment and all were assembled in proper order into a complete car. Every worker accomplished a small and specialized task, infinitely repeated. This technique Ford would explain as one that "lifted the hard work off the backs of men and laid it on steel and motors." When the car reached the end of the line, it was driven off. Assembly time was cut from almost twelve and one-half hours to slightly over one-and-one-half, production skyrocketed, and prices dropped. The Model T was so popular that Ford produced it for almost twenty years, offering it in any color "so long as it's black." Increased car sales spurred the growth of the petroleum industry and improved the processing of rubber used for tires. Soon standardized interchangeable parts and the assembly line were making complicated machinery and machine tools for American industrial plants that were rapidly mechanizing.

Steel and Chemicals Between 1899 and 1919 innovation in machinery and electrical engineering tripled the horsepower in factories and significantly increased the output per worker. The development in the 1890s of hydroelectric power and the invention of the steam turbine made possible the production of cheap and abundant electrical power. Electric motors, which had supplied only five percent of factory power in 1899, generated fifty-five percent in 1919. A wage earner who produced eighty-five tons of finished steel in 1900 would produce 114 in 1920.

Steel manufacture expanded greatly in the Progressive Era. By 1900 the open hearth furnace had replaced the older Bessemer process for more than half the production of steel and made a tougher, less brittle metal. Steel production is basically a chemical process, and manufacturers produced a variety of alloys adaptable to numerous needs. The modernizing of railroads consumed steel for heavier rails and larger cars, and wooden bridges gradually gave way to steel. Western cattlemen increasingly used wire fencing and barbed wire. Wire nails, naval vessels, and the beams and girders of modern skyscrapers also used steel.

Innovations in the relatively new chemical industry raised the value of its products from \$48 million in 1899 to \$158 million in 1914. In 1911 Americans began production of "artificial silk," later called rayon. An electrolytic process for refining aluminum made this hard but light metal increasingly popular for kitchen utensils, automobile parts, and electrical equipment. Research into chemistry financed by commercial concerns insured that manufacturing would continue to be innovative in the years to come.

Corporations and Capital

Corporations In 1898 there were just eighty-two relatively small trusts. By 1904, 318 large combinations with a total capital of \$6 billion ran such industries as railroads, meatpacking, steel, copper, tobacco, and petroleum. In 1901 J.P. Morgan had formed United States Steel, the nation's first billion dollar corporation, absorbing 158 companies. By 1909 one percent of all the industrial firms in the country were producing forty-four percent of the nation's manufactured goods.

Many of the new combinations were themselves organized by investment banking firms like J. P. Morgan and Company and Kuhn, Loeb and Company, which emerged when heavy industry turned to Wall Street for credit. Finance capital meant that a few titans virtually controlled the credit resources of the country. In both 1893 and 1907, when the nation was at the brink of financial collapse, it was the Morgan firm that came to the rescue.

Responding to charges of a "money trust" circulating widely in the press, Congress decided to launch an investigation of the financial markets in the United States. A subcommittee of the House Committee on Banking and Currency, led by Representative Arsene Pujo of Louisiana, undertook the investigation during the spring of 1912. Dozens of leading financiers and bankers, including Morgan, were called to testify before the committee. When the hearings were concluded, the Pujo committee reported that the concentration of money and credit was increasing in the United States, and that such investment banking practices as interlocking directorates, stock purchases, the use of consortiums, and banking investment in railroads, insurance companies, and public utilities were likely to make the problem worse. Pujo also claimed that J. P. Morgan and Company had enough power to cause a major financial panic and industrial depression.

The Pujo Committee hearings were taking place just when the National Monetary Commission was making its report. After the panic of 1907, Congress had passed the Aldrich-Vreeland Act to give the money supply a measure of flexibility. The legislation also established the National Monetary Commission, under the chairmanship of Senator Nelson Aldrich of Rhode Island, to study the currency system. In 1912 the commission recommended the creation of a national reserve association with branches around the country. The associations would have the authority to issue currency during times of economic contraction. Such a program, commission members believed, would prevent future financial panics or at least make them less severe. The National Monetary Commission report, along with the Pujo Committee investigations, helped create a political momentum that was to lead to the Federal Reserve Act of 1913 during Woodrow Wilson's administration.

The Newly Rich Such enormous power frightened people. Though the new way of doing business gave order to several important industries, small local competitors increasingly lost out to large national—in some cases international—companies. Finance capitalists were accused of manipulating other people's money, and making great profits without producing any tangible goods or services. They lived somewhere, most of them in the East, far away and unconnected to the communities and sections their actions vitally affected. Their great wealth, displayed in monumental mansions surrounded by landscaped estates, overshadowed the moderately comfortable local gentry who composed most small-town elites. There was but limited comfort in learning of the bad taste with which the rich spent their money. But middle-class readers might feel a bit less awed when they read *House Beautiful's* description of a room in a typical mansion:

> Passing from the Hall you enter the Drawing-room. More money; less taste. The upholstered ceiling, the tortured walls, the bedecked and be-gilded furniture, the costly and trumpery ornaments wage a continual battle. All the nations of Europe are represented in this apartment and they keep up an international warfare. . . . the French furniture hurls invectives at the German draperies. . . .

Workers

Along with the rise of organized capital came a similar, if less spectacular, growth of organized labor. The growing number of industrial workers, some thirty-five percent of the labor force in 1900, toiled—when there were jobs—an average of fifty-nine hours a week for wages of less than $2 a day. And many workers' real income actually declined in the period. Wives and children also entered the factories, contributing even lower wages to the precarious maintenance of their families. In 1910 some two million children and about one in four American women held jobs, many in agriculture but also in industry. Few of these children attended school. Life for working-class families was hard, hazardous, and insecure. The United States still had the highest rate of industrial accidents in the world. In 1917 over 11,000 workers were killed, and nearly 1.4 million injured. Increasing numbers of immigrants, composing the majority of workers in many major industries like steel, contributed more than their share to these statistics. Many of them were single men willing to take manual and unskilled jobs for minimal compensation. Even skilled workingmen, the elite in many industries, began to find themselves replaced by new machinery. Others found that Frederick Taylor's scientific management was redesigning their time-honored informal craft skills. Taylor personally alienated many labor leaders with his description of his prize pig-iron shoveler as a man "more or less of the type of an ox."

Labor Unions Although the ranks of unionized workers had been decimated in the setbacks of the 1890s, the American Federation of Labor—founded in 1886 to represent the interests of skilled workers in national trade unions—survived and expanded rapidly during the prosperous years of the Progressive Era. In the seven-year period from 1897 to 1904, its membership grew from 250,000 to 1,670,000. Perennially led by Samuel Gompers, who preached and practiced a partnership with capital, the AFL regarded the strike and boycott as last resorts and tried to avoid partisan political action. Gompers worked to free organized labor from such legal restraints as injunctions issued by courts against strikes and boycotts. But he preferred to win tangible, practical benefits, such as higher wages, shorter hours, and safer jobs. The way to achieve these, he thought, was to force business to engage in collective bargaining with unions. Labor unions and employers entered into agreements for the improvement of working conditions. Such unionism was "craft, job conscious, business and wage conscious," not class conscious. AFL unions were sometimes distinctly anti-foreign. One manifestation came in the Progressive Era when an AFL group told its members:

> If you are an American at heart, speak our language.
> If you don't know it, learn it.
> If you don't like it, MOVE.

New unions appeared during the early 1900s and some of the older unions began to gain ground. The International Ladies' Garment Workers Union was formed in 1900 to organize female workers in the garment industry, and in 1914 the Amalgamated Clothing Workers Union appeared to organize male workers in the same industry. The railroad brotherhoods continued to add membership in the early 1900s, as did unions like the United Mine Workers and the Amalgamated Association of Iron, Steel, and Tin Workers.

Initially, the AFL did little to organize women. From about 1910 on, it made more serious efforts, but the AFL leadership remained committed to the convention that, under normal circumstances, men should earn wages and women should stay at home. The Women's Trade Union League, which had been founded in 1903 at an AFL meeting, attempted to organize women workers. For its first decade, the WTUL worked closely with the AFL, but eventually relations between the two organizations became strained. In 1915 the WTUL, apparently acquiescing in the AFL view of woman's place, abandoned direct organization and turned to pressuring for state and local government regulation of the conditions of women's work. The history of the WTUL captures the difficulty of organizing women workers as the nation industrialized. Much of its female leadership held middle-class ideas of reform that looked to rational "social housekeeping," as it has been called, and failed to perceive women as full wage-laborers. Much of the male leadership of the AFL remained fixed on the goal of winning gains for male workers, for whom the good life meant having a wife at home and not facing the competition of female labor hired at low wages.

Socialism Many socialist labor leaders argued instead that workers should develop class consciousness, organize a labor party with candidates supporting their own interests, and fight capitalism. Some even opposed working for improved conditions and shorter hours because these were palliatives that perpetuated the inherently evil capitalist system. Always a minority of organized workers, socialists were influenced by European radical ideologies or by evidence that the real miseries of industrial life were not yielding to the policies of "business unionism." This was the term they derisively gave to the conventional American union movement in its dependence on bargaining over wages and working conditions. Although Gompers fought socialists who wished to influence the AFL—"economically, you are unsound; socially, you are wrong; industrially, you are an impossibility"—by 1912 socialists led about one-third of AFL affiliates and controlled unions of miners and machinists. Socialist Party candidates won office in more than 300 cities across the nation, including Milwaukee, Schenectady, and San Francisco. Eugene V. Debs, former President of the American Railway Union, polled over 900,000 votes as the Socialist candidate in the 1912 presidential election.

Debs and most other moderate socialist leaders, like the New York lawyer Morris Hillquit and Milwaukee editor Victor Berger, never advocated violent revolution. Yet in

IN THE CONFLICTS *between capital and labor, labor has always had the best music.*

THE PREACHER AND THE SLAVE

Long-haired preachers come out ev'ry night,
Try to tell you what's wrong and what's right,
But when asked about something to eat,
They will answer with voices so sweet:

Chorus
You will eat (you will eat), bye and bye (bye and bye),
In that glorious land in the sky (way up high).
Work and pray (work and pray), live on hay (live on hay),
You'll get pie in the sky when you die (that's a lie!).

1905, after a series of bloody strikes in the West that the AFL failed to support, they helped create the militant Industrial Workers of the World, led by "Big Bill" Haywood. The Wobblies organized migratory laborers and lumbermen, western miners, northeastern textile workers, and other laborers who did not conform to the craft-worker model favored by the AFL. They sought to create a united labor organization of all trades, skill levels, and races and ethnic groups: One Big Union. Organization of the whole labor force was to build a new voluntary cooperative human society even as its strikes and sabotage destroyed the capitalist and governmental structures of the old.

The Wobblies lived the free, anarchic style that symbolized the society they hoped to bring about. One of their tactics was to go to town, begin reading the Declaration of Independence in public, and then protest when any attempt was made to stop them. When they took their fight for free speech to the streets of Spokane, Fresno, and San Diego, they were bitterly repressed, and established labor leaders representing the best-paid sector of the work force opposed them for their disruptive tactics and their concern for the unskilled. The IWW gained few victories. The outstanding and successful deviation from their practice of operating outside the system of mainline labor disputes was the 1912 wage increase won for 30,000 textile workers in Lawrence, Massachusetts. Even at its peak the IWW probably never had more than 60,000 members, and after 1913 its membership declined. Vigilante action and federal prosecution for pacifism during World War I finished it as a visible force by 1920. Yet its interest in immigrants, blacks, and the marginal and unskilled workers spawned by modern mass industry made it a forerunner of the Congress of Industrial Organizations of the 1930s.

By 1917 membership in 133 national unions reached a total of 3,104,000, representing about twenty percent of all industrial workers. Unionized women, particularly in the clothing industries, grew in numbers from 76,700 in 1910 to 386,900 in 1920. Most of the national unions were in the AFL, the vast majority of them amalgamated unions of workers in interrelated trades rather than pure craft unions. The four railroad brotherhoods of over 400,000 skilled workers remained independent of the AFL. Unions gained in mining, the building trades, and the clothing and transportation industries. Spectacular strikes—like that of the United Mine Workers under John Mitchell in 1902 and the International Ladies' Garment Workers' "Uprising of the Twenty Thousand" in 1909—consolidated union power in important industries.

Big business was inclined to see the virtues of Gompers' conservative unionism, and corporate leaders like George Perkins of the House of Morgan and Andrew Carnegie joined with him in 1900 in the National Civic Federation to promote industrial peace. But other businessmen rallied under the banner of the National Association of Manufacturers, organized in 1895 to resist all unionization, or joined the American Anti-Boycott Association, which went to the courts to oppose labor's strikes and boycotts. In an effort to discourage unionization and promote loyalty and efficiency among workers, some businessmen turned to welfare schemes. Corporation welfare frequently meant amenities like restrooms, recreation areas, and classes in language, music, and the arts, but some businesses also introduced benefit associations for the sick and injured, pension funds for the disabled and aged, and group insurance. A few offered profit-sharing plans. Company unions instituted welfare capitalism by giving employees a voice, sometimes more apparent than real, in running the plant.

Many members of the middle class, too, feared the violence and "conspiracy" of strikes and boycotts and feared foreign agitators. They also felt caught, and helpless, between big business and big labor.

New Americans

New and strange and frightening to many Americans was the flood of immigrants who arrived in the United States during the Progressive years and after. Between 1900 and 1930, 19,000,000 newcomers came in the largest migration in American history. In the peak year of 1907 alone, over 1,285,000 people disembarked at American ports. The majority, like most of those who had arrived toward the end of the nineteenth century, were "new immigrants"—so these late nineteenth- and early twentieth-century waves of migration were called—of the kinds that fascinated some Americans and startled others. Between 1896 and 1915 Italy sent over 500,000 annually, while 2,700,000 Russians, two-thirds of them Jews, settled in the United States. By 1914 a million Poles had come. Some immigrants migrated to American jobs in the spring and returned home in the fall, but most stayed. Many Jews brought their families with them, but the majority of Italian men came alone, sending for their families when they could.

Like most of the old immigrants, the new were drawn to the United States by both hardship at home and American economic opportunity. Pogroms—anti-Semitic violence—and economic restrictions pushed Jews out of their east European villages or *shtetlekh*. Italians, particularly in the parched southland of their country, could scarcely eke out a living on the small, barren plots. Polish peasants also suffered overcrowding on their lands. Some emigrants had seen their countrymen returning from America "well dressed, with an overcoat, a cigar in the mouth," and others received word of successful friends and relatives. Agents of employers in search of cheap labor recruited many with the promise—the reality was often far different—of good jobs and comfortable lives. *Padrones* rounded up gangs of willing Italians to go to work on the railroads, mines, and farms. And steamship companies induced millions to undertake the arduous journey. By 1890 the Hamburg-Amerika line and others like it had networks of thousands of European and American agencies to ensure regular supplies of passengers. By 1900 two-thirds of immigrants traveled on prepaid tickets, the money remitted from the United States.

Almost all immigrants started at the bottom as manual or unskilled workers. By the turn of the century they formed the bulk of the labor force in each of the nation's basic industries. Italians worked in construction and railroads; Jewish men, although few had been tailors in Europe, flocked into the garment factories or did sweat piecework at home, many with the help of their wives and children. Poles and Slavs concentrated in iron and steel. Exploiting enmities among nationalities, and even among different groups from the same countries—northern Italians often hated southern, assimilationist German Jews wanted nothing to do with Orthodox eastern European Jews—employers sometimes hired a variety of ethnic groups to discourage unionization. Almost all newcomers earned shockingly low wages: eight cents an hour, thirteen hours a day, six days a week, was not uncommon. At the slightest expression of discontent they might be replaced by even more recent immigrants. Their inability to understand warnings of danger shouted in an unfamiliar tongue contributed to the appalling rate of industrial accidents.

Immigrants in the Cities Immigrants lived where they could get work and few traveled beyond the Altantic ports and major industrial cities. About two-thirds of the Jews settled in New York, Chicago, Philadelphia, and Boston. The lower East Side, "in the shadow of the Brooklyn Bridge," was the largest Jewish community in the world. Italians also concentrated in the industrial Northeast, while large numbers of Poles lived in Chicago. The investigator Robert Hunter found in 1904 that thirty-five percent of the people in New York were foreign-born, and over eighty percent of foreign parentage. In thirty-three of the largest cities the immigrant population outnumbered the native-born. Most immigrants settled in dense ethnic communities, segregated in the inner cities and isolated from the mainstream of American life. One immigrant from Poland wrote:

> I am polish man. I want to Be American citizen . . . But my friends are polish people—I must live with them—I work in the shoe-shop with polish people—I stay in all the time with them—at home—in the shop—anywhere. I want to live with american people, but I do not know anybody of american . . .

The major cities were mosaics: New York's East Harlem had twenty-seven different

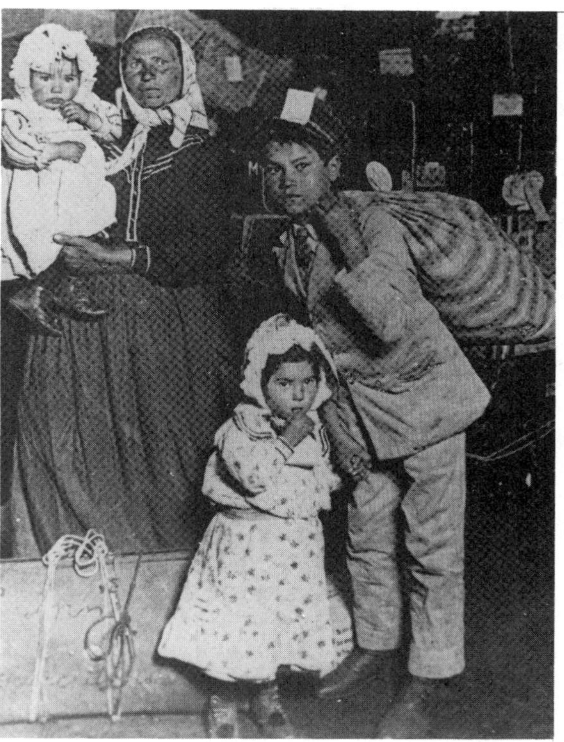

Immigrants arriving at Ellis Island, New York, ca. 1900. *(Courtesy, Scribner's Archives)*

groups, including blacks and Chinese, while Bohemians, Germans, Italians, Irish, Jews, Syrians, and Poles all peopled Chicago's Nineteenth Ward.

Packed into tenements and slums abandoned by Americans of earlier immigrant stock who had moved up and out of the central city, the new arrivals suffered many miseries. Boarders and relatives crowded into already inadequate quarters:

> A family with two children rents an apartment of three rooms and then goes ahead and rents out the kitchen and the living room to two or three boarders. Sometimes there would be shifts, people would sleep in the daytime, and the same place would be used by somebody else at night.

Privacy, even for birth, sickness, and death, was virtually unknown. In the absence of sanitation and ventilation, such diseases as tuberculosis, diphtheria, and scarlet fever spread. Infant and maternal mortality were high. Hunger, language barriers, and the desire for an easier life lured young girls into prostitution. In many cities few children attended school full time, and many who did sat in overcrowded classrooms, read battered books, and afterward played in the streets. Working children labored in factories and sweatshops, work that stunted their growth and sometimes robbed them of vitality forever. Family ties were strained or broken, but many immigrant wives—notably among Italians and Jews—chose to work at home to maintain family life. Filthy streets and exorbitant street railway fares assaulted the new strangers outside their homes. In the industrial cities immigrants could live and die in squalor.

Yet immigrant experience also evoked a rich variety of social and cultural institutions in response to the bewildering new environment. Papers for ethnic communities were found everywhere. Some, like the Jewish daily *Forverts* and the Italian *Il Proletario*, spoke for labor. Others, probably most, simply expressed in a familiar language the attitudes and aspirations of their readers, informed them about community activities, and introduced them to American ways. Cafés and saloons gave a respite from toil and functioned as communications centers for the neighborhood. Mutual aid societies provided sickness and death benefits. Members of fraternal orders like the Odd Fellows, and of service organizations like the Sons of Italy and the Ancient Order of Hibernians, helped one another through hard times. Religious feast days were occasions of colorful celebration. Hebrew schools passed on Old World language, history, and customs to new generations. Although leisure time was limited, immigrant wards supported an energetic popular culture. East Harlem had Yiddish theaters and Italian marionette shows, not to mention movie and vaudeville houses. In some of the smaller industrial towns, nickelodeons and libraries provided relaxation for tired workers and their families. In many places, settlement houses were neighborhood centers with men's and women's clubs, day nurseries, gyms, art, music, and language classes, meeting halls, and discussion groups.

Nativism Many Americans greeted their new countrymen with little enthusiasm and blamed the ills of the cities on them. Some argued that cleaning up the slums and improving city services required getting rid of corrupt ward politicians, who bought the immigrant's vote for a turkey at Christmas or a little money when

Cartoon delineating the movement for immigration restriction. It culminated in congressional laws of 1921 and 1924 limiting new immigrants to three percent of each group living in the U.S. in 1920 and 1890 respectively.

times were bad. Child-savers, prison reformers, and charity workers noted the high proportion of foreigners among juvenile delinquents, criminals, paupers, and the insane. Organized labor charged the new arrivals with being strike-breakers who lowered wage levels and reduced living standards to their own "pigsty mode of life." Complaining that immigrants were hard to organize, labor sought laws to restrict the employment of unnaturalized aliens in factories.

Despite an increasingly rigorous checklist of physical, social, and mental characteristics that officials at the new Ellis Island depot used to detain undesirables after 1898, some Americans continued to worry about social and biological degeneration. The Immigration Restriction League asked:

> Do you want this country to be peopled by British, German, or Scandinavian stock, historically free, energetic, progressive, or by Slav, Latin, and Asiatic races, historically down-trodden, atavistic, and stagnant?

Restrictionists proposed literacy tests to keep out the "unassimilables." They buttressed their beliefs with scholarly arguments. One professor intoned:

> The recent immigration from eastern and southern Europe, however, will, it seems agreed, decrease the average stature of the American. It is said that the skull will become shorter and broader. There will also be psychological changes resulting from the mixture of races. What the final man will be no one can foretell. . . .

Even respected sociologists and economists like Edward A. Ross and John R. Commons worried about "race suicide" and the "harmful" effects of the high immigrant birth rate. The House-Senate Dillingham Report in 1911 declared the "new immigration" to be "unassimilable," and suggested the need for a quota system. Many old-stock Yankee Protestants shared these fears. The well-known poet Thomas Bailey Aldrich set the fears to meter:

> Wide open and unguarded stand our gates,
> And through them presses a wild, motley throng—
> Men from the Volga and the Tartar steppes,
> Featureless faces from the Huang-Ho,
> Malayan, Scythian, Teuton, Kelt and Slav,
> Flying the old World's poverty and scorn;
> These, bringing with them unknown gods and rites,
> Those, tiger passions, here to stretch their claws,
> In street and alley what strange tongues are these,
> Accents of menace alien to our air,
> Voices that once the Town of Babel knew!
> O Liberty, white Goddess! Is it well
> To leave the gates unguarded?

An alternate view came from abroad, from the British playwright Israel Zangwill, who urged Americans to regard the new immigrants as a challenge. In his 1908 play, *The Melting Pot*, Zangwill wrote:

> America is God's Crucible, the great Melting Pot where all the races of Europe are melting and reforming. . . . God is making the American. . . . He will be the fusion of all races, the coming superman.

But the Americans who wanted nothing to do with Zangwill's "races of Europe" pressed for laws restricting immigration. Labor unions also clamored for a legislative cap on the influx. In 1896 President Grover Cleveland had vetoed a bill imposing a literacy test as a prerequisite to entering the United States, and President William Howard Taft did the same in 1913. Congress passed another literacy test measure in 1915, which President Woodrow Wilson vetoed. In January 1917 Congress revived the literacy test and Wilson once again vetoed it, but this time Congress overrode the veto, making the literacy test the law. It required new immigrants to demonstrate their ability to read in English or in their native language. Those who could not read were denied entry.

"Americanization" Making their contribution to this future, progressives in the settlement houses sought, in the words of Mary Simkhovitch, to "get the slant of the neighbors" while easing newcomers into American life with language courses and civic instruction. Randolph Bourne, a young disciple of John Dewey, celebrated their diversity and predicted a "cosmopolitan federation, national colonies of foreign cultures" in a future "Trans-National America." Considerably less appreciative of European cultures were groups like the North American Civic League for Immigrants, which was originally formed to provide help in adjusting to the new environment, but eventually concentrated on steering newcomers away from threatening radical groups. The YMCA ran perhaps the most successful Americanization programs.

Still many immigrants who sensibly wanted to know better English to advance themselves could not solve the problem of

Learning a strange language was one of the greatest problems new immigrants faced. Many attended night-school classes after a full day's work at their jobs. *(Courtesy, Erving Galloway, New York)*

being members of an immigrant group and being Americans:

> Better job to get is very hard for me, because I do not speak well english and I cannot understand what they say to me. The teacher teach me—but when I come home—I must speak polish and in the shop also. I can live in your country many years—like my friends—and never speak—write well english—and never be good American citizen. I know here many persons, they live here 10 or more years, and they are not citizens, they don't speak well english, they don't know geography and history of this country, they don't know constitution of America.

Many immigrants themselves responded ambivalently to efforts to Americanize them. Abraham Cahan's fictional David Levinsky gradually abandoned all the outward signs and observances of Judaism. Many Americanized second-generation children, like the hero in *The Odyssey of a Wop,* experienced excruciating embarrassment at the trappings of the Old World in their homes: "I am nervous when I bring friends to my house: the place looks so Italian." Yet others suffered from the condescension with which the Americanizers approached their cultures. For all their good will, in the end they imposed a standard of immigrant performance that made those who did not conform look like the deviants of whom some nativists warned. In the wake of World War I, hostility to foreigners surfaced again in a particularly virulent form.

Mass Culture and Assimilation

Some authoritarian patriots hoped the Americanization crusade would make the new immigrants more like themselves. But subtle forces at work in the American cities were far more effective in encouraging assimilation.

Except for a few massive concentrations of immigrants—the Jews and Italians of New York, the Irish of Boston and New York, the Poles of Chicago, the Chinese of San Francisco—these neighborhoods were becoming more mixed. In the mill towns of New England, for example, the Irish, Italians, Portuguese, and French-Canadians worked together in the factories and lived within a few blocks of one another. The same was true of the Slavs, Italians, and Irish in the Pennsylvania mines; of the Italians, Slovaks, and Romanians in the Cleveland steel mills; the Jews, Syrians, and Italians in the needle trades of New York City; or the Poles, Irish, Lithuanians, Germans, Czechs, and Italians in the Chicago packinghouses. In the immigrant cities, churches, synagogues, businesses, public schools, parochial schools, and ethnic societies were concentrated spatially, and people were able to see clearly the difference between their own and other ethnic communities. But at the same time, the immigrants and their children had contact with people from other ethnic groups, and in those meetings in the mixed neighborhoods the forces of assimilation worked their magic. Soon their children learned to speak English and communicated freely with one another.

Immigrants and their children were on the move. The idea of a stable population, with the same people spending their whole lives trapped in urban ghettoes, does not explain urban life in the United States. Poor immigrants were highly mobile people, moving from city to city or neighborhood to neighborhood. In older pedestrian times the rich had lived downtown, close to the seats of political, religious, and economic power, while the poor were near the warehouses and railroad terminals where they worked. But as factories appeared downtown and streetcars, subways, and elevated trains crisscrossed the city and reached outside its limits, the rich relocated to the suburbs. The poor then filled the vacuum, often turning the large abandoned single-family homes of the rich into multifamily tenements. Even then the immigrants did not live out their lives in one neighborhood. As quickly as they could save enough money, they purchased homes in the outskirts of the city or in the suburbs and travelled downtown to work. Although the Irish, Italian, German, Slavic, and Jewish neighborhoods survived in the cities, they were rarely occupied by the same people for more than a few years. New immigrants would crowd into the same tenements while older immigrants and their children moved to newer neighborhoods. Those new neighborhoods were even more likely to be mixed ethnically, with even more contact among different groups in the markets, stores, workplaces, and public schools.

The new industrial economy, with its mass production of goods, was creating a consumer culture in which all Americans—native-born as well as immigrants—participated. Companies competed to sell their products, and advertisements in newspapers, magazines, and billboards bombarded consumers with one message: buy. As Americans of all ethnic backgrounds purchased the same clothes, shoes, and appliances, their styles became more similar. The new film industry, with its nickleodeons, storefront theaters, and movie palaces, created more standardized forms of entertainment. These trends, which would accelerate in the 1920s, especially after the invention of the radio, had their beginnings in the Progressive Era.

A New Middle Class: Ideas for Progress

The New Professions

A major part of the middle class was a creation of industrial society. It included the new bureaucratic, salaried middle class, clerical workers and salespeople, professionals and technicians, government workers, and service employees. These were the consumers ravaged by inflation to whom progressives—particularly in the cities—appealed. They also included the social workers, teachers, government scientists, and public officials whose professional activities often brought them in direct touch with the problems of poverty, sickness, exploitation, and corruption that the politics of the era struggled to address.

The older middle class of independent professionals and entrepreneurs had their own grounds for uneasiness. Small businessmen, in particular, were often enthusiastic progressives. They worried over the large corporations that seemed in control of their supplies and goods, fretted over railroad rates, feared unions, and distrusted the creaky national banking system heavily dominated by private bankers, many of them located on New York City's Wall Street. Independent professionals—lawyers, doctors, ministers—saw their independence erode and their world change. Ministers unable to match the styles of their rich parishioners or the expertise of secular authorities feared that they were being replaced as social arbiters. Salaried employees gradually took over such mechanical jobs as title-searching that had enabled many a lawyer to survive while waiting for more interesting work. The middle class professions were prepared to defend the integrity of their specialized kinds of knowledge. The medical profession, for example, crusaded in the Progressive Era against quacks armed with bottled cures for diseases like diphtheria—as well as against midwives with folk knowledge that many male doctors lacked. A sharp upgrading of medical education, the rapid spread of immunization and antiseptic surgery, and great advances in public health made the Progressive Era formative years of American medicine.

Progressivism A better-educated middle class faced the major task of squaring its inherited moral standards with the social and economic world it encountered. Its members still retained the sense of personal responsibility that had characterized nineteenth-century American religion and culture. Yet they recognized that the increasingly complex society around them required large-scale organization and flexible, collective action. Immigrants and uprooted country folk new to the cities had to be fitted into an interdependent society. Reformation of dubious ethical practices in politics and business required detailed investigation, and practical solutions needed the careful formulation of practical alternatives. Earlier reformers had been repeatedly accused of being soft-headed, abstract, impractical. The progressives would seize intellectual weapons from the new arsenals of progressive thought, the universities. The most persuasive description of this new intellectual landscape came from the Harvard University philosopher and psychologist William James, whose essays enjoyed wide influence.

William James James, elder brother of the great novelist Henry James, was at Harvard for thirty-five years. A serious knowledge of art, a degree in medicine, travel in Europe, and even early experience on a scientific expedition to the Amazon went into the profile of this scholar with a rare flexibility of mind. His charm, vivacity, and urbanity sparkled in his lectures and his popular prose. He was the most widely known American intellectual since Ralph Waldo Emerson.

James's seminal work, *Principles of Psychology* (1890), was an extraordinarily effective critique of the determinism and pessimism that characterized Social Darwinism, with its view that evolution and change were a process over which human beings had no control. In this and his later work, he presented a way of looking at existence that came increasingly to be known as pragmatism. Founded in the writings of several philosophers, among them Chauncey Wright and Charles Saunders Peirce, pragmatism holds that an idea is to be tested not by some abstract inner logic but by its ability to give order and clarity within the flux of human experience. James, in a well-known phrase, spoke of the "cash value" of ideas.

James's version of pragmatism made use of the concept of the stream of consciousness, the stream of thoughts and sensations that flows through us. As James saw it, this gushing river is an unending source of uniqueness and creativity. Each of us is free to impose moments of order on the stream, seeking ideas that give form to some cluster of sensations and thoughts within it, relentlessly testing out and recycling ideas that do not provide a satisfactory order. For James balanced freedom with a rigorous method of examining the usefulness of ideas. True ideas, in effect, are true not in having some kind of inner coherence or truth but in helping their possessor to negotiate the endless detail presented in consciousness. In this sense, James was the exemplar of the Progressive Era, in which both social theorists and practical reformers strove to order what seemed an unending and chaotic flow of social and economic events.

The New Scholarship John Dewey's development of progressive education was a prime example of the new ways of thinking. Pragmatism invited a young generation of social critics to view a particular social problem not as formal textbooks would describe it, but by means of continual experimentation. They were urged to try out one theory or practical reform after another until the reformer finds a program that exactly answers to the detail of the problem. Dewey's way of teaching children sounds like training them to do precisely that kind of experimentation. Children learn, Dewey argued, by constant encounter with their environment, constant adjustment to its facts and demands. How could their education teach them to gather data about the world around them, to form and modify hypotheses, and to apply these to practical tasks?

Dewey began, of course, by experimenting. In 1896 at the University of Chicago, he and his wife, Alice Chipman Dewey, founded their Laboratory School. There students, by pursuing the activities required in agriculture, crafts, and industry under the supervision of subtle and effective teachers, discovered their need for the various kinds of knowledge that make up the subjects usually taught in schools. In the progressive school students discovered directly what they needed to know about their social environment, just as others had once discovered such things as part of their farm chores, their encounters with nature, their dealings with other people. Progressive education, which has influenced American educational practice ever since, did not meet all the goals Dewey had charted. Nonetheless, it enabled schools to introduce an increasingly diverse and foreign-born school population to enduring parts of the American ethos, and to motivate students by showing them that their curriculum could relate itself concretely to their future lives.

In the field of law, the pragmatic ferment was apparent in the writings of Oliver Wendell Holmes, Jr., who later served thirty years on the United States Supreme Court. Holmes, from the 1880s onward, expounded what came to be called "legal realism," interpreting the law as a practical instrument for dealing with public and private disputes rather than as a body of sacred, immutable principles passed down in awesome splendor from Roman and medieval times. The job of lawyers, according to Holmes, was to predict as best they could what judges would decide in particular cases and to advise their clients accordingly. A knowledge of legal reasoning and precedent was valuable in the service of that utilitarian purpose rather than as an end in itself. Similarly, a judge's decisions ought to reflect the practical situation. The law, like everything else in the world, changes with the changing times. The legal past is a guide to society's expectations and therefore important in making decisions, but so are the statistics, the data, the empirical information about the present that ought to be taken into consideration in deciding a case. The great "people's lawyer" of the Progressive era, Louis D. Brandeis, took this doctrine seriously in the case of *Muller v. Oregon*, which he argued before the Supreme Court in 1908. Brandeis was defending state laws limiting hours of labor for women, and in this defense—its presentation is known as the Brandeis brief—he emphasized the sociological and economic effects on women of long working hours. And he made little reference to legal precedent. The court was persuaded in this case, although for many years such "Brandeis briefs" were more popular in law schools than before judges.

Oliver Wendell Holmes, whose belief that the law should be treated as a utilitarian tool rather than a body of immutable principles, captured the pragmatic spirit of the Progressive Era. *(Courtesy, Scribner's Archives)*

Political scientists moved away from theoretical issues of natural rights or the character of sovereignty. They turned their attention to the actual workings of institutions like

Congress—as in Woodrow Wilson's *Congressional Government*—or the activities of pressure groups, explored in Arthur F. Bentley's *The Process of Government*. At Columbia University, the political scientist John W. Burgess began to examine the economic motives behind political decision-making. Instead of deducing correct economic behavior from the laws of classical theories, economists like John R. Commons and Richard T. Ely at the University of Wisconsin began to collect economic statistics and to study in close detail corporations, railroads, and the banking system. Thorstein Veblen, the renowned economist, argued in such works as *The Theory of the Leisure Class* (1899) and *The Theory of Business Enterprise* (1904) that businessmen were motivated by greed, that the economic system did not regulate itself by natural laws, and that government experts should develop policies for giving direction to the economy. *An Economic Interpretation of the Constitution of the United States*, a 1913 study of that revered document by historian Charles Beard of Columbia University, interprets it as the product not of pure and virtuous political philosophy but, at least in part, of late eighteenth-century financial interests hoping to profit from a stronger central government.

Sociologists studied urban life, prostitution, labor organizations, and poverty. Lester Frank Ward, a Brown University sociologist, rejected the older theories of laissez-faire and Social Darwinism. The evolution of society, he argued in books like *Dynamic Sociology* (1883), was not controlled by fate or cosmic natural laws. Human beings, through rational planning, could change the course of social evolution and guarantee human progress. Other sociologists made similar claims. The *Hull House Maps and Papers* (1895), a study of Chicago's Nineteenth Ward by a group of economists, socialists, and social workers connected with the activities of Jane Addams' settlement work, exemplified the many studies of American life that provided the basis for reform. With its chapters on working conditions, schools, housing, charities, settlements, and other institutions, this volume was a guidebook for progressivism.

As the academic study of politics, economics, and social conditions began to center on the actual crowded facts of living social systems, practical legislators and administrators learned to consult scholars for help in designing policies. Theodore Roosevelt in the White House, Woodrow Wilson as governor of New Jersey and then as President, Robert M. La Follette in Wisconsin, and other progressives would turn to academic experts for detailed studies of problems and for the drafting of legislation and programs.

The Muckrakers

A new journalism arose around the start of the twentieth century to make a vast public aware of society's problems. Technological innovations in publishing—cheap, high-quality paper, improvements in the printing of photographs—allowed inexpensive, mass-circulation magazines to flourish, beginning in the 1890s. New currents in literature also encouraged the realistic portrayal of American society. A creative and enterprising publisher, Samuel S. McClure, assembled a stable of ambitious, college-educated journalists and gave them the time and expense money for thorough research on articles about American life. In *McClure's* magazine they produced a series of startling exposés.

Lincoln Steffens wrote articles later collected in his book *The Shame of the Cities;* Ida M. Tarbell revealed the questionable practices that had created the Standard Oil trust; Ray Stannard Baker investigated railroads, labor unions, racial problems; Burton J. Hendricks exposed the inner workings of the insurance companies; Samuel Hopkins Adams attacked medical frauds. All listed names and carefully described illegal or immoral activities; the absence of successful libel suits against them attested to their journalistic accuracy. Theodore Roosevelt attacked these new journalists, recalling the passage in Bunyan's *Pilgrim's Progress* about the "Man with the Muckrake, the man who could look no way but downward with the muckrake in his hand"; but his attack gave them the name that they accepted as a badge of honor: "to muckrake" became a common verb for the art of exposing social wrongs.

In the decade after 1902 over 2,000 muckraking articles were written by journalists, professors, reformers, ministers, public officials, and the like. Muckraking dominated the magazines particularly from 1902 to 1906. *McClure's* continued to be the leading journal, but important articles appeared as well in *Collier's Weekly, American Magazine, Everybody's, Cosmopolitan, Arena, Pearson's*, and many other magazines selling for between five and fifteen cents a copy.

The typical article combined a careful accumulation of facts with heavy Protestant moralizing, rather than concrete suggestions for reform. The basic tactic was to induce shame. "The spirit of graft and of lawlessness," wrote Lincoln Steffens, perhaps the greatest of the muckrakers, "is the American spirit. The people are not innocent. . . . My purpose was. . . . to see if the shameful facts, spread out in all their shame, would not burn through our civic shamelessness and set fire to American pride." The tactic worked: Steffens's exposures of American cities left a trail of civic renewal in their wake as respectable citizens mobilized—for a while at least—to throw the rascals out.

Americans enjoyed their orgy of guilt and reveled in the discovery of how bad things were because they believed themselves capable of setting things right. Mr. Dooley, Peter Finley Dunne's fictional saloonkeeper, caught the spirit:

> This country, while wan iv th' worst in th' wurruld, is about as good as th' next if it ain't a shade betther. But we're wan iv th' gr-reatest people in th' wurruld to clean house, an' th'way we like best to clean th' house is to burn it down.

This appetite for learning the worst was gradually sated and, partly in response to some prodding by advertisers, muckraking faded from American magazines after 1912. By then national politics had caught up with the issues the magazines exposed. The muckrakers had focused the diffuse uneasiness of the American public on concrete problems. The progressive crusades of the times had their goals defined and explained by the muckrakers.

Woman Reformers

Throughout the age of muckrakers and early twentieth-century progressivism, the women's movement gained strength, although in a variety of ways and with disagreements over the goals for which women should work. The fight for political and civil rights gathered force following 1890, culminating in the 1920 passage of the Nineteenth Amendment. But during the final three decades of the nineteenth century, women's participation in general movements for social and cultural reform both for themselves and for society at large would be more extensive than their engagement in the fight for political rights.

European visitors, such as this woman, found the social activism of American women very unsettling:

> Since American women are emancipated from the time they are twelve—from that age they can testify and marry without their parents' consent!—since you hear them everyday demand the same privileges as men in political matters; since you even see some who covet the soldiers' knapsacks and trousers—or rather the officers' bars and feathered hats, along with the command of a regiment.

Prohibition, Settlement Houses

Crusades largely supported by the work of women aimed to eradicate drinking and prostitution, to improve family life and childrearing, to make education compulsory, to stamp out pornography, and to educate the young in the scientific but proper knowledge of sex. The Women's Christian Temperance Union (WCTU), founded in 1874 following a series of local women's crusades against saloons and drinking, achieved a special status among all women's organizations. By the 1920s, it would attain a membership of over a half million, which made it one of the three largest women's groups. In the late nineteenth century, the WCTU organized women from all over the country but especially the Midwest in defense of sobriety and the protection of the home. Frances Willard, leader

Women parading for suffrage. *(Courtesy, Library of Congress)*

of the organization, became increasingly interested in political rights for women so that they could force respect for their causes and implementation of their policies, notably prohibition. Ultimately, the WCTU as a whole came to favor granting women the vote so that they might carry their special domestic values into the public sphere. In this respect, it followed a path similar to that of the other groups that began with an interest in "social housekeeping," or subjecting public institutions in general and the unmanageable cities in particular to the high standards of domestic purity and order. Cleaning up the city and its social and political corruption became a project comparable to cleaning a house. New forms of women's activities resulted in a significant politicizing of even otherwise conservative or nonmilitant American women, and contributed to the emergence of a unified suffrage movement at the end of the century. They also frequently pitted middle-class women and their values against immigrant and working-class Americans and theirs.

In 1899 Jane Addams and her friend Ellen Gates Starr, borrowing the idea of settlement houses from Great Britain, opened Hull House in Chicago's run-down Nineteenth Ward in 1889. Settlement houses, arising in many cities, made careers for women in social service, education, and political activism. The settlements provided nurseries and playgrounds for children, adult education for parents, and opportunities for study for visiting experts. Woman and men residents entered reform politics and used their education in the settlements to develop plans for sanitary legislation, factory reform, labor legislation, and a host of municipal programs. One Christmas, the residents at Hull House were puzzled when neighborhood children refused gifts of candy, until they learned that the children were working six days a week in a candy factory. From the settlements, middle-class Americans could learn to appreciate the culture of the new immigrants and become aware of the armies of working women and children whose labors made life more comfortable for the favored classes.

Work in settlement houses provided middle-class women with a firsthand introduction to the problems of urban society. For all their sympathy for immigrants, these settlement workers normally sought to help the immigrants to adapt to American life, which meant in some measure to adopt American values. Settlement women tried to teach poor immigrant women how to keep house properly, how to feed their children, and how to provide them with health care. In their efforts, the settlement workers frequently came into conflict with the urban political bosses who sought to organize the immigrant communities according to different principles. Settlement workers like Jane Addams decided that women must have the vote in order to implement correct public standards. In this respect, settlement workers were of one mind with Frances Willard, who argued that women must do everything—including things that had previously been viewed as unfitting for women—to bring their own values to society.

Women's Clubs In this same period another large movement of middle-class women organized the General Federation of Women's Clubs. The movement originated in New York in 1868 when a group led by Jennie June Croly organized a club to provide themselves with the intellectual stimulation they had missed by being excluded from men's clubs. It rapidly expanded to include more than literary circles. Women throughout the country organized into groups to participate in a variety of interests and good causes. By 1910 these local clubs, linked through the national organization but pursuing separate activities, included more than 800,000 members. Ex-President Grover Cleveland, writing in *The Ladies' Home Journal,* echoed the sentiments of many men when he insisted that women should not join clubs other than those with "purposes of charity, religious enterprise, or intellectual improvement." But thousands of women who had joined clubs for just those purposes were slowly led to demand more and more rights for themselves and other women simply to guarantee the success of their charitable, intellectual, and religious purposes. The General Federation of Women's Clubs was drawn farther into the public sphere when it lobbied for progressive causes such as conservation, consumer legislation, child labor laws, and other legislation benefiting children. One club campaign produced over a million letters in support of the Pure Food and Drug Bill in 1906.

The National Consumer's League—modeled after an English organization—became a powerful lobby for legislation protecting women and children. Under the able leadership of Florence Kelley, the league boycotted manufacturers employing children, and pushed through the Ten Hour Law in Oregon that Louis Brandeis would defend successfully before the Supreme Court. The Women's Trade Union League paired wealthy women and reformers to aid working women in their efforts to organize unions.

In 1915 Margaret Sanger formed the National Birth Control League to work for the improvement and legalization of birth control. Middle-class, educated people had access to birth control information, but most poor people did not. Laws made it illegal on grounds of obscenity to distribute birth control literature. In 1923 Sanger set up the first birth control clinic in New York City, staffed by women volunteers and women doctors. Other clinics were soon opened in cities outside New York. Women were interested in birth control because they saw it as a way toward happier and healthier family life; they also believed it would reduce poverty and disease. Supporters of birth control understood that their message would appeal to those who advocated a strict immigration policy. Yet the combined work of the woman reformers and the clinics forged one of the few links between the poor working woman and the more affluent middle-class woman.

Middle-class women's groups in general were instrumental in pushing for protective legislation for women workers. In their view, all women shared biological characteristics that made them gentler and more fragile than men, but also more moral. They insisted that women be recognized and treated as a special social group. Women needed protection, not equality with male workers. It is not entirely clear how completely working women, who needed to make as much money as possible, agreed with these women's groups. If protective legislation brought important benefits to women, it also imprisoned them in a segmented labor market. But it is impossible to exaggerate the contributions that middle-class women's organizations contributed to the passage of protective legislation for women workers. In this respect, as in so many others, organized middle-class American women were developing considerable skill in assuring the triumph of some of their own values in American society.

Suffrage Gradually the women's groups and the constituents of their reform movements coalesced around the issue of votes for women, convinced not only that it was right but that it would improve political and social life. But there was much resistance. One suffragette remembered:

> A student at Vassar tried to get up a suffrage meeting, and the college President refused to let her hold the meeting. So she organized a little group, and they jumped over a wall at the edge of the college and held the first suffrage meeting at Vassar in a cemetery. Imagine such a thing happening at a women's college so short a time ago. You can hardly believe such things occurred. But they did.

That liquor interests and large corporations financed the fight against suffrage reinforced the women reformers' sense that their movement and progressivism were vital to each other. After 1914 the General Federation of Women's Clubs came out squarely for women's suffrage, giving the cause fresh respectability.

Two women who had journeyed to England and admired the militant struggle women were waging there, Alice Paul and Lucy Burns, formed the Congressional Union to oppose President Woodrow Wilson on the suffrage issue in 1916. Starting in January 1917, Union members picketed in front of the White House for a year and a half in behalf of a constitutional amendment requiring all states to allow women the vote. Shortly after the picketing began, the United States entered World War I. The women were faced with a difficult decision. Would it be unpatriotic to continue their protest? When they chose to continue to work for the vote, police arrested many picketers and while some newspapers were sympathetic, most were not. By the end of the year 218 women had been charged and ninety-seven went to jail. Many of these women were prominent. Stories circulated about physical abuse and forced feeding; these drew more attention to the cause and gained some further sympathy. Not all of the women's organizations agreed with these militant tactics. Carrie Chapman Catt, president in 1915 of the National American Woman's Suffrage Association, counseled moderation. She supported the slow process of educating and changing public opinion.

Many women worked hard in the state legislatures. The movement finally managed to persuade President Wilson to support a constitutional amendment. Wilson's decision was not altogether altruistic. In states that had already given women the vote, women's rights groups were urging them to cast their ballots against local Democratic candidates until the President decided to support a constitutional amendment providing suffrage for all adults, regardless of sex. The political pressure mounted on Wilson until he finally, but reluctantly, lent his support to the amendment.

In 1920 the Nineteenth Amendment became part of the Constitution: the right of citizens of the United States to vote could never again legally "be denied or abridged by the United States or by any State on account of sex." The struggle had taken over seventy years. The effects of the political victory went far beyond politics. With the vote, women had the means to enlarge their world outside the home and the church. Yet little immediate change occurred. Many women did not vote; many who did simply followed the political advice of their husbands or fathers.

Points To Think About

1. In 1904, Robert Hunter, a settlement worker, explained that poverty was related to the life cycle for working-class families. Hunter supposed the most favorable conditions: steady work, no accidents or disabling diseases, no unusual expenses of any kind. Even in this best case the average worker at three points in his life would fall below the level at which income or property matched expenses: as a young child, when his family was dependent solely on his father's income; as a young parent, when his family depended solely upon his income; and as an old person, when he was becoming too old to earn much and his children had married and moved away.

Most of the working class did not have even the advantages Hunter's illustration in his book *Poverty* presumed. The business cycle of the last third of the nineteenth century featured two major depressions and numerous lesser downturns; so employment was far from steady. Work accidents, moreover, were appallingly frequent, leaving many families without the primary breadwinner. Disease too claimed a horrendous number of victims with results equally calamitous to the family's economic well-being.

2. Richard Hofstadter, in *The Age of Reform*, argues that the significance of muckraking was largely symbolic. Crusading journalists would spell out the excruciating details of political corruption or economic exploitation for middle-class readers who believed, Hofstadter claimed, that the mere exposure of these wrongs somehow expiated them. Hence, he argued, muckraking led to few practical reforms.

An extension of this analysis could note the largely symbolic character of many progressive-era reforms. Sociologist Joseph Gusfield describes the prohibition movement as a *Symbolic Crusade* more interested in enshrining old-fashioned virtues like sobriety and striking out at immigrants than in controlling the use of alcohol.

There is a tendency to denigrate the importance of symbolic actions, to imply that they are not as meaningful as nuts-and-bolts changes. But, as Gusfield points out, people attach great significance to symbols. In that sense they are perfectly real and worth pondering.

3. The effort of Frederick Winslow Taylor to discover economies in the daily labors of factory workers not only furthered the industrial revolution but in a sense symbolized its very essence. Taylor was attempting to identify in the smallest movements of the worker precisely the principles that inventors had for centuries been attempting to achieve in machinery: simplicities of motion, exact applications of force, coordination of separate functions. From the beginning of modern technology and politics, engineers and scientists had been treating the world as a vast workplace, and political theorists had defined human beings as worker-citizens within it. The modern idea of political equality, in fact, has as one of its foundations the concept of the individual as a worker. So Taylorism, in its small and entirely unintentional way, belongs to the joint history of politics and technology. When politicians of the Progressive Movement considered ways of remaking society in the interest both of justice and of material progress, they were carrying to a logical conclusion much the same kind of thought that Taylor addressed to the factory floor and engineers to the design of machinery.

Suggested Readings

Recent books on the social history of the Progressive Era include Moses Rischin, *Grandma Never Lived in America; The New Journalism of Abraham Cahan* (1988), Beverly Beeton, *Women Vote in the West* (1986), Ruth Rosen, *The Lost Sisterhood* (1982), Alice Kessler-Harris, *Out to Work* (1982), Alan Kraut, *The Huddled Masses: The Immigrant in American Society, 1860–1921* (1982), and Louis Harlan, *Booker T. Washington* (1983). Allen F. Davis wrote the perceptive *American Heroine: The Life and Legend of Jane Addams* (1973).

Robert Wiebe's interpretation of the Progressive Era is an essential work: *The Search for Order* (1968) makes progressivism a response to the breakdown of the "island communities" in American society, the emergence of an industrial economy of interdependent parts. The progressive social critics, as Wiebe explains them, believed that the new economy, with its technological sophistications and its capacity for change, needed to be subject to continual administration by experts, and the reform they advocated was toward giving government this role. For a case study, see Daniel Nelson's *Frederick W. Taylor and the Rise of Scientific Management* (1980). Hofstadter's *The Age of Reform* (1955) represented at its time of publication a break with the tradition of scholarship that grouped together differing reform movements in American history as expressions of a common and virtuous democratic impulse. Hofstadter, who liked to conjecture that the opposite of received truth is the fact, is still full of insights for the receptive reader.

The work of the muckrakers is anthologized in Harvey Swados, ed., *Years of Conscience* (1962). David M. Chalmers, *The Social and Political Ideas of the Muckrakers* (1964) and Harold S. Wilson, *McClure's Magazine and the Muckrakers* (1970) are useful studies. Bradley Robert Rice examines the working of the commission system, a plan that a number of American cities adopted early in the twentieth century as a means of bringing efficiency to city government. In *Progressive Cities: The Commission Government Movement in America, 1901–1920* (1977), Rice claims that the commissions did not respond sufficiently to the need for social reform and the provision of welfare services. Henry F. May, in *The End of American Innocence* (1959), finds the beginnings of "modern" America in the years just before the First World War.

On feminism see Lois Banner, *Women in Modern America* (1974) and William O'Neill, *Everyone Was Brave: The Rise and Fall of Feminism in America* (1969). Aileen Kraditor studies the arguments both for and against woman suffrage in *The Ideas of the Woman Suffrage Movement* (1981). Thomas Reed West's *Flesh of Steel: Literature and the Machine in American Culture* (1967) defines in the culture of modern technology an element of discipline and one of energy and force. Thomas Haskell in *The Emergence of Professional Social Science* (1977) describes a division in the American Social Science Association between older members who saw a simple causation in social events and a younger generation convinced that causes are complex and hidden.

☆ ☆ ☆ POINTS OF VIEW: ☆ ☆ ☆

In Search of Progressivism

Peter G. Filene

"What was the Progressive Movement?" This deceptively simple question, posed in different ways, holds prominent rank among the many controversies which have consumed historians' patient energies, spawned a flurry of monographs and articles, and confused several generations of students. [O]ne may suspect that it is a false problem because historians are asking a false question. This essay seeks to prove the latter suspicion—more precisely, seeks to prove that "the progressive movement" never existed. . . .

As soon as some . . . issues are examined in detail, the progressive profile begins to blur. The most familiar debate focused on federal policy toward trusts and has been immortalized in the slogans of "New Nationalism" versus "New Freedom." In 1911 Theodore Roosevelt bitterly rebuked those of his alleged fellow-progressives who wanted to split industrial giants into small competitive units. This kind of thinking, he claimed, represents "rural toryism," a nostalgic and impossible desire for an economic past. . . .

Another example of progressive disunity concerns the struggle to achieve women's suffrage, a cause that has generally been attributed to the progressive movement. Yet progressive Presidents Roosevelt and Wilson entered late and grudgingly into the feminists' ranks. More general evidence emerges from a study of two Congressional votes in 1914 and 1915, both of which temporarily defeated the future 19th Amendment. Using a recent historian's list of 400 "progressives," one finds progressive Congressmen almost evenly split for and against women's suffrage.

[T]he intellectual atmosphere before World War I consisted of a faith in moralism and progress—and almost everyone breathed this compound eagerly. In order to distinguish progressives from others, then, one must specify their values more strictly. Activism . . . at first seems to serve well. Unlike conservatives of their time, progressives believed that social progress could and should come at a faster rate via human intervention, particularly governmental intervention. Yet this ideological criterion works paradoxes rather than wonders. It excludes not simply conservatives, but Woodrow Wilson and all those who subscribed in 1913 to his "New Freedom" philosophy of laissez faire and states rights. In order to salvage Wilson as a progressive, one must expand the definition of progressivism beyond optimism and activism to include a belief in popular democracy and opposition to economic privilege.

Historians have discovered numerous businessmen who qualify as progressive by their support for federal economic regulation and civic improvement. But these same individuals diverged sharply in ideology. They doubted man's virtuousness, believed that progress comes slowly, trusted in leaders rather than the masses as agents of progress, and generally preferred to purify rather than extend democracy. In short, their progressive activism blended with a nonprogressive skepticism and elitism. Do these reform-minded businessmen deserve membership in the progressive movement? [The historians James] Weinstein and Gabriel Kolko go further, arguing that these businessmen formed a salient, if not dominant, thrust of influence and ideas within progressivism; they were not merely supporting actors. . . .

The present state of historical understanding seems to deny the likelihood of a synthesis as convenient and neat as "the progressive movement." In their commitment to making sense of the past, however, historians will continue to search for conceptual order. Perhaps, after further studies of specific occupations, geographical areas and issues, a new synthesis will appear. But if that is to occur, the "progressive" frame of reference, carrying with it so many confusing and erroneous connotations, must be put aside. It is time to tear off the familiar label and, thus liberated from its prejudice, see the history between 1890 and 1920 for what it was—ambiguous, inconsistent, moved by agents and forces more complex than a progressive movement.

Reprinted by permission of *American Quarterly* XXII (Spring 1970), 20, 21, 22, 23, 25, 26, 34.

Daniel T. Rodgers

[P]rogressives did not share a common creed or a string of common values, however ingeniously or vaguely defined. Rather what they seem to have possessed was an ability to draw on three distinct clusters of ideas—three distinct social languages—to articulate their discontents and their social visions. To put rough but serviceable labels on those three languages of discontent, the first was the rhetoric of antimonopolism, the second was an emphasis on social bonds and the social nature of human beings, and the third was the language of social efficiency. . . .

Of these languages, antimonopolism was the oldest, the most peculiarly American, and, through the first decade of the century, the strongest of the three. When Tom Johnson took on the streetcar franchises, when Frederic Howe plumped for municipal ownership of natural monopolies, when the muckrakers flayed the trusts, there was nothing essentially new in the grievances they dramatized or the language they employed. The disproportionately large number of single taxers in the early progressive crusades was clue enough that this line of attack on "privilege" and "unnatural" concentration of wealth ran back through the Populists, through Henry George, and on at least to Andrew Jackson. But this understanding of economics and politics in terms of graft, monopoly, privilege, and invisible government had almost always before been the property of outsiders: workers, farmers, Democrats, Populists. What was new in the Progressive years was that the language of antimonopolism suddenly gained the acceptance of insiders: the readers of slick magazines and respectable journals, middle class family men, and reasonably proper Republicans. . . .

[T]he most common explanations most Americans gave to political, economic, and social questions at the end of the century were couched in terms of largely autonomous individuals: poverty and success were said to hinge on character; the economy was essentially a straight sum of individual calculations; governance was a matter of good men and official honesty. Part of what occurred in the Progressive era was a concerted assault on all these assumptions, and, in some measure, an assault on the idea of individualism itself. That was what the era's "revolt against formalism" was all about: not a revolt against formal categories of thought, for progressive intellectuals were full of them, but against a particular set of formal fictions traceable to Smith, Locke, and Mill—the autonomous economic man, the autonomous possessor of property rights, the autonomous man of character. In its place, many of the progressives seized on a rhetoric of social cohesion.

The last of the three clusters of ideas to arrive—so very different in outward form from the other two—was the one we associate with efficiency, rationalization, and social engineering. The language of social efficiency offered a way of putting the progressives' common sense of social disorder into words and remedies free of the embarrassing pieties and philosophical conundrums that hovered around the competing language of social bonds. . . . [I]t was the merger of the prestige of science with the prestige of the well-organized business firm and factory that gave the metaphor of system its tremendous twentieth-century potency—and it was presumably for this reason that that metaphor flourished more exuberantly in the United States, along with industrial capitalism itself, than anywhere else. . . .

What made progressive social thought distinct and volatile, if this reading is correct, was not its intellectual coherence but the presence of all three of these languages at once. If we imagine the progressives, like most of the rest of us, largely as users rather than shapers of ideas, this was the constellation of live, accessible ways of looking at society within which they worked, from which they drew their energies and their sense of social ills, and within which they found their solutions. It did not give those who called themselves progressives an intellectual system, but it gave them a set of tools which worked well enough to have a powerful impact on their times. To think of progressive social thought in this way is to emphasize the active, dynamic aspect of ideas. It is also to admit, finally, that progressivism as an ideology is nowhere to be found.

Daniel T. Rodgers, "In Search of Progressivism," *Reviews in American History* 10 (December 1982), 123, 124, 126, 127.

Upton Sinclair's graphic description of conditions in the Chicago Stockyards upset the public more for what it revealed about the meat Americans consumed than for the plight of the workers. The meat packers, it was said, used "everything about the hog except the squeal." *(Courtesy, Scribner's Archives)*

CHAPTER 22

The Politics of Progressivism 1900–1917

THE JUNGLE

Upton Sinclair's novel *The Jungle* (1906) is remembered chiefly as an exposé of the packing houses and for its role in the passage of the Meat Inspection Act of 1906. The Beef Trust was an obvious target. The emergence of the packing houses and the refrigerated railroad car had rapidly transformed the sale of meat from one of the most local of industries to a nationwide enterprise. The old-time butcher who slaughtered and dressed his own meat had been a familiar figure in American life. Most butchers were, according to American folklore, rotund and ruddy, walking testimonials to the quality of the meat they sold. People talked knowingly of Butcher Watson's or Butcher Smith's chops, convinced that in watching the man carefully cutting up the animals, they had a guarantee of quality. A label reading "Armour" or "Swift" evoked no such confidence.

Exposing the meat-packing industry was not Upton Sinclair's main purpose for writing *The Jungle.* A recent convert to socialism, he had received a $500 advance from *The Appeal to Reason,* the nation's leading socialist newspaper. Choosing to write about packing-house workers who had just lost a strike in the summer of 1904, he went to Chicago, infiltrated the stockyards, and wrote a novel exposing their workers' miseries.

Sinclair's socialist connections gave him access to workers' homes, and by dressing poorly and toting a dinner-pail like them he could wander at will through the packing houses. He soon had the material for a tract, though not the characters for a novel. Then, one Sunday afternoon, wandering through the "Back of the Yards" neighborhood, Sinclair chanced on a wedding party in the rear of a saloon and joined the group as an observer of the festivities: "There were my characters—the bride, the groom, the old mother and father, the boisterous cousin, the children, the three musicians, everybody."

The Jungle is the story of struggling immigrants destroyed by American industry. The hero, Jurgis Rudkus, goes through a series of industrial horrors that wrecks his entire life and finally brings him to socialism. The book ends hopefully—the socialists have shown their first strength:

> There were telegrams to the national office from enthusiastic individuals in little towns which had made amazing and unprecedented increases [in the Socialist vote] in a single year: Benedict, Kansas, from 26 to 260; Henderson, Kentucky, from 19 to 111; Holland, Michigan, from 14 to 208; Cleo, Oklahoma, from 0 to 104. . . .

But it was not Sinclair's plea for socialism that impressed the public. What made the book a best seller, quickly translated into seventeen languages, was its graphic description of the packing house in which Jurgis works:

> There was never the least attention paid to what was cut up for sausage; there would come all the way back from Europe old sausage that had been rejected, and that was moldy and white—it would be doused with borax and glycerine, dumped into the hoppers, and made over again for home consumption. There would be meat that had tumbled out on the floor, in the dirt and sawdust, where the workers had tramped and spit uncounted billions of consumption germs. There would be meat stored in great piles in rooms; and the water from leaky roofs would drip over it, and thousands of rats would race about on it. It was too dark in these storage places to see well, but a man could run his hand over these piles of meat and sweep off handfuls of the dried dung of rats. These rats were nuisances, and the packers would put poisoned bread out for them; they would die, and then rats, bread, and meat would go into the hoppers together. . . . there were things that went into the sausage in comparison with which a poisoned rat was a tidbit. There was no place for the men to wash their hands before they ate their dinner, and so they made a practice of washing them in the water that was to be ladled into the sausage.

President Theodore Roosevelt quickly responded to the public outcry aroused by *The Jungle*. Reading the book and inviting Sinclair to the White House, he worked out a plan to investigate Sinclair's charges against the packers. Then the President held off the impatient Sinclair for months ("Mr. Sinclair," he once wrote, "you *must* keep your head.") while the investigation confirmed all that Sinclair had written.

The packers had made large contributions to Roosevelt's campaign fund in 1904 and could not believe that he would go through with strict legislation. But Roosevelt had the goods on them and released the tamer part of his investigators' discoveries. The Beef Trust senators began negotiating; and the President—who did not actually want to hurt the industry or overly damage its sales of meat products abroad—compromised rather more than Sinclair liked.

Still, Roosevelt had achieved a significant piece of legislation. In his memoirs he takes full credit for the Meat Inspection Act of 1906 and makes no mention of Sinclair. As a socialist, Sinclair was at odds with Roosevelt's ideology, and he had a bumptious way of giving unwanted advice: Roosevelt wished that the writer would "go home and let me run the country for a while." Sinclair himself said that the passage of the act "was some satisfaction to me, but not my main interest. . . . I aimed at the public's heart and by accident hit it in the stomach."

The Progressive Movement

The Nature of Progressivism In 1914 the journalist and political commentator Walter Lippmann wrote that it was the task of his generation "to substitute purpose for tradition; and that is, I believe, the profoundest change that has ever taken place in human history." Speaking for those born after the Civil War, for those who had grown up in an industrializing, urbanizing, and polyglot nation, Lippmann gave voice to the people of his generation's optimism that they could control the pace and direction of social change:

> We can no longer treat life as something that has trickled down to us. We have to deal with it deliberately, devise its social organization, alter its tools, formulate its method, educate and control it. In endless ways we put intention where custom has reigned. We break up routines, make decisions, choose our ends, select means.

Americans, Lippmann said, needed to substitute "mastery" for "drift." Just what "mastery" would mean was a matter of dispute among Lippmann's politically active contemporaries. But most shared his conviction that a new nation had come into existence, his certainty that old ways of doing things no longer worked, and his confidence that his generation would invent new and better ways.

To label someone or something progressive was to pay a high compliment. There were progressive business methods, progressive political reforms, progressive farming techniques. There was even progressive dancing and, of course, progressive education.

Politicians and political activists of various sorts appropriated the term to describe themselves and their favorite programs. Any word as overused as "progressive" inevitably loses much of its meaning. And historians have largely despaired of coming up with a single definition that will fit the very diverse kinds of progressive reforms of the years between 1901 and 1917, the period conventionally referred to as the Progressive Era. Some progressives campaigned to increase popular participation in politics and government; they called, for example, for the direct election of senators. Until the Seventeenth Amendment to the Constitution was adopted in 1913, senators had been chosen by state legislators. Still other progressives tried to remove certain issues from electoral politics altogether, preferring instead to create independent commissions, staffed by experts, to regulate railroad rates or the cost of electricity.

One conviction that progressives, for all of their differences, shared was a belief that they possessed the scientific and management skills necessary for them to bend the future to their moral will. National leaders like Theodore Roosevelt and Woodrow Wilson, colorful mayors like "Golden Rule" Jones and Hazen Pingree, dynamic reformers of the calibre of Robert M. La Follette and Jane Addams, social thinkers like Simon Patten, such labor leaders as John A. Mitchell believed in common that the conscience of the people and the skills of experts could fuse into public policies. These would meet society's major needs: to alleviate the suffering of the poor, safeguard the health and lives of workers, regulate commerce, protect consumers, and preserve opportunity. Some believed that progressive American values could set an example for other nations.

The progressives shared a joy in combat, a relish for debate, a high capacity for moral indignation that made public life exhilarating to literate Americans. Politics, now far more oriented to issues than had been customary in the nineteenth century, enlisted the middle class even when it discouraged many poorer citizens and new immigrants from voting. In some ways, the Progressive Movement was the culmination of a series of responses to industrialism reaching back half a century. In other ways, it marked the beginning of a twentieth-century age of reform that was to continue later with the New Deal in the 1930s and the Great Society of the 1960s. It resembled earlier reform in its moralism and yearning for social justice, but was more experimental and practical, more concerned with detailed investigation, quicker to apply the findings of scholarship to social policy.

Progressives were also much taken with the organizational and managerial triumphs of business corporations. While they often worried at the unprecedented power these transportation and industrial giants exercised, they deeply admired the efficiency and productivity that enabled the New York Central Railroad, for example, to keep track of millions of tons of freight. Paul U. Kellogg, a reform-minded journalist and the director of the first major investigation of industrial society, the Pittsburgh Survey of 1907–1909, contrasted the energy and invention of Pittsburgh's business enterprises with the carelessness of its social and governmental institutions.

Progressives thus sought to look beyond the ills of modern society, including those associated with technology and modern business, to commit themselves to the larger spirit of modernity: its insistence on expert knowledge, its will to bring exact and productive order to the world. In attempting to live up to that commitment they invented many of the characteristic features of the modern polity. These include the social welfare state, the imperial presidency, consumer protection, regulation of working conditions and business practices, and government mediation of disputes between labor and management.

Urban Progressivism

The Cities Most of the initial efforts of the progressives were directed to cities. That was where were posed the greatest challenges to the progressive faith in scientifically managed social change. And it was the cities that seemed the most resistant to political reform.

British commentator Lord Bryce delivered a common view in 1889 when he wrote that its cities were the "one conspicuous failure" of American civilization. At the heart of this failure, or so Bryce and other critics believed, was the rise of machine politics.

Lincoln Steffens' *The Shame of the Cities* was the most famous progressive indictment of urban corruption. Steffens insisted that municipal corruption depended upon the active support of the most respectable and wealthiest citizens and upon the passive acquiescence of the middle class. One machine politician, Tammany Hall's George Washington Plunkitt of New York City, described good government campaigns as "morning glories" that faded in the noonday sun when the public wearied of the battle. Progressives knew this and went beyond goals of "good government" and devoted themselves to making urban government more efficient and serviceable. Unlike earlier reformers who concentrated primarily on reducing the cost of government by eliminating graft and bribery, the progressives had positive programs that might as easily expand government as streamline it.

Reformers began to modernize the nation's cities in the 1890s. One of the earliest of these urban leaders was Hazen Pingree, who became mayor of Detroit in 1889. He built schools and parks, forced reductions in gas rates and streetcar fares, reformed the local tax structure, and even introduced work relief during the depression of the 1890s. In Toledo, Samuel M. Jones, better known as "Golden Rule" Jones, built playgrounds and golf links, promoted municipal concerts, and established kindergartens in schools. He introduced the eight-hour day for some municipal employees and removed the police force from political influence. In Cleveland, Tom Johnson won his fight for the three cent fare on streetcars, passed effective public health ordinances, built recreational facilities, improved municipal garbage collection, reformed the police department, upgraded the city water works. These three men, whose example spread to cities across the country, were all successful businessmen who had turned to political reform. More than contenting themselves with simply being crusaders against the party machines, such reformers had a vision of government as a public business, to be run efficiently by skillful and educated men and women providing services and social justice for a wide range of citizens.

Many of the younger progressives, fresh out of college or the new graduate schools, entered public life hypnotized by these older reformers. Notable among Johnson's protégés was Frederic C. Howe. One of the first Americans to earn the Ph.D. degree, from Johns Hopkins, Howe was a young attorney in Cleveland when he joined Johnson's administration. He served on the city council and then in the Ohio state senate before returning to Cleveland and a position on the city's tax commission. Later he would be-

The exponential increase in the number of automobiles required the paving of city streets. Before asphalt came into wide use, cobblestones or bricks were commonly used.

come United States Commissioner of Immigration. In 1905 Howe wrote a book that became the bible of urban progressivism, *The City: The Hope of Democracy*. The progressively governed city, Howe believed, would significantly broaden the services it offered to residents. It would collect garbage, supply water and electricity, extend the reach of the public schools through kindergartens, and open new parks and playgrounds. It was to regulate housing through model tenement laws and ensure the public health by inspecting milk. It would take over ownership of so-called natural monopolies, "the street railways, gas, water, electric-lighting, telephone, power, and heating companies." The rule, wrote Howe, should be "that whatever is of necessity a monopoly should be a public monopoly."

No city, not even Cleveland, fully measured up to Howe's ambitious reform agenda, but a great many made significant progress. New York took the lead in establishing minimum standards for housing, Detroit in operating public utilities. As reform mayor Hazen Pingree summarized his administration's achievements, the city was "no longer lighted by gas, but has its own electric lighting plant and is magnificently illuminated at less than half the old rates. The gas furnished to its citizens has been reduced at least one-third in price and much improved in quality." Streetcar fares had come down, telephone rates reduced, parks improved, schools built, and the city's wharfs rebuilt. Many American cities were quite well governed during the Progressive Era, especially middle-sized and small cities that rarely had to deal with machine politics.

The Social Gospel The spiritual soul of urban progressivism was the Social Gospel movement. In huge urban slums like Hell's Kitchen in New York City, Protestant clergymen built neighborhood churches in an attempt to proselytize the largely Catholic and Jewish immigrant masses. But traditional religion somehow seemed out of place in the tenements. Poverty, disease, unemployment, family strife, and crime assumed a greater urgency than the conversion of souls. Much of urban Christianity in the late nineteenth and early twentieth centuries became committed to improving the economic plight of poor people.

The idea of having churches actually implement the Christian charity they were talking about had one of its origins in an 1876 book by Washington Gladden. *Working People and Their Employers* is an indictment of modern industrial capitalism, laissez-faire, and Social Darwinism. Gladden argued that poverty was neither a result of vice on the part of the poor nor the inevitable product of social evolution. People were often victimized by social and economic forces beyond their control. The government and the churches should join hands, Gladden urged, to provide assistance to the urban poor. Walter Rauschenbusch, a Baptist minister working in Hell's Kitchen, widened the argument. The Kingdom described in the Gospels, he insisted, is to be an earthly as well as a heavenly kingdom, a reign of justice and virtue.

The Social Gospel also found expression in the rise of Roman Catholic progressivism. Prominent priests and Catholic laymen like Patrick Ford, John Ryan, and Raymond McGowan wrote widely and called for a variety of governmental and trade union solutions to the problem of poverty. The official church hierarchy was more cautious. It worried that any show of support for the Social Gospel would indirectly associate the Catholic church with the disruptiveness of groups like the Industrial Workers of the World, or with the radical economic schemes of the socialists.

Middle-Class Urban Reform Urban progressives came largely from the middle class that had long felt shut out of power in the cities, creating alliances with of the churches, the settlement houses, the social workers, teachers, lawyers, doctors, and small businessmen. They usually rejected the decentralized, ward-based government that had characterized the old regimes. In place of a council or board of aldermen, with each member controlling a little fiefdom in his neighborhood, they wanted a strong mayor supported by the middle class of the entire city. In many smaller cities progressivism went farther, obliterating the old political structure and centralizing executive and legislative functions in a commission form of government, or hiring a professional manager to run the city. Progressives sought to separate governing from politics; their reforms looked more to modernization and efficiency than toward the democracy of which they so glibly spoke. Indeed, in many cities fewer citizens voted after these progressive reforms than before. On the other hand, all classes in the cities received more services, and the quality of government improved. The Progressive Era initiated a long period in which city schools, hospitals, parks, police and fire departments, welfare agencies, and city-owned utilities made life better for generations of urbanites.

Woman Progressives Women were prominent in many of these progressive reforms. Through the settlement house movement and their various organizations, they promoted and undertook a variety of projects to improve the quality of urban life. Their concerns ranged from temperance to lighting and sewer systems to art museums. They brought to taming the urban jungle their own special advocacy of domestic virtues, the virtues, so they thought, that were in the keeping of women. Jane Addams and Florence Kelly are notable among the many American women who saw community building as a special female responsibility.

Black women were every bit as active on behalf of their communities as white women were in aid of theirs. Lugenia Hope in Atlanta pioneered in clearing and supervising playgrounds for black children. The National Federation of Colored Women's Clubs undertook a vast array of activities. The Women's Convention of the Black Baptist Church raised money for dormitories so that young black women could attend colleges far from their homes. The Young Women's Christian Association had black chapters that were especially active among young black college women, who were expected to use their educations for the "uplift" of their families, their communities, and their race. In important respects, progressive reforms can be seen as attempts to make industrial society safe for women and their children. Much of the progressivism that required state inter-

THE SHAME OF THE CITIES *by Lincoln Steffens*

One of the most prominent muckrakers, Steffens stressed the link between business and politics, maintaining that privilege was the enemy, not city bosses alone.

"Philadelphia: Corrupt and Contented"

All our municipal governments are more or less bad. . . . Philadelphia is simply the most corrupt and the most contented. Minneapolis has cleaned up, Pittsburgh has tried to, New York fights every other election, Chicago fights all the time. Even St. Louis has begun to stir (since the elections are over), and at the worst was only shameless. Philadelphia is proud; good people there defend corruption and boast of their machine. . . .

The machine [in Philadelphia] controls the whole process of voting, and practices fraud at every stage. The assessor's list is the voting list, and the assessor is the machine's man. "The assessor . . . padded his lists with fraudulent names registered from his house. . . . The constable of the division kept a house [of prostitution]; a policeman was assessed as living there. . . . The election was held in the disorderly house maintained by the assessor. . . . The man named as judge had a criminal charge for a life offense pending against him. . . . Two hundred and fifty-two votes were returned in a division that had less than one hundred legal votes within its boundaries." These extracts from a report of the Municipal League suggest the election methods. The assessor pads the list with the names of dead dogs, children, and non-existent persons. One newspaper printed the picture of a dog, another that of a little four-year-old negro boy, down on such a list. A ringing orator in a speech resenting sneers at his ward as "low down" reminded his hearers that that was the ward of Independence Hall, and naming . . . signers of the Declaration of Independence, he closed his highest flight of eloquence with the statement that "these men, the fathers of American liberty, voted down here once. And," he added, with a catching grin, "they vote here yet."

---

vention in civil society and foreshadowed the welfare state of the twentieth century resulted from women's special concerns and campaigns.

For many of her generation Florence Kelley exemplified the best of the progressive spirit. After a failed marriage, in 1891 she left New York for the Hull House settlement in Chicago. She has left a remarkable account of her introduction to that remarkable place:

> On a snowy morning between Christmas 1891 and New Year's 1892, I arrived at Hull-House, Chicago, a little before breakfast time, and found there Henry Standing Bear, a Kickapoo Indian, waiting for the front door to be opened. It was Miss Addams who opened it, holding on her left arm a singularly unattractive, fat, pudgy baby belonging to the cook, who was behindhand with breakfast. Miss Addams was a little hindered in her movements by a super-energetic kindergarten child, left by its mother while she went to a sweatshop for a bundle of cloaks to be finished.
>
> We were welcomed as though we had been invited. We stayed, Henry Standing Bear as helper to the engineer several months, when he returned to his tribe; and I as a resident seven happy, active years until May 1, 1899, when I returned to New York City to enter upon the work in which I have since been engaged as secretary of the National Consumers' League.
>
> I cannot remember ever again seeing Miss Addams hold a baby, but that first picture of her gently keeping the little Italian girl back from charging out into the snow, closing the door against the blast of wintry wind off Lake Michigan, and tranquilly welcoming these newcomers, is as clear today as it was at that moment.
>
> Henry Standing Bear had been camping under a wooden sidewalk which surrounded a vacant lot in the neighborhood, with two or three members of his tribe. They had been precariously employed by a vendor of a hair improver, who had now gone into bankruptcy leaving his employees a melancholy Christmas holiday. Though a graduate of a government Indian school, he had been trained to no way of earning his living and was a dreadful human commentary upon Uncle Sam's treatment of his wards in the Nineties.

Florence Kelley's work at Hull House

helped lead to the creation in 1893 of the first state law regulating the hours and working conditions of women and children, and Governor John Peter Altgeld appointed her the first chief of factory inspection. Altgeld, Kelley later wrote, wanted the law enforced to the hilt, but the district attorney for Cook County, which includes Chicago, refused to prosecute any of the cases Kelley and her staff brought. Kelley thereupon acted in conformity with her approach to social reform, and to life in general. She enrolled in Northwestern University's Law School, completed her law degree by 1894, and successfully prosecuted the factory safety law violators herself.

When Governor Altgeld was defeated for reelection in 1897, Kelley lost her job of chief factory inspector. She proceeded to help organize a new kind of public interest lobby, the Illinois Consumers' League in 1898. The League published a "white list" of companies that lived up to the law and urged its members, most of them middle and upper-class women, to boycott manufacturers who did not earn the League's seal of approval. There was scarcely a progressive cause in which Florence Kelley did not play a leading role. Newton D. Baker, a fellow reformer and later Woodrow Wilson's secretary of war during World War I, summed up her ability to inspire a whole generation of young women, and men: "Everybody was brave from the moment she came into the room."

State Progressivism

Urban progressives quickly found themselves at the state legislatures demanding new laws to carry out their programs, including various forms of home rule. State franchise laws might restrict what a city could do in dealing with its utilities and streetcar lines, and laws passed in the state legislature might undo reforms achieved in the cities. In 1902, for example, the Ohio legislature, seeking to defeat Samuel "Golden Rule" Jones's campaign against police brutality, removed from the mayor's jurisdiction the police and the police courts of the city of Toledo.

The city reformers found allies in the state government among rural and small-town reformers seeking to control railroad rates, reduce tariffs, improve rural life, increase farm credit, and attack trusts and banks. Rural progressivism became a powerful force in the Midwest and Far West, as well as in parts of the South, and eventually even entered eastern states, among them Massachusetts and New Jersey.

Progressives, both urban and rural, recoiled against the emergence of new and, in their eyes, dangerous sources of power. These included urban political machines, which through voter fraud and other corrupt practices seemed to make a mockery of the idea of self government, and giant corporations, which appeared to have the power to control both wages and prices. Progressives labeled these giant businesses and their political allies "the interests," while they called themselves the defenders of "the public" or "the public interest." Some, unlike their political cousins of a later age, were also hostile to labor unions, seeing them as another of the large concentrations of power that warred against simple democracy.

Political Reforms

While some progressives were pressing, especially at the city level, for clean and efficient mechanisms of government administration removed from the clash and vices of democracy, others worked to expand popular participation in the political process. Progressives stocked their arsenal for this campaign with a number of weapons. The Australian or secret ballot dated from the 1880s in the United States; by the end of the Progressive Era every state had adopted it. Laws limiting the uses and amounts of money spent in campaigns also spread in the first decade of the new century. The direct primary gave all members of a political party the opportunity to participate in the choice of the party's candidates, and was popular among innovations designed to make politics a more open and less boss-ridden process. The direct primary soon replaced the system of local conventions, which the bosses could easily manipulate. The initiative, referendum, and recall were experiments in direct democracy. The initiative is a process in which a number of citizens, by signing a petition, can offer a new law for consideration. The referendum is a direct popular vote on whether to accept a proposed law. The recall refers to a popular vote that can remove officials from office before the expiration of their terms.

The ultimate effect of these structural reforms has been a subject of controversy. Some political scientists believe that in loosening party organization the direct primary actually weakened the democratic process and increased the importance of money in elections. The initiative and referendum, they point out, can serve conservative as well as progressive purposes and can require expensive organizing and lobbying campaigns. Yet these reforms have in fact lent themselves predominantly to progressive and liberal causes.

State Governors State-level progressivism began as a major force in 1900, when Robert M. La Follette became governor of Wisconsin. A central issue in Wisconsin was the way the state taxed railroads. They were the largest property owners in the state, and their taxes were based upon their annual earnings rather than upon the assessed value of their property. This meant that during the depression following the panic of 1893 the railroads' tax burden dropped, from seventy-two percent of the state's tax revenues in 1892 to forty-seven percent in 1897. For all other property owners, however, taxes remained the same or went up. So La Follette was able to tap into deep pools of popular resentment when he made the railroads' privileged position a major issue. After legislative opponents defeated his initial moderate reform package, La Follette, stamping, demanding, and scolding, created a majority for reform and then ruled it tightly. Stubborn, humorless, and fiercely independent, La Follette became a reform boss, ruthless in the use of patronage, absolute in his demand for loyalty, implacable in dispatching his enemies in the good cause of honest government.

La Follette pushed through a wide range of political reforms: the direct primary, anti-lobbying laws, and civil service acts. Determined to make state government efficient and useful as well as honest, he called on outstanding academic experts to draft legislation, sit on commissions, and generally improve the quality of government. And there was a lot to do in Wisconsin. La Follette's reform program included a strong railroad-rate commission, sharp increases in the taxes paid by corporations and railroads, conservation and water power measures, state banking regulation, and a host of other social and economic reforms. Under his prodding, Wisconsin became the first state to pass a graduated income tax. Theodore Roosevelt, always ready with an apt phrase, called Wisconsin "the laboratory of democracy."

Where Wisconsin led, other states followed. Albert Baird Cummins in Iowa, Joseph Folk in Missouri, Jeff Davis in Arkansas, Hiram Johnson in California, Hoke Smith in Georgia, Charles Evans Hughes in New York, and Woodrow Wilson in New Jersey were among the governors of the era who adopted the Wisconsin Idea, as it was labeled, and in various degrees succeeded in modernizing their state governments and passing political and economic reform legislation. During much of the nineteenth century, state government had addressed little energy to the development of large social and economic policy. Revitalization of state government was one of the major achievements of the Progressive Era.

Theodore Roosevelt Becomes President

As the nationwide economy became increasingly close-knit, there were still other reforms that only the federal government could undertake. Only it could effectively guarantee the safety of medicines; only it could regulate interstate commerce. Working against these progressive hopes was a century-long tradition of hostility to strong central government strengthened by a series of Supreme Court decisions that had substantially weakened the Interstate Commerce Commission and virtually destroyed the Sherman Anti-Trust Law. Early in the new century, the leadership of a national progressive movement began to emerge. A number of progressive governors like "Fighting Bob" La Follette entered the United States Senate, and in 1901 Theodore Roosevelt became President.

The Last Nineteenth-Century President

President William McKinley's election victories in 1896 and 1900 established the Republicans as the majority party in national political life. Democrats and Republicans were no longer fighting with the narrow partisan intensity of equal competitors. That, along with the divisions within the Democratic Party that the Bryan campaign had brought, turned politics away from the old partisan issues that had grown out of the Civil War and Reconstruction. New publics—the concerned citizens of the cities and towns eager to assume more control of their surroundings, women active in social movements, the new professionals, the increasingly self-aware immigrant groups—could support a new national politics fixed on the issues of industrialism, urban life, and the growing interdependence of all communities across the nation. McKinley remained in some sense a politician of the old kind. Standing close behind him, however, cautiously nursing hopes for the presidential nomination in 1904, Vice President Theodore Roosevelt was eager to enter the twentieth century.

Then a cloudy-minded young man, Leon Czolgosz—whose knowledge of anarchism scarcely extended beyond the popular information that anarchists had a habit of assassinating rulers like czars and kings—pumped two bullets into McKinley. A black man courageously seized the assassin's gun, but he was too late. The President, shot on September 6, 1901, while attending the Pan-American Exposition at Buffalo, died on September 14. Roosevelt, informed while in Vermont, sped by special train to Buffalo. His ambition, and the great difference between the two men in age and ideology, impressed contemporaries. Rumors circulated of a cursing J. P. Morgan, his face a flaming red, staggering to his desk in fear that the government might wage war on his interests. A song stressed Roosevelt's eagerness for the White House, his aristocratic background, and his reputation for horsemanship:

> He jumped on his horse and pulled down through Maine:
> He said to his horse you've got to outrun this train [carrying McKinley's body];
> Buffalo to Washington.
> Now Roosevelt's in the White House drinking out of a silver cup.
> McKinley's in the graveyard, he'll never wake up.
> He's gone; he's gone.

McKinley was gone, and national progressivism had its leader.

The First Twentieth-Century President

Just under forty-three years old when he took office, Theodore Roosevelt was by far the youngest President in American history up to that time. He contrasted sharply with the staid chief executives of the previous quarter century. Articulate, excitable, and energetic, with a range of interests extending far beyond politics, he and his young family, particularly his beautiful daughter Alice, lent a glamour and excitement to national events. Already famous as a military hero, he immediately captured a vast public, becoming its beloved "Teddy." A young girl in the 1870s had written in her diary of the adolescent Theodore: "He is such fun . . . the most original boy I ever knew." Throughout his life, he remained fun for millions of his adorers. Perhaps, too, he remained a most original boy as well: "You must always remember," wrote a friend, "that the President is about six." The ebullient man with the thick pince-nez glasses over his large nose, the face as square as his moralism, the gleaming teeth, the vigorous gesturing style was a cartoonist's delight. A college classmate long before had wondered "whether [Roosevelt] is the real thing, or only the bundle of eccentricities he appears." The public soon discovered that he was the real thing, a skillful leader and shrewd politician as well as a colorful character.

Theodore Roosevelt had been born in 1858, the first child of a public-spirited New York merchant and a southern lady. The Roosevelts' Manhattan brownstone was scarcely a log cabin, and the young Roosevelt was hardly an instinctive democrat. Even at Harvard he chose his company carefully. Graduating twenty-first in his class of 158—a creditable showing—he wrote his sister that "only one gentleman stands ahead of me." His precocious interest in nature and love of the outdoors almost led him to a career in science. Perhaps he was too much the dilettante for such a calling. Young Theodore needed a career to satisfy his enthusiasms for literature, sports, society, and nature, to meet his father's high ideals of public service, and to give him a limitless field in which to compete. For he was one of the most competitive of men, whether in boxing, hunting, politics, or literature.

With time out for exploring the Dakotas and for literary endeavors, Roosevelt pursued a career of elitist public service. He received appointment to various offices for which his energy and connections made him suitable: the United States Civil Service Commission, the Board of Commissioners of the New York City Police, and assistant secretary of the navy (1897–98). Meanwhile, he was available when the Republican machine needed a reform candidate, as happens periodically to every political machine however wicked its usual behavior. In 1886 he was an unsuccessful Republican candidate for mayor of New York City. In 1898, after he had become famous in the war with Spain for leading the Rough Riders in their charge up San Juan Hill, and with the state party facing a scandal, he was elected governor of New York.

Roosevelt acquitted himself well as governor, just as he had in his other offices. Well organized, hard working, and with a flair for the dramatic, he was successful and popular. He showed that he could battle to improve the public service without wholly alienating the professional politicians. His New York State progressivism was a modest eastern version of the Wisconsin Idea.

Reformers put in office by machine politicians rarely serve more than one term. New York Republican boss Tom Platt, thoroughly tired of struggling with the moralistic governor that fate and scandals had forced on him, easily maneuvered Roosevelt out of the statehouse and into the vice presidency, a usually trivial office and to Roosevelt's mind maddeningly dull for a "comparatively young man." McKinley's previous Vice President, Garret A. Hobart, had died in office.

Roosevelt was superbly suited for the presidency. He was ready to preach to a nation that wanted a new kind of secular preacher. He had advanced ideas about the needs of an industrial society, but he would couch them in words of a plain and traditional morality. His zest for competition led him to revive disused powers of the office. He was in touch

As President, Roosevelt became a kind of secular preacher whose plain and traditional morality greatly appealed to the American middle class. *(Courtesy, Brown Brothers)*

with the new generation and its new ideas, yet he was a Republican regular in an age of clear Republican majorities. Most of all, he was a good speaker at the end of a period of great American oratory, a telling phrasemaker in an age of popular literacy, and good copy in the finest age of American journalism.

"I wish to say that it shall be my aim to continue, absolutely unbroken, the policy of President McKinley for the peace, prosperity, and the honor of our beloved country," Theodore Roosevelt promised his cabinet just before taking the presidential oath. Roosevelt had many good reasons to avoid any sudden upsets at the beginning of his accidental administration. The McKinley Administration's identification with prosperity, after the harsh depression of the nineties, meant that any upset of business confidence would be blamed directly on the White House, which might then get a new occupant after the 1904 election. The focus of power in

Washington was, meanwhile, not in the White House, but at the other end of Pennsylvania Avenue, especially in the United States Senate.

Roosevelt vs. the Senate The Senate was the keystone that joined and held together the overarching powers of business and the Republican Party. Organized under tight party discipline to a far greater extent than it had been earlier or would be later, the upper House was ruled by a handful of powerful Republicans. Nelson W. Aldrich of Rhode Island, John C. Spooner of Wisconsin, Orville H. Platt of Connecticut, and William B. Allison of Iowa—called "The Four" by contemporaries—ran the formal machinery of the Senate. Mark Hanna of Ohio had been the administration's man in the Senate during the McKinley presidency and was the party's great fundraiser. All directly represented the major industries, frankly seeking subsidies and favors for their pet interests while standing firm against any reforms that might disturb "confidence," meaning the happiness of big business. Roosevelt worried them; they could see his assertive personality, knew his active governorship of New York, and were old enough to remember that the presidency could be transformed into an immensely powerful office, as during the Civil War.

Roosevelt had no intention of remaining within the mold the leadership had cast for his office. But he wisely refrained from hopeless confrontation with The Four. He saw that he would have to begin with activities remote from legislation in order to develop a public and to exercise the long-disused muscles of the office. He would turn the presidency—as he wished to turn all life—into drama. Even his everyday routine was designed to invoke wonder and fasten attention on the White House. At his desk every morning by 8:30, he saw dozens of groups each day, not just senators and other party dignitaries, but writers, reformers, social workers, scientists, even labor leaders. The great Spanish cellist Pablo Casals performed in the White House, as he would do again sixty years later when John F. Kennedy was in office. And Roosevelt saw people during breakfast, lunch, and dinner, and during his daily horseback ride through Rock Creek Park. Scarcely a month after moving into the White House he defied white supremacist custom, inviting the most celebrated black leader of the era, Booker T. Washington to sit down at lunch with him. When white southerners protested the symbolic gesture bitterly, Roosevelt announced that he would have Dr. Washington "to dine just as often as I please"—though the politic President was never again pleased to do so.

The Roosevelt Leadership

Roosevelt and the Trusts Five months after taking office, the President took his first large action. It was on the "absolutely vital question," as he would later call it, of government regulation of the large corporations. J. P. Morgan provided Roosevelt's opportunity when, late in 1901, he formed the Northern Securities Company. The new holding company controlled the Northern Pacific Railroad and the Great Northern Railroad. This $400 million combination was essentially a peace treaty that Morgan imposed on all the groups competing for rail traffic in the Northwest. The first important holding company, it brought together the Hill, Harriman, Rockefeller, and Morgan interests and inflated their holdings by one-third. It extended across the country the Morgan rail monopoly of the eastern lines, bringing unified management and the threat of higher rates to a large part of the nation's shippers. Though unpopular with the public, it seemed safe from attack, since in *United States v. E. C. Knight Company* (1895) the Supreme Court had sharply restricted the scope of the Sherman Antitrust Act. Roosevelt, consulting only Attorney General Philander C. Knox, ordered him to file suit for the dissolution of the holding company. The Supreme Court, in effect reversing the Knight decision, would uphold the President in *Northern Securities Company v. United States* (1904).

The image of trustbuster that Roosevelt gained in his confrontation with Northern Securities and other companies was more important than any particular antitrust actions he undertook. There is little question that

TR's aversion to trusts was sincere. Just before the election of 1904 he had written in a private letter:

> Corporation cunning has developed faster than the laws of nation and State. Corporations have found ways to steal long before we have found that they were susceptible of punishment for theft. Sooner or later, unless there is a readjustment, there will come a riotous, wicked, murderous day of atonement. There must come, in the proper growth of this nation, a readjustment. If it is not to come by sword and powder and blood, it must come by peaceful compromise. These fools in Wall Street think that they can go on forever! They can't!
>
> I would like to be elected President of the United States to be the buffer between their foolishness and the wrath that is surely to come—unless they sober up.

But as a weapon with which to attack shrewd and powerful businessmen, the Sherman Act was largely inefficient, and Roosevelt did not necessarily believe in breaking up most large corporations. Rather, he wished to use the threat of antitrust action to establish the precedent of regulation and to assure the public that the presidency stood above the demands of any one economic interest group. Roosevelt objected to Morgan's attempt to treat the government, in effect, as an equal and rival party during the edgy negotiations between the government and the Northern Securities Company. It offended Roosevelt that Morgan could apparently not see the moral distance between a business and the government of the United States. Yet once the regulatory power of government was accepted in principle, he was eager to negotiate a "gentlemen's agreement" to approve in advance new acquisitions to the vast Morgan empire. Running with both the hounds and the hares, Roosevelt made his point without alienating either the Senate or the business community.

After the Northern Securities case, Roosevelt had considerable success with Congress. It agreed to establishing within the Department of Commerce and Labor, which was then being organized, a Bureau of Corporations that would collect statistics and investigate the activities of corporations. The Elkins Act, passed with railroad support in 1903, outlawed rebates to large shippers and increased the powers of the Interstate Commerce Commission. Together these acts created an enduring American legend. A song written during his second administration presents the popular Roosevelt image:

> Not long ago the railroads owned the whole United States,
> Their rates were high to farmers, but a trust could get rebates,
> Who stopped this crime of freight rebates among the railroad men?
> Who fixed it so the railroads carry people now and then?
> It's Theodore, the peaceful Theodore;
> Of all the rulers great or small
> He is the greatest of them all.

TR and Labor Roosevelt sought to find moral grounds for distinguishing good corporations that increased services and efficiency or lowered prices from bad ones that limited competition and raised prices. He reached the same position on labor unions, which had also flourished in the years of trust building and inflation after 1897. In 1902, when old conflicts between the operators and the workers again erupted in the coal fields, Roosevelt had an opportunity to push the presidency into relations between labor and management in a way that

"The President's Dream of a Successful Hunt"
(Courtesy, Library of Congress)

would establish his conception of a "square deal" for all sides. The Square Deal was the first of a number of twentieth-century administrative slogans, a precedent for the New Deal, the Fair Deal, the New Frontier, and the Great Society.

In 1900 the anthracite coal workers had threatened a massive strike. Anthracite was the hard coal used to heat houses and workplaces, and despite the ready availability of a usable substitute, bituminous or soft coal, Americans feared for the misery that might come once the coal cars stopped rumbling over the Pennsylvania hills. To head off this election-year threat, Mark Hanna persuaded the operators to make concessions to the union. Two years later, however, when John Mitchell, the United Mine Workers' president, called for a new wage scale, the operators determined to crush the union. They rejected all overtures for negotiation, refusing not only a wage increase but any recognition, formal or informal, of the union.

Despite the rising bitterness of his men, whose gains of two years before had vanished with inflation, Mitchell remained moderate in his demands and restrained in his tactics. Told that the miners had to contend with miserable conditions, the leader of the operators, George F. Baer, insisted that the miners "don't suffer; why, they can't even speak English." On May 12, 1902, the miners began the largest strike to date in American history. Mitchell kept his men in order, also seeing to it that the soft-coal workers stayed in the mines digging coal to compete with anthracite and contributed part of their paychecks to the strike fund.

Roosevelt hoped at first to bring an antitrust prosecution against the six railroad corporations that owned seventy percent of the mines and controlled the movement of the coal to market, but Attorney General Knox did not consider the case strong enough. As summer dragged into fall with the price of coal soaring and the public in fear of a cold snap, first Mark Hanna and then Roosevelt made efforts to end the strike. But the operators steadily rejected all overtures. The New York City schools closed down for lack of fuel. Finally Roosevelt, "at my wits' end how to proceed," and supported even by conservative Republican leaders, took the novel step of inviting to the White House the leaders of both the operators and the union.

It was a dramatic scene as these men who were not speaking to each other assembled, and Roosevelt, in a wheelchair from a recent accident, pleaded for a settlement. Mitchell offered to accept binding arbitration, but Baer, a few months before having announced that "God in his infinite wisdom" had appointed the coal owners to their post, vilified Mitchell and (in Roosevelt's careful prose) "in at least two cases assumed an attitude toward me which was one of insolence."

Threatening a military seizure of the mines unless the owners agreed to arbitration, Roosevelt got J. P. Morgan, the most influential American financier, to agree to back arbitration. The men went back to work and the threat of warfare in the coal country faded. The board of arbitration Roosevelt set up gave the workers a ten percent pay hike and corrected some minor abuses, but on the larger issue of recognition the union lost totally. The board passed on the cost of the settlement to the public by granting the operators a ten percent increase in prices.

Nonetheless, Roosevelt had broken decisively with the federal practice of intervening only in the interests of public order, and therefore on the side of management. Government as a third force in disputes between labor and management was now an accomplished fact. Roosevelt had at last provided a response to the middle-class fear of being squeezed to pieces between labor and capital. Whether or not he had made the system work better, he made labor and the public feel better.

The Second Term

The Election of 1904

Roosevelt's nomination for a term on his own was a foregone conclusion. He had won the hearts of the people and the heads of the leaders. The Democratic opposition, having nowhere to go, went nowhere. Outflanked on the left by Roosevelt's initiatives, they turned away from William Jennings Bryan to nominate a colorless New York judge, Alton B. Parker. The Republican

National Committee collected almost three-quarters of its gifts from large corporations, and Roosevelt swept to an overwhelming victory. Flawless political management simply added to Roosevelt's huge personal acclaim. His one blunder came on election night when, as part of his victory statement, he announced that "under no circumstances will I be a candidate for or accept another nomination." Roosevelt, who would be only fifty years old when he left office, was to have abundant cause to regret this noble pledge.

The second Roosevelt Administration was quite different from the first—in some ways far more successful, in other ways less so. Roosevelt's initiatives grew bolder, while opposition within his own party rose. As he widened the national agenda of reform, he began to strain the Republican alliance.

In the months after his election, Roosevelt announced a comprehensive set of goals. Noting that the Elkins Act of 1903 had failed to end the rebate evil, he called for the strict regulation of railroads; he wanted greatly to increase the power of the Interstate Commerce Commission and limit court review of its actions. He also proposed employers' liability laws, a minimum wage for railroad workers, and for the District of Columbia—which the federal government directly ruled—a variety of regulations, covering child labor, factory inspection, and slum clearance, designed to make it a model of progressive legislation for the states.

The Hepburn Act

The Republican Congress wanted none of this. "Congress will pass the appropriation bills and mark time," predicted Speaker Joseph G. Cannon, the plain-spoken autocrat who ruled the House of Representatives. Roosevelt quickly decided to concentrate on regulation of the railroads, one of the two questions then exciting the Middle West and the West. The other was the tariff, a sensitive economic issue all over the country that the Republican leadership, happy with the current high rates, refused to touch.

Roosevelt's strategy was to threaten the leadership with a tariff bill in order to force concessions on railroad regulation. Cannon eventually swallowed his distaste for railroad regulation and allowed the House to pass stringent bills by huge majorities. But the Senate was more conservative. As yet no constitutional amendment provided for direct election of senators, and senators chosen by state legislatures could afford to give their services freely to big business. Senator Aldrich used all his formidable parliamentary skills to block a strong bill. But the President, continuing to whip up the wrath of the small shippers and farmers and rallying middle-class opinion to the cause, kept a steady pressure on the Senate. He played off radicals and conservatives against each other, finally accepted a few painful compromises, and got a useful bill.

The Hepburn Act, as passed in 1906, allowed the Interstate Commerce Commission to set railroad rates on the complaint of a shipper, these to be subject to court review. It permitted the ICC to examine the railroads' books and prescribed bookkeeping standards. What it did not do was to permit the ICC to conduct valuations of the worth of a road's physical property, a power that Robert La Follette had argued was essential to the fixing of fair rates. The judicial review permitted under the act was broad: the courts could pass not only on the procedures of the commission but on whether the rates set were "reasonable." The act was nonetheless epoch-making. For the first time, a governmental body was empowered actually to set rates, and for the first time such an agency could open the books of the companies.

Consumer Legislation

The whole question of consumer protection also had its origins in the Progressive Era. The quality of processed food and drugs had never before been much of an issue.

Most Americans traditionally lived on farms in rural areas; they raised, cooked, and ate their own food. All that changed in the cities. Urban dwellers purchased food in local stores, and they knew little about where it had come from, how it had been processed, or how long it had been on the shelf. That problem of food processing was especially acute in the marketing of meat. Rural Americans had always raised, processed, and preserved their own beef, pork, and poultry. They knew which animals had been sick, which ones had been healthy, and how much time had passed since the animals had been slaughtered. But buyers of meat in city stores or butcher shops had none of that information. New preserving processes and the introduction of artificial flavorings and colorings in food and meat had made it increasingly uncertain what exactly the public was purchasing. In the cities food poisoning, from salmonella to the deadly botulism, became increasingly common.

City people experienced a similar problem with drugs. Back on the farm, they had used herbs and folk medicines, family healing practices handed down from one generation to another. The real efficacy of the potions, of course, was debatable, but at least the cures were usually not worse than the diseases. Rural Americans might from time to time hear marvelous claims from snake-oil peddlers selling magic medicine from the backs of wagons. But in the cities people were more vulnerable to the mass marketing and mass advertising techniques of pharmaceutical companies. It was not uncommon for those companies to exaggerate the potency of certain drugs, market veterinary products for human use, or distribute new drugs that had not been adequately tested, or even tested at all.

For years the lone voice in the consumer wilderness had been that of Dr. Harvey W. Wiley, the chief chemist for the Department of Agriculture. He regularly tested food and drug products and was appalled at what he considered to be unsafe chemical tampering with the public health. Wiley demanded federal regulation of the food processing and drug manufacturing industries.

With the support of President Theodore Roosevelt and the public impact of Upton Sinclair's muckraking novel *The Jungle*, Congress addressed the problem and in June 1906 passed landmark legislation. The Pure Food and Drug Act prohibited the manufacture, sale, or transportation across state lines of foods and drugs that had been adulterated or carried fraudulent labeling. The Meat Inspection Act was targeted at cleaning up the packinghouses. It established sanitary regulations for meatpacking plants and provided for federal inspection of all companies selling meats in interstate markets.

Origins of the Conservation Movement Several important conservationists of the nineteenth and early twentieth century had been well in advance of the thinking of President Roosevelt, whose own ideas were in turn ahead of those of most Americans. Frederick Law Olmsted, a landscape architect most famous for planning New York's Central Park, had promoted the creation of city parks because they fostered health and offered a refuge from the growing pace of urban life. John Wesley Powell, an adventurer who sailed down the Colorado River, mapped and classified the resources of much of the West and offered a plan to develop arid regions responsibly. George Perkins Marsh wrote in the pathbreaking *Man and Nature* (1864) about the "improvident waste" of natural resources. Once nature was dominated by man, Marsh believed, it could not revert to its primitive condition and so remained forever impoverished. John Muir decried the dominance of man over nature and offered a theory of biocentrism as a value far superior to a rampant man-centeredness.

George Catlin, a painter and one of the earliest environmentalists, envisioned

> a Nation's Park, containing man and beast, in all the wild and freshness of nature's beauty

Catlin wished no other memorial than credit for having elaborated the concept of a park for the nation. Yellowstone in the northwest corner of Wyoming Territory first realized his dreams in 1872 when President Grant gave the nation a great treasure of lakes, clear rivers, forests, geysers, and incredible beauty all around. Sequoia Park and Mount Ranier Park followed in the 1890s. By the turn of the century the conservation movement was ripe for national leadership.

From his founding of the "Roosevelt Museum of Natural History" in an upstairs bookcase sometime before he reached the age of ten, Theodore Roosevelt had maintained a continuous passion for nature. His interest was both scientific and romantic. In his public life it translated into a concern for the conservation of natural resources. The government should "make the streams and rivers of the arid region useful by engineering works for water storage," he wrote in supporting what became the Newlands Act of 1902 to reclaim arid lands in the West. The goal of conservation policy was to insure that the use of natural resources would be "in such manner as to keep them unimpaired for the benefit of the children now growing up to inherit the land." Always the emphasis was on use, on policies that would employ the country's natural wealth efficiently and without destruction of it. After centuries of reckless exploitation of a seemingly inexhaustible treasury of land, water, plants, animals, and minerals, making conservation a national movement was TR's most decisive precedent for the new century. He established national parks, wildlife refuges, and monuments, set aside hundreds of millions of acres as national forests and nationally controlled mineral lands, and put federal land and water policy on a solid and coherent basis.

"Is there any law that will prevent me from declaring Pelican Island a Federal Bird Reservation?" President Roosevelt inquired in 1903. Told that there was not, he announced, "Very well, then I so do declare it." In the next six years, he so declared fifty more times, establishing a substantial network of federal wildlife refuges. Congress, particularly westerners, reacted harshly to his setting aside 150 million acres of land as national forests, imposing limits on their exploitation while his chief forester developed stringent regulations on their cutting. In 1907 an amendment to the Agricultural Appropriations Act (which Roosevelt had to sign to keep the Forestry Service going) forbade the laying aside in six western states of any additional forest reserves. Roosevelt and Pinchot hurriedly established twenty-one new forest reserves totaling sixteen million acres while the bill sat on the President's desk. Only after officially proclaiming the new reserves did Roosevelt sign the appropriations bill, amid rising protest against "executive usurpation" and complaints from the Far West that the policy was retarding the region's economic development.

Toward the end of his second term Roosevelt—noting the continued rise of labor, the growing strength of socialism, the clear distrust of the wealthy in the public mind, the discomfort over rising prices, and the desire for reform—preached an increasingly radical message. He called for "industrial reform" to give the workingman a "larger share of the wealth." Yet the battle over forest reserves was one of the last successes of Roosevelt's second administration. Only Teddy's indomitable good spirits and self-righteousness saved him from discouragement, for his legislation proceeded no further.

Nor were Roosevelt's actions always in harmony with his inflamed words. He gave informal approval to the Morgan interests when they proposed having United States Steel purchase the Tennessee Coal and Iron Company, a financially troubled competitor whose acquisition would give the House of

Theodore Roosevelt's daughter Alice added to the aura of glamour and excitement surrounding the President. *(Courtesy, Library of Congress)*

Morgan control of over sixty percent of iron and steel production. Unlike Standard Oil or the Santa Fe Railroad, U.S. Steel was a good trust in Roosevelt's mind because it had cooperated with his Bureau of Corporations.

Despite his increasingly broad denunciation of the corporations, Roosevelt did not want to destroy them; he wanted them to be orderly, predictable, rational, and moral. What this meant was clear to him, but to scarcely anyone else.

Roosevelt remained by far the most popular man in American life. He had succeeded in convincing millions both that he understood the new bustling world of giant industry, big labor, international rivalries, and mass immigration and that he retained and found applicable to this new world the moral values of a simpler time. His hand-chosen successor, the portly William Howard Taft, whom Roosevelt billed as a stout defender of "my policies," would have to be far more nimble than he looked to meet the demand for reform that Roosevelt had evoked.

Taft

"Get on the Raft with Taft, Boys" As secretary of war, Taft had become an informal "assistant President," carrying out presidential policies close to Roosevelt's heart, particularly in supervising the construction of the Panama Canal and in completing various initiatives in foreign policy. "If only there were three of you!" he had exclaimed to Taft upon appointing him. That would have been just under a half-ton of William Howard Tafts, for he weighed comfortably over 300 pounds. The one Taft available to Roosevelt performed many functions in addition to his duties at the War Department.

Yet for all his closeness to Roosevelt and his administrative experience, Taft was in some ways a curious choice. He had, as one historian puts it, risen "to the presidency through the appointive route." A loyal Republican lawyer from a distinguished Cincinnati family, Taft became the first governor general of the Philippines, a role in which he achieved outstanding success in quieting Filipino unrest and establishing limited self-government. In 1904 Roosevelt brought Taft into his cabinet, where he quickly became the first among equals. But his ability to lead the Republican Party and to provide the public with the image of presidential leadership that Roosevelt had created was far more questionable. "Politics, when I am in it, makes me sick," Taft admitted in 1906. William Jennings Bryan's energy at the head of the Democratic ticket was no match for Taft's well-financed campaign of 1908, and the Ohioan rolled up a million-vote popular margin.

Taft was a lackluster campaigner. A popular song written for the campaign of 1908 sang more loudly of Roosevelt than of the candidate:

> The greatest man that ever ran the greatest land on earth
> Is Teddy R., whose shining star is only in its birth.
> We'd like some more of Theodore, but Theodore has said,
> That TAFT was meant for President to follow in his stead.
>
> CHORUS:
> Get on the raft with Taft, boys
> Get in the winning boat,
> The man worthwhile, with the big glad smile,
> Will get the honest vote. . . .

At state and local levels, the Republicans did not fare quite so well. Taft ran ahead of the local Republican tickets. In all but a few states in which progressive Republicans dominated the party, the Democrats, though defeated in the presidential race, demonstrated renewed strength. And the progressive Republicans would be demanding that the new President continue Roosevelt's pressure against the standpatters in the House and Senate.

New Reforms Taft received little credit from contemporaries for carrying out Roosevelt's reform policies. He deserved much recognition for doing just that. Taft enforced the Sherman Act with far more vigor, if less drama, than had Roosevelt. Roosevelt in eight years had brought forty-four antitrust suits; Taft's Attorney General George W. Wickersham in four years brought sixty-five. Roosevelt had carefully avoided

President Taft enjoying a round of golf.
(Courtesy, Library of Congress)

the issue of tariff revision, but Taft plowed into this thicket, securing an unsatisfactory—and politically disastrous—bill, the Payne-Aldrich tariff, which in fact did reduce some rates. If the Hepburn Act of 1906 was the first measure to put some teeth into railroad regulation, then the Mann-Elkins Act of 1910, which Taft supported and helped lobby into law, was a great white shark. "Bully! Bully!" Taft, for once in a Rooseveltean mood, exclaimed to reporters upon hearing that the bill had passed. Mann-Elkins enabled the Interstate Commerce Commission to initiate rate changes and to regulate telephone, telegraph, cable, and wireless companies, and placed squarely on a railroad seeking to raise a rate the burden of proof that the old rate was inequitable. The act's practical effect for some years was to prevent the railroads from raising rates. Liberal historians have praised Mann-Elkins for its securing effective control of rates. As a conservationist, Taft set aside forest reserves even more rapidly than had his predecessor.

Taft's record on labor issues was one that he could vigorously and correctly defend during the 1912 campaign:

> We passed a mining bureau bill to discover the nature of those dreadful explosions and loss of life in mines. We passed safety appliance bills to reduce the loss of life and limbs to railroad employees. We passed an employers' liability act to make easier recovery of damages by injured employees. We have just passed through the Senate a workman's compensation act . . . requiring the railroads to insure their employees against the accidents of a dangerous employment. We passed the children's bureau bill calculated to prevent children from being employed too early in factories. We passed the white phosphorus match bill to stamp out the making of white phosphorus matches which results in dreadful diseases to those engaged in their manufacture.

Taft might have added that he had appointed as chief of the new Children's Bureau a veteran labor reformer, Julia Lathrop, the first woman in American history to be appointed a bureau chief.

Perhaps most important of all was Taft's initiating of the process that resulted in the adoption of the Sixteenth Amendment, which in effect allowed the federal government to impose graduated personal income taxes that would rise proportionately with income. It is hard to see how without this levy any of the welfare state measures of later years could have been financed.

Nonetheless, Taft has gone down in history as both a conservative and a failure as President. (He would be more successful later as chief justice of the United States, from 1921 to 1930.) He carried out far too many progressive reforms to rank as a successful conservative, while his political ineptitude and his personal style made him a stranger to the progressives. Taft signed the Payne-Aldrich Tariff Bill of 1909 containing modest increases and infuriated the progressives. But Taft's most dramatic clash with progressives, dramatic because it pitted him directly against one of Roosevelt's closest friends, was in the Ballinger-Pinchot controversy.

The Ballinger-Pinchot Controversy

Richard A. Ballinger, Taft's new secretary of the interior, was a western lawyer sympathetic to the western view that favored making lands available for immediate development. Though committed to upholding federal law on conservation, he began soon after he took office to reverse what he considered to be illegal Roosevelt Administration actions in withdrawing public lands. Taft, referring tartly to the "transcendentalists" in Chief Forester Pinchot's office who had exceeded the law, had Ballinger return over a million acres to private hands. Pinchot, in retaliation, publicized the findings of an investigator in the General Land Office that Ballinger, before becoming secretary of the interior, had been involved in a shady land transaction that delivered an enormous windfall in Alaskan coal lands to a Morgan-Guggenheim syndicate.

Taft bought none of this; he exonerated Ballinger, although he went out of his way to state his continuing desire that Pinchot remain as chief forester. Pinchot, however, was not appeased, and he began a surreptitious press war against Ballinger and the President. Then he had a progressive senator read on the Senate floor a letter from Pinchot accusing Ballinger of being an enemy of conservation. Taft now had no choice but to fire Pinchot, and he then had to defend his action before a joint congressional committee investigating the affair. As he had feared, his defense of the secretary of the interior came across to the public as opposition to conservation and therefore to Roosevelt's policies.

Roosevelt returned from a much publicized African hunting trip in June 1910 bearing the hides of dozens of large animals and the hopes of the thousands of progressives now in conflict with Taft. Conservationists smarting over the Ballinger-Pinchot affair, progressive editors disappointed in Taft and angered as well by his plans to raise sharply the second-class postal rates that magazines paid, westerners disappointed with the Payne-Aldrich tariff, all looked to Roosevelt for an alternative. The ex-President promised that he would "make no comment or criticism for at least two months." But a vow of silence was the hardest possible promise for Roosevelt to keep. Within a week the newspapers were full of his opinions, and in less than two weeks they would note that he had conferred with both Pinchot and Senator La Follette, Taft's worst enemies.

The "New Nationalism" Late that summer Roosevelt, fearing an "ugly" party split, delivered two major speeches designed, he claimed, to provide "a common ground upon which Insurgents and Regulars can stand." But the speeches, particularly one at a gathering of Civil War veterans at Osawatomie, Kansas, had everything to horrify the regulars and cheer the progressives. Calling for a "New Nationalism" that would greatly extend the powers of the federal government, particularly over the corporations, and sharply criticizing the courts that stood in the way of such a program, the address made it obvious that Roosevelt had grown more radical. Taft complained that the speech "frightened every lawyer in the United States" and began identifying himself as a conservative.

With the Republicans in disarray, divided between western progressives and eastern conservatives, between Roosevelt men and Taft loyalists, the 1910 congressional elections warned of the dangers the party would face two years later. The House of Representatives went Democratic for the first time since 1892; state and local victories introduced to the public a fresh set of attractive, reform-minded Democrats such as Woodrow Wilson, a Virginian who had been president of Princeton University and was now governor of New Jersey. Among Republican candidates, it was western progressives who fared well, and Taft already considered progressives "assistant Democrats" rather than true members of his party.

The last act in this curious drama of personal and ideological division came in 1911, when Taft ordered an antitrust suit against the United States Steel Company. One prominent piece of evidence for the monopolistic character of U.S. Steel was the corporation's acquisition in 1907 of the Tennessee Coal and Iron Company, a deal that Roosevelt had tacitly approved and, so Teddy recalled, he had discussed with his secretary of war several times. Privately he excoriated Taft's "small, mean and foolish" act; publicly he attacked Taft's "archaic" attempt to break up the trusts when a better policy would be to regulate them effectively. So it was an issue on which Taft seemed more the progressive opponent of business than did Roosevelt, that put the two at irreconcilable odds.

The Election of 1912

A Four-Party Race

In 1912 progressive energies were surging. Of the four candidates who took the field in 1912—Taft for the Republicans, Woodrow Wilson for the Democrats, Roosevelt for the newly established Progressive Party, and Eugene V. Debs for the Socialists—even the most conservative among them, President Taft, could claim large credit for progressive ideas. By 1912, Roosevelt and Taft were publicly accusing each other of broken faith, dishonesty, and hypocrisy. As Roosevelt swept the presidential primaries (he even won Taft's home state of Ohio) and Taft used his patronage to pick up the delegates in the nonprimary states, the party split widened. The belligerent Roosevelt, confident that he had the support of the majority of Republicans, personally attended the national convention decked out in his Rough Rider outfit, topped by a giant sombrero. But the President's men, who controlled the party machinery, awarded themselves all the many disputed delegate seats and nominated their man with ease—while Roosevelt's supporters began to plan a new party.

The emergence of alternative parties—and in 1912 there would be two, the Socialists and the Roosevelt forces—can signify and make for political vigor, when ideas and programs are too insistent and various to be contained within the older organizations. So it was to be in 1912.

Furious at his loss to these "political thugs," and convinced that it was due to corruption in the selection of delegates, Roosevelt was ready to forsake the allegiance of a lifetime and bolt the Republican Party. When supporters guaranteed financial backing for a new party, the Progressive Party was born. Adopting the symbol of the bull moose—Roosevelt had once described himself as being as fit as a bull moose and the remark stuck—the party's national convention had the flavor of a religious revival. Roosevelt offered a "confession of faith"; delegates sang "Onward Christian Soldiers" and "The Battle Hymn of the Republic." The platform endorsed a wide range of progressive reforms, including unemployment insurance and old age pensions, woman suffrage, a tariff commission, tight regulation of the trusts, and national presidential primaries. The platform was stating the agenda for a generation of reform; by splitting the Republican Party, however, it was insuring that the Democratic Party would be the agent of reform.

After forty-six ballots interspersed with furious negotiations, the Democratic Party finally managed to nominate its ideal candidate, Woodrow Wilson, a native southerner who was attractive to many different elements within the party. As an intellectual, he was a fit match for Roosevelt. He had been a Gold Democrat in 1896, which pleased some, and had become a progressive by 1912, which pleased others. Most of all, he had been a Democratic executive who carried out a progressive program in New Jersey, a state that was eastern and Republican as well as infamous for its corruption and conservatism.

While Taft defended his record and Debs made earnest pleas for socialism, Roosevelt and Wilson clashed over a question that had been shaping itself during the progressive years: should the nation accept the increasing centralization of its economic and political life or should it break up concentrations of power?

Theodore Roosevelt, "Strong as a Bull Moose," became the candidate of the Progressive Party in the 1912 election. *(Courtesy, Roosevelt Memorial Association, New York City)*

The "New Nationalism" vs. the "New Freedom" Borrowing language from Herbert Croly's *The Promise of American Life* (1909), Roosevelt argued that Americans should recognize that the increasing organization and interrelatedness of their society was both inevitable and good. The trusts were good insofar as they could impose order on the nation's economy, and should therefore not be broken up. Instead, the government ought to regulate them more tightly and therein bring still more order and purpose to national life. In that spirit the government should take on responsibility for social welfare and for relations between labor and management. This New Nationalism, as the campaign termed it, was in a Republican tradition that as early as the party's founding had envisioned a unified country, its economy nourished by the federal government, as opposed to a country that was no more than a collection of states and localities.

Wilson's response—the product of long hours of discussion with "the people's lawyer," Louis D. Brandeis, a great legal mind of the age—was the New Freedom. Wilson demanded vigorous, effective antitrust activity that would open the avenues of commerce to new talent and energy. The rules of fair business dealing would be carefully established, and violators subjected to harsh penalties. Wilson was somewhat vague on how he would accomplish this restoration of competing small units, but the idea appealed to people frightened by bigness both in industry and in government.

Ex-President Taft escorting Woodrow Wilson to his inauguration. *(Courtesy, Underwood-Stratton, New York City)*

In the election Republican voters split, the progressives going for Roosevelt and the regulars for Taft. The Democrats won forty-two percent of the popular vote—not a majority, but a sizable plurality. Roosevelt gained a little over a quarter of the voters, and Taft a little less than a quarter. Even the Socialist candidate won nearly a million voters. Wilson had slid between two halves of a majority party to win the presidency. But even as a minority President he possessed a clear mandate for reform.

Woodrow Wilson

Like his great rival, Thomas Woodrow Wilson had decided while still a boy that he wanted to be a member of the governing class, but unlike TR he had no relish for the rough and tumble of politics. Instead he longed "to do immortal work." As a youth growing up in a South devastated by war and then embittered by Reconstruction, he found his models of greatness not in state or national leaders but in his father, a Presbyterian minister, and in the British prime minister, William Gladstone. Raised in relative comfort and able to move in the highest circles of southern society because of his father's calling, Wilson dreamed of becoming a great public figure, an American Gladstone. Wilson memorized speeches and practiced delivering them in his father's empty chapel. His Presbyterian background sometimes contributed to making him rigid in dealing with Congress, most notably in the later dispute over the League of Nations.

Wilson's college career, first at Davidson and then at Princeton, followed this same pattern. As he polished his oratorical skills, he read British and American history with great interest. He lamented "the decline of American oratory." The cause, Wilson wrote in a senior essay, was that in Congress decisions were made in committees whose members negotiated the contents of bills. In the British Parliament, to the contrary, bills were approved or rejected in open debate. Wilson's preference for what he thought to be the British system was lifelong, and it meant that he would disapprove of much of the American political machinery even when he was actively seeking to lead his state or country.

After Princeton Wilson studied law at the University of Virginia. But he had no desire to try cases "in an atmosphere of broken promises, of wrecked estates, of neglected trusts, of unperformed duties." So he returned to school, this time to the new graduate school at Johns Hopkins University, where he earned a doctorate in 1885. His dissertation, published as *Congressional Government* (1885), is a striking clue to the way Wilson's mind worked: he wrote this study in Baltimore, just a short train ride from Washington, but never attended a single congressional session or committee hearing. He praised the British system for uniting the legislative and executive powers in the person of the prime minister and extolled the superiority of parliamentary to congressional debate.

After a teaching career, in 1902 he became president of Princeton, a position from which he could address a national audience on the issues of the day. A believer in Anglo-Saxon superiority, he supported efforts to segregate public facilities in the South and criticized the "mongrel" races of southern and eastern Europe who formed the majority of the new immigration.

At Princeton Wilson recruited an outstanding faculty. In these respects Wilson succeeded brilliantly. But he soon found himself embroiled in a series of battles that would virtually drive him out of the university by 1910. One of the most important involved Princeton's exclusive eating clubs, which functioned snobbishly as fraternities. Wilson wanted to build a series of quadrangles where students from each class and some resident faculty members would live, eat, and study together. Many alumni voiced their disapproval, and, since their contributions were essential to the financial well-being of the university, their opposition convinced the trustees to withdraw support for Wilson's plans.

At the same time a new opportunity beckoned. If New Jersey's Democrats could find the right candidate, a candidate with a national reputation who could appeal to progressives while still able to work with the machine, they could win the gubernatorial contest in 1910. Wilson was able to appeal to progressives, but he broke his alliance with the conservative bosses, and as governor accomplished an impressive string of progressive legislative triumphs. Wilson's successes made him a plausible candidate for the Democratic presidential nomination in 1912.

Another Reform President

In the election of Woodrow Wilson, as in that of Theodore Roosevelt, progressivism triumphed nationally. Wilson's inaugural address called for reform of the tariff and the banking and currency system, for regulation of industry, and for conservation. Under conservation Wilson included the preservation of human resources. This notion that the government was to treat human beings as resources, promoting their health and development as assets to the national economy and society, was common among progressives.

Early in his administration Wilson, having called Congress into special session for reform of the tariff, did something that no President since George Washington had done: he appeared before Congress to present his program. The Underwood Tariff that he thereupon got through the national legislature cut rates; the same bill also imposed a federal graduated income tax—a progressive measure that the newly adopted Sixteenth Amendment to the Constitution made possible. Wilson kept Congress in session through the summer in order that it could achieve reform of banking and currency. The product was the Federal Reserve Act of 1913.

The Wilson Legislation The Act was the most impressive domestic measure of Wilson's administration. Yet its scope indicates something of the lim-

Woodrow Wilson. *(Courtesy, Library of Congress)*

its of American reformist ambitions when they translated themselves into actual legislation.

A major contributor to the popular sentiment for the reform had been an investigation by a congressional committee, with Representative Arsene Pujo as its chairman, of the "money trust," the forces that managed finance and credit. The Federal Reserve Act did make large changes. It set up a Federal Reserve system of twelve banks that would issue currency to private banks in exchange for secured notes that those banks received from their borrowers. A Federal Reserve Board, its members appointed by the President, was to set the rediscount rate that private banks would pay in trading their notes for Federal Reserve bills. All this provided for a more flexible currency, somewhat less dependent on the price of gold, than currency had been; and it established some public control over the banking system. But it was not a radical measure. It accepted and left almost completely intact the institution of private banking, and Wilson appointed to the Reserve Board bankers sympathetic to the banking business.

Other policies of the Wilson years had, in their application, a similar character of both reforming and accepting the basic nature of American business institutions. During Wilson's first term Congress passed several pieces of legislation designed to assist farmers in increasing production, improving the marketing of their crops, and gaining access to new sources of credit. These programs, in effect, treated farmers not as manual workers on the land but as business people, mini-capitalists.

The Smith-Lever Act of 1914, as an example, greatly strengthened the Department of Agriculture's extension services by creating a cooperative program with the state land-grant colleges. The federal government provided matching funds to state governments to build extension agencies in each county and help educate farmers in the latest techniques of scientific agriculture. But by working with the more prosperous farmers and by encouraging mass production on the farms, it unintentionally pointed agriculture in the direction that New Deal policies, again unwittingly, would later take it: toward consolidation into larger farming businesses.

Two other major pieces of farm legislation were adopted during Wilson's administration. The Warehouse Act of 1916 permitted licensed, bonded warehouses to store various commodities for farmers. The federal government designated the warehouse receipts as negotiable financial instruments that could serve as collateral for loans. Giving farmers a reliable source of working capital made it possible for them to hold crops off the market until prices were favorable. The Federal Farm Loan Act, also passed in 1916, created a Federal Farm Loan Board and twelve regional Federal Land Banks, which were designed to provide long-term loans to farmers at interest rates well below those offered by commercial banks.

The Federal Trade Commission Act, which Congress passed in 1914, was one of two laws that, in the spirit of Wilson's New Freedom, strengthened the federal government's power to break up trusts that were thought to squeeze out small businesses. The legislation dissolved Theodore Roosevelt's Bureau of Corporations and replaced it with a new Federal Trade Commission. The FTC had the authority to investigate corporate operations and issue rulings outlawing unfair and monopolistic business practices.

Three weeks after creating the FTC in September 1914, Congress passed the Clayton Antitrust Act. It contained stronger provisions for breaking up business trusts than the Sherman Antitrust Act had embodied. It outlawed interlocking corporate directorates among companies capitalized at more than $1 million as well as stock purchases and price discriminations in which the major objective was to lessen competition. It held corporate officials personally liable when companies violated federal antitrust laws. The Clayton Act also exempted labor unions from its provisions, outlawed most federal court injunctions in labor disputes, and legalized labor's right to strike and engage in picketing and boycotts. Although subsequent court decisions would weaken the Clayton Act, for the moment its provisions protecting organized labor appeared to promise fundamental change in the relations between workers and employers. Samuel Gompers termed it the "Magna Carta of Labor."

Wilson's first administration passed a series of laws designed to protect consumers and workers. The Harrison Narcotic Act of 1914 identified a number of pharmaceutical products that were not to be sold without a doctor's prescription. With the President's blessing, Senator Robert La Follette of Wisconsin pushed the Seaman's Act through Congress in 1915. At the time maritime workers were among the most exploited members of the country's labor force. The legislation established rules for fair treatment of the workers and for improving safety conditions. The Adamson Act of 1916 established the eight-hour day for railroad workers and guaranteed them time-and-a-half pay for overtime. To provide more jobs, to eliminate the exploitation of children, and, according to some historians, to make northern industries more competitive with southern industries where child labor was common, Congress passed the Keating-Owen Act in 1916. It outlawed child labor in enterprises engaged in interstate commerce. In 1918 the Supreme Court would find the law unconstitutional. The Workmen's Compensation Act of 1916 set up an insurance program for federal government employees. The insurance would compensate workers for injuries related to their jobs and provided death benefits to the families of workers killed on the job.

The Progressive Record

What emerged from Roosevelt's and Wilson's progressivism, and from the actions of President Taft's administration, was a collection of federal programs that imposed on business a degree of social responsibility and made it an active partner of government. This was not an entirely new concept. The nineteenth-century grants of federal lands to railroads for the building of lines needed by the nation as a whole had constituted a somewhat similar partnership. Presidential progressivism did, however, much expand the practice of putting business to the service of the public, adding some fairly sharp restraints on private enterprise. But the Wilson Administration did little for black Americans; and in fact this Democratic administration, tied to a party that had the white South as one of its major bases, extended segregation in government.

Black Americans

The Oppression of Blacks

In the postwar decades of Reconstruction and the rebuilding of the "New South," slavery was replaced by other forms of economic and social bondage. Sharecropping and peonage, along with the tightening of racial segregation in the form of Jim Crow laws, assured white southerners of continued control over the black population.

Throughout the late nineteenth century about one hundred blacks each year were lynched in the South, and the practice continued in significant numbers into the mid-1920s. The ostensible reason for this mob violence was usually attempted rape, but in most cases the lynch mob was functioning to maintain white control of blacks. The federal government, including the Supreme Court, ignored this abuse, as well as the practice of leasing black prisoners to road building contractors in states like Georgia. One survivor of that system called it "hell itself." As late as 1931–32 the "Scottsboro boys" were imprisoned in Alabama for rape on the testimony of two white prostitutes, one of whom later recanted her testimony. The last Scottsboro boy, Andrew Wright, got free at the age of thirty-nine, remarking then of Alabama justice:

> I am just like a rabbit in a strange wood, an the dogs is after him and no place to hide.

The poll tax, a tax on voting, discouraged blacks from exercising the franchise. Another device for turning blacks away from the polls was the "grandfather clause." A state might impose certain requirements stiff enough to exclude from the polls both blacks and a substantial portion of the white population; at the same time it would set aside those requirements for anyone whose grandfather would have possessed the right to vote—and that waiver meant, of course, that whites could vote. In these years of oppression arose three major black figures who defined the ideological perceptions of American black society from 1880 to 1930.

Booker T. Washington, founder of Tuskegee Institute in Alabama in 1881. Some criticized his gradualist, conciliatory approach to race relations, but he was very much a man of action who often defied traditional racial conventions. *(Courtesy, Library of Congress)*

Booker T. Washington The period from 1880 to 1915 has been characterized as the age of Booker T. Washington—a period when his ideology of self-help and accommodation to the fact of segregation held ascendance. Black church life, business, family, and organizational activities adapted easily to Washington's philosophy, which offered a means of dealing with the extremes of discrimination and segregation that blacks faced. The life of Booker T. Washington was itself an epic of self-help in which the black leader pulled himself from the depths of poverty and persecution in the postwar South to a position of power and influence. Throughout his life, Washington exemplified what was then required of a successful American black—to wear the mask, to play the expected role. For a time, it would become common to dismiss Washington as an Uncle Tom currying favor with whites by accepting a subordinate position for his race. But recent scholarship depicts him as a man of action, a political in-fighter often defiant of racial conventions.

Born in 1856 in Virginia, the son of a slave woman, Washington never knew the identity of his white father. At first he mined salt and coal. Then Mrs. Lewis Ruffner, a well-to-do white woman in whose home he worked, encouraged and helped him to attend Hampton Institute in Virginia, which stressed vocational skills for its black student body. Washington arrived at Hampton footsore, dirty, and penniless; on his graduation three years later, he was endowed with a basic education and a high moral commitment. Washington taught school, becoming increasingly convinced of the necessity of teaching young black men and women practical skills and a belief in self-help and the dignity of labor.

In 1881 Washington became the founder and principal of Tuskegee Institute in Alabama. He acquired the land, built buildings, raised money for books, equipment, and salaries. For fifteen years Washington worked tirelessly to establish an all-black teachers' college with goals similar to those of Hamp-

Theodore Roosevelt with Booker T. Washington. *(Courtesy, Tuskegee Institute, Alabama)*

ton. Graduates of Tuskegee went on to be teachers throughout the South and in Africa.

In 1895 Washington became nationally known. That year, at the opening of the Cotton States and International Exposition in Atlanta, he stood before blacks and whites and enunciated his accommodationist doctrines to the cheers of his audience and the acclaim of the nation. In 1901 his autobiography, *Up From Slavery,* became a bestseller. Disillusioned by the failure of the political process during Reconstruction and committed to a morality of work and self-discipline, Washington believed that the black community could progress only by careful and laborious accumulation of skills, education, and property.

Yet it was a political incident, Theodore Roosevelt's luncheon with him in 1901, that may be taken as a symbolic climax of Washington's career. This incident of social mingling between a President and a black man offended southern whites as had President Cleveland's meeting with Frederick Douglass a few years before. The larger implication of the meeting was the political power it implied. Washington acted as a presence-behind the scenes in American political life, influencing both Roosevelt's and Taft's appointments and racial policies. He also enjoyed the acquaintance of industrialists and financiers and could tap them for powerful philanthropic support for black projects. Washington had gained his influence among the wealthy and politically powerful through much the same strategies of care and discretion that he had urged black Americans to adopt in their daily life and work. He consolidated power in the black community, offered political favors to Republicans, and cultivated friendships among whites.

Black opposition to Washington is represented by William Monroe Trotter and his militant newspaper, *The Guardian;* W. E. B. Du Bois's Niagara Movement; and the NAACP and its publication *The Crisis*. Trotter bitterly reproached Washington for obstructing black opportunity in the South, and

Du Bois complained that Washington "practically accepts the alleged inferiority of the Negro races." Northern whites, however, regarded him as a "genius" (Teddy Roosevelt) and "wonderful" (Andrew Carnegie). Few contemporaries were willing to look behind his optimistic, conciliatory demeanor. Washington, in fact, was not averse to applying whatever tactic was necessary to stifle critics. He was a powerful figure constantly seeking to strengthen the Tuskegee Machine, a network of black political and business organizations throughout the country.

The Great Migration

Booker T. Washington's program would have black Americans build up their economic and educational resources but accept, for the moment, the bulk of existing social and political arrangements. These were designed especially to help the millions of southern blacks who found themselves suffering from abject poverty and constant discrimination from the white majority. But at the same time, the African American community was changing. On the eve of World War I, the vast majority still lived in the South, but the beginnings of the great black migration were already under way. Between 1870 and 1890 some 80,000 African Americans had moved out of the South, and 200,000 more left between 1890 and 1910. That year there were more than 850,000 black people living in the northern cities. Large African American communities appeared in the North complete with their own elite groups of lawyers, teachers, ministers, doctors, nurses, social workers, businessmen, and business women. Successful black newspapers appeared, such as the Chicago *Defender*, the Pittsburgh *Courier*, and the New York *Amsterdam News*.

Migration to the North accelerated when the South was hit by an economic recession in 1914 and by the cotton-destroying boll weevil attacks in 1915. Thousands of jobs disappeared in the South just as northern and midwestern industries were booming during World War I. Black people headed north by the hundreds of thousands. Between 1910 and 1920 the black population of the North increased from 850,000 to 1.4 million people, and by 1930 it had grown to more than 2.3 million. Two million more were to leave the South during the Great Depression and World War II, and African American ghettoes would appear in cities throughout the Northeast and Midwest.

Despite white hostility, African Americans in the North lived in their own communities without constant intervention by whites, and slowly they developed into a force that white politicians had to take into account. Because of the great migration, there were now two African American communities in the United States, one rural and southern and the other northern and urban. Booker T. Washington represented southern blacks; new African American leaders appeared whose primary constituency consisted of the urban, northern community. The two most prominent of them were W.E.B. DuBois and Marcus Garvey.

W. E. B. Du Bois

The year of Washington's death, 1915, marked a significant point in American black history. Events in Europe, discrimination and segregation at home, and the black exodus to northern cities prepared the way for W. E. B. Du Bois's challenge to the established progressive gospel of Washington. Militant rhetoric, legal and political aggressiveness, and a commitment to a black elite distinguished Du Bois from Washington. An exceptional student and a descendant of an old, established black family, Du Bois encountered little blatant racial discrimination. Not until his student years at Fisk University in Nashville, Tennessee, did he develop any real racial identity. At this black institution, Du Bois began to perceive the implications of the race situation and to adopt a faith in the role of black intellectuals.

In 1889 Du Bois began a socially isolated life at Harvard College and graduate school. He found satisfaction in scholarship and was influenced and stimulated by William James and George Santayana. He earned a doctorate in history, the first American black to be awarded such a degree from Harvard. Travel and study in Europe completed his education and confirmed Du Bois's view of himself as an American black with a special destiny.

A sociological survey conducted for the University of Pennsylvania, Du Bois's *The Philadelphia Negro* is still noted today as a significant piece of research. It emphasizes the need for the black upper class to encourage the progress of the race. In this extensive study Du Bois called for the "the mastery of the art of social organized life." Du Bois's ideology, along with Booker T. Washington's doctrines, prompted middle-class black urban women to take up club work as a means to self-help. Among such women were Ida

William Edward Burghardt Du Bois, 1869–1963. *(Courtesy, National Portrait Gallery)*

Wells Barnett, Fannie Barrier Williams, and Josephine St. Pierre Ruffin. Black women joined clubs to administer to the needs of the poor, the sick, the old. The groups also promoted the idea of the black woman as an important social and moral force in the black community. In their adoption of the formula of opportunity, ambition, frugality, and perseverance, these women seemed closer to Washington. Yet in their commitment to social organization, which recalls the ideology of *The Philadelphia Negro*, they were in the spirit of Du Bois.

At Atlanta University in 1897 Du Bois supervised sociology programs and directed conferences on blacks sponsored by the university. Through this program, he published a series of monographs aimed at social reform and insisted on the cultivation and promotion of a "talented tenth." College-trained young black people would become community leaders, business organizers, and members of a cultural avant-garde.

In a collection of essays, *The Souls of Black Folk*, Du Bois in 1903 presented black Americans in all their variety to the white public. The black poet James Weldon Johnson described it as having "a greater effect upon and within the Negro race in America than any other single book published in this country since *Uncle Tom's Cabin*."

In his biography of John Brown, in his response to the Atlanta race riot of 1906, and in his lectures, Du Bois spoke not in the measured tones of *The Souls of Black Folk* but with the fervor of a forceful propagandist impatient for the attainment of equality. Under Du Bois's leadership, the Niagara Movement, which argued against the accommodationist tactics of Washington, was founded in 1905 at Niagara Falls, Ontario. The organization's "Declaration of Principles" demanded suffrage and civil rights, and called attention to southern peonage. The next year the delegates made a barefoot pilgrimage to the site of John Brown's execution. The movement's elitism thwarted its founder's hopes for wide support, and by 1911 it had petered out. Du Bois continued to agitate.

The Niagara Movement provided the groundwork for the establishment in 1911 of the National Association for the Advancement of Colored People, which contained an interracial membership. The social workers Lillian Wald and Jane Addams and *Nation* editor Oswald Garrison Villard were among the prominent whites involved. The organization took a radical position on matters of racial equality and segregation, denouncing the political and economic subordination of blacks. In association with the NAACP, Du Bois edited *The Crisis*. Both the organization and the magazine increased his prestige and influence. Throughout the 1920s and 1930s Du Bois increasingly articulated a socialist ideology that many NAACP board members could not accept.

As a member of the black intellectual elite, Du Bois was an integral part of the cultural phenomenon known as the Harlem Renaissance. Representing in part an integration of white and black culture during the 1920s, it was an assertion of black pride, an expression of white fascination with Africa, and a part of the larger American cultural upheaval of the time. The Harlem Renaissance demonstrated a new awareness of blacks by whites and an opportunity for intellectuals of both races to mingle in salons (many of them organized by wealthy white women), studios, and theaters. Countee Cullen, James Weldon Johnson, Claude McKay, Zora Hurston, and Langston Hughes were prominent within the Harlem

Renaissance, which also included black literary and political magazines—*Harlem, The Messenger, Fire*—theater and art groups, and political associations.

An important radical who wrote for *The Messenger* (1917–28) was A. Phillip Randolph, who urged blacks to join unions and to vote for socialist candidates. In 1925 Randolph would found the Brotherhood of Sleeping Car Porters and become its president. During the New Deal of the 1930s the Brotherhood won a good union contract with the Pullman Company. In 1941 Randolph threatened a mass march on Washington to protest the boycotting of blacks from defense jobs. President Roosevelt promised to prevent such discrimination and that march was never held. But Randolph lived to preside over the March on Washington of 1963, a high point of the civil rights movement.

Marcus Garvey and Pan-Africanism Pan-Africanism, a special vision of Du Bois, was particularly popular after World War I. Du Bois dreamed of a great free central African state to encompass a "unity of the colored races." An NAACP session in 1919 endorsed Du Bois's grand scheme, but it received no popular support. Du Bois's movement eventually clashed with that of Marcus Garvey, whose showmanship, flash, and ability to evoke emotion won him a following. Garvey has been described as a "charlatan" and a "crook" and as "the greatest thing that happened to a black man."

Born in Jamaica in 1887 of peasant parents, Garvey attended local secondary schools. A youthful experience of rejection by the white daughter of a Methodist minister taught Garvey that "there were different races, each having its own separate and distinct social life. . . ." Garvey pursued a short-lived printing career, then became involved in the Jamaican labor movement.

Before he came to the United States, Garvey's most significant achievement was the founding in Jamaica of the Universal Negro Improvement Association. Its purpose was to unite "all the Negro peoples of the world into one great body to establish a country and government absolutely their own." Arriving in the United States, Garvey proceeded to raise funds and interest other blacks in his plan for the formation of a black economic community. This visit coincided with harsh events in the American black experience: the emergence of the second Ku Klux Klan, a continued tightening of Jim Crow laws, and a boll weevil infestation that damaged the southern cotton crop and caused southern blacks to flock to northern cities, there to suffer from unemployment, bad living conditions, and the economic and social discrimination that prevailed. Garveyism appealed to these displaced, unhappy rural people as well as to the disillusioned urban workers. By 1919, Garvey's UNIA claimed thirty branches in American cities and the organization flourished until 1927.

Garvey spread his ideology through the publication of a weekly newspaper, *The Negro World.* Printed in Spanish, French, and English, the paper celebrated black heroes of the past, recalled slave rebellions, and promoted the grandeur of Africa. Garvey's insistence on racial pride had a tremendous impact on the black community.

Garvey in 1919 established a steamship company, the Black Star Line. Only blacks were entitled to buy shares in the company and thousands made the investment. Garvey announced that "the Black Star Line will sail to Africa if it sails in seas of blood." The three ships of the line eventually were lost at sea, and the company went bankrupt. But Garvey then established a Negro Factories Corpora-

---

SHARE-CROPPERS *by Langston Hughes*

Just a herd of Negroes
Driven to the field,
Plowing, planting, hoeing,
To make the cotton yield.

When the cotton's picked
And the work is done
Boss man take the money
And we get none.

Leaves us hungry, ragged
As we were before.
Year by year goes by
And we are nothing more.

Than a herd of Negroes
Driven to the field—
Plowing life away
To make the cotton yield.

During the early twentieth century large numbers of blacks left the rural South for northern cities. *(Courtesy, Library of Congress)*

tion, along with another steamship company, and plans for the settlement of American blacks in Liberia testify to Garvey's unflagging spirit.

One of Garvey's most impressive accomplishments was the organization of three conventions. Thousands of delegates came to Harlem and drafted a Declaration of the Rights of the Negro Peoples of the World. The document planned a free Africa under a black government.

New York City's Assistant District Attorney questioned Garvey in 1919 about the sale of unincorporated stock in the Black Star Line. The Jamaican was also involved in libel suits instigated by comments printed in the *New World*. His legal problems culminated in a trial for using the mails with intent to defraud. Found guilty, Garvey lost an appeal in 1925 and the Supreme Court refused to review his case. He served three years of a five-year sentence and was deported to Jamaica, where he continued his efforts toward fulfillment of his grand scheme. In 1935 he moved to London, dying there in poverty five years later.

The Great Migration

The war-fueled economy created a great migration of blacks to northern cities during and after World Wars I and II. This movement of peoples had enormous consequences for American politics, cities, and culture. Black northern newspapers served as a source of information to southerners, as exemplified in this letter to the Chicago *Defender*:

> Sherman, Ga., Nov. 28, 1916.
>
> Dear sir:
>
> This letter comes to ask for all infirmations concerning employment. . . . Now I am in a family of (11) eleven more or less boys and girls (men and women) mixed sizes who want to go north as soon as arrangements can be made and employment given places for shelter and so on (etc) now this are farming people they were raised on the farm and are good farm hands I of course have some experience and qualefication as a coman school teacher and hotel waiter and along few other lines.
>
> I wish you would write me at your first chance and tell me if you can give us employment at what time and about what wages will you pay and what kind of arrangement can be made for our shelter. Tell me when can you best use us now or later.

Will you send us tickets if so on what terms and at what price what is the cost per head and by what route should we come. We are Negroes and try to show ourselves worthy of all we may get from any friendly source we endeavor to be true to all good causes, if you can we thank you to help us to come north as soon as you can.

The longings expressed in letters like these are as important a part of black history in the first half of the twentieth century as the activities of such leaders as Washington, Du Bois, and Garvey.

The South during the Progressive Era was rigidly segregated. One black woman who moved to the west coast recalled:

You could not go to a white restaurant; you sat in a special place at the movie house; and, Lord knows, you sat in the back of the bus. It didn't make any difference if you were rich or poor, if you were black you were nothing. You might have a hundred dollars in your pocket, but if you went to the store you would wait at the side until all the clerks got through with all the white folks, no matter if they didn't have change for a dollar. Then the clerk would finally look at you and say 'Oh, did you want something? I didn't see you there.'

They did want our money, that was true enough, but otherwise we were dirt in the street. If you'd go in to get some shoes, some stores would not let you try them on before you bought them. If you wanted to have a new hat, they might make you put a handkerchief on your head before you tried it out. They thought we were dirty; they thought we leave stains, maybe that was it; and they didn't want to drink out of the same water fountain. There were women who would go into stores to buy a fur coat but they couldn't use the rest room.

A black man in Philadelphia recounted his new life there:

Well Dr. with the aid of God I am making very good I make $75 per month. I am carrying enough insurance to pay me $20 per week if I am not able to be on duty. I don't have to mister . . . every little white boy comes along I havent heard a white man call a colored a nigger you no now—since I been in the state of Pa. I can ride in the electric street and steam cars any where I get a seat. I dont care to mix with white what I mean I am not crazy about being with white folks, but if I have to pay the same fare I have learn to want the same acomidation. and if you are first in a place here shopping you dont have to wait until the white folks get thro tradeing yet amid all this I shall ever love the good old South and I am praying that God may give every well wisher a chance to be a man regardless of his color.

Points To Think About

1. Progressivism is one of those terms, like liberalism or conservatism, that seem clear enough until you attempt to define them. Then what had seemed a reasonably coherent movement fragments into a troubling multiplicity of progressivisms. It may help to define some minor questions over which political activists of the day divided. One of them had to do with the exercise of political power. A number of the reforms of the day, like the direct election of senators or the referendum, aimed at giving the citizenry a more direct voice in government. Other reforms sought just the opposite goal: to remove certain issues from the uncleanness, the deal-making, the inefficiency of electoral politics. The various independent regulatory commissions and the city manager movement are examples. As progressives divided over who would exercise power, they argued about the ends its exercise should achieve. Some, like Woodrow Wilson, thought of government mainly as a referee. Its primary role was to guarantee the fairness of the free market system. Others, like Theodore Roosevelt, believed that government should seize an active role in planning the American economy and society. His conservation proposals are examples. Yet all "progressives" did hold certain values in common. All believed in making government more efficient. All were committed to ending the excesses of the industrial revolution such as the high accident rate. And all shared, as the late Richard Hofstadter put it, a "good-natured" faith that the American people could take control of events and improve their lives.

2. Theodore Roosevelt's decision to run as a third-party candidate in 1912 did for the Democrats what they were unable to do for themselves—capture the presidency. Mere words cannot express the outrage of Republican party regulars at Roosevelt for his Bull Moose campaign. Yet Roosevelt remained perhaps the most popular politician in the country, and he also remained determined to regain the White House.

As 1916 approached Roosevelt had to decide whether to run as a third-party candidate once more or to seek the Republican nomination. The third-party route seemed merely a way of guaranteeing Wilson's reelection, so he turned to the Republicans. The problem was that the Republican Party regulars were not about to forgive him for 1912 so easily. Roosevelt had little choice but to go over the heads of the party officials and appeal directly to the people. If he could find a volatile enough issue, he might inspire such popular support that the party would be forced to nominate him. For his issues, Roosevelt chose preparedness and "100 Per Cent Americanism" (this theme was directed at immigrant Americans who were, in his opinion, insufficiently patriotic). Roosevelt did attract enormous crowds, but party regulars still refused him the nomination. This time Roosevelt accepted the party's decision and campaigned vigorously for the nominee, Charles Evans Hughes. Hughes lost a very close race; Roosevelt managed to make immigrants a popular political target; and he put himself back in the party's good graces. There's every likelihood that had he not died unexpectedly in 1919, he would have won the nomination in 1920 and then carried the general election. Whatever a Roosevelt administration would have been like in the 1920s it would have sought something different from the national placidity that Harding termed "normalcy."

3. We normally contrast the reform legislation of the Progressive Era with the complacency of the 1920s. The contrast is perfectly valid, but it is important not to ignore the many important continuities between the Progressive Era and the twenties. The prohibition movement is one. Calls for restriction of immigration is another. And the active participation of business in the process of government is a third.

Some may have difficulty accepting these as legacies of an age of "reform," but this is largely because we tend to limit the term "reform" to those measures we favor ourselves. Prohibition is still widely viewed as a disaster. Tight restrictions are now seen as having reflected all too faithfully the racism of the day. And many though not all Americans view with suspicion the idea of a partnership between business and government. But we should learn to recognize what reforms mean to people at the moment they are enacted, and by that standard prohibition, for example, was a progressive measure.

Suggested Readings

Recent works on progressivism include Nick Salvatore, *Eugene V. Debs* (1982), Arthur S. Link and Richard McCormick, *Progressivism* (1983), Dewey W. Grantham, *Southern Progressivism* (1983), and John Milton Cooper, Jr., *The Warrior and the Priest: Woodrow Wilson and Theodore Roosevelt* (1983).

Gabriel Kolko, in *The Triumph of Conservatism* (1963), argues that much of the support for regulation of business came from big business itself, which wished for a safe and orderly existence under government regulation in place of the discomforts of uncontrolled competition. In *The Corporate Ideal in the Liberal State, 1900–1918* (1968), James Weinstein stresses the role of corporations in drafting reform legislation. R. B. Nye, *Midwestern Progressive Politics* (1951) and R. S. Maxwell, *La Follette and the Rise of Progressives in Wisconsin* (1956) analyze progressivism on a state level. James Green's *Grass Roots Socialism* (1978) is perceptive.

Good studies of Roosevelt include John M. Blum, *The Republican Roosevelt* (second edition, 1977), and George E. Mowry, *The Era of Theodore Roosevelt, 1900–1912* (1958). Standard on their subjects are D. F. Anderson, *William Howard Taft: A Conservative's Conception of the Presidency* (1973) and Arthur S. Link, *Woodrow Wilson and the Progressive Era, 1900–1917* (1954).

William Harris is excellent on *A. Phillip Randolph* (1981). C. F. Kelley, *NAACP: A History of the National Association for the Advancement of Colored People* (1970) and E. M. Rudwick, *W. E. B. Du Bois: Propagandist of the Negro Protest* (1960) are informative. Louis Harlan's exhaustive study of Booker T. Washington is definitive: *Booker T. Washington: The Making of a Black Leader, 1856–1901* (1972) and *Booker T. Washington: The Wizard of Tuskegee, 1901–1915* (1983). On Marcus Garvey, see E. David Cronon, *Black Moses: The Story of Marcus Garvey and the Universal Negro Improvement Association* (second edition, 1969). A new study is Nicholas Lemann, *The Promised Land: The Great Black Migration and How It Changed America* (1991).

Stephan Thernstrom pursues *The Other Bostonians: Poverty and Progress in the American Metropolis, 1860–1970* (1973); see also Tamara K. Hareven and Randolph Langenbach, *Amoskeag: Life and Work in an American Factory City* (1978).

☆ ☆ ☆ **POINTS OF VIEW:** ☆ ☆ ☆

Booker T. Washington: A Great Compromiser?

Louis R. Harlan

It is ironic that Booker T. Washington, the most powerful black American of his time and perhaps of all time, should be the black leader whose claim to the title is most often dismissed by the lay public. Blacks often question his legitimacy because of the role that favor by whites played in Washington's assumption of power, and whites often remember him only as an educator or, confusing him with George Washington Carver, as "that great Negro scientist." This irony is something that Washington will have to live with in history, for he himself deliberately created the ambiguity about his role and purposes that has haunted his image. And yet, Washington was a genuine black leader, with a substantial black following and with virtually the same long-range goals for Afro-Americans as his rivals. . . .

Washington's bid for leadership went beyond education and institution-building, however. Symbolic of his fresh approach to black-white relations were a speech he gave in 1895 before a commercial exposition, known as the Atlanta Compromise Address, and his autobiography, *Up from Slavery* (1901). As Washington saw it, blacks were toiling upward from slavery by their own efforts into the American middle class and needed chiefly social peace to continue in this steady social evolution. Thus, in the Atlanta Compromise he sought to disarm the white South by declaring agitation of the social equality question "the merest folly" and proclaiming that in "purely social" matters "we can be as separate as the fingers, yet one as the hand in all things essential to mutual progress." . . .

Washington's concessions to the white South, however, were only half of a bargain. In return for downgrading civil and political rights in the black list of priorities, Washington asked whites to place no barriers to black economic advancement and even to become partners of their black neighbors "in all things essential to mutual progress." Washington saw his own role as the axis between the races, the only leader who could negotiate and keep the peace by holding extremists on both sides in check.

Washington sought to influence whites, but he never forgot that it was the blacks that he undertook to lead. He offered blacks not the empty promises of the demagogue but a solid program of economic and educational progress through struggle. It was less important "just now," he said, for a black person to seek admission to an opera house than to have the money for the ticket. Mediating diplomacy with whites was only half of Washington's strategy; the other half was black solidarity, mutual aid, and institution-building. He thought outspoken complaint against injustice was necessary but insufficient, and he thought factional dissent among black leaders was self-defeating and should be suppressed.

Washington brought to his role as a black leader the talents and outlook of a machine boss. He made Tuskegee Institute the largest and best-supported black educational institution of his day, and it spawned a large network of other industrial schools. Tuskegee's educational function is an important and debatable subject, of course, but the central concern here is Washington's use of the school as the base of operations of what came to be known as the Tuskegee Machine. It was an all-black school with an all-black faculty at a time when most black colleges were still run by white missionaries. Tuskegee taught self-determination. It also taught trades designed for economic independence in a region dominated by sharecrop agriculture. . . .

Washington did try to change his world by other means. Some forms of racial injustice, such as lynching, disfranchisement, and unequal facilities in education and transportation, Washington dealt with publicly and directly.

Louis R. Harlan, "Booker T. Washington and the Politics of Accommodation," in *Black Leaders of the Twentieth Century*, John Hope Franklin and August Meier, eds. (Urbana University of Illinois Press, 1982), p. 2–4, 12.

Manning Marable

Popular and powerful, [Booker T. Washington] symbolized the strengths and critical weaknesses within the Afro-American community at the turn of the century.

Washington's sudden emergence as a major figure came in September 1895, when he delivered a short address at the Cotton States and International Exposition in Atlanta. Little in the speech, which Du Bois later termed the "Atlanta Compromise," represented a radical departure from what other moderate black educators and elected officials had already argued. He observed that one-third of the South's population was black, and that any "enterprise seeking the material, civil, or moral welfare" of the region could not disregard the Negro. Blacks should remain in the South—"Cast down your bucket where you are"—and participate in the capitalist economic development of that area. During the Reconstruction era, blacks had erred in their priorities. "Ignorant and inexperienced," blacks had tried to start "at the top instead of at the bottom"; a Congressional seat "was more sought than real estate or industrial skill." To the white South, Washington pledged the fidelity of his race, "the most patient, law-abiding, and unresentful people that the world has seen." And on the sensitive issue of racial integration and the protection of blacks' political rights, Washington made a dramatic concession: "In all things that are purely social we can be as separate as the fingers, yet one as the hand in all things essential to mutual progress. . . . The wisest among my race understand that the agitation of questions of social equality is the extremest folly." Washington's "compromise" was this: blacks would disavow open agitation for desegregation and the political franchise; in return, they would be permitted to develop their own parallel economic, educational, and social institutions within the framework of expanding Southern capitalism.

White America responded to Washington's address with universal acclaim. President Grover Cleveland remarked that the speech was the foundation for "new hope" for black Americans. More accurate was the editorial of the Atlanta *Constitution:* "The speech stamps Booker T. Washington as a wise counselor and a safe leader." Black reactions were decidedly mixed. . . . [B]lack editor W. Calvin Chase described the speech as "death to the Afro-American and elevating to the white people." A.M.E. Bishop Henry M. Turner believed that Tuskegee's principal "will have to live a long time to undo the harm he has done our race." The Atlanta *Advocate* condemned Washington's "sycophantic attitude." . . .

Through Washington's patronage, his black and white supporters were able to secure posts in the federal government. Washington's influence with white philanthropists largely determined which Negro colleges would receive funds. The Tuskegee Machine never acquiesced in the complete political disfranchisement of blacks, however, and behind the scenes Washington used his resources to fight for civil rights. In 1900 he requested funds from white philanthropists to lobby against racist election provisions in the Louisiana state constitution. He privately fought Alabama's disfranchisement laws in federal courts, and in 1903–04 personally spent "at least four thousand dollars in cash" to promote the legal struggle against Jim Crow. Nevertheless, the general impression Washington projected to the white South was the Negro's subservience to Jim Crow, lynchings, and political terror. One of Washington's strongest critics in this regard was Alexander Crummell. The black scholar disliked Washington's emphasis on Afro-American industrial training at the expense of higher education. But more important, he viewed Washington's entire accommodationist political program as opportunistic, and believed that Tuskegee's principal was nothing but a "white man's nigger."

Charles A. Lindbergh. *(Courtesy, AP/Wide World)*

CHAPTER 23

The Great War and the Buoyant Twenties

LINDBERGH'S TRANS-ATLANTIC FLIGHT

At almost 8:00 a.m. on May 20, 1927, after a sleepless night, Charles A. Lindbergh, carrying five sandwiches, climbed into the cockpit of his small plane, which was loaded with as many extra containers of gasoline as it could carry. He left his parachute on the ground to conserve twenty pounds of fuel. The engine seemed sluggish as he slowly maneuvered down the muddy runway of Roosevelt Field, New York, and his wheels left the ground dangerously late. He managed to clear a steamroller at the end of the field and then missed some telephone wires by less than twenty feet. As he crossed Long Island Sound and Connecticut, Lindbergh's speed reached only one hundred miles an hour. Chasing the horizon, the plane used more and more fuel, which eased the strain on the engine and the trembling wings. It was when he left Massachusetts and headed toward Nova Scotia that Lindbergh first sensed the danger of his unique solo flight—he had never before passed over a large body of water. Below him lay the awesome span of the Atlantic. His single propeller droned on.

Suddenly, over the rugged countryside of Cape Breton Island, the weather turned bad. Cross winds, driving rain, and turbulence buffeted the tiny craft; the primitive weather forecasts had suggested nothing of this. But just as unpredictably the sky cleared. Lindbergh dipped his wings over St. John's, Newfoundland, before heading out over two thousand miles of rough ocean. Night came on swiftly, and now he had to fly with a compass and an altimeter, but no lights, no flares, no means of reaching human beings. Fog descended along with wintry gusts, and Lindbergh climbed to 10,000 feet. He became sharply aware of the cold. Using a flashlight, he saw ice forming on the wings and knew he was in an ice cloud. Lindbergh's autobiography observes:

> They enmesh intruders. They are barbaric. . . . They toss you in inner turbulence, lash you with hailstones, poison you with freezing mist. It would be a slow death, a death one would have long minutes to struggle against . . . climbing, stalling, diving, whipping, always downward toward the sea.

Lindbergh soon emerged into clear air under a dome lighted by stars.

Twenty-six hours after leaving Long Island, the young flyer sighted a land bird and knew he was approaching Ireland. He swooped down over a fishing boat and asked for directions, but received no response from the astonished crew. At last, there it was: a rocky shore and green fields. But the aviator flew on—over England, over the Channel, over France—until he saw the lights of the Eiffel Tower dead ahead. Lindbergh circled it to mark his victory and, thirty-three hours after takeoff, set down at Le Bourget Field, where a mob engulfed his plane even before the propeller stopped. After a night's sleep he called his mother 4,000 miles away to confirm his safe arrival.

Greeted at home by massive ticker-tape parades, he was America's last hero. "He has displaced," orated Charles Evans Hughes at a dinner for Lindbergh in New York, "everything that is petty, that is sordid, that is vulgar." Lucky Lindy had shown a decade that it was not rotten to the core, that it could put ethics and achievement above wealth, that modesty and courage were really the great virtues after all.

Lindbergh entitled his story of flying solo across the Atlantic *We*—the aeronautical "we," the flying pronoun—for his achievement depended on a machine, his airplane the *Spirit of St. Louis*. Lindbergh symbolized an earlier time, but at the same time became an emblem of change, yoked to the new technology that was remaking the nation. That the machine, in all its metallic impersonality, could also be a partner in danger represented the complexity of the American encounter with modern technology. Americans were calling the Ford car the Tin Lizzie.

Massive ticker-tape parade in New York City for America's new hero, "Lucky Lindy."

Neutrality 1914–1917

The War in Europe

Military people and intellectuals, including Wilson, assumed that those "great watery moats" of the Atlantic and Pacific protected their country from major international troubles. But the war in Europe, which broke out in 1914, worried Americans when trench warfare stalemated in northern France. German predominance over continental Europe might harm American economic interests and be the basis for an attempt later at world dominion. An Anglo-French victory, on the other hand, might freeze Americans out of vast markets in the Allies' growing empires.

The American public preferred neutrality. "Our people," Wilson later said, "did not see the full meaning of the war. It looked like a natural raking out of Europe's pent-up jealousies." Orders for war goods stimulated an American economic boom. Why, then, did the United States change from a determined neutral in 1914 to a belligerent in 1917? The answer lies in considerable part in the way that the Germans had to fight the war.

Both the Central Powers—Germany, Austria-Hungary, and later Turkey and Bulgaria—and the Entente or Allied nations—Britain, France, Russia until the Bolsheviks commandeered its revolution, and eventually Italy—had planned for a quick, decisive war. After the murder of the Archduke Franz Ferdinand of Austria on June 28, 1914, the need to keep armies mobilized one step ahead of potential enemies accelerated into a general war by early August. A huge German army plunged through Belgium and into northern France, trying to outflank French troops and capture Paris from behind. Rather than hold fast on the Rhineland border, French generals moved their units westward. As each army tried to get beyond the other, a virtual race to the North Sea resulted. Thereafter, both sides settled into trench warfare, a tactic particularly favorable to the defense. The war stalemated: battles became a bloody attrition. On the huge plains of eastern Europe, armies found more room for maneuver, but here, too, the forces became locked together. Poorly trained Russian troops moved ponderously against smaller but better-equipped German and Austrian armies. Neither side was gaining a victory, though the Kaiser's troops slowly advanced.

Submarine Warfare

Britain declared the entire North Sea a military region and mined its waters. The captains of neutral ships had to stop for sailing directions at Dover, where British officials often found pretexts to keep them there: the usual device was a greatly expanded notion of what constituted contraband. Germany retaliated by declaring its own war zone in the North Sea, where its submarines, or U-boats, would attack any vessel. The British armed their merchant marine and prepared it to fight. Thereby they trapped the Germans in a dilemma. The fragile submarines, so small they carried a crew of only a few men, could not obey the rule that a warship must give warning to the merchant vessel and must take on its passengers: steel merchant ships could easily ram the U-boats. Successful use of the submarine required breaking principles adopted before this stealthy but frail craft existed; otherwise the Germans would have to allow the Allies a commerce that could provide for a German defeat.

Early in 1915, when Germany prepared for unrestricted submarine warfare in the North Sea, Wilson responded with a warning, holding the Germans "strictly accountable" for the property and lives of any American citizens lost as a result. Then, on May 7, 1915, came news that a German U-boat had sunk the famous *Lusitania,* grandest ship of Britain's Cunard Lines. (A torpedo set off secondary explosions in the ship's hold, where a large amount of munitions was stored. This, not the torpedo itself, caused the vessel to sink rapidly.) Twelve hundred people drowned, 128 of them American citizens. The act outraged Americans. "The torpedo which sank the *Lusitania,*" *Nation* magazine editorialized, "also sank Germany in the opinion of mankind." A wave of anti-German hysteria victimized innocent Germans living in the United States. Wilson protested the sinking so vigorously that Secretary of State William Jennings Bryan, an advocate of peace, resigned. Germany backed down, ordering U-boat captains not to attack passenger liners in the future. Still, damage to German prestige was immense. President Wilson himself told his cabinet:

Gentlemen, the Allies are standing with their backs to the wall fighting wild beasts.

The year 1916 tested American neutrality even more. Stalemated land war prompted leaders in Berlin to expand the ocean war. About fifty U-boats swarmed into the North Sea, attacking naval patrols and armed merchant ships. On March 24, 1916, an overeager German commander torpedoed an unarmed French channel ferry, the *Sussex.* Wilson reacted with a virtual ultimatum: the United States would break diplomatic relations if Germany ever again attacked civilian ships. Though furious at Germany, Wilson was also angry with Britain. During the summer of 1916, the British Cabinet issued a blacklist of neutral firms that had traded with the Central Powers. The British announced that they would confiscate whatever goods of such firms their ships could seize. It was a blatant violation of rights. Peeved with both sides and anxious about the presidential election in the fall, Wilson took up peacemaking. His close adviser Colonel House traveled several times to Europe, where he hinted that if one side refused an armistice, the United States would join forces with its enemy. Both sides thereupon presented peace proposals, but they were so far apart that reconciliation was impossible.

Peace and Preparedness President Wilson's attempts to secure an armistice in Europe did not inspire confidence among his critics. They viewed Germany as a threat to American security, and they insisted that the country at least prepare militarily for war that might come in spite of the President's peacemaking. Theodore Roosevelt accused Wilson of weakness, and General Leonard Wood, head of the National Security League, began organizing volunteer militia units throughout the country and putting his soldiers through weekend training programs. Congress responded to the campaign by passing preparedness measures. President Wilson initially opposed the preparedness campaign, but with the presidential election looming, he decided to be prudent: he talked peace and prepared for war.

It was a successful strategy. Mediation efforts did sustain Wilson as the peace can-

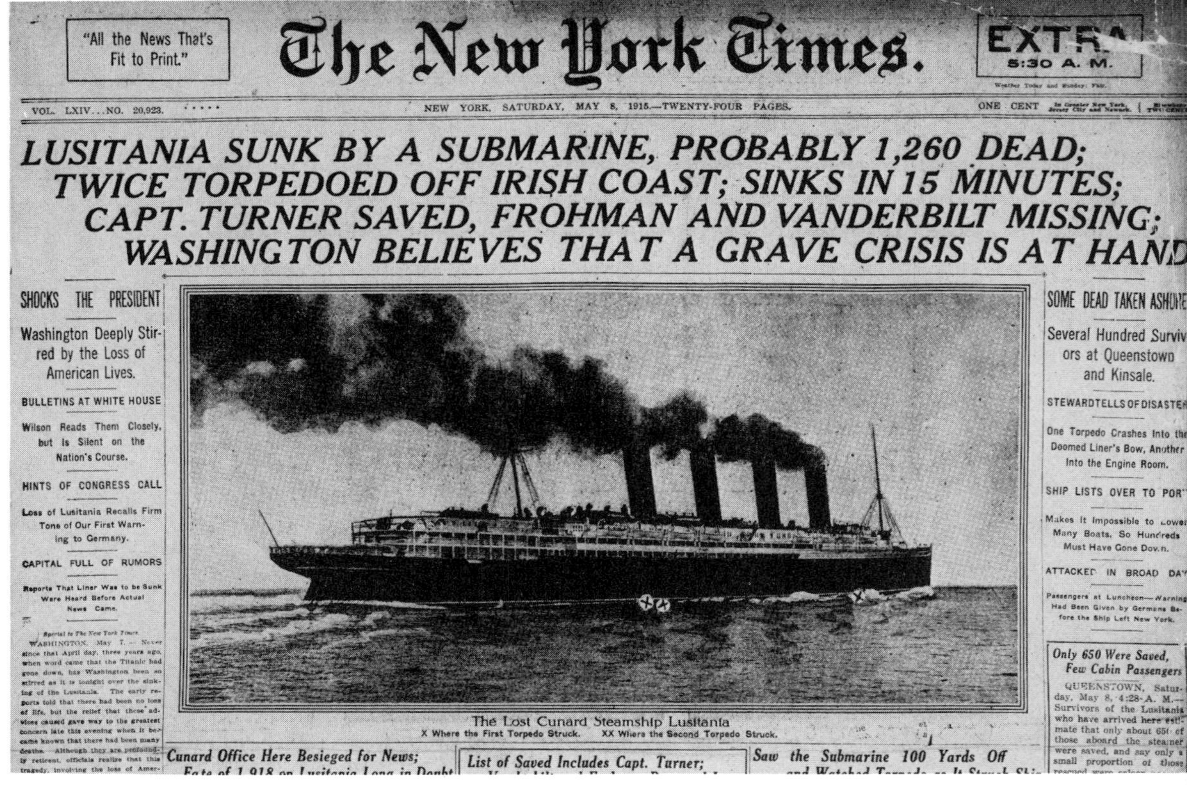
"All the News That's Fit to Print."

The New York Times.

EXTRA 5:30 A. M.

VOL. LXIV...NO. 20,923. NEW YORK, SATURDAY, MAY 8, 1915.—TWENTY-FOUR PAGES. ONE CENT

LUSITANIA SUNK BY A SUBMARINE, PROBABLY 1,260 DEAD; TWICE TORPEDOED OFF IRISH COAST; SINKS IN 15 MINUTES; CAPT. TURNER SAVED, FROHMAN AND VANDERBILT MISSING; WASHINGTON BELIEVES THAT A GRAVE CRISIS IS AT HAND

SHOCKS THE PRESIDENT

Washington Deeply Stirred by the Loss of American Lives.

BULLETINS AT WHITE HOUSE

Wilson Reads Them Closely, but Is Silent on the Nation's Course.

HINTS OF CONGRESS CALL

Loss of Lusitania Recalls Firm Tone of Our First Warning to Germany.

CAPITAL FULL OF RUMORS

Reports That Liner Was to be Sunk Were Heard Before Actual News Came.

Special to The New York Times.

WASHINGTON, May 7.—Never since that April day, three years ago, when word came that the Titanic had gone down, has Washington been so stirred as it is tonight over the sinking of the Lusitania. The early reports told that there had been no loss of life, but the relief that these advices caused gave way to the greatest concern late this evening when it became known that there had been many deaths. Although they are profoundly reticent, officials realize that this tragedy, involving the loss of Amer-

The Lost Cunard Steamship Lusitania

X Where the First Torpedo Struck. XX Where the Second Torpedo Struck.

SOME DEAD TAKEN ASHORE

Several Hundred Survivors at Queenstown and Kinsale.

STEWARD TELLS OF DISASTER

One Torpedo Crashes Into the Doomed Liner's Bow, Another Into the Engine Room.

SHIP LISTS OVER TO PORT

Makes It Impossible to Lower Many Boats, So Hundreds Must Have Gone Down.

ATTACKED IN BROAD DAY

Passengers at Luncheon—Warning Had Been Given by Germans Before the Ship Left New York.

Only 650 Were Saved, Few Cabin Passengers

QUEENSTOWN, Saturday, May 8, 4:28 A. M.—Survivors of the Lusitania who have arrived here estimate that only about 650 of those aboard the steamer were saved, and say only a small proportion of those

Cunard Office Here Besieged for News;

List of Saved Includes Capt. Turner;

Saw the Submarine 100 Yards Off

didate. The Republicans passed over the bellicose Teddy Roosevelt and selected a moderate—former New York governor Charles Evans Hughes. The Democrats praised Wilson's progressive reforms and proclaimed that he had kept the country out of war. Hughes had a difficult time convincing the electorate that his views were much different from Wilson's. In a close vote, Wilson defeated Hughes.

The German Imperial Government announced that unrestricted submarine warfare would resume on February 1, 1917; two days later, Wilson severed diplomatic relations. A determined antiwar group in Congress blocked the President's call for arming merchant ships, but by late February a rush of events compelled most of them to accept the inevitable. German submarines sank a British Cunard liner, the *Laconia,* and torpedoed three American freighters, killing several Americans. Soon after, British intelligence officers made public a startling secret. Germany's foreign minister, Arthur Zimmermann, had promised the Mexicans a chance "to reconquer lost territory in New Mexico, Texas and Arizona" if they declared war on the United States. Stunned, angry Americans now eagerly followed where Wilson reluctantly led. On April 2, 1917, the President asked Congress for a declaration of war. The resolution passed four days later. "The Yanks are coming!" a newspaper headlined. But would they arrive in time?

Isolationism Isolationists were Americans who wanted their country to keep isolated from the politics and ambitions of Europe. The United States, they believed, had a particular task, to perfect social and political democracy, which other nations might then profit from. Isolationism had considerable sway among the progressives, and a part of progressive isolationism was the strength that the progressive movement had possessed among midwestern German Americans. In later years, isolationism would become increasingly a creed among conservatives. Akin to isolationist thinking about the war was that of the socialists—again, many were of German background—who looked on the conflict as a reactionary capitalist and nationalist war that was merely setting workers to killing their brother workers on the battlefield, when all the world's working class should be sharing in the creation of a new just order.

At War 1917–1918

The Arsenal of Democracy While some progressives had embraced isolationism, the war enlisted the services, and beyond these the spirit, of progressivism. That movement, as a political and ideological force, embodied an appetite for central planning. The war offered that appetite a feast. Despite the years of fighting in Europe, the United States was not ready for war. No one in government had plans for mobilizing an American army or for converting industry to military production. Treasury officials and bankers paled at the complexities of war finance. If America was to become an arsenal of democracy, the nation must organize its economic power and invigorate its morale. That is exactly what progressives would do.

Raising an army proved easier than equipping one. Wilson and most members of Congress wanted a national army, not a collection of volunteer corps gathered locally as during much of the Civil War. A conscription law—the "draft," Americans have become accustomed to calling it—garnered nearly twenty-five million men between the ages of eighteen and forty-five into a national pool of potential soldiers, nearly twenty-five million. Of these, nearly three million were inducted and another two million volunteered. Yet the army had stockpiled in April 1917 only 600,000 rifles and 900 heavy guns, field weapons critical to trench warfare. American industrialists quickly converted their plants to munition and small arms production, but the British and French had to supply almost eighty percent of the artillery used by American forces. Nor did Yankee ingenuity meet the challenge of the war's new weapons, the tanks and the airplane. By the armistice, just sixty-four tanks had rolled off American production lines, and poor design and even worse management plagued aircraft construction.

The Allies, though, needed money more than military knowledge, and here the Americans responded hugely. War finance at first set off a bitter dispute in Congress: conservatives wanted high taxes on consumer goods, while progressives in both parties fought for large inheritance, personal income, and excess profits taxes. Congress in the War Revenue Acts settled for taxing away nearly two-thirds of large personal and corporate income. Radicals in Congress were not appeased; they pushed for confiscation of all earnings above $100,000. The extraordinary taxes brought in about $10.5 billion, some one-third of the war's total cost. The government borrowed the rest. The Treasury sold to the public some $25 billion of liberty bonds. This Niagara of dollars financed the American armies, of course, but billions poured overseas to pay for armaments for the Allies and to prop up British and French currencies.

Attention!

ALL MALES between the ages of 21 and 30 years, both inclusive, must personally appear at the polling place in the Election District in which they reside, on

TUESDAY, JUNE 5th, 1917

between the hours of 7 A.M. and 9 P. M. and

Register

in accordance with the President's Proclamation.

Any male person, between these ages, who fails to register on June 5th, 1917, will be subject to imprisonment in jail or other penal institution for a term of one year.

NO EXCUSE FOR FAILURE TO REGISTER WILL BE ACCEPTED

NON-RESIDENTS must apply personally for registration, at the office of the County Clerk, at Kingston, N. Y., AT ONCE, in order that their registration cards may be in the hands of the Registration Board of their home district before June 5, 1917

Employers of males between these ages are earnestly requested to assits in the enforcement of the President's Proclamation.

Signed,

BOARD OF REGISTRATION
of Ulster County
E. T. SHULTIS, Sheriff
C. K. LOUGHRAN, County Clerk
Dr. FRANK JOHNSTON, Medical Officer

After the declaration of war on April 2, 1917, the Selective Service Act was passed in May.

The Bureaucratic State

When the United States entered World War I in 1917, few people had any idea of the impact the war would have on the economy and public policy. The war brought the federal government into the economy in ways that had been unimaginable only a few years before.

Together, the Lever Act of 1917 and the Overman Act of 1918 gave the President absolute authority over farm production, commodity prices, and the uses and prices of industrial raw materials. To guarantee the uninterrupted shipment of goods, President Wilson created the Railroad Administration and virtually assumed complete control over American railroads. The Food Administration supervised rationing programs and helped augment American food production, while the Fuel Administration stimulated coal production by bringing marginal mines into service.

To prevent debilitating labor strikes that would disrupt war production, Wilson created the National War Labor Board and gave it the power to arbitrate disputes between management and labor. His War Labor Policies Board guaranteed labor's right to bargain collectively and set minimum wages and maximum hours in defense industries. The War Industries Board was given broad authority over industrial prices, allocation of raw materials, and production priorities so that it could guarantee sufficient war goods and meet domestic economic needs. The War Finance Corporation was to make loans to war industries. The modern American political economy, with its abundance of government agencies, had its beginnings during World War I.

The war was enormously profitable to the United States. Able to sell huge amounts of war goods in Europe but protected by the Atlantic Ocean from the ravages of war, the economy blossomed. By the end of the war the United States had become the greatest economic power in the world.

"The Yanks Are Coming"

The United States contributed a boisterous morale to the war. The spirit of the Yankee doughboys rekindled hopes for victory that the long lethal grind of trench warfare had dulled. At home, too, Americans steeled themselves for the unfamiliarity of vi-

President Wilson portrayed the Germans as "wild beasts." *(Courtesy, Imperial War Museum, London)*

olence with an enforced gaiety and a harsh patriotism. George M. Cohan, the Broadway star, had earlier written a stirring musical, composing one song "You're a Grand Old Flag!" so spirited that Congress awarded him a Medal of Honor. Another ballad, "Over There," cheerfully promised, "The Yanks are coming, the drums rumtumming," and "We won't come back until it's over, over there!" But dark bigotries clouded the nation's thoughts. Hatred of Germans and all things Germanic swept across the country, particularly in Pennsylvania and the upper Middle West where millions of German ancestry lived. Mobs stormed German language newspapers: some closed permanently. Schools and universities dropped courses related to the "enemy's" culture, even classes in German literature and music. Town elders changed street names; ball park vendors rechristened their frankfurters "hot dogs"; cooks spoke of "liberty cabbage," not sauerkraut. The government meanwhile waged, in such forms as the Sedition Act, something of

World War I soldiers in the trenches. *(Courtesy, AP/Wide World)*

A POOR AVIATOR LAY DYING. *This song of World War I was a favorite.*

A poor aviator lay dying.
At the end of a bright summer's day.
His comrades had gathered about him.
To carry his fragments away.

The airplane was piled on his wishbone,
His Hotchkiss was wrapped round his head;
He wore a spark-plug on each elbow,
'Twas plain he would shortly be dead.

He spit out a valve and a gasket,
And stirred in the sump where he lay,
And then to his wondering comrades,
These brave parting words he did say:

"Take the magneto out of my stomach,
And the butterfly valve off my neck,
Extract from my liver the crankshaft,
There are lots of good parts in this wreck."

"Take the manifold out of my larynx,
And the cylinders out of my brain,
Take the piston rods out of my kidneys,
And assemble the engine again."

a campaign of repression against socialists, draft resisters, anyone who could be seen to be obstructing the war effort.

The Eastern Front

The Central Powers pushed forward. In late October 1917 an Italian army disintegrated under hellish artillery fire and hand-to-hand combat near Caporetto. Submarine warfare mauled British shipping all that fall. Only after months of hard lessons did the Allies have enough ships and enough knowledge to convoy merchantmen safely to port. On the Eastern Front, meanwhile, Russia's ability to stay in the war seemed less and less likely. Battles there had wiped out much of the country's fledgling industry; only large munitions shipments from Britain and the United States kept dispirited, poorly led Russian troops in the field.

In February 1917, socialists and middle-class liberals had taken over the government of Russia from Tsar Nicholas. When the Tsar called for troops to oust the usurpers, none responded; they were too disillusioned by military failures, and autocracy was no longer acceptable. Americans at first regarded the overthrow of the tsars in a positive light. But radical groups demanded from the new democratic government an immediate peace and sweeping economic reforms. Germans abetted the growing chaos by slipping Lenin, leader of the revolutionary Bolshevik party, back into the capital city. Once there, he orchestrated the chant, "Peace, Land and Bread," into a program for revolution. The prospect of an anti-capitalist Russia abandoning the war panicked the Allies. Wilson and Prime Minister Lloyd George pressured Russian leaders such as Alexander Kerensky to keep on fighting, regardless of public sentiment. But more and more Russian troops—nearly one-third of them virtually unarmed—simply deserted. The Eastern Front would soon disintegrate.

The German High Command, now under the leadership of Erich Ludendorff, massed its troops for a decisive assault. German troops overran the Baltic provinces and occupied much of Ukraine. Already discredited and disillusioned by the war, moderates quietly gave in to a palace revolution staged by the Bolsheviks in November 1917. Lenin then capitulated to the Germans. A peace treaty, signed at Brest-Litovsk in March 1918, surrendered nearly half of European Russia to the Kaiser.

The Western Front

Soon after the Russians withdrew, the Germans attacked violently all along the Western Front. Their dangerous offensive lasted five months. During March and April Ludendorff's most battle-ready troops stormed across Allied lines in northern France and Belgium. British counterattacks stopped their advance, but only after Germans had penetrated some thirty miles, more ground than either side had gained since the beginning of trench warfare in 1914. This near disaster prompted the Allies to set up a unified command under French general Ferdinand Foch and accelerated the movement of American troops into the war. Soon nearly 250,000 fresh, hastily-trained American soldiers were taking to the lines every month, over two million by the fall of 1918. One soldier wrote of finding

> a country of flat plowed field, pollard willows and deep muddy ditches. Then we come along, and in military parlance 'dig ourselves in.' That is, with the sweat of the brows of hundreds . . . working by night narrow trenches five feet deep at least and with the earth thrown up another two and a half feet as a bank on top. These trenches are one and a half to two feet wide, and curl and twist about in a maddening manner to make them safer from shell-fire. Little caves are scooped in the walls of the trenches, where the men live about four to a hole, and slightly bigger dug-outs where two officers live. All the soil is clay, stickier and greasier than one could believe possible. It's like almost solid paint, and the least rain makes the sides of the trenches slimy, and the bottom a perfect sea of mud—pulls the heels off your boots almost.

Meanwhile, the Germans attacked again, this time east of Paris. In just three days, the enemy reached the strategic village of Chateau-Thierry on the Marne River, only fifty miles from the capital. A French army, now well fleshed out by American divisions, blocked further advance; then the Americans by themselves pushed the Germans out of Belleau Woods, reestablishing the front. By midsummer 1918, the grand German offensive was broken. With Americans streaming up to the lines, the military advantage shifted permanently to the Allies. That fall, Foch launched a counterattack along a 200-mile front, aimed at destroying Germany's supply lines behind the Meuse River. General John Pershing, now commander of an exclusively American army, fought on the easternmost flank, for five weeks slugging through the Argonne Forest. The Yanks finally triumphed, wiping out German armies long entrenched in the difficult terrain. In late October Pershing's forces captured the railways that had supplied German forces. British and French troops had already destroyed German positions north of Paris, and German armies everywhere reeled back across France into Belgium. As the Western Front crumbled, the German High Command surrendered any hope of victory. "Open armistice negotiations as soon as possible," Ludendorff telephoned the Kaiser. The belligerents agreed to the armistice on November 11, 1918. Guns along the Western Front fell silent.

The Fourteen Points Wilson's war message to Congress, designed to rally domestic public opinion, had pledged "to make the world safe for democracy." Such generalities had little to do with secret Allied agreements that granted to Britain a dominant role in the Middle East and to France its long-coveted frontier on the Rhine. Even before the United States entered the war, Wilson had called for "a peace without victory," a peace between equals that avoided mutual hatreds and the seeds of future war. Then partly to counter Bolshevik propaganda, partly to thwart his Allies' imperialist schemes and partly to reinvigorate

---

I HAVE A RENDEZVOUS WITH DEATH *by Alan Seeger*

This was John F. Kennedy's favorite poem. Seeger died in the First World War.

I have a Rendezvous with Death
At some disputed barricade,
When Spring comes back with rustling shade
And apple blossoms fill the air—
I have a rendezvous with Death
When Spring brings back blue days and fair.

It may be he shall take my hand,
And lead me into his dark land,
And close my eyes and quench my breath—
It may be I shall pass him still.
I have a rendezvous with Death
On some scarred slope of battered hill,
When Spring comes round again this year
And the first meadow-flowers appear.

God knows 'twere better to be deep
Pillowed in silk and scented down,
Where Love throbs out in blissful sleep,
Pulse nigh to pulse, and breath to breath,
Where hushed awakenings are dear . . .
But I've a rendezvous with Death
At midnight in some flaming town,
When Spring trips north again this year;
And I to my pledged word am true,
I shall not fail that rendezvous.

Western morale, Wilson presented an attractive set of war aims. In a speech to Congress on January 8, 1918, he outlined his Fourteen Points, which defined a new world order of justice, peace, and prosperity: freedom of the seas, removal of trade barriers, disarmament, national self-determination in central and eastern Europe, and a new era of collective security. This last idea, institutionalized in a League of Nations, was supposed to lessen the prospect of any future wars. All countries would pledge to resist any single nation guilty of aggression, and the prospect of certain defeat would deter the potential wrongdoer. Critics pointed out that such provisions masked Anglo-American movement toward global domination. But Wilson's ringing rhetoric thrilled public opinion at the time on both sides of the Atlantic. A new dawn seemed close to breaking.

The League of Nations

A Grand Vision Woodrow Wilson's League of Nations was a grand vision. It was to be a social contract among nations, leading the peoples of the world out of an old age of wars and fragile peace. The United States, in fulfillment of its historic mission, would be the agent of regeneration. Because America was the embodiment and champion of humane and libertarian values, its pursuit of its own safety and eminence was for the good of the world community it sought to renew. Or so the Wilsonians believed. Wilson's great importance for twentieth-century foreign affairs lies in his casting of the American national interest in a rhetoric of liberal internationalism.

Postwar policy was as anti-Bolshevist as it was anti-German. Bolshevism was the enemy in Siberia, where in the winter of 1919 the United States joined Britain, France, and Japan in an unsuccessful intervention and suffered considerable casualties. Against Lenin's vision of a world revolution, Wilson set a vision of a world system of parliamentary republics and unhindered international commerce—ordered by the League and led by the United States.

Wilson was probably wise to go to Paris to negotiate the Treaty of Versailles that ended the war and divided the former German and Austrian empires in eastern Europe into a number of new nations. He displayed more vision and greater energy at the peace table than did any other major world leader, and he took with him a host of intellectual advisers to provide him with timely analyses of problems to be solved.

Yet he did not, perhaps could not, prepare the Senate and the American people for acceptance of his work, particularly for the many compromises between ideals and European national interest. Wilson lost in his attempt to scale down to reasonable size the reparations from Germany demanded by the Allies, but thought that a future American presence on the reparations commissions would insure a fairer settlement. He was perhaps most effective in resisting excessive territorial encroachments on Germany by the Allies, and setting political boundaries that conformed in the main to lines of nationality. Wilson did not support Japan's demand for a racial equality clause in the Treaty and lost face among liberals by agreeing to let that country keep the Chinese province of Shantung. A paternalistic mandate system gave to modern countries a number of presumably backward and unwesternized territories they were to govern and prepare for eventual self-rule. Though the mandate system was partly a means of dividing among the victors the spoils of war, it subjected the governing powers to various restrictions and demanded of them responsible administration of the mandated territory. On balance Wilson achieved a reasonable treaty redeemed, in his estimate, because it contained the Covenant of the League of Nations.

The Fight Over the League At the end of the war the vast majority of Americans favored some form of a League. But this support splintered when they had to agree on a particular League.

Republicans were the first to be estranged. By his appeal on October 25, 1918, for a Democratic Congress, Wilson invited a partisan response on postwar policies. By failing

The "Big Four"—Prime Minister Lloyd George of England, Premier Orlando of Italy, French Premier Clemenceau, and President Wilson—who forged the Treaty of Versailles ending World War I. *(Courtesy, Library of Congress)*

to take senior Republicans with him to Paris, and by leaving them ignorant of his progress there, he widened the gulf. The off-term elections produced a Republican Congress. Wilson assailed anti-League Senators, calling them "bungalow minds" whose heads were "knots tied to keep their bodies from unraveling." Wilson apparently assumed at Versailles and thereafter that it was the Senate's duty to stamp its formal approval on such momentous presidential negotiation. It is therefore not surprising that the Republicans—led by Senator Henry Cabot Lodge, majority leader and chairman of the Foreign Relations Committee—insisted on modifications of the League Covenant. And Wilson's willingness to barter away advantage at Versailles in exchange for a secure League lost him the support of many fellow idealists. Unwilling to accept Wilson's argument that a League could correct inequities in the treaty, they became convinced that the President had betrayed his famous Fourteen Points outlining the basis for a just peace.

The issue of Versailles divided the President's own party. The immigrant vote, much of it traditionally Democratic, became as bitterly opposed to the treaty as the most intractable isolationists. Several nationalities resented its impact on their motherlands. The heavily Democratic Irish saw the League as an instrument for oppression at the hands of the British, who, through the membership of their dominions, such as Australia or South Africa, would control a sizable number of votes in the League Assembly. German-Americans sought revenge against Wilson for the war and the reparations settlement. Americans of Italian descent resented the award of the city of Fiume to the new state of Yugoslavia. Jews disliked the eastern European territorial settlements, the failure at

Versailles to create a Jewish homeland, and the administration's treatment of Jewish radicals.

By the fall of 1919 wartime idealism had fallen victim to the continuing and fruitless League debates in and out of the Senate. By the time Senator Henry Cabot Lodge finished his Foreign Relations Committee hearings, much of the public thought of the League not as an instrument for peace but largely as a vehicle for unending war. For the Republicans argued that Article X of the League Covenant—a statement guaranteeing national boundaries—would simply mean one police action after another, with the United States obliged to contribute. Wilson invited Republican senators to the White House and tried to reason with them; he even drew up four reservations to the Covenant, which he planned to offer if needed.

Opposition to President Wilson's League of Nations mounted, and the Senate finally defeated the plan that would have allowed the United States to join. *(Cartoon by Rollin Kirby,* New York World, *April 14, 1921)*

Going to the People

Wilson had a final strategy. Following the British tradition, he would go to the people. Although weakened by influenza, he began a speaking tour in September to generate support for his League. He delivered some thirty major speeches, pointing out the economic benefits the League would bring, arguing that Article X was a moral rather than a legal commitment, and generally portraying the League as man's best hope. On September 25 he suffered a physical breakdown in Pueblo, Colorado, and shortly after that he had a paralyzing cerebral hemorrhage. Had Wilson died in 1919 and become a martyr, his dream of American participation in a League might have become a reality. As it was, secluded in the White House, he became an object of gossip and slander.

The Versailles Treaty with the League Covenant attached first came before the Senate in November 1919. The critical vote was on whether to accept entrance with reservations, which protected Senate prerogatives and such traditions as the Monroe Doctrine. Loyal Wilsonian Democrats opposed to the reservations joined their votes to those of isolationists opposed to the treaty as a whole, and it was defeated. The Senate voted again: perhaps enough members in favor of a League would finally accept compromise. Three of the first four Democrats previously in opposition voted for the Treaty. The final vote was forty-nine in favor and thirty-five against—just seven short of the necessary two-thirds.

Wilson asked that the election of 1920 be a "solemn referendum" on the League. But the candidacy of a handsome Ohio senator, Warren Harding, overwhelmed the Democratic ticket of Ohio governor James Cox and vice-presidential candidate Franklin Delano Roosevelt. Senator Harding rode an anti-Wilson tide and won the election by almost a two-to-one popular margin. The new Republican Vice President, Calvin Coolidge, observed that the election marked "the end of a period which had seemed to substitute words for things." The League was dead.

Women at Work and in the Voting Booth

The war had accelerated important changes in women's role in the labor force. The decline in the importance of the farm sector, together with the growth of the corporation, the expansion of such forms of white collar employment as advertising, and the coming of electrical industries had altered the employment of women as well as men. The war itself brought only a modest increase, 6.3 percent, of women in the labor force, but it did deepen new patterns of female employment. Female clerks, secretaries, advertising employees, and telephone operators increased significantly in numbers. And the number of white women in service jobs, especially domestic service, declined significantly. Black women remained heavily concentrated in service and agricultural labor. But a small percentage of black women workers did break into manufacturing jobs that had previously been rigidly closed to them. Although business did not force women altogether out of the labor force to make way for returning veterans, many were dismissed from some of the higher-paying jobs related to the war. The war years confirmed the steady, if still slow, growth in female participation in the labor force.

The Nineteenth Amendment The adoption of the Nineteenth Amendment, which guaranteed women the right to vote in federal and state elections, like other political events of the period benefited from the spirit engendered by the war. Before the nation's entry into the war, the campaign for woman suffrage had received new vigor under the lead-

Most women voted for the first time, in the 1920 elections, following passage of the Nineteenth Amendment. *(Courtesy, Brown Brothers, New York City)*

IN THIS ERA OF EMERGING WOMEN'S RIGHTS, *a woman wrote to a friend about the summer she did the haying:*

Dear Mrs. Coney:

Mr. Stewart had been too confident of getting men, so that haying caught him with too few men to put up the hay. He had no man to run the mower and he couldn't run both the mower and the stacker, so you can fancy what a place he was in.

I don't know that I ever told you, but my parents died within a year of each other and left six of us to shift for ourselves. Our people offered to take one here and there among them until we should all have a place, but we refused to be raised on the halves and so arranged to stay at Grandmother's and keep together. Well, we had no money to hire men to do our work, so had to learn to do it ourselves. Consequently I learned to do many things which girls more fortunately situated don't even know have to be done. Among the things I learned to do was the way to run a mowing-machine. It cost me many bitter tears because I got sunburned, and my hands were hard, rough, and stained with machine oil, and I used to wonder how any Prince Charming could overlook all that in any girl he came to. For all I had ever read of the Prince had to do with his "reverently kissing her lily-white hand," or doing some other fool trick with a hand as white as a snowflake. . . .

I almost forgot that I knew how until Mr. Stewart got into such a panic. If he put a man to mow, it kept them all idle at the stacker, and he just couldn't get enough men. I was afraid to tell him I could mow for fear he would forbid me to do so. But one morning, when he was chasing a last hope of help, I went down to the barn, took out the horses, and went to mowing. I had enough cut before he got back to show him I knew how, and as he came back manless he was delighted as well as surprised. I was glad because I really like to mow.

Elinore Stewart

ership of Carrie Chapman Catt and was beginning to score important victories in winning women the vote in specific states. But in 1917 women had still not gotten the vote in any of the big industrial eastern states or in any state in the South. The suffrage leaders recognized the importance of gaining passage of a federal bill or constitutional amendment. The mainstream suffrage movement made every effort to support the war effort and to demonstrate women's loyalty to American values, a position reminiscent of the social feminism that had sought the vote for women as the moral element in American society. The more radical current of the movement, under the leadership of Alice Paul, refused any compromise with American institutions until women received the vote, a stand in the tradition of the militant feminism that placed issues of women's rights above all else. But when in 1919 Woodrow Wilson moved from opposing to supporting the suffrage campaign, he said that he was doing so in acknowledgment of women's contribution to the war effort. The perception that women had won the vote through their support for dominant American institutions and values, and through their continued acceptance of a proper female role, helps to explain why woman suffrage did not, in the short run, bring a strong feminist presence to American politics. Women won the vote under conditions that made it appear to be primarily a tool of middle-class white women who accepted the status quo and who had no special ties to black or working-class women.

Demobilization and the Red Scare

Conversion to Peace The end of the First World War left the government with the problem of how to return the country's economy and society to a peacetime basis. The President said that "people would go their own way." They would want a relaxation of wartime restraints and Wilson, who viewed the public as the final repository of support for his League of Nations, had no wish to alienate them.

Demobilization, when it came, was rapid. Almost immediately following the armistice the government discharged 600,000 veterans. Four million more returned to the peacetime economy during the next year; most of them reached their homes by the summer of 1919, some carrying gas masks or helmets as souvenirs. Commitments to government war spending inevitably continued into peace, and no early postwar deflation occurred. In 1920 Congress did pass legislation that helped demobilize the economy from its wartime footing and also represented a final burst of Wilsonian progressivism. But it was a progressivism of a character less of Wilson's New Freedom than of Theodore Roosevelt's New Nationalism, a concern not for dismantling large enterprises but for bringing them under close federal regulations.

The Transportation Act, also known as the Esch-Cummins Act, returned the nation's railroads to private control but at the same time expanded the powers of the Interstate Commerce Commission, allowing it to set minimum and maximum railroad rates. By establishing a Railway Labor Board, the law also came close to requiring government arbitration of disputes between labor and management in the railroad industry. The Merchant Marine Act, also termed the Jones Act, repealed the wartime legislation giving the federal government much authority over the shipping industry. The Shipping Board helped the industry make the transition to private control. And the Water Power Act brought the federal government into the hydroelectric power industry. Progressives had long been demanding government regulation of monopolies, and the Water Power Act represented a beginning. The legislation created the Federal Power Commission and gave it authority over all public land water as well as over navigable streams, lakes, and rivers.

The economy was unsettled. As industries once bloated by war shrank, many people moved from one job to another. The high cost of living was a constant irritant; consumer prices had almost doubled between 1914 and 1920 and rose fastest in the postwar period. It was a time not of high unemployment but of economic dislocation.

The "Red Scare" The emotion of a modern war, the perfect fusion of lofty idealism with the baser feelings of chauvinism, had settled easily upon a nation technologically advanced enough for total mobilization and still naive enough to believe in splendid adventures with noble goals. The aftermath of the war was an assault on that innocence. Having finished a war it had thought it could handle on the simplest and purest moral terms, the nation discovered that those terms meant little to Europe. The war passion had been orchestrated by the Committee on Public Information, which had set professors from the best universities to writing propaganda. The organization and George Creel, the Denver progressive who directed it, shared in the popular enthusiasm they elicited. When the war ended and the committee dissolved, the emotion remained and sought out new enemies on which to spend its aggression. Among them was Bolshevism.

The Socialist Party, once a thriving progressive organization under the leadership of Eugene Debs, had fallen into disrepute for its opposition to the war. Debs himself, prosecuted under Wilson's harsh Sedition Act, remained silent in jail. Mobs and wartime legislation crushed the more radical Industrial Workers of the World or Wobblies. By 1919 many socialists had joined either the native Communist Party of America or the Communist Labor Party, composed mainly of foreign-born urban Americans. Both parties combined amounted to considerably less than one percent of the population. Their very existence, however, provided some business groups, anxious to keep labor from extending its wartime gains, with a convenient image to fix on to the labor movement and social protest as a whole.

In the winter of 1919 the city of Seattle, Washington, experienced something almost totally unfamiliar in American history, a general strike. In sympathy with striking longshoremen, the unions that ran the city—streetcar employees, clerical workers, even firemen—walked off their jobs, leaving Seattle paralyzed. A Committee of Public Safety, which sounded vaguely foreign and revolutionary, maintained essential services. But the strikers could not agree on demands, public opinion turned against them, and Mayor Ole Hanson brought marines into the city to end the strike.

After the Seattle strike Mayor Hanson's office received a package wrapped in brown paper. Since the mayor was in Colorado selling war bonds that were still being issued after the end of the war, it was put aside and some liquid leaked out, burning a wooden table. The package was a homemade bomb. A similar missive went to the home of a southern senator favoring more stringent immigration restriction—and blew the hands off his black maid. A New York City postal employee read about the packages and remembered putting some others aside for insufficient postage. Marked with a "Gimbel's Brothers" return address, they were found at the main post office in New York City or in transit. Newspapers compiled a "bomb honor list" that included Supreme Court Justice Oliver Wendell Holmes, financier J. P. Morgan, and Attorney General A. Mitchell Palmer. Whoever mailed the packages apparently intended that they should arrive around May Day, the Communist holiday. In June a bomb-thrower blew himself to smithereens with his own missile on the steps of Palmer's house in Washington. After this incident Palmer, once known as a progressive, became notorious for rounding up aliens and endeavoring to deport them.

In the summer of 1919 a bloody race riot occurred in Chicago, where 600,000 blacks would move in the decade beginning in 1917. A black youth unable to swim had clung to a railroad tie that drifted into an area of Lake Michigan reserved for whites. Whites swam menacingly toward him: he moved away for a few strokes, then sank and drowned. When police refused to arrest any whites and instead took a protesting black into custody, a riot ensued, killing twenty-three blacks and fifteen whites. Riots occurred in other cities, and in the course of 1919 some seventy blacks were murdered, including at least ten veterans of the recently ended World War.

In September the whole Boston police force went out on an unprecedented strike. The mayor fired the strikers, the President called the strike "a crime against civilization," and Governor Calvin Coolidge said that there was "no right to strike against the public safety by anybody, anywhere, anytime." In Washington state that November an IWW member provoked into shooting an American Legionnaire was taken from prison by a mob that beat and castrated him, hanged him from a bridge, and riddled his body with bullets. In early January 1920, the New York State Assembly refused to seat five legally elected Socialists. For once in a period when law and mobs were persecuting radicals, distinguished citizens did protest an act of repression. A number of them denounced the Assembly's action.

Labor Strife Friction between labor and management heated after the war. Labor unions, which had been granted some government protection during the hostilities, determined to maintain collective bargaining and to push the closed shop, an arrangement whereby a business would hire only union members. Leaders of management, resolved to restore their earlier dominance, denounced the closed shop as an assault on liberty, and promoted the "American Plan," the open shop. Over 4,000 strikes ensued during the year 1919.

The men who ran the steel industries were among the least enlightened in all management. In 1910, thirty percent of the labor force in steel had worked a seven-day week; seventy-five percent had worked a twelve-hour day, some even laboring on two consecutive twelve-hour shifts every other Sunday when they changed from day to night work. The average work week for the whole industry was sixty-eight hours. During the war the industry, to avoid government intervention, agreed to pay time-and-a-half for work beyond an eight-hour day, and a severe labor shortage raised wages faster than inflation could erode the gains. Unions flourished; by the war's finish, more than 100,000 steel workers belonged. The great steel strike began on September 23, 1919. Management, which refused to meet with union leaders at all, knew it held the upper hand. The national organization was unready, lacking money and adequate preparation for a venture thrust upon it by militant locals. By January the strike was dead.

The Palmer Raids The Red Scare culminated in the Palmer raids of January 2, 1920, when Justice Department agents, striking simultaneously in dozens of cities, rounded up thousands of aliens. Held incommunicado for days in violation of their civil rights, they would have been shipped to Europe had Palmer got his way.

Sonia Kaross would remember what happened to her during the Palmer Raids:

> We were living in Philadelphia and had been at a chorus rehearsal. We came home—it must have been eleven or twelve—and went to bed. One o'clock, there was banging on the doors. It woke up the whole building. There were police cars and all kinds of detectives all over the street. They came in and took all my books, all my letters, whatever they found.
>
> Then they took my husband and me away. I was almost seven months pregnant. The police threw me in the wagon. And I was locked up with five or six prostitutes. I got sick from all the excitement and the way the police handled me. Those prostitutes, I want to tell you, were the nicest people. I didn't fully understand what was going on. I thought: Well, I'm just getting sick. But they realized that I might lose the baby. They raised an awful rumpus. They were screaming, hollering, knocking on the door. They were yelling, "This woman is dying! Get her an ambulance!" But nobody responded. All night they banged the door while I lay there suffering. Well, my companions in jail saved my life, but they couldn't save the baby's. Before the ambulance came it was morning, and the baby was dead. . . .
>
> We were charged with being undesirable. . . . I was elected a delegate . . . from the Young Socialist League, and they had found that out. . . . We had no rights. . . . There was such a wide gap between the native Americans and the foreign-born.

The opposition of Acting Secretary of Labor Louis F. Post, a political progressive who now held technical power over deportations, saved many of Palmer's victims from being thrown out of the country. When nativist congressmen sought to impeach Post in the House, he reminded them of the Bill of Rights and refused to budge. At the same time that Post was declining to effect Palmer's will, the nation was tiring of its attorney general and his repeated warnings against the Reds. By the spring of 1920 the Red Scare was on the wane, soon to be replaced by concern over a serious depression that lasted until 1922 and then by the revolution in customs and values that occupied the nation in the 1920s. A bomb that killed dozens in Wall Street in 1920 was correctly regarded as the work of cranks, and there was no widespread attempt to associate it with a conspiracy of radicals.

Lingering Effects The Bolshevik revolution and the establishment of a one-party Communist regime added a burden that has pressed upon American socialists ever since. Now a system calling itself "socialist" was manifestly imposing centralization and repression on Russia and the other lands under the control of the Bolshevik Communists. Not even the relentless war of words and bullets that Communists and democratic socialists have waged upon each other since then, in country after country, has managed to reveal to the American public the irreconcilable opposition between socialism and the thing that in Russia took that name.

This conviction that radicalism and socialism are alien to the nation's culture, this absence of a longstanding and fairly sizable political left, is a peculiarity of American politics. The decline of the Socialist Party after the First World War and the ferocity with which Americans came to reject the very idea of a radical left meant that their politics would lack the diversity, the sharpness and intelligence of philosophical debate that have prevailed among other Western nations.

Traces of the Red Scare itself flecked the twenties. The newly-formed American Legion grew rapidly, preaching "one country, one language, one flag." While the Legion was a legitimate organization of veterans, some of its members collected themselves into such mobs as the one that lynched the Wobbly in Washington state. A burgeoning Ku Klux Klan reached a membership of some two to four million by 1924. The trial of two Italian anarchist immigrants, Bartolomeo Vanzetti and Nicola Sacco, for the robbery and murder in 1920 of a paymaster in South Braintree, Massachusetts, was reminiscent of the Red Scare. While modern ballistics study indicates that Sacco was probably guilty, the

Tornado Over Kansas **by John Steuart Curry, one of the regionalist painters who celebrated rural American life.** *(Courtesy, Muskegon Museum of Art)*

fish peddler Vanzetti was perhaps innocent. What is memorable about the trial is its xenophobic atmosphere. The judge privately referred to the defendants as "those anarchistic bastards," and his conduct of the trial was scarcely less prejudiced. Before his execution in 1927 Vanzetti delivered a moving oration:

> We were tried during a time that has now passed into history. . . . I am suffering because I am a radical and indeed I am a radical. I have suffered because I was an Italian, and indeed I am an Italian; I have suffered more for my family and for my beloved than for myself; but I am so convinced to be right that if you could execute me two times, and if I could be reborn two other times, I would live again to do what I have done already.

City vs. Country in the 1920s

For traditionalists from the farms and the small towns, the city stood for all that was alien to American life. Descended from many generations of Americans, they worried about the communities of "foreign" stock and identified the city with the vice of alcohol.

Prohibition For a short time, the alcohol question came close to being the single most intoxicating ingredient in American politics on the national level. In 1919 the nation adopted the Eighteenth Amendment to the Constitution, and it went into effect the next year. The measure prohibited the manufacture, sale, transportation, import, and export of liquor. By the mid-twenties, the defenders and opponents of prohibition were at angry odds over whether the Amendment should be repealed. Each side connected the issue with larger cultural matters. Many though not all prohibitionists associated alcohol with Roman Catholics, immigrants, corrupt worldliness and pleasure-seeking: with a whole range of forces that were centered in the big cities and threatened the nation's plain old-fashioned morals. Numbers of immigrant-stock Catholics in turn associated prohibition with nativist prejudice and Protestant bigotry. New York City gave the country Alfred E. Smith, a Catholic of Irish descent who opposed prohibition and as governor of New York State signed bills legalizing Sunday baseball and the bloody sport of boxing.

Prohibition in Practice Prohibition's history dates back to the mid-nineteenth century and before, when Americans consumed huge amounts of liquor. During the Progressive Era the dry organizations drew support from the eugenics movement, which argued the banning of alcohol for improving the race; from women who saw their husbands spend wages in saloons or wished to "uplift" the urban poor; and from nativists who viewed the movement as a symbolic battle against the new immigrants as well as the Irish. Then came the war. Along with wartime hostility to German-American brewers came more serious considerations: alcohol was a wasteful use of grain that could feed the army and war-torn Europe; the purchase of whiskey was a luxury diverting money from the war effort; and alcohol, so it was thought, interfered with the efficiency of the labor the war so desperately needed. And so, with the passage of the Eighteenth Amendment after the war, the country went dry.

In many cities prohibition popularized drinking by forcing it to be secretive and therefore romantic. While the immigrant poor could make their own home brews, the young middle class—both male and female—had fun in dark speakeasies. Movies depicted drinking by the hero and his girlfriend. But the quality of available liquor declined as well as the quantity. Now there came mixtures called Old Stingo or Cherry Dynamite, concocted often with a dash of iodine, sulphuric acid, creosote, or embalming fluid. Poisoned liquor occasionally killed someone who could not afford the steady flow of Canadian Club that entered from the North, sometimes on sleds drawn by dog team, or spirits brought in by Caribbean and Atlantic rum-runners.

Organized crime had existed well before the twenties: by taking over the illegal distribution of liquor the gangs flourished. Prohibition's fairest flower was Al Capone, a Chicago mobster responsible for hundreds of deaths. The St. Valentine's Day Massacre, which culminated a gang war in Chicago, Capone called "bad public relations." For some Americans of immigrant background a life of crime was a route to higher status.

Part of the folklore of the period is that prohibition did not work. Statistics reveal that prohibition did cut down the amount of drinking, and alcoholism also declined. The problem is that this came at a great price. Prohibition made for an increase in organized crime in the dank criminal underworld. It put a strain on the resources of the police. It deprived the government of the tax revenues that might have been collected on legal alcohol. It deepened the hostility between Catholics and Protestants, between immigrant-stock and old-stock Americans. It gave the prohibitionist and hate-mongering Ku Klux Klan one more issue to feed on.

By the later 1920s, then, the social and financial costs of prohibition were outrunning its apparent benefits. Drys had promised that it would empty jails and mental institutions, and therefore lower taxes. Local taxes did not fall, and some wealthy Americans began to spend money to get the Eighteenth Amendment repealed. As the Great Depression cast its shadow the public was turning against the great experiment. An increased need for tax revenue and a turning of public attention to grim realities brought in 1932 the Twenty-First Amendment, repealing the Eighteenth.

Fundamentalism The politics of traditionalism also drew fundamentalists, those Protestants who hold to belief in the literal meaning of Scripture. The preachers and lecturers of fundamentalism would talk about the growing power of the Catholic Church, drawing its strength from the immigrants and their offspring in the urban centers. Or they would announce that the great cities were the place of skepticism and agnosticism, and warned of modernist Protestant theologians who refused to accept the Bible in its clear and simple sense. Hinterland moralists were convinced that the cities, infected with atheism and false religion, had gone also into more general decadence. New York City housed cultural enterprises like the opera and the ballet that many rural Americans thought snobbish and unmasculine. More particularly, traditionalists identified the city with Tammany Hall.

Fundamentalism had its own particular public event in the decade. In the small town of Dayton, Tennessee, John Scopes had taught his public high-school biology students, in disobedience of state statute, that man had descended from an ape-like creature. William Jennings Bryan—hopelessly naive about religion—offered himself as a witness for the prosecution and was intellectually pounded by the great criminal lawyer, Clarence Darrow, an agnostic. A witness for Scopes remembered later:

> The important question he [Darrow] asked was whether Scopes' teaching for evolution had affected my religion in any way. He asked if I still attended church and Sunday school and believed in the Bible. I said I was still religious.

In one sense, the encounter of 1925 merely pitted authority against authority—"the Bible teaches" against "Science says"—for many street-corner evolutionists, like much of American society, took science to be a giver of revelations rather than a complex method of doubt, inquiry, and tentative hypothesis.

Immigration Restriction Hostility to immigrants was reinforced during the First World War, which brought violence against German Americans. And the activities of antiwar radicals evoked the old image of the immigrant revolutionary, a large specter during the Red Scare of 1919. Native labor, suffering hard times in the depression of 1920–1922, complained that competition with immigrants was pulling down wages. Even among businessmen who were interested in cheap labor, there was some distrust of immigrants as being open to labor radicalism. Social workers sometimes betrayed a subtle distaste for their clients. One reformer's guide recommended for tenement flats:

> wood-stained and uncluttered furniture surfaces, iron beds with mattresses, and un-upholstered chairs. . . . Walls must be painted not papered . . . screens provide privacy in the bedrooms; a few good pictures should grace the walls.

The white-sheeted, anti-immigrant fraternal order of the Ku Klux Klan flourished during the decade. Founded in 1915 in Georgia as an imitation of the Reconstruction Klan, the new organization gathered its two to four million members chiefly during the early twenties. In the South it directed much of its fury against blacks; over the country as a whole it was militant against Catholicism and immigration. The Klan's popularity came from the lure of secrecy and from association with religious and patriotic institutions. One of the Klan's most popular songs, sung to the tune of "The Battle Hymn of the Republic," combined symbols of both:

> We rally round Old Glory in our robes of spotless white,
> While the Fiery Cross is burning in the silent, silv'ry night,
> Come join our glorious army in the cause of God and Right,
> The Klan is marching on.

One of the Klan's triumphs came in helping to insure that Governor Al Smith of New York would not win the Democratic presidential nomination in 1924. The Klan did its part to spread anti-Catholic rumors that the Pope, crowded in the Vatican, aspired to new headquarters in the Mississippi Valley and that his minions were tunneling their way under the Atlantic Ocean to give orders to Smith in New York. The Klan declined when financial and sexual scandals struck some of its leaders in the mid-twenties.

Another ground of nativism, quite urban and academic in character, was the pseudoscientific racism that was having its vogue at this time. The social psychologist William McDougall of Harvard studied results of World War I intelligence tests, which showed lower I.Q. scores for southern Europeans. Having little knowledge of the distortions that differences in environment and cultures make in such tests, he concluded that they demonstrated the superiority of northern Europeans over other peoples.

The immigration law of 1921 imposed an annual nationality quota: three percent of the number of each group in America in 1920. The Johnson Act of 1924 legislation reduced the quota from three to two percent, and set the date back to 1890 for computing it. The thrust was against the cities and the recent immigrant. The Japanese were badly treated in the 1924 law; through a diplomatic bungle the Gentleman's Agreement with Japan, by which unskilled workers were barred except for those with families already here, was abrogated and Japanese immigration totally banned. It was an insult to a proud people, and an incident in a continuing history of insults to Japan that prepared the ground for World War II.

The Jazz Age

The Idea of the "Twenties"

People have a way of thinking by decades, as though "the twenties," "the thirties," or "the sixties" each defines by some logic of numbers a distinct cultural situation. The 1920s was especially susceptible to this, for the decade is marked off nearly at its edges by the Great War and the Great Depression. It was a colorful time that became quickly and heavily stereotyped. Under a rhetoric of individualism, the United States was collectivizing its productive and financial institutions. An ideology of calling for economy in government coexisted with an expansion of bureaucracy. The country talked isolationism and extended its influence abroad.

Defined by some of its most striking qualities, the "twenties" did not even open with 1920 or 1921, but was launched well before then. There had been bohemians in Greenwich Village, Chicago, and San Francisco as early as 1910. American women had begun to assert themselves, leading in the field of social work, entering a few of the professions, and demanding the vote. As early as 1914, H. L. Mencken coined the term "flapper" for a new, less inhibited type of woman. Unsettling literary influences were coming in from abroad: D. H. Lawrence in England, the decadent symbolists in France, the mystic novelists and short story writers in Russia. Experiments in poetic form were particularly notable. Some young people began to think of themselves as "modern" and as a new generation, and to denounce their elders as puritans. World War I sped these and other changes. Before 1914 people had read Freud and interpreted him as blaming sexual repression for neuroses, but the war—seen in retrospect as a mad and reckless slaughter—made Freudians take notice also of his emphasis on human irrationality. After the experience of the conflict, and later the Great Depression, the influential Protestant theologian Reinhold Niebuhr would begin his lifetime advocacy of the need for social reform to mitigate the effects of man's unending potentiality for evil.

Literature and Popular Culture

The decade was a triumphant time in art and literature. The 1920s introduced or continued the work of durable figures: Eugene O'Neill, Gertrude Stein, Ezra Pound, e. e. cummings, Sinclair Lewis, Sherwood Anderson, Ernest Hemingway, F. Scott Fitzgerald, John Dos Passos, Theodore Dreiser, Robert Frost, Hart Crane, Robinson Jeffers, Edna St. Vincent Millay, and many others. And there was a rich flowering of the arts in Harlem: the Harlem Renaissance, which included the works of James Weldon Johnson and Zora Neale Hurston. The American theater enjoyed a highly creative period, and there was active experimentation, both artistic and technical, in the young medium of the movies.

I'll Take My Stand (1930), a book of essays by twelve southern writers, was a counter-attack against modernity. The Agrarians, as the contributors were called, agreed with the modernists that tradition had ceased to exist as a guide or anchor for human life. In contrast to the modernists, however, they lamented this loss and advocated the restoration of tradition. A farm or a community can be loved, the Agrarians observed, but the intangible world of credit and production cannot. And when a person loses touch with the folk, with nature, and with tradition, the way is lost to a meaningful aesthetic and religious existence.

Towns in Literature

The culture of the American people in the 1920s was richer in traditions, in a sense of community, and in sustaining vir-

King Oliver's famous Creole Jazz Band of the 1920s poses for a striking picture. *(Courtesy, Hogan Jazz Archives, Tulane University)*

tues than some of commentators supposed. It possessed in the novelist Sinclair Lewis an observer who satirized it stingingly—and came to reveal his love for it. As Lewis indicates in his preface to *Main Street* (1920), the town of Gopher Prairie could be found anywhere—in the Middle West, the South, or upstate New York. The story, set early in the twentieth century, is about the efforts of the mildly feminist Carol Kennicott to bring a higher culture to Gopher Prairie, or at least to survive her own boredom there. *Main Street* depicts a town still untouched by the upheaval of values that followed World War I; Carol thinks of the wives of American villagers as part of the oppressed classes of the world. Possessed of a phonographic as well as a photographic memory, Lewis was able to reproduce the monotonous tones and platitudinous content of everyday speech, along with the town's routinized life and drab appearance. The same authenticity in talk and manners, and in the small feelings that make up the surface of consciousness, gives strength to *Babbitt* (1922), a satirical novel about a businessman in a much larger midwestern city, the fictional Zenith.

Another avenue to an understanding of the American town is advanced in a sociological work, *Middletown* (1929), a study of Muncie, Indiana, by Robert and Helen Lynd. Middletown was no longer a Gopher Prairie, if it had ever been one; it was closer to the Zenith of *Babbitt*, and indeed hinted at what much of American society would soon become. The idea of the small town survived the reality. Suburbs, residential and industrial, metropolitan areas, and new demographic categories like neighborhood and region, created by the automobile and other forms of transportation, were replacing the older, simpler categories of town and city. The role of Middletown's women was changing. Of 446 girls in the three upper high school classes in 1924, eighty-nine percent were planning to work after graduation. The whole family structure and the dominance of the home were giving way under the influence in part of the automobile, as the ride in the country replaced the visit in the parlor.

Alice B. Toklas with Gertrude Stein, who labeled the disillusioned writers of the 1920s the "Lost Generation." *(Courtesy, Scribner's Archives)*

Radio The radio had long been in use by ship operators and amateurs, but the first station to do regular broadcasting was WWJ in Detroit, which in 1920 began covering election returns. Radio was an instant hit in the United States. More than 500 new radio stations began broadcasting in 1922. The Radio Act of 1927 brought the airwaves under federal control. By the late 1920s, radio networks like the Columbia Broadcasting System (CBS) and the National Broadcasting Company (NBC) had established local affiliated stations, linked them by telephone to network headquarters in New York City, and were broadcasting soap operas, situation comedies, sports, and news programs across the country. Americans everywhere began listening to the same programs, laughing at the same jokes, hearing the same advertisements, and recognizing the same personalities. Radio did more than any other medium to create a mass culture in the United States.

Silent Movie Classics Long before television's domination of the mass media, audiences of the twenties were living vicariously through the larger-than-life images that flickered enticingly across the screens of movie theaters throughout the United States. The burgeoning film industry became big business. True to the spirit of American industry, films became a commodity valued according to their box office success. By the end of the decade at least one ornate movie house could be found in town after American town. White-gloved doormen and uniformed ushers, baroque lobbies, balconied theaters—all testified to the public's total enthusiasm for the country's favorite form of entertainment.

The film-makers picked subject matter that would attract all classes. Movies of the twenties reflected the transformation in social values that prevailed in the years following World War I. Scenes of sex and drinking were frank and tolerant. Yet the heroes and heroines of movies embodied the virtues: courage, generosity, kindness, honesty, and responsible conduct. Particular actors and directors in Hollywood films seized the imagination of American moviegoers. Charlie Chaplin advocated dramatic revisions of the social structure. Chaplin became a star in 1914 with *Tillie's Punctured Romance*, and he continued to dominate silent comedy throughout the 1920s. In *The Sheik* Rudolph Valentino embodied the romantic, sensual hero. Among other European stars whose passionate images stirred American fantasies, Greta Garbo was legendary. During the 1920s Garbo played numerous roles as the temptress. A Mrs. B.I.H. of Cheyenne, Wyoming, wrote a typical letter to her local paper protesting the emphasis on sex in the movies:

> I just wonder why all actresses wear so little. Don't they have shame? They go so near naked there is nothing left to the imagination. I don't object to love scenes, but let the ladies keep their bodies covered.

At the end of the decade, talkies—Al Jolson's *The Jazz Singer* (1927) was the first major one—transformed the experience of moviegoing, at once depriving it of the verbal imagination that the public had needed to bring to it and adding to the artistic resources of the film.

Charlie Chaplin, who dominated film comedies in the early days of the industry, in *The Gold Rush*. *(Courtesy, Scribner's Archives)*

Republican Ascendancy

Warren Harding: Strengths and Weaknesses

In 1920 the Republican President Warren Harding, likeable and hardworking, had inherited from Woodrow Wilson a disintegrating presidency and a drifting foreign policy. He also faced a severe postwar depression, growing out of tight money policies and cutbacks in federal spending, that was worsening as he entered the White House. Harding appointed three important progressives to his cabinet: Charles Evans Hughes to State, Henry C. Wallace to Agriculture, and Herbert Hoover to Commerce. Astute programs from these three helped him to recreate confidence among businessmen. A President's Commission on Unemployment, called by Hoover, marked the first time in United States history that the federal government acted in a considerable way as though it had a responsibility to curb hard times. By the end of 1922 there was a consensus that good times for business lay ahead. The Fordney-McCumber Act of that year restored high tariffs. In his first two presidential years, Harding by his bland, reassuring manner gave the nation a respite from factional strife and a sense that old values were still alive.

But Harding's personal cronies brought his downfall. Secretary of the Interior Albert Fall accepted sizable "loans" from oilman Edward L. Doheny, who sought advantages in the stock market from leasing government oil lands in Elk Hills, California, and Teapot Dome, Wyoming. Fall eventually went to jail, but nothing was proven against Attorney General Harry Daugherty, who was also implicated. Beginning in 1923 there were suicides and resignations among Harding appointees below the cabinet level. Charles R.

Forbes, head of the newly-formed Veterans' Bureau, made off with $250,000 and was sentenced to Leavenworth prison for two years. If Harding had not died of heart disease in August 1923—a death hastened perhaps by his knowledge of the impending scandals—he would have had a hard time winning reelection. Calvin Coolidge, the Vice President who succeeded to the presidency on Harding's death, muted the effect of the scandals by appointing an independent investigating committee under the chairmanship of a Democratic senator, Thomas J. Walsh.

A born compromiser, Harding had tried to maintain some moderation in his ideological position; Coolidge almost always sided with big business. He encouraged Secretary of the Treasury Andrew Mellon to reduce taxes, especially on the wealthy. Mellon, a wealthy industrialist from Pittsburgh, also worked to reduce both the national debt and government expenditures.

Conservative Coolidge Coolidge slept a lot, suffered indigestion, and enjoyed his reputation for being the spare, laconic Yankee who took as his motto "Don't hurry to legislate." His ideal day, H. L. Mencken remarked, was one on which nothing whatever happened. He would not permit economic and social problems to intrude much on his equanimity or his moral sense. He honestly thought they would go away. Some did. Pungently honest, Coolidge was a good symbol of rectitude in an era that was experimenting with pleasure: a "Puritan in Babylon," he has been called. At a press conference he said:

> We have got so many regulatory laws already that in general I feel that we would be just as well off if we didn't have anymore.

The Coolidge era venerated business. People credited it with providing the appliances, radios, cars, electricity, and indoor plumbing that finally became commonplace in the decade. Coolidge asserted: "The man who builds a factory builds a temple . . . the man who works there, worships there." Bruce Barton, an advertising executive, compared Jesus Christ to a great business executive whose parables are effective advertisements. Jesus also embodied the ideal of public service. Business was, in fact, no longer publicly looking like the expression of ruthless and competitive forces that during the nineteenth century had not bothered to disguise their character. It was now articulating ideas of welfare capitalism that had been maturing for at least two decades. Large corporations began pension plans and early forms of unemployment insurance.

The Teapot Dome and Elk Hills oil scandal rocked the Republican administration in 1924, resulting in the prosecution or resignation of several of Harding's appointees. *(Cartoon by Clifford Berryman, Courtesy, Library of Congress)*

The predominance of big business almost assured that its traditional opponent, organized labor, would suffer in the twenties. It did. Membership in the AFL declined sharply to a scant three million. The Railway Brotherhoods felt the sting of an unfriendly government: the Railway Labor Board approved a twelve percent reduction in the wages of railway shopmen, and Attorney General Daugherty ended the resulting strike with an injunction. Hardest hit of all were soft-coal miners. Highly competitive market conditions brought union-busting and bloodshed, particularly in the Appalachian South. The Jacksonville Agreement, engineered in 1924 by John L. Lewis of the miners and Secretary of Commerce Hoover, broke down after bringing a brief interlude of peace. The Supreme Court added its weight against labor in *Bailey v. Drexel Furniture Company* (1922), which declared unconstitutional a federal tax on products manufactured by children. The next year in *Adkins v. Children's Hospital* the Court decided against a District of Columbia law setting minimum wages for women.

Public finance also reflected the conservatism of Coolidge's administration. Secretary of the Treasury Andrew Mellon was convinced that fiscal responsibility on the part of the federal government would inspire business confidence and strengthen the economy, so he implemented budget cuts that by 1928 had created a net surplus of $8 billion. Mellon used the money to reduce the national debt. He believed that tax cuts on the rich would also benefit the economy, since the well-to-do would tend to reinvest the money. Congress in the 1920s passed special revenue acts that reduced corporate income tax rates, personal income tax rates, gift taxes, inheritance taxes, and luxury excise taxes.

Farmers In 1920 the government's wartime price support for farmers ended at the same moment the European market was shrinking. Large operators bought out small ones, and three million people left the farms between 1921 and 1928. Price levels varied immensely from one crop to another. Wheat suffered precipitous price cycles and grave problems of surplus; tobacco and dairying flourished. Cattle and hog prices fluctuated. Shifts in consumption away from breads and toward dairy products and in international demand away from wheat and cotton in particular threatened special groups of farmers, as did severe droughts or flooding.

In the twenties one half of the farmers produced over ninety percent of the agricultural product. What about the lower half? They owned small farms, sometimes of submarginal land, or were tenants or sharecroppers. Many were deficient in skills and unable to adjust to new tools or changed demands of the market, while others simply could not afford tractors. The real bottom of agriculture, and a huge one, included southern sharecroppers, farm laborers, and migratory workers. These forgotten Americans had no political power, and remained practically invisible.

All politically successful ideas for agriculture reform in the twenties promised one thing—higher price levels. A number of laws designed to help agriculture passed Congress in the early twenties. They provided higher tariffs, more government credit, regulation of the grain exchanges, packers, and stockyards, and the freeing of farm cooperatives from prosecution under antitrust laws. Sweeping plans dominated the debates in the middle and late twenties, each conceptually subtle and mechanically complicated.

The idea of controlling the marketing of farm goods abroad was the most important scheme. Its authors were George N. Peek and Hugh S. Johnson, two farm machinery industrialists of Moline, Illinois. In the form of several slightly divergent bills all called McNary-Haugen after congressional sponsors, this proposal remained before Congress from the mid-twenties to 1929. Two such bills survived both houses of Congress, only to be vetoed by President Coolidge. The McNary-Haugen bills provided for a government-owned marketing corporation to purchase all surplus agricultural production in major crops at a high price level. In its original form, the plan defined this level as being that of an established "parity" price comparable to prewar prices. In compensation for

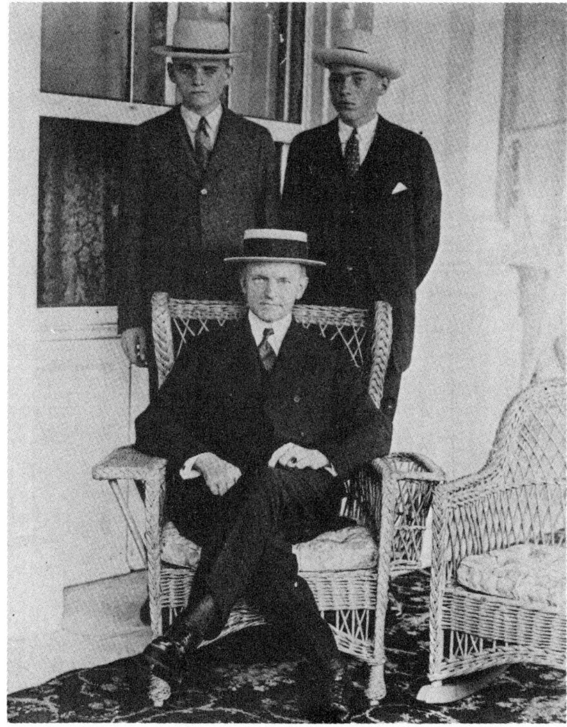

President Calvin Coolidge flanked by his two sons, one of whom died from an infection while his father was in the White House. *(Courtesy, Library of Congress)*

losses the government might incur in selling its surpluses abroad, the processors were to pay the government an equalization fee making up the difference between the home price and the world price. Tariffs would protect the farmer against foreign competition. The artificially created scarcity at home would impose higher prices on consumers. The plan could have worked only in an expanding world market; in the existing, contracting one it would have forced retaliatory tariff action by foreign governments and would have added to inflation at home.

Herbert Hoover offered an alternative proposal: cooperative marketing. He wished not only to leave many managerial decisions to the farmers, but also to leave price determination to the free market. Yet Hoover wanted farmers to rationalize their production, and to control their marketing in behalf of both higher and more stable prices. He advocated government aid for large marketing cooperatives—similar to trade associations in other industries—made up in each case of farmers producing a given commodity. He hoped that a given cooperative could successfully recommend annual production quotas to individual farmers, make marketing agreements with purchasers, rationalize marketing by calculated storage and by better processing, and possibly even expand markets by advertising. In 1929 Congress passed the Agricultural Marketing Act, which authorized a Federal Farm Board to implement it. The Board made loans to cooperatives. After the collapse of farm prices in 1930, stabilization corporations purchased to the limits of their funds in a vain attempt to hold up wheat and cotton prices. By 1932 they were broke. But as minor price-support programs they set a precedent for supports in the New Deal, and it is hard to say how effectively they would have worked in more prosperous times.

Power and Peace: Diplomacy, 1921–1929

East Asian Problems

The most vexing foreign problem for the new Republican administrations of the 1920s came in East Asia, where Japanese ambitions challenged both China's integrity and America's security. The Bolshevik revolution had destroyed Russia's traditional check upon Japanese expansion, while world war had weakened the area's major colonial powers, Britain, France, and the Netherlands. Japan's alliance with England forestalled unilateral action by the United States. In this favorable diplomatic circumstance, ministers around Japan's emperor began to fashion a sea-based empire in the western Pacific and dreamed of still grander glories on the mainland: dominion over the industrial heartland of East Asia, Manchuria, and the huge populations of central China.

Disarmament

Disarmament readily attracted the public imagination. In the aftermath of war, many people thought that weaponry itself created a climate for violence.

At the Washington Naval Conference of 1921–22 Secretary of State Charles Evans Hughes made skillful use of the political hunger for disarmament and created a temporary strategic balance in the Pacific. The conference produced three major agreements, each named after the number of countries participating in it. The Five-Power Pact embodied Hughes's proposal that the five great naval powers limit future building so as to preserve their battle fleets at a constant ratio of total tonnage: Britain and the United States, 525,000 tons each; Japan, 315,000 tons; France and Italy, 175,000 tons each. In the Four-Power Pact, Britain, France, Japan, and the United States each promised to respect the insular possessions of the other signatories in the Pacific and to consult, presumably for joint action, in the event any outsiders challenged this status quo. The Nine-Power Pact, signed by all the major colonial powers in East Asia, pledged each to respect the principles of the Open Door in China, including that country's right to self-determination.

The three agreements distributed losses and gains. The United States won naval equality with Britain and formal recognition of the Open Door principles, but both Western powers had to agree not to fortify most of their island possessions in the west Pacific, effectively ceding to Japan naval superiority there. Britain jettisoned its centuries-old naval dominance but gained guaranteed security for its extensive Pacific possessions and

In this visual equivalent of later sound bite journalism, Coolidge epitomizes the traditional rural identification of the presidency. *(Courtesy, National Archives)*

escaped from any trouble its alliance with Japan, now formally abrogated, could have brought. The Japanese lost territorial prerogatives in China but won secure control over an island empire in the Pacific. A newspaper remarked that the secretary of state had "frozen over the Pacific."

Hughes also dealt with many diplomatic questions left over from war. Not until the end of 1921 did Hughes begin to answer letters from the League of Nation's headquarters in Geneva, Switzerland. Two years later he sent an American delegation to an opium conference sponsored by the League. His successors broadened this policy of joining in non-political functions, and by 1932 the United States had participated in fifty such gatherings. The Senate in 1926 approved a treaty for United States membership in the World Court, a body that ruled in controversies that disputing nations agreed to bring before it. But the Senate adopted reservations so sweeping that other members refused to accept them.

At the beginning of his full presidential term, Calvin Coolidge appointed Frank Kellogg to replace the retiring Hughes. Kellogg deftly handled a tricky negotiation with his French counterpart, Aristide Briand. Peace factions in the United States, long discontented at their country's cautious foreign policy, persuaded an all-too-willing Briand to publish an open letter on the tenth anniversary of the entry of the United States into World War I. The letter called for a Franco-American treaty renouncing war between the two countries. Kellogg and his advisers quickly realized that the proposal would in fact bring the two nations close to a military alliance that he did not want. Kellogg cleverly countered with an offer to all nations to join in "outlawing war forever." Some sixty-four powers in 1928 ultimately signed what became known as the Kellogg-Briand Pact, which deepened the illusion of international stability.

Latin America Kellogg dealt less convincingly with difficulties in Nicaragua. Bickering over the presidency there descended into a fierce struggle, and Coolidge sent several thousand marines into the small country in 1926. When the puppet ruler supported by Coolidge's administration seemed more intent upon looting the public treasury than in building democracy, troops from the United States policed a national election. Then the marines trained a local militia, a job they did so well that after they left in 1933 its chief, the ruthless Anastasio Somoza, seized power. Meanwhile, Nicaragua under Augusto Sandino had waged against the invaders an armed resistance that left Sandino a national hero and martyr from whom the later Sandinistas took their name.

The Republicans navigated an even stormier course in Mexico, where social revolution continued. A new constitution in 1917 had claimed all subsoil wealth as the property of Mexico's people. The secretary of state finally denounced Mexico as "a center of Bolshevik activity," but Coolidge sent to Mexico City Dwight Morrow, a friendly, skillful negotiator who restored a measure of amity between the two nations. Morrow's compromises postponed a clash between foreign oil and Mexican nationalism until the late 1930s, when Mexico seized all concessions with only modest compensation.

Despite such episodes, Coolidge and Kellogg moved generally toward greater neighborliness with Latin America. In 1924 the occupying troops sent by Washington left the Dominican Republic, though United States administrators supervised government finances there until 1940. The United States paid Colombia an indemnity of $25 million for its loss of Panama. Late in his term Coolidge asked J. Reuben Clark, an official in the State Department, to outline the precise limits of the Monroe Doctrine. His brief, published in 1930 as the Clark Memorandum, argued that "the Doctrine states a case of the United States versus Europe, not of the United States versus Latin America." This was a repudiation of Roosevelt's Corollary to the Monroe Doctrine, which had justified unilateral intervention in Latin American countries.

War Debts and Reparations High United States tariffs blocked sales of many European goods and kept debtors from earning dollars, so what could they use to repay wartime era loans? The Allies also argued that the money represented the contributions of the United States to the war effort and an unequal one at that: Americans had lost dollars, but Europeans lost millions of lives and suffered frightful physical destruction. Most of the money had been spent in the United States, where it stimulated industry and kept employment high. American Presidents and public opinion bluntly rejected pleas for cancellation. Coolidge said, "They hired the money, didn't they?"

Worried by rumors of default, Congress early in 1922 created the World War Foreign Debt Commission, headed by Secretary of the Treasury Mellon, to negotiate specific repayment schedules. This group adjusted interest rates and other technical details to each debtor's capacity to repay. Most European leaders, privately supposing they could simply collect reparations from Germany and pass them along to the United States, went along with this proposal. Overall, the Debt Commission reduced by about half the combination of original debts and accrued interest.

Meanwhile, foreign officials together with private American bankers stabilized the German economy and set up a schedule of German reparations to European countries that were supposed to go in step with European war debt payments to the United States. In 1924, following the trying French occupation of the Ruhr Valley after a German default on reparations payments, Germany and its former enemies ratified the Dawes Plan. Germany pledged to put into reparations its profits from railroads and mines. British and American bankers promised loans to speed recovery in the Rhineland, the center of German industry. In late 1928, Germany and its creditors reorganized reparations again under the guidance of the banker and industrialist Owen D. Young. The Young Plan limited payments to the next fifty-nine years on a sliding scale determined by Germany's economic health. Still, nothing changed the underlying nature of such rickety agreements: reparations, like war debts, could be paid only if countries allowed an influx of foreign goods.

The Election of 1928

The Democratic Party, badly split between its rural and its urban component, went nowhere in the 1920s. At the famous 1924 Convention in New York City, delegates voted for 103 ballots before turning to a colorless compromise candidate, John W. Davis. Only a third party of progressives led by Senator Robert La Follette gave ideological variety to the 1924 campaign; he won almost twenty percent of the vote, nearly as much as Davis.

Some three years later, at about noon on a showery day in South Dakota, August 2, 1927, thirty or so reporters in attendance on President Calvin Coolidge filed into the mathematics classroom of the Rapid City High School. Coolidge was already there, and when the door was closed he told the newsmen "the line forms on the left." As they passed by, the slight man from Vermont who had recently lost his son to sudden death handed each a slip of paper that read: "I do not choose to run for President in nineteen twenty-eight." The country by and large accepted the statement at face value, and Secretary of Commerce Herbert Hoover came correctly to mind as the likely Republican presidential nominee in 1928.

"Al" Smith But the more familiar story of the 1928 campaign concerns not Hoover—who went on to become President—but Governor Alfred E. Smith of New York, the unsuccessful Democratic nominee. Al Smith, born on New York's lower East Side, was a faithful Roman Catholic, a practicing opponent of prohibition, and a product of New York City's Tammany Hall. In the thinking of many Americans, a more threatening combination could not be imagined. Smith's presence on the ticket sparked the worst bigotry in any recent presidential campaign, especially but not exclusively in the South.

One voter complained to Franklin D. Roosevelt, who had made a nominating speech for Al Smith at the Democratic Convention:

> Birds of a feather flock together, and if you uphold Smith and help him get in it is obvious you are in Tammany's pay. Of course he may be better than the ordinary man but Tammany has not become honest. . . . Everyone knows that Tammany uses Public School surplus to supply parochial schools so god knows what they will do when he gets to be President. . . . If you ever heard the Knights of Columbus oath I am sure you a Protestant would be through with [Roman Catholics]. They say it is all right to steal or cut out the bellies (the exact words used) of Protestants. . . . Why people are saying that he will make us have war with Mexico and he will so he can kill off some Protestants. . . . We can't trust them, don't you know that their church and the Pope come first, and they will be subject as it was to them first, and

Al Smith, Catholic and anti-prohibitionist, many perceived as the candidate of New York City and the corrupt political machine Tammany Hall. *(Cartoon by Gale, August 31, 1928. Courtesy, the* Los Angeles Times, *Los Angeles, California)*

> to America and her ideals second. . . . You ought to know the corruption there is in New York with Smith having a private telegraph wire to Tammany Hall, so of course he'll have a private wire to Tammany if he is made President. . . . An eyewitness saw him carried on the train dead drunk after his mother's funeral. He'd make a fine President, getting the Protestants drunk like he did when he was speaker or leader of the floor, in Albany, just so they would vote his way. And everyone knows his sons had to get married. And what kind of a woman would that be in the White House? Some difference from Mrs. Coolidge, who is educated and refined, and cultured. Mrs. Smith's father was a saloon keeper, and kept Prostitute Houses and yet you'd help those kind of people get in. Well, all I can say is God help you and all of us, if they do get in.

Smith, an amateur and a provincial in national politics, was not entirely without responsibility for the manner in which the issue of religion became inflamed. He displayed his Catholicism in ways that were irrelevant to the core of his faith but could offend Protestant sensibilities. He was public in his Catholicism: he kept an autographed picture of the Pope in his Albany office, publicly kissed the ring of a visiting papal prelate, and received words of political encouragement from the pope himself by way of his talkative wife, who visited Rome in 1925. Smith, moreover, drank and served liquor in the Albany executive mansion during prohibition. When the governor appointed as his presidential campaign manager John J. Raskob, an outspoken anti-prohibitionist closely identified with the Catholic church, many Americans assumed that he wished to flaunt what was most controversial about his candidacy. John F. Kennedy in 1960 would be at once more open and more reassuring in addressing the religious issue.

Herbert Clark Hoover had none of Smith's disadvantages and a large career already behind him: a Quaker orphan who had made himself into a millionaire working on the frontiers of five continents, a supplier of relief to Belgium and later to much of Europe and the Soviet Union. During the twenties Hoover had converted his Commerce Department into an instrument for promoting a free-flowing international trade intended to replace the relationships of force and war. It was also a center of communication among manufacturers, and a purveyor of a concept of socially responsible business self-regulation in the public interest. Hoover was the Great Engineer and the Great Humanitarian. In an era of prosperity the nominee of the party in power would undoubtedly win by a wide margin—and he did. With his Middle American background and his success in technology, Hoover was an agreeable blend of tradition and progress. People expected much of him: "He sweeps the horizon of every subject. Nothing escapes his view," a delegate had observed. But Hoover worried about

> the exaggerated idea the people have conceived of me. . . . if some unprecedented calamity should come upon the nation, I would be sacrificed. . . .

Hoover and the Great Depression

For many years before Herbert Hoover became President, he had been warning against the "crazy and dangerous" stock market, while President Calvin Coolidge to the contrary told press conferences that stock prices were not high enough. As Hoover feared, much was wrong with the American economy. While it resisted inflationary temptations and increased the real income of all classes, a larger proportion of the new wealth went into the hands of the very rich. When the stock market average ended its dazzling ascent and slumped downward, vast quantities of consumer goods now beyond the purchasing power of average householders quickly piled up in warehouses and factories.

What is striking about the Great Depression—which lasted until the Second World War—is that we still are not precisely sure of its origins. Was the Depression a crisis in confidence as Hoover grimly assumed and as a modern school of economists argues? Was the chief cause the weak banking system, another culprit singled out by Hoover? Did a shrinking in the supply of money in circulation cause the Depression? Or as John Kenneth Galbraith suggests in his witty account *The Great Crash*—a book rarely to be found in airport terminals—was the market crash an intricate effect and cause of economic instability? These explanations need not be in conflict with one another. Confidence did collapse and banks did fail and the money supply did shrivel as the stock market collapsed. The probable effect of each of these conditions was to accelerate the others. And together they worsened the Depression. But the illness of the economy did not begin with the Wall Street crash of 1929.

A host of new consumer goods industries that had emerged during the decade would run into problems of overproduction well before the stock market crashed. Vacuum cleaners, linoleum, and washing machines made the lives of homemakers more convenient; the automobile and airplane improved the mobility of people and goods; telephones, radios, and motion pictures bolstered communications and recreation. These products, in turn, stimulated such producer goods industries as steel, rubber, oil, glass and textiles, as well as government building of highways and airports. But this economic growth fed on consumers, intrigued by the newness of these products and willing to pay for many of them in installments. As consumers went more deeply into debt, they could not continue to purchase; and by the later 1920s, many who could afford durable consumer goods already had them. The postwar consumer spree began to level off. Yet many durable goods producers were basing their production projections on their previously escalating sales. As consumption leveled in the period from 1925 to 1929, these industries soon found themselves overproducing.

A sight that became more and more prevalent during the Great Depression: unemployment and food lines stretching along city blocks throughout the country. *(Courtesy, Scribner's Archives)*

A recession began, with the resultant layoffs and further drops in consumption. Some 5,000 banks failed before 1929.

These events not only preceded the stock market crash but helped cause it. Speculation in stock prices had begun in the mid-1920s on the solid basis of profits and the stock dividends that companies paid to investors. But in time it turned to sheer gambling. People bought stocks at high prices on the assumption that everyone else would then want to buy them at higher prices on the assumption that others would thereupon be happy to buy them at still higher prices. To raise the money for purchase of stocks, people bought on margin: paying in cash as little as ten percent of the price of a stock and being indebted for the rest. Businessmen, finding few profits in expanding production, flooded their wealth onto the market, and this drew money away from investment in the fundamental production that constitutes the health of an economy.

After serious collapses in late October 1929, the stock market staged a recovery, particularly early in 1930. Not until mid-1930 did prices fall steadily, week by week, until their low point in 1933. Employment began to drift downward in 1930 and reached very serious proportions in the winter of 1930–31; by 1933 almost one-quarter of the labor force was without work.

In 1930, meanwhile, President Hoover had signed a staggeringly high tariff in order to repay a campaign promise to farmers. By the time it passed Congress, the Hawley-Smoot tariff had raised to well over fifty percent tariff rates that the Fordney-McCumber schedules had already put at more than thirty-eight percent. This unilateral American protectionism stunned Europe. Already pressed by the drying up of American loans following the Wall Street crash, Europeans found themselves unable to sell in the American market. Their retaliatory tariffs damaged American exports, especially farm products. Europe and the United States were stifling international trade and further battering productive industries already badly pounded. The inability of Europeans to sell on the American market also deprived them of the funds to pay debts to both European and American banks, including loans that American institutions had made to the Allies during the World War. When Austria's largest bank, itself indebted to American banks, folded in the spring of 1931, Hoover got a one-year agreement on both sides of the Atlantic for a moratorium on all war debts and on the reparations payments that Germany in defeat had been forced to make to the victors. The moratorium became permanent, and had the effect of nearly complete defaults. Five thousand American banks closed their doors between 1929 and 1932.

Hoover was more willing and quicker than most politicians, including the Democratic Congress that met in 1931, to use the government to cushion the fall. Right after the crash he urged business to maintain wages. He increased spending for public works at all levels of government. Within the limits of economic solutions then entertained by leading economists Hoover moved swiftly; but he refused to step outside these boundaries. And as chief executive at the outset of the Great Depression, Hoover could hardly present himself as the solution to it. This shy President, who knew the importance of confidence, could not bring himself to manufacture it.

A popular song, "Brother, Can You Spare a Dime," carried the lament of a World War veteran:

> Once in khaki suits,
> Gee, we looked swell,
> Full of that Yankee Doodle-de-dum.
> Half a million boots were sloggin' through Hell,
> And I was the kid with the drum.
> Say, don't you remember, they called me Al—
> Al it was all the time.
> Say don't you remember I'm your pal—
> Brother, can you spare a dime?

Hoover's opposition to direct federal relief programs furnishes our worst memory of him. He accused progressive senators of "playing politics at the expense of human misery" by recommending expensive relief programs, and he hinted darkly at the evils of the public dole as practiced in Great Britain. In fact, it was some of the best things in Hoover's past that stood in his way. His relief projects in the era of World War I had trained him to believe that people voluntarily contribute their money and time, that good will and expert knowledge could solve the most enormous problems of logistics and supply. He feared hordes of government subsidy seekers, who would indeed crawl out of the woodwork during the New Deal. He believed that more fortunate Americans would come to their neighbors' aid. Not selfishness or indifference but a misplaced faith in public generosity kept Hoover from engaging in the more extensive programs of relief that were in fact necessary.

Reconstruction Finance Corporation Hoover set up government agencies to encourage and coordinate private and local relief efforts. But his main measures to combat the Depression were the Agricultural Marketing Act, the Reconstruction Finance Corporation, and the Federal Home Loan Act.

The agricultural legislation, which was passed in the spring of 1929, was not intended for relief. Once the Depression began, however, the fund was used to stabilize the market, and it had the helpful effect of slowing the descent of farm prices. It was, in fact, largely a relief agency.

The Reconstruction Finance Corporation was a grander vision, adopted late in 1931 after a similar private scheme had failed. Patterned after the War Finance Corporation that had made loans to industries during World War I, the RFC could loan up to $2 billion to banks and other agencies. For once, Hoover had overcome his fear of the duplication, slowness, and wastefulness of bureaucracy. But he worried that business interests would wish to manipulate it. Under Hoover, in 1932, the RFC began to loan substantial sums to the states for relief, loans he knew would never be repaid.

To relieve what was fast becoming a catastrophic unemployment problem in the construction industry, Hoover had Congress pass the Federal Home Loan Bank Act. Adopted in July 1932, it created a system of federal home loan banks to discount home mortgages. The Federal Home Loan Banks received $125 million in capital to discount the home mortgages of building and loan associations, insurance companies, and savings banks. Hoover believed that the ability of private lending institutions to secure new sources of capital would encourage them to make more construction loans and revive the industry. But it had little effect.

Hoover was not the grumbling reactionary that New Dealers later portrayed. Depression forced him to abandon a host of reforms that he had planned to pass into law. One radical piece of legislation that he did achieve was a steeply graduated income tax. Many of Hoover's programs, such as the RFC, anticipated the New Deal, though Roosevelt was to go much farther. Hoover gave private enterprise a chance to cure the Depression, and its timidity in the face of the crisis revealed that the government was going to have to take the initiative. By 1932 the election of a Democrat was inevitable.

The new governor of New York, Franklin D. Roosevelt, beat out his predecessor Al Smith for the Democratic presidential nomination in 1932. To demonstrate that the polio that had crippled him in 1921 could not scar his vitality, Roosevelt delivered sixty speeches on a national tour by railroad. His talks, vague in substance and dynamic in delivery, were well received by Depression audiences. One telegram to Hoover at the end of the campaign captured the voters' sentiment: "Vote for Roosevelt and make it unanimous." One quatrain caught a popular contempt for the outgoing President:

O 'Erbert lived over the h'ocean
O 'Erbert lived over the sea;
O 'Oo will go down to the h'ocean,
An drown 'Erbert 'Oover for me?

Depression Diplomacy: Hoover and the World, 1929–1933

As international problems became more complex, the American people turned inward, preoccupied by greater worries of their own. President Hoover dreamed of further disarmament, economic collaboration, conciliation in Latin America, even modest collective security efforts. Yet obstinate Congresses and Depression stymied Hoover's internationalism. The times and the man were uniquely mismatched.

An Economic House of Cards The international economy collapsed with surprising swiftness during the first eighteen months of 1930–31. National banks in central Europe

Though Herbert Hoover made sincere efforts to end the Depression, his opposition to direct federal relief programs convinced the voters that he was insensitive to their suffering. In 1932, they sent him fishing. *(Courtesy, National Archives)*

had borrowed funds from private banks in New York and London to re-lend to domestic businesses. As depression ruined sales both at home and abroad, the German and Austrian central banks discovered that on many of their loans they could collect neither interest nor principal. Scared by the prospect of financial collapse, foreign investors sold property and securities. Others frantically tried to exchange paper marks for gold or other currencies that popular mythology conceived as being solid. These pressures forced Germany to default on all its loans, public and private, and to abandon the gold standard—meaning that holders of German marks could no longer exchange them for gold—during the summer of 1931. Many British banks had invested heavily in high-risk, high-yield German ventures that now were worthless. Depositors rushed to withdraw their money from London banks, and soon Britain too had left the gold standard. Prime Minister J. Ramsay MacDonald decided to devalue the pound—to reduce its worth compared to that of other currencies. This made British goods cheaper in foreign currencies and stole markets from other countries still burdened by expensive gold currencies.

Hoover believed in a sound currency in which paper money was solidly backed by gold reserves. Britain's aggressive, unorthodox use of monetary devices frightened him into financial alliance with the only other major gold power, France. During talks with French Premier Pierre Laval in October 1931, Hoover secured a pledge from the Bank of France to support the dollar with its own gold. In return, the President had hinted that he might cancel war debts entirely if the Allies canceled German reparations. This arrangement temporarily strengthened the dollar. And the Allies soon gathered at Lausanne, Switzerland, where they pared German reparations to a token $700 million. This chain of events embarrassed both Hoover and Roosevelt, now in the midst of a presidential campaign. Both men realized that canceling German reparations and Allied debts was economic good sense, but both appreciated equally the political folly of saying so. Even after the election they shied away from decisive action, so all America's debtors except Finland defaulted during 1933.

The Hoover Doctrine Economic crisis also upset the delicate naval and political balance in East Asia. On September 18, 1931, Japanese armies in Manchuria, stationed there to guard the strategic South Manchurian Railway owned by

Japan, attacked around Mukden and soon routed the Chinese. This early triumph emboldened local commanders to begin a systematic conquest of all Manchuria. Victory there, they hoped, would discredit moderate leaders at home and commit Japan to armed expansion in China proper. Aircraft bombed villages and raided China's largest city, Shanghai, early in 1932. All Manchuria fell to the invaders that spring, when a puppet ruler signed a protective alliance with Japan. Its generals next assaulted the provinces of north China. Chiang Kai-shek, the leader of the ruling Nationalist Party, could not stop the Japanese advance. A weak political base and a persistent Communist rebellion led by Mao Zedong inhibited Chiang's ability to resist. He turned to the United States and the League of Nations for help.

Peace machinery clanked slowly into motion. Faced with the first serious challenge to collective security, the League dispatched a fact-finding group to Manchuria under Lord Lytton. While its members tramped over rough terrain and interviewed village elders, Britain's foreign secretary, Sir John Simon, endeavored to put pressure on Japan. France and Italy nervously offered token help; Simon did not even ask Germany and the Soviet Union. The issue became starkly simple: would the United States and Great Britain in defense of the Nine-Power Pact and the principle of collective security risk war with Japan? Secretary of State Stimson hinted that the answer might be "yes," but Hoover overruled him. The Quaker from Iowa sensed what Americans would later learn: conventional land warfare in East Asia was beyond United States power. Hoover politely declined Simon's idea, taking up instead the device of refusing to recognize the Manchurian regime installed by Japan. Stimson notified the signatories of the Nine-Power Pact only that the United States "can not admit the legality of conquests in violation of treaty commitments." Most other countries rallied to this Hoover-Stimson Doctrine. Late in 1932, the Lytton Commission Report found Japan guilty of aggression; the League of Nations formally condemned Japan; Japanese delegates left Geneva. But wrist-slapping did not halt Japan's aggression against China. Maneuverings and plots continued there intermittently until 1937, when a local skirmish near Peking grew into a full-scale war of conquest.

Good intentions led Hoover into ineffective efforts at disarmament. Early in his term, he invited British Prime Minister MacDonald to Washington for wide-ranging talks that soon began to look like an Anglo-American effort to settle the world's major problems. As they sat on a log near a stream at Hoover's private retreat in the hills of northern Virginia, the two rhapsodized about peace and disarmament. They agreed on details for another naval limitations conference to be held in London during 1930. That meeting granted ocean tonnage parity to the United States for all classes of ships, long an American objective, but isolationist senators worried that secret clauses might ally the country with England. They demanded all documents pertaining to the negotiations. Hoover refused, citing executive privilege.

The Senate eventually ratified the work of the London Naval Conference, but the new treaty was far less effective than its predecessors. France and Italy did not join, and an escalator clause allowed building past agreed limits under certain circumstances. Japan did sign, but in Tokyo the ratification fight was so bitter it was only a matter of time before that country pulled out of the agreement. The signatories altogether ignored enforcement measures.

Points To Think About

1. The Red Scare was at least in part a continuation into peacetime of wartime demands for political conformity. During the war the Justice Department and the Post Office, which could censor the mails and ban "unsound" publications, waged a determined campaign against the Industrial Workers of the World and the Socialist Party. The government sought to whip up patriotism to a controlled frenzy. Criticism of the government, which in peacetime was a favorite national pastime, became defined as sedition. Pacifists, conscientious objectors, radicals of all sorts, and critics of

the war found themselves with the choice of keeping their opinions to themselves or running the risk of spending the rest of the war in jail.

So fervid had the national mood become that some measure of intolerance was bound to carry over into peacetime. White-hot patriotism does not cool in a day. But the various dislocations that came in the absence of planning for demobilization worsened the situation. Millions of servicemen returned to the labor market before industries had time to convert to peacetime production. Employers geared up to crush the unions that with federal backing had organized their workers during the war. The unions in turn were determined to consolidate and extend their gains. Inflation was fueled by pent-up consumer demands and scarcities brought on by the war. Returning servicemen organized in the newly formed American Legion blamed immigrants for grabbing their jobs. Employers accused unions of being Bolshevik-inspired, and portrayed every strike as the opening shot in a leftist revolution. Many politicians saw a popular issue and joined in the denunciations of foreigners and radicals.

2. It is always hazardous to describe a period as the "beginning" of anything. Historians have a genius for finding still earlier manifestations of the condition in question. So it is with the claim that mass consumption society in the United States had its beginnings in the 1920s. Traces of all of the developments associated with mass consumption could be found in the preceding decade or two. Even so, these developments reached maturity in the twenties.

American industry during the nineteenth century was preoccupied with the problems of production. The chief tasks were to find new ways of making goods. Clothing aside, few of these products passed directly to the consumers. They went more often into building railroads and factories. As production expanded, however, an ever-growing list of new products designed for the individual consumer emerged. Business had to find ways of marketing these new products, and this involved inventing the basic elements of the consumer society. They included a system of allowing consumers to pay in installments; an increase in advertising—the radio was an advertiser's playtime; and the cultivation of a new national consciousness that equated consumption with personal worth.

America had worshiped the Horatio Alger myth that anyone, through luck and pluck, could achieve success. Popular magazines had featured success stories encouraging readers to believe that they could do likewise. During the twenties the ideal of personal fulfillment through individual achievement was in no way disputed, but it did begin to share the field with a new set of ideas. Advertising told people that personal fulfillment would come to them through consuming various goods. They could drive the same cars, smoke the same cigarettes, use the same mouthwash as did those who occupied positions of power. Success would consist in consuming rather than in occupying a self-sufficient position in society.

This development touches on a continuing contradiction in American society. Americans pride themselves on having a work ethic. They also assume that work is the origin and justification of property and wealth. But wealth rarely has any clear relationship to a given quantity or excellence of work. Luck and tricks of the market have as much to do with wealth as do effort and skill. And wealth, once acquired, often becomes an occasion for substituting luxury and consumerism for any further work. The work ethic has succeeded in short-circuiting itself.

Suggested Readings

New books on the era include Paul K. Conkin, *The Southern Agrarians* (1988), Nancy Cott, *The Grounding of Modern Feminism* (1987), Carole Marris, *Farewell—We're Good and Gone: The Great Black Migration* (1989), Michael C. C. Adams, *The Great Adventure: Male Desire and the Coming of World War I* (1990), Cary D. Wintz, *Black Culture and the Harlem Renaissance* (1988), and Lloyd Ambrosius, *Woodrow Wilson and the American Diplomatic Tradition: The Treaty Fight in Perspective* (1987).

Still standard on the First World War is Ernest R. May, *The World War and American Isolation* (1959). A briefer treatment can be found in Ross Gregory, *The Origins of American Intervention in the First World War* (1971). An excellent study is Frank E. Vandiver, *Black Jack: The Life and Times of John J. Pershing*, (1977). Black soldiers who fought in the war are depicted in A. E. Barbeau and F. Henri, *The Unknown Soldiers* (1974), while David Kennedy treats the home front in *Over Here* (1980). On the Versailles Treaty, see

Charles L. Mee, Jr., *The End of Order: Versailles 1919* (1980). Ralph A. Stone, in *The Irreconcilables: The Fight Against the League of Nations* (1970), investigates the reasons that motivated each of the sixteen senators who refused to ratify the treaty. Woodrow Wilson's vision is presented in Arthur S. Link, *Woodrow Wilson: Revolution, War, and Peace* (1979) and N. Gordon Levin, *Woodrow Wilson and World Politics* (1968). See also Link's multivolume biography, *Wilson* (1947–).

A good general survey of the twenties is William E. Leuchtenburg, *The Perils of Prosperity, 1914–1932* (1958). David Burner has written two books on the era's politics: *The Politics of Provincialism: The Democratic Party in Transition, 1918–1932* (1968) and *Herbert Hoover: A Public Life* (1979). Francis Russell's *The Shadow of Blooming Grove: Warren G. Harding in His Times* (1968) and Donald R. McCoy's *Calvin Coolidge: The Silent President* (1967) each to some extent rehabilitates the reputation of its subject.

On the importance of the automobile, see J. B. Rae, *The Road and the Car in American Life* (1971) and James J. Flink, *The Car Culture* (1975). For the literature of the era, see Alfred Kazin, *On Native Grounds* (1942) and F. J. Hoffman, *The Twenties* (1955). Nathan J. Huggins portrays *The Harlem Renaissance* (1972), as does David Levering Lewis, *When Harlem Was in Vogue* (1981). Mark Schorer's *Sinclair Lewis* (1961) is definitive. Other studies of twenties literary figures include Carlos H. Baker, *Ernest Hemingway: A Life Story* (1969) and Henry D. Piper, *F. Scott Fitzgerald: A Critical Portrait* (1972). Robert Sklar, *Movie-Made America* (1975) and Larry May, *Screening Out the Past* (1980) discuss the rise of motion pictures.

☆ ☆ ☆ POINTS OF VIEW: ☆ ☆ ☆

Wilsonian Internationalism: Curse or Blessing?

Thomas J. Knock

Thus, on the evening of April 2, 1917, Wilson asked Congress to recognize that a state of war existed between their country and the German empire. . . .

After outlining the measures necessary for getting the country's war effort underway, he turned to more transcendent matters. His thoughts, he said, were still the same as when he had addressed the Senate on January 22; "Our object now, as then, is to vindicate the principles of peace and justice in the life of the world as against selfish and autocratic power and set up amongst the really free and self-governed peoples of the world such a concert of purpose and of action as will henceforth insure the observance of those principles." Yet he emphasized several times, in all of this, the United States had no quarrel with the German people themselves; it was not they, but their military masters, who had brought on the war. "A steadfast concert of peace can never be maintained except by a partnership of democratic nations. No autocratic government could be trusted to keep faith within it or observe its covenants."

He continued: "The world must be made safe for democracy. Its peace must be planted upon the tested foundations of political liberty. We have no selfish ends to serve. We desire no conquest, no dominion. We seek no indemnities for ourselves, no material compensation for the sacrifices we shall freely make. We are but one of the champions of the rights of mankind. We shall be satisfied when those rights have been made as secure as the faith and the freedom of nations can make them."

Then in words that one observer compared to Shakespeare's for their rhetorical grace and power, Wilson compressed into a final peroration his vision of the American historical mission, in all its arrogance and innocence—a summons to the New World to return to the Old to vindicate the creed for which it had broken away a hundred and forty years before: "It is a distressing and oppressive duty, Gentlemen of the Congress, which I have performed in thus addressing you. There are, it may be, many months of fiery trial and sacrifice ahead of us. It is a fearful thing to lead this great peaceful people into war, into the most terrible and disastrous of all wars, civilization itself seeming to be in the balance. But the right is more precious than peace, and we shall fight for the things which we have always carried nearest our hearts—for democracy, for the right of those who submit to authority to have a voice in their own governments, for the rights and liberties of small nations, for a universal dominion of right by such a concert of free peoples as shall bring peace and safety to all nations and make the world itself at last free. To such a task we can dedicate our lives and our fortunes, everything that we are and everything that we have, with the pride of those who know that the day has come when America is privileged to spend her blood and her might for the principles that gave her birth and happiness and the peace which she has treasured. God helping her, she can do no other."

Of all the outpouring of public commentary, none better captured the thoughts and emotions of Wilson's admirers and critics at that moment than the *New Republic*, "Our debt and the world's debt to Woodrow Wilson is immeasurable," the editors wrote. "Only a statesman who will be called great could have made American intervention mean so much to the generous forces of the world, could have lifted the inevitable horror of war into a deed so full of meaning. . . . Through the force of circumstance and through his own genius he has made it a practical possibility that he is to be the first great statesman to begin the better organization of the world."

Reprinted from Thomas J. Knock, *To End All Wars: Woodrow Wilson and the Quest for a New World Order* (New York: Oxford University Press, 1992).

Shari Osborn

Only after much soul searching did Woodrow Wilson call Congress into special session on April 2, 1917, to hear his message of war. What he was asking contradicted much that he stood for. In his May 1914 address to the same body he had recalled George Washington's advice to avoid entangling alliances. That summer of 1914 the European war broke out. For a time, Wilson tried to keep his country out of it. The ideals of the Founding Fathers afforded him—and more particularly the isolationists who warned more strongly than he against siding with the Allies—a solid ground on which to base their argument. Isolationists wanted the United States to remain aloof from the rest of the world, or at least from the corruption that they associated with reactionary and imperialist European regimes. But events pressed Wilson—or, so historians hostile to him would argue, he pressed events—to so angry a confrontation with Germany that by April 1917 he saw no way out of entering the war. His decision probably stemmed from his increasing recognition of the significance of European power relationships to American security. He was never convinced, even after the April 2 speech, that war was the answer. He had become certain, however, that it was inescapable. To salvage the situation, he set out to convert the savage bloodletting into a crusade to make the world safe for democracy. War, in Wilson's thinking, was to be justified now for its moral result.

Throughout the twentieth century, isolationism would continue to attract many Americans. In its later forms, isolationism has gotten a bad reputation, and that is in good part the fault of isolationists themselves. Hostility to impoverished immigrants, hostility to foreign aid aimed at relieving suffering abroad, surliness toward any possibility of intervention that might ease the lot of other peoples but at some expense to the United States: these have been more recent isolationist postures.

That mentality is not to be confused with that of the isolationists who tried to prevent our country's entrance into the First World War. Progressive isolationists who opposed Wilson did not have the antagonism to foreigners displayed by later advocates of staying within our own borders. Nor did they adopt for domestic issues the right-wing Republican economics favored by late twentieth-century isolationists, an economics designed to protect the wealth of the wealthy. To the contrary, progressive isolationists of the time of the First World War wished to put government actively to nourishing the well-being of the people and to strengthening the institutions of democracy. It was not, they believed, in siding with capitalist and imperialist Britain against capitalist and imperialist Germany that the United States could make its contribution to the world. Our best course instead was to serve as a peaceful example of social and political democracy.

The words of President Wilson's war address to Congress are indeed powerful and sincere. But their warning of "civilization . . . in the balance," its fate hanging on the outcome of the conflict, belongs to the inflated and self-delusionary mind that comes with all wars. In the hands of early twentieth-century Germany and Austria-Hungary, civilization would have continued to do quite nicely. In the United States, the Wilson administration in time of war was conducting perhaps the most extensive repression in the nation's history. Civilization was not the winner. Wilson's prose, his driven conscience, and his capacity for generous vision deserved a better cause than that to which he had committed his country.

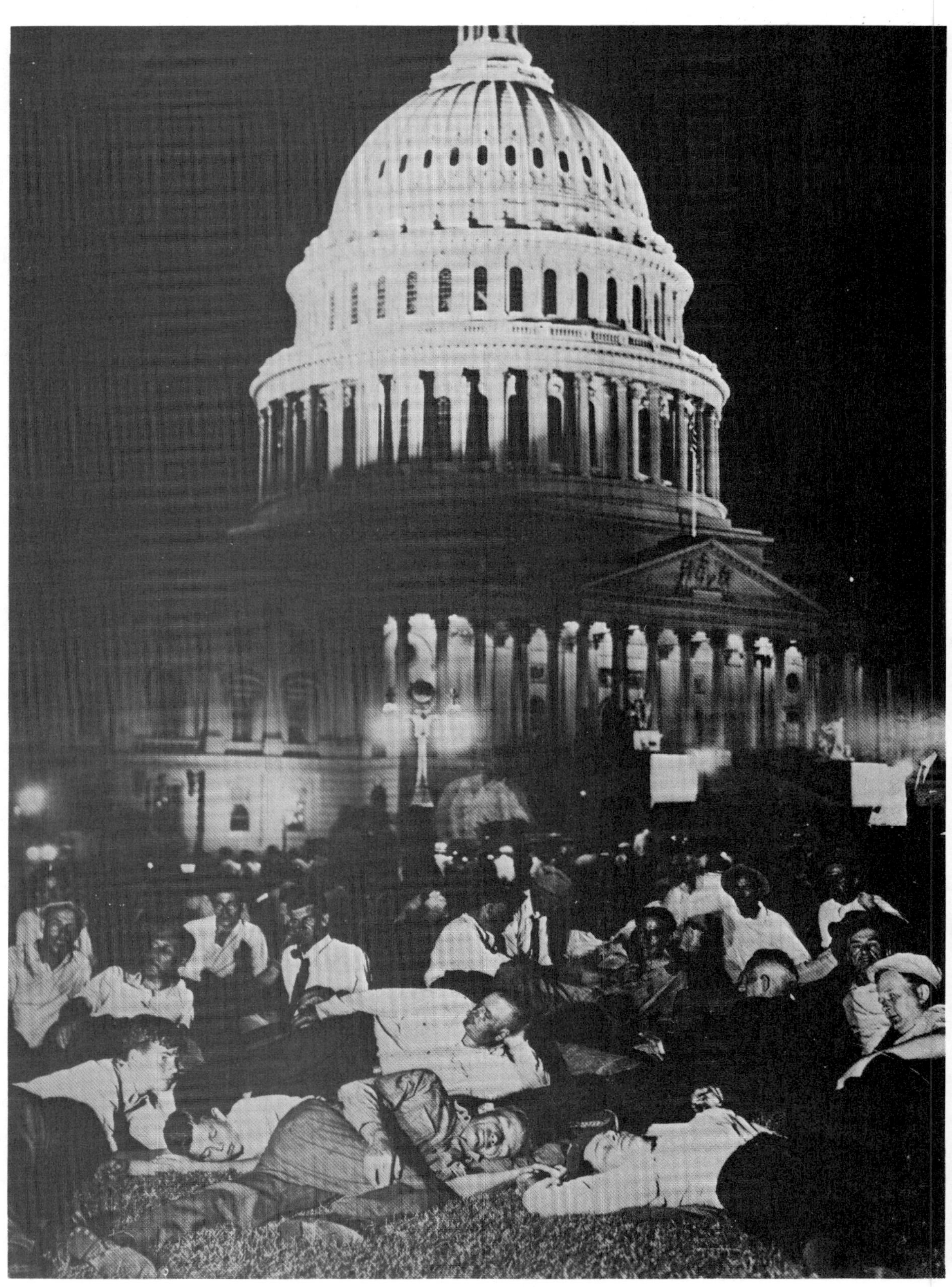

The Bonus Marchers of 1932. *(Courtesy, Library of Congress)*

CHAPTER 24

The New Deal

THE BONUS ARMY OF 1932

In the spring of 1932 few newspaper readers paid much attention to reports that some 300 unemployed First World War veterans were traveling in Union Pacific freight cars rocking and swaying over the Rockies from Portland, Oregon, to Pocatello, Idaho. Some accompanied by their families, they were headed for Washington, D.C., to persuade Congress to approve early payment of a soldier's bonus not scheduled for distribution until 1945.

Congress had ignored their pleas. Now the Bonus Army picked up fresh recruits at almost every city, and finally became national news when the B & O Railroad tried to stop it in the "Battle of East Saint Louis." Local railroad union leaders averted bloodshed by moving truckloads of men, women, and children across Illinois to the Indiana border. Then each state governor hurried the band as swiftly as possible across his territory, and so the travelers crossed Indiana, Ohio, Pennsylvania, and Maryland until they reached the District of Columbia. There they met other veterans from every state in the Union, a total of more than 20,000 people.

President Herbert Hoover allowed the veterans to settle in abandoned buildings, and on the largest site, Anacostia Flats. He quietly provided them with army food, clothing, beds, tents, and even medical supplies—characteristically keeping his humanitarian acts secret.

Like Hoover, Governor Franklin D. Roosevelt of New York disapproved early payment of the bonus. He offered his state's veterans both transportation home and guaranteed employment. While the bonus bill passed the House on June 5, 1932, two days later the Senate defeated it. Hoover thereupon initiated federal loans to provide transportation home to any veteran who applied. But some 10,000 stayed on, waiting for something to happen.

On July 9 some 250 Californians arrived, led by a navy veteran, Roy W. Robertson, who camped out with his men on the Capitol lawn. While in the service Robertson had broken his neck falling out of a hammock. Wearing a brace supported by a tall steel column rising almost a foot above his shoulders, he gave the eerie impression of a man with his head perpetually in a noose. For three days and four nights his men took turns slowly walking single file in a "Death March" vigil around the Capitol building. His head held high in the rigid brace, Robertson was a study in determination. While an angry mob of fellow veterans occupied the building's steps, Congress adjourned and its members escaped by subterranean passageways.

Army Chief of Staff General Douglas MacArthur stood ready for trouble with a sizable regular army force. The moment came when the administration on July 28 forced the eviction of veterans from a small downtown area of government buildings scheduled for demolition. A riot ensued between a gathering of as many as 5,000 veterans and fewer than 800 police. One veteran was dead; another lay fatally wounded.

MacArthur ordered his troops to assemble at the Ellipse behind the White House. Hoover specifically directed MacArthur only to move the rioting veterans out of the business district and back to their camps. But MacArthur saw "revolution in the air." Ignoring the President's orders, he sent his troops across the bridge into the Anacostia Flats. The whole Anacostia camp became ablaze with light: setting fire to their own huts was the veterans' final symbolic act of defiance. Eisenhower would recall "a pitiful scene, those ragged, discouraged people burning their own little things." Soldiers fired the remaining empty huts. Fleeing the capital, the veterans became refugees from a government more immobile than heartless, more ignorant than cruel. Hoover, the great humanitarian who had fed the starving Belgians during World War I, received all the blame in the election—and Depression—year of 1932. The incident helped assure an overwhelming victory for the Democratic candidate, Franklin Roosevelt, in the presidential election of 1932.

General Douglas MacArthur disobeyed President Hoover's orders and engineered a confrontation that ended in the burning of the Bonus Army shacks in the muddy Anacostia Flats. *(Courtesy, National Archives)*

The Roosevelts

FDR

The Democrat who defeated Hoover in the 1932 election possessed a personality suited to the times. Franklin Delano Roosevelt would speak of the nation's troubles only to express confidence that they could be banished. He did not hold himself back from the people, but seemed eager to meet each one personally. One woman, trying to express to her grandchildren in later years her feeling toward Roosevelt, has remarked that if the President had come into her kitchen for morning coffee she would have been perfectly comfortable and not the least bit surprised. A young soldier, standing outside the White House at night after hearing of the President's death, said, "I felt as if I knew him. I felt as if he knew me—and I felt as if he liked me." In 1932 this personal charm contrasted sharply with the aloofness of the reserved, unsmiling Hoover. Someone remarked that Roosevelt could say "my old friend" in ten languages while Hoover could say it in none. While the programs put forward in their campaign speeches differed in only a few respects, Roosevelt took all but six states—with a margin in the popular vote of seven million—against an incumbent President himself elected overwhelmingly four years earlier.

Born in 1882 to a wealthy and aristocratic family in Dutchess County, New York, Franklin grew up as the sheltered only child of an aging, indulgent father and a domineering but intensely loving mother. His monopoly on parental affection, and the luxury and material comforts of the family estate at Hyde Park, made him secure and self-assured. At the Reverend Endicott Peabody's Groton School Roosevelt learned the values of the "better" classes: patriotism, public service, and a simple and unobtrusive Christianity. Both at Groton and later at Harvard, he lived a life of gentility, manners, and fellowship rather than of serious intellectual effort. But he was competitive. As friends of his youth have recalled, he took his cousin Theodore as a model and planned to follow TR's career to the presidency.

Franklin began well by winning election to the New York state legislature and then, before the First World War, achieving TR's old job of assistant secretary of the navy. He accepted the 1920 Democratic nomination for Vice President. The defeat of the ticket that year was only a temporary check to Roosevelt's ambition. But the following year he contracted an illness that could have broken him: a case of polio that left his legs badly and permanently crippled. Even this the buoyant aristocrat met gallantly. It would even become something of an asset during the 1932 campaign. FDR's optimism and courage in the face of his disability suggested that he was equal to combating the Depression, while the disability itself helped to make the public more comfortable with his wealthy background. Four years before the presidential campaign Roosevelt had won election for governor of New York, following Al Smith into the office. There he backed important if not drastic reforms in agriculture, public utilities, welfare, and conservation, making New York one of the states most vig-

Franklin Roosevelt as a boy. *(Courtesy, F. D. R. Library)*

orous in its attempts to cope with the Depression. By 1932 he had experience in governing and a national reputation for being a reformer.

While Roosevelt's gubernatorial program, like those he would later initiate or support in the presidency, were never organized into a logical, coherent philosophy, they gave an impression of energy and action. The pursuit of pet programs, frequent, last-minute meetings with advisers, and quick responses to emergencies were to comprise whatever platform is detectable in his presidential years. The essence of the New Deal to come was perhaps best summed up by a revealing bit of FDR's campaign wisdom: "The country needs bold, persistent experimentation. It is common sense to take a method and try it. If it fails, admit it frankly and try another. But above all, try something." Whatever else it did, this approach promised movement in a country mired in despair.

Roosevelt managed repeatedly to seem bold and innovative by breaking with traditional behavior, at the same time affirming the values in which he and most of the country believed. After being nominated on the fourth ballot by the Democratic convention, he surprised and thrilled the delegates by flying through stormy weather from New York State to Chicago in a Ford Trimotor to accept their nomination in person. Almost immediately after his election he won an important ally, the press, by opening his news conferences to offhand questions and joking with reporters, rather than simply delivering answers to written questions as his predecessor had done. Using radio as a new political tool, Roosevelt in the presidency delivered "fireside chats" to the nation, explaining his policies and plans in a conversational, easily understood manner, and projecting his personality into millions of homes.

Eleanor Roosevelt. *(Courtesy, F. D. R. Library)*

Eleanor Roosevelt The First Lady also lent a special aura to the administration. Eleanor Roosevelt involved herself more deeply in public life than any previous President's wife had done, establishing a personality that competed for public attention with that of her remarkable husband.

Anna Eleanor was also a Roosevelt, niece of Theodore and distant cousin of Franklin. Perceiving herself as unattractive and awkward, the young Eleanor had been extremely shy. Her beautiful mother called her "Granny" and made fun of her in front of visitors. The mother died when Eleanor was eight. Her father Elliott, though kind, soon drank himself to death. Her parents' early deaths, which left her to grow up with a grandmother and without many playmates, deepened her withdrawal. After marrying her confident and attractive cousin Franklin in 1905, Eleanor gave birth in rapid succession to six children who, in upper-class fashion, were brought up by servants. As the years passed, however, she gradually gained greater self-confidence; and she began to take a more and more active interest in her husband's career and in public affairs generally. Mrs. Roosevelt's public role became increasingly visible as Franklin proceeded from office to office.

After the Roosevelts settled into the White House in 1933, Eleanor shocked those who expected another in the tradition of virtually invisible first ladies. With her husband unable to walk or to travel easily, she often became the President's eyes and ears. Although their relationship was no longer intimate, and her dearest friends were female social activists, Eleanor had Franklin's respect and trust;

he encouraged her to see people and problems firsthand and report to him. She showed up in so many places that her adventures became legendary. One cartoon of the period showed coal miners deep underground looking up to say, "Here comes Mrs. Roosevelt."

She produced after 1935 a newspaper column called *My Day*, which purposefully remained rather chatty and trivial although it occasionally floated a political balloon, and she published several books on her life and on broad political questions. Ordinary people responded to her evident sympathy for their plight. One woman wrote from Troy, New York, in 1935:

> About a month ago I wrote you asking if you would buy some baby clothes for me with the understanding that I was to repay you as soon as my husband got enough work. Several weeks later I received a reply to apply to a Welfare Association so I might receive the aid I needed. Do you remember?
>
> Please Mrs. Roosevelt, I do not want charity, only a chance from someone who will trust me until we can get enough money to repay the amount spent for the things I need. As a proof that I really am sincere, I am sending you two of my dearest possessions to keep as security, a ring my husband gave me before we were married, and a ring my mother used to wear. Perhaps the actual value of them is not high, but they are worth a lot to me. If you will consider buying the baby clothes, please keep them (rings) until I send you the money you spent.

From the first months of her husband's administration, Eleanor Roosevelt's activities provoked criticism. Her involvement in public affairs seemed improper to some, especially to those opposed to her liberal ideas and attitudes. Later Eleanor defied the segregation customs of her time and intervened personally when prejudice barred the black singer Marian Anderson from Constitution Hall, owned by the Daughters of the American Revolution. She supported the American Youth Congress, which a red-hunting House committee claimed to be dominated by Communists. When challenged, Eleanor was quick to assert her independence and to deny any responsibility to the electorate since "I have never been elected to any office." Yet had she been in an elective post, she would not have needed to fear being unseated. A January 1939 Gallup poll reported that sixty-eight percent of the population approved of Mrs. Roosevelt, a higher rating than her husband achieved. Repeatedly, ordinary people remarked on how neighborly she seemed. In 1939 she raised a stir by roasting hot dogs for the King and Queen of England.

The Hundred Days

By the time of Roosevelt's inauguration the Depression of course had been under way for more than two years. Millions were now unemployed. The daughter of a railroad worker in Cleveland recalled her own family's experience:

> I remember all of a sudden we had to move. My father lost his job and we moved into a double-garage. The landlord didn't charge us rent. . . . We had a coal stove, and we had to each take turns, the three of us kids, to warm our legs. It was awfully cold when you opened those garage doors. We could sleep with rugs and blankets over the top of us [and] dress under the sheets. . . . In the morning we'd get out and get some snow and put it on the stove and melt it and wash around our faces. . . . [We] put on two pairs of socks on each hand and two pairs of socks on our feet, and long underwear and . . . Goodwill shoes. Off we'd walk, three, four miles to school.

In his inaugural address the new President proclaimed that "the only thing we have to fear is fear itself" and promised "to wage a war against the emergency." The so-called Hundred Days from March 4 to mid-June 1933 marked the first major campaign in that war.

It was one of the most productive bursts of lawmaking in American history. Perhaps the only element that unified the legislation of the Hundred Days and beyond was the personality of the President. Roosevelt brought to Washington a "Brains Trust" of college professors including Raymond Moley, Adolf A. Berle, Jr., and Rexford G. Tugwell from Columbia University, and Felix Frankfurter of Harvard Law School. But none of these intellectuals put his stamp on the New Deal as a whole; nor did they collectively give order and system to the administration's programs. Roosevelt's cabinet reflected the President's penchant for variety. Secretary of the Trea-

Stateswoman Frances Perkins. *(Courtesy, National Portrait Gallery)*

sury Henry Morgenthau was a model of caution. At Agriculture was Henry A. Wallace and at Interior Harold C. Ickes, both Republican progressives. And running the Department of Labor was an urban liberal, Frances Perkins, the first woman cabinet officer in United States history. Untroubled by either philosophical or personality conflicts, Roosevelt freely mixed diverging ideas and interests.

The Banking Crisis

On assuming the presidency, Roosevelt had to address immediate concerns. The nation's paramount and paralyzing trouble was the condition of its banks. Between Roosevelt's election in November 1932 and his inauguration on March 4, 1933, the American economy had slid even lower. During this interregnum more than a quarter of the labor force was out of work. Neither the defeated President nor the waiting President-elect could initiate major policies. The banking system, under pressure since 1931, collapsed in the first months of 1933. Depositors stood in line at banks in every part of the country to demand their savings; such runs emptied the cash drawers of more and more weaker institutions, forcing them to close. On February 14 the governor of Michigan closed that state's banks for eight days. By Roosevelt's inauguration, state governments had closed or placed under restriction nearly all the nation's financial institutions.

The banking crisis eased Roosevelt's task. Everyone from the conservative businessman to the most liberal reformer admitted the need for drastic action; for a time all bowed to his lead almost without question.

On March 6 the President dramatized his new leadership by declaring a four-day national bank holiday. On March 9, the first day of the special session of Congress called by Roosevelt, the Emergency Banking Relief Act was introduced, passed, and signed within hours, with congressmen shouting their support before the final version was complete. The act confirmed the President's power to do as he had already done, provided guidelines for reopening sound banks, and strengthened federal authority over the currency. These measures, backed by Roosevelt's firm public insistence on the soundness of the banking system, enabled about seventy-five percent of member banks in the Federal Reserve System to reopen within three days, and boosted stock market prices fifteen percent in the next two weeks.

Despite threats in Roosevelt's inaugural address about driving the money changers from the temples, the new banking laws were drafted in collaboration with the big banks. As would happen again and again, Roosevelt's angry speeches produced safe legislation. Other financial laws of the Hundred Days included the Economy Act—a futile effort to reduce federal expenditures and to balance the budget; the Federal Securities Act, requiring full disclosure to investors of information on new securities issues; and the second Glass-Steagall Act (Banking Act of 1933), creating the Federal Bank Deposit Insurance Corporation (FDIC) to guarantee a minimum amount of bank deposits up to $5000 and expanding the membership and authority of the Federal Reserve System. The panic eased as the public began returning its money to the banks.

The Alphabet Agencies

One of Roosevelt's favorite programs addressed the problem of unemployment among young men. The Civilian Conservation Corps (CCC) employed men aged eighteen to twenty-five in reforestation, highway, anti-erosion, and national park projects under the direction of army officers. At its peak the CCC payroll contained the names of 500,000 conservation soldiers, and by 1941 it had employed a total of over 2,000,000 young men. One aging enrollee recalls:

> I was sent to Utah. I'll never forget the ride up the mountains in this battered old truck. We had an old grizzled army sergeant in charge. When we got to the area, it was just thick woods. 'Where's the camp?' I asked. The sarge waved his hands around the trees. 'This is it. Break out the axes and chop like hell if you don't want to sleep on the ground.' We chopped and built cabins and even a mess hall. For the next three years I grew up, physically and mentally and spiritually, in that beautiful country. It was one of the most rewarding experiences of my life. Before I left I was offered a job as a ranger. To this day I wonder whether I was a fool in turning it down and coming back east. A large number of the CCCs stayed on. Some own ranches today.

Among the most striking New Deal programs passed during the Hundred Days was a sweeping experiment in regional planning for the valley of the Tennessee River. During the First World War the federal government had constructed a large hydroelectric power facility and two munitions plants at Muscle Shoals, Alabama. When, after the war, the government was unable to obtain a reasonable price for these facilities from private interests, Senator George W. Norris twice shepherded through Congress, in 1928 and 1931, legislation allowing the federal government to operate the plants to provide power and fertilizer for the region's inhabitants. Republicans Coolidge and Hoover vetoed these measures on the grounds that such a project would compete with private enterprise. But Roosevelt, who visited Muscle Shoals in January 1933, saw the possibilities for a broad development of the valley through the careful control and use of water resources. Con-

In this very unusual picture of Franklin Roosevelt showing his leg braces, he is flanked by his wife and mother. *(Courtesy, Scribner's Archives)*

gress in that year created the Tennessee Valley Authority (TVA), an independent public corporation with the authority to build dams and power plants, to produce and sell electric power and nitrogen fertilizers, and to sell explosives to the federal government. The TVA was to provide a yardstick for judging the rates charged by privately owned utilities. But its planners had larger ambitions. Roosevelt and Norris hoped to further the entire social and economic well-being of the region through erosion and flood control, land reclamation, reforestation, recreational development, and the encouragement of mixed industry. By 1944 nine dams on the main river and many on tributaries had greatly improved the economic outlook in six states. The TVA was for many years one of the most successful of all planning programs except for its lack of concern over polluting the environment.

The Agricultural Adjustment Act, creating the Agricultural Adjustment Administration (AAA), aimed at restoring the security and the purchasing power of farmers. After an unhappy experiment in plowing under crops and killing piglets to cut surpluses and raise prices, the administration attempted to accomplish reductions by paying subsidies to farmers for the voluntary reduction of acreage and production in certain basic commodities. The AAA would obtain funds for these subsidies from a tax on the processors of listed farm products. The act also provided funds for refinancing farm mortgages through Federal Land Banks. The Farm Credit Act, also of 1933, went much farther, offering loans for agricultural production and marketing and allowing farm mortgages to be refinanced on longer terms, at low interest. Together, these two laws did for farmers what another act of the Hundred Days—the Home

The New Deal programs quickly made Roosevelt the hero of the working class. *(Cartoon by Burris Jenkins, January 30, 1934)*

Owners Refinancing Act, which created the Home Owners Loan Corporation (HOLC)—did for other debtors. Within less than two years, the government had refinanced about twenty percent of all home and farm mortgages, offering both immediate relief and some hope of future security.

At the heart of Roosevelt's plans for reviving industry was the National Industrial Recovery Act (NIRA). One part of this broad legislation created the Public Works Administration (PWA) for direct public employment in the construction of roads and public buildings and a variety of other projects. The PWA, under Interior Secretary Harold Ickes, spent over $4 billion on some 34,000 ventures. Another section of the NIRA attempted to stimulate business activity by halting the downward spiral of prices and wages. It encouraged representatives of various industries to draw up "codes of fair competition" establishing fair wages, working conditions, and prices. Once created and approved by the President, these codes were to be exempt from antitrust actions and enforceable by law. The National Recovery Administration (NRA), for the first year headed by the brash General Hugh Johnson, had the difficult task of policing the codes and encouraging consumers to buy only from those businesses that participated.

One small part of the NIRA gave labor unions a long-desired legal basis. Section 7-A guaranteed workingmen the right "to organize and bargain collectively through representatives of their own choosing." A National Labor Relations Board, with Senator Robert Wagner of New York at its head, was charged with assuring the right of collective bargaining. Organizers cleverly, if not entirely accurately, used this legal prop to persuade workers that the President wanted them to join a union, and an era of intensive unionization and labor-management strife got under way. A labor organization not by crafts but by entire industries, a form of organization that had gained infrequent success in the past, was characteristic of the labor movement of the 1930s. Its leader was John L. Lewis of the mine workers. Despite resistance within the AFL toward this more daring strategy, that older federation did allow the establishment of the Committee on Industrial Organization; before the Depression was over it would split from the AFL and became the Congress of Industrial Organizations, retaining the familiar initials CIO.

After the Hundred Days

More Help from Washington

The First Hundred Days brought excitement to the national government and a sense of movement to the country as a whole.

The repeal of prohibition contributed to the new mood. The First World War had provided for prohibition the argument that the nation had better uses for grain than to make spirits; now the Depression furnished against it the argument that the sale of alcoholic beverages would bring desperately needed tax revenues. On December 5, 1933, the Twenty-first Amendment to the Constitution achieved ratification, repealing the Eighteenth Amendment. People stood in saloons with glasses raised awaiting the hour of new era, crowds sang "Happy Days Are Here Again," and bootleggers went out of business.

Congress continued to churn out legislation all through 1933 and 1934. Many new laws simply expanded the legislation of the Hundred Days. The AAA had depended on voluntary crop reduction, but the Bankhead Cotton Control Act of 1934 and the Tobacco Control Act of 1934 required cutbacks for these specific crops, fixing a national production limit and then providing farmers with individual allocations. A number of federal agencies now long familiar to Americans were the products of congressional activity in 1934. The Securities and Exchange Commission (SEC) was established to regulate the trading of stocks and bonds and to discourage the manipulation of values or overspeculation. The Federal Communications Commission (FCC) had the task of overseeing all interstate and foreign uses of telegraph, cable, and radio. Each of these agencies has directly or indirectly affected millions of Americans.

Saving the Money Markets

In at least one component of the economy—the financial system—the New Deal possessed conviction and pursued a relatively consistent set of policies. Adolf Berle, who was to be among the most brilliant members of the Brains Trust, in a 1932 memorandum to Roosevelt as governor of New York created an image. On one side of a plate glass window are crowded a mass of accumulated goods and the capacity to make goods. On the other are gathered an equally enormous volume of poverty and suffering. The money markets, the one instrument capable of smashing the window, are in paralysis. Berle was convinced, and he convinced Roosevelt, that the country's "greatest single need was to undergird the credit of the operations which were the basis of the . . . economy." With millions of Americans unemployed and with tax revenues way down, thousands of American financial institutions and local governments faced bankruptcy. Those bankruptcies had to be stopped.

Millions of farmers were unable to make their mortgage payments in the early 1930s, and in 1933 President Roosevelt issued an executive order creating the Farm Credit Administration. Within eighteen months, the FCA had refinanced more than twenty percent of all farm mortgages in the country. Again, New Dealers stressed the aid they were giving to poor people, but they had saved thousands of rural banks from disaster. If those farmers had not been able to make their payments, the banks would have foreclosed on all of that property and then sold it off at tremendous losses. The New Deal did the same for city dwellers. Millions of homeowners were unemployed and unable to make their mortgage payments. To assist them, Congress in 1933 created the Home Owners' Loan Corporation. Eventually, the HOLC would refinance countless home mortgages. The HOLC certainly helped millions of American homeowners, but it also saved thousands of building and loan associations from bankruptcy by reducing the numbers of properties they had to repossess and try to sell. To stimulate the construction industry, Congress passed the National Housing Act in June 1934 establishing the Federal Housing Administration. The FHA had the authority to insure loans made by banks and savings and loan associations to middle-income families who wanted to repair their homes or build new ones.

The Depression Persists

And yet, despite this rich harvest of legislation, the Depression refused to fade away under the brilliance of Roosevelt's smile. The economy did revive somewhat, but there was little long-term recovery. Manufacturers, for instance, increased their inventories, driving up industrial production, because they expected labor costs to rise under the NIRA; this gave an appearance of rapid success for the New Deal while actually providing no sustained improvement. By the spring of 1935, when Roosevelt had been in office two years, nearly 20 percent of the labor force remained unemployed and national income had risen only slightly from the depths of 1933.

Any administration and any plan of action would have faced great difficulty in ending the Depression, but Roosevelt's policies met special problems. Some portions of hastily drafted New Deal legislation failed to withstand legal challenge. Roosevelt's taste for a balanced budget got in the way of his desire to increase purchasing power and put people to work through spending on public works. Many programs simply did not work, and some conflicted with others.

The NRA eagle became a national symbol, displayed in storefronts and businesses throughout the country.

For a time, the NRA was a popular institution signifying national cooperation in the face of the Depression. Its emblem, the Blue Eagle, proudly appeared in windows of stores and businesses that were adhering to the NRA codes. And some Americans still remember the Blue Eagle as a badge of the New Deal. But the NRA faced particularly substantial problems. It produced codes for separate industries, written largely in isolation and usually under the influence of big corporations. Progressives worried about this revival of monopoly; small businessmen resented the power it gave to big business. Company unions continued to flourish despite the NIRA's Section 7-A. General Hugh Johnson, for all his enthusiasm, proved to be an incompetent administrator, and was removed after a year. The NRA did much to end child labor and encouraged labor unions. But as a device to bring economic recovery it had clearly failed even before May 1935, when the Supreme Court in *Schechter v. United States* declared unconstitutional the legislation creating the NRA. That law, claimed the Court, had conferred on the executive branch powers to regulate the economy that under the Constitution could belong only to Congress.

The AAA encountered similar difficulties. Farmers did reduce acreage in order to receive federal subsidies, but they took out of production their poorest land and on their better acreage actually increased the size of their crops. Farm income rose, but marginal farmers and farm tenants were pushed off the land. The AAA, administered in the South by local appointees, did little for blacks.

Roosevelt himself harbored conflicting ideas. He was unable to instill in business leaders the confidence that has so much to do with stimulating commercial activity. Yet while he frightened them, his legislation never came close to the rhetoric with which he denounced them. Despite the TVA, he remained cautious about putting the federal government into competition with private industry and refused to allow wages in public projects to match those in the private sector. Later, when private industry began to revive, Roosevelt, to prevent that competition, would drop even the most successful federal programs. The Banking Act was a bankers' act. The NRA was a dramatic initiative but in fact built on the trade-association movement of the 1920s among big industries. The selection of an old Wall Streeter, Joseph P. Kennedy, as first chairman of the Securities and Exchange Commission insured the investment community a voice in its own reform.

FDR's dilemma was real. Many of the nation's economic institutions required serious reform, and public bitterness toward the corporations made the political demand for reform overwhelming. Yet recovery required a renewal of business investment, while serious changes in regulations and policies would frighten the rich away from investment.

Down and Out in the Land of Opportunity

On the Road Many people tried to escape family tensions and an unpromising future. Americans once again moved about in numbers that recall the days of the frontier. In the course of the decade the rural populace declined by more than a fifth; by 1940 about sixty percent of the people lived in urban areas. Drought and a slump in commodity prices prodded many midwesterners toward California or into middle-sized towns. Whole families, unable to find work or to continue paying rent or the mortgage, piled into the old car and took to the highway, bewildered driftwood carried from town to town by a tide of unemployment. Migratory workers usually moved with the seasons, but some simply rushed into regions where rumor pointed to jobs. For nearly a sixth of the population, depression meant permanent emigration, always leaving someplace, never really going anywhere. Perhaps as many as five million people became vagrants, perpetually unemployed, perpetually hounded out of towns. These hoboes gathered together in camps remote from state troopers. Woody Guthrie wrote a famous social protest song about his own "Hard Travelin' ":

> I've been doin' some hard travelin',
> I thought you knowd

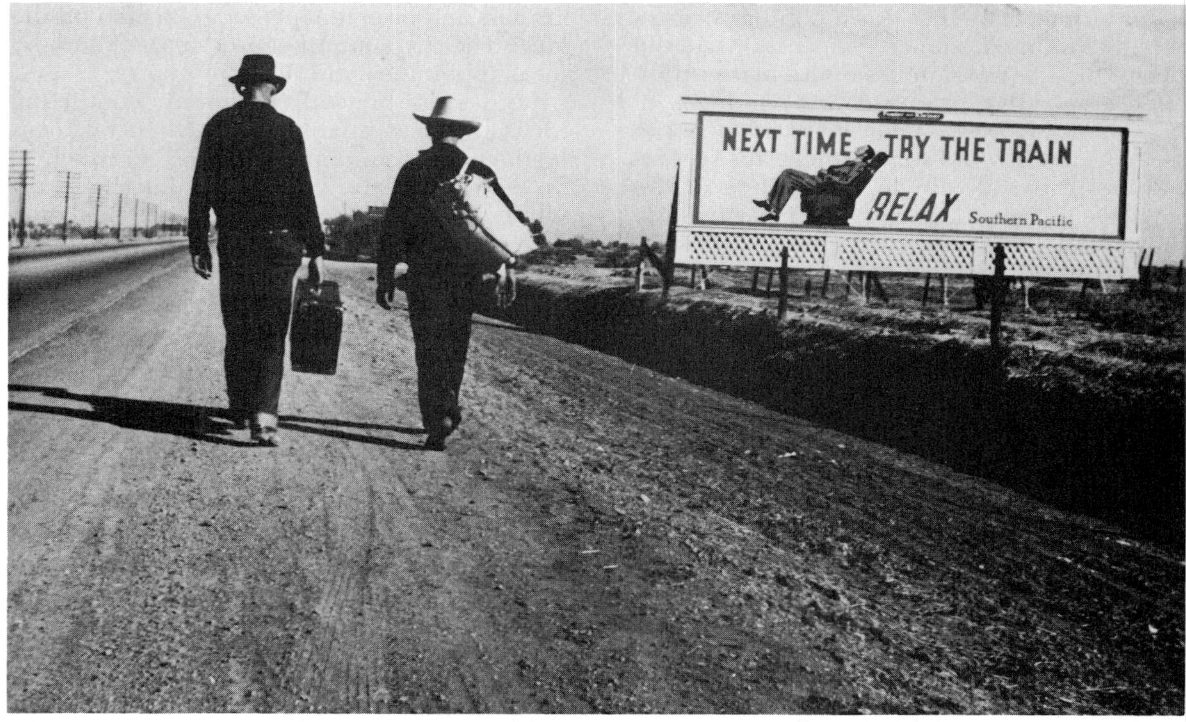

(Courtesy, Library of Congress)

I've been doin some hard ramblin'
Away down the road. . . .
I've been layin in a hard rock jail,
I thought you knowd
I've been out ninety days
Way down the road.
The damned old judge, he said to me,
It's ninety days for vagrancy,
And I've been doing some hard travelin',
Lord.

"It's the big trouble," a young girl explained. "That's why I'm on the rails." Nearly two million youngsters like her understood the slang: depression had turned them into twentieth-century nomads riding steel trails. The Union Pacific Railroad reported in 1933 that freight cars had killed hundreds of boys and girls. Joe Morrison, a coal miner, described riding the rails:

> In '30 and '31 you'd see freight trains, you'd see hundreds of kids, young kids, lots of 'em, just wandering all over the country. Looking for jobs, looking for excitement. . . . That one thing that was unique was to see women riding freight trains. That was unheard of, never had been thought of before. But it happened during the Depression. Women gettin' places by ridin' freight trains. Dressed in slacks or dressed like men, you could hardly tell 'em. Sometimes some man and his wife would get on, no money for fare.
>
> You'd find political discussions going on in a boxcar. Ridin' a hundred miles or so, guys were all strangers, maybe two or three knew each other, pairs. There might be twenty men involved. They would discuss politics, what was happening. What should be done about this, that and so forth.

Pictures of poor farm workers Dorothea Lange or Walker Evans photographed impart something of what poverty did to people. Hard times lashed out first at the unskilled, those with the least resources to tide them over. Some areas suffered more than others: the southern Appalachians with its depleted mines; the Great Plains made barren by wind erosion and drought; the old southern cotton belt with too many people on too little good land. Grayness and worry settled over the poor and the lower middle class.

Family Tensions Loss of employment, or the threat of it, altered the fundamental form of the nuclear family, The equation of home and family diminished when banks foreclosed mortgages. Parents became so discouraged

A lineup of jobless men on a park bench. *(Courtesy, International Museum of Photography at George Eastman House)*

that between 1935 and 1940 the numbers of new babies fell below the rate of zero population growth. Young couples postponed children until times should improve, and the number of marriages decreased by nearly one fourth. Only because of a drop in the death rate to eleven per thousand—boosting life expectancy to sixty-three years—did the population increase as much as seven percent in the course of the decade. The number of divorces dropped sharply, perhaps because legal costs, child support, and alimony were beyond the reach of so many people.

The Depression burdened family life in less tangible ways. Across the country, indigent relatives moved in with more fortunate aunts or brothers or cousins. Generations crowded in on one another, grandmothers and mothers arguing over how to raise children or run the household. Youngsters were suddenly confronted with orders from many adults, not just two. Most available jobs for men went to unskilled laborers at low wages; railroads, for example, paid only $10 a week for work on road gangs. As a result, many fathers sat at home, losing their traditional authority over the family while their sons worked.

During the Depression, dominant American values strongly opposed married women's participation in the labor force at a period in which so many male heads of families were without jobs. But by the 1930s, middle-class American families also had developed a strong consumer ethos—a belief that the constant purchase of goods is a mark

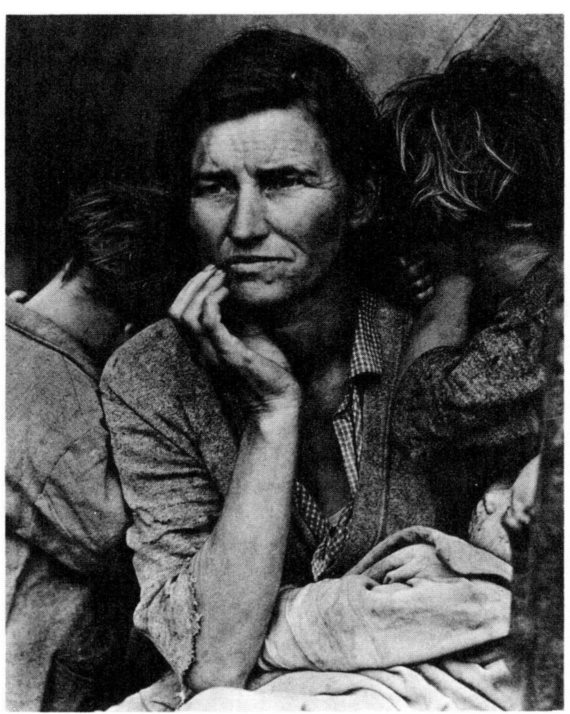

***Migrant Mother, Nipomo, California*, by Dorothea Lange.** *(Courtesy, The Museum of Modern Art, New York)*

of worth—that made a married woman's extra income appear indispensable to the well-being and standard of living of the family. These attitudes did not present married women's work as good in itself, nor did they result in campaigns for equal pay for women. But they expanded the notion of woman's role to include bringing in enough extra money that the family could afford a car, college for children, and small luxuries that were increasingly being redefined as needs. Under these conditions, many middle-class women remained in the labor force during the Depression, normally in jobs that had already been defined as female, and frequently in jobs that had previously belonged to lower-class or black or Hispanic women. There was a general tendency for white women to push other women out of the labor market. In addition, the labor of women of all classes, especially their unpaid labor in the home, more and more became crucial to the very survival of their families. Women made small budgets stretch further by making things that they had previously bought: food, clothing, home furnishings. And many women bore the main share of the burden of taking in relatives who were out of work, or young or elderly people who could not get work, or young couples who could not afford to set up independent households.

Inventive Americans discovered new ways to earn a living. During the twenties, people had avoided jury duty; now they shoved their way into court buildings eager for the allotted $4 a day. An army of new-fledged salesmen went from door to door, peddling everything imaginable, and in cities they spread out their wares along the street curbs. Arguments went on over whether permanent investment in a shoeshine kit would produce more income than hawking apples or newspapers. The International Apple Shippers Association, faced with a large surplus, sold its product on credit to the unemployed; some 6,000 people sold apples on New York City streets in 1930. Sunday papers sold from door to door in apartment houses offered an income, and more and more newsboys walked the city streets. Enterprises given up earlier as an uneconomical use of labor—vegetable and fruit pushcarts, for example—reappeared.

Middle- and Upper-Class Americans in the Depression

Even in the worst Depression years, most American workers had jobs. Essential skilled laborers, both farm and factory, or those in the few powerful unions, generally rode out the decade with few scars. Clerks, typists, and many white-collar workers fared less well as business activity slowed. Professionals like lawyers and doctors lost income as the earnings of their clients lagged. Schoolteaching, especially in college, was usually a stable, much-prized job, even when some salaries dropped. Government work became the most desirable of all: Washington, D.C., possessed the healthiest economy of any city

In the cities, unemployed workers selling apples on streetcorners became an all-too-common sight. *(Courtesy, AP/Wide World Photos)*

in the nation. If such workers bought few luxuries, they seldom worried about the necessities.

For small businessmen lucky enough to survive, the Roosevelt era restored a measure of stability. Though banks hoarded money, making long-term expansion almost impossible, grocers, druggists, and oil dealers, for example, could rely upon a small but stable income and assets slowly rising in value. Many merchants, in fact, took advantage of abysmally low prices to invest in land or the stock market.

The Rich

Except for the worst months at the end of 1932 and the beginning of 1933, the Depression scarcely touched the very rich, that top five percent of the population who owned three-fourths of the nation's wealth. The stock market crash had wiped out plungers more often than those with carefully diversified investments. Dividends and rents shrank during those long, weary years, but prices also declined. Ice cubes still tinkled against cut glass at cocktail parties, which with the repeal of the Eighteenth Amendment had now moved away from speakeasy brownstones and back into expensive apartments. Well-dressed women copied Parisian styles, wearing long scarves, low hemlines and close-fitting hats. The rich collected objects of art during the thirties. Porcelain, antique silver, paintings, French furniture, and jewelry flooded into the United States as the wealthy bought treasures from Europe's harder-pressed upper classes. Winter vacationing on the shores of the Caribbean became popular, Miami and Havana being the new watering holes for the very fashionable. More and more islands built resort hotels and legalized casino gambling. On the mainland, conspicuous consumption revived, though not the public lavishness of the twenties. General Motors reported large declines in its sales of Chevrolets, but none at all for Cadillacs.

Class Themes in Depression Movies

The Great Depression put fifteen million people out of work, brought businesses to a standstill, and sent banks to the brink of disaster. It is therefore astonishing that, broke or not, tens of millions of Americans every week proved

Paul Muni's role in *I Am a Fugitive from a Chain Gang* suggests the despair encountered by many Americans during the Great Depression.

that for them film-going was not a luxury but a necessity.

The classic gangster movies, such as *Little Caesar* (1930), *Public Enemy* (1931), and *Scarface* (1932), were all propelled by a single dynamic. They emphasized the individual—the self-made man who seeks somehow to transcend his environment. The disorder of the heroes' lives reflected the turmoil and confusion of the early Depression years. *Little Caesar* (played by Edward G. Robinson), the first of a long succession of films in this genre, is the story of Rico, a man outside the law and at the same time a personification of the American dream. Rico's life follows the pattern of a nineteenth-century Horatio Alger success story. Starting his career as a nobody, he climbs to the pinnacle of achievement in his own milieu. Once at the top, however, he dies—the only acceptable ending for a man who lives outside the law. In the sordidness and frustrations of their lives, the characters depicted in these movies represented the many victims of widespread social chaos and deterioration.

The films of the Depression, even when they featured "fallen women," did echo women's values as they had emerged from the progressive period. Frequently women's failings are shown to result from the collapse of responsible male roles. Husbands, fathers, boyfriends are portrayed as disoriented, incapable of providing properly for their families, and, if rich, irresponsible in their use of their social position. Under these conditions, women frequently are forced to enter the public sphere and to go to work, thus risking the dangers a woman alone confronts in the public space. Many of these working heroines are depicted as strong and attractive. But if they need strength, a film might suggest, it is because the social order in which males did the work and provided strength has collapsed.

Depression movies had a lighter side. The Marx brothers, W. C. Fields, and Mae West all represented versions of the anarchic character in comic guise. W. C. Fields in *The Fatal Glass of Beer* mocks the family. Mae West jokes irreverently about sex in *I'm No Angel.* In *Duck Soup* (1932) the Marx Brothers do away with logic and sequence. In the mid-1930s screwball comedies appeared, at once teasing about social conventions and romantic about love. Perhaps none did it better than the very first of this type, Frank Capra's *It Happened One Night* (1934). Two dozen or so of these comedies appeared during the later part of the decade, with such stars as Cary Grant, Carole Lombard, Katherine Hepburn, Irene Dunne, and Clark Gable. Musicals of the 1930s also presented romantic escapism and one or another version of the success story. Three of the most popular, *Forty Second Street, Gold Diggers of 1933,* and *Footlight Parade,* were all constructed around Depression themes.

The escapist screwball comedies and musicals contrasted with other films of the period that emphasized social and economic problems. Labor dissension, slum conditions, and, of course, unemployment were among the issues facing the country and appearing on screen. John Ford's filming of John Steinbeck's novel *The Grapes of Wrath* (1939) was notable for its sympathetic portrayal of farm workers—"Okies" driven by dust storms from Oklahoma.

Opponents of the New Deal

Although the Democrats picked up a total of nine seats in the House and Senate in the 1934 elections, an uncommon gain for the party in power in a non-presidential year, the New Deal had acquired a variety of enemies. Some, out of either principle or pigheadedness, refused from the beginning to accept Roosevelt's programs, while others who began as supporters, or at least neutrals, turned sour when the New Deal failed to meet their particular expectations. The crisis of the Depression led voters to entertain both cure-alls and prejudices that they would have dismissed in normal times.

The Right On the far right stood American fascists, lavishing hatred on Jews, blacks, Communists, and foreigners, and talking of saving democracy, Christianity, free enterprise, and America. William Dudley Pelly's Silver Shirts won a temporary and unsavory fame.

Unlike the fascists, who desired sweeping changes that would institutionalize their prejudices, political conservatives wanted little change of any kind. Conservatives made up a substantial portion of the business community, the professions, the press, and the Republican Party. By the autumn of 1933 conservatives, after having cooperated during the crisis of the Hundred Days, began to organize in opposition to Roosevelt. They charged the New Deal with extravagant spending, overtaxation, and meddling bureaucracy. They warned that the administration was trampling on the Constitution and marching to socialism. Many conservatives charged that recovery had been about to occur when Roosevelt took office, and that his foolish programs were unsettling the economy and prolonging hard times. The well-financed Liberty League issued anti-New Deal propaganda, attracting several prominent Democratic conservatives, including the former presidential nominee Al Smith.

Communists and Socialists The American Communist Party extended its membership and influence in the early thirties while using the militant rhetoric of hostility to capitalism that the Soviet Union was then demanding of its puppet parties throughout the world. By the mid-1930s the new Soviet strategy of the Popular Front—cooperation with liberal democracies against Hitler—had turned the Communists to a more restrained rhetoric. Yet beneath their strategies of restraint they continued in their conviction that liberals, progressives, and the non-communist left were self-deluded servants or ineffectual critics of a dying capitalist order and would have to be crushed or remade when communist resolution came. Other sectarian groups on the left pursued their private versions of Marxism, each convinced that it alone spoke for the future.

The First World War and the Red Scare had decimated the Socialist Party, but it continued to exist in the thirties under the leadership of Norman Thomas. Roosevelt, thought the Socialists, was a decent and well-meaning man though not a strong leader, and the New Deal presented merely a conglomeration of weak measures. Roosevelt was wasting a precious historical moment, when a major reshaping of the system was possible. As Norman Thomas put it, the New Deal was like an attempt "to cure tuberculosis with cough drops."

In 1934 Upton Sinclair, author of *The Jungle* and other muckraking novels, left the Socialist Party and with the help of the unemployed obtained the Democratic nomination for governor of California. In a program known as "End Poverty in California" (EPIC), Sinclair called for turning silent factories and fallow farmlands into nonprofit cooperatives that, he hoped, while operating inside the capitalist system would provide large-scale relief and convert millions to socialism. Although Sinclair at first had strong support and the implicit approval of the White House as the party nominee, California interests and state Democratic leaders soon organized a modern advertising campaign to tar him as communistic, atheistic, and un-American. Sinclair was badly defeated at the polls. Other protest movements rose to champion agricultural interests. Milo Reno, a longtime agricultural radical, supported the traditional populist solution of currency inflation, and demanded government guarantees of the farmer's production costs and a further extension of farm mortgages. His Farm Holiday movement proposed agricultural strikes, and his followers attracted attention by blocking highways, dumping milk on the roads, and forcibly preventing eviction sales.

Meanwhile, national movements for social reconstruction were gathering in opposition to the New Deal. The sentiments were evident in mail to the White House:

Dear Mrs. Roosevelt:

I do hope our dear President will start to divide among the people of this country the billions of dollars of the Duponts, Rockefellers, Morgans, and their kind. My children need so many little things that my husband and I are anxious to get our share. My husband says that President Roosevelt got a mandate from the people . . . to redistribute wealth. He says the common people have woken up, and are not going to be slaves any more to keep the Duponts and Rockefellers and Morgans in luxury. And he says, too, that the mass of the people . . . demand their share, and they are going to get it, or they will give the multimillionaires a bloody revolution. . . . We are entitled to our home, and money for our children just the same as the Rockefellers, Duponts and Morgans. Yes, and we are entitled to have just as much money as they have got. My husband says that anyone who trifles with the people at this time had better be careful. . . . I do hope you will ask our dear President to divide the wealth as soon as possible.

Yours very truly
Mrs. M. B.

Huey Long Huey P. Long, from the hard-scrabble hills of northern Louisiana, was a formidable opponent. Long had gone from traveling salesman to lawyer to railroad commissioner to governor at the age of thirty-five, and finally United States senator in 1930. Possessing an intelligence unburdened by scruples, he taxed oil profits as governor and used the taxes (after keeping a share for himself) to provide school books, health services, and other benefits to the people of Louisiana, including poor blacks. By 1934 he held virtually dictatorial power in Louisiana, establishing a base for national ambitions. He aimed at forming a coalition of the poor, black as well as white; his slogan was "Every Man a King."

An early supporter of Roosevelt, Long quickly moved away to advance his own program, which he termed "Share Our Wealth," and denounced Roosevelt as a stooge of Wall Street. He suggested seizing all private assets above $5 million and taxing at one hundred percent the portion of annual incomes over $1 million. The money collected would be redistributed to provide every American family a "homestead" and a yearly income of between $2000 and $3000 as well as pensions and educational benefits. The uninhibited, brash but clever "Kingfish" gleefully gained as an associate Gerald L. K. Smith, a shouting evangelical preacher who helped build his

IN HIS NOVEL *Of Time and The River* Thomas Wolfe evoked the folk nationalism that helped America through the Depression. Wolfe sang

the thunder of imperial names, the names of men and battles, the names of places and great rivers, the mighty names of the States. The name of The Wilderness; and the names of Antietam, Chancellorsville, Shiloh, Bull Run, Fredericksburg, Cold Harbor, the Wheat Fields, Ball's Bluff, and the Devil's Den; the names of Cowpens, Brandywine, and Saratoga; of Death Valley, Chickamauga, and the Cumberland Gap. The names of the Nantahalahs, the Bad Lands, the Painted Desert, the Yosemite, and the Little Big Horn; the names of Yancey and Cabarrus counties; and the terrible name of Hatteras.

Then, for the continental thunder of the States: the names of Montana, Texas, Arizona, Colorado, Michigan, Maryland, Virginia, and the two Dakotas; the names of Oregon and Indiana, of Kansas and the rich Ohio; the powerful name of Pennsylvania, the name of Old Kentucky; the undulance of Alabama; the names of Florida and North Carolina.

In the red-oak thickets, at the break of day, long hunters lay for bear—the rattle of arrows in laurel leaves, the war-cries round the painted buttes, and the majestical names of the Indian Nations: the Pawnees, the Algonquins, the Iroquois, the Comanches, the Blackfeet, the Seminoles, the Cherokees, the Sioux, the Hurons, the Mohawks, the Navajos, the Utes, the Omahas, the Onondagas, the Chippewas, the Crees, the Chickasaws, the Arapahoes, the Catawbas, the Dakotas, the Apaches, the Croatans, and the Tuscaroras; the names of Powhatan and Sitting Bull; and the name of the Great Chief, Rain-In-The-Face. . . .

The rails go westward in the dark. Brother, have you seen starlight on the rails? Have you heard the thunder of the fast express?

Of wandering forever, and the earth again—the names of the mighty rails that bind the nation, the wheeled thunder of the names that net the continent: the Pennsylvania, the Union Pacific, the Santa Fé, the Baltimore and Ohio, the Chicago and Northwestern, the Southern, the Louisiana and Northern, the Seaboard Air Line, the Chicago, Milwaukee and Saint Paul, the Lackawanna, the New York, New Haven and Hartford, the Florida East Coast, the Rock Island, and the Denver and Rio Grande. . . .

The names of the mighty rivers, the alluvial gluts, the drains of the continent, the throats that drink America (Sweet Thames, flow gently till I end my song). The names of men who pass, and the myriad names of the earth that abides forever: the names of the men who are doomed to wander, and the name of that immense and lonely land on which they wander, to which they return, in which they will be buried—America! The immortal earth which waits forever, the trains that thunder on the continent, the men who wander, and the women who cry out, "Return!"

Finally, the names of the great rivers that are flowing in the darkness. . . .

The names of great mouths, the mighty maws, the vast, wet, coiling, never-glutted and unending snakes that drink the continent. Where, sons of men, and in what other land will you find others like them, and where can you match the mighty music of their names?—The Monongahela, the Colorado, the Rio Grande, the Columbia, the Tennessee, the Hudson (Sweet Thames!); the Kennebec, the Rappahannock, the Delaware, the Penobscot, the Wabash, the Chesapeake, the Swannanoa, the Indian River, the Niagara (Sweet Afton!); the Saint Lawrence, the Susquehanna, the Tombigbee, the Nantahala, the French Broad, the Chattahoochee, the Arizona, and the Potomac (Father Tiber!)—these are a few of their princely names, these are a few of their great, proud, glittering names, fit for the immense and lonely land that they inhabit.

following. By 1935 twenty thousand Share-Our-Wealth clubs claimed several million members, and Long was taking aim at the presidency—actually writing a book entitled *My First Days in the White House*. Some believe that Long hoped to achieve the presidency in 1936, but more likely he sought to lay the basis for a triumph in 1940. The question became moot when, on September 8, 1935, an assassin fatally wounded Long in the marble corridors of the Louisiana state capitol, destroying both Long and his movement.

Father Coughlin and Doctor Townsend

Rivaling Long in national influence during the early thirties was the "Radio Priest," Father Charles Coughlin. In his mellifluous voice he had been broadcasting a weekly religious message since 1926, but in the thirties his messages became increasingly political. At first an enthusiastic supporter of the New Deal, he came to dislike Roosevelt's financial policies and was soon searching for sensational topics to hold his audience among low-income people, particularly urban Catholics in the Midwest. Coughlin called Roosevelt a "great betrayer" and a "liar," and he eventually gave expression to an anti-Semitism suggestive of European Fascism. Coughlin, his audience estimated at between thirty and forty-five million listeners, seemed a major political threat.

The New Deal had another challenger less menacing than Long or Coughlin: a white-haired, retired doctor living in California, Francis E. Townsend. Disturbed by the terrible effects of depression and unemployment on the elderly, Townsend proposed that the government give each person over sixty a pension on the conditions that the recipient refrain from a paying job and spend the entire amount within the month. The presumption was that such spending would create jobs for younger workers and stimulate economic recovery. Critics noted that Townsend's plan would require the expenditure of about $25 billion, or half the national income, to support ten percent of the population. Yet Townsend had tapped an important new interest group in politics, the elderly, who made up an increasingly large segment of the population.

Huey P. Long might have combined his virtually dictatorial power in Louisiana and his theme of "Share Our Wealth" to challenge Roosevelt in the 1936 or 1940 elections had he not been assassinated. *(Courtesy, United Press International Photos)*

In 1936 the Townsendites, Coughlin's National Union for Social Justice, and the remnants of Long's movement came together in the Union Party to oppose Roosevelt. Although the Union Party won only a few hundred thousand votes in the election, these protest movements reflected serious dissatisfactions with the New Deal's progress in ending depression. The despair of 1932 had turned to hope in 1933, and that hope had bred frustration. But Roosevelt was a political master. By early 1935 he was moving to expand the New Deal dramatically in ways that would confound all his opponents in 1936.

The Second Hundred Days

The Works Progress Administration (WPA) At the beginning of 1935, Roosevelt's annual message to Congress called for new initiatives in resources policy, provision of relief, slum clearance, and some form of social legislation to protect against sickness, unemployment, and penniless old age. Yet by the time Congress prepared to adjourn for the summer, it had passed only the Emergency Relief Appropriation Act. This important bill established the Works Progress Administration (WPA), which, universally called by its initials, became the very symbol of the New Deal. To some a giant boondoggle, to others it was a vast, imaginative use of federal dollars to provide work for the unemployed. In eight years, the WPA spent $11 billion—then a giant sum even for the federal government—employing over eight million people in nearly one million projects. It constructed and repaired roads, bridges, parks, airports, and public buildings, hired artists and writers to spread culture to even the tiniest villages, and performed a bewildering array of services, some priceless when the project was well designed, some doubtless a waste. But however humanitarian, however useful in pump-priming the economy, the WPA remained essentially a relief measure.

Then Roosevelt seized the moment. A series of executive orders established several important agencies: the Resettlement Administration, to help poor farm families and to establish greenbelt towns for low-income city-dwellers; the Rural Electrification Administration (REA), an extraordinary success that vastly speeded the use of modern appliances by farm families; the National Youth Administration (NYA), which offered jobs to young people, helping millions to survive and hundreds of thousands to complete college. The President also demanded that Congress remain in session during the sweltering summer of 1935. Congressmen prodded and driven from the White House entered upon the "second hundred days," enacting laws that have had a permanent effect on American society.

The Wagner Act The National Labor Relations Act of 1935, long pressed by Senator Robert Wagner of New York but only now supported by FDR, radically shifted the balance of power in labor-management relations by guaranteeing labor's right to organize. The Wagner Act reestablished and even strengthened labor rights gained under the NRA and lost at the hands of the Supreme Court. The National Labor Relations Board established by the act could supervise elections among workers, certify duly elected unions as bargaining agents, and collect data on management's unfair labor practices, including refusal to bargain.

Thereafter the rise of organized labor, while still tested in bloodshed as well as court battles, proceeded without serious interruptions. The newly powerful mass unions quickly became an essential element of the New Deal coalition.

The Social Security Act The Social Security Act of 1935 had consequences equally far-reaching. It established a vast system providing a very modest cushion for most Americans against unemployment, dependency, and old age. Coverage was limited: domestics, agricultural workers, and people working in businesses of fewer than eight employees were excluded. Nonetheless, the act signaled a basic change in the country's direction and outlook—the United States was becoming a welfare state. It had at last joined other industrial nations in providing social insurance against the worst shocks of modern economic life.

Additional Legislation The Banking Act, the Holding Company Act, and the Wealth Tax Act were all aimed squarely at Roosevelt's opponents, and they represented his response to the public hostility toward big business and banks reflected in the popularity of Long and Coughlin. The Banking Act opened the way for closer central control over the banking system. The Holding Company Act and the Wealth Tax Act aroused some of the fiercest controversy in that summer of 1935. The newspaper baron William Randolph Hearst decreed that all his editors should henceforth refer to the New Deal as the Raw Deal because of the wealth tax, and the public utilities invested over a million dollars on bogus telegrams to Congress opposing the Holding Company Act.

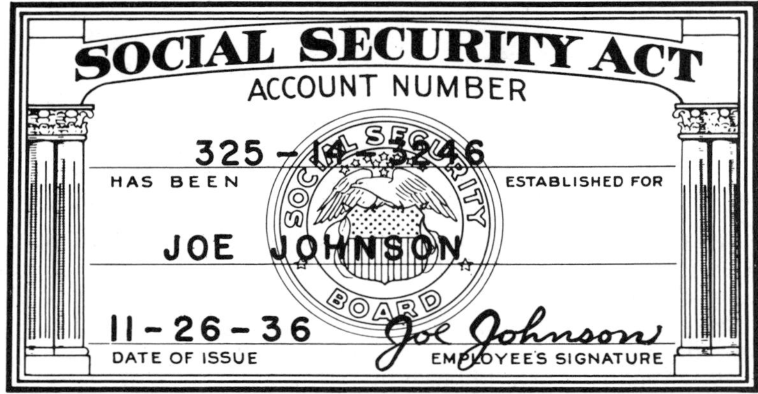

The Social Security Act of 1935 ultimately established a vast system of pensions and unemployment insurance, providing a modest cushion against unemployment, dependency, and old age.

Some historians have referred to the second hundred days as a second New Deal fundamentally different from the first. They see the first New Deal as more conservative and sympathetic to business and the second New Deal as a coalition against business. But whatever elements of planning, or regulation, or basic safeguards for individuals Roosevelt championed and experimented with, his thinking and that of most of his public never went beyond seeking adjustments within the system of private enterprise, within the system that had produced both the nation's wealth and its Great Depression. New Deal or raw deal: most critics now agree that he continued to deal from the same deck.

The Election of 1936

In 1936 the Democrats renominated Roosevelt at their convention in Philadelphia and promised more reform. If the Supreme Court blocked economic regulation by the government, the platform hinted darkly, Congress and the people must seek "a clarifying amendment" to the Constitution. Then on the evening of June 27 the President delivered to a radio audience of millions one of the great speeches of American political history. "In the place of the palace of privilege," he told his excited listeners, "we seek to build a temple out of faith and hope and charity." Castigating "economic royalists," he grandly called the country to its mission: "There is a mysterious cycle in human events. To some generations much is given. Of others much is expected. This generation of Americans has a rendezvous with destiny."

Not all Republicans were ready to concede a Roosevelt triumph. Despite the severe drubbing of the 1934 congressional campaign, those who survived thought that the welfare politics of 1935 and 1936 had alienated conservatives in the border South and Far West. Townsend, Coughlin, and Gerald L.K. Smith all pumped out anti-Roosevelt propaganda to their followers in critical states like California and Michigan, and Republicans could hope that the three would draw votes away from Roosevelt. The Depression continued with persistent double-digit unemployment that also gave the Republicans hope of winning. The GOP finally turned to Governor Alfred Landon of Kansas, a man with few enemies and one of the few Republicans still in office. Best known for fiscal caution—Landon had balanced the Kansas budget every year—the nominee along with his party platform nevertheless boldly approved unemployment relief, farm subsidies, collective bargaining, and antitrust action. But Republicans still denounced the style, if not the substance, of the New Deal as "socialistic" and as "unconstitutional dictatorship."

Almost everyone realized that the popularity of the New Deal and Roosevelt's personal magnetism guaranteed a Democratic sweep. But few could believe the election eve prediction of James Farley, the President's campaign manager: "Roosevelt will carry every state except Maine and Vermont." He was exactly correct. That coalition of farmers, workers, blacks, and middle-class wage earners who had voted against Hoover in 1932 now even more strongly validated New Deal reforms. Roosevelt won over sixty percent of the popular vote, and all the electoral college votes but eight. Only eighty-eight Republicans remained in the House of Representatives. The election of 1936, like its counterpart in 1896, transformed national politics for a generation. It institutionalized the New Deal, cementing a coalition of Democratic voters that insured the party's dominance in the United States for many years thereafter. In only four years out of the next forty would the Republicans hold a majority in Congress.

Roosevelt and the Supreme Court

Even as Roosevelt's reelection was appearing more and more certain, the Supreme Court was striking broadly at the government's legal power to regulate the economy. Early in 1936 the justices in *United States v. Butler* wrecked the administration's agricultural policy by declaring the AAA unconstitutional. Congress had overextended its taxing power, the Court charged, and had interfered with states' rights. Then, in June, the "nine old men," as some angry Democrats called them, vetoed a New York law that legislated minimum wages for women: the state, they said in *Morehead v. New York ex rel. Tipaldo,* had encroached upon the exclusive federal jurisdiction over interstate commerce.

The Court-Packing Scheme

Roosevelt decided to remove the obstacle that had blocked the will of President, Congress, and people. Early in 1937, he suddenly released a White House plan to reform the entire federal judiciary. Thirty-five additional district judges could speed decisions in lower courts. The age of six Supreme Court justices—all over seventy—slowed its deliberations, the proposal argued. Unless each retired, Congress should allow the President to appoint another judge to assist him. The Court's numerical makeup had shifted several times in its history. The ill-disguised purpose of the maneuver was clear: Roosevelt wanted to add to the Court liberals certain to approve New Deal reforms.

The popular President now encountered a sudden barrage of opposition. Most Republicans and many conservative Democrats condemned Roosevelt, some publicly, as a dictator. They feared that the court-packing scheme might subordinate the judiciary to the executive. But Roosevelt's abrupt manner on this issue angered many liberals as well. Chief Justice Charles Evans Hughes testified during Senate hearings that the Court regularly completed some ninety percent of its docket every year. Additional justices, he charged, would slow the Court's work, for "more must discuss, more must decide." The Court, which had already approved a minimum wage law, then made a series of unexpected decisions: it accepted social security benefits, then startled even labor leaders with a confirmation of the Wagner Act. A conservative justice, Willis Van Devanter, retired during the spring; Roosevelt's replacement, presumably, would tilt the Court toward a five to four liberal majority. The final blow to Roosevelt's plan came that summer with the death of Joseph T. Robinson, floor manager for the bill in the Senate. Thwarted by the politically astute chief justice, his own clumsy tactics, and congressional independence. Roosevelt quietly admitted defeat.

The President later claimed that he had "lost a battle but won the war." Between 1937 and his death, Roosevelt appointed seven new justices, all liberals. For the first time since the Civil War, the judges widened the scope of government activity, particularly its right to regulate the economy. The Court also vigorously expanded those First Amendment freedoms so eloquently defended by Oliver Wendell Holmes some forty years earlier, and hastened the great judicial revolution in civil rights that was to result in the destruction of the system of Jim Crow in the ensuing decades. During the middle third of the twentieth century, in fact, the Court would become the most reformist branch of government.

The American people rejected President Roosevelt's "court-packing" scheme to obtain Supreme Court rulings more sympathetic to the New Deal. *(Courtesy, F. D. R. Library)*

The Waning of the New Deal

A substantial number of Americans, including some who voted for FDR, had never lost their inbred conservatism. One Indiana woman wrote to Mrs. Roosevelt in 1937 of the "pampered poverty rats":

> I suppose from your point of view the work relief, old age pensions, slum clearance and all the rest seems like a perfect remedy for all the ills of this country, but I would like for you to see the results. . . .
>
> We have always had a shiftless, never-do-well class of people whose one and only aim in life is to live without work. I have been rubbing elbows with this class for nearly sixty years and have tried to help some of the most promising and have seen others try to help them, but it can't be done. . . . let each one paddle their own canoe, or sink.
>
> There has never been any necessity for any one who is able to work, being on relief in this locality, but there have been many eating the bread of charity and they have lived better than ever before. I have had taxpayers tell me that their children came from school and asked why they couldn't have nice lunches like the children on relief.
>
> The women and children around here have had to work at the fields to help save the crops and several women fainted while at work and at the same time we couldn't go up or down the road without stumbling over some of the reliefers, moping around carrying dirt from one side of the road to the other and back again, or else asleep.

The Court fight, a sharp economic downturn, and the approach of war in Europe largely halted liberal efforts at social engineering. In Congress an alliance of southern Democrats, determined to protect economic and social practices, and northern Republicans, equally determined to preserve business prerogatives, effectively blocked further challenges to the status quo. Debate raged between isolationists and interventionists over the nation's role in world affairs. Reform lost some of its public, and much of its urgency.

The Sit-down Strikes

While the government was less active, labor's drive in 1936 and 1937 toward national organization had a permanent success that both gave the New Deal an institutional base and solidified opposition to it. At the end of 1936, CIO workers at the General Motors Fisher Body plant in Flint, Michigan, seized the factory, sitting down instead of walking out. The new strategy of the sit-down strikes spread across the nation, achieving more success for unionization in a year than labor had accomplished in decades. Businessmen were fearful of having their equipment damaged along with their hopes of industrial recovery, and both the federal and the state governments were resistant to the traditional use of force to put down such disruption. So industry after industry yielded to the workers' new militancy. Some workers threw pop bottles or nuts and bolts, and in a few incidents heads were cracked and blood flowed. Four people were killed in the Republic Steel strike of 1937. But much of American industry was organized in scarcely a year.

The CIO even managed to help some black workers. Jim Cole remembered when the Congress of Industrial Organizations came to the packinghouses:

> I'm working in the Beef Kill section. Butcher on the chain. Been in the place twenty years, I believe. You got to have a certain amount of skill to do the job I'm doing. Long ago, I wanted to join the AFL union, the Amalgamated Butchers and Meat Cutters, they called it. They wouldn't let me in. Never said it to my face, but reason of it was plain. Negro. Just didn't want a Negro man to have what he should. That's wrong—you know that's wrong.
>
> Long about 1937 the CIO came. Well, I tell you, we Negroes was glad to see it come. Union asked for fifteen extra men on the killing floor, on the chain. Company had enough work for them, just tried to make us carry the load. After we had a stoppage, our union stewards went up to the office of the company and talked turkey. We got the extra help.
>
> I don't care if the union don't do another lick of work raising our pay, or settling grievances about anything. I'll always believe they done the greatest thing in the world getting everybody who works in the yards together, and breaking up the hate and bad feelings that used to be held.

In 1936 before the great strikes began, scarcely four million workers belonged to unions. By the end of 1937, the figure was over seven million. The nation entered World War II with over eleven million workers organized. The workers had found a home; the New Deal had found its steady base both in funds and in votes.

The Depression Worsens

The Depression intensified during the winter of 1937–1938. Record crops glutted markets, and many farmers stopped buying manufactured goods. Federal spending and taxation policies also affected the economy. The Social Security Act had been passed in 1935, but the program was not going to pay any benefits until 1940. In order to build up its reserve fund, however, the Social Security Administration began collecting taxes late in 1936. Also, Roosevelt's administration, anticipating a continuing strengthening of the economy, slashed federal relief programs. Both of these measures together pulled down to only $800 million in 1937 the net federal contribution to the national income; in 1936 the sum had been more than $4.1 billion. As federal spending declined and taxes went up, consumer purchasing power fell sharply and the economy slipped badly.

Between October 1937 and May 1938, industrial production fell more than a third, durable goods production more than half, and business profits more than three-quarters. National income was down by 13 percent, employment by 20 percent, payrolls by 35 percent, and industrial stock averages by 50 percent.

The economic decline precipitated an intense debate within the administration. For several months Roosevelt wavered, doing nothing. Why return to deficit spending if it apparently had failed to restore prosperity? Inactivity, however, seemed the greater error. Several of the President's economic advisors now urged a fresh round of relief spending. Influenced by the theories of the great

British economist John Maynard Keynes, they argued that government spending could compensate for a fall in private purchasing and thereby encourage fresh private investment. Others pressed Roosevelt to reduce expenditures and thereby to calm businessmen holding to the orthodox conviction that government's role in the economy should be small. Roosevelt compromised by calling for a $3 billion public works program. This was too small to be a major boost to the economy, but it was the right size for Congress, which passed it in just two months.

A new farm bill, the second AAA (1938), allotted acreage quotas to individual farmers; in return for confining their production to only a part of their land, the Department of Agriculture bought up their crops at artificially high prices. These subsidies, called parity payments, aimed at boosting income to the levels that had obtained between 1909 and 1914, known as a time of agricultural prosperity. Most farmers willingly joined the voluntary program. To reduce its own surplus holdings and to alleviate the effect of higher food prices on the poor, the government distributed food stamps to the unemployed.

Then, after a long struggle, the administration finally pushed through Congress the Fair Labor Standards Act of 1938, which set the minimum wage at twenty-five cents per hour and limited the work week to forty-four hours. The law also barred from interstate commerce goods manufactured by child labor. The Wagner-Steagall National Housing Act—complementing the earlier Federal Housing Administration Act, which guaranteed home mortgages for the middle class—sought to fill the huge demand for low income housing and to revive the long depressed construction industry. Local governments received $600 million in loans and built nearly 150,000 units over the next three years.

The sleek, clean lines of the modern factory are caught in Charles Sheeler, *River Rouge Plant* (one of a series). *(Courtesy, Henry Ford Museum, Dearborn, Michigan)*

Assessing the New Deal What had the New Deal accomplished? Its relief programs had taken the raw edges off the Depression. The New Deal welfare measures cannot claim credit for recovery. What did restore the economy were the purchases government made of military supplies as the nation prepared to face the Axis powers and then fought them. War orders put farms, factories, and shops to work, and that created jobs, and the wages got spent on consumer goods, which gave industry further productive work to do. But Roosevelt's temporary jobs program gave the dignity of work to victims of the Depression, along with money that they could pump into the economy, just as wartime wages were later pumped. As acts of government spending, moreover, the military purchases that ended the Depression may be thought of as continuations of the federal quickening of the economy that the relief programs had been intended to do. The public emerged from the Depression with the understanding that thereafter the government had a responsibility to prevent depressions and stimulate recoveries. But the New Deal gave to the government a role in the economic and social life of the nation far more intense than that. Washington became a regulator of the stock market, an insurer of banks, a protector of labor unions, and a collector of funds for unemployment insurance and retirement pensions.

Ignoring It All

Leisure at Home Americans did not gloom their way through ten years of depression. Economic troubles were so common and widespread that a kind of camaraderie sprang up. People took up a variety of pastimes.

Parlor games changed to meet the need and the opportunity for inexpensive, readily available entertainment. Card-playing, especially the new game of contract bridge, became immensely popular. After Ely Culbertson and his wife beat Sidney Lens and Oswald Jacoby in a 150-game "Battle of the Century" on radio, over twenty million people learned the Culbertson system of point count and bidding. Other inexpensive crazes—jigsaw puzzles, Monopoly, Ping Pong—helped many adults keep their minds off their problems.

Radio For American stay-at-homes the most ubiquitous entertainment came over the air waves. The number of radio sets quadrupled during the decade to over forty million. Most households listened three or four hours each day to a wide range of programs. Dance music from New York City nightclubs or popular singers like Kate Smith filled many hours, but most popular of all was comedy; after all, what was more needed? George Burns and Gracie Allen drew laughs with their routines about a dizzy but insightful housewife; Jack Benny and Mary Livingstone joked about his stinginess. Ethnic comedies like *The Goldbergs* introduced millions to the habits and cultures of one of the country's many minorities. One program above all fascinated Americans during the thirties: *Amos 'n' Andy*. While this series about two black men, played by whites, presented stereotyped racial attitudes, it had the general aim of poking fun at the dilemmas of individuals caught in situations beyond their control. President Hoover's fears about "air waves chocked full with advertising chatter" had come true. As radio broadcast major-league baseball contests and Broadway show tunes, it did much to homogenize the nation, to create universal symbols.

Outside the home, bingo games, slot machines, pinball boards, and prize contests offered a chance to win something for (almost) nothing. A lucky bingo card, often selling for only a penny, might win a ham or a new shirt. Slot machines, then legal throughout most of the country except the East Coast, returned on the average seventy-five cents on each dollar. Thousands danced on weekends in local "hippodromes" to the sounds of swing music—happy tunes with a quick beat—made famous by Benny Goodman. Doing the Big Apple or the Lindy under twirling specks of light reflected overhead from hundreds of little mirrors calmed worries about the next paycheck. When Rudy Vallee sang "Life is just a bowl of cherries," he was counseling his listeners not to take the Depression too seriously:

> Life is just a bowl of cherries,
> Don't make it serious,
> Life's too mysterious.
> You work, you save, you worry so,
> But you can't take your dough when you go-go-go,
> So keep repeating, it's the berries. . . .

Getting Away From It All As the Depression lengthened the free time that American technology had already begun providing more and more of, the country still spent about ten percent of its national income on vacationing and recreation. Even more than the new streamlined trains with air-cooled Pullman cars, the country's highways took people to inexpensive vacation spots such as national parks and seashores. Automobile ownership actually increased during the thirties, as the appearance of modest tourist camps and motels enticed millions onto the roads, their cars burning the cheap fuel of the times. Auto trailers also began to appear in large numbers.

The Works Progress Administration (WPA) spent huge amounts on local parks, swimming pools, tennis courts, and beaches. States contributed as well to the nearly $1 billion lavished on new recreation areas. In New York, Public Works Commissioner Robert Moses opened for public use miles of bathing beaches on Long Island and built roads and bridges to reach them. Depression weakened the popularity of spectator football, of necessity a costly amusement, although some institutions took advantage of cheap labor to construct enormous stadiums such as the Yale Bowl, built to hold fifty-five

Yankee Stadium, New York, 1935. Baseball and other spectator sports continued to attract city dwellers in search of diversion. *(Courtesy, AP/Wide World Photos)*

thousand people. Among spectator as opposed to participant sports, big-league baseball remained important. But the athlete of the decade was the black boxer, Joe Louis. Son of an Alabama sharecropper, the "Brown Bomber" turned pro in 1934 and defeated the former heavyweight champion Max Baer the next year. Millions followed his career on the radio as he won bout after bout, losing only to Max Schmeling, the great German fighter. In 1937 only three years after his debut, Louis knocked out James Braddock to win the world heavyweight championship. The next year, Louis again met Schmeling. Patriotic Americans, and especially blacks, hoped ardently to see him defeat the white man who, Hitler bragged, had proved Nazi theories about the Aryan "master race." Their hopes were realized. Louis destroyed Schmeling in the first round.

Crime

Despite the solace of religion, sports, and parlor games, a sense of decline afflicted the daily life of most citizens. The ending of prohibition and the onset of hard times sliced in half the revenue from organized crime. But crimes against property increased during the thirties, as did arrests for vagrancy and drunkenness. Personal assaults declined, although an old American type reappeared, the bandit or outlaw who panicked whole regions with sprees of violent revenge against society. Some outlaws, like Clyde Barrow and his moll Bonnie Parker, were pathetic people too buffeted by depression and ignorance to understand why they compulsively, happily robbed banks and killed. John Dillinger reveled in the notoriety of being J. Edgar Hoover's FBI "Public Enemy Number One." Federal agents or state police staged elaborate ambushes of such figures, gunning down Dillinger outside a movie theater in Chicago and assassinating the Barrow gang along a back road in Louisiana.

Persistent Optimism Americans still dreamed of a better future. Twenty million people visited the Century of Progress exposition in Chicago during 1933 and 1934 to stare at the technological gadgetry and wonder over the possibilities of science. Five years later, an even more ambitious undertaking, the Golden Gate International Exposition in San Francisco, looked to a future of swift transportation and near-simultaneous communication. These *papier maché* fantasies had their grandest expression at the gigantic New York World's Fair of 1939. Nearly fifty million people strolled around the "Trylon and Perisphere": a 728-foot needle pyramid and a 180-foot globe that symbolized "The World of Tomorrow." Huge exhibits, sponsored by businesses and governments from all over the world, portrayed the panorama of a future built around cooperation and the rational use of the earth's resources for the benefit of all mankind. These earnest hopes were shortly dashed by the beginning of yet another war among the great powers—a war that, in one of history's profound strokes of irony, would finally bring to an end the decade-long Great Depression. The Trylon and the Perisphere were soon melted down to make war weapons.

Points To Think About

1. Supporters of the Soviet Union attacked the New Deal as an effort to prop up capitalism and save it from popular revolution. Right-wingers assaulted the New Deal for being Muscovite Communism in an American guise. The New Deal, in fact, represented an attitude toward property alternative both to the Communist attitude and to that of strict capitalism.

Communism aimed to abolish private property and make all material and financial wealth the collective possession of the people (which turned out, of course, to mean the possession of the ruling party and bureaucracy). Capitalism has been content to allow property to be distributed however circumstance or the market distributes it: to one family, a fortune of millions; to another, a tarpaper shack. The New Deal chose in effect to strengthen property by measures insuring that as many Americans as possible would have some of it. This it did in its efforts to promote ownership of homes and farms; in its provision of wages through public works; in its Social Security scheme, which gives participants something of the individual stake in it that a subscriber has in an insurance program. This solicitude for the wide distribution of small property puts the New Deal in a long tradition of homegrown American radicalism. Still, the question of what constitutes property is complicated in a modern industrial society, which replaces tangible property with wages and salaries and pulls separate jobs into close interconnections. Perhaps the most satisfactory answer would lodge property and independence in the possession of an education, or a skill.

Still, conservatives attacked the New Deal distribution of property. The most primitive claim among opponents of the New Deal was that property in a market system is the exact award for hard work, and that the poor are always poor only because they have not worked hard. But no demonstration exists that the market passes out its awards chiefly on the basis of work or any other kind of merit. In any event, the American habit of identifying property with work has had the effect of shifting attention from the virtues of work to the virtues of wealth. The New Deal, in assuming that every family should have a solid slice of property as a means to a full and productive life, could have been a beginning to rescuing the work ethic from the American fascination with wealth.

2. The New Deal sponsored a number of reforms such as the social security system and unemployment compensation that together formed the building blocks of the welfare state in the United States. Controversy yet stirs over these and other welfare programs and their supposed incompatibility with the traditional American commitment to free enterprise.

In fact, however, every industrial nation in the

world provides the same welfare programs. Every industrial society has had to come to terms with the industrial revolution. The Great Depression of the 1930s was simply the occasion for the United States to come to this same recognition. Even today the United States is the only industrial nation that does not provide comprehensive national health insurance. And the United States spends less of its total wealth on welfare programs than any other country except Japan, whose employers traditionally do not lay off workers during bad times.

The point of these comparisons is not to defend the American welfare state from all of its critics, but to point out that some of these criticisms have no basis in reality. It can be argued that the American welfare state is wasteful or ineffective but not so easily that it is too large. It is proportionately the smallest in the world.

3. The Wagner Act of 1935, also known as the National Labor Relations Act, had been hailed as the "Magna Carta" of American labor because it required employers to recognize unions as legitimate bargaining agents once a majority of the workers in a plant had voted for a union. The law was an enormous benefit later in the decade to the Congress of Industrial Organizations (the CIO), which was battling to organize the basic industries—steel, auto, rubber, and so on. Previously employers had been able to refuse to recognize or bargain with unions. They had been able to count on the support of the courts and the government when facing strikers. The combination of the CIO's aggressive organizing campaigns and the legal protections afforded by the Wagner Act led to an enormous growth in union membership.

With the unions came higher wages, shorter work weeks, and a host of other benefits. Organized labor also became one of the major elements in the Democratic Party, claiming and receiving a major voice in party policy decisions. In return, the CIO consistently supported Democratic candidates even after John L. Lewis, the CIO's first President, broke with FDR in 1940.

For all of these reasons the Wagner Act was among the most important laws of the 1930s. But it is worth remembering that all the Wagner Act did was permit unions in the United States to gain the kind of influence they already had achieved in other industrial nations. The Wagner Act simply brought American labor relations into the twentieth century.

Suggested Readings

Some new books on the 1930s include Richard Brestman and Alan M. Kraut, *American Refugee Policy and European Jewry, 1933–1945* (1987), Susan Ware, *Partner and I: Molly Dewson, Feminism, and New Deal Politics* (1987), Maurine Beasley, *Eleanor Roosevelt and the Media* (1987), Pening Migdal Glazer, *Unequal Colleagues: The Entrance of Women into the Professions, 1890–1940* (1987), George M. Jimsen, *Harry Hopkins* (1987), Robert Eden, ed., *The New Deal and Its Legacy* (1989), the very readable Frank Freidel, *Franklin D. Roosevelt: A Rendezvous with Destiny* (1990), and the anti-New Deal book by Gary Dean Best, *Pride, Prejudice, and Politics: Roosevelt Versus Recovery* (1990).

William Leuchtenburg's *Franklin D. Roosevelt and the New Deal, 1932–1940* (1963) is an excellent comprehensive survey; his *In the Shadow of FDR* (1983) is an interesting account of Roosevelt's influence on subsequent administrations. Paul Conkin's *The New Deal* (rev. 1975) is critically alive and surrounds the period with controversy. On the Depression itself a readable study centers on the stock market crash, John Kenneth Galbraith, *The Great Crash* (rev. 1979); *Robert Sobel's The Great Bull Market* (1968) is more analytical. Donald Lisio is thorough on the Bonus Army: *The President and Protest: Hoover, Conspiracy, and the Bonus Riot* (1974). Joseph P. Lash has written a sympathetic biography of the widely admired Eleanor Roosevelt, *Eleanor and Franklin* (1971). Alan Brinkley looks at opposition to the New Deal in *Voices of Protest: Huey Long, Father Coughlin, and the Great Depression* (1982). Thomas K. McCraw goes thoroughly into the fortunes of the Tennessee Valley Authority, one of the most important New Deal innovations: *TVA and the Power Fight, 1933–1939* (1971). Elliot A. Rosen questions the generosity of some recent historians to Herbert Hoover. In *Hoover, Roosevelt and the Brains Trust* (1977), Rosen claims that Hoover had a commitment to individualism that his ideas of cooperation did not at all modify. Rosen also argues that before Roosevelt took office he and the Brains Trust had thought out a general coherent public policy for coping with the economic crisis. Rosen's claim contradicts the familiar belief that the New Deal had no consistent ideas and made itself up from one moment to the next. Otis Graham analyzes the important topic of federal economic planning in *Toward a Planned Society: From Roosevelt to Nixon* (1976).

See also Robert S. McElvaine, ed., *Down and Out in the Great Depression* (1983), Arthur M. Schlesinger, Jr., *The Age of Roosevelt*, 3 vols. (1957–1960) on Roosevelt, Harvard Sitkoff, *A New Deal for Blacks* (1978), Lois Scharf, *To Work and to Wed* (1980), and Susan Ware, *Beyond Suffrage* (1981), Richard Pells, *Radical Visions and American Dreams* (1973), Warren Sussman, ed., *Culture and Commitment* (1973), and Richard Wright, *Native Son* (1940).

☆ ☆ ☆ **POINTS OF VIEW:** ☆ ☆ ☆

A New Deal But Not a New Deck?

William Leuchtenburg

In eight years, Roosevelt and the New Dealers had almost revolutionized the agenda of American politics. . . . In 1932, men of acumen were absorbed to an astonishing degree with such questions as prohibition, war debts, and law enforcement. By 1936, they were debating social security, the Wagner Act, valley authorities, and public housing. The thirties witnessed a rebirth of issues politics, and parties split more sharply on ideological lines than they had in many years past. . . .

Franklin Roosevelt re-created the modern Presidency. He took an office which had lost much of its prestige and power in the previous twelve years and gave it an importance which went well beyond what even Theodore Roosevelt and Woodrow Wilson had done. Clinton Rossiter has observed: "Only Washington, who made the office, and Jackson, who remade it, did more than [Roosevelt] to raise it to its present condition of strength, dignity, and independence." Under Roosevelt, the White House became the focus of all government—the fountainhead of ideas, the initiator of action, the representative of the national interest.

Then Roosevelt greatly expanded the President's legislative functions. In the nineteenth century, Congress had been jealous of its prerogatives as the lawmaking body, and resented any encroachment on its domain by the Chief Executive. Woodrow Wilson and Theodore Roosevelt had broken new ground in sending actual drafts of bills to Congress and in using devices like the caucus to win enactment of measures they favored. Franklin Roosevelt made such constant use of these tools that he came to assume a legislative role not unlike that of a prime minister. He sent special messages to Congress, accompanied them with drafts of legislation prepared by his assistants, wrote letters to committee chairmen or members of Congress to urge passage of the proposals, and authorized men like Corcoran to lobby as presidential spokesmen on the Hill. By the end of Roosevelt's tenure in the White House, Congress looked automatically to the Executive for guidance; it expected the administration to have a "program" to present for consideration. . . .

If the test of good administration is not an impeccable organizational chart but creativity, the Roosevelt must be set down not merely as a good administrator but as a resourceful innovator. The new agencies he set up gave a spirit of excitement to Washington that the routinized old-line departments could never have achieved. The President's refusal to proceed through channels, however vexing at times to his subordinates, resulted in a competition not only among men but among ideas, and encouraged men to feel that their own beliefs might win the day. . . . Most of all, Roosevelt was a successful administrator because he attracted to Washington thousands of devoted and highly skilled men. . . .

[T]he New Deal added up to . . . more than an experimental approach, more than the sum of its legislative achievements, more than an antiseptic utopia. It is true that there was a certain erosion of values in the thirties, as well as a narrowing of horizons, but the New Dealers inwardly recognized that what they were doing had a deeply moral significance however much they eschewed ethical pretensions. Heirs of the Enlightenment, they felt themselves part of a broadly humanistic movement to make man's life on earth more tolerable, a movement that might someday even achieve a co-operative commonwealth. Social insurance, Frances Perkins declared, was "a fundamental part of another great forward step in that liberation of humanity which began with the Renaissance."

Franklin D. Roosevelt and the New Deal (New York: Harper and Row, 1963). Reprinted by permission.

Paul Conkin

The welfare legislation [of the New Deal], large in hopes generated, often small in actual benefits, hardly represented a social revolution. Except for temporary relief, it added only a small burden to the national budget and none of the welfare programs significantly redistributed the wealth of the country. . . . Welfare, by stilling the voice of dissent and by stimulating consumption and higher profits, represented a type of government insurance for a capitalist economy. . . . But the meager benefits of the early Social Security system were insignificant in comparison to the building system of security for large, established commercial farms. . . .

The story of most New Deal frustration remains untold. The thirties was indeed a reform decade, a period when sensitivity to injustice, to vast structures of privilege, to the terribly empty life of most people, prevailed as never before. Much of the concern remained outside government, in critics of the New Deal, in radical political movements, in artists of varied mediums, in a few philosophers. But many reformers worked in or with New Deal agencies, particularly the relief and rehabilitation agencies. They were always in the minority and had to fight an unending battle within their own agencies. But the outside battle was the main one. As they struggled to carry out their programs, dealing directly with the exploited people who loved Roosevelt, they often found their task impossible. The economic and social institutions of a Democratic South, as an example, presented a continuing source of frustration, particularly in the treatment of blacks. . . .

The enemies of the New Deal were wrong. They should have been friends. Security was a prime concern of the insecure thirties. Concern for it cut across all classes. Businessmen, by their policies, desperately sought it in lowered corporate debts and tried to get the government to practice the same austerity. Even when ragged and ill-housed, workers opened savings accounts. The New Deal, by its policies, underwrote a vast apparatus of security. . . . But like stingy laborers, the frightened businessmen did not use and enjoy this security and thus increase it. New Dealers tried to frame institutions to protect the economy from major business cycles and began in an unclear sort of way to underwrite continuous economic growth and sustained profits. Although some tax bills at least hinted at restrictions on high profits, the New Deal certainly never attacked profits. During the thirties, taxes did not contribute to any leveling of income. Because of tax policies, even relief expenditures were disguised subsidies to producers, since future taxes on individual salaries or on consumer goods would pay for most of the relief. Thus, instead of relying on higher wages to create increased consumer demand, possibly at the short-term expense of profits, the government created the demand through relief expenditures, without taking the cost out of the hides of businessmen in the way they expected and feared.

The crusade almost always ended in some degree of futility. . . .

But nothing in [Roosevelt's] leadership was capable of transforming the desires of these loyal reformers into a new structure of political power. It may have been impossible, even had he tried. Master of politics, he was also captive to politics. Thus the story of many New Deal agencies was a sad story, the ever recurring story of what might have been. . . .

The New Deal, 3rd ed., 1992. Reprinted by permission of Harlan Davidson, Inc. pp. 58, 66, 73–76 passim.

Der Führer–Adolf Hitler.

CHAPTER 25

Diplomacy and War 1933–1945

KRISTALLNACHT

On October 28, 1938, the German government suddenly rounded up about 18,000 Polish Jews living in Germany. Thousands of stormtroopers snatched children from the streets, plucked the ill out of hospitals, herded both young and old into trains and trucks. Allowed only to take the clothes on their backs and ten marks ($4), they were dumped across the Polish border to find shelter in the no-man's-land between these hostile nations' frontier outposts.

The deportees suffered terrible hardship, particularly those at Zbaszym, whose plight attracted worldwide attention. One of them, Zindel Grynszpan, described his family's suffering in a letter to his seventeen-year-old son, Herschel, who had escaped from Germany to Paris. Wild with grief, the young man bought a pistol and went to the German embassy in Paris. He was sent to the desk of a minor official, Ernst vom Rath—himself under investigation for suspected Jewish ancestry. Convinced he could not see the ambassador, Grynszpan shot Vom Rath.

As the German official lay dying, it is said, the German S.S. teletyped orders to cities throughout Germany for a "spontaneous" pogrom. Vom Rath's death on the afternoon of November 9 was the signal; at 2:00 the next morning began *Kristallnacht*, the "night of broken glass." Some two hundred synagogues were burned, thousands of shops looted or destroyed, and twenty thousand Jews thrown into concentration camps. Thirty-six Jews were murdered, and many Jewish women were raped. While the destruction continued, the German government issued a set of decrees that essentially expropriated all property of German Jews and barred Jews from virtually all but the most menial employment.

American religious and civic groups and hundreds of newspapers demanded that something be done. German propaganda minister Josef Goebbels replied coolly to worldwide protests: "if there is any country that believes it has not enough Jews, I shall gladly turn over to it all our Jews." The United States government retorted with a mild diplomatic gesture of calling back its ambassador to Germany "for consultation" (a gesture less serious than a formal recall). President Roosevelt expressed his shock at a news conference, but was evasive on the question of whether the United States would accept more refugees. Trade with the Third Reich continued.

In response to the "night of broken glass" the Netherlands, Belgium, and Great Britain admitted several thousand refugee children, inspiring a movement among clergymen to do the same in the United States. Senator Robert F. Wagner of New York and Representative Edith Nourse Rogers of Massachusetts proposed the Wagner-Rogers Bill, which would have admitted up to 20,000 German refugees under the age of fourteen as an addition to the next two years' regular German quota. Advocates of the bill assured a joint House-Senate Committee that "none will come here save those who are, in the opinion of trained specialists, good material for American citizenship." They pointed out how few refugees the United States had recently absorbed and gave assurances that there was a surplus of good homes for these children. Mrs. Calvin Coolidge and Herbert Hoover were among the people offering to sponsor these children.

The bill, however, was in trouble from the start. The congressional hopper was crammed with sixty different anti-alien bills, including one—officially endorsed by the American Legion—to abolish all immigration to the United States for ten years. Patriotic societies opposed immigration generally. One hostile witness saw the children as the entering wedge "to break down the whole quota system." Another characterized the refugees in question as "thousands of motherless, embittered, persecuted children of undesirable foreigners." Republican Senator Robert A. Taft of Ohio echoed a common argument: "20,000 American children could profit if such nice homes were available."

The Roosevelt Administration retained a tomblike official silence. The President was then struggling to pry from Congress funds to build naval bases and to expand the Army Air Corps in preparation for the country's possible involvement in another world war. Despite Roosevelt's genuine concern over the fate of all of central and eastern European Jewry, whose future he described at this very time as "exceedingly dark," he let the Refugee Bill and many of the refugees die.

Sophia Litwinska remembered Auschwitz, largest of the Nazi extermination camps, which began to operate in 1940; estimates of the numbers who died at Auschwitz vary from one to two-and-one-half million:

> There was a big selection in Block No. 4, the hospital block. Over 3000 Jewish women had to parade in this selection, which was under the charge of Hoessler. We had to leave our beds very quickly and stand quite naked to attention in front of him and the doctors, Enna and Koenig. All those who could not leave their beds had their numbers taken, and it was clear to us that they were condemned to death. Those whose bodies were not very nice looking or were too thin, or whom those gentlemen disliked for some reason or other, had their numbers taken, and it was clear what that meant. My number also was taken. We stayed in Block No. 4 for a night and the next day were taken to Block No. 18. About half-past five in the evening trucks arrived and we were loaded into them, quite naked like animals, and were driven to the crematorium. . . .
>
> The whole truck was tipped over in the way they do it sometimes with potatoes or coal loads, and we were led into a room which gave me the impression of a shower-bath. There were towels hanging round, and sprays, and even mirrors. I cannot say how many were in the room altogether, because I was so terrified, nor do I know if the doors were closed. People were in tears; people were shouting at each other; people were hitting each other. There were healthy people, strong people, weak people and sick people, and suddenly I

> saw fumes coming in through a very small window at the top. I had to cough very violently, tears were streaming from my eyes, and I had a sort of feeling in my throat as if I would be asphyxiated. I could not even look at the others because each of us concentrated on what happened to herself.
>
> At that moment I heard my name called. I had not the strength to answer it, but raised my arm. Then I felt someone take me and throw me out from that room. Hoessler put a blanket round me and took me on a motor-cycle to the hospital, where I stayed six weeks. As the result of the gas I had still, quite frequently, headaches and heart trouble, and whenever I went into the fresh air my eyes were filled with tears. I was subsequently taken to the political department and apparently I had been taken out of the gas chamber because I had come from a prison in Lublin, which seemed to make a difference, and apart from that, my husband was a Polish officer.

The United States never met Goebbels's challenge. The American public believed not only that it had enough Jews, but that it had more than enough aliens in general. Not until 1944 did American policy against the atrocities become vigorous, and by then there were pathetically few refugees to save. In December 1944, after American troops had already reached some of the death camps, a public opinion poll showed that most Americans still believed that the Nazis had killed fewer than 100,000 Jews instead of some six million—or probably more—Jews, gypsies, and homosexuals. The United States admitted about 250,000 Jewish refugees in the entire period. The American government, which made military detours to preserve the art of the Japanese city of Kyoto, and the architecture of the German city of Rothenburg, sent no bombers to destroy the ovens at Dachau and Auschwitz or train trackage to them, although the administration had evidence available that amply suggested what the ovens were being used for.

The World Economic Conference

Foreign affairs were but an afterthought on March 4, 1933, a windy, steel-gray day in Washington, D.C., as silent, anxious Americans gathered on Capitol Hill or listened on the radio to a new President. Recovery at home, the problem of unemployed workers, closed factories, bankrupt banks—it was these that preoccupied Franklin Delano Roosevelt, not distant drums in the Far East or continental Europe. "I favored as a practical policy," Roosevelt said, "the putting of first things first." Certain of his country's impregnable security, he girded up for a war mainly against depression at home, not enemies overseas.

Yet the new leaders in Washington were not true isolationists. Roosevelt and the Democrats, long identified with Wilsonian internationalism, repeatedly glanced abroad for cures to the nation's economic ills. While Congress debated New Deal recovery measures, a debate that lasted until early summer, Roosevelt restlessly took up a proposal left over from the Hoover Administration for a world economic conference.

Ever since a financial panic forced Great Britain off the gold standard in 1931, world leaders, especially in France and the United States, had groped after an international solution to the spreading economic crisis. By the time the World Economic Conference convened in London on June 12, 1933, no coherent strategy had emerged. The delegates knew that Roosevelt's experimental plans were at odds with those of the so-called Gold Bloc, those nations whose economic interests required continuation of the gold standard. Discussions in London drifted on for a few weeks, but the gathering that could have ended the crisis of confidence only worsened it by spoiling the hopes it had raised. Even Secretary of State Cordell Hull, a devout Wilsonian committed to expanding world trade by lowering tariffs, decided that "The best contribution America can make to world prosperity is its own domestic recovery."

And so the country turned inward to seek its economic salvation—a luxury the United States thought it could afford in the impregnable security behind the world's great oceans. Still, the New Deal did make several modest attempts at easing the effects of the Great Depression by addressing international economic issues. To make American goods more competitive in world markets, Roosevelt in his first year in office devalued the dollar by approximately forty percent. At the insistence of Secretary of State Hull, Congress passed the Reciprocal Trade Agreements Act of 1934, which provided for negotiated, bilateral tariff reductions. During the 1920s, tariff increases around the world had stifled international trade and contributed to the global economic decline, and the effort to reduce tariff rates was designed to stimulate world production. For an added stimulant Roosevelt established the Export-Import Bank in 1933, and restructured it in 1934, to provide new credit sources for American companies doing business abroad. But by and large, the immensity of the Depression simply forced international matters into the background.

Recognizing the Soviet Union

Ever since Woodrow Wilson refused to recognize the Communist regime in 1918, Americans had found many justifications for ignoring the Soviet Union. Wilson himself doubted that a new government that made such radical pronouncements would survive in a country so wedded to a feudal past. Then, too, the Russians had angered the West in many ways. Lenin signed a separate peace with Imperial Germany early in 1918, releasing large numbers of German troops for an onslaught against the Western Front. The Communists brooked no opposition to their plans for a proletarian paradise; police murdered thousands of potential subversives, including the Tsar and his family. And the Soviet leaders announced the start of a world revolution against capitalism.

The idea of world revolution collapsed quickly after brief coups in Hungary and Germany; by the thirties, Stalin was committed to "building socialism in one country." Soviet financial sins seemed less offensive when France, and later almost all of the countries owing money to the United States, defaulted on their public debts. Roosevelt himself thought it foolish to continue to withhold recognition from a regime that was stable; he also calculated that a rapprochement between the Soviet Union and the United States might restrain Japan in the Far East. As businessmen had once dreamed of the China market, so others now looked to the Russians. Stalin had been dumping Soviet grain on world markets at absurdly low prices in a desperate effort to pay for expensive technological equipment; a trade agreement might boost sales for Yankee industry and keep Russian grain at home, to the benefit of both countries.

Roosevelt's first overtures to the Russians brought Stalin's Commissar for Foreign Affairs, Maxim Litvinov, to Washington for talks. On November 16, 1933, the President and Litvinov reached an accord that formalized relations between the two countries. Wall Street bankers wanted payment of Russia's prewar bonds; the representatives from the Soviet Union sought compensation for damages caused by American troops during Wilson's intervention in their civil war. The Roosevelt-Litvinov accord also included a pledge by the Russians not to "spread Communist propaganda" in the United States, and guaranteed religious freedom and the right to a fair trial to Americans living in the Soviet Union. Roosevelt sent William Bullitt as his first ambassador to the Soviet Union. Litvinov stayed on in Washington as the Soviet ambassador. But negotiations about claims collapsed, and Stalin ignored both the civil liberties of Americans (as he did those of Russians) and his promise to halt subversive activities in the United States. Bullitt unsuccessfully tried to interest the Russians in American culture; at one point he distributed baseball bats and gloves to the somewhat bewildered citizens of Moscow. Businessmen and farmers, too, were disappointed: Soviet-American trade actually declined after 1933, and the Russians continued to dump huge amounts of grain on world markets.

Lenin and Stalin, ca. 1920. The United States formally recognized the Soviet Union in 1933, sixteen years after the Bolshevik revolution. *(Courtesy, Brown Brothers)*

The Good Neighbor

"In the field of world policy," Roosevelt had pledged during his inaugural address, "I would dedicate this nation to the policy of the good neighbor—the neighbor who respects the rights of others." Hoover already had turned away from the interventions in Caribbean affairs characteristic of Theodore Roosevelt, William Howard Taft, and Woodrow Wilson. At the Seventh International Conference of American States, which met at Montevideo, Uruguay, during December 1933, Latin American leaders challenged the Roosevelt Administration to renounce unilateral intervention in the Western Hemisphere. Cordell Hull, chairman of the delegation from the United States, was expected to do what his predecessors had always done in such situations: veto the agenda. But instead the secretary of state proclaimed that "No state has the right to intervene in the internal or external affairs of another," and signed a formal convention condemning intervention, while retaining a loop-hole permitting the United States to move against "outlaw" regimes.

Alarmed by Hitler's rhetoric and by the rise of fascism in Japan and Europe, Roosevelt concocted the practice of "consultation": whenever an outside force threatened "the peace and independence" of the Western Hemisphere, the nations of the New World would attempt to react in concert. Most Latin-American states, already frightened by events elsewhere, welcomed the implied protection almost as much as they rejoiced in the ending of a unilateral Monroe Doctrine.

Consultation worked smoothly during the tense years of World War II; on three occasions before 1942 the countries of the New World met together, the last time to declare war against the Axis powers. (The Argentines alone held to neutrality until early 1945, seeing in fascism both a possible solution to their economic troubles and an opportunity for hemispheric leadership.)

The Caribbean Roosevelt's concern for national security made it hard for him to be a good neighbor to Cuba. This 700-mile-long-island commands the defense of the nation's southern coasts; instability there had always prompted intervention. A treaty of 1904 formally obligated the United States to maintain internal order and when President Gerardo Machado's dictatorial ways threatened to bring civil war, Roosevelt sent diplomat Sumner Welles to calm the island. Machado was forced to resign, but this failed to restore order, and Roosevelt then sent warships into the area. The confident Welles made plans with local army officers, themselves trained by Yankee advisers, to foist upon Cuba an "acceptable" President. More in the spirit of the good neighbor, the Senate in 1935 ratified a new treaty that abrogated this country's control over Cuban affairs, although the United States Navy retained its huge base at Guantanamo Bay.

Elsewhere in the Caribbean, where United States security concerns were less pressing, Washington's diplomats acted with more restraint. By late 1934 Roosevelt, following a plan laid down by Hoover, withdrew the last contingent of marines from Haiti. A "fiscal representative" stayed behind to insure repayment of debts to creditors in the United States. A customs supervisor from this nation also controlled revenue in the Dominican Republic, as did a supervisor in Nicaragua. In Puerto Rico, Roosevelt's governors-general—especially former brains-truster Rexford Tugwell—diversified the island's economy and struggled against widespread illiteracy. A mini-New Deal, emphasizing public works, relieved some of the Depression gloom in the largest city, San Juan. But not until the postwar years would tourism, together with large-scale emigration to the mainland, invigorate the Puerto Rican economy.

Mexico Roosevelt's good-neighborliness survived its greatest interwar test, which came in Mexico. In 1934 Mexican voters elected as president Lazaro Cardenas, who wanted to accelerate the mildly socialist revolution begun in 1912. He nationalized most foreign-owned land suitable for farming, turning it over to local communities, and organized industrial workers into a single giant union. Then early in 1938, Cardenas confiscated most major oil lands in Mexico from their British and Yankee owners. In theory, he was acting to force the companies to accept a new labor contract that with some justification they had rejected. But Cardenas almost at once offered to buy out the oilmen. Although the companies conducted private negotiations with the government, Roosevelt refused to pressure the Mexicans, and just two weeks before Pearl Harbor the two nations settled all outstanding differences.

The Good Neighbor policy, so richly praised since the early 1930s, was more than rhetoric, yet less than revolution. Roosevelt withdrew the remaining symbols of his country's dominance, those marines stalking the streets of small Caribbean capitals, and resisted temptation in Mexico. In return, despite Argentina's opposition, the Latin Americans followed Washington's careful steps toward war in the early 1940s. The Monroe Doctrine now became a multilateral device for deflecting threats from the Old World. The Americas could live as good neighbors, though only as long as Washington felt its interests to be secure.

Neutrality and the Descent into War

The World Economic Conference, the recognition of the Soviet Union, the Good Neighbor Policy—all these were merely adjustments to present realities rather than any sort of New Deal in foreign affairs. Roosevelt shrank from adventures abroad that might jeopardize economic recovery or his new political coalition. In those days before the Cold War with the Soviet Union, Presidents shared decision-making about foreign affairs with Congress, and legislators reflected the attitudes of their constituents. Probably a majority of Americans who thought about the question at all during the thirties were steadfast isolationists, believing involvement overseas to be futile and dangerous.

Reassessing the Great War George Norris, a progressive Republican from Nebraska, persuaded his colleagues in the Senate to investigate the role of "those merchants of death," the munitions makers, in the country's decision to enter World War I. Norris, like many progressives in both parties, believed that big businessmen started wars for their own profit. So Norris maneuvered the unknown, and therefore presumably neutral, Senator Gerald P. Nye of North Dakota into the chairmanship of a special committee named in 1934 to ferret out the truth.

In months of highly visible hearings, Nye and his colleagues proved the obvious: American businessmen had made millions selling arms during the war. It seemed far-fetched to suggest that a great nation would go to war solely to protect the investments of a few citizens, yet much of the American public accepted this interpretation. Revisionist historians like Charles A. Beard and Walter Millis added academic prestige and the authority of footnotes to a dubious hypothesis. The complex legalities of neutral rights, the novelty of submarine warfare, Wilson's own fierce moralism, the country's national interests, all were ignored by people now certain that businessmen had tricked the United States into a needless war.

The Neutrality Acts Congress reacted predictably, and speedily, to the isolationist mood. No doubt happy at last to take the initiative in national affairs, the legislators passed a series of neutrality acts.

The first, passed in 1935, provided that whenever the President proclaimed that a state of war existed anywhere in the world, United States arms shipments to belligerents on both sides had to cease. No American ships could transport war material, and Americans might be warned against traveling on neutral ships. Roosevelt himself thought the act would "drag us into war instead of keeping us out," but still he signed the bill rather than risk making the presidential election of 1936 a fight over isolation instead of a referendum on the New Deal. Congress quickly added a second neutrality act, extending all the provisions of the first and adding another: American bankers could not lend to belligerents.

In 1937 a third act forbade Americans to travel on belligerent ships, even at their own risk. Nations at war might purchase nonmilitary goods in the United States, but only on a basis of what became known as "cash and carry." That same year Roosevelt did officially ignore the outbreak of hostilities between China and Japan in order to ship munitions to the Chinese, America's traditional friend in the Far East.

The Rise of Fascism While Congress talked a rhetoric of neutrality, totalitarian regimes in Germany, Italy, and Japan glorified war as man's greatest enterprise, oppressed the individual to advance the state, and fostered racial hatreds. In the depressed thirties fascism was seductive. Germany's prosperity mocked the persisting depression in England, France, and the United States. The future, many thought, lay with ordered regimes and not with outdated notions of personal liberty. Adolf Hitler in Germany, Benito Mussolini in Italy, and Francisco Franco in Spain would triumph amid the decline of the West, establishing a new order.

In Italy, Mussolini boasted, "We have buried the putrid corpse of liberty." In Germany, fascism was early coupled with an intense racism. Writing in *Mein Kampf,* a book that roughly sketched out his dreams and his hatreds, Hitler had blamed "subhuman" Jews for defeat in World War I. In the utopian future as the Nazis envisioned it, "mongrel" races would serve their natural superiors, a master race of Germans who would rule a European empire for a thousand years. The nation must earn this magnificent destiny by obedience and sacrifice.

Fascist regimes gained their successes while their rivals were inactive. Though possessing the greatest standing army in Europe, France feared war. Germany's demographic advantage, its greater population and birth rate, meant that a fresh conflict could end in

Italy's Benito Mussolini (center) was the first fascist dictator, taking power in the 1920s. *(Courtesy, Strazza Photo)*

Francisco Franco achieved another victory for fascism in the Spanish Civil War of the late 1930s. *(Courtesy, United Press International)*

France's defeat. A vast empire spread over a quarter of the globe on six continents drained Britain's power away from Europe. Depression and popular sentiment distracted the United States from world affairs. Stalin sought mainly to stabilize the Soviet revolution with blood purges and massive coercion of his people. With potential opposition so fragmented and the world so disillusioned, the Fascists easily persuaded themselves that they could remold society. The failure of the West to project any alternate vision made Hitler's monomaniacal schemes almost plausible.

Capitalist leaders in some Western countries openly proclaimed their preference for Hitler over Stalin. The long-term success of the Bolshevik revolution in Russia had alarmed Europe's propertied classes. Fascists played on these anxieties, accusing the Communists of destroying religious values and robbing the middle class of its modest wealth. Stalin's cruelty and his ruthless collectivization of rural lands created its own horror. British prime ministers often argued that a strong central Europe would serve to prevent Soviet expansion. Paris conservatives chanted at rallies, "Better Hitler than Blum"—Blum being a moderate socialist who became premier of France in 1936.

Adolf Hitler

The Rhineland and Spain

Adolf Hitler, possibly the most sophisticated or most gambling German diplomat since Bismarck, steadily maneuvered his way toward imperial domination in Europe. Gradually he destroyed those parts of the Versailles Treaty that had forced Germany into a position of inferiority. He began to rearm on both land and sea; he meddled in Austrian affairs, bringing that country closer to Germany; then, in 1936, he marched his new though still small army into the Rhineland, which the victors in World War I had forbidden Germany to rearm. Hitler further isolated France in 1937 when he signed an alliance with Mussolini's Italy. Then the two Axis powers intervened in the Spanish civil war on behalf of Francisco Franco. In Spain, the dictators experimented with new techniques of war, especially air attacks designed to demoralize civilian populations. Airplanes had replaced ships at sea as the dominant strategic weapons, a development that would work to Britain's disadvantage. Britain and France refused to aid the Spanish republicans, and the American Congress applied its neutrality legislation to civil as well as international wars, thereby depriving the United States of any role at all. The republicans in Spain had no foreign power to help them but the Soviet Union, which gave aid to Communists within the republican coalition. And the Spanish Communists, when they had the chance, brutally asserted their dominance over the non-Communist forces within the coalition. By 1939 the Fascists had won the conflict in Spain.

Certain that the Western democracies would not block him, the Nazi chancellor was continuing his war of nerves elsewhere. Just across German frontiers, he wailed, millions of Germans languished under oppressive regimes. Until they could rejoin the fatherland, Europe could have no peace. Nazi agents sparked pro-German rallies in these areas, and many ethnic Germans responded enthusiastically. Austrians saw union with Germany both as economic salvation and as a return to former imperial glory; Germans living in the Sudetenland, a part of Czechoslovakia bordering Germany, longed to escape what they perceived to be second-class citizenship in a second-class country; Germans in Poland protested that country's treatment of its minorities. For eighteen dramatic months, Hitler exploited these discontents.

Austria and Czechoslovakia

In early 1938 Nazi sympathizers so bedeviled the regular government in Austria that its leaders called for a plebiscite. The people, they thought, would reject union with Germany. Hitler reacted quickly, sending an army into Austria before the voting in March. Storm troopers marched through Vienna, reinforcing a martial image abroad as well as terrorizing the Austrian populace. The powers had not really recovered from this coup—which at one stroke made Germany the leading nation in Europe—when Hitler began to pressure the Czechs. He wanted the Sudeten Germans and the mountain areas where they lived. The minority Germans refused Czech offers of negotiation while Hitler's speeches became more and more hysterical and his armies gathered along the frontier. By early fall, war seemed inevitable: if Hitler attacked, the Czechs would fight back, and the French and Russians would have to come to their aid. British ministers sought to head off a war between Germany and the Western democracies. Prime Minister Chamberlain flew several times to meet Hitler in Germany, where he finally secured an agreement at Munich in late September. Hitler immediately occupied the Sudetenland, but promised to settle all future disputes without war. But the "peace in our time" that Chamberlain announced soon collapsed. Four months later Hitler marched into the rest of Czechoslovakia and then, during the summer of 1939, took up a refrain that had become commonplace within his regime. "So long as Germans in Poland suffer grievously, so long as they are imprisoned away from the Fatherland," he said, "Europe can have no peace."

The War Begins

Everyone realized now that Hitler was determined upon great conquests, not mere revisions of the status quo. Hitler told his commanders:

> When you start a war, it does not matter who is right, but who wins. Close your hearts to pity. Act with brutality. Eighty million Germans must get what is their due. Their existence must be made secure. The stronger man is in the right.

But an odd twilight lingered over Europe; everyone, even the Germans, hesitated about going the final distance to war. Chamberlain's government issued a unilateral guarantee of Polish independence. This maneuver, probably designed to bring the Russians closer to Britain, failed. By late August 1939 Stalin had signed a nonaggression pact with Hitler, thereby spurning Anglo-French offers for a formal alliance. Days later, on September 1, the Nazis attacked Poland with the new weapons of *Blitzkrieg*, "lightning war." Airplanes strafed Polish troops and urban

The principal conferees in the historic Munich Conference, intended to address the dispute between Germany and Czechoslovakia: Prime Minister Neville Chamberlain (left), Adolf Hitler and Benito Mussolini (third and fourth from left). *(Courtesy, United Press International)*

centers, while German motorized divisions sped across eastern Europe's wide plains; badly organized and poorly equipped, the Poles fell back on all fronts. Then the Russians invaded from the East, and within six weeks Stalin and Hitler were dividing the country between them. Britain and France had declared war a few days after the German invasion, but they could scarcely save Poland or, for that matter, take up an offensive. French generals, remembering the lessons of World War I, worshiped at the altar of defensive warfare. A hastily gathered British army did land in western Europe, but it numbered only about 300,000 soldiers.

Still hoping for a negotiated settlement and not yet ready for war in the West, both sides stalled for time. Then the *Sitzkrieg,* or "sitting war," ended abruptly in 1940. Hitler attacked Denmark, then Norway. A new British prime minister, Winston Churchill, pledged to destroy the Nazis, not negotiate with them. But the revered Maginot Line—a defensive system the French had set up along part of their border with Germany and thought to be unbreachable—crumbled against a new *Blitzkrieg,* and within six weeks Hitler had conquered France, trapping its armies in a great semicircular sweep through Belgium and driving the British off the continent in an improvised evacuation at Dunkirk. Hitler was master of Europe, and only England fought on against him.

The Far East The Far East had also descended into war. Leaders in Japan, a militarist state where philosophers glorified war and political and military leaders hungered for a self-sufficient, and therefore secure, Japanese Empire, dreamed of dominating all Asia. Raw materials from the European colonies there and control over all China could satisfy even the most ambitious imperialism. Soon after consolidating their control in Manchuria, the Japanese stepped up pressure against Chiang Kai-shek's Nationalist government in Nanking. An American teacher in Shanghai wrote in a letter on January 29, 1932:

> Today the Japanese have been bombing Shanghai. We're getting our first sample of what war on populations can mean,—non-combatants blown up by bombs, shot down in the street, or burned alive in the great fires the battle has set. These may destroy the city before they can be checked. What part will be taken by Americans and British is uncertain. Eventually these events of the last week or so will lead to war,—if not this year, then in ten years, or twenty. When I was a college student writing orations, I thought we should soon come to permanent peace. Now I know we won't, in my lifetime.

The Chinese rallied against this new threat of foreign invasion—Chiang and Communist leader Mao Zedong even agreed to suspend their civil war—and leaders in Tokyo backed down. Yet the presence of Chinese and Japanese troops in north China guaranteed that incidents which might lead to war could be triggered at any time. The future depended upon which of two factions came to dominate Japan's aristocratic government, the moderates who favored only economic expansion or the militarists who promoted war. For the moment, however, everyone in the West was transfixed by Hitler's adventure in Europe.

From Neutrality to Undeclared War, 1937–1941

From these climactic events the American people only wished to retreat. When the Japanese sank the United States gunboat *Panay* in December 1937, on the Yangtze River in China, the reaction of over seventy percent of Americans asked in an opinion poll was that the United States should withdraw from the Far East. Roosevelt was convinced that his country eventually must join Britain and China in the fight against fascism in Europe and Asia. But he had to cope with an isolationist public. In any case, the United States possessed only a tiny army, and its navy, though growing, was spread over two oceans. Still, the country drifted toward war, nudged by Roosevelt's convictions, a reinvigorated interventionist movement, and the reality of the fascist menace.

Isolationists vs. Interventionists

Roosevelt sounded a warning. On October 5, 1937, during a speech delivered in Chicago, he denounced Japan's war against China and likened the spread of violence to a disease that peace-loving nations must halt. His call to "quarantine the aggressors," such as Italy in the invasion of Libya, led to questions about exactly what he meant. The President refused any clarification. This was perhaps just as well, for two-thirds of the legislators on Capitol Hill opposed sanctions, most agreeing that economic retaliation was only "a back door to war."

Yet Americans began to attend to military matters. Only three weeks after Hitler's invasion of Poland in September 1939, representatives of all the republics in the Western Hemisphere gathered at Panama. Pledging joint action against any threat to their security, they issued the Declaration of Panama, which marked out a war-free zone three hundred miles out to sea, surrounding the neutral Americas. Meanwhile, Roosevelt had succeeded in modifying some of the neutrality acts. He believed that Britain and France could defeat the Nazis if the United States supplied them generously. In this way, outright American participation in any hostilities could be avoided. The Neutrality Act passed in November 1939 repealed the embargo on arms shipments abroad—a considerable gain for the Allies—although no loans could be extended to fund the purchase of American goods: the "cash and carry" policy remained intact. Over the next six months, the British bought several billion dollars worth of munitions.

Then the Nazi *Blitzkrieg* of May 1940 shocked American politicians into action. Roosevelt asked for increases in the army and navy and huge expenditures for military equipment—capped by a pledge to build 50,000 planes a year. Congress passed the necessary appropriations. But where was the army? Widespread anti-militarist sentiment, the army's reputation for harsh treatment, and new openings in private industry discouraged volunteers. A Selective Service Act became law on August 25, 1940, but was limited in effect to only one year. In the summer of 1941 the House extended the draft by only one vote. Nonetheless, about 1,600,000 men were conscripted during the next year under the first peacetime draft in American history.

Rick Blaine, played by Humphrey Bogart, deserts isolationism and his romantic love Ilsa, played by Ingrid Bergman, to serve his country selflessly. *Casablanca* (1942).

The Election of 1940

The debate over the war became part of the presidential campaign of 1940. Meeting in Philadelphia only days after the French surrender, the Republicans nominated Wendell L. Willkie of Indiana, a progressive Midwestern businessman who turned his back on the strong isolationist bloc within the GOP. A former Democrat, Willkie himself supported most New Deal reforms and approved aid to Britain. Roosevelt, who wanted an unprecedented third term but was worried about being accused of excessive ambition, maneuvered the Democratic convention into drafting him.

Roosevelt shunned active campaigning for two months. He stayed in the White House, directing a large-scale buildup of American defenses. Then, shortly after Hitler launched a massive air attack against England, Churchill asked for United States destroyers. Roosevelt was anxious to help, but isolationists had amended a naval appropriations bill to forbid any transfer of equipment unless the service chiefs certified that it was not needed for national defense. So Roosevelt made a deal: fifty aged destroyers went to Britain in exchange for long-term American leases on military bases in Newfoundland, Bermuda, and the Caribbean. This trade vastly improved the country's defense posture, outflanking the isolationists, and at the same time ended neutrality. Now the United States was neither at war nor at peace with Nazi Germany: it was supplying to Britain short of war.

At this point, Willkie shifted his campaign strategy against Roosevelt, charging that the President's policy "surely meant wooden crosses for sons and brothers and sweethearts." Suddenly Willkie's crowds grew more and more enthusiastic, and Democrats around the country worried about the rise in anti-war sentiment. Roosevelt, who had shrewdly appointed two prominent Republicans to his cabinet, then toured the Northeast, repeating in New York City the rationale for aid to Britain and finally pledging in Boston, "I have said this before, but I shall say it again and again and again: Your boys are not going to be sent into any foreign wars." These words blunted Willkie's charges. The President also said that a defense of the United States required the defense of Britain. Roosevelt won another term by another landslide, but Willkie did reduce the President's popular vote margin.

Lend-Lease

Just after his victory, Roosevelt faced a strategic situation of great complexity. Feisty British pilots and a new invention, radar, had denied Hitler that superiority in the air necessary for a cross-channel invasion. But victory in the Battle of Britain did not signal defeat for the

Prime Minister Winston Churchill inspects the ruins at Coventry Cathedral, bombed by the Luftwaffe in October 1941. President Roosevelt's Lend-Lease program helped the British survive while they fought alone against Germany from June 1940 to December 1941. *(Courtesy, British Information Services)*

Germans, now the masters of central and western Europe. Hitler loosed "wolf packs," patrol after patrol of submarines, against Britain's merchant marine. Slow strangulation, he hoped, could achieve what the quick blow had not. Strangulation loomed from still another source: the cash-and-carry provisions of American neutrality acts under which the British could not buy goods here on credit, but must pay cash only. British dollar resources had dwindled to about $2 billion.

Roosevelt reacted strongly and swiftly. Recalling the simple human duty to "lend a garden hose" to a neighbor whose house "had caught fire," the President declared that "We must be the great arsenal of democracy." The United States would supply the material, Britain the men, for the war against fascism. In January 1941 Roosevelt laid his "Lend-Lease" proposal before Congress, along with an impassioned declaration of the need to preserve the "Four Freedoms": freedom of speech, freedom of worship, freedom from want, and freedom from fear. By March 1941

Lend-Lease—under which the United States was to lend Britain some $7 billion in goods—had passed Congress.

So began a period of involvement that in time brought the United States into open war. Hitler marked off a huge area of the North Atlantic between Iceland and Britain as a war zone, where submarines aided by aircraft "spotters" attacked merchant shipping headed for Britain. Almost 500,000 tons of ships a month disappeared beneath the waves. When the Nazis sank an American freighter, the *Robin Moor*, on May 21, 1941, the President ordered the Navy to convoy American ships across the "neutral" area almost to Iceland. Congressman Robert Taft of Ohio protested: "Convoys mean shooting and shooting means war." In August 1941 Churchill met with Roosevelt in Newfoundland. After secret meetings aboard a United States cruiser and a British battleship, the two leaders issued a communique, soon dubbed the "Atlantic Charter." A blueprint of sorts for the postwar world, this document pledged self-determination for all people, freedom from want and fear, freedom of the seas, equal commercial opportunities, and disarmament. By September fifteen nations including the Soviet Union had endorsed the principles of the Atlantic Charter.

On September 4, 1941, the Germans attacked another destroyer, the *Greer,* in Icelandic waters, and the President announced a policy of "active defense." The navy now would guard the sea lanes all the way to Iceland for all ships, opening fire on sight at any German vessels or aircraft. When another destroyer was sunk in October with 100 lives lost, Woody Guthrie wrote a ballad about it: "What were their names, tell me, what were their names? Did you have a friend on the good *Reuben James*?" Roosevelt then pushed through Congress a measure that armed American merchant ships and permitted them to carry cargo directly to British ports. Isolationists protested, but public sentiment now agreed with the President that the nation must aid Britain at all costs. That cost was indeed high: by the fall of 1941 the United States had abandoned its neutrality laws and joined in the Battle of the Atlantic. The "arsenal of democracy" already had entered a shooting war. "Never before since Jamestown and Plymouth Rock," said Roosevelt in a fireside radio chat, "has our American civilization been in such danger."

Japan

Tension with Japan During 1938, and well into 1939, Japan and the United States had tried to ignore each other. Tokyo continued its military adventure in China, certain that the economic health of its empire required exclusive access to resources there; the United States still insisted upon the traditional Open Door policy. Events in Europe diverted attention from this deadlock for many months.

The outbreak of war in Europe forced Britain to cut back its commitments to Chiang Kai-shek. Almost at once, Roosevelt moved to take on a stronger role in Asia. Convinced that Japan's leaders would never dare fight the United States, he adopted a policy of firmness, pressuring them constantly to withdraw from China. For two years, from late 1939 until late 1941, the United States gradually severed its commercial and financial relations with Japan in a slowly escalating economic war. Embargoes on scrap iron and steel, industrial chemicals, and oil, aid to China's war effort, and the freezing of Japanese assets in the United States all reflected Roosevelt's grim determination. Most of the leadership in Tokyo was not yet prepared to go to war against the Americans, especially since the Soviet Union remained a potential danger on Japan's flank.

Hitler's conquests in Europe made the Japanese less cautious. The fall of France and the Netherlands bewitched most of Prime Minister Fumimaro Konoye's cabinet: raw materials from French Indochina and the Dutch East Indies could replace those embargoed by the United States. Still, moderates in Japan and many naval leaders shrank from action that could provoke war. So when Roosevelt widened the embargo, Konoye temporarily turned to diplomacy.

Konoye suggested a face-to-face meeting with Roosevelt, but the President refused unless, as Secretary Hull insisted, the issue of China was settled beforehand. This requirement, amounting in effect to a demand that

Japan retreat from all its conquests since 1937, toppled Konoye and brought to the premiership a militant expansionist, General Hideki Tojo. Like many of his fellow army officers, he sought war.

Pearl Harbor, December 7, 1941 A huge fleet of aircraft carriers had left the Kurile Islands on November 25 for Pearl Harbor, and a massive army mobilized in southern Indochina for an attack on British Malaya, the strategic key to Southeast Asia. American intelligence, both in the Pacific and in Washington, had predicted an attack on Singapore, while fog and the absence of radar camouflaged Japanese ships moving toward Hawaii. At the same time the American naval commander there, Admiral Husband E. Kimmel, ordered all American aircraft carriers out to sea and grouped airplanes together on runways as a safeguard against sabotage. Then, a little before 8 a.m. local time on December 7—just as the Japanese ambassador was supposed to be cutting off negotiations in Washington—hundreds of Japanese planes attacked America's greatest naval installation, destroyed most of the planes bunched on the ground, and then turned toward the fleet. One dive bomber intentionally crashed into a ship. A second wave of bombers appeared an hour later to continue the assault almost unopposed, so completely were the Americans surprised. The United States's eight battleships were disabled, the *Oklahoma* and *Arizona* sunk outright. More than 2300 Americans died.

One witness to Pearl Harbor was

> sixteen years old, employed as a pipe fitter apprentice at Pearl Harbor Navy Yard. On December 7, 1941, oh, around 8.00 a.m., my grandmother woke me. . . . I was four miles away. I got out on my motor-cycle and it took me five, ten minutes to get there. . . . I was asked by some other officer to go into the water and get sailors out that had been blown off the ships. Some were unconscious, some were dead. So I spent the rest of the day swimming inside the harbour, along with some other Hawaiians. I brought out I don't know how many bodies and how many were alive and how

Pearl Harbor, December 7, 1941. A United States ship burns and lists following the Japanese attack. *(Courtesy, AP/Wide World Photos)*

many dead. Another man would put them into ambulances and they'd be gone. . . .

The following morning, I went with my tools to the *West Virginia*. It had turned turtle, totally upside down. We found a number of men inside. The *Arizona* was a total washout. Also the *Utah*. There were men in there, too. We spent about a month cutting the superstructure of the *West Virginia*, tilting it back on its hull. About three hundred men we cut out of there were still alive by the eighteenth day.

Still, the survival of the American aircraft carriers meant that the attack on Pearl Harbor, a major Japanese tactical victory, was in effect a strategic defeat for Japan. Since the Japanese attack on Pearl Harbor, while laying waste to the American battleship fleet, had left the carrier fleet untouched, the United States would be able to counterattack long before Japan could greatly strengthen its defensive positions. On a political level, the attack on Pearl Harbor was in another way also a strategic disaster for Japan. It inflamed American public opinion to a desire for revenge that bordered on blood lust. That rage would eventually lead to the detonation of atomic bombs over the Japanese cities of Hiroshima and Nagasaki.

On the day after the attack on Pearl Harbor, President Roosevelt, appearing before the jointly assembled House and Senate, called the attack "a day which will live in infamy," and Congress declared war against the Empire of Japan. FDR reacted in the same way he had during the banking crisis of 1933. He started at once to do the things he had to do—and with perfect assurance that the country would be able to meet any situation whatever. Hitler and Mussolini, joined to Japan in the Tripartite Pact, declared war on the United States three days later. Americans were now at war with the three largest Axis powers as they were called. Almost all Americans, including the isolationists, at once closed ranks behind the President; "the only thing to do now is to lick hell out of them," isolationist Senator Burton Wheeler wrote, catching the national mood.

As in the first world war the countries opposed to Germany became known as the Allies. The three major Western Allies—the United States, Britain, and the Soviet Union—came together in a great alliance. The Soviet Union had been Hitler's ally until June 1941, when Nazi Germany had suddenly launched a massive invasion of Russia, and the Russians were now bearing the full weight of a German attack. On New Year's Day 1942, the United States, Britain, and Russia, together with twenty-three other nations at war against the Axis powers, signed the Declaration of the United Nations, each committing itself to uphold the Atlantic Charter and promising not to make a separate peace.

The Home Front

The Nation Begins to Fight

War and the preparations of war revived to some extent a reform impulse in American society that had withered in the late 1930s. Global conflict not only honed the skills of government bureaucrats and academic intellectuals, making both more expert in social planning, but also changed radically the status of blacks and women. The population shifted northward to industrial centers in Chicago, Cleveland, Pittsburgh, New York, and New Jersey, and westward to defense plants in southern California. A new sense of noble purpose and community replaced the malaise of the Depression years. War saddened but also invigorated the nation.

In the first months of war, while American newspapers spoke with a chatty optimism, Hitler's troops were camped outside Moscow, almost in sight of the golden glint of the Kremlin's ancient churches. In North Africa the Nazi legions of General Rommel, the "Desert Fox," had by midsummer swept almost to the gates of Alexandria, Egypt, threatening to seize the Suez Canal that connected Britain with much of her empire. German submarines infested the Atlantic, their skilled commanders sinking ships far more rapidly—nearly 750,000 tons a month—than the Allies could replace them. In 1942 the Germans destroyed 1,664 ships. Elated by success, Admiral Doenitz wanted to send every U-boat he had to the eastern seaboard of the United States, where a mere dozen subs had sunk fifty-seven percent of American tankers in a few weeks. But Hitler preferred to rely on his attacks of intuition. "Norway," he said emphatically, would be his "zone of destiny." "Norway?" the admiral asked incredulously. The Führer rolled his eyes toward the map. Nonetheless, Germany had accomplished the amazing feat of waging war effectively on three fronts.

Meanwhile, the Japanese descended upon the British, Dutch, and American possessions in Asia. An army moving overland down the Malay Peninsula captured the key British naval base of Singapore. Now the Japanese roamed almost at will across East Asia, conquering Burma, most of the East Indies, and the Philippines, where General Douglas MacArthur, commander of United States forces in the Pacific, directed a gallant but futile defense. When the Philippine stronghold of Bataan fell after a three-month siege, Japanese soldiers forced Filipinos and Americans to evacuate quickly and without adequate food or water. Thousands died on this infamous Bataan death march. Donald Knox lived through incidents like this one:

> We moved down the ridge a ways when we saw this GI. He was sick. I figured he had come out of the hospital that was in the tents out under the trees. He was wobbling along, uneasy on his feet. There were Japanese infantry and tanks coming down the road alongside us. One of these Jap soldiers, I don't know whether he was on our side or if he deliberately came across the road, but he grabbed this sick guy by the arm and guided him out across the road. Then he just flipped him. The guy hit the cobblestone about five feet in front of a tank and the tank pulled on across him. Well, it killed him quick. There must have been ten tanks in that column, and every one of them came up there right across the body. When the last tank left there was no way you could tell there'd ever been a man there. But his uniform was embedded in the cobblestones. The man disappeared, but his uniform had been pressed until it had become part of the ground.

Last-ditch battles on Bataan Peninsula and Corregidor, together with a rearguard naval action in the Java Sea, could do no more than slow the Japanese advance. By summer, both Australia and India lay open to attack. A few Japanese fishing vessels even shelled Los Angeles in early 1942, but the Pacific's vast expanses protected the American west coast from any serious assault. The United States had now to gear up its industrial might for a war of attrition.

Mobilizing the Economy Mobilization proved a cumbersome task. The experiences gained in depression were no guide. In the years of economic hardship the nation had worried about unemployment; now it worried about labor shortages as industries expanded to produce war goods and workers were drained into the military. Inflation, not falling prices, now bedeviled government economists. Congress again granted the President sweeping powers to organize the economy.

Roosevelt immediately set up a central agency, the War Production Board, to oversee all industry. WPB chief Donald Nelson faced a difficult problem. Most businessmen did not want to make heavy investments in military plants that would probably be useless at war's end, yet business would never accept any suggestion that the government itself manufacture war goods. Nelson finally swung private industry toward conversion with the carrot of guaranteed profits and the stick of banning all nonessential production. Even then, bottlenecks appeared, so he organized a committee to allocate scarce raw materials. A scrap-rubber campaign aroused popular enthusiasm—a set of rubber galoshes appeared in the White House mail—but produced little usable rubber; not until 1943 did a massive expansion of synthetic rubber plants, together with wartime rationing, make it possible to meet industrial demands.

On April 18, 1942, Roosevelt created the War Manpower Commission to see that priorities were established and enforced on the use of human resources during the war. The President also directed that until the war was over, the normal work week would be forty-eight hours. The government soon became extremely concerned about the possibility of crippling labor strikes. Not wishing simply to outlaw strikes and leave workers subject to the whims of management, President Roosevelt created the War Labor Board in January 1942. The board established guidelines for wages, hours, working conditions, and collective bargaining rights, and under this federal protection union membership expanded rapidly to more than fifteen million people. The War Labor Board decided that wage increases would be scaled to the cost of living. The board first implemented that decision in

1943 when 180,000 workers of Bethlehem, Inland, and Republic steel companies—called "Little Steel"—asked for a dollar-a-day increase and were instead given a fifteen percent raise, which the War Labor Board determined was the increase in the cost of living from January 1, 1941, to May 1, 1942. This became known as the "Little Steel" formula.

Women entered the war industries in full force. Between 1940 and 1944, five million women joined the labor force to help meet the demands of war production and to replace the men who had gone overseas. During this period, women entered jobs that had previously been barred to them, especially in heavy industry. The government waged massive campaigns to encourage women, including married women, to join the labor force. The image of Rosie the Riveter gained widespread appeal. One woman found that wartime work was changing her life:

> My mother warned me when I took the job that I would never be the same. She said, 'You will never want to go back to being a housewife.' She was right, it definitely did. At Boeing I found a freedom and an independence I had never known. After the war I could never go back to playing bridge again, being a clubwoman and listening to a lot of inanities when I knew there were things you could use your mind for. The war changed my life completely.

Women working on an airplane shell. *(Courtesy, McDonnell Douglas)*

But after the war, women withdrew from many of the jobs they had held during it.

The massive federal spending and shortages of consumer goods led inevitably to serious inflation during the early years of the war. On January 30, 1942, the Emergency Price Control Act went into effect, establishing the Office of Price Administration to fix prices, except on farm products, and to control rents in areas where defense needs were creating housing shortages. Leon Henderson was appointed to head the agency. The rationing of tires had already started at the end of 1941, and during the rest of the war a number of other products—sugar, rubber, butter, coffee, gasoline, meat, cheese, processed foods, and shoes—were added to the rationing program to prevent inflation and black marketeering. Each citizen received a quota of special ration stamps; retail goods cost both dollars and stamps.

World War II had a great impact both on the size of the American economy and on the role of the federal government in regulating and stimulating it. Between 1941 and 1945, federal spending added up to more than $321 billion, twice as much as all federal spending from 1789 to 1941. The Gross National Product grew by more than seventy-five percent. In only a matter of a few years, the federal government became the premier sector of the economy. Although there were some labor strikes during the war, the time lost constituted only one tenth of one percent of total working time. The American economy produced an extraordinary volume of goods during the war—275,000 military aircraft, 75,000 tanks, 650,000 pieces of artillery, 55,239,000 tons of merchant shipping, and more than 1.5 million tons of synthetic rubber. General prices increased only thirty-one percent during the four years of the war, compared to sixty-two percent during the less than two years of World War I.

The Citizen Army In all, nearly twenty million American men and women went into uniform. Huge training camps transformed farmland outside cities and towns into miniature battle fronts or vast barracks for citizen-soldiers.

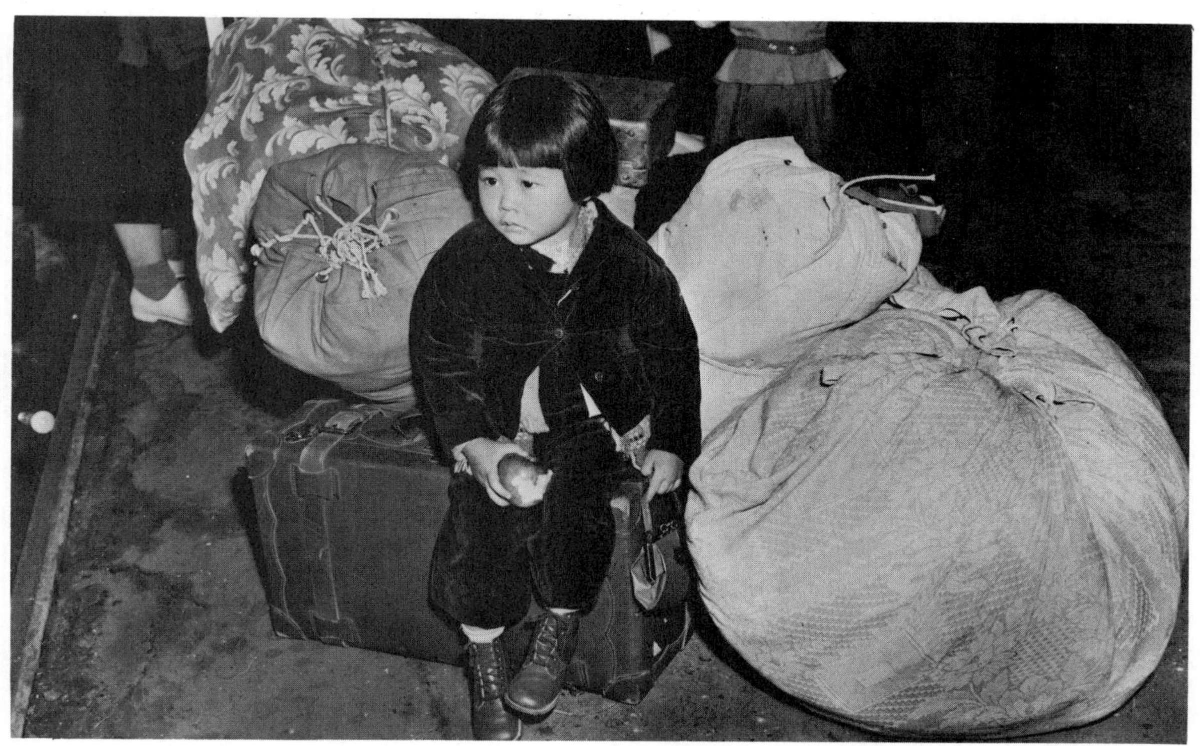

Although engaged in a war to defeat racist regimes in Japan and Germany, the United States succumbed to wartime hysteria, interned Japanese Americans living in California, and relocated them far inland. *(Courtesy, National Archives)*

The Depression had made physical training doubly difficult. Poverty had condemned many to inadequate diets and so to weak bodies; and few doctors, nutritionists, or physical trainers had gone through college during the 1930s. The only people accustomed to handling large numbers of young men, it turned out, were the nation's high school coaches. Thousands of them left local playing fields for basic training camps in the South and California, so many that for several years the traditional Saturday football and basketball games disappeared in small towns. GIs—so called because everything they owned was government-issued—received four to six months of physical conditioning, good food, and patriotic propaganda.

Critics worried that this mass experience in military uniformity might weaken America's individuality and diversity. The citizen army, though, quickly dispelled such fears. Soldiers spoke of "SNAFU": "situation normal, all fouled up." Officers rounded up for service—"ninety-day wonders" hastily trained in special camps—did not glorify war. (Some commanders forgot this character of their armies. George Patton, a dynamic general whose bold tank maneuvers destroyed the enemy in Africa and southern Italy, once struck and humiliated a young soldier suffering from combat fatigue. Public anger temporarily forced him from his command, and he later publicly apologized.) Military service, Americans assumed, was a temporary thing, a necessary duty to be abandoned at the moment of victory. They were fighting a war to preserve American liberties, not weaken them.

Though millions of Americans left familiar jobs or the unemployment lines to work in weapons factories or for wartime bureaucracies and all citizens paid swollen tax bills, the fighting itself was far distant. In the Pacific, battles on oddly named atolls invisible on most maps erupted sporadically; in Europe, the Allies avoided any decisive move against Hitler's entrenched Fortress Europe until well into 1944. No bombs fell on American cities, no armies threatened invasion. War was work: many adults held one full-time and one part-time job. War was also scarcity:

guns, ships, aircraft, bombs, and ammunition spilled into distant battle fronts, leaving few goods behind for ordinary consumers. Americans worked harder and longer and earned more than they had in years, but they found little to buy in department stores or groceries or car lots. Shortages sometimes had unexpected consequences. Disappearing supplies of cloth, for example, prompted government officials to order a reduction of yardage in women's clothes, whereupon the skimpy two-piece bathing suit replaced the one-piece skirted model popular during the 1930s.

Discrimination Against Blacks and Japanese Americans Although struggling to defeat racist regimes in Germany and Japan, white American civilians extended into the war effort their own bigotry against blacks. Many defense contractors hired blacks only when whites were unavailable. New Deal bureaucrats pledged not to challenge "local social patterns."

The armed forces segregated blacks into separate barracks and units, and excluded them from all but menial tasks. Here was a typical experience for a young black:

> I was drafted into the Army at the age of nineteen through the Selective Service. . . . They segregated us, and when we went into basic training we had to eat separately, we were put into separate barracks, and separate uniforms from the white soldiers, but we always had a white soldier as commander. We did have some Negro officers, but they always had a white commander over them.
>
> Everything was segregated, and they kept it that way until 1943, when I was overseas in Germany, then they began integrating the troops. General Eisenhower was the Supreme Allied Commander in Europe, and actually we were losing the war, all because of segregation. Those German soldiers would sneak upon American soldiers, kill them and take their equipment, then disguise themselves by using Americans uniforms to get into the camps—they killed many soldiers that way. The white soldiers were so prejudiced they trusted anything with a white face, yet they would not trust their own fellow Negro American soldiers.

And the Air Corps and Marines—self-styled elite forces—accepted very few blacks.

Urban blacks suffered unfamiliar harassments in small towns near training camps. Another black soldier, Lloyd Brown, has written of an incident in Salina, Kansas. He and several friends, all in uniform, entered a restaurant. "You boys know we don't serve colored here," the waiter told them. Brown remembers:

> We just stood there, staring. For sitting at the counter having lunch were six German prisoners of war. The people of Salina would serve these enemy soldiers and turn away black American GIs.

Another stunning instance of discrimination against blacks occurred at a navy depot north of San Francisco. In the segregated armed forces of the day all-black units loaded arms and ammunition on ships. In 1944, in the worst homefront disaster of the war, 202 black men were blown to bits doing this dangerous assignment. Some white workers died, too, but the white officers, responsible for the unsafe working conditions, survived.

Japanese Americans living in California, along with others of Asian origin there, had long endured discrimination. Tokyo's attack on Pearl Harbor set off hysteria against them as subversives. Local army commanders ruthlessly rounded up some 100,000 Japanese and corralled them into "relocation centers" hundreds of miles inland. "A Jap's a Jap . . . whether he's an American citizen or not," General John DeWitt explained. Many lost all their property and their businesses, an injustice unremedied for decades until Congress in the 1980s compensated some of those still living.

"Relocation" was the polite term for the policy of rounding up all of the Japanese and herding them into concentration camps. The ostensible justification for this policy was the need to protect American naval and other military installations from espionage. Most of the Japanese in this country had settled along the West Coast, and many were fishermen and so had small boats and short-wave radio sets. The real basis for "relocating" the Japanese, it is clear in retrospect, was continuing prejudice against Asians, which was especially strong in California. The Supreme Court refused to intervene even though the policy amounted to imprisoning tens of thousands of American citizens without trial or even formal accusation. All second-generation Japanese Americans were citizens; every person born in the United States is by that very fact a citizen. Thus the Bill of Rights was, in effect, suspended for the duration of the war, and even afterward the Japanese

MS. YOSHIYE TOGASAKI, *a Californian, recalled her wartime imprisonment in a concentration camp for Japanese Americans:*

We could not go to public swimming pools in San Francisco, and they tried to segregate the schools, you know. It was not quite the same discrimination as the blacks in the South experienced, because we were not excluded from most public facilities, but we were definitely set apart. We might have white friends in school, but they did not socialize with us outside of school. We did not date whites, we did not go to parties or dances with them.

They thought of us as inferior, at least many of them did. We were called J-A-P-S. And of course there was the problem that nobody recognized you as a citizen. So we had to struggle that much harder to reach our goals. I certainly had to do my share of struggling to become a doctor. . . .

The rule was that everyone was evacuated who was at least one-sixteenth Japanese. . . .

I went to Manzanar. It was built from scratch by the military, and so it resembled a military place. Families had no privacy, and they were split apart. I was particularly upset with that aspect of it. A mother and children might be in one place, the father in another, and maybe teen-age daughters would be thrown in with four or five bachelors.

It was also a very dirty place. Manzanar at one time had been a pear orchard, before Los Angeles took over all of the water rights of the area. When that happened, the orchard went dry, and the place became very dusty. The wind would blow from the south, and then it would turn around and blow from the north, and it was a very fine grit that covered everyone and everything. It was in the beds and in the food. We took showers, of course, but that was an unpleasant task. The showers were all open, and you can imagine how the women were embarrassed with that. . . .

Many of the older people had lived in the United States most of their lives, and the nisei (second-generation Japanese-Americans) were full citizens. They were law-abiding people, they were hard-working, they loved the United States, and now they were treated like traitors. . . .

All of Manzanar was a stockade, actually—a prison. We were in jail. There was barbed wire all around, there were great big watch towers in the corners, and there were spotlights turned on during the night. You could not cross the boundaries, unless you were authorized on a work detail or something. The guards carried rifles. There was a teen-ager at Manzanar who walked out into the desert one day. He was not running away, he just walked in plain sight. Who in God's name would try to escape in broad daylight? He was mentally deranged. And he got shot. They shot him in the back. So we all knew exactly where we stood.

Americans faced sometimes insurmountable obstacles in reacquiring lost property.

Wartime Entertainment Film and radio brought the war home. Americans watched and listened. One young American girl was enthralled watching newsreels of Roosevelt and Churchill:

> We thought they were our great, great friends. I mean it was wonderful to see Churchill . . . and Roosevelt sitting together. . . . We thought they were precious men. They'd sit there and smile and laugh and both were jolly and fat. They were taking care of us.

MovieTone news clips preceded double features everywhere. Edward R. Murrow won overnight fame for his dramatic broadcasts that, as German bombs exploded eerily in the background, he would begin with the words, "This . . . is London." Hollywood filmmakers produced a record 982 movies in three years. No *All Quiet on the Western Front* caught the spirit of the war; instead, a wearying genre of patriotic films repeated a litany of American virtue, enemy perfidy, and the final triumph of a righteous people. Still, movies like the Humphrey Bogart-Ingrid Bergman classic *Casablanca* made effective drama of war. And the oppressive atmosphere lent itself to such masterpieces of film noir as *Double Indemnity* (1944) and *Mildred Pierce* (1945). In that day of radio, schoolchildren looked forward to an afternoon fare that included *Terry and the Pirates* (also a comic strip), *Hop Harrigan,* and *Jack Armstrong* (the All-American Boy), featuring small bands of heroes who in adventure after adventure took on the Axis foe.

Superman, going to war like the other comic-strip heroes, gave his audience satisfying images of invincible power. Joe Palooka, formerly a boxer, enlists in the army in 1941: "No, I ain't gonna be an officer," he tells his girlfriend, Rosie, "just a buck private. I don't deserve t' be an' don't know enuff t' be." The next year, as Joe stands with a pal on dangerous anti-sniper duty, their dialogue sums up a nation's recent conversion: "Yeah, Joe, I was an isolationist. I really believed I was right then." "A man's certainly entitled to 'is b'lifs, George." "But when the big test came I realized how wrong I was. . . . "

In *Terry and the Pirates,* an older pilot, Colonel Flip Corkin (loosely based on an authentic Army air hero, Colonel Philip G. Cochran), lectures Terry in the strip of October 17, 1942: "You'll get angry as the devil at the army and its so-called red tape . . . but be patient. . . . Somehow, the old eagle has managed to end up in possession of the ball in every war since 1776—so just humor it along . . . remember, there are a lot of good guys missing from mess tables in the South Pacific, Africa, Britain, Asia and back home who are sorta counting on you to take it from here. Good night, kid!" (Terry salutes as Corkin waves.) And the leader of the "pirates" in the strip, the sinister sexpot known as the Dragon Lady, turns after years of crime to patriotism: "Follow me against the invader [Japan] who threatens to engulf China!" Her band replies, "We fight for Dragon Lady! We march with Dragon Lady against foreign armies!"

The nation's young people indulged themselves with fads: yo-yos, mismatched shoes, slumber parties, and bubblegum. Then Frank Sinatra gave teenagers a singing idol. On the night before New Year's Eve 1942, Sinatra appeared at New York's Paramount Theater, where the audience, mostly high school girls, alternately shrieked and swooned as "the Voice" crooned favorites like "Fools Rush In" and "Night and Day." Wherever he appeared, girlish screeching created pandemonium; souvenir hunters tore his clothes and preserved his footprints in mud; a concert in 1944 required some 400 police to control a crowd of 30,000. Parents and psychiatrists professed bewilderment: this puny kid with greased hair and flamboyant antics so completely contradicted the all-American image of helmeted, soft-spoken GIs. Well-publicized love affairs and a garish life in southern California made Sinatra an American celebrity entertaining as much offstage as on.

Some attributed the wacky Sinatra craze to an anomaly of war: few young men remained at home. College women worried about their prospects for a "MRS. degree," then one of the major reasons parents sent daughters to colleges. One coed at the University of Nebraska complained, "They're all either too old or too young or too sick." (Men not drafted for physical reasons, even if quite legitimate, often suffered unjust scorn as "4-F'ers.") Most women did not use the opportunity of war for feminist reform. They did not adopt the image of "Rosie the Riveter," so cultivated by business leaders desperate for labor. Women yearned for normal times. Hasty trips to the altar produced a growing number of divorces, then a severe social stigma. Yet the birthrate increased. American women, then, continued to value most the traditional roles of wife and mother.

The Early War in Europe and the Pacific

The Pacific War Vice-Admiral William F. "Bull" Halsey struck at the Marshall and Gilbert Islands, held by the Japanese. Army Air Corps bomber squadrons, led by Jimmy Doolittle, raided Tokyo itself on April 18, 1942. Only a month later, aircraft from the *Lexington* and *Yorktown* thwarted an attack on Port Moresby, New Guinea, in the Battle of the Coral Sea. These reverses prompted navy leaders in Tokyo to send a huge armada into the central Pacific. The capture of Midway

Island, they thought, would cut American communications with Asia. Admiral Chester Nimitz, commander of the Pacific forces, ordered Rear Admirals Ghormley and Spruance to meet the Japanese on June 3, and for three days a giant battle raged in the air: the fleets themselves were some 400 miles apart. American pilots sank four carriers and two heavy cruisers, and put four destroyers out of commission. Admiral King, in charge of all American naval forces, called the battle "the first decisive defeat suffered by the Japanese Navy in 350 years." And by the end of January 1943, after some of the most difficult fighting in the war, Papua, New Guinea, was in Allied hands.

An even more difficult battle was occurring in the nearby southern Solomons, where Ghormley ordered an assault on Guadalcanal and Tulagi island by the First Marine Division. The marines landed on August 7, 1942, but within forty-eight hours the naval force that had landed them was attacked and smashed in the most decisive defeat ever suffered by the United States Navy, the Battle of Savo Island. In several other minor engagements in the ensuing two months the American navy could not relieve the marines. Cut off from supplies and untrained for the kind of fighting they faced, the marines hung on grimly against three attempts by the Japanese to drive them into the sea. Casualties were heavy, supplies dwindled, and defeat seemed certain.

Then, on November 12, a naval task force moved against the Japanese naval units enveloping the island of Guadalcanal. In a three-day battle the Japanese lost two battleships, a cruiser, two destroyers, and ten transports. The Americans also lost heavily: two cruisers and seven destroyers; two admirals were killed. But the battle prevented the landing of Japanese reinforcements and so weakened the position of the Japanese that they had to begin evacuating Guadalcanal. The army's Americal Division moved in, and by mid-February, 1943, the Japanese had left the island.

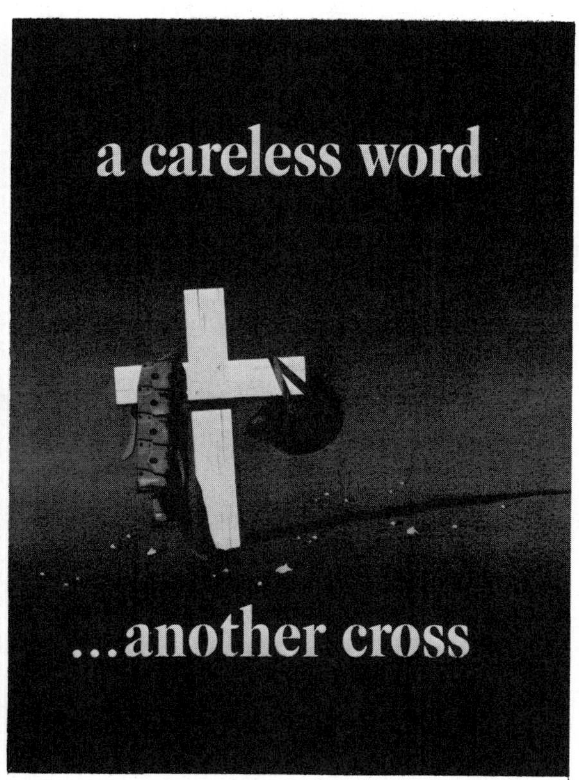

John Atherton, *A Careless Word, Another Cross.*
(Courtesy, The Museum of Modern Art, New York)

War in North Africa and Russia

In June 1941 Hitler had launched a huge offensive against Russia. Leningrad was encircled and the Sixth Corps under General Paulus ramrodded south into Ukraine and beyond, toward the oil fields of central Asia. As the war dragged on, Stalin appealed urgently to his allies for some action to counter German strength in Russia, preferably an invasion of France across the English Channel. Lower echelon military planners in the United States agreed, but their chiefs knew that the British and Americans could at best secure a beachhead in France, not open a major front there. Some indirect evidence suggests, also, that they hoped Hitler would exhaust Germany's armies against Stalin, and thereby considerably ease their own task. Worried that an early assault with American supplies might bog down into a stalemated front reminiscent of World War I, Churchill flatly rejected any scheme to invade France. His concern, instead, was to preserve the British Empire and its lifeline in the Mediterranean.

Rather than risk decisive action on the continent, the British Eighth Army in Egypt, under General Bernard Montgomery, and a hastily-trained American force commanded by Dwight Eisenhower attacked German positions in North Africa. The giant pincer movement of Operation TORCH began in

WORLD WAR II
PACIFIC THEATER
1941–1945
Allied Nations
Japanese Empire 1933
Neutral Nations
Japanese Conquests to
December 7, 1941
Maximum Extent of
Japanese Control
U. S. S. R.
Neutral until
Aug. 8, 1945
MANCHUKUO
SEA OF
JAPAN
CHOSEN
(KOREA)
JAPAN
YELLOW
SEA
Tokyo
Osaka
Hiroshima
Aug. 6, '45
Nagasaki
Aug. 9 '45
CHINA
"Flying the
Hump"
Chungking
Ledo
Stilwell Road
44–'45
Burma Road
Kunming
INDIA
Lashio
BURMA
EAST
CHINA
SEA
RYUKYU
OKINAWA
Apr.–June '45
ISLANDS
Formosa
IWO JIMA
Feb.–Mar. '45
HONG
KONG
(Br.)
PHILIPPINE
SEA
FRENCH
INDO-
CHINA
THAILAND
SOUTH
CHINA
SEA
PHILIPPINES
Oct. '44–Aug. '45
Luzon
PHILIPPINES
Manila
PHILIPPINE SEA
June '44
Saipan
Guam
(U.S.)
LEYTE GULF
Oct. '44
Mindanao
PALAU
Sept. '44
BR.
NORTH
BORNEO
MALAYA (Br.)
SARAWAK
(Br.)
Singapore
Sumatra
Borneo
Celebes
NETHERLANDS EAST INDIES
Java
Timor
New
Guinea
PAPUA
(Austr.)
Port
Mores
INDIAN OCEAN
AUSTRALIA
Sakhali
Karafut
U.S. air
Nov.
BONIN
ISLAND
VOLCA
ISLAN
CAROL
NEW GUINEA
June '43–Ju
TERR. OF
(Austr. N
(Jap

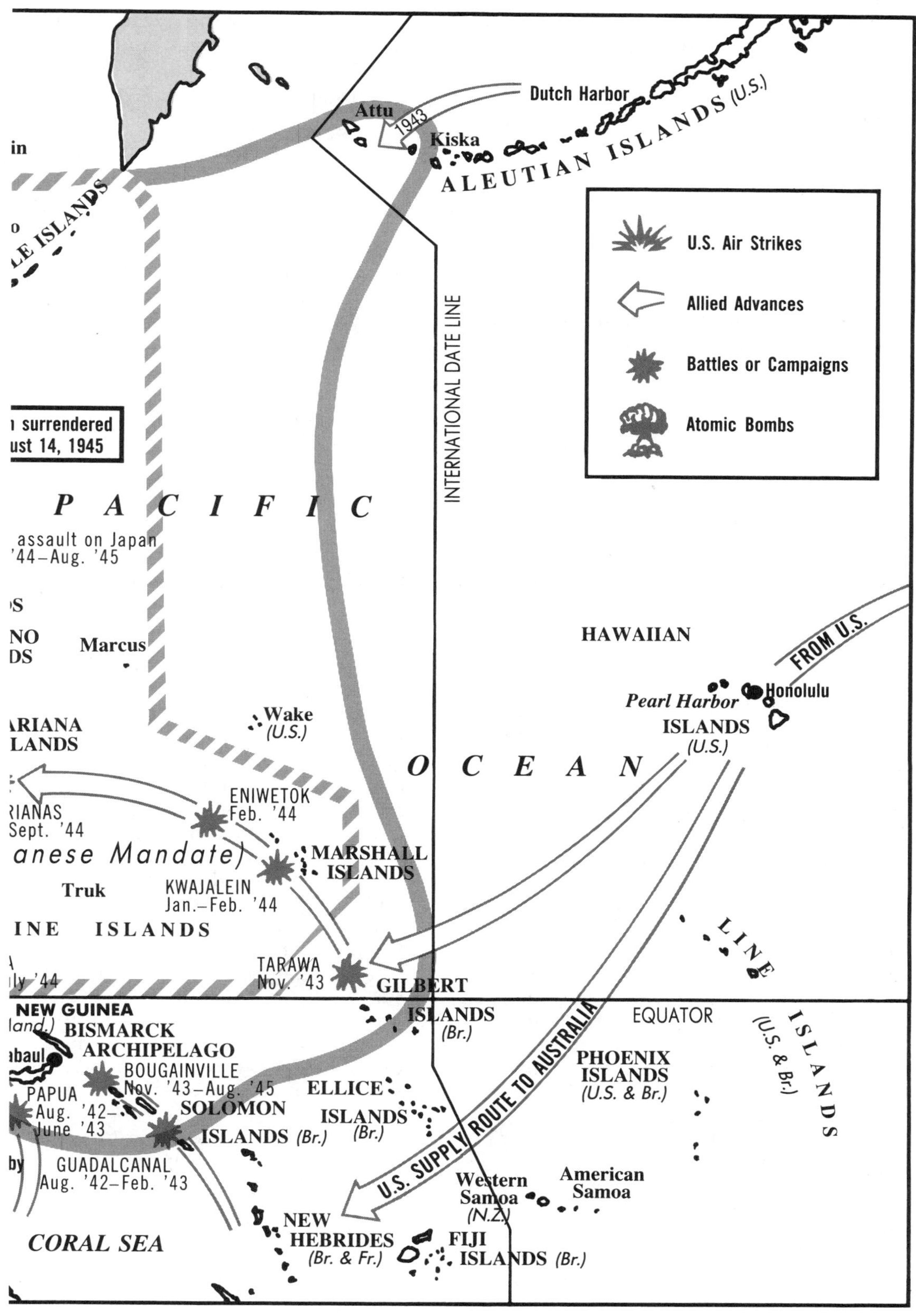

Dutch Harbor
Attu
1943
Kiska
ALEUTIAN ISLANDS (U.S.)
U.S. Air Strikes
Allied Advances
Battles or Campaigns
Atomic Bombs
INTERNATIONAL DATE LINE
surrendered
ust 14, 1945
PACIFIC
OCEAN
assault on Japan
'44–Aug. '45
Marcus
HAWAIIAN
ISLANDS
(U.S.)
FROM U.S.
Pearl Harbor
Honolulu
Wake
(U.S.)
ENIWETOK
Feb. '44
Sept. '44
anese Mandate)
MARSHALL ISLANDS
Truk
KWAJALEIN
Jan.–Feb. '44
INE ISLANDS
TARAWA
Nov. '43
GILBERT ISLANDS
(Br.)
LINE ISLANDS
(U.S. & Br.)
EQUATOR
NEW GUINEA
BISMARCK ARCHIPELAGO
BOUGAINVILLE
Nov. '43–Aug. '45
PAPUA
Aug. '42–
June '43
SOLOMON ISLANDS (Br.)
ELLICE ISLANDS
(Br.)
PHOENIX ISLANDS
(U.S. & Br.)
U.S. SUPPLY ROUTE TO AUSTRALIA
GUADALCANAL
Aug. '42–Feb. '43
Western Samoa
(N.Z.)
American Samoa
NEW HEBRIDES
(Br. & Fr.)
FIJI ISLANDS (Br.)
CORAL SEA

early November 1942, Montgomery moving west, Eisenhower landing in Morocco. General Rommel slowly retreated, conserving his forces to defend Tunisia—since Roman times, the strategic key to North Africa and the Mediterranean Sea. But British and American tanks relentlessly closed around him, and his troops surrendered on May 12, 1943.

Elsewhere, too, during the fall and winter of 1942 to 1943, the Allies halted the Axis advance and took the initiative. In the most important theater of war, the Russian front, Hitler's legions had driven rapidly forward, reaching the Caucasus in the South and the Volga River in the East. But immensely long supply lines, a foolishly harsh occupation policy that used many soldiers for garrison duty, and a devastatingly cold winter slowed, then stopped, German armies. The turning point came at Stalingrad. General Paulus laid furious siege to the city throughout the fall, but the Russians staved off the Germans in hand-to-hand, building-by-building fighting. At the peak of winter Stalin, buoyed by the arrival of American lend-lease from Iran, launched a surprise counterattack. The Russians encircled the Sixth Army, and the Germans lost 600,000 soldiers, some killed and the remainder captured. The great victory came on February 2, 1943—now a national holiday throughout Russia—and marked the beginning of a Soviet offensive that ended in Berlin. In lives lost Russia bore by far the largest cost of the war: some twenty million compared to only half a million Americans.

Coalition Diplomacy, 1943–1945

In early 1943 the British and American leaders met at Casablanca, and decided that Germany must surrender unconditionally. This promise probably reassured the Soviet Union, already suspicious that the Western powers planned to impose on it the chief burden of the fighting. Some commentators have argued that the prospect of total defeat encouraged the Germans to fight to the bitter end, so that the demand for unconditional surrender needlessly prolonged the war. Yet the alternative—a negotiated settlement with Hitler—was neither realistic nor morally desirable.

In 1943 George Patton's Third Army and Montgomery's British troops swept across Sicily and part way up the Italian peninsula; both commanders received secret offers of surrender from King Victor Emmanuel. Ignoring Russian protests, Roosevelt and Churchill negotiated separately with these agents, finally accepting surrender terms insuring that moderate capitalists and their allies would dominate post-war Italy. Already suspicious of every Anglo American move, Stalin was infuriated.

Arguments broke out even between the Americans and the British. Churchill insisted that the western Allies should first invade "the soft underbelly of Europe"—strike northward through the Balkans and Italy into Austria and Czechoslovakia. Churchill was thinking of slicing across the path of a Soviet advance into eastern Europe on which he could guess the U.S.S.R. had designs. American Army Chief of Staff George C. Marshall angrily replied that "No American is going to land in that god-damned [region]." Instead, the Americans argued, an invasion across France into the Rhineland would more quickly end the war, and more surely keep the industrial heartland of western Europe out of Russian control. After several particularly strained meetings among Big Three planners and foreign ministers, Churchill, Roosevelt, and Stalin agreed to meet at Teheran. On their way to the Iranian capital, Churchill and Roosevelt stopped at Cairo, where they conferred briefly with Chiang Kai-shek. The three leaders demanded unconditional surrender from the Japanese, vowing to deprive that country of all its empire. Manchuria and Formosa would be returned to China, the islands of the Pacific handed back to their former imperial masters, or given to the United States.

At Teheran during the last days of November 1943 the world's leaders discussed both military strategy and postwar relations. The Americans outlined their campaign against Japan in the Pacific, and the Soviet Union promised to join the war there after Germany's defeat. Stalin pressed the other leaders vigorously for an invasion of France, now code-named OVERLORD, but he was unable to obtain firm commitments. Agreement came more easily on less immediate matters. The three men pledged to partition Germany, reducing it to a third-rank military power. To prevent future wars, a United Nations would oversee collective security. The Allies would jointly administer all liberated countries until representative institutions were set up.

1944: The Final Struggle

Bombs rained on German cities as the Anglo Americans during 1944 opened an immense three-pronged campaign against Hitler's western stronghold. Their air war, which had carried destruction to Germany itself as early as 1942, entered a new phase. Radar bombsights tripled the destructive power of nighttime raids, and new long-range fighters permitted daytime sorties. Round-the-clock bombing, made possible by immense amounts of equipment and men from the United States, targeted German aircraft plants, communications systems, and chemical factories. Incessant bombing may have discouraged many Germans, already fatigued by years of warfare, but its strategic effectiveness remains questionable. Some attacks, like those against Düsseldorf and Dresden, nearly destroyed entire cities; a total of almost three million tons of bombs fell on Hitler's Reich from 1942 to 1945.

In those pre-atomic days, however, wars were still decided on the ground. The battle for western Europe began in earnest on January 22, 1944, when an Anglo American army landed at Anzio behind the German front in Italy. But this effort soon bogged down. That spring a slow, hard advance began against the German divisions south of Rome. It linked up with the Anzio beachhead and then, on June 4, captured Rome itself. The Germans retreated to their so-called Gothic Line, some 150 miles north of the city, where the fighting stabilized.

Overlord On June 6, "D-Day," just two days after the fall of Rome, began Operation OVERLORD, the biggest amphibious landing in history. Supreme Commander Dwight Eisenhower had planned the attack well. Air bombardments softened up beach defenses (Hitler's famous "Westwall") and disrupted German communications; three airborne divisions landed the night before behind German lines, there to disrupt defense strategy; finally, at 7 a.m., some 125,000 soldiers scrambled onto the beaches of the French region of Normandy. The Allies had gone to great lengths to convince Hitler, successfully, that their principal landing site would instead be farther north, around the city of Calais, with the result that the main German force, General Rommel's Seventh Army, stayed away for several critical days. Despite enormous casualties, which sometimes reached a hundred percent at places like Omaha Beach, the Allies established their beachhead. Within five days, sixteen more divisions landed. The invaders now occupied some eight miles of coastline.

A government poster urging the conservation of gasoline. *(Courtesy, National Archives)*

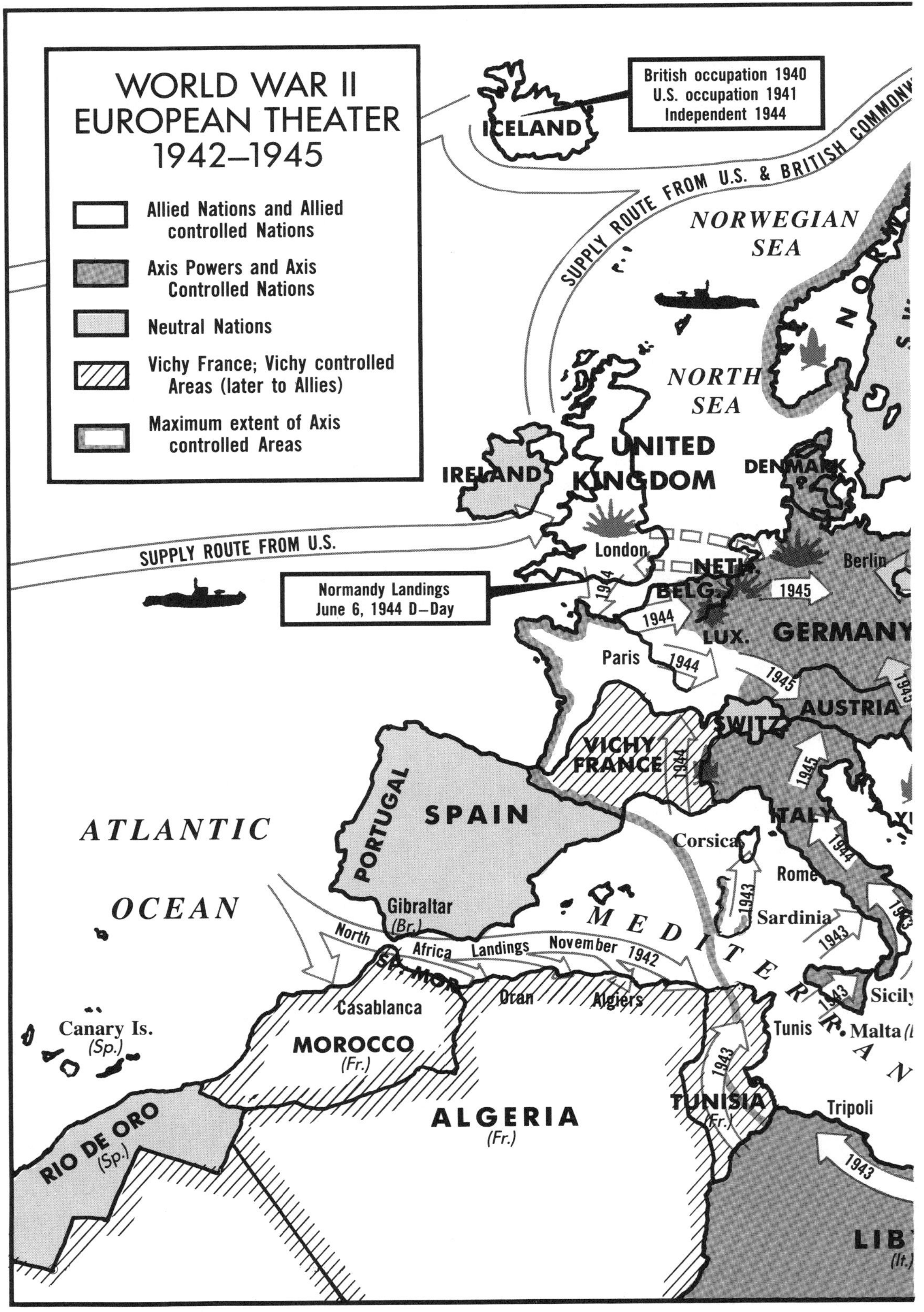
WORLD WAR II
EUROPEAN THEATER
1942–1945
Allied Nations and Allied controlled Nations
Axis Powers and Axis Controlled Nations
Neutral Nations
Vichy France; Vichy controlled Areas (later to Allies)
Maximum extent of Axis controlled Areas
British occupation 1940
U.S. occupation 1941
Independent 1944
ICELAND
SUPPLY ROUTE FROM U.S. & BRITISH COMMONW
NORWEGIAN SEA
NORTH SEA
UNITED KINGDOM
IRELAND
DENMARK
London
Berlin
NETH.
BELG.
LUX.
GERMANY
SUPPLY ROUTE FROM U.S.
Normandy Landings
June 6, 1944 D–Day
Paris
AUSTRIA
SWITZ.
VICHY FRANCE
PORTUGAL
SPAIN
ATLANTIC
OCEAN
Corsica
ITALY
Rome
Sardinia
Gibraltar
(Br.)
North Africa Landings November 1942
MEDITERRANEAN
Casablanca
Oran
Algiers
Tunis
Sicily
Malta
Canary Is.
(Sp.)
MOROCCO
(Fr.)
ALGERIA
(Fr.)
TUNISIA
(Fr.)
Tripoli
RIO DE ORO
(Sp.)
LIBY
(It.)
1943
1944
1945

Allied Air Strikes
German Air Strikes (Flying Bombs V1, V2)
Battle of "The Bulge"
Guerrilla Actions
Allied Advances
Western Front
Eastern Front
Murmansk
FINLAND
SWEDEN
Leningrad
EST.
LATVIA
LITH.
Moscow
UNION OF SOVIET SOCIALIST REPUBLICS
Stalingrad
POLAND
Ukraine
SLOVAKIA
HUNGARY
RUMANIA
Ploesti
UGOSLAVIA
BULGARIA
GREECE
BLACK SEA
CASPIAN SEA
ALLIED SUPPLY ROUTE TO U.S.S.R.
IRAN
TURKEY
Neutral until Feb. 1945
SYRIA
(Fr.)
IRAQ
Cyprus
(Br.)
Crete
PALESTINE
(Br. Mandate)
TRANS-JORDAN
(Br. Mandate)
El Alamain
Cairo
EGYPT
SAUDI ARABIA
Neutral until Mar. 1945
Persian Gulf
1942
1943
1944
1945

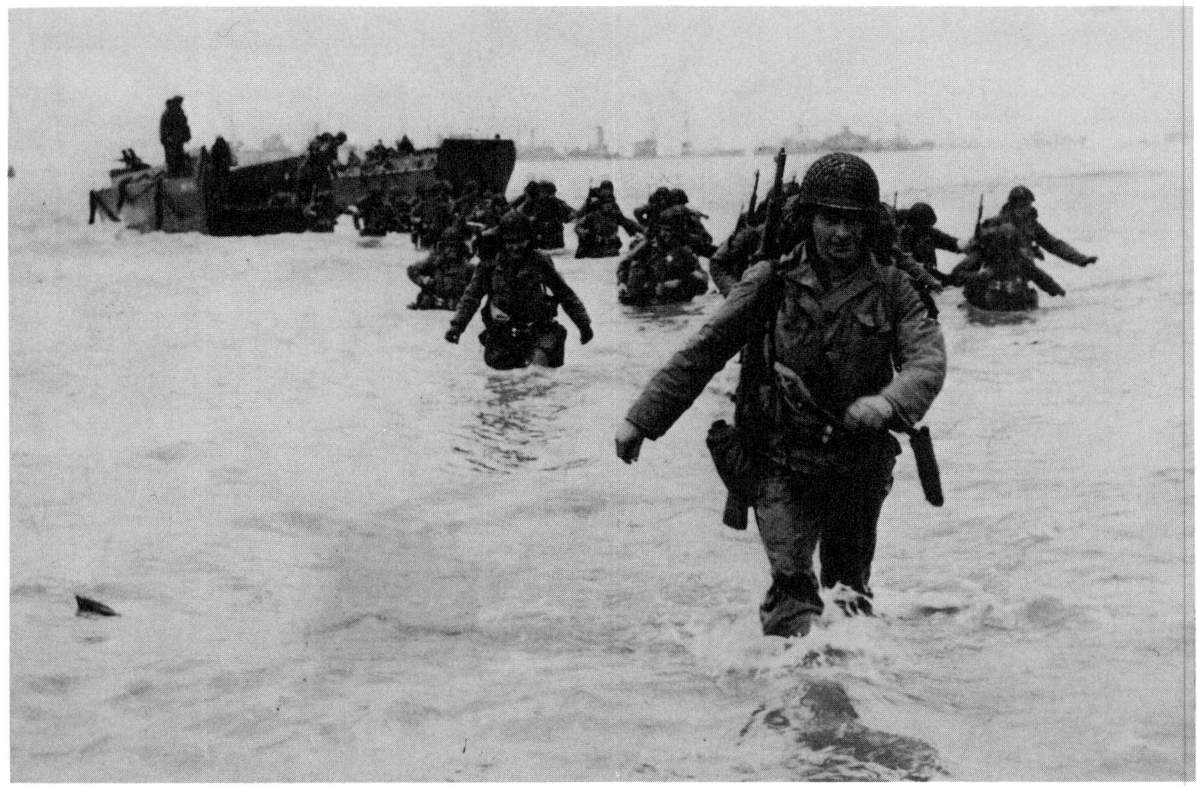

The Normandy beachhead, June 1944. *(Courtesy, Acme Photo)*

One American medic had more than his share of work:

> By the time I got to Normandy, several villages had already been captured. We'd just set up a tent hospital. It was unbelievable. . . . A sergeant came in and said, 'Captain, you better come out and take a look at this.' I went out, and as far as the eye could see, for miles up the highway, there were ambulances waiting to get in. We had a four-hundred-bed hospital and we were already filled. Then he said, 'I want you to look out there, too.' I looked around and there lying in the field are several hundred wounded. So I said, 'Sergeant, get me about twenty syringes and twenty shots of morphine and we're goin' out for a walk.' It was a bright, beautiful summer day. The two of us wandered from group to group. I had a vision in my mind of the Civil War, with all the wounded in the fields. In little groups. Those Mathew Brady photographs. Relived on this field.

Unlike the Italian campaign, that in France quickly took on the character of a *Blitzkrieg* in reverse. There General Patton's Third Army raced into Brittany and down the Loire Valley, while another Allied force under Montgomery drove eastward to Paris. Under orders not to retreat, the German Seventh Army counterattacked, was trapped at Falaise, and managed to extricate only a few of its troops as Polish, Canadian, British, and United States soldiers snapped shut the jaws of the trap. Now the road to Paris lay open, and on August 25 its citizens rebelled against the Nazis. British and Canadian troops streamed along the coast into Belgium and the Netherlands; American soldiers headed for Luxembourg. The Allied rush halted in early September at the Siegfried Line, a string of powerfully defended forts protecting Germany against a Western invasion.

Germany's Final Offensive

On December 16, 1944, General Gerd von Rundstedt, Rommel's successor, attacked along the thinly held front in the Ardennes Forest. Spearheaded by tanks, the offensive carried rapidly forward. Then a column of American troops blunted the advance and rescued the besieged city of Bastogne. This Battle of the Bulge was a very near thing for the Allies, although it proved to be Germany's last major effort on the Western Front. The Germans tenaciously defended their Rhineland cities that winter against the Allied troops across the river, but on March 7, 1945, the Allies captured the strategic bridge at Remagen. Their armies crossed over the Rhine into Germany. The end was near.

Meanwhile, the Soviet Union had destroyed Hitler's main force on the plains of eastern Europe, where the Nazis had concentrated nearly eighty percent of their military strength. Despite huge losses at Stalingrad, Hitler launched still another offensive against Russia in July 1943. But increasingly scarce supplies and poor morale robbed his legions of their elusive victory. The Eastern Front became a vast war of attrition. American equipment and Russian blood guaranteed Allied triumph. As his dreams faded, a monomaniacal Hitler threw every possible unit, every possible weapon, against the Soviet advance. Nothing availed. Russian soldiers pushed the Germans out of Ukraine in March 1944 and then that summer drove into Poland. The people of Warsaw, like those in Paris, rebelled at the approach of their liberators. But Stalin halted his advance supposedly to regroup his scattered forces, while the Nazis slaughtered the Polish patriots, having already wiped out the city's fiercely resisting Jewish ghetto. Stalin welcomed this outcome, for it killed many who might otherwise have battled a Communist seizure of the country. That fall, the Red Army drove into the Balkans, routing German armies in Romania and Bulgaria. By the end of 1944 Soviet troops were inside East Prussia and at the gates of Budapest. All that remained was the final drive on Berlin.

A Two-Pronged Strategy in the Pacific

Guadalcanal and Papua had been more than the first successful offensive actions by American ground forces in the Pacific. They had proved that amphibious landings backed by naval concentrations and heavy air support could work, that Americans could learn jungle fighting and fight the Japanese on such ground. The battle intensified a major and long-continued debate in the American high command. Admiral Nimitz used the example of Guadalcanal to argue that taking the islands one by one would be too risky and costly, that such Japanese island fortresses as Rabaul in the Bismarcks and Truk in the Carolines were impregnable, and that the logistic problems of such a campaign were insurmountable. He argued in favor of an attack on Japan by the Central Pacific route—straight across the open reaches of the ocean, relying on carriers rather than ground-based aircraft for attacks on the less heavily fortified islands of the Central Pacific: the Gilberts, the Marshalls, and the Marianas. MacArthur, on the other hand, insisted that the effort should be concentrated in the southwest Pacific area, where ground-based aircraft could support a drive from Papua and the Solomons along New Guinea through the Netherlands East Indies to the Philippines, and from there to Japan. The Joint Chiefs were also divided, but eventually, largely because it was becoming apparent that the American economy was producing enough to support two offensives, President Roosevelt decided to accept both recommendations.

This "two roads to Tokyo" offensive began in 1943. By September the Americans had pushed their front to a line running from the western Pacific in the North through the Marshall Islands to the Coral Sea. In November the campaign began with the landing of 14,000 men on Bougainville, the northernmost island of the Solomons. An American air base there would provide bombing access to Rabaul. The Japanese tried in two naval assaults in eight days to drive the Americans from the island, but each time the Americans won handily. In four months Rabaul was ringed and neutralized. In November the Gilbert Islands were captured with amphibious landings of a total of 108,000 American troops. In January and February 1944, Kwajalein in the Marshalls capitulated after a bitter struggle and Truk was neutralized from the air. By May, American forces had also reached the western end of New Guinea.

In June 1944 the American Fifth Fleet, under Admiral Raymond A. Spruance, supported one army and two marine divisions at Saipan Island in the Marianas. Within one week of the initial assault, the counterattacking Japanese fleet was destroyed in the Battle of the Philippine Sea and other related air actions. Carrier aircraft from Vice Admiral Marc A. Mitscher's fast carriers destroyed over five hundred Japanese planes. Having crushed the Japanese air force in the Central Pacific and turned back Japan's fleet, American forces completed the capture of Saipan and neighboring Tinian and Guam. From these

The USS *Yorktown* under attack during the Battle of Midway, June 1942. The American victory permanently ended Japanese naval superiority. *(Official United States Navy photo)*

islands, very long range American B-29 strategic bombers could reach Japan.

Meanwhile, in the China-India-Burma theater—designed at first only to keep China in the war, and later to provide bases for B-29 attacks against Japan—Allied troops were attempting to open the Burma road so that supplies could be taken into China by land. But geography, weather, and logistics worked against the Allies, and the Burma campaign bogged down. It would be 1945 before effective land communication replaced the flights of Americans over "the hump" from India as the principal means of access to China. Chinese troops under Chiang Kai-shek had not been pulled together into a single effective army. By the late summer of 1944 it was clear that not even effective bomber bases could be maintained and supplied in China, and late in the year the Japanese made it doubly clear by a massive attack that demolished the airfields that had been so laboriously constructed the preceding year.

On October 20, 1944, MacArthur's forces landed in the Philippines along a twenty-mile beachhead at Leyte. A Japanese naval force moved in to attack the Americans, and the greatest naval battle in history ensued. The Americans sank four Japanese carriers, two battleships, and nine cruisers.

While MacArthur's forces were mopping up in the Philippines, Nimitz's forces were pressing north toward Japan. In early February the air forces began softening up another tiny steppingstone to Japan, the island of Iwo Jima, lying only 750 miles southeast of Tokyo—close enough to allow the bombers the fighter support necessary for making heavy attacks on Japan. An intensive naval and air bombardment of Iwo Jima was conducted, and three days later the Americans landed. On February 23, 1945, the famous American flag-raising on Mount Suribachi took place. Iwo Jima was the bloodiest battle in United States Marine history: 4,189 killed and 15,308 wounded. The American high command reckoned that the advantage they gained had been worth the cost, for in March American B-29's began receiving fighter support from Iwo Jima airfields for their bombing missions over Japan.

Yalta and the Postwar World

Diplomacy acquired an urgency until now reserved for the battlefield. Despite preliminary agreements about unconditional surrender, the partition of Germany, and a joint occupation of liberated areas, troubles among the Allies intensified as their armies approached one another. The western Allies worried about the principles of self-determination in eastern Europe, where the Red Army was prepared to install regimes controlled by the Kremlin. Since the British and Americans were sure to dominate the industrialized parts of Germany, the Soviet Union wanted reparations; yet reparations presumably must come principally from the Rhineland and Bavaria, precisely the areas under Western control. United States military experts calculated that the war against Japan required Soviet help. Another meeting of the Big Three was necessary for sorting out these complicated and increasingly political postwar issues.

Planning for the Postwar World

Churchill, Roosevelt, and Stalin came together once again, in February 1945 at the Black Sea resort of Yalta, for eight days of difficult talks about the future. Each wanted something from the others. Worried by military estimates that the Pacific war might require two more years and a million American casualties—MacArthur predicted 50,000 casualties on the first day of the invasion of Japan—Roosevelt sought help from his Allies. Stalin was determined to erect pliant if not subservient governments along Soviet borders, especially in eastern Europe, Iran, and China. Churchill looked forward to an enlarged British Empire, perhaps in the Middle East, and financial aid from the United States. Churchill and Stalin already had mapped out spheres of influence in the Balkans, a plan that Roosevelt was not fond of. Nevertheless, a spirit of amity—signaled by the appearance of carafes of vodka at the breakfast table—prevailed. On broad declarations of principle, there was ready accord. All agreed that Germany would never again cause war. All agreed that a conference would meet in San Francisco on April 25, 1945, to work out institutional arrangements for a United Nations. All agreed that the liberated countries would have self-determination. But no friendship came out of Yalta.

Many Americans at times since 1945 have blamed Roosevelt for dooming eastern Europe to Communist slavery. But both the presence of the Red Army and Stalin's demands for security in that region made it unlikely any regime could exist there that the Soviet dictator considered unfriendly. The President understood, as other Westerners did not, that the area by and large did not contain the conditions for a middle-class, democratic alternative to Stalinist domination. The three leaders issued a Declaration on Liberated Europe, which guaranteed free elections and self-determination. This solved a public-relations problem in England and the United States, but just as clearly opened the way for Stalin.

The conference's determinations on Germany and on the Pacific both presented great problems for the postwar era. His country desperately weak, Stalin was greedy for Germany's industrial plants, those factories that lay almost exclusively in the Western zones. He accepted an Anglo American plan that divided the country into four sectors—north-central Germany for Britain, the south for the United States, the Rhineland for France, and the pastoral east for the Soviet Union—on condition that Moscow receive $10 billion in reparations "in kind," that is, in goods rather than money. The Western Allies accepted this sum as a basis for discussion. All four powers would garrison the capital, Berlin, although it lay deep within the Soviet sector, and would jointly decide Germany's future. Stalin promised Roosevelt that the Soviet Union would enter the war against Japan as soon as possible, but his price was high: virtually the return of that Russian dominance in northern China exercised by the tsars before 1905. The Yalta agreements—bargainings by distrustful victors—did not work out as their planners had hoped. Without the cooperation that war had forced among the powers, the compromises of Yalta would soon collapse into the conflicts of the Cold War.

The End of the War

Within three months both a symbol of Allied unity, Roosevelt, and the common danger, Nazi Germany, were gone. During that early spring of 1945, Anglo-American and Soviet troops closed in on Hitler's last

The "Big Three"—Churchill, Roosevelt, Stalin—together for the last time, at Yalta, February 1945. *(Courtesy, British Imperial Museum)*

strongholds. General Eisenhower vetoed Montgomery's plan to drive straight for Berlin. The Americans, more interested in winning the war than in politicking about the future, considered this British plan likely to prolong the conflict if Nazi armies escaped to a southern redoubt in Bavaria. Instead, they wanted to surround and destroy German armies in the Rhineland, then push south of the capital toward the Elbe River. Churchill argued furiously with Eisenhower that "We should shake hands with the Russians as far to the east as possible." Roosevelt did not resolve the issue, for the exhausted President was now in Warm Springs resting for the coming United Nations Conference. Around noon on April 12, he complained of a terrible headache; that afternoon he lay dead of a cerebral hemorrhage. Eisenhower now followed his own plan. Soviet and American troops met at the Elbe, some 200 miles south of Berlin, on April 27. That same day Hitler committed suicide, and Russian soldiers raised the hammer-and-sickle flag over his command post. German armies in Italy, Austria, Holland, and Denmark, some one million men, stopped fighting during the next week. On "V-E Day," May 7, 1945, General Alfred Jodl on behalf of the German high command surrendered unconditionally.

On April 1 Nimitz's forces had moved to within 370 miles of Japan by invading Okinawa, a sixty-five-mile long island in the Ryukyus, near the Japanese homeland and close enough to open all Japan's skies to American fighters as well as bombers. The Japanese fought desperately at Okinawa, and the United States Navy, covering the land assault, took a heavy beating from some 3,500 Japanese kamikaze pilots, who dived their explosive-laden planes directly into American vessels in a glorious sacrifice of life for the emperor. Total American casualties were 11,260 killed, 33,769 wounded.

Then, in August, 1945, came the dropping of atomic bombs on the 6th and 9th. Japan offered to surrender on August 10. The young GIs waiting for the invasion of Japan realized that their futures had suddenly changed:

> When the bombs dropped and news began to circulate that the invasion of Japan would not take place, that we would not be obliged to run up the beaches near Tokyo, assault-firing while being mortared and shelled, for all the fake manliness of our façades, we cried with relief and joy. We were going to live. We were going to grow up to adulthood after all.

When Japan's formal surrender was announced on August 15, "V-J Day," Americans at home went wild with joy. A Mexican American girl in Corpus Christi, Texas, heard a sound that a year earlier would have meant a warning:

> When the war ended the sirens sounded again. Corpus Christi has a bluff. There's uptown and there's a downtown. The sailors that were there were in white because it was hot and they rolled. They would roll down this bluff on to the street and nobody was stopping them. The whole city went wild.

A boy from Union, New Jersey, was in the midst of the celebrating:

> I can remember going into New York City and the whole harbor was one great big banner. In those days there were a lot of piers along Manhattan Island where the ships came in . . . and when they would come in the tug boats would run around and they'd be spraying water up. They'd shoot this water way up in the air and blow the whistles and all of the docks had great big banners on them—'welcome home' and 'victory'.Everything was red, white and blue. The troop ships came in with thousands and thousands of guys jammed on them. These are the old luxury liners, the ships that before the war used to carry passengers back and forth to Europe. They tore out all of the luxury suites and crammed these guys in them and painted them gray. . . . We used to have a railroad track fairly close to our house and at night we'd hear the troop trains come through and they'd stop there and everybody would run out with bottles of wine and trade them for souvenirs.

"Any girl . . . in downtown San Diego got kissed and thrown in Horton Plaza Fountain," recalled Patricia Livermore. "I got thrown in ten times."

Harry Truman was sworn in as President following the death in April 1945 of Franklin Roosevelt, who did not live to see the end of the war. *(Courtesy, UPI)*

Points To Think About

1. The Gentlemen's Agreement, by which Japan pledged to ban the emigration of laborers to the United States in return for an end to discriminatory practices against Japanese already in this country, represented an honest effort by both parties to prevent the anti-Japanese hysteria in California from precipitating an international crisis. The Agreement did serve this purpose until Congress in effect disowned it in the Restriction Act of 1924, which barred all immigration from Asia. This treatment accorded Japanese in the United States remained a sore point between the two countries until World War II.

Anti-Japanese sentiment ran deep in American culture, and its consequences were disastrous. Japan never questioned the right of the United States to regulate or bar immigration. What it objected to were policies which singled out the Japanese for special discriminatory treatment. It was especially offensive that Japanese immigrants were ineligible for American citizenship. Japan bitterly resented all such measures that asserted that its people were inferior. It held that these policies were unnecessary even from the point of view of the biased Californians. After all, the Gentlemen's Agreement was sufficient to prevent further Japanese immigration. What would it cost the United States to treat fairly the hundred thousand or so Japanese already in the country? It is a good question.

2. World War I, though hailed by Woodrow Wilson as a struggle to make the world safe for democracy, actually was in part a war to settle European imperial rivalries. In some respects World War II was a continuation of this same contest. Japan sought an Asian empire and, in so doing, threatened not only American possessions and interests in the Pacific but also the French empire in Indochina, the Dutch control of Indonesia, British holdings in India, Burma, Malaysia, and China, and Russian ambitions in Korea and Manchuria. Italy's forays into Africa jeopardized both British and French possessions. And Germany sought a European empire for itself.

The Japanese, Italian, and German threats were all beaten back, though at a terrible cost. The old imperial powers found themselves no longer able to hold on to their empires. The so-called Third World was born.

The United States attempted to control the process of independence in a variety of places. But the dissolution of the old empires proceeded too rapidly, and in too many places, for even the United States to do much. And so the old colonial possessions need to be counted among the victors of twentieth-century war. None of the major European powers intended that victory, of course, but much that happens has the impudence to do so without the consent of the major powers.

Suggested Readings

Recent works on the era include Stephen E. Ambrose, *Eisenhower: Soldier, General of the Army, President-Elect, 1890–1952* (1983), Forrest C. Pogue, *George C. Marshall* (1987), Ruth Milkman, *Gender at Work: The Dynamics of Job Segregation by Sex During World War II* (1987), Waldo Heinrichs, *Threshold of War: FDR and American Entry into World War II* (1987), and William Klingman, *1941* (1988).

For American policy toward the persecution of the Jews, see Henry L. Feingold, *The Politics of Rescue: The Roosevelt Administration and the Holocaust, 1938–1945* (1970) and David S. Wyman, *Paper Walls: America and the Refugee Crisis, 1935–1941* (1968). Albert U. Romasco, *The Politics of Recovery* (1983), studies the politics of international economic reform. On Latin America see Irwin Gellmen, *Good Neighbor Diplomacy* (1979). Various strains of isolationism are studied in Manfred Jones, *Isolationism in America, 1935–1941* (1966).

Robert Dallek's *Franklin D. Roosevelt and American Foreign Policy, 1932–1945* (1979) is a balanced study. America's road to the Second

World War is the subject of William L. Langer and S. Everett Gleason's monumental volumes, *The Challenge to Isolation, 1937–1940* (1952) and *The Undeclared War, 1940–1941* (1953). On wartime battles and strategy there is Richard Ernest and Trevor N. Dupuy, *Encyclopedia of Military History* (revised edition, 1977). The best account of the confusion surrounding the day of infamy is Roberta Wohlstetter, *Pearl Harbor: Warning and Decision* (1962). John J. Stephen, *Hawaii Under the Rising Sun* (1984) studies Japanese planning for an invasion of Hawaii. A good survey of wartime diplomacy is Gaddis Smith, *American Diplomacy during the Second World War* (1965). Richard Polenberg argues that the war made for great changes in American society, among them a further mechanization of agriculture, an increase in the membership of labor unions, a weakening of the ideology of racism, and a growth in government: *War and Society: The United States, 1941–1945* (1972). Roger Daniels gives a survey of the persecution of Japanese Americans during the war in *Concentration Camps, USA* (1971); see also Jacobus ten Broek *et al., Prejudice, War and the Constitution* (1954).

☆ ☆ ☆ POINTS OF VIEW: ☆ ☆ ☆

Did the United States Provoke the Japanese into World War II?

Hosoya Chihiro

Hard-liners in the U.S. government such as Stanley Hornbeck, Cordell Hull, Henry Stimson, and Henry Morgenthau, who favored economic sanctions against Japan in the years immediately preceding the Japanese attack on Pearl Harbor, seriously miscalculated the impact of such a policy on Japan. Instead of deterring the Japanese from pursuing an expansionist policy, these economic sanctions exacerbated U.S.-Japanese relations, encouraged Japan's southward expansion, and provoked Japanese hard-liners to risk war with the United States. The advocates of the hard-line policy toward Japan misunderstood the psychology of the Japanese, particularly the middle levels of the military, the Japanese decision-making process, and Japanese economic realities. They also rode roughshod over the prudent proposals of the soft-liners in the U.S. State Department such as the director of the Far Eastern Division, Maxwell Hamilton, and Ambassador Joseph Grew in Japan.

The demand of the hard-liners for economic sanctions against Japan played into the hands of the ultranationalists in the Japanese government. The latter argued that the imposition of economic sanctions by the United States necessitated risk and expansion by Japan. In such a climate Japanese moderates found it impossible to counsel caution and accommodation. Their counterparts in the U.S. government similarly learned that they were no match for those who foolishly believed that Japan would not dare attack the United States and that economic reprisals would so cripple Japan that she would acquiesce to American pressures. . . .

The American hard-liners' policy of first proposing and then imposing economic sanctions to deter a Japanese southern advance and war failed badly. To understand how it produced the opposite effect it is necessary to consider two miscalculations about the Japanese made by the hard-line faction of the U.S. government. One was that Japan would seek to avoid war with the United States at all costs. The other assumption followed from the first, namely that Japan would inevitably submit to unbending American resolution. However, economic pressure did not restrain Japan from a southern advance. Instead it accelerated a Japanese southern policy even at the risk of possible war with the United States. . . .

The hard-line faction concluded that, in light of the disparity in strength between Japan and the United States, Japanese decision makers could not rationally decide on war. In this regard they made the mistake of applying to the Japanese in unaltered form the western model of decision making based upon rational behavior. Lack of knowledge about the psychology of the Japanese people and especially of the middle-echelon military officers in the period immediately preceding the war led the hard-line faction to miscalculate Japanese psychology. That psychology was marked by a predisposition to making crucial decisions in the face of extremely great, even illogical, risks—as was expressed in Tōjō Hideki's often quoted statement that "sometimes a man has to jump with his eyes closed, from the temple of Kiyomizu into the ravine below." This predisposition was also characterized by an absolute abhorrence of submission.

Hosoya Chihiro, "Miscalculations in Deterrent Policy: U.S.-Japanese Relations, 1938–1941," in *Pearl Harbor Reexamined: Prologue to the Pacific War,* eds. Hilary Conroy and Harry Wray (Honolulu: University of Hawaii Press, 1990), pp. 51, 60, 61, 62.

Michael Barnhart

Stanley Hornbeck, chief of the State Department's Far Eastern Division and, after 1938, political adviser for East Asian affairs, has often been the object of criticism, even derision, for his role in America's relations with Japan before Pearl Harbor. . . .

These arguments are wide of the mark. Nearly alone among the top American policymakers, Hornbeck had a clear sense of what America's interests were in East Asia, what power the United States could wield in that corner of the world, and what policies could best use that power to achieve those interests. Moreover, Hornbeck was consistently correct in his assessments of Japan's aims in the Far East.

Hornbeck believed that his country's interests were best expressed by the Open Door policy. For Hornbeck, the chief principle of that policy was respect for the territorial and administrative integrity of all nations. This was no high-sounding altruism. As long as no nation achieved hegemony over East Asia, the fundamental security of the United States would not be endangered.

Hornbeck realized that the United States was not likely to use military force to uphold this tenet. The nation's direct stake in Asia, unless hegemony actually threatened, was too small. Hornbeck maintained, however, that any effort to influence Japan or China had to be backed by a strong military. Hornbeck did not approve of bluffs. The United States, he argued throughout the decade before Pearl Harbor, ought to make clear its positions and be prepared to support them. Military force was the ultimate, but not the only, instrument of support. Hornbeck recognized that the enviable economic strength of America—and the economic vulnerability of Japan—gave another weapon of great potency to the government he served. . . .

Hornbeck's watchful concern grew to alarm. After literally scores of new laws, including the powerful National General Mobilization Law, were passed by the Japanese Diet, Hornbeck rightly concluded that the military and expansionist elements were using the patriotism generated by the war in China to revolutionize the Japanese economy and place it firmly under martial control. He feared that the result would be a militaristic Japan that would devote all its energies to aggression. This in turn would compel the United States to enlarge its own naval forces in self-defense. Hornbeck fully realized the expense that would be involved and was all the more appalled that the Japanese buildup was fueled largely by exports of American scrap iron, machine tools, and petroleum products to Japan. . . .

Until 1940 he labored largely in vain. After Japan used American-made equipment in the bombings of Chinese civilians, public pressure compelled the Roosevelt administration to call for a "moral embargo" on exports of aircraft, air munitions, and aeronautical equipment to Tokyo. The embargo did not, however, have the force of law. . . . Shipments of all types of scrap iron and an array of exotic alloy metals were stopped after Japan allied with Nazi Germany and Fascist Italy in September. Embargoes on machine tools and industrial equipment shortly followed. . . .

Informal negotiations, going on since April [1941], still offered some hope for avoiding armed conflict. These reached their end in the final offer, called Proposal B, from Japan in late November. The Japanese asked for a restoration of U.S.-Japanese trade relations before the asset freeze of July (meaning a resumption of American oil shipments), American help to enable Japan to procure materials, including oil, from the Dutch East Indies, and an American promise not to "hinder" peace efforts between Japan and China (meaning an end of American aid to the Chinese). In exchange, the Japanese offered to withdraw their troops from the southern half of Indochina.

Hornbeck opposed acceptance. Proposal B, if agreed to, promised the virtual defeat of China while the United States provided Japan with additional stockpiles of oil! The United States government rejected Proposal B.

The result was the unforeseen attack on Pearl Harbor and the equally unforeseen Japanese victories of the spring of 1942. Nevertheless, historians should not allow perfect hindsight to cloud their judgments of the past. . . .

Frequently the argument is raised that the United States ought to have pursued a less hard-line policy so to have encouraged the resurgence of Japanese "moderates." These moderates, it continues, then would have redirected Japanese policy back toward a closer alignment with the West or, at the least, have agreed to some sort of *modus vivendi* that would have averted war.

This reasoning does not stand scrutiny. . . . The sad fact is that there were no Japanese moderates with the will or ability to deflect their country from the course chosen for it by the military and the aggressive civilian leaders. . . . Hornbeck was right.

Michael Barnhart, "Hornbeck Was Right: The Realist Approach to American Policy toward Japan," in *Pearl Harbor Reexamined: Prologue to the Pacific War,* eds. Hilary Conroy and Harry Wray (Honolulu: University of Hawaii Press, 1990), pp. 65–66, 67, 68, 69, 70, 71.

The atomic bomb explodes over Hiroshima, August 6, 1945. *(Courtesy, United States Air Force Photo)*

CHAPTER 26

Truman

HIROSHIMA AND NAGASAKI

Hiroshima—the name means "broad island"—had never suffered conventional bombing during the war. On the morning of August 6, 1945, a lone American bomber, the *Enola Gay*, approached the city, lazy in the sky, from the Southeast. As the B-29's bombardiers released the five-ton atomic bomb it carried, the sky above Hiroshima was blue and serene, the air flooded with glittering sunlight. An all-clear air raid signal had just sounded, and the inhabitants were going about their daily business. Suddenly there came a great flash of light, "brighter than a thousand suns," followed by the lacerating heat of a giant fireball, then the sound of a blast bringing the force of hurricane winds, and finally, the now-familiar multicolored mushroom cloud rising high above the city.

The bomb, with a destructive force equivalent to that of twenty thousand tons of TNT, exploded at a height of 1,800 feet near the center of the flat city built mostly of wood. Within a radius of two miles of ground zero, the destruction was total: metal and stone melted, and human beings were incinerated. Then fire spread everywhere. The nine-square-mile city almost disappeared. As many as 200,000 Japanese died, either immediately or some time after, as a result of the dropping of the bomb on Hiroshima. Human suffering from burns was terrible. The trimmed and nurtured landscape that the Japanese have loved so much was scorched to dead soil and rubble, and with its scorching survivors felt as though nature itself had died.

Three days later, another atomic bomb was dropped on Nagasaki, Hiroshima's neglected historical sister. The captain who piloted the plane wrote: "Does one feel any pity or compassion for the poor devils about to die? Not when one thinks of Pearl Harbor and of the Death March on Bataan." Mass open cremations followed; perhaps 100,000 more people died then or later. Life and death went out of cycle with each other.

Only gradually did the world come to realize that an even more wretched curse had been visited on the two cities in the form of a slow, painful, invisible

Hiroshima after the blast. *(Courtesy, United States Air Force Photo)*

contamination—radiation poisoning. The course of the disease consisted of vomiting; diarrhea with large clots of blood in the stool; fever; loss of hair; ulceration and purple spots on various parts of the body from bleeding into the skin. Some deaths came from cancer years later.

Why had the political and military leaders of the United States sanctioned using the atomic bomb on Japan? For President Harry Truman, the decision was plain: its use might save many thousands of American lives by shortening the war, and, after all, the Japanese had struck us at Pearl Harbor without warning. Some advisers had suggested exploding a demonstration bomb in an uninhabited area in the Pacific to convince the Japanese of the new weapon's terrible power. But government scientists feared that the bomb might prove a dud, and there existed a very limited number of bombs to detonate.

On August 10, the day after Nagasaki was destroyed, the Japanese agreed to surrender.

The use of the atomic bomb deprived the United States of some of the position of moral superiority it had held through most of the war. No longer could we speak of totally evil Axis powers confronting totally righteous Allies. The United States was the first and only country to commit such an act of monumental devastation. "O, it is excellent," Shakespeare writes, "To have a giant's strength; but it is tyrannous/To use it like a giant." Critics have argued that the violence the world has accepted since World War II would not have been countenanced but for this earlier use of atomic bombs. Some have even suggested that the principal reason the United States used the bomb was its desire to demonstrate its military superiority to the Soviet Union, that it was thus the first act of the Cold War as much as the last of the war against Japan.

One argument deserves some measure of consideration: perhaps these actual demonstrations of even these miniature atomic bombs' awesome power served to instill a degree of caution in the world's leading powers. The proliferation of atomic weapons and the availability of nuclear raw materials, however, put that restraint at risk.

Harry S Truman

A Missouri Democrat One of President Roosevelt's closest aides, Steve Early, said only: "Harry, please come over to the White House right away." Several hours before on that day, April 12, 1945, in Warm Springs, Georgia, President Franklin D. Roosevelt had died of a massive cerebral hemorrhage.

Almost a legend by 1945, Roosevelt, through his reassuring manner no less than his virtuoso leadership, had guided a nation through depression and global war. Now, when Vice President Harry Truman arrived at the White House, he was met by Eleanor Roosevelt, who said simply, "Harry, the President is dead." "I felt," Truman was to remark a little later, "like the moon, the stars and all the planets had fallen on me."

Harry S Truman of Missouri considered himself a plain man, taking pride in his honesty and self-reliance. His mother had inculcated a resoluteness in this middle-class child: do your best and don't worry about it afterwards. The family farm prospered during the Progressive Era; he served creditably as an artillery captain in World War I; the postwar recession ruined a haberdashery venture in Kansas City. Out of work, Truman gratefully accepted an endorsement from the Pendergast political machine to run for county judge. A reputation for integrity and a folksy campaign style won the election, and Truman settled into the comfortable life of presiding over a quiet court.

A dispute among Democratic bosses in Missouri later gave Truman a chance to run for United States senator. His political finesse and a workmanlike record carried him to Washington, where he vigorously supported Roosevelt and the New Deal. Senate leaders back in Washington put Truman in charge of a watchdog committee on the conduct of the war, a difficult job he performed with sober dispatch. But no aura of destiny surrounded him, at least not before 1944.

In that year, a bitter squabble broke out in the Democratic party over the vice-presidential nomination. Liberal Democrats supported the incumbent, Henry A. Wallace. But many midwesterners thought Wallace too quixotic, too radical. Busy with the war, and not wishing to offend, an ailing Roosevelt allowed the labor and urban bosses who controlled the 1944 Democratic Convention to pick Truman, a good campaigner from an important border state. The election that fall made Truman Vice President; Roosevelt's death five months later made him President.

A Quicksilver Peace: From Allies to Adversaries

Truman and the World The new Chief Executive faced giant problems. As Vice President he had been excluded from any role in policy and decision making. Now, inexperienced in foreign affairs, and surrounded by advisers far more knowledgeable than he, Truman had somehow to gather the reins of government into his own hands. Events tumbling over one another in the last months of the war and the first days of peace enabled Truman to establish his authority almost immediately.

The United Nations Charter reflected the President's determination. At the Dumbarton

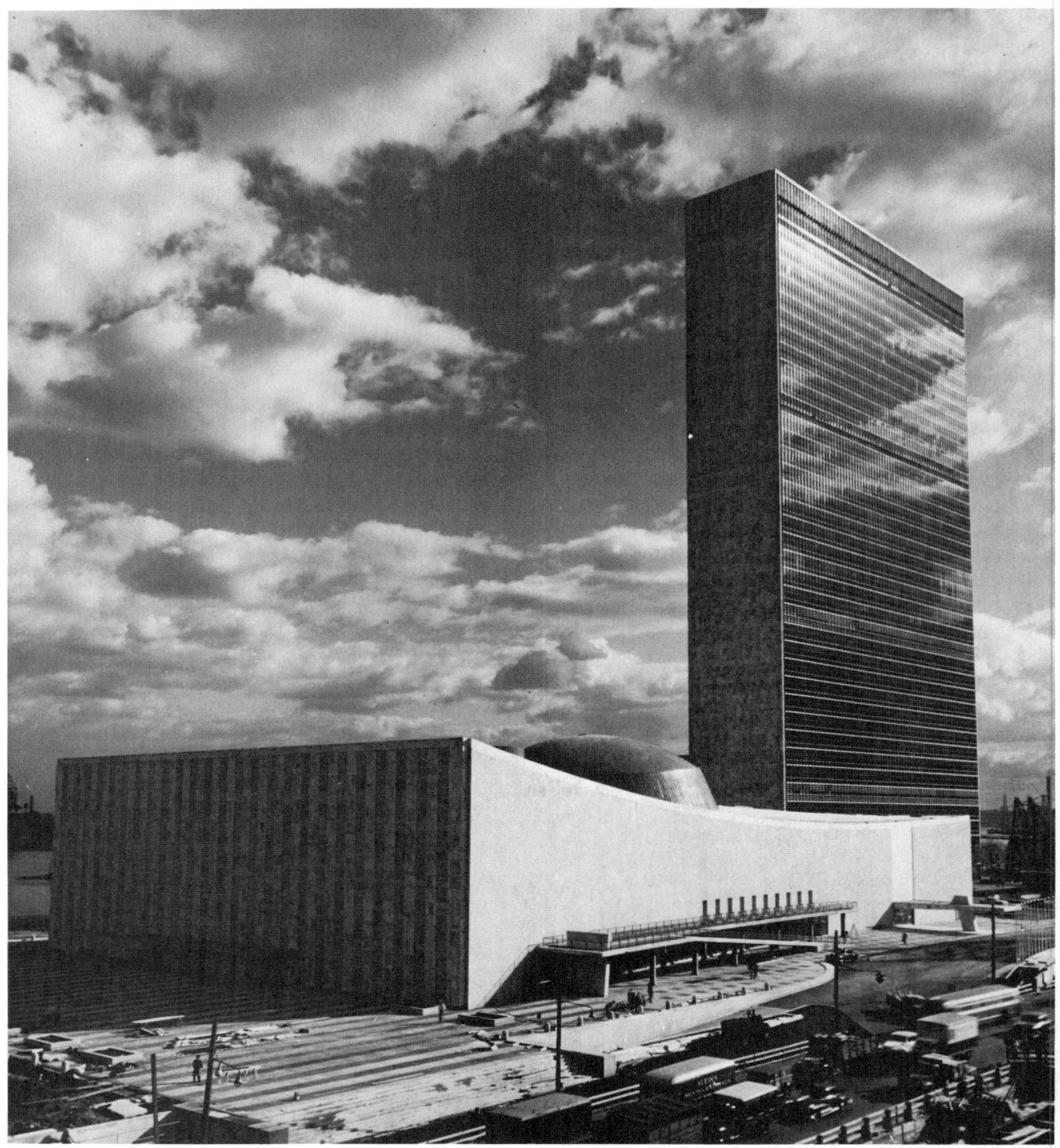

The United Nations General Assembly Building, New York, completed in 1952. *(Courtesy, United Nations)*

Oaks Conference in 1944 and again at the Yalta Conference early the following year, the powers had pledged to replace the discredited League of Nations with a new, more effective instrument of collective security. But when they gathered in San Francisco during April 1945, negotiations turned unpredictable and difficult. Friction over Poland and disputes over procedure led Truman abruptly to inform Stalin that the United States would go ahead with the United Nations project with or without the Soviet Union. Stalin relented. The Charter allowed all member nations to discuss any question and vote in the General Assembly, but the Assembly's recommendations required approval from the Security Council. This supercabinet, with five permanent members—the United States, Britain, France, the Soviet Union, and China, each with a veto—and six temporary members elected by the General Assembly, would meet to take action in times of crisis. A Secretariat administered dozens of economic, social, financial, and relief agencies, all to have their headquarters with the rest of the UN in New York City.

The Potsdam Conference New rivalries quickly crushed hopes for worldwide cooperation. At a meeting in July 1945 of the Big Three at Potsdam, near Berlin, Truman, Stalin, and Clement Attlee (who replaced Churchill as British prime minister halfway through the conference) pondered the future of eastern Europe, the occupation of Germany, and the war against Japan. They demanded an unconditional surrender from the Japanese, and Stalin again promised to send Soviet troops against the Japanese in Manchuria and North China. In other areas, the problems proved intractable. Huge Soviet armies in the Balkans and eastern Europe added compelling force to Stalin's demand for "friendly regimes" there. Unable to compromise, the three men simply postponed decisions about Poland, Hungary, Romania, Austria, Yugoslavia, Bulgaria, and Greece. The future of Germany proved an even more divisive issue. Stalin, already angered by Washington's refusal of a postwar loan to rebuild his war-shattered country, demanded a joint occupation of all Germany and immense reparations. The British and Americans succeeded in reaffirming a zonal occupation, coinciding roughly with the distribution of Allied troops at the time. Stalin satisfied himself with a promise from the other Allies to turn over twenty-five percent of western Germany's factories and movable equipment as reparations in kind.

Harry Truman wrote his impressions of Stalin:

> July 17, 1945
>
> Just spent a couple of hours with Stalin. . . . He'll be in the Jap War on August 15th. Fini Japs when that comes about. . . . I can deal with Stalin. He is honest—but smart as hell. . . . I invited him to come to the U.S. Told him I'd send the Battleship *Missouri* for him if he'd come. He said he wanted to cooperate with U.S. in peace as we had cooperated in war but it would be harder. Said he was grossly misunderstood in U.S. and I was misunderstood in Russia.

Eleven years later Truman recorded his memories of Stalin at Potsdam:

> A large number of agreements were reached only to be broken as soon as the unconscionable Russian Dictator returned to Moscow! And I liked the little son of a bitch. . . .

Domestic Whirlwinds: Demobilization and Reform

Conversion to Peacetime Roosevelt's death and the end of the war threw American politics into prolonged uncertainty. Democrats argued among themselves over civil rights, labor policy, and demobilization. Yet the Republicans, deeply divided over foreign policy and weakened by so many years of defeat, seemed unlikely to provide a strong, effective alternative. Some Americans wanted to dismantle what they called "the welfare state" and "government interference with business." Others looked forward to still more reform in health care, distribution of income, and race relations. Everyone feared the return of depression once the war ended. And everyone hoped for a new era of peace, achievement, and growing affluence. As soon as Japan surrendered, Americans demanded foremost a return to normal peacetime pursuits. Some twelve million soldiers wanted to come home as soon as possible.

The flood of veterans complicated the task of converting the nation's economy to peacetime production without a return to high prewar rates of unemployment. Congress soon passed the GI Bill of Rights. Veterans took advantage of a wide range of its benefits: hospital services and vocational training, favorable mortgage terms for houses and small businesses, payments for college attendance, weekly unemployment checks if necessary. Four out of five GIs went back to school, many to colleges that welcomed them gratefully after fifteen years of half-empty classrooms. For the first time in American history, many middle-class males now looked forward to a university education as a matter of course. Few noted that since the GI bill applied almost exclusively to males, it was a thoroughgoing act of sexual discrimination.

Initially the postwar period seemed to strengthen traditional gender relations, and certainly the media preached the virtues of domesticity and women at home. In fact, many women continued to drift in and out of the labor force during their lives. But despite the strength of domestic values, which severely circumscribed their participation in the labor force, the percentage of married women and mothers who worked for a wage or a salary climbed steadily. Many women worked to contribute extra income to their families. Many other women, notably black women who in growing numbers were now facing life in northern urban centers, worked when and how they could for survival. Even during the conservative 1950s, the numbers of women in the labor force would increase steadily. What was not to change swiftly were popular attitudes that endorsed inequality of pay, approved segregation of the labor force by gender, and expected women to assume full responsibility for domestic work and child care. Not until the maturation of the new women's movement at the end of the 1960s and beginning of the 1970s would these questions even be frequently raised, and mostly by and for women who were not poor, not black, and not Hispanic. And even then, the needs of poor, black, and Hispanic women would not receive widespread attention.

Throughout United States history, at least until the years of the New Deal, the federal government had assumed a very small role in regulating the functioning of the economy. Few Americans even believed it was the responsibility of government to guarantee full employment and stable prices. The Great Depression and World War II changed all that, especially after Keynesian economics made it clear that the federal government, through spending and taxation policies,

Chrysler workers on strike. Relations between management and labor deteriorated in the postwar period, as inflation and unemployment rose. *(Courtesy, United Auto Workers)*

could affect the course of the economy. At the end of World War II, Truman's administration wanted to make the transition to a peacetime economy as well as continue the social and economic safety-net programs inaugurated by the New Deal. Liberal Democrats also wanted the federal government to assume permanent responsibility for guaranteeing full employment in the United States.

The legislation designed to achieve those goals was the Employment Act passed by Congress in 1946. It created the Council of Economic Advisers to assist the President in developing economic policy, established a Joint Economic Committee of Congress to monitor those policies, and gave the federal government responsibility for maintaining full employment. It was tacitly understood that the government should use spending and taxation policies to stimulate employment and to control prices.

Labor Trouble, Inflation, and Intraparty Bickering Labor-management relations deteriorated rapidly. Union members, worried about job security and declining purchasing power, demanded pay hikes. President Walter Reuther of the United Automobile Workers argued that if workers' real wages did not increase, they could not buy the increased production of American factories. Large peacetime profits, he insisted, could and should finance higher pay without any boost in retail prices. In November 1945 workers walked off their jobs in all General Motors plants. Electrical workers, meatpackers, and steel workers followed during January 1946. That spring John L. Lewis ordered out the United Mine Workers, threatening to close down a wide range of satellite industries dependent upon soft coal. These strikes were settled, but in late May a strike shut down the country's railroads. Faced with the prospect of economic chaos, Truman reacted quickly. The President promised a nationwide radio audience that he would draft the strikers and order the army to run the trains unless they returned to work. The railway brotherhoods relented at once.

The congressional elections of 1946 rebuked those who wanted to maintain Roosevelt's legacy. The Republicans turned popular dissatisfaction into a stunning victory that gave them control of both the Senate and the House of Representatives for the first time in sixteen years. After the Republicans triumphed in November, everyone expected a difficult two years in domestic politics—with a progressive President now confronting conservative legislators. Nonetheless, Senator Robert Taft, the Republican leader, did indicate that Congress might address at least one progressive concern. "You don't get decent housing from the free enterprise system," he observed. And in foreign affairs bipartisanship made for action and innovation.

Atomic Diplomacy

The American atomic monopoly reinforced an American sense of total security. It also must have made Stalin even more insecure. More than ever he thought he needed compliant regimes in those nations that bordered the Soviet Union in eastern Europe, central Asia, and the Far East. His maneuvers in these areas strengthened American hostility. Truman and his new secretary of state, James Byrnes, labored on proposed peace treaties to resurrect a unified but neutral Germany as a buffer state against Stalin. Remembering two world wars, Stalin disrupted, postponed, and ignored these negotiations. By the middle of 1947, the two opposing sides had tacitly divided Europe: Italy and the heavily industrialized western portions of Germany in the Western sphere of influence; eastern Europe and most of the Balkans in the Soviet sphere.

The Baruch Plan In June 1946, Bernard Baruch, on behalf of the Truman Administration, submitted a daring plan to the United Nations for the international control of atomic energy. An agency independent of any country would operate all uranium mines and production plants. It was also to oversee nuclear research, monitor all explosions, and administer the peaceful use of atomic energy. Composed of scientists from many lands, the new body would inspect unhampered all atomic installations everywhere and punish violators. No veto could block its decisions.

Stalin rejected this idea. Aware that his own scientists would soon be exploding atom bombs, he preferred the more familiar if more dangerous path of rivalry. Stalin saw a Soviet bomb as a great equalizer, necessary given the huge lead of the United States in industrial output and its dominion over the world's resources. He was convinced that the Americans were determined to exploit their economic and political power. Hence the lack of any Soviet veto in the Baruch Plan made the plan doubly objectionable to him. Allies had now become relentless adversaries.

Containment of Communism Secretary of War James V. Forrestal outlined plans for American naval bases scattered throughout the Mediterranean. During a visit to the United States in 1946 Winston Churchill publicly warned of Soviet imperialism in eastern Europe, charging in a speech at Fulton, Missouri, that an "iron curtain" had descended across the continent "from the Baltic to the Adriatic." (Forty-six years later another Russian leader, Mikhail Gorbachev, would return to Fulton to speak of the raising of the iron curtain.)

In Moscow, George Frost Kennan, a counselor at the United States Embassy there, reported an ominous warning from Stalin: "The present capitalist world order makes peace impossible." Kennan drafted a long dispatch to the State Department, describing Russian paranoia about the outside world. The Soviet leaders, he concluded, "are committed fanatically to the belief that it is necessary to disrupt the internal harmony of our society and to break the international authority of our state, if Soviet power is to be secure." The proper response—which Kennan anonymously proposed in a famous article of 1947 by Mr. "X" in the prestigious journal *Foreign Affairs*—was for the United States to "contain" Communist power by rebuilding American military might as a "counterweight" to Soviet "expansive tendencies." The Soviet Union was like

> a toy automobile wound up and headed in a given direction, stopping only when it meets with some unanswerable force . . . a fluid stream which moves constantly, wherever it is permitted to move . . . [until] . . . it has filled every nook and cranny available to it in the basin of world power.

Since early 1945, the Soviet Union had given moral support to local Communist guerrillas in Greece, while England had aided the embattled Greek monarchy with money and troops. But in 1947 the British ambassador told Truman that his country could no longer sustain the financial burden. At the same time, Stalin was leaning heavily on Turkey to gain control of the Bosporous Straits. The Soviet Union seemed likely to replace the British throughout the eastern Mediterranean. Thereupon, Truman boldly went to Congress for $400 million in military assistance for Greece and Turkey. "It must be the foreign policy of the United States," he explained, "to support free peoples who are resisting attempted subjugation by armed minorities or by outside pressures." A new secretary of state, former Army Chief of Staff George Marshall, heartily approved this so-called Truman Doctrine. Greece and Turkey survived and became firm allies of the Western powers. The Truman Doctrine fully engaged the United States in a Cold War against the Soviet Union. No longer would our foreign policy be a matter of sallies beyond our borders, to which we would then return. We were committing ourselves to a complex and steady course of diplomatic, economic, and military engagement.

Containment in Action

The Marshall Plan Economic catastrophe and a growing sense of frustration in western and central Europe seemed likely, many feared, to push the whole continent into Stalin's embrace. The war's destruction made recovery in western Europe appear remote, and the unusually harsh winter of 1946–47 edged the suffering populace toward despair. Already French and Italian Communists had demonstrated impressive voting strength.

The administration within two months radically altered American foreign policy. In a commencement address at Harvard University, Marshall proposed the rescue of Europe's economic health. "There can [otherwise] be no political stability and no assured peace," he declared. "Our policy is directed against . . . hunger, poverty, desperation and chaos." Instantly applauded throughout a troubled Europe, Marshall's project for massive aid was a breathtaking act of policy and imagination.

Within three weeks, British, French, and Soviet leaders gathered in Paris to work out specifics for the European Recovery Program. But the Russians, angered by what they saw as a scheme to undermine their control over eastern Europe, quickly left the conference, denouncing the ERP, or Marshall Plan, as "an imperialist plan to subjugate independent nations."

Certainly Truman had many motives for this spectacular scheme: humanitarianism blended almost imperceptibly with hopes for anti-Communist and American advantage. A prosperous Europe would provide markets for United States manufacturers; successfully democratic societies in the West would halt any drift toward Communism there and dampen the appeal of that ideology elsewhere in the world. Still, the Marshall Plan encountered significant opposition from the new Congress. Some internationalists considered unilateral action a dangerous affront to the Russians. At the other pole was isolationism, an attitude once associated with a number of political progressives but now tilted to the Republican right. Determined to lower taxes and reduce the role of government in American life, conservatives wondered about the long-term result of massive aid to Europe, and feared alliances and commitments that would compromise American independence. Nonetheless the Marshall Plan moved steadily through Congress. In this as in other policies of the postwar years, the American confrontation of international Communism was chiefly a liberals' rather than a conservatives' enterprise.

In early 1948 sixteen western European nations submitted a comprehensive report, outlining their specific needs and asking for $20 billion during the next four years. Hearings began several months later before Senator Vandenberg's sympathetic Foreign Relations Committee. Suddenly, on February 25, 1948, Communists staged a successful *coup d'etat* in Czechoslovakia. The seizure of this industrialized country convinced Congress and many officials of Stalin's aggressive designs. Within six weeks, the legislators had voted $17 billion in Marshall aid. American money and materials flooded western Europe for the next four years, creating a recovery so fast and so complete that Communist parties, strong at the war's end, rapidly declined in political power.

Secretary of State George C. Marshall (left), seen here with U. S. Ambassador to Britain Lewis Douglas. The Marshall Plan rebuilt western Europe's economy. *(Courtesy, United Press International)*

Even before Congress passed the Marshall Plan, the administration had toyed with ideas for a permanent, peacetime alliance. Then action by the U.S.S.R. thrust the United States into another radical departure from its past diplomatic practice.

The Berlin Airlift All during 1947 the Soviet Union had bickered with the British and Americans over Germany's future. Stalin—understandably after losing twenty million soldiers to the Nazis—aimed for a weak, neutral Germany, forever unable to wage modern war, while the West stubbornly insisted upon a strong democratic state. The Soviet Union advocated joint control over Germany's industrial areas, not just a regional division into east and west. But as the Marshall Plan moved toward adoption, Britain, the United States, and later France made plans to merge their three zones into a single political and economic unit. A furious Stalin then impeded Western ground access to Berlin, isolated some 110 miles inside the Soviet occupation zone. In response the western Allies speeded up plans for a single regime. On June 25, the Red Army blocked all ground access to Berlin. Soviet propaganda clarified Stalin's aims: to force the West to give up its plan to unify Germany or risk losing its advanced position in Berlin.

For nearly a year, the Soviet military cut off Western ground contact with Berlin. Realizing that a mistake might precipitate a third world war, Truman responded with a sophisticated use of air power. Hundreds of British and American planes flew in all essential supplies to some two million people trapped behind the blockade. The technical skills of the pilots and flight crews, together with the great courage of the Berliners, matched the determination of Moscow.

The commander of American troops in Europe, Lucius D. Clay, announced that the U.S.S.R. "can't drive us out by any action short of war." Eleven months passed. Suddenly Stalin proposed a scheme that in effect masked his surrender, promising to respect Berlin's independence in return for the resumption of regular meetings of the largely ceremonial Council of Foreign Ministers.

NATO

The Berlin crisis of 1948 and 1949 had a tremendous impact upon the United States. The State Department quickly opened talks aimed at establishing a defensive alliance with Britain, France, Italy, the Netherlands, Denmark, Norway, Portugal, and Canada. Despite the continuous prod of the Berlin

Berlin children gaze hopefully at the sky near a runway approaching Tempelhof Airport, Berlin, Germany, Oct. 4, waiting for candy bars to be dropped from the occupants of an airlift C.54 Skymaster passing overhead. This is the spot where Lt. Gale S. Halvorsen of Garland, Utah, dropped candy to the youngsters by way of a handkerchief parachute on each of his trips to Tempelhof. *(Courtesy, AP/Wide World Photos)*

blockade, opposition to a comprehensive alliance developed in the Senate. Senator Taft opposed the idea because it "committed this country to the policy of a land war in Europe." Nonetheless, the North Atlantic Treaty Organization (NATO) passed in the British and American legislatures, primarily because of the immediacy of the Soviet threat. Article 5 provided that "an armed attack against one or more of the signatories . . . shall be considered an attack against them all." Truman spoke of NATO's new strategic dimension, that of deterrence: "If we can make it sufficiently clear in advance that any armed attack affecting our national security would be met with overwhelming force, the armed attack might never occur."

This formula made explicit the need for a standing American army. The National Security Act of 1947 brought all the armed forces under the administrative control of a new Department of Defense. James Forrestal became its first secretary and began the long task of molding the rival services into a cooperative military enterprise. A Joint Chiefs of Staff worked under the secretary, although at times its members leap-frogged over him by appealing to sympathetic congressmen or directly to the public. Intelligence functions and personnel were brought together in the Central Intelligence Agency (CIA). The secretaries of state, defense, and the treasury became members—with a large number of experts and special assistants—of the newly formed National Security Council, which coordinated decision making about pressing questions of military intervention.

Rearmament, the Marshall Plan, and the NATO alliance revolutionized United States foreign policy. A nation that had never had a standing army of any substance in peacetime, and had not entered a formal military treaty alliance since the compact with the French during the Revolution, now took on heavy overseas commitments, both economic and political. The United States boasted the muscle to defend those interests with force if necessary. In a faraway place few Americans cared about, that resolve would soon be tested.

Politics as Usual: The Eightieth Congress and the Election of 1948

Congress and the President, together fashioning precedent-shattering military and diplomatic policies, continued to quarrel on domestic issues. Truman confronted an alliance of conservatives on Capitol Hill, who not only blocked future reform but also aimed at undoing important parts of the New Deal. Its leader, Senator Robert Taft of Ohio, argued that "We have got to break with the corrupting idea that we can legislate prosperity, equality and opportunity." Southern Democrats, seriously alarmed by Truman's increasing commitment to civil rights, often joined with the Republicans. "The New Deal is kaput," gloated the conservative New York *Daily News*, like

> the Thirty Years' War or the Black Plague or other disasters. . . . [Its demise] is like coming out of the darkness into sunlight. Like feeling clean again after a long time in the muck.

The Taft-Hartley Act

A battle erupted early in 1947, almost as soon as the new Eightieth Congress convened, over the future of labor unions. Many Americans were blaming both high prices and scarcities on the greed of big unions. That militant leaders like John L. Lewis, chief of the United Mine Workers, called for strikes in defiance of court orders added to the unpopularity of unions. Many conservatives were philosophically opposed to unions, believing that they wielded unwarranted power over American labor and that they disrupted the free market. The antilabor mood of the postwar 1940s, combined with conservative control of Congress, produced the Taft-Hartley Act of 1947.

This complicated statute outlawed major tools of the labor movement: the closed shop, which required workers to join a union before taking a particular job; the secondary boycott, in which a union picketed firms not directly involved in a labor dispute; and the check-off, which directed employers to deduct union dues from paychecks. In addition, the act banned contributions to political campaigns and required workers to notify management of a strike in advance and to postpone any walkout for eighty days if it "affected an entire industry" or "imperiled the national health or safety." Taft-Hartley thus blunted labor's only really powerful weapon, the strike, and limited the control of union leaders over the rank and file. Truman vetoed the bill at once, arguing that it would "encourage distrust and suspicions and . . . threaten our democratic society." The next day, Congress overrode his veto. Republicans everywhere were elated: Taft-Hartley redeemed a major campaign promise, reversed the course of New Deal reform, and humiliated Truman. But labor unions pledged a struggle to repeal what they called "the slave labor law."

Congress and the President battled as well over inflation and tax policy. The GOP wanted to lower income taxes, maintaining that the money left in the private economy would go into investment and consumer spending. Twice during 1947 Congress passed bills reducing taxes by some twenty percent; Truman vetoed both of them. The President argued that a tax cut would aggravate inflation. Although most economists agreed with him, political pressures during the election year of 1948 enabled Congress to override Truman's veto of a third tax cut bill. The angry President noted that the reductions benefited the upper classes more than working people, and that Congress still had not acted on proposals for control of wages and prices. These immediate economic issues were rapidly becoming the stuff of an exciting presidential election.

Thomas E. Dewey, who some said looked like the man on a wedding cake, was heavily favored to defeat President Truman in the 1948 election. But Truman's whistle-stop campaign won the day. *(Courtesy, AP/Wide World Photos)*

The Election of 1948—the Republicans

Few observers gave the embattled President—or any Democrat, for that matter—much of a chance in the 1948 election. The Republican primary battles gradually narrowed to two men: Senator Taft and Governor Thomas E. Dewey of New York, the nominee in 1944. Though at ease with Taft's more conservative philosophy, most Republicans worried that the stilted oratory and unyielding views of the "somber senator" might needlessly risk GOP defeat. Dewey had been a successful governor of a large state, and still carried a certain glamour from his earlier role of racket-busting district attorney who had prosecuted Murder, Incorporated, an organized gang of assassins for hire. Dewey campaigned effectively, stressing a moderation that essentially embraced the New Deal while suggesting that few further reforms should be initiated. Sophisticated politicking quickly isolated Taft, who withdrew on the third ballot, making Dewey's nomination unanimous.

The GOP platform, influenced by the Berlin crisis which broke out during the convention, readily took up internationalist foreign policy, lauding "collective security against aggression." The party routinely took credit for the Taft-Hartley Act as "a sensible reform of the labor law," and promised more tax reductions and stronger civil rights legislation. The Republicans did not attack the New Deal, and even called for federally sponsored slum clearance and low-cost housing projects.

The Election of 1948—the Democrats

As the lure of victory unified Republicans on a strategy of moderation, Democrats were battling over ideology. While Henry Wallace pushed for conciliation with the Soviet Union, liberal Democrats who supported containment of the Communists gathered round the Americans for Democratic Action. Its leaders, particularly the mayor of Minneapolis, Hubert H. Humphrey, struggled to commit the party to civil rights. Southern Democrats protested this attack on local traditions and countered with a tough rejoinder: respect states' rights or risk destroying the party. A vicious battle over the platform broke out during the convention. The liberals won what would prove a historic victory: the platform pledged the party "to eradicate all racial, religious and economic discrimination." They also pushed through promises of federal aid to education, national health insurance, repeal of Taft-Hartley, and increases in the minimum wage and in social security coverage. The 1948 Democratic platform was an agenda for reform. The convention nominated Truman unanimously.

Other Political Parties Angered by the antisegregation platform, the Alabama and Mississippi delegations walked out of the convention and at a meeting in Birmingham several days later organized a States Rights Party. This convention, attended primarily by reactionary elements long familiar to the South, nominated for President the governor of South Carolina, James Strom Thurmond. A blunt platform declared opposition to any force that threatened to interfere with local "social custom," which meant, of course, white supremacy. Dixiecrat leaders controlled local election machinery in some states.

Meanwhile, Henry Wallace, running as the candidate of the newly formed Progressive Party, denounced containment and the Marshall Plan. The Communist organization in the United States officially endorsed Wallace during August.

The Whistle-Stop Campaign Few expected Truman to win except the President himself and his intimate political advisers. Ever a fighter, Truman called the Eightieth Congress back into session during late July, challenging the Republicans to enact their own platform. GOP congressmen at first vacillated and then blundered, when several senators proposed ending farm price supports as a means of reducing taxes. Throughout his grueling thirty-thousand mile whistle-stop campaign Truman laced into the "party of privilege" and "old mossbacks in a do-nothing Congress." He spoke plainly and directly just as he had when he wrote a famous letter denouncing a critic's review of one of his daughter's musical performances:

> I have just seen your lousy review of Margaret's concert. . . . It seems to me that you are a frustrated old man. . . . Some day I hope to meet you. When that happens you'll need a new nose, a lot of beefsteak for black eyes, and perhaps a supporter below.

From the platform of his train's rear car, Truman reminded his audience of his own country background; appealing to the working class and the farmers, he hammered at the theme that only the Democrats cared about ordinary Americans. Organized labor supported Truman vigorously, if only because of his veto of Taft-Hartley, and farmers everywhere recalled the "Hoover" Depression. To Roman Catholic audiences Truman spoke of his tough anti-Communist policies. He courted Jews by quickly recognizing the new state of Israel.

His own convictions, along with a desire to appeal to African-American voters in the coming presidential election of 1948, led President Truman to implement a federal civil rights program that for its time was the most comprehensive in United States history. Late in 1946 he had established the President's Committee on Civil Rights to study discrimination in the United States. The committee published its report—*To Secure These Rights*—in 1947, and Truman accepted

"Give-em-hell" Harry drew increasing criticism from Republicans and others, but for the most part their efforts to control Truman were ineffective. *(Courtesy, Library of Congress)*

its recommendations. He asked Congress in 1948 to establish a permanent federal civil rights commission, a permanent fair employment practices commission, a congressional committee on civil rights, and a civil rights division in the Justice Department. He also proposed a federal antilynching law and legislation prohibiting discrimination in interstate transportation and in voting rights.

The proposals were way ahead of their time and made little progress through a Congress in which southerners had considerable strength. But Truman moved ahead with his own civil rights program, using executive orders. In July 1948 the President prohibited discrimination in the hiring of federal employees, and later that year he established the President's Committee on Equality of Treatment and Opportunity in the Armed Services. As a result of its 1950 report entitled *Freedom to Serve,* Truman would largely desegregate the armed forces.

Dewey badly underestimated the sophistication of Truman's strategy, and polls predicted a Republican landslide. Early returns on election night seemed to confirm Dewey's anticipated victory. The New Yorker won the Northeast, except the Democratic bastions of Massachusetts and Rhode Island. The Dixiecrat Thurmond would almost surely capture South Carolina, Alabama, Mississippi, and Louisiana. The headline of the conservative Chicago *Tribune's* late edition read, "Dewey Sweeps Nation." At home in Independence, Missouri, Truman simply told his family not to worry and went to bed. As the President slept, ballot-counters recorded a startling trend. Not only did Truman win all the border South and Texas, but also, in the early morning, the rural vote in Ohio, Illinois, and Iowa put these states into the Truman column. Now the candidates were running even. Still, Dewey seemed a sure winner, for the Far West traditionally supported the GOP. Yet California and Washington went for Truman and gave him the election.

The Fair Deal, 1949–1952

New Reforms Now President in his own right, Truman left no one in doubt about his liberalism. His State of the Union message in January 1949 announced a sweeping agenda of domestic change: aid to education, national health insurance, a revised farm program, regional development projects, civil rights legislation, wider coverage for social security, public housing, a reorganization of the federal bureaucracy, and repeal of Taft-Hartley. Truman labeled this whopping list of social welfare proposals the Fair Deal. At the time prospects for its passage seemed good. A thriving economy disposed many Americans to help the unfortunate. And the Democrats had recaptured control of both houses of Congress.

Even before the outbreak of war in Korea some eighteen months later, however, the Fair Deal faltered. Truman, so skillful with voters, proved inept in his dealings with Capitol Hill, and special-interest groups sidetracked many specific reforms. Yet on some issues Truman enjoyed a clear popular support that overwhelmed his congressional opponents. New social security laws covered nearly eleven million more people, and doubled benefits to offset postwar inflation. The administration pushed through an increase in the minimum wage from 40 cents to 75 cents per hour. Desperate shortages prompted Congress to pass the National Housing Act of 1949, which subsidized slum clearance projects and built almost one million houses for low-income families. Legislators also granted Truman authority to streamline the federal bureaucracy. Following the recommendations of a commission headed by former President Herbert Hoover, Truman reduced the number of agencies and improved staff work.

The Nation at Mid-Century

By 1950, statistics told of prosperity. Gross national product nearly doubled between 1940 and 1950, to some $350 billion; real personal income increased by half; unemployment rarely reached five percent of the work force.

The distinctively American pace of innovation speeded up after the war. New industries such as plastics emerged in the Northeast, southern California, and in the Great Lakes region. Giant chemical corporations, spurred by government contracts during the war, prospered even more as synthetics created a rush of new consumer goods: plastics often replaced wood and metal; detergents and insecticides eased housework; drugs cured illness. The appliance and electronics industries in particular galvanized the postwar economy. Always entranced by gadgets, Americans welcomed air-conditioners, electric blankets, advanced gasoline-powered and electric lawn mowers, and automatic washing machines. Television sets, some three million by 1950, could unify the country instantly and at the same time persuade viewers to buy the fruits of technology. An infant computer industry promised a future of startling efficiency and frightening centralization. Rapid advances in aviation shrank the country.

The Suburbs The sense of place that had traditionally reassured Americans gave way to the restlessness that has also been a mark of American culture. Together, mobility and affluence created the suburb, that mode of living so characteristic of the postwar era. As early as 1947, some twenty miles outside New York City, a Long Island builder put up ten thousand homes, all identical except for their front doors. Each house in Levittown sold for $7500, including appliances and landscaping, well within the financial resources of most of the working middle class. Another Levittown rose near Philadelphia the next year, and by 1950 suburbs had exploded around major cities. The population pressures of a baby boom that had begun at the war's end quickened their growth. During the 1930s economic conditions had limited families, but now three or even more children seemed normal. Since many cities prolonged wartime rent controls, landlords refused to build new apartments. Federal tax benefits for homeowners and liberal mortgage terms for veterans soon turned meadowlands into suburbs.

The long rows of matchbox houses were more than shelters; they became a new way of life. Clustered together, Americans soon organized themselves into a bewildering variety of groups. Scout troops multiplied, and Little League baseball engaged children; local politics preoccupied many adults; church membership increased substantially; PTAs brought parents into school activities; small

Levittown, New York, 1949. After the war came the rise of the suburbs.

businessmen joined chambers of commerce; hobbyists gathered monthly or weekly; fraternal orders like the Elks and Masons spread rapidly. Soon enough, strip zoning created massive corridors of storefronts, drive-ins, and used-car lots. Critics spoke of the intellectual sterility of the homogeneous suburbs, their conformity, their materialism. Yet millions of workers were rescued from city tenements, while educational standards improved and entertainment appeared in unparalleled varieties. Some Americans hoped that the spread of suburbia and its values might soon erase poverty altogether as new industries hired more and more workers to produce more and more consumer goods. In fact, many suburbanites forgot about that other nation of urban blight, racial bigotry, organized crime, and regional poverty. More aware of taxes and their own local interests, they largely shunned progressive reforms and big government.

Spanish-Speaking Immigrants

By mid-century, when middle-class whites were settling into what was supposed to be a life of singular progress and contentment and a civil rights movement was soon to gather blacks, it was increasingly apparent that a population of Latin American people had become an integral part of the United States. By convention and convenience, citizens of this country who are Mexican in background are termed "Mexican American." It is an instance of the troublesome practice of using "American" to refer exclusively to citizens of the United States. Mexican citizens, Guatemalans, and the rest of the peoples south of the Rio Grande, being inhabitants of the American continent, speak of their homelands as American. But the awkwardness of "United States" as an adjective has dictated that for certain purposes "American" will designate the northern republic alone.

Mexican Americans

Mexicans have a longer history in the United States than many of the European groups that immigrated during the late nineteenth century. Citizens of Spain and then citizens of Mexico were the first Europeans to settle what is now the southwest United States. When the Treaty of Guadalupe Hidalgo was signed in 1848, the United States acquired the land of California, Arizona, New Mexico, Colorado, and parts of Utah and Nevada while at the same time annexing Texas. As many of the place names in California and the southwestern states bear out, there was already a significant Mexican presence in the Southwest by the time the first citizens of the United States arrived. With the coming of the Yankee transcontinental railroad after the Civil War, Mexican Americans ceased to live in isolation. Conflicts between Mexican Americans and "Anglos," as they referred to all whites in the United States, intensified while Anglo American numbers increased. Many Mexican Americans lost their land and mines and fell to second-class citizenship.

Violence was sharpest in Texas, particularly near the Mexican border. As the open range gradually became fenced, cattlemen clashed with sheepmen and farmers. Anglos often found legal means to invalidate land claims held by their Hispanic neighbors. American courts, presided over by Anglo American judges, usually awarded disputed land claims to those of their own ethnic kind. Mexican Americans resisted registering titles and paying taxes on lands their families had held for generations. In the more violent encounters, outlaws of both ethnic backgrounds attacked and retaliated for past wrongs. Besides feeding on a biased court system, violence had the support of Juan Cortina, a high Mexican official who had resolved to make Texans pay for their thefts. This made the Texas-Mexican border unsafe for decades after the Civil War.

In New Mexico, conditions were similar, but there was no Juan Cortina to generate border wars. Numbers of Mexican Americans lost their landholdings as the federal government invalidated their claims, appropriating some of their land for national forests, granting some to railroads, and opening still more to homesteaders. These actions forced many Mexican Americans either to move to more obscure places or to become laborers. A few Spanish aristocrats maintained their holdings and old customs while becoming sufficiently involved in New Mexican politics to deliver votes and thereby maintain bilingualism—the presence of both Spanish and English—in their laws and schools. When New Mexico became a state in 1912, its constitution guaranteed the equality of the Spanish and the English languages.

Although in California Mexican Americans succeeded in holding onto important political positions longer than their cousins did elsewhere, they too lost political and economic power. Their lands also fell to court interpretations of titles or to bankruptcies caused by the legal costs of defending those titles.

Between 1900 and 1930, the numbers of Mexican Americans in the United States increased from 100,000 to between one and 1.25 million. Many were pushed from Mexico by the revolution there; others came seeking jobs. Railroad construction in the Southwest, combined with the Chinese Exclusion Act of 1882, left openings for railroad crews. The railroad also expanded economic competition and opportunities. As the Colorado irrigation project poured water into the Southwest, fruit, vegetable, and cotton agriculture increased, and until 1930 about sixty percent of all Mexican Americans in the country were farm workers. Many moved north into the fruit valleys of Yakima and Wenatchee in Washington, while others went to the mills and packing plants of St. Louis and Washington.

As early as the 1920s, the largest number of immigrants were crossing the open border between the United States and Mexico illegally. They crossed the border illegally because they could not afford the head tax and visa or feared they would not pass the required literacy test in English for work in this country. Contracted haulers who avoided border patrols delivered many of them to crop growers, who preferred them because they worked for lower wages. Small growers especially became dependent on them as unions later formed. Life for the undocumenteds—or "wetbacks" as they came to be called in slang—has been particularly tenuous. They not only suffer private discrimination against "Mexes" and wetbacks but live in constant fear of local and immigration authorities and even of the schools and social services agencies. They have therefore been afraid of staying long in one place or becoming involved in local communities, on school boards or in public offices.

The demand for the labor of Mexican Americans increased during World War I: many of them enlisted in the armed forces. But Mexican Americans became much less welcome during the Great Depression. Other Americans, out of desperation, took the labor-intensive jobs in agriculture as well as the industrial jobs that the Mexican Americans had formerly held. New Deal jobs programs prohibited employment of noncitizens, which further threatened the income of the undocumenteds. The government deported half a million of them.

Those who remained in the United States continued to face the same kind of discrimination that blacks endured in such privately-

---

ABELARDO DELGADO, *born in Chihuahua, Mexico, emigrated to the United States in 1943. He was a leading figure in the Chicano political movement of the late 1960s and early 1970s. His poem "Stupid America" was published in 1969.*

Stupid america, see that chicano
with a big knife
in his steady hand
he doesn't want to knife you
he wants to sit on a bench
and carve christfigures
but you won't let him.
stupid america, hear that chicano
shouting curses on the street
he is a poet
without paper and pencil
and since he cannot write
he will explode.
stupid america, remember that chicanito
flunking math and english
he is the picasso
of your western states
but he will die
with one thousand masterpieces
hanging only from his mind.

---

owned businesses as restaurants and theaters and in public transportation and swimming pools. In the summer of 1943, riots broke out in Los Angeles—the "zoot suit" riots. The disturbances were provoked by American servicemen who prowled the streets looking for Mexican Americans dressed in the zoot-suit fad of the time—baggy pants, long coats, and wide-brimmed hats. The media characterized these young Mexican Americans as shiftless gangsters who were not giving their fair share to the war effort. The victims were arrested; their attackers were not.

During World War II, the demand for labor increased and again the United States encouraged Mexican labor. Between 1942 and 1947, the United States and Mexican governments arranged the *bracero* program, which recruited a quarter of a million field hands on annual contracts. The program lapsed for a year and then revived between 1948 and 1964, bringing 4.5 million Mexican citizens temporary employment here.

After 1945 undocumented immigrants came in greater numbers than before, probably outnumbering those entering legally as immigrants or under the *bracero* program. Deportation was stepped up in the early 1950s, as hostility to the foreign-born attended the Red-hunting of the era. Between 1950 and 1955 nearly four million left the country. Most of them were "persuaded" to leave; few were formally deported under legal due process. Congress in the 1980s adopted stiff penalties for those who hired illegal aliens and gave amnesty to some who had been in the country for a specified period.

Puerto Ricans

Since 1917 Puerto Ricans have been citizens of the United States. But since the culture of Puerto Rico is substantially different from that of the mainland, their migration more closely resembles that of earlier European immigrants. When, as a result of the Spanish-American War, Puerto Rico was ceded to the United States, a slow movement to the mainland began. After World War II, the economic boom on the mainland attracted unskilled and semiskilled workers from the island, where unemployment was high and wages low. Between 1940 and 1950 the Puerto Rican population on the mainland of the United States quadrupled to 301,000. Throughout the 1950s, recruiters went to the island seeking workers for industries, often sweatshops. Communities began to grow in Pennsylvania, Illinois, New Jersey, Connecticut, and New York.

Several influences have pulled Puerto Ricans to the continental United States. Improved medical services at home brought down the death rate while the birthrate continued high. Population was increasing rapidly in an economy based on the seasonal production of sugar, tobacco, and coffee, all of which left the majority of workers unemployed for a great part of the year. Transportation has also been an important factor in migration to the mainland. Before World War II, the journey was expensive and unpleasant. After the war, commercial air travel enabled individuals to fly between the island and the states for relatively modest sums.

Cubans

Few Cubans lived in the United States when the island nation, ninety miles off Florida's coast, became separate from Spain in 1898. While Cuba gained technical independence, the United States was to dominate it politically and economically. Yet this did not lead to a great movement of Cubans to the mainland. The island was able to employ most of its population in urban areas, mining, or the large sugar industry.

After World War II the number of Cuban immigrants began to increase greatly. In the decade from 1951 to 1960 almost 79,000 Cubans came to the United States mostly through Miami or New York City. An unsteady political situation impelled these Cubans to seek a new home. The corrupt Batista government was challenged during this decade and finally overthrown by a new dictator, Fidel Castro, and his followers in 1959. What began in that year as a trickle of Cuban refugees, mostly strong Batista supporters such as police and army officials, was by the middle of 1962 a flood. Between 1961 and 1970 some 208,000 Cubans left their homeland to seek refuge in the United States.

The United States and East Asia, 1945–1953

Reconstructing Japan Denied raw materials and geared almost exclusively for military production, the Japanese economy collapsed in late 1945. Catastrophic defeat in war disgraced the governing military clique that had long ruled the country. Americans moved swiftly, methodically, to crush the old elite. Democratic ideals and capitalist profits must replace feudal values and Japan's monopoly industry. Although authority after the surrender was nominally in the hands of a four-power commission, it was General Douglas MacArthur, commander of the only Allied armed forces in the region, who made all decisions. Ruling almost without restraint for several years, MacArthur reformed the educational system, rewrote the Japanese constitution, broke up the great cartels, and encouraged trade unions and a two-party political system. The Japanese, realizing the totality of their defeat and ready to abandon the past, eagerly accepted these changes. Western styles swept the nation; businesses welcomed American methods and investment; and citizens enjoyed a civil liberty and social mobility that traditional Japan would never have provided.

The Fall of China, 1945–1949 Control of the Pacific, the ambition of many Presidents, was supposed to be in the late 1940s a preliminary to keeping China in the American camp. The Chinese revolution, begun in 1911 by intellectuals and urban leftists, entered its last stages after World War II. During the interwar period traditionalists, led by Chiang Kai-shek, had maintained control over most of China, warding off the Communist challenge. Largely suspending their civil war during the war against Japan, the adversaries after 1945 entered their final struggle. Chiang and his Nationalist regime relied upon military and financial aid from the United States, while the Communists took comfort in Marxist predictions of inevitable triumph.

Chiang's ramshackle, corrupt regime alienated both peasants and urban workers. Persistent inflation convulsed the economy. Mao Zedong's Communist guerrilla armies rooted themselves deep in the village structure of rural China, where Communist promises of peace and land won many converts. The Soviet Union had withdrawn from Manchuria, the industrial heartland of mainland East Asia, in such a way that Mao fell heir to Japanese positions and agreements there. With sophisticated propaganda and a dedicated, well-trained fighting force, the Communists slowly penetrated southward. Truman and most Asian experts in the State Department believed that Mao and his Communists would probably win any prolonged conflict.

The United States, Truman decided, must mediate. In late 1945, he sent Army Chief of Staff George C. Marshall, recently retired, to secure a ceasefire. Promises of vast reconstruction aid, it was thought, could persuade the two sides to join in a coalition regime. Marshall arranged a truce that winter but in the spring, when military operations could resume, both sides broke the agreement. Discouraged, Marshall was recalled to the United States at the end of 1946. Truman was by that time preoccupied by events in Europe, but several months later he sent to China another general, Albert C. Wedemeyer. Only far-reaching administrative reforms, Wedemeyer reported, could end the corruption that so alienated the Chinese people. Yet the nationalists rejected all of Wedemeyer's suggestions. Like Marshall before him, Wedemeyer told Truman that only direct military intervention, perhaps millions of American soldiers, could rescue the Nationalist cause. Largely because of propaganda by the "China Lobby"—a collection of anti-Communist conservatives in Congress and industry—Truman did continue to send money and equipment to Chiang. But after 1947 Washington concentrated upon containing Communism in Europe. No one was ready for a war in Asia.

Less than two years later, newspapers across America trumpeted the "fall" of China. Mao captured Peking in 1948 and crossed the Yangtze River early in 1949. Chiang's armies disintegrated, many of the troops surrendering without a fight or simply melting away into the countryside. The mainland became the People's Republic of China—or "Red China," as Americans nicknamed it. Chiang set up an exile regime on the island of Taiwan off the shores of China, vowing to return someday to the mainland. The "fall" of China shocked Americans. The very word "fall" implied loss, defeat. Who

Mao Zedong and Chiang Kai-shek in happier times. *(Courtesy, United Press International)*

was to blame? The China Lobby vitriolically denounced the President and called for "a holy crusade against godless Communism in the Far East." Senator Taft even attacked some experts in the State Department as "pro-Communist." Dean Acheson, who had succeeded the ailing Marshall as secretary of state in 1949, outraged such critics with his suggestion that the United States recognize the new regime. "We are all on the same planet," he declared, "and must do business with each other." Many Americans, inexperienced in the complexities of foreign affairs, looked for scapegoats—a search that quickly degenerated into a quest for "subversives" within the United States. Conservatives, having lagged behind liberals in committing the country to military and economic confrontation of Communism, were rushing ahead in verbal anti-Communism.

National Security Council Paper Number 68

The Truman Administration in the spring of 1950 finally put together a new blueprint for Cold War strategy. National Security Council Paper No. 68 claimed that the Communists were aiming at world domination. They were seeking to achieve their goal, the paper argued, by a process of gradual, step-by-step conquest. It followed that American national security could be preserved only through maintenance of the global status quo, and so the United States was now obliged to patrol the world. This new mission, in turn, required a huge increase in military force. Rearmament must proceed regardless of cost, even if it consumed as much as a fifth of the nation's production. The Democrats also realized that NSC 68, whether its assumptions were sensible or not, was good politics: its hard line offset Republican criticism, and the heavy defense it called for stimulated the economy.

In response to the ending of its atomic monopoly and to the Communist victory in China, the United States determined to confront Communism in any form, Soviet, Chinese, or local at any point on the globe where it threatened to expand. That there might come to be not one Communism but many scarcely occurred to Americans. It had occurred to the State Department, which for a time wanted to pull Mao away from the Soviet Union and into a friendship with the United States. But a militant anti-Communism that owed as much to a reflexive American antagonism to radicalism as to the growth of Communist power abroad discounted the possibility.

Yet even the implacable anti-Communism of Truman, Secretary of State Dean Acheson, and the liberals in general was not enough for emerging militant conservatives. The policy of containment, they complained, was a cowardly acceptance of the existence of Communism in the regions it already controlled. American policy must commit itself to the destruction of Communism on every square foot of the globe. For this policy conservatives had few specific suggestions. And they did not seriously entertain the idea of crashing American troops through the Iron Curtain in a war of global liberation. What they really wanted was ideological spotlessness: a rejection of friendship with even non-Communist regimes on the left, a national renunciation of the welfare state, which some conservatives perceived as Communism itself in a pale form.

A World War II veteran was hurt in 1949 in what was coming to be a crusade for superpatriotism:

> During the war I was wounded. When I came back, I worked for the Veterans Administration in New Jersey. It was about a year and a half later when the attorney general, Tom Clark, issued a list of organizations that were supposed to be "subversive." These were organizations that, according to him, advocated the overthrow of the government by unconstitutional, violent means. . . .
>
> I received a letter from the Veterans Administration saying that because of my membership in the Socialist Workers Party, my employment was to be terminated. The notice that I was to be fired stunned me more than anything I experienced during the war. As jobs go, I guess mine was nothing to brag about, routine, even dull. . . . The thing that made it ridiculous was that I had no access to any kind of confidential information that could in any way benefit the enemies of this country.

The Korean War, 1950–1953

In early January 1950, Secretary of State Acheson spoke of America's "defense perimeter," those areas the United States considered vital to its own security. Attacks against Alaska, Japan, the Ryukyu Islands, or the Philippines, he explained, would mean instant retaliation. The secretary of state pointedly excluded from this umbrella of protection two former Japanese holdings on the Asian mainland, Korea and French Indochina (Vietnam, Cambodia, and Laos). Both countries seemed likely to follow China's example: populist coalitions, calling for reform and backed by outside Communist powers, were challenging local dictators financed and armed by the United States. French soldiers had already fought unavailingly for four years against a guerrilla rebellion in Indochina led by Ho Chi Minh. Korea, too, had disappointed leaders in Washington. By late 1948 the United States was supporting a pro-Western regime under a reactionary President, Syngman Rhee, while the U.S.S.R. countered by establishing a Communist government in the North. Although the Americans and then the Soviet Union withdrew their troops, skirmishes broke out constantly along the 38th parallel, the dividing line between the two Korean states. Both North and South dreamed of a reunited country, and civil war seemed likely at any time.

North Korea Invades the South

North Korea now boldly asked for Soviet aid in a war of liberation against the South. Stalin apparently calculated that the United States would not fight to rescue Rhee, so he encouraged the North Koreans, shipping them arms and food. Soviet advisers trained a sophisticated ground force of ten divisions, one motorized. On June 25, 1950, these troops attacked along a broad front. Truman quickly implemented NSC 68, telling the American people that "to conquer independent nations, Communism has now resorted to armed invasion and war." He responded along a wide front. The Seventh Fleet steamed toward Taiwan to protect it from possible Communist Chinese attack. American money and military equipment flooded into Indochina to help the French preserve their colonial authority there. And in Korea itself, an American army landed to repulse the North Korean invaders. Congress passed huge appropriations not only for the war in Korea but also for massive rearmament. This determined, wide-ranging response caught Stalin off guard: the Soviet Union was boycotting Security Council sessions when Truman pushed a resolution through the United Nations calling for joint action to punish "unprovoked aggression in Korea." In the three years of fighting that fol-

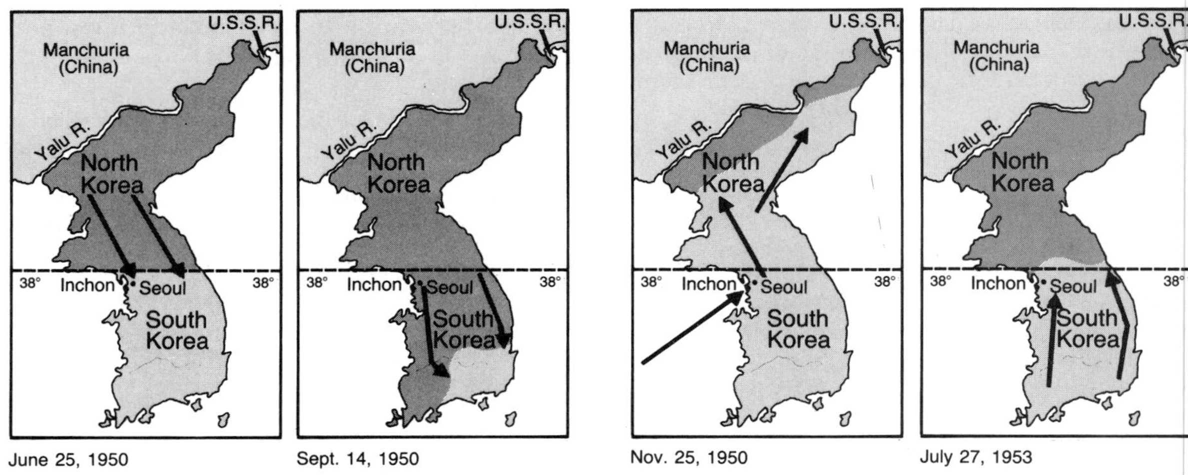

Military advances and stalemate in the Korean War, June 1950 to July 1953.

lowed, a United Nations force, composed mostly of South Korean and American troops but supplemented by contingents from many other nations, would conduct this largest venture in international peacekeeping that the UN was ever to undertake.

Counterattack and Stalemate The military situation in Korea at first looked bleak. The North Koreans rapidly pushed southward, overwhelming Rhee's ill-trained troops. Although GIs from Japan quickly joined in defense of the South, the North Koreans had conquered most of the peninsula by mid-August, trapping the United States Eighth Army in a 140-mile semicircle around Pusan. On September 15 General Douglas MacArthur launched a brilliant amphibious assault at Inchon, a port well behind enemy lines. Meanwhile, the newly supplied Eighth Army, commanded by General Matthew Ridgway, punched its way out of the Pusan perimeter. By early October, American forces had cleared all South Korea of Communist troops.

This rapid success elated Truman, who now, however, overreached himself. Once again turning to the United Nations, the President received approval for "steps to insure stability throughout Korea"—that is, to destroy the North Korean regime altogether. American armies rushed northward. "All resistance," MacArthur told Truman at a meeting on Wake Island on October 14, "will end by Thanksgiving."

This time the general's calculation proved disastrous. North Korea bordered China's industrial heartland, Manchuria. For weeks Chinese Premier Chou En-lai had been warning the West that his people would not "supinely tolerate seeing their neighbors invaded by imperialists." Still the American troops drove forward. Then, on October 26, Chinese troops were discovered across the Yalu River and in November they attacked MacArthur's widely scattered armies. The Communists skillfully retook much lost territory, until the Eighth Army in January 1951 finally stopped their advance at a rough line that divided the two Koreas into much the same territories that the 38th parallel had done. Here the front stabilized and the war became a stalemate, although hard fighting continued for many months over the rocky terrain.

Medics struggled with the cold:

> Everything was frozen. Plasma froze and the bottles broke. We couldn't use plasma because it wouldn't go into solution and the tubes would clog up with particles. We couldn't change dressings because we had to work with gloves on to keep our hands from freezing.
>
> We couldn't cut a man's clothes off to get a wound because he would freeze to death. Actually, a man was often better off if we left him alone.

An incident in Korea suggests many in the Vietnam War:

> There was the crack of carbines, a burst or two of automatic fire, somewhere away to the right, and a peasant woman crumpled into the ditch by the roadside with her two babes crawling upon her. . . . One babe sat on her belly, small hands

reaching up to her face, stroking, pulling at her lips, growing frantic, inconsolable, its screams agonizing, as it knew, as it tried to suckle the warm still heavy breasts, to wake the dead. The other child sat in a kind of torpor of dejection at his dead mother's feet.

Someone tried to divert the young child with an apple. Nothing could stem this infant grief. It smote us all down, reminding us of the unforgettable meaning of war. A medical truck had been ordered up, and a corporal took the children in his arms to the beginning of their orphan lives, and the woman was alone in the ditch.

MacArthur Oversteps His Authority Driven to destroy what he called "an alien, despised Communism," MacArthur wanted to bring all possible force to bear against Chinese troops in Korea: bombing the bridges across the Yalu, opening a second front with Nationalist troops from Taiwan—even, if necessary, using atomic weapons. If this brought war with China, so much the better. MacArthur began urging this course in the face of the administration's own policy.

On April 11, 1951, Truman relieved MacArthur of his command for what appeared to be a determination to change the government's strategy. The immediate issue was clear: "If I allowed him to defy the civil authority," Truman said, "I myself would be violating my oath to uphold and defend the Constitution." Many citizens, including generals in the Pentagon, agreed that MacArthur had overstepped the line that for long had preserved American politics from interference by the military. But some Republican politicians raised a larger issue; they used MacArthur as a foil to attack the whole notion of containment. Congressional hearings, televised across the nation, broadcast their aim: the destruction of Communism in the Far East.

"A wider conflict in Korea," General Omar Bradley told a Senate committee, "would involve us in the wrong war, at the wrong place, at the wrong time, and with the wrong enemy." MacArthur enjoyed a hero's welcome at first, but the excitement of his homecoming soon diminished. Although the old soldier himself faded away, the larger issue raised by the Truman-MacArthur controversy remained: should America merely contain its adversaries or go farther to liberate those "captive nations," as Senator Taft melodramatically phrased it, "struggling under the yoke of Communist tyranny."

A Second Red Scare

After 1945 Americans never recaptured the sense of normality that had followed World War I in the 1920s. Strategic security evaporated in a nuclear age. Oceans no longer isolated the New World from troubles in Asia and Europe. Mao Zedong's victory in China, the news of Soviet nuclear weaponry, and the frustrations of limited war in Korea all provoked dread. Many Americans simply could not understand how a nation endowed in 1945 with a mighty army, navy, and air force and a fully operating industrial plant amid a world in ruins could, in such a short space of time, find itself facing such threats and feeling so insecure. Surely something must be wrong; sinister and mysterious forces inside the country must have subverted the easy security that was an American birthright. Mickey Spillane has his hard-boiled detective hero Mike Hammer say in 1951 in *One Lonely Night*, which sold three million copies:

I killed more people today than I have fingers on my hands. I shot them in cold blood and enjoyed every minute of it. . . . They were commies . . . red sons-of-bitches who should have died long ago. . . . They never thought that there were people like me in this country. They figured us all to be soft as horse manure and just as stupid.

The House Un-American Activities Committee This second Red Scare—the first had been just after World War I—began slowly. Early in 1947, Truman set up regional loyalty boards to unmask "radicals" within the sprawling federal bureaucracy. Over the next six years, however, only 384 alleged "security risk" employees were dismissed, most of them homosexuals. The House Un-American Activities Committee (HUAC) grilled suspected Communists about their presumed efforts to infiltrate American society. Trade unions, colleges, and the Hollywood movie

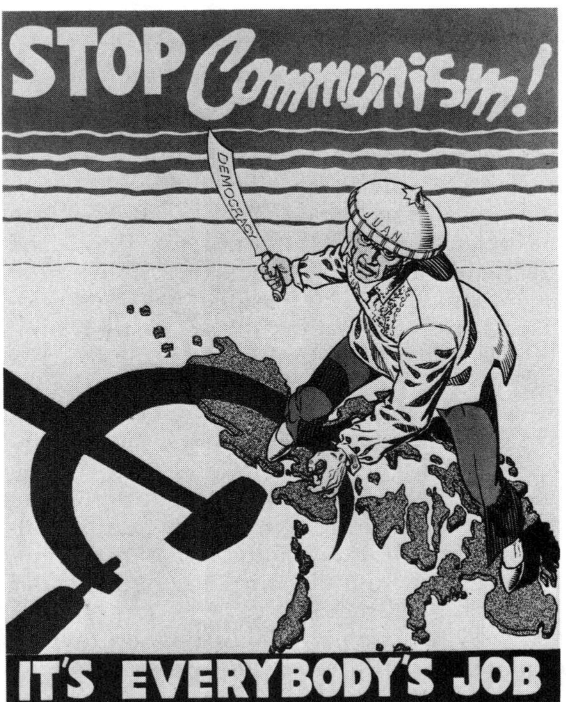

Stop Communism in the Philippines. A U.S. government poster. *(Courtesy, Library of Congress)*

industry were all thought to be jammed with Communists and "fellow travelers," a popular term for anyone who seemed to be in any degree of collaboration with Communists. Truman's attorney general warned that American Reds "are everywhere—in factories, offices, butcher stores, on street corners."

Private citizens and organizations also engaged in the Red Scare. Entertainment moguls blacklisted performers accused of holding unpopular opinions; anti-labor politicians called for tighter regulation of unions. Red-hunters looked for political dissenters among college teachers. Truman lambasted "subversives" during his 1948 presidential campaign. *Marvel Comics* warned: "Beware, commies, spies, traitors, and foreign agents—Captain America is looking for you yellow scum." A gumball machine in Wheeling, West Virginia, was quickly impounded when it was found to dispense geography lessons under the hammer-and-sickle Soviet flag, reading: "U.S.S.R. population 211,000,000. Capital Moscow. Largest country in the world."

The American Legion Reader warned of "slick tricks of the Commies":

> Got commie trouble in your organization? Here's how they operate . . . to seize power and frustrate Americans from running their own groups.
>
> As the Reds in any meeting seldom exceed 7 or 8 per cent of those present, the problem of exerting maximum parliamentary pressure with such slender forces is solved through use of the 'Diamond' seating scheme, a most effective Communist device. An anti-Communist union member arises to denounce the Reds. Or he criticizes Russia. Instantly the 'Fraction' members surrounding him jump up, angrily denouncing him as a 'Red-baiter'. . . . If the chairman is a Red stooge or a weak character, the wolfpack will collectively torpedo the 'Red-baiter.'

The Hiss Case In the midst of the frenzy, a sensational testimony provided some limited evidence of a Soviet espionage network. Whittaker Chambers, a senior editor of *Time* magazine, told of his membership in the Communist Party for many years before the war. He named seven people who might be still active in the Soviet underground. One of the accused, Alger Hiss, then president of the prestigious Carnegie Institution for International Peace and a former official in the State Department, denied the charge. While under oath, he said, "I have never been a member of the Communist party. . . . I have never laid eyes on Chambers." Hiss then sued Chambers for libel. But the former Communist produced evidence that lent credence to his charge that Hiss had given him copies of secret government documents during the 1930s. Chambers claimed to have microfilms of these papers composed on Hiss's typewriter hidden in a pumpkin on his farm in Maryland, and he dramatically revealed them to a startled court. This disclosure prompted a federal grand jury to indict Hiss for perjured testimony before a congressional committee. Hiss was convicted, and he went to jail. The evidence for Hiss's guilt was overwhelming.

Before the eighteen-month furor about Hiss died down, British agents arrested Klaus Fuchs, a physicist who had evidently supplied the Soviet Union with information about Anglo American atomic research during the war. Many blamed Fuchs's treachery for the Soviet Union's unexpectedly rapid development of nuclear power. During his

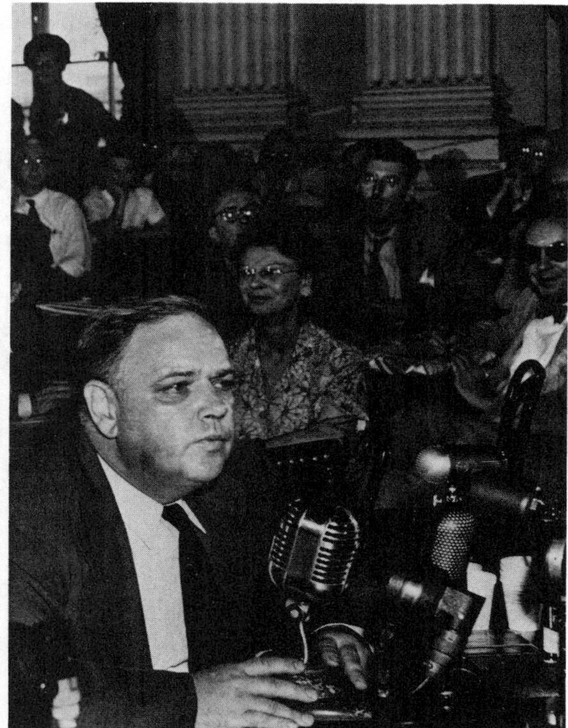

Whittaker Chambers testifying against Alger Hiss before the House Un-American Activities Committee, August, 1948. *(Courtesy, United Press International)*

trial, he implicated several Americans, including Julius and Ethel Rosenberg, two members of the New York City Communist Party. Ethel's brother, David Greenglass, who had been an army sergeant at Los Alamos, had supposedly turned over detailed diagrams of America's first atomic bomb to the Rosenbergs, who in turn, Greenglass charged, had given them to the Soviet consul in New York City. The Rosenbergs made moving declarations of their innocence, but after a sensational trial both were sentenced to die.

Whatever the actual degree of Soviet infiltration, the reaction of many people was out of proportion. "How much more are we going to take?" orated Homer Capehart, a conservative Republican senator. "Fuchs and Hiss and hydrogen bombs threatening outside and New Dealism eating away at the vitals of the nation. In the name of Heaven, is this the best America can do?" Jack Warner of Warner Brothers Studios wrote:

> Ideological termites have burrowed into many American industries, organizations, and societies. Wherever they may be, I say let us dig them out and get rid of them. My brothers and I will be happy to subscribe generously to a pest-removal fund. We are willing to establish such a fund to ship to Russia the people who don't like our American system of government and prefer the communistic system to ours.

Senator Joseph R. McCarthy

Into the frenzy strode a bizarre figure from the Midwest: Senator Joseph McCarthy of Wisconsin. A crude bully, McCarthy had scored upset victories for local and national office with campaigns of innuendo against his opponents. As a senator, he had not distinguished himself. But on February 8, 1950, he addressed a meeting of the Republican Women's Club in Wheeling, West Virginia. Waving a piece of paper, he charged that some 279 subversives had "thoroughly infested" the State Department. "The reason we find ourselves in a position of impotency," he explained to his receptive audience, "is because of traitorous actions by those who have been treated so well by this nation." McCarthy expanded on this theme throughout the spring and summer of 1950, accusing both high officials and simple clerks of Communist sympathies. He never proved any of these "documented cases." Culling old, mostly outdated information about Soviet spy rings, some of it from discredited sources, McCarthy relied upon his gifts of rhetorical embellishment.

During the next four years, the junior senator from Wisconsin verbally abused Presidents, the much-respected George C. Marshall, and many skilled experts in government service. Charge followed charge so fast and in a voice so tight with conviction, so mesmerized by its own message, that critics hardly knew how to begin to respond. Richard Rovere, a reporter for *The New Yorker,* dismissed McCarthy as "a pool room politician grandly seized with an urge to glory." Many others, including intellectuals like Daniel Boorstin and politicians like Senator Robert Taft, endorsed McCarthy. He condemned the Democrats for "twenty years of treason," and many Americans believed him. How else, they wondered, could Communism have triumphed in eastern Europe and China? GOP conservatives especially lauded McCarthy's cause, and various Republican newcomers won major elections by smearing opponents with the charge that they were soft on Communism. Richard Nixon destroyed the reputation of his opponent, Helen Gahagan Douglas, during the 1950 race for the Senate in California by permitting underlings to refer to "the pink lady." (Her lieutenants in turn labeled him a fascist and an anti-Semite.) McCarthy himself mercilessly attacked Senator Millard Tydings of Maryland, an early foe of Red-baiting, and was probably responsible for Tydings's defeat. More and more, McCarthy's critics silenced themselves.

Sensationalist newspapers played up the senator's cause; he was, after all, good copy, and publishers learned that publicity insured protection from his vitriolic attacks. In reality McCarthy never commanded quite the mass following that he seemed to have. His main supporters were conservative Republicans. And in 1954, after he claimed that the army "coddled" Communists, he lost support and earned the censure of the Senate. His heavy drinking had made him reckless, and he died of liver disease in 1957.

The Election of 1952

The Democrats' Liabilities

By 1952 the country seemed stagnant, mired in limited war in Korea and, many thought, betrayed by subversives at home. Then political corruption darkened the shadows of mistrust. A Senate subcommittee unearthed evidence that a presidential aide, Harry Vaughan, had influenced the awarding of government contracts, directing business to several friends. In gratitude, one of them had sent him a freezer, then a glamorous new appliance, worth $500. Some other bureaucrats, the Senate committee discovered, charged a flat five percent fee for favorable action. Truman, never personally involved in any of these scandals, vigorously prosecuted the wrongdoers, firing his attorney general. Corruption also surfaced in the cities, where organized crime prospered under the official blindness of politicians. An investigating committee headed by Democratic Senator Estes Kefauver of Tennessee exposed widespread prostitution, illegal gambling, and shakedown rackets. Television beamed the dramatic testimony of underworld figures like Frank Costello—who endlessly "took the Fifth" (Amendment) while nervously tapping his fingers—to a nation both fascinated and repelled by real-life gangsters.

The issues of Korea, Communism, and corruption all afflicted the country. Truman's popularity rating plunged to less than thirty percent.

Many midwestern Republicans again vigorously supported the candidacy of the conservative Robert Taft. But Republicans from urban states along the East Coast worried that Taft's outspoken hostility to New Deal reforms and his anti-labor reputation might alienate millions of voters. They persuaded General Dwight D. Eisenhower to resign his command of NATO forces in Europe and enter the race.

General Dwight Eisenhower

Born in Texas and reared in the modest surroundings of Abilene, Kansas, Dwight D. Eisenhower was a product of the American frontier town. The young Eisenhower had secured entrance to West Point and, despite a mediocre academic record, distinguished himself in campus leadership. At Command and General Staff School in Fort Leavenworth, Kansas, he graduated first in his class after a year's study in 1925-26. As a soldier, Eisenhower did not affect the bluff arrogance and the disdain for civilian direction that can go with the military temperament. Eisenhower's military and strategic skill was demonstrated during the Second World War by his conduct during the 1942 North African invasion and later when he was supreme commander of Allied forces in Europe.

After the war, Eisenhower served as Army Chief of Staff and then as President of Columbia University. There he instituted the American Assembly, a forum for discussion of major national problems, and, as he would recollect with some pride, an academic "Chair of Peace." Late in 1950 President Truman appointed him military commander of NATO.

The general at first resisted those who urged him to enter the race for the presi-

Ike and Mamie Eisenhower at the Republican Convention, 1952. *(Courtesy, Scribner's Archives)*

dency. He believed that a military man was unsuited for national politics. Ultimately, Eisenhower's decision in 1952 to resign his post of NATO commander and seek the presidency—so his *Memoirs* assert—came from a fear that the foreign policy commitments of Senator Robert A. Taft of Ohio might otherwise prevail. Taft, still holding to the isolationism that many conservative Republicans had argued for a few years earlier, denied that America had a duty to extend its institutions abroad. The delegates nominated the easygoing and politically promising "Ike." For Vice President the Republicans chose Richard M. Nixon, whose success in prosecuting Alger Hiss had won him national fame.

Adlai Stevenson The Democrats settled on a presidential candidate at least as cerebral as Taft: Governor Adlai E. Stevenson of Illinois. As governor he had increased funds for schools and roads, wiped out downstate gambling operations, and modernized the state bureaucracy. The 1952 campaign sparkled with Stevenson's cultivated, witty speeches that he wrote himself. But though the governor campaigned hard, he could not hope to overcome Eisenhower's popularity.

Stevenson actually had wanted Eisenhower to win the Republican nomination, fearing the effect of Taft's foreign policy ideas on the Western alliance. For Stevenson, like Eisenhower, represented an internationalist position that the Truman Administration had itself sustained. That internationalism was in part a benign acceptance of the nation's responsibility to enter the world community. But even in the language of the mild and hesitant Stevenson it could ring with what today sounds like an archaic belligerence. Speaking standard foreign policy to a Kansas audience, for example, Stevenson explained that we were fighting in Korea "so we wouldn't have to fight in Wichita"; Korea was "a crucial test in the struggle between the free world and Communism."

Eisenhower worked to heal wounds in the Republican Party. He welcomed Taft to a breakfast at Morningside Heights, Columbia University, after which they agreed on the essentials of domestic policy. Easily projecting his folksy style across the land, the general spent more time campaigning in the South than had any previous Republican candidate. And he deleted from an important speech a remark criticizing Senator Joe McCarthy; Eisenhower did little to support his old boss, General Marshall, against his attacks. A storm broke when the *New York Post* charged Senator Nixon with accepting money from friendly businessmen for personal expenses. Nixon rebutted the claim—Stevenson had a similar fund to supplement the salaries of public officials—and in a highly sentimental and effective speech demonstrated a command of television politics. Both major candidates seemed ready to accept the accomplishments of the New and Fair Deals, though neither was anxious to promote civil rights in the spirit of the 1948 Democratic Convention.

The results on election day shocked no one. After October 24, when Eisenhower promised that if he won he would "go to Korea," the polls showed his margin to be widening. On November 7 Eisenhower won fifty-five percent of the popular vote, and even carried the southern states of Virginia, Florida, and Texas. He received a majority vote from all income groups and drew unexpected support from normally Democratic Roman Catholics. What Eisenhower offered in the 1952 campaign, and would achieve in the first term of his presidency, was something the country needed rather desperately: an easing of tensions after the hectic recriminations of the Truman years.

Soon after the new President took office, a time of political calm began with the Korean armistice in midsummer 1953 and the Senate censure of McCarthy for his increasingly outrageous charges in 1954. So confidently stable did the national temper become, under the tranquil leadership of this most unbelligerent statesman, that the name of Eisenhower is remembered as defining an era. Eisenhower continued most of the policies of economic regulation, social welfare, and internationalism associated with his Democratic predecessors. He did more. By removing these policies from partisan debate, first in the campaign and then later in relations with congressional Democrats (who often supported him more strongly than did his own party), Eisenhower the Republican made of internationalism and the Democratic New Deal a permanent part of the national consensus.

Points To Think About

1. Postwar American foreign policy was based on a doctrine known as "containment." Truman and his successors determined to hold back the Soviet Union, and then Communist China, by preventing Communist "aggression" no matter where it broke out. This policy rested upon a number of assumptions that ultimately proved to be incorrect.

One was that all Marxist-oriented movements were part of an international Communist conspiracy directed from Moscow. This seriously overestimated the ability of the Soviet Union to control events beyond its borders, and seriously underestimated the importance of nationalism in the so-called "Third World." The United States never understood that figures like Ho Chi Minh were as opposed to Russian control as they were to American control.

The nation also assumed that it actually had the economic and political resources to shape the direction of change all over the world. Truman, Eisenhower, Kennedy, and Johnson all had a fatal willingness to extend American commitments beyond the country's real power to honor them. Vietnam proved the point.

2. Historians generally agree that the New Deal really came to an end by the middle of Franklin Roosevelt's second term. By then the administration had run out of fresh ideas for coping with the Depression. By then too the court-packing fight had seriously weakened FDR's influence over Congress. Conservative Democrats and Republicans formed a coalition that effectively blocked further reform.

Yet in several important ways the New Deal did not end. Specific programs, like the WPA, were abandoned, but the responsibility of the federal government to take an active role in solving the nation's problems was firmly established. Succeeding administrations, including Republican administrations, were forced to honor this commitment. And the spirit of the New Deal continued to provide the ruling ethos of the Democratic Party.

President Truman's Fair Deal was designed to extend the New Deal. John Kennedy spoke of a "New Frontier" and the "new generation of Americans" his administration had brought to power. But much of their agenda consisted of items Roosevelt and Truman had first proposed. The Alliance for Progress, for example, was a clear elaboration of FDR's Good Neighbor Policy. And Kennedy's manpower training programs drew elements from old New Deal programs like the Civilian Conservation Corps and the Works Progress Administration. Lyndon Johnson, although he invoked the Kennedy name, made it clear that his Great Society was inspired by the New Deal. The Economic Opportunity Act that launched the "war on poverty" represented the high point of New Deal liberalism in American politics.

The New Deal, in other words, provided the framework in which American politicians debated the issues of the day. And Franklin Roosevelt dominated the imagination not only of his own but of succeeding generations. One measure of this dominance is the laudatory references to FDR in Ronald Reagan's campaign speeches in 1980. Even conservative Republicans have learned to praise Roosevelt, just as Democrats of an earlier day had to learn to praise Abraham Lincoln.

3. The First World War was followed by a period of intensive domestic reaction known as the Red Scare. The years after World War II had an even more intense and long-lasting witch hunt. This second Red Scare is usually named after the most flamboyant and irresponsible Red-baiter, Senator Joseph McCarthy. McCarthy blamed every reverse suffered by the United States on a "Red Menace" boring from within the American power structure.

There were some Communist agents in the government, although never as many as claimed by McCarthy or the House Un-American Activities Committee. The key to McCarthy's career is that he was less interested in catching actual spies or traitors than in making charges. McCarthy, in fact, took particular joy in claiming to find Communists in high places like the State Department. McCarthy actually tried to do what he charged the Communists with intending—tear down the American power structure. He finally overreached himself when he decided to hunt for Reds in the Army. General Eisenhower was not about to sit still for that, and he and the Democratic leader in the Senate, Lyndon Johnson, quietly worked together to engineer McCarthy's censure by the Senate.

4. If Richard Nixon's career began spectacularly, it almost ended in scandal during the 1952 campaign. At issue was a fund allegedly set up for Nixon's personal use out of campaign contributions. Eisenhower, who apparently had little love for Nixon anyway, was seriously considering dumping him. Nixon's last chance to save his spot on the ticket—and his career—was a television speech to the nation. This was the famous "Checkers" speech.

Nixon claimed total innocence. He spoke of his hard-working father, his saintly mother, his own record of working for everything he had. He spoke movingly of his wife's Republican cloth coats, implying that the absence of furs proved his integrity. Finally, Nixon, near tears, did admit that he had accepted a personal gift from a political supporter. It was a puppy, the famous Checkers. He would not give the dog back, he said: his two young daughters loved Checkers. There was not a dry eye in the house. Of such hokum is politics sometimes made. And Nixon saved his career, only to destroy it in far more spectacular fashion twenty years later.

Suggested Readings

Books published lately on this period include Michael J. Hogan, *The Marshall Plan* (1987), Burton Kaufman, *The Korean War* (1986), Robert James Maddox, *From War to Cold War: The Education of Harry S Truman* (1988), William E. Pemb, *Harry S. Truman* (1989), Kenneth T. Jackson, *Crabgrass Frontier: The Suburbanization of the United States* (1985), and M. J. Heale, *American Anti-Communism: Combatting the Enemy Within, 1830–1970* (1990).

Alonzo Hamby gives a rather favorable interpretation of Truman's domestic policies in *Beyond the New Deal: Harry S Truman and American Liberalism* (1973). Maeva Marcus examines the events of Truman's seizure of the steel mills during the Korean War, and goes into the constitutional issue that the Supreme Court confronted in its invalidation of Truman's act: *Truman and the Steel Seizure Case: The Limits of Presidential Power* (1977). See also Robert J. Divine, *Conflict and Crisis: The Presidency of Harry S Truman, 1945–1948* (1977). Allen Weinstein in *Perjury: The Hiss-Chambers Case* (1979) goes over the evidence bearing on the guilt or innocence of Alger Hiss, convicted of perjury for having falsely denied to a congressional committee the charge made by Whittaker Chambers that Hiss had engaged in espionage for the Communists. The author concludes that Hiss was probably guilty.

Martin Sherwin writes with insight of *A World Destroyed: The Atomic Bomb and the Grand Alliance* (1975). Barton J. Bernstein also studies this critical issue in *The Atomic Bomb* (1976) while Gregg Herken in *The Winning Weapon: The Atomic Bomb in the Cold War, 1945–1950* (1980) analyzes the importance of nuclear weapons in making policy. Thomas G. Paterson presents an illuminating study of the problems and policies that led to the Cold War and the continuing antagonism between the United States and the Soviet Union: *Soviet-American Confrontation: Postwar Reconstruction and the Origins of the Cold War* (1973). John Lewis Gaddis also explores these issues carefully in *The United States and the Origins of the Cold War, 1941–1947* (1972). Joyce and Gabriel Kolko, covering the same period, strongly condemn American policy: *The Limits of Power: The World and United States Foreign Policy, 1945–1954* (1972). John W. Spanier reviews *The Truman-MacArthur Controversy and the Korean War* (1959).

POINTS OF VIEW: Why Did We Drop the Atomic Bomb?

Paul Fussell

Most of those with firsthand experience of [World War II] at its worst were relatively inarticulate and have remained silent. Few of those destined to be destroyed if the main islands had had to be invaded went on to become our most eloquent men of letters or our most impressive ethical theorists or professors of history of international jurists. The testimony of experience has come largely from rough diamonds like James Jones and William Manchester, who experienced the war in the infantry and the Marine Corps. Both would agree with the point, if not perhaps the tone, of a remark about Hiroshima made by a naval officer menaced by the kamikazes off Okinawa: "Those were the best burned women and children I ever saw." . . .

On the other hand, John Kenneth Galbraith is persuaded that the Japanese would have surrendered by November without an invasion. He thinks the atom bombs were not decisive in bringing about the surrender and he implies that their use was unjustified. What did he do in the war? He was in the Office of Price Administration in Washington, and then he was director of the United States Strategic Bombing Survey. He was 37 in 1945, and I don't demand that he experience having his ass shot off. I just note that he didn't. In saying this I'm aware of its offensive implications *ad hominem.* But here I think that approach justified. What's at stake in an infantry assault is so entirely unthinkable to those without experience of one, even if they possess very wide-ranging imaginations and sympathies, that experience is crucial in this case.

The dramatic postwar Japanese success at hustling and merchandising and tourism has (happily, in many ways) effaced for most people important elements of the assault context in which Hiroshima should be viewed. It is easy to forget what Japan was like before it was first destroyed and then humiliated, tamed, and constitutionalized by the West. "Implacable, treacherous, barbaric"—those were Admiral Halsey's characterizations of the enemy, and at the time few facing the Japanese would deny that they fit to a T. One remembers the captured American airmen locked for years in packing-crates, the prisoners decapitated, the gleeful use of bayonets on civilians. The degree to which Americans register shock and extraordinary shame about the Hiroshima bomb correlates closely with lack of information about the war.

And the savagery was not just on one side. There was much sadism and brutality—undeniably racist—on ours. No Marine was fully persuaded of his manly adequacy who didn't have a well-washed Japanese skull to caress and who didn't have a go at treating surrendering Japs as rifle targets. Herman Wouk remembers it correctly while analyzing Ensign Keith in *The Caine Mutiny:* "Like most of the naval executioners of Kwajalein, he seemed to regard the enemy as a species of animal pest." And the enemy felt the same way about us: "From the grim and desperate taciturnity with which the Japanese died, they seemed on their side to believe they were contending with an invasion of large armed ants." Hiroshima seems to follow in natural sequence: "This obliviousness on both sides to the fact that the opponents were human beings may perhaps be cited as the key to the many massacres of the Pacific war." Since the Japanese resisted so madly, let's pour gasoline into their emplacements and light it and shoot the people afire who try to get out. Why not? Why not blow them all up? Why not, indeed, drop a new kind of big bomb on them? Why allow one more American high school kid to see his intestines blown out of his body and spread before him in the dirt while he screams when we can end the whole thing just like that?

On Okinawa, only weeks before Hiroshima, 123,000 Japanese and Americans *killed* each other. "Just awful" was the comment not of some pacifist but of MacArthur. One million American casualties was his estimate of the cost of the forthcoming invasion. . . .

Experience whispers that the pity is not that we used the bomb to end the Japanese war but that it wasn't ready earlier to end the German one.

Martin J. Sherwin

[L]et us move from combat experiences to historical research and inquire what *Truman was experiencing* and what he was thinking about as he sat behind his desk in the Oval Office in the spring and early summer of 1945.

Research in the President's Official File, and in the diaries, correspondence and records of his closest wartime advisers, reveals that while the war was an ever-present consideration, its conduct was not among Truman's primary tasks. The record of military successes, Roosevelt's deteriorating health, a growing concern with postwar problems and Truman's inexperience had shifted much of the daily management of the conflict away from the White House during 1945. The new President would officiate over victory, but he would not be credited with having led the nation to it. The problems of the postwar world loomed larger before Truman than they ever had before Roosevelt, and they occupied more of his time. *His* performance would be judged on what he accomplished *after* the war.

The Soviet Union was the primary postwar problem. Joseph Stalin was breaking the Yalta Agreement, the Secretary of State reported to the President at their first meeting on April 13, and soon after, Averell Harriman, Ambassador to Moscow, characterized Soviet behavior as nothing less than a "barbarian invasion of Europe. . . ."

As the bomb moved toward completion, a dangerous (though now familiar) illusion was nurtured in the White House: the idea that the bomb was a panacea for America's diplomatic as well as its military problems. As preparations for the Potsdam Conference got underway, assurances that the weapon would work became increasingly important to the President. . . . And then, Truman agreed, in an early linkage of arms control and diplomacy, that after the first bomb had been successfully used against Japan, a fitting exchange for an American offer to the Russians for the international control of atomic energy would be "the settlement of the Polish, Rumanian, Yugoslavian, and Manchurian problems." And even before this discussion, Secretary of State-designate James F. Byrnes had told Truman that the bomb "might well put us in a position to dictate our own terms at the end of the war."

Truman inherited the basic policy that governed the atomic bomb, just as he inherited every other policy related to the war, a point that commentators on both sides of the debate often ignore. It was therefore *possible* to use the bomb only because Roosevelt had made preparations to do so. Truman was *inclined* to use the bomb because of those preparations. But he *decided* to use it because there seemed no good reason not to. On the contrary, the bombs were available and the Japanese fought on; the bombs were available and precedents of burned cities were numerous; the bombs were available and $2 billion had been spent to create them; the bombs were available and revenge had its claim; the bomb was available and the Soviet Union was claiming too much. Its use held out not only the hope of shocking Tokyo into submission but also the possible dividend of jolting Moscow into cooperation.

But a critical question remains: Were the bombings of Hiroshima and Nagasaki the quickest way to end the war? A considerable body of evidence suggests that the decision to use the bomb, which involved a decision to reject another recommended initiative, *delayed* the end of the war.

American cryptographers had broken the Japanese diplomatic code before the war, and senior members of the Administration were aware of a struggle between peace and war factions within the Japanese government. Based on this privileged information, and on his knowledge of Japanese politics gained from long experience as Ambassador to Japan, Acting Secretary of State Joseph C. Grew urged Truman during the final days of May to modify the unconditional-surrender policy. It was an insurmountable barrier for the peace faction, he explained, for no Japanese government would surrender without assurances that the Emperor would not be deposed or the dynasty eliminated. But Truman decided to reject Grew's advice, and an important question is *why*?

One answer is that he would not accept the political consequences that were likely to result from a public retreat from a policy that had become a political shibboleth since Roosevelt introduced the idea in 1943.

Another answer is that he preferred to use the atomic bomb.

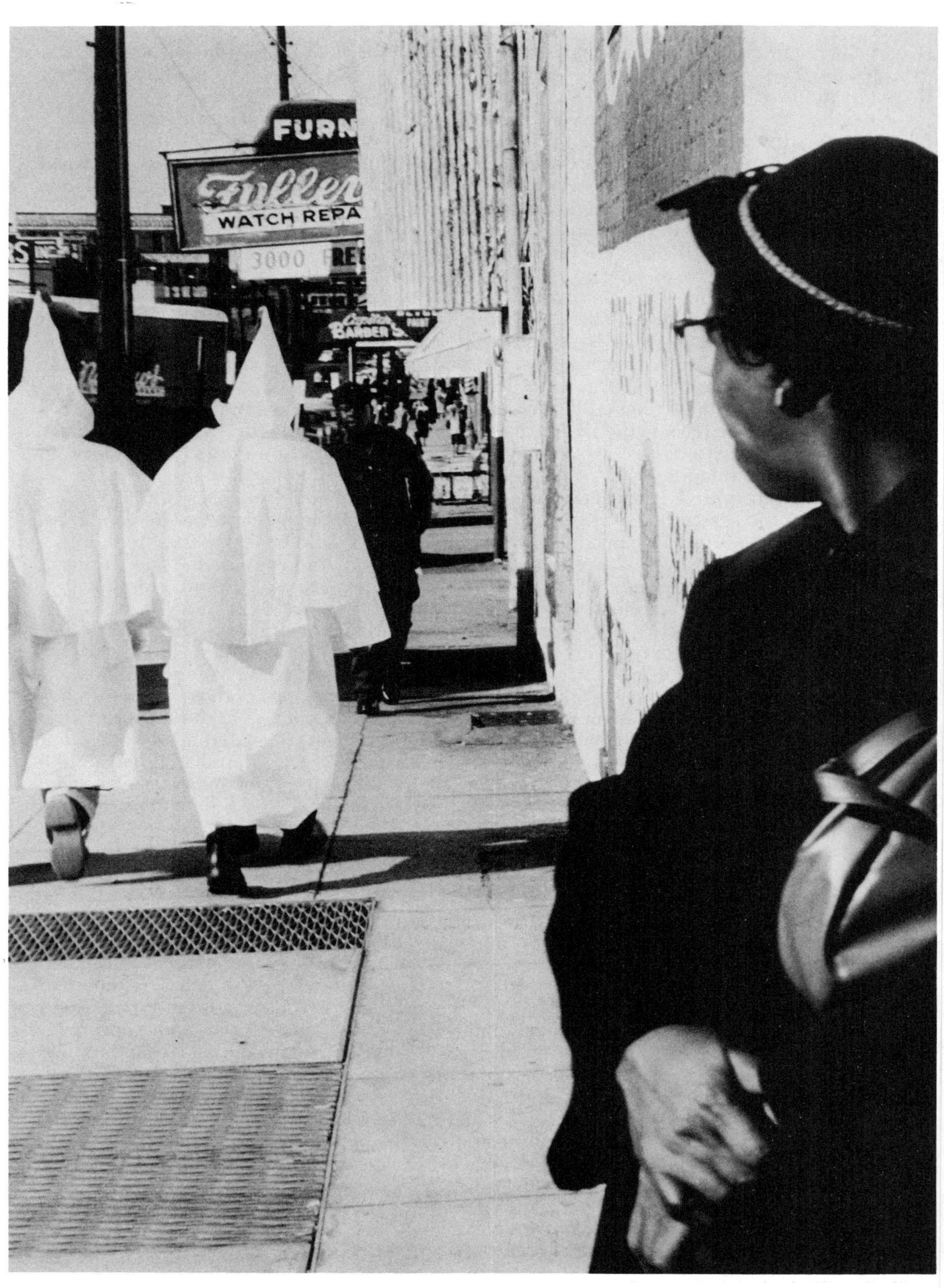

A black woman in a southern town during the 1950s watches Klansmen in full regalia. *(Courtesy, AP/Wide World Photos)*

CHAPTER 27

New Frontiers

THE GREENSBORO SIT-INS (1960)

None of them was over eighteen. Ezell Blair, Jr., David Richmond, Franklin McCain, and Joseph McNeil were younger than the youthful American revolutionaries of the 1770s. Their carefully planned revolutionary act was polite: they asked for Coca-Cola. Customers in range of the Woolworth's department store lunch counter noted their neat clothes and grooming. To all appearances they were normal American college students straight out of the 1950s. Some were to employ Cold War rhetoric to justify their act, suggesting that racial justice at home would enhance their nation's struggle against Communism in the Third World, and later one of them, as a veteran of the Vietnam war, would heatedly defend his country's engagement in that conflict. But on Monday, February 1, 1960, the relatively progressive city of Greensboro, North Carolina, was still segregated, and at Woolworth's the four freshmen from the black North Carolina Agricultural and Technical College did not get their Cokes.

After leaving Woolworth's they formed a circle on the sidewalk and said the Lord's Prayer. Their return the next day with sixteen fellow students brought national wire service attention. On the third day, there were sixty-three. An elderly white woman seeking the white ladies' room encountered two black girls and exclaimed, eyes wide with alarm, "Nigras, Nigras everywhere!" On Thursday three white students from North Carolina Women's College joined the sit-ins. After that white youths mobbed the aisles and heckled the demonstrators, and in a mild departure from the original character of the event the A & T football team confronted gangs who waved Confederate flags. "Who do you think you are?" asked an angry white. "We the Union army," a player responded. On Friday, with more than 300 students participating, the movement started to spread to other stores, and within a few days it had traveled to other cities. In response to Greensboro a network of civil rights activists already in place began marching into the combat it had been planning and waiting for. Within two months the sit-ins had invaded fifty-four segregated establishments in nine southern states. The activists, most of them black but including numbers of white students, were taking up leadership of the civil rights movements from traditional older figures. John F. Kennedy, increasingly an inspiration to the young, endorsed the sit-ins during that year's presidential campaign.

The civility of the Greensboro demonstrations did not reassure respectable southerners. North Carolina's governor Luther Hodges, soon to be appointed secretary of commerce in the Kennedy Administration, told the press that the sit-ins threatened law and order. The Chancellor of the Women's College, having persuaded the female demonstrators to refrain from participating, convened a meeting with the local black colleges that, after Woolworth's temporarily closed its doors, resulted in an unproductive truce. Moral privileges, a Greensboro business leader explained, could not "be obtained by force or intimidation, but must be secured through the medium of orderly negotiations, reason and mutual respect." It took a resumption of the demonstrations to desegregate the Woolworth's lunch counter.

The Greensboro sit-ins did not mark an increase in resolve on the part of the southern civil rights movement: a number of sit-ins had already occurred in the late fifties without benefit of the national attention that was to add confidence to the later action. But 1960 was precisely the time when the movement accelerated into the relentless, unbroken assault of the following years on southern and northern racism, its confrontations and setbacks and victories reported in the press like dispatches from the battlefield.

Eisenhower Diplomacy

The Cold War Wanes Eisenhower's efforts in foreign policy were more impressive than his work at home. A peace-loving man, he quickly ended the Korean War on terms that Truman had found unacceptable. The President settled for a truce that divided the country where the opposing armies had stopped, not far different from the old division of Korea into North and South. The threat to use atomic weapons that he had employed to bring the Communists into peace negotiations was pure Cold War stridency. But the truce itself meant that the country's most successful recent general had become the first President to halt a modern war short of victory.

At the same time, the Soviet Union moved toward improved relations with the West. Freed of Stalin's arbitrary cruelty by his death in March 1953, and perhaps sobered by Truman's determined containment politics and the unexpected strength of decadent capitalism, Georgi Malenkov, Stalin's nominal successor, sought detente. He received support from Foreign Minister Vyacheslav Molotov, Defense Minister Nikolai A. Bulganin, and Nikita Khrushchev, first secretary of the Communist Party. A three-year struggle for dominance ensued among Stalin's successors, a contest Khrushchev won largely because of timely support from Marshall Zhukov, a war hero who controlled the Red Army. Khrushchev's triumph over his rivals seemed to increase the possibility of a more stable world order. He would later announce the doctrine of peaceful coexistence and economic competition, both direct repudiations of Bolshevik militancy. An atomic standoff (in 1953 the Soviet Union exploded its first hydrogen bomb), the decline of McCarthyism in America, and new faces on both sides of the Iron Curtain seemed to be putting the world on a more peaceful course.

In Washington, a new tenor and even a new substance entered the making of foreign policy. The President's immense following and his military reputation made it possible for him to pursue a policy of armed and edgy but civilized truce with the Communist world. Eisenhower knew the horrors of war:

he recalled the harrowing experience of entering the Falaise Gap zone in Normandy in 1944:

> It was literally possible to walk for hundreds of yards at a time, stepping on nothing but dead and decayed flesh. . . . I hate war as only a soldier who has lived it can, only as one who has seen its brutality, its futility, its *stupidity*.

Eisenhower turned over the day-to-day control of foreign affairs to the somber John Foster Dulles. The secretary of state's vocabulary of unbending anti-Communism, his rhetorical willingness to go to the brink of nuclear war in order to contain Communism went counter to the details of his actual foreign policy, which did not bring the nation anywhere near to any brink.

Not long into his presidency, Eisenhower managed to complete a real peace between West Germany and France. Dulles negotiated the Paris Accords, which guaranteed French security and at the same time brought West Germany into the NATO alliance. This act provoked the Soviet Union into the Warsaw Pact, an alliance system in eastern Europe. This clear organization of the continent into two blocs actually appeared to make for an increase not in danger but in stability.

Both Eisenhower and Dulles relied heavily on the deterrent power of nuclear weapons as opposed to conventional forces. Admiral Arthur Radford, chairman of the Joint Chiefs of Staff, called it the "New Look" defense policy. This strategy produced "more bang for a buck" in the colorful words of economy-minded Charles Wilson, the secretary of defense. Yet the nuclear approach generally restricted the United States either to doing nothing or to threatening catastrophe, and the Soviet Union's acquisition of nuclear weapons blunted the device. However perilous the nuclear standoff might be in the years to come, it too for the moment made for stability, diplomacy, and mutual retreat.

President Eisenhower and Soviet Premier Nikita Khrushchev at Camp David, 1959. *(Courtesy, AP/Wide World Photos)*

Summit Meeting

In the most dramatic departure from the techniques of the Truman and Acheson years, Eisenhower sought direct meetings with Soviet leaders—a diplomatic device unused since 1945. Meeting at Geneva in late July 1955, the United States, the Soviet Union, Britain, and France discussed disarmament, an increase in communication between East and West, and German unification.

Not just the Soviet Union but every nation in Europe feared a revival of German militarism. Many West Germans, particularly in the Rhineland and Bavaria, questioned whether the prosperous West should bail out the depressed East. Germany remained divided until 1990. The greatest disappointment was the failure to achieve progress toward disarmament. At Geneva Eisenhower had outlined his "open skies" proposal: mutual aerial surveillance and an exchange of military blueprints so that arms reductions, when negotiated, could be reliably verified. The U.S.S.R. politely scuttled the idea. Yet the summit launched the hopeful "spirit of Geneva."

Throughout 1956 and 1957 caution dominated American foreign policy. Both the Communist and the Western blocs suffered internal dissension during the summer and fall of 1956.

The Hungarian Rebellion

In 1956 the Soviet empire in eastern Europe nearly collapsed. Some 15,000 impoverished Polish factory workers revolted in Poznan on June 28. While the Kremlin hesitated, the Poles demanded that Wladyslaw Gomulka take over the government. A patriot and Communist who opposed hasty collectivization, Gomulka refused to compromise with Soviet leaders clearly caught off guard. After a series of maneuvers, he forced Moscow to accept a government under his leadership. Gomulka's success triggered the devastating Hungarian rebellion, which sought political independence as well as economic reform. On October 23, a demonstration supporting Polish liberation quickly changed into a huge crowd of workers, soldiers, and students who demanded the return of Imre Nagy, a former minister. Nagy, a Communist who opposed Soviet economic methods and Moscow's political domination, formed a new government on the Polish model. But demonstrations turned into armed rebellion; the provinces almost immediately went over to the rebel cause and Budapest soon followed. Encouraged by signs of support from the West, the revolutionaries opted for complete independence. When the Hungarians persisted in trying to escape its orbit, Moscow brought in a heavy military force to crush the rebellion.

Worried about nuclear confrontation and tacitly recognizing Soviet dominance in eastern Europe, the West never considered intervention. In any case, events elsewhere had dissolved Western unity into barely disguised animosity.

Suez

On November 5, 1956, England, France, and Israel launched a joint attack on Egypt, ostensibly to reopen the Suez Canal, which President Gamal Abdul Nasser had nationalized in July. Other issues lay behind the question of the canal. To the Israelis, the operation was a preventive war against Egypt, which along with other Arab nations had been in a standing conflict with the Jewish state. France hoped to recoup its prestige after frustrations in Vietnam and Algeria. Only Britain hesitated. Though anxious to topple Nasser, whose action against British interests in the Suez created a dangerous example to other Arab states, London understood the enormous military risks. British officials misread Eisenhower's mild warnings and concluded that he would not object. The United States, anxious to avoid identifying itself with European colonialism, abruptly condemned the attack. Eisenhower even threatened to bankrupt the British pound unless Prime Minister Anthony Eden withdrew British troops. Beset on all sides—the entire Arab world had broken off diplomatic relations—the prime minister accepted a proposal by Canada and the United States for a United Nations peacekeeping force in the Sinai peninsula.

Sputnik

The next jolt occurred outside the field of politics. On October 4, 1957, the first space satellite, the Russian Sputnik, beeped the beginning of the space age and seemed to tip the technological balance in favor of the Soviet Union. Economies in the Defense Department, together with an exaggerated reliance upon manned bombers, had limited the American missile development program. Despite the quiver that ran through the Western world, the new earth satellite had little strategic significance; the United States far surpassed the USSR in military technology and gross national product. Yet Soviet rocket engineers had given their government a strong propaganda weapon.

In 1957 Dulles enunciated the Eisenhower Doctrine for the Middle East, offering not only economic assistance but American soldiers to governments protecting their territorial integrity against Communism. The new policy resulted from the rapid erosion of the West's position throughout the strategically significant Near East. Egyptian leader Gamal Abdul Nasser's attempt to unify the region politically accelerated the trend toward militant nationalism.

Lebanon

In Lebanon during 1958, a confused, intricate civil war erupted setting Christians against Moslems, opponents of Egypt's President Nasser against his supporters, and urban Beirut with its Western flavor against the culture of the hill areas. The pro-Western president of Lebanon asked the United States for military support to end the civil war. Eisenhower invoked his new doctrine and dispatched 3,500 marines, a force that eventually grew to 14,000. The intervention, so brief, bloodless, and well-executed, deserved commendation at least for its technical skill. While American troops helped keep peace, American diplomats aided in hammering out an accord that would restore harmony and balance to Lebanon for the next fifteen years. But a larger purpose of the landing failed; the attempt to set up an alternative to Nasser in the Middle East collapsed around Arab fears of renewed colonialism and the reluctance of Arab countries to combine with outside powers against one another.

Eisenhower deftly handled another crisis, potentially the most serious of the decade, when the Soviet Union sealed off East Berlin in the late summer of 1958 to thwart black market currency operations by West Berliners and to halt an embarrassing exodus from East Germany. The President's determination to stand firm without overreacting quickly diminished tension. As if to reiterate the common resolve to avoid war, Khrushchev paid a successful visit to the United States in 1959, and met a cordial Eisenhower at Camp David, Maryland. Observers spoke of the "spirit of Camp David," the dissipation of mistrust.

Economic and Social Policy in the 1950s

Unemployment Unemployment was the central economic issue of the decade; up to 7.7 percent of workers were without jobs, and recessions of growing severity marred the times. The end of the Korean War and a sharp cut in military expenditures brought on the first recession in 1953–54. An easy money policy adopted by both the Treasury and the Federal Reserve Board, combined with a tax cut and an increase in old age and unemployment payments, eventually managed to offset the economic decline resulting from postwar layoffs. But the administration, worried over inflation, reacted slowly to another recession in 1957–58. When unemployment rates remained at seven percent during the congressional elections, Republicans suffered disastrous consequences. Even in 1960, though a presidential campaign hung in the balance, inflation troubled Eisenhower more than unemployment. What the economy needed, according to the Democrats, was growth. Growth would pull down prices by flooding the market with goods. And it would provide new jobs even as technological improvements cut down the number of workers needed for a given operation. But that growth did not occur; the national economic growth rate remained below levels then prevailing in western Europe.

Eisenhower's administration no doubt wanted to curb rising prices, but it could not do it with voluntary restraints, especially since the steel industry resisted. Large firms aimed not for competition at home and abroad, but for secure growth based on rising prices in a carefully planned market, or for an "administered price." During the 1950s American investments in new plants and equipment shrank well below that in European economies. In the 1950s, business-oriented Republicans appeared fearful of stimulating more rapid economic growth, while at the end of the decade, Democrats,

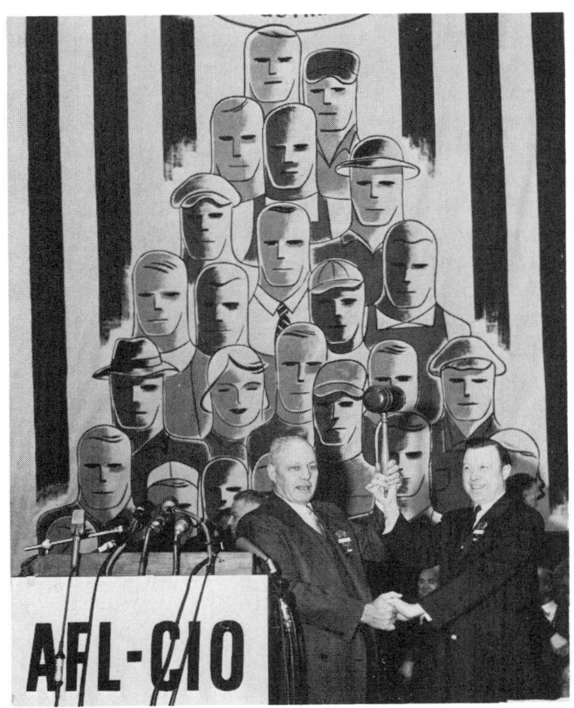

The merger of the American Federation of Labor and the Congress of Industrial Organizations in 1955 created a sixteen-million member labor union. *(Courtesy, AP/Wide World Photos)*

less frightened by inflation, made growth their major objective.

As usual, the poor suffered most during the economic doldrums. Blacks, Indians, Mexican Americans, and growing numbers of the elderly were, in Michael Harrington's apt word, "invisible"—physically shut away and forgotten in slums, on reservations, in migrant workers' camps, and often in filthy nursing homes as medical indigents. Mass-produced clothing, which replaced the rags of earlier generations of the poor, hid their true economic condition. These same groups were also politically invisible, lacking a voice even in the Democratic Party, which had its institutional base in the unions.

Aid to public education was so popular, and the need for classrooms so great, that most people expected Eisenhower to implement his campaign pledge of direct federal aid to schools as "the American answer." Yet he failed to do so. Congress did pass one important education measure, the National Defense Education Act of 1958. But both the act's provisions and Congress's motivation seemed far removed from concern over the quality of local education. During the anxious period following the 1957 Russian launching of Sputnik I, the national government had quickly decided to improve college-level education, primarily in the applied sciences and engineering. Implementing this decision, NDEA provided loans, scholarships, and fellowships directly to students and a lesser amount in grants to the colleges themselves. The NDEA did mean that education had now become a concern of the federal government.

A most important domestic achievement of the Eisenhower Administration was the program to build a system of interstate highways. After World War II, when trucks became the preferred method of freight shipment in the United States and automobiles the most desired means of travel, traffic problems grew especially severe. Congestion in cities made it particularly difficult, and expensive, to ship goods across the country. Urban planners and transportation engineers began proposing the construction of limited-access, high-speed expressways. President Eisenhower endorsed the idea, and in June 1956 Congress passed the Interstate and Defense Highway System Act. The law provided for $32 billion over a thirteen-year period to construct a 41,000 mile interstate highway system and for improvements on other federal highways.

A Philosophy of Conservatism Eisenhower's determination not otherwise to expand the federal budget expressed itself in the struggles over environmental bills. In 1960 the President vetoed a water pollution bill that would have established federal grants to build sewage treatment plants. He argued that pollution was "a uniquely local blight," and that responsibility rested with state and local governments. Soon Rachel Carson would awaken environmental concerns about worldwide pollution of the oceans in *Silent Spring* (1962). Caution and philosophical objections guided Eisenhower's approach to social and ecological issues; the Republican President varied in his response to other kinds of federal spending. Public works projects that promoted the economic development of the country—what economists call the "capital infrastructure"—received quick, almost enthusiastic approval despite often costly drains on government funds. The Middle West welcomed plans for construction by Canada and the United States of the Saint Lawrence Seaway, a dream of Herbert Hoover's brought to fruition in 1959, thirty years after he recommended it to Congress. Massive highway building programs, justified to a frugal Congress as an aid to "national defense," gained support from local businessmen and commuters as well as construction companies and unions.

The Eisenhower Administration, then, was not in the reformist grain of the Democratic years that had preceded it. But it is equally important that the President made no attempt to repeal the New Deal. Quietly, in the very absence of any pronouncement on the subject, the Eisenhower presidency allowed the welfare state to become a permanent part of the American consensus. As Ike bluntly cautioned his conservative brother Edgar:

> Should any political party attempt to abolish social security and eliminate labor laws and farm programs, you would not hear of that party again in our political history. There is a tiny splinter group, of course, that believes that you can do those things. . . . a few Texas oil millionaires, and an occasional politician and businessman from other areas. Their number is negligible and they are stupid.

The Elections of 1956 and 1958

Stevenson Again The 1956 campaign featured the same presidential candidates as in 1952. Stevenson presented a vision of possible disengagement from the Cold War; he recommended a unilateral halt to nuclear testing and an end to the draft. At the same time, however, he implied that Eisenhower had sacrificed our national security in exchange for a balanced budget and had failed to answer Soviet ideology with an articulate program and philosophy. Early in 1956 Stevenson told a Los Angeles audience that the use of federal troops to enforce school desegregation court orders would be "a fatal mistake." He explained: "That is exactly what brought on the Civil War. We must proceed gradually, not upsetting habits or traditions that are older than the Republic." Like his hero Abraham Lincoln, Stevenson put national unity before racial justice. Many black newspapers backed Eisenhower, who later ran well in black precincts. Stevenson's shining reputation for articulateness has been preserved as in amber, but he was a man far removed from the issues that would prevail in the mid-sixties.

In the last days of the campaign the crisis in the Middle East, in which the country looked to presidential leadership, further strengthened Eisenhower. His margin of victory did not reach the fabled triumph of FDR twenty years before, but a tally of 457 to 73 electoral votes and a nine million popular vote margin gave the Republicans much reason for self-congratulation. It was a far more conclusive triumph than that of 1952. Even the Democratic Solid South crumbled; Stevenson lost Virginia, Florida, Louisiana, and Texas.

Had they read the congressional returns more carefully, however, the Republicans might have been somewhat less jubilant, for they had not built a lasting national majority. In 1956 Eisenhower ran 6.5 million votes ahead of the Republican congressional candidates. All through the fifties, in fact, the Democrats gradually regained congressional seats they had lost in 1952.

A Democratic Resurgence The congressional elections of 1958 produced a landslide for the Democrats. The 1957 recession suggested that perhaps only under the Democrats could a stable prosperity be sustained. The Republicans unwisely chose 1958 to push "right to work" or open shop laws forbidding any kind of compulsory union membership. The Eisenhower agricultural program favored large farms that employed the latest technology and indirectly forced more and more small farmers to sell their holdings and to become tenants or move into the cities. The Soviet Union had launched two Sputniks in October 1957; the second one demonstrated that it had perfected the rocket fuel necessary for space exploration, and that the booster rocket could propel a nuclear weapon at high speed to a radius of 4,000 miles. These developments shocked those who presumed that under a military man the United States would naturally hold its own in competition against the Soviet Union. Questions about the ad-

Adlai Stevenson, though he won enormous loyalty from his followers, could not overcome Eisenhower's popularity and lost both the 1952 and 1956 elections. *(Courtesy, Wide World Photos)*

ministration had also appeared with the dismissal of Eisenhower's closest adviser, Sherman Adams, for accepting gifts.

The era, moreover, was stirring from its torpor with the publication of muckraking articles about automobile safety, air and water pollution, the need for better schooling, and the neglect of equal treatment of minorities.

The Warren Court and Civil Rights

An Activist Court Himself cautious on domestic issues, Eisenhower appointed one of the most activist of chief justices. Earl Warren presided over the Supreme Court from 1953 to 1969, a time of increasingly militant confrontations over race relations and, in the later years, of unprecedented dissent from American foreign policy. The Court majority headed by Warren repeatedly intervened in American social life, and critics claimed that the Court was usurping legislative power and willfully imposing its own blueprints of reform. Yet the Warren Court was not unique in its energy. The great chief justices beginning with John Marshall had gained renown not for the elegance of their constitutional arguments but for their involvement in social or political transformation. Surely the Court's enunciation of the doctrine in *Plessy v. Ferguson* (1896) that public facilities—could be "separate but equal"—that states could impose segregation as long as both races enjoyed comparable facilities, savored much more of political motivation than the Warren Court's rejection of that position in *Brown v. Board of Education* (1954). Defenders and critics of the Warren Court divided ultimately not over the Court's methods but over the social wisdom of its decisions.

The National Association for the Advancement of Colored People (NAACP), through a team of lawyers headed by Thurgood Marshall, had been hammering away at school segregation for fifteen years before 1954, but the Supreme Court responded only by tightening the requirement for equality within the concept of "separate but equal." Then the Warren Court, overturning that doctrine of *Plessy v. Ferguson,* unanimously held in *Brown v. Board of Education* that "separate educational facilities are inherently unequal." In its unanimous decision the Court mentioned psychological damage to black children forced into separate schools. The basic constitutional issue, Chief Justice Earl Warren wrote, was whether segregation on the basis of race, even though all other factors were equal, deprived the minority group of equal educational opportunity. "We believe that it does," the nine judges asserted. Since the Fourteenth Amendment guaranteed the "equal protection of the laws," segregation was clearly unconstitutional. Aware that desegregation was not a simple matter, the Court ordered the following year that steps be taken to implement the decision "with all deliberate speed."

Little Rock Eisenhower never put the moral prestige of his office clearly behind the Court's decision. He believed that the battle against intolerance had to be won in "the hearts of men," not in legislative chambers. Yet when violent resistance to school desegregation erupted in Little Rock, Arkansas, in 1957, Eisenhower did not hesitate to enforce federal supremacy. A state court had blocked an integration plan approved by the Little Rock School Board, claiming that violence would break out if it went into operation. After a federal court ordered integration, Governor Orville Faubus mobilized the Arkansas National Guard to bar entrance to black students. In response Eisenhower placed the National Guard under federal authority and also ordered paratroopers from the United States Army into Little Rock. With bayonets fixed, the troops broke up a segregationist mob and stood guard while the integration plan went into effect.

Eisenhower was not acting out of a strong commitment to integration. He was a conservative—more temperamentally conservative than the many excitable ideologues who go by the title—and he had a conservative's belief in the unbending authority of the Constitution. That document as the courts had interpreted it forbade public school segregation. The governor of Arkansas was disobeying the federal court, and so Eisenhower acted. But his action was more radical than he. It implied an overturning of what had been the relationship between federal and state government on the issue of race. Not since the end of Reconstruction had the federal government imposed its authority upon the southern states in their pursuit of white supremacy. Until Little Rock if a state wished to disobey the Constitution in matters of racial equality it had been at liberty to do so. President Eisenhower settled that issue. Thenceforth, civil rights lawyers knew that they had a potential ally in the federal government.

The Civil Rights Act of 1957 In 1956 Attorney General Herbert Brownell had transmitted to Congress arguments for a strong civil rights bill. Eisenhower himself approved only two sections—one calling for an investigatory commission, the other reorganizing the civil rights unit in the Justice Department. The President withdrew his support from the critical Part III; at a news conference he answered "no" on whether the attorney general should be allowed to bring about school desegregation suits if local authorities did not request such action. In spite of pleas from prominent blacks to veto a weakened measure and demand something better, the President signed it. Nevertheless, the Civil Rights Act of 1957 was the first federal civil rights legislation in more than eighty years.

Far more revolutionary in its effect on the future of civil rights was the Montgomery, Alabama, bus boycott of 1955. It was not a sudden and spontaneous event, a reaction to a single incident led from the beginning by the Reverend Martin Luther King, Jr. For some time the leadership of the black community in Montgomery had planned a protest against the insulting details of racial segregation on the city's buses, by which black people were required to sit in the rear section of a bus and the driver could order them about. Black women such as Jo Ann Robinson had taken much of the initiative in planning for resistance. Rosa Parks, whose arrest for refusing to move from her bus seat was the immediate cause of the boycott, had been a committed civil-rights activist. King's eloquence strengthened the subsequent struggle in Montgomery, and his conversion to nonviolent resistance gave the boycott a character that would influence other protest movements. But the boycott, which after about a year of black abstention from bus-riding was followed by a court victory that forced the end of segregation on the city's buses, was wide in its leadership.

JFK

The Kennedy Promise Millions of Americans remember the hope and energy that attended the presidency of John Kennedy. He possessed intelligence, good looks, a Harvard education, a war hero's record, and a beautiful wife. For all its overuse, the word "image" is inescapable in any discussion of the Kennedy years. Perhaps the clearest achievement of his administration was his projecting a crisp energy and purposefulness that influenced for the better a generation of Americans.

The Massachusetts senator of the 1950s gave clues to the later man. In an obvious effort not to antagonize his Irish Catholic supporters, he kept silent on Joseph McCarthy in the early 1950s. When Eleanor Roosevelt at the end of the decade asked him to go on record against the late senator—an act that would have brought him needed convention support—Kennedy had the honesty to recognize that to do so then, after his years of silence, would be hypocritical. He was refreshing and unpredictable. Yet his Roman Catholicism made him a political underdog.

When he first entered national politics in 1956 as a candidate for the vice presidency, Kennedy allowed his adviser Ted Sorensen to leak a memorandum arguing that a Catholic candidate would strengthen rather than harm a national ticket. Kennedy also let himself be cast as a northerner friendly to the South and willing to let that section move slowly on the race issue. Though he lost his vice-presidential bid in 1956 to Senator Estes Kefauver of Tennessee, in 1958 he won reelection in Massachusetts by 875,000 votes, the largest majority in the state's history.

Jacquelyn and John F. Kennedy, the first Catholic and the youngest man to be elected to the White House.

The Election of 1960

Shrewd political methods and an able staff gave Kennedy by 1960 a commanding lead in the race for the Democratic presidential nomination. Party leaders worried about his religion and his youthfulness, but he proved himself in the primaries.

Many northern Democrats and labor leaders were chagrined at Kennedy's choice of Lyndon B. Johnson of Texas as his running mate, but they had nowhere to turn. The Republican party had nominated their old enemy, Vice President Richard Nixon.

Condemning Kennedy on religious grounds, Norman Vincent Peale, Nixon's own pastor, in effect gave credence to the view that the Catholic candidate was a victim of prejudice. Methodist leaders gave Kennedy a dramatic opportunity to prove to a skeptical audience of Houston ministers—and by way of television to the nation at large—that they had no religious reasons to fear him. Here Kennedy stood in sharp contrast to Al Smith. Smith had rejected as bigotry the very question of whether his faith might interfere with obligations to the country's laws and institutions; Kennedy welcomed queries and responded openly and at length.

In the course of the campaign Kennedy appeared the more activist candidate. When Kennedy endlessly said it was time "to get moving again," he referred principally to the national economy. But economic expansion also had its implications for foreign policy. Kennedy repeatedly charged that the Soviet Union held a lead over the United States in the development of missiles. He managed to link the issues of national prestige and economic growth, implying that Nixon, as a high official in the decent but placid Eisenhower Administration, could bring the country neither. Kennedy's charm and confident handling of the complexities of public problems cast him as a man who would handle the nation's problems with imagination and dash. Nixon agreed to a series of television debates in which Kennedy appeared fresher and more vibrant, thus confirming in the minds of voters the contrast between him and the exhausted Republican candidate. Kennedy won the election narrowly and became the youngest President to be elected in American history.

Kennedy's inaugural address is the subject of much controversy. Did it set the tone for his administration as few such addresses have ever done? Or do its measured cadences suggest a belligerence at odds with his more prudent conduct of foreign policy. Here are some of his more famous words:

> . . . Let the word go forth from this time and place, to friend and foe alike, that the torch has been passed to a new generation of Americans—born in this century, tempered by war, disciplined by a hard and bitter peace, proud of our ancient heritage—and unwilling to witness or permit the slow undoing of those human rights to which this nation has always been committed, and to which we are committed today at home and around the world.
>
> Let every nation know, whether it wishes us well or ill, that we shall pay any price, bear any burden, meet any hardship, support any friend, oppose any foe to assure the survival and the success of liberty.
>
> This much we pledge—and more.

A Darkening Plain: Kennedy Foreign Policy

Limited War Kennedy foresaw an end of direct superpower confrontation and the coming of an age of wars of national liberation in the course of which Communists would try to wrest control in the Third World. Kennedy joined General Maxwell Taylor in calling for a more mobile and technically skilled armed forces capable of fighting in limited wars. Kennedy's background made him especially receptive to the new brand of warfare: a naval hero, a reader of James Bond stories, the creator of the Green Berets, he combined a fascination for military technology with a feeling for military dash and style. Yet at the same time Kennedy seemed to believe that he could bring about an easing of international confrontation. That belief was not exactly contradictory to an interest in building a more sophisticated and mobile armed forces. The Kennedy people shared with earlier Cold War Democrats a conviction that conservative Republicans had brought primitive anticommunist emotions to the conflict with the Soviet Union. They saw themselves as substituting for those emotions the cooler and more controlled temper appropriate to a technically advanced military and society. This notion contributed to that phenomenon that is remembered as the Kennedy style.

That concept of what the twentieth century, the United States, and the new administration were all about gained its best expression in the Peace Corps. The idea was to send dedicated and knowledgeable Americans to impoverished regions of the world, there to apply to practical projects their skills in nursing, teaching, agriculture or engineering. Volunteers were supposed to understand that their work would be difficult, under conditions of physical discomfort unfamiliar to middle-class Americans. The implicit assumption was that in the Third World cool technical expertise, as opposed to crude anti-Communist ideology and to crude military dominance, would be the appropriate American response both to Communism and to poverty.

The Bay of Pigs In April 1961 President John F. Kennedy, relying on a plan developed by the Central Intelligence Agency under the Eisenhower administration, gave orders for an assault on Cuba. The invasion force was made up of Cuban refugees. The CIA trained the men, some 1,400 of them, high on a coffee plantation in the Guatemalan mountains. It was a fool's dream. Cubans were overwhelmingly content under Fidel Castro. After overthrowing in 1959 the longtime dictator, Fulgencio Batista, Castro had alleviated suffering caused by decades of right-wing corruption. While Castro was himself a dictator, increasingly Communist in orientation, who imprisoned and executed his political enemies, the Cuban people had no interest in joining an insurrection against him. Yet most people in the United States and Kennedy's administration mistakenly believed that any people who had lived under Communism yearned to overthrow the yoke of tyranny.

The CIA chose the landing spot, the *bahia*

de cochinos. It was a swampy area separated by eighty miles of jungle from the Escanaba mountains, where the "freedom fighters" had been instructed to hide in the event of trouble. (Maps of the area contained the little grasslike symbols for swampland that any Boy or Girl Scout could have read.) Most of the ammunition and radio equipment was carried in a single ship, which was blown up before it landed. Freighters supplied by the United Fruit Company—famous symbol of Yankee imperialism—had their hulls ripped by coral reefs at the landing area. Castro's troops quickly defeated the landing attempt, and Kennedy displayed enough restraint not to involve the United States military more deeply in an effort to rescue the operation.

One of Kennedy's responses to problems in Latin America was to press for an Alliance for Progress, a $10 billion, decade-long program of economic aid to Latin America. He pushed harder for greater military spending, and in 1961 Congress responded with an increase. Kennedy discounted the argument that building up an arsenal of new weapons would provoke the Soviet Union into its own buildup. Nevertheless, the U.S.S.R. did respond with a similar increase in its defense expenditures.

The Berlin Crisis of 1961 In June 1961 Kennedy and Khrushchev met in Vienna, where they accomplished little except an exchange of views. As Kennedy judged his rhetoric, Khrushchev seemed intransigently committed to disrupting world order, for he threatened to sign a peace treaty with East Germany.

The encounter discouraged Kennedy. Upon returning home he increased draft quotas, called up the reserves, and demanded a civil defense program that led to a popular frenzy for bomb shelters. When Khrushchev in August acceded to the construction of the Berlin Wall, sealing off East Berlin from the Western sector and preventing inhabitants of East Germany from going to the West, Kennedy sent 1,500 troops from West Germany down the Autobahn to West Berlin, and Vice President Johnson came to pledge American lives to the defense of the city. But Kennedy was careful to restrict American reaction to gestures not calculated to bring war.

In September 1961 Russia began to detonate nuclear bombs of enormous power; the United States followed in the spring of 1962. The older policy of massive retaliation established chiefly by Dulles now existed perilously alongside a new Kennedy policy of "flexible response," which envisioned a willingness to use conventional weapons in wars against Communist forces. On every continent ambitious third powers threatened to upset the world balance and precipitate the ultimate conflict between the Soviet Union and the United States.

In distant Southeast Asia, the existing regimes in both Laos and South Vietnam were endangered by native Communist forces. In Laos the President, remembering the Bay of Pigs, avoided direct intervention.

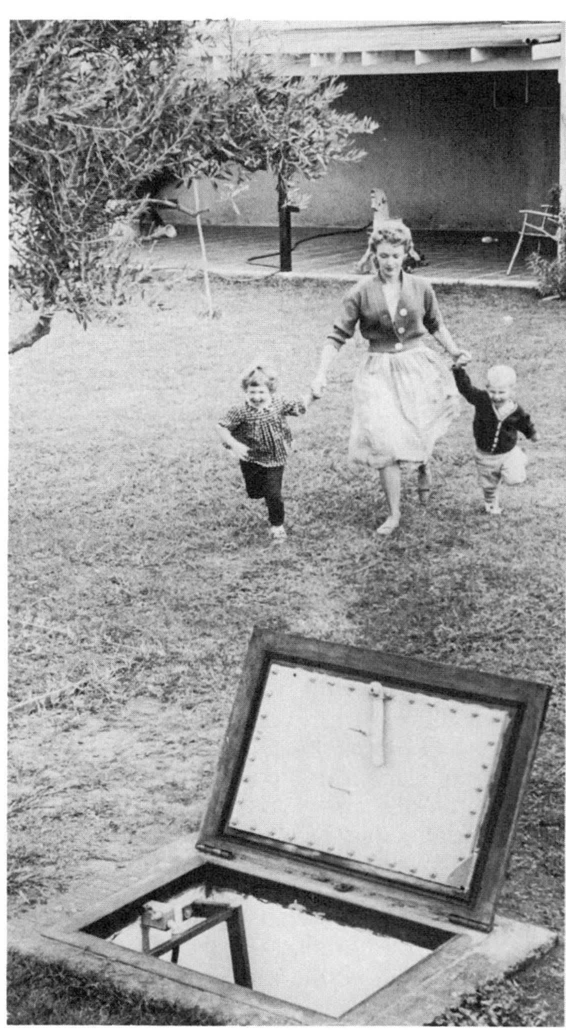

The Family Fallout Shelter. *(Courtesy, AP/Wide World Photos)*

The Cuban Missile Crisis In Cuba, Khrushchev was anxious to provide a semblance of defense for the island. Under pressure from the Soviet military, in the late spring of 1962 the U.S.S.R. placed intermediate-range missiles in Cuba. United States air surveillance first revealed the sites as their construction neared completion. Kennedy quickly decided that he could not tolerate interference in an area so patently within his country's sphere of influence. Although quite congruent with international law, and no real military threat to the United States, the placing of missiles was a major challenge to the political and diplomatic status quo. Khrushchev's justification was that the missiles would protect a sovereign Cuba against a United States invasion—a possibility Kennedy's Bay of Pigs venture made believable even in the opinion of our allies. But his act brought the world in October 1962 close to nuclear war.

The President's military consultants recommended an immediate air strike, which would inevitably wipe out Soviet advisers along with the missiles. But the military and Attorney General Robert Kennedy, the President's brother, disagreed. He argued that it was not in the American grain to launch an air attack against a small island unable to retaliate. The United States would be faithless to its past if it attacked Cuba much as the Japanese had attacked Pearl Harbor.

The President decided on a less drastic course; he instituted a naval blockade against Russian ships bringing additional missile equipment to Cuba. The United States permitted a harmless tanker to penetrate the quarantine area, but then, as millions waited breathlessly, the first ship carrying technical equipment turned back. During the week Khrushchev and Washington engaged in a series of exchanges, each party careful neither to back fully down nor to push the other too

When intelligence photos revealed that the Russians were placing intermediate-range missiles in Cuba, the United States and the USSR apparently stood at the brink of nuclear war. *(Courtesy, Department of Defense)*

far. By the end of the week Moscow had agreed to remove the missiles, while Washington promised not to invade Cuba. That crisis was over.

Some critics blamed Kennedy for bringing the world to the edge of nuclear war. Khrushchev, they said, had displayed the greater maturity by accepting humiliation. But Kennedy, too, had exercised restraint in the face of a reckless Soviet provocation. Before his countrymen Kennedy appeared a courageous and mature statesman.

An Easing of Tensions After the fall of 1962, the antagonism between the Soviet Union and the United States shifted to the Third World. There confrontation would continue but with less immediate risk of incinerating the globe. Direct relations between the two superpowers underwent a kind of thaw. A "hot line" insured instantaneous communication between the Kremlin and White House for times of crisis. Kennedy, in a speech at American University in June 1963, looked to a new era of cooperation between the two countries. In that year, too, the Soviet Union rejected a Chinese call to global militance and proposed instead peaceful coexistence. By now it was clear that Communist China and the U.S.S.R. were not allies but potential enemies. That too calmed Cold War militancy in the United States. For it meant that the West was not facing a dangerously unified Communist bloc, and it demonstrated that Communism was not a single indivisible ideology. Finally, the Test Ban Treaty of 1963 outlawed atmospheric testing of nuclear weapons. Ratification by the necessary two-thirds of the Senate came with the aid of a conservative Republican Senator Everett Dirksen, whose support broke the opposition by rightist senators. The treaty repudiated the relentless confrontation that right-wingers had been hoping for all through the 1950s.

Kennedy and the Civil Rights Movement

On the major domestic issue of the era, that of civil rights, John F. Kennedy brought to the presidency a record of compromise. He had voted twice to weaken the 1957 Civil Rights Act. But Title III of the act, which promised decisive action in school desegregation, received his vote. From 1956 to 1960 he sought support from the most segregationist governors.

During the presidential campaign Kennedy castigated Eisenhower for tolerating segregation in federally financed housing, and his telephone message of sympathy to Mrs. Martin Luther King while her husband sat in an Atlanta jail was an important symbolic gesture. He appointed a black, Robert C. Weaver, to be federal housing administrator. But Kennedy, fearful of losing support for other programs, sent no new civil rights legislation to Congress in 1961 and 1962.

Bloody incidents in 1961 involving freedom riders at Birmingham and Montgomery, Alabama—whites and blacks desegregating interstate transportation—forced Washington into action. Attorney General Robert Kennedy, the President's brother, told the Birmingham office of the Greyhound Bus Company to get in touch with "Mr. Greyhound" and said (this was quoted widely throughout the South): "I am—the Government is—going to be very much upset if this group does not get to continue their trip." The government sent 400 federal marshals to Montgomery to protect the contingent of freedom riders, some of whom had been beaten, and obtained an injunction against the Ku Klux Klan and other groups that were interfering with the rides. And the attorney general decreed that the Interstate Commerce Commission ban segregation in bus terminals that served out-of-state passengers.

In the fall of 1961 and the summer of 1962 civil rights efforts stalled in Albany, Georgia. Black demonstrators there learned some of the limits of nonviolence. When Martin Luther King came to that city, he told the largest gathering yet assembled at Shiloh Baptist Church: "Don't stop now. Keep moving. Don't get weary. We will wear them down with our capacity to suffer." And in harmony with Gandhi's precepts activists filled the jails. But the shrewd police chief Laurie Pritchett confined most of them in neighboring towns where they were nearly invisible, also

This Greyhound bus carrying the first Freedom Riders into Alabama was set afire by a mob outside the town of Anniston. *(Courtesy, AP/Wide World Photos)*

instructing his force in the methods of nonviolence and making arrests across racial lines. Among his tactics was to get down on his knees and pray with the demonstrators, then lock up every one of them. He thereby deprived the demonstrators of the scenes of white-supremacist violence, enacted before the national media, that elsewhere his more primitive southern compatriots happily supplied.

Coverage by the media made the nation aware of this time of confrontation, of violence from segregationists, of the posing of absolute moral issues. Forward momentum continued in the fall of 1962 with the enrollment at the University of Mississippi of its first black student, James Meredith. A white mob took over the campus, and when federal marshals were besieged in their attempt to enroll Meredith, Kennedy sent in federal troops. Vivian Malone entered the University of Alabama under milder conditions in the spring of 1963.

The only strategy that worked for blacks in Birmingham, Alabama, during May 1963 was the forcing of massive arrests. The city met the demonstrators with fire hoses, police dogs, and electric cattle prods. Later a bomb went off in a black church just before Sunday school, killing four little girls. Kennedy, foreseeing the "fires of frustration and discord . . . burning in every city, North and South," responded with legislative proposals. The President requested a partial ban on discrimination in public places, asked that the Justice Department be given powers to sue for school desegregation upon request, and urged broader powers to withhold funds from federally assisted programs in which discrimination occurred. Congressional civil rights leaders pushed Kennedy farther, persuading him to give the attorney general power to intervene in all civil rights cases.

The young folk singer Bob Dylan caught the spirit of the civil rights demonstrations in one of his songs:

> Come mothers and fathers
> Throughout the land
> And don't criticize
> What you can't understand.
> Your sons and daughters
> Are beyond your command
> There's a battle
> Outside and it's ragin'
> It'll soon shake your windows
> And rattle your walls . . .
> For the times they are a-changin'.

LETTER FROM BIRMINGHAM CITY JAIL *by The Reverend Martin Luther King, Jr.*

King's attack on white moderates who counseled patience is a classic.

MY DEAR FELLOW CLERGYMEN, While confined here in the Birmingham City Jail, I came across your recent statement calling our present activities "unwise and untimely." Seldom, if ever, do I pause to answer criticism of my work and ideas. If I sought to answer all of the criticisms that cross my desk, my secretaries would be engaged in little else in the course of the day and I would have no time for constructive work. But since I feel that you are men of genuine good will and your criticisms are sincerely set forth, I would like to answer your statement in what I hope will be patient and reasonable terms. . . .

You deplore the demonstrations that are presently taking place in Birmingham. But I am sorry that your statement did not express a similar concern for the conditions that brought the demonstrations into being. I am sure that each of you would want to go beyond the superficial social analyst who looks merely at effects, and does not grapple with underlying causes. I would not hesitate to say that it is unfortunate that so-called demonstrations are taking place in Birmingham at this time, but I would say in more emphatic terms that it is even more unfortunate that the white power structure of this city left the Negro community with no other alternative.

In any nonviolent campaign there are four basic steps: (1) collection of the facts to determine whether injustices are alive; (2) negotiation; (3) self-purification; and (4) direct action. We have gone through all of these steps in Birmingham. There can be no gainsaying of the fact that racial injustice engulfs this community. Birmingham is probably the most thoroughly segregated city in the United States. Its ugly record of police brutality is known in every section of this country. Its unjust treatment of Negroes in the courts is a notorious reality. There have been more unsolved bombings of Negro homes and churches in Birmingham than any city in this nation. These are the hard, brutal, and unbelievable facts. On the basis of these conditions Negro leaders sought to negotiate with the city fathers. But the political leaders consistently refused to engage in good faith negotiation.

Then came the opportunity last September to talk with some of the leaders of the economic community. In these negotiating sessions certain promises were made by the merchants—such as the promise to remove the humiliating racial signs from the stores. On the basis of these promises Reverend [Fred] Shuttlesworth and the leaders of the Alabama Christian Movement for Human Rights agreed to call a moratorium on any type of demonstrations. As the weeks and months unfolded we realized that we were victims of a broken promise. The signs remained. As in so many experiences of the past, we were confronted with blasted hopes, and the dark shadow of a deep disappointment settled upon us. So we had no alternative except that of preparing for direct action, whereby we would present our very bodies as means of laying our case before the conscience of the local and national community. . . .

The March on Washington The role of Martin Luther King in the movement is debated. He was the most widely recognized of the civil rights leaders, many of them ministers in black evangelical churches who in the late fifties had organized themselves into the Southern Christian Leadership Conference. But unknown or lesser-known individuals within and outside SCLC performed acts of equal heroism in lonelier isolation than King. Still, in his promotion of the idea of nonviolent resistance, and in his eloquence, King held a special place in the rights movement. King, wrote one white woman, had captured the

> devotion of the masses of Negroes. . . . My wash lady tells me every week about how she hears the angel's wings when he speaks, and God speaks directly through him and . . . he speaks directly to God.

When 250,000 people, about one-third white and the rest black, marched on Washington in August 1963 to be counted for civil rights legislation, King addressed them:

I have a dream that one day on the red hills of Georgia the sons of former slaves and the sons of former slaveholders will be able to sit down together at the table of brotherhood. I have a dream that one day even the state of Mississippi, a desert state sweltering with the heat of injustice and oppression, will be transformed into an oasis of freedom and justice.

The President's assassination that November brought an outpouring of grief in black communities. Construing civil rights legislation as a memorial to Kennedy aided its passage; Congress easily approved the first major law in 1964, and others followed in 1965 and 1968.

The New Frontier: Substance or Style?

In his handling of economic problems Kennedy had some success. In the 1960 campaign he had charged the Eisenhower Administration with failing to maintain as high a national growth rate as that of western Europe. Until the third quarter of 1962 Kennedy's policies held the cost of living steady, bringing neither substantial new unemployment nor inflation. A severe drop in the stock market began in May 1962. It threatened the somewhat shaky prosperity and persuaded Kennedy to embark upon a venturesome new policy. The patient counsel of Kennedy's chief economic adviser, Walter Heller, had convinced Secretary of the Treasury Douglas Dillon, a Republican in the Democratic administration, of the need for federal action. For the first time during a period of relative prosperity, an administration proposed a budget deficit through reduction in taxation, which was much more acceptable to business than new spending. The Congress concurred. Under President Lyndon Johnson in 1964 the cut went into effect.

John F. Kennedy. *(Courtesy, John F. Kennedy Library)*

Businessmen had already profited enormously from the Kennedy policies. The President signed tax credits and a generous depreciation allowance in 1962, and reduced corporate income taxes by twenty percent in 1963. But in April 1962 Kennedy so confronted the steel industry that, for many businessmen, his name would join that of the despised Franklin Roosevelt. Late in the afternoon of April 10, Roger Blough of United States Steel told Kennedy that even as they spoke press releases were announcing a steel price rise. The President was furious. He had persuaded the unions to settle for a modest wage hike on the understanding that prices would remain steady. Blough seemed both to deceive and to insult the President of the United States. Kennedy privately quoted his father's denunciation of businessmen as "sons of bitches" and launched an unprecedented government attack on the industry. The Defense Department threatened to switch its contracts over to the small companies that had not yet raised prices; the Justice Department and the Federal Trade Commission spoke of antitrust measures; the Treasury hinted at a tax investigation. Kennedy himself spoke on television:

> In this serious hour in our nation's history, when we are confronted with grave crises in Berlin and Southeast Asia . . . , the American public will find it hard, as I do, to accept a situation in which a tiny handful of steel executives whose pursuit of private power and profit exceeds their sense of public responsibility can show such utter contempt of the interests of 185 million Americans.

It was a massive application of presidential power. Big steel canceled the increase in prices, at least for the moment.

Kennedy gave promise later in 1963 of responding to more domestic needs in the next years of his administration. Then he went to Dallas. Riding unprotected in an open car, Kennedy was an easy target for an assassin's bullet. Lee Harvey Oswald, confused and angry in his politics, was evidently the killer. The presidential plane promptly flew the body home to Washington. Chief Justice Earl Warren directed a comprehensive but hurried report on the killing, which uncovered no evidence of conspiracy. Subsequent efforts to link Oswald with one or more additional marksmen or conspirators remain merely speculative.

The achievement of the Kennedy Administration lay elsewhere than in a relatively meager legislative record. Kennedy's ultimate success with the economy and the fruitful negotiation of the Test Ban Treaty brightened the end of his thousand days. But like some other Presidents he gave something intangible to the country. He gave a style that could invite trivialization but also invited its admirers to fresh hope and purpose. By the end of Kennedy's administration many college students were uninterested in a life of mere security and accumulating of material goods; they desired something more idealistic and therefore more rewarding. At that moment that might mean the Peace Corps. In the years to come, those desires would splinter, seizing here on some radical political vision, looking there to an alternative community, or slipping into drugs, or returning to hitherto forsaken material goals.

LBJ

President Kennedy once told an off-the-record press conference that he did not have much hope for solving America's problems. Kennedy's pessimism about what was possible for mankind, a side of his intellectual sophistication not sufficiently appreciated, inevitably narrowed his perspective and his goals. Lyndon Johnson's strength—and his weakness—lay in a faith that America could accomplish anything. Johnson's pride, daring, and technical skill reached their greatest effectiveness in attacking stubborn domestic ills. During his years in office Congress passed more laws than in any earlier era for civil rights, health, education, the arts and sciences, the eradication of poverty, and aid for the cities.

Lone Star Rising

Johnson's confidence originated in the New Deal of Franklin Roosevelt. Raised in the hill country of central Texas, Johnson himself had witnessed poverty at first hand. His calculating ambition was evident at Southwest Texas State Teachers College, where he dominated the student body. Afterward he taught briefly in a rural school and learned of the needs of poor Mexican Americans. He campaigned successfully for a congressional seat in 1937.

With the coming of the Eisenhower era Johnson, now in the Senate, moved to the political center; in 1953, by virtue of his impressive legislative skill and bland ideology he won the post of Senate majority leader. Everything he did was the work of a masterful politician. In 1960 he became a presidential candidate. After Johnson's candidacy failed, Kennedy thought it desirable to have the popular southerner as a running mate.

In the days following the assassination of Kennedy, Johnson behaved with skill and

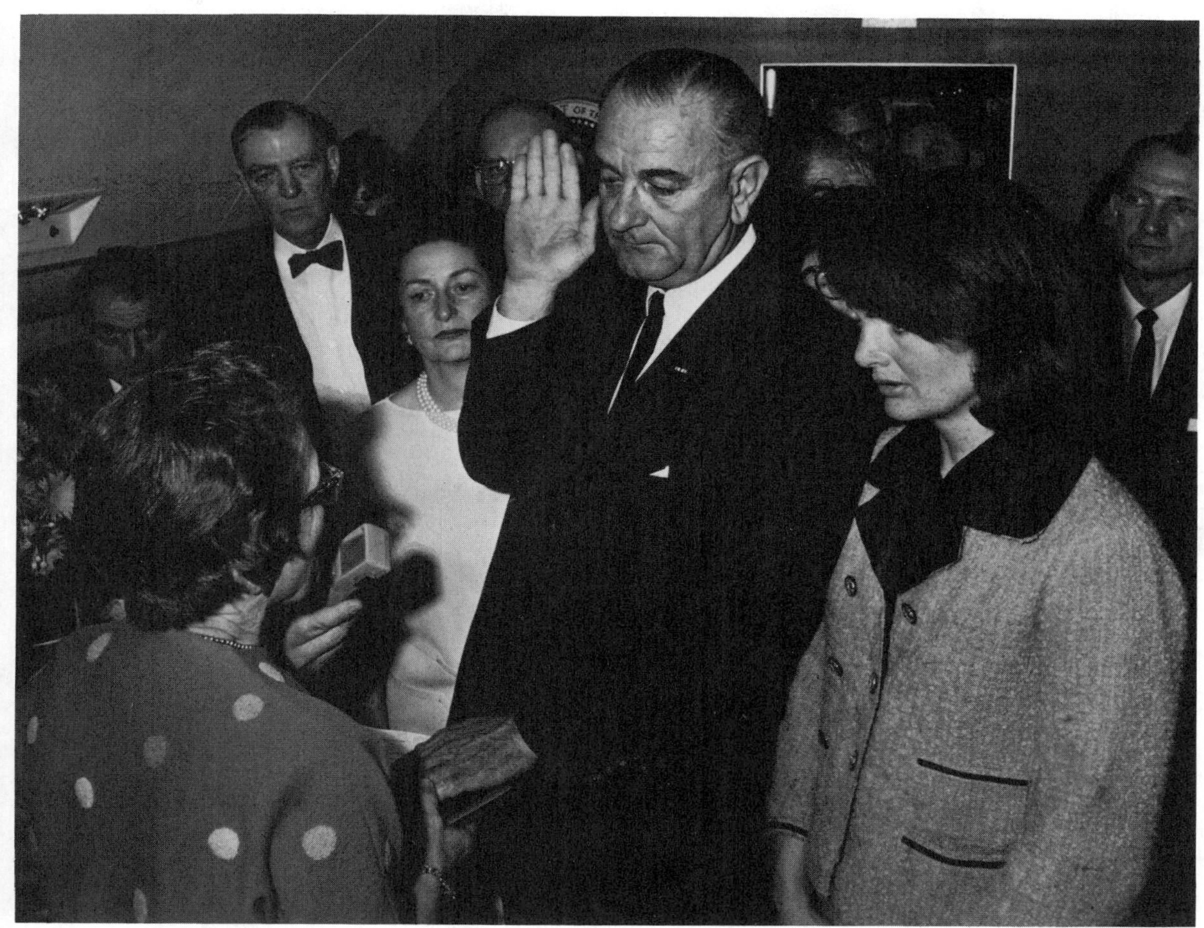

Lyndon Baines Johnson receiving the oath of office following President Kennedy's assassination in Dallas, November 22, 1963. *(Courtesy, AP/Wide World Photos)*

tact. He persuaded all of Kennedy's advisers to stay on, at least for the moment. Johnson's aggressive political mastery carried social programs much farther than Kennedy would most likely have taken them. He gathered into his policy much of what had latently existed for a decade, and he completed and presided over a powerful liberal coalition. Such coalitions as Johnson's are familiar in American history, accomplishing in a few years of intense activity what reformers had wanted for many years.

The Election of 1964 To Republican Party leaders the nomination of Barry Goldwater for President in 1964 was a calculated risk. A year so bleak for the Republicans could put to the test a proposition, long held by the political right wing, that there was a large potential electorate made up of nonvoters and working-class Democrats who would awaken and come to the polls for a belligerently conservative candidate. Goldwater accepted the nomination in the spirit that would dominate his campaign:

> Anyone who joins us in all sincerity we welcome. Those who do not care for our cause, we don't expect to enter our ranks. . . . Extremism in the defense of liberty is no vice. . . . Moderation in the pursuit of justice is no virtue.

During the course of the campaign Goldwater revealed a knack for making a handicap of honesty. In Appalachia he insisted on attacking the poverty program; in Knoxville,

Tennessee, he declared in favor of selling part of the Tennessee Valley Authority; in St. Petersburg, Florida, a city filled with retired people, he criticized social security; in North Dakota he told farmers that a decline in price supports would be good for them. Before an audience composed chiefly of first- and second-generation immigrants, vice-presidential candidate William Miller on Labor Day criticized liberal immigration policies.

All the pollsters agreed that November 4 would be a cold day for Goldwater. He carried only his home state of Arizona, in addition to Mississippi (where he won 87 percent of the vote), Louisiana, Alabama, South Carolina, and Georgia. The Democrats maintained their margin of two to one in the Senate and picked up thirty-eight seats in the House. Such were the immediate results of the Republican candidate's strategy of working to bring the still largely Democratic South solidly into the Republican Party. Yet the candidacy may have marshaled a set of emotions that would find a more effective political voice in later years. The race issue had not yet ripened to cause a backlash against the Democrats among whites in the North.

The first landmark of the Great Society was the tax reduction bill of 1964, which had been in the works for some time. Reducing income tax rates a total of $11 billion gave individuals and corporations an increase in spending power. The theory was that the resulting growth in investment and consumer demand would spur production, slacken unemployment, and ultimately swell federal revenues since the government would have a wealthier economy to tax. Unemployment fell in 1965 to the lowest level in eight years, and federal revenues actually rose, revenues that the Democratic administration put in part into measures for the relief of poverty. On the other hand, the tax cut, along with other incentives to activate business and the pressures of massive spending for the war in Indochina, contributed to the inflationary economy of the late 1960s and the 1970s.

The Economic Opportunity Act

President Johnson had seen much of poverty during his youth; its alleviation became a major goal. Kennedy's poverty programs had included the retraining and rehabilitation of the unemployed, area redevelopment, youth employment, the eradication of illiteracy, and accelerated public works in poverty regions. Early in 1964 Johnson brought together these programs and others, declaring a "war on poverty," an attractive theme for a presidential campaign. After hearing from the Council of Economic Advisers that twenty percent of all American families were poor by standard measures, Congress passed the Economic Opportunity Act of 1964, appropriating $800 million for the first year. Programs under the Office of Economic Opportunity (OEO) differed from past efforts in design as well as in size. Local community action agencies, the central innovation of the program, received $300 million. In each community, advisory boards, comprised of local business and political interests and representatives of the poor themselves, administered the funds. Another major emphasis of OEO programs was on the young. The Job Corps, an urban version of the New Deal's Civilian Conservation Corps, established for young slum-dwellers facilities offering remedial education and vocational training. The Neighborhood Youth Corps provided summer jobs paying $50 a week for high school students, with an eye toward pacifying edgy ghetto youth. A work-study program assisted many college students. Volunteers in Service to America (VISTA), a domestic equivalent of Kennedy's Peace Corps, sent teams of idealistic people into communities across the country to assist in government programs.

Following the 1964 election came an ingenious manipulation of Congress by the President, who continued to capitalize on the memory of Kennedy as well as on his own legislative skills. Johnson showered Congress with Great Society proposals.

Education and Medicare

Aid to public education was next on Johnson's list. The President effectively steered the legislation through Congress. For the first time Congress passed $1 billion in aid for elementary and secondary schools, concentrating on districts with pupils from low-income families. Johnson flew to the small Texas schoolhouse where he had once taught and there signed the bill.

Another of Johnson's major legislative goals was Medicare, health care for the elderly funded through social security. Despite continued opposition from the American Medical Association, the legislation passed rather easily. The basic plan provided funds for hospitalization and doctors' fees for people over sixty-five; a supplemental voluntary plan permitted individuals to enroll for coverage of doctors' bills and laboratory fees. Within two years, seventeen million Americans had taken advantage of this opportunity. Legislation in 1965 and 1966 set up the Medicaid program, which extended federal medical care to other large categories of needy people—dependent children, the blind and disabled, and many low-income families. Although Medicare and Medicaid laws set upward limits of coverage and required patients to assume responsibility for a deductible amount, they constituted a major victory for the administration.

Environmental Legislation Not satisfied with the Water Quality Act of 1965, which provided demonstration grants for sewage control, Johnson demanded $6 billion for a six-year national program with the federal government ultimately imposing water purifying standards. The Clean Water Restoration Act of 1966 authorized $3.5 billion to be spent over five years. (Presidents Johnson and Nixon would use less than one-third of these funds.) Under Johnson legislation set standards for exhaust emission on combustion engines, but left the enforcement date to government discretion. The deadline for nearly fume-free combustion engines was later advanced to the twenty-first century. Johnson's environmental bills set important precedents that later administrations, after considerable resistance from various industries, were to extend somewhat in scope and in rigor of enforcement.

Civil Rights and Civil Liberties

In June 1964 the Senate voted 71 to 29 to end a southern filibuster; it was the first time Congress had invoked cloture during a civil rights debate. Then a new civil rights law passed by an even wider margin. Only five Republicans from outside the South, including Barry Goldwater, and even fewer nonsouthern Democrats, opposed the bill.

The Civil Rights Acts of 1964 and 1965 The new law covered a wide range of subjects, generally promising more than it could deliver. The most controversial portion, Title II, outlawed discrimination in hotels, motels, restaurants, theaters, and all other public accommodations engaged in interstate commerce; a provision exempting "private clubs" without defining "private" made evasion of the law fairly simple. The law also created an Equal Employment Opportunity Commission with broad powers to investigate and review complaints but with little power to enforce compliance. Despite its weaknesses, the Civil Rights Act of 1964 represented a signal victory for the activists and friends of the civil rights movement. The provisions covering public accommodations were generally obeyed.

In 1965 Congress strengthened the guarantee of voting rights that the 1964 Civil Rights Act had promised. The Voting Rights Act empowered the attorney general to appoint federal examiners to supervise voter registration in states and counties that had used such devices as literacy tests to exclude potential voters. By the end of 1965, examiners had been appointed in thirty-five counties, and within five months black registration in deep South states increased forty percent. The Voting Rights Act worked in tandem with the Twenty-fourth Amendment, ratified in 1964, which eliminated poll taxes in federal elections. Together they provided a base of voters in some areas for the election of the first black officials since Reconstruction.

Black Power and Ghetto Riots Johnson made his most controversial civil rights request in January 1966. He wanted laws prohibiting discrimination in the sale or rental of all housing and punishing interference with the rights of Americans in education, employment, jury service, and travel. Congress responded with legislation, but resistance was hardening. When Martin Luther King led a group of demonstrators into a white ethnic suburb of Chicago, a mob met them filled with a rage King claimed never to have en-

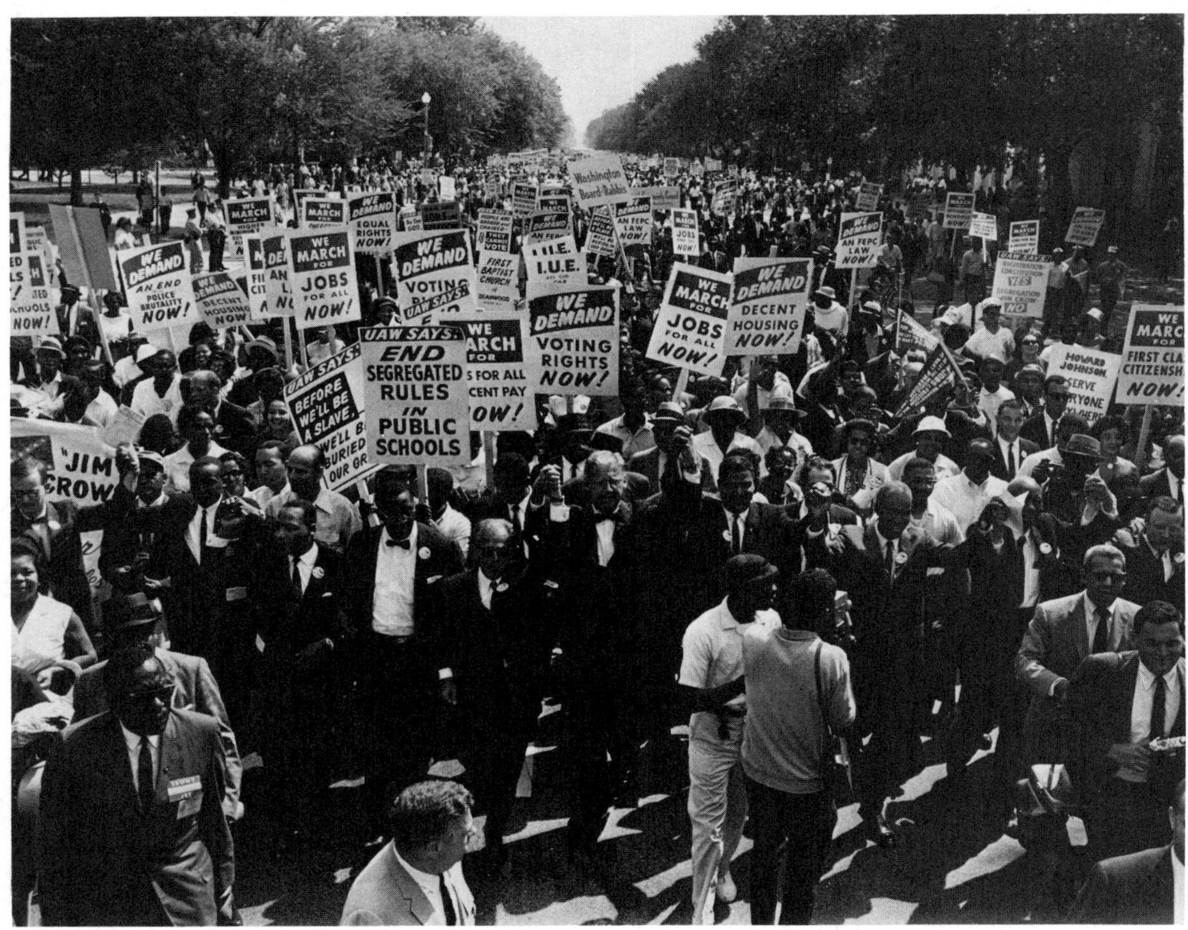

The civil rights movement of the 1960s marched onward, seeking equality in schooling, voting, employment, and housing. *(Courtesy, AP/Wide World Photos)*

countered before, even in Mississippi or Alabama.

At the same time a militant black power movement, expressing at moments a hostility to whites that sounded similar to white racism, was coming to replace in the public consciousness the civil rights movement of the early 1960s. Its hero was the martyred Malcolm X, killed by assassins in 1965. Malcolm had written against the ideas of King:

> There is no such thing as a nonviolent revolution. The only kind of revolution that is nonviolent is the Negro revolution. The only revolution in which the goal is loving your enemy is the Negro revolution. It's the only revolution in which the goal is a desegregated lunch counter, a desegregated theatre, a desegregated park, and a desegregated public toilet; you can sit down next to white folks—on the toilet. That's no revolution. Revolution is bloody, revolution is hostile, revolution knows no compromise, revolution overturns and destroys everything that gets in its way. And you, sitting around here like a knot on the wall, saying, 'I'm going to love these folks no matter how much they hate me.' No, you need a revolution.

Ghetto rebellions, most notably those in Los Angeles in 1965 and in Detroit two years later, frightened even voters who lived far from black neighborhoods. Later in his life Malcolm X himself renounced racial hatred.

One of the most radical of the civil-rights organizations of the 1960s began as the Student Nonviolent Coordinating Committee (SNCC). By the mid-sixties SNCC was turning against Martin Luther King. On a Missisippi March in 1966 Stokely Carmichael of SNCC appropriated the cry "black power" and took a shot at one of King's followers with a water pistol. One white youth from the University of Michigan remembers the anger of Carmichael's adviser, Willie Ricks, who

> lashed out at whites. As he talked . . . there was a feeling of a rising storm. [The black power chant] seemed like a hit on well-intentioned whites like me, that the message from Willie Ricks was 'Go home, white boy.'

In accord with its new temper, SNCC dropped "Nonviolent" from its title, substituting "National" and thereby keeping the acronym "SNCC," customarily pronounced "snick."

But another SNCC member, John Lewis of Georgia, recalls of the period:

> The civil rights movement that I was a part of has, in a short time, changed this region. There are still problems, no question about it, but when you go around this area, you see people working together in a way that is simply amazing. It's a different climate.

One of the most admirable of all civil rights ventures had occurred under SNCC's leadership at a time when it was still friendly to white allies. In the early and middle 1960s, black activists in Mississippi worked under risky conditions to encourage and help blacks to register to vote. Local authorities attempted to frighten blacks away from voting, and dozens lost their lives amidst the most murderous repression in the country. In the summer of 1964, Freedom Summer as it was called, about a thousand northern volunteers of college age, most of them white, went to the state at the invitation of SNCC to aid in the voter registration campaign. More specifically, that campaign was enrolling black Mississippians in the Mississippi Freedom Democratic Party (MFDP) as an alternative to the state's regular Democratic Party, which was under white control. In the most widely publicized killing of the summer a black activist, James Chaney, along with the northern white volunteers Michael Schwerner and Andrew Goodman were killed by a local white death squad. A legendary figure of the movement, Robert Parris Moses, returned to a SNCC office in Greenwood, Mississippi, to find it empty and ransacked by Klansmen. Exhausted from his day's work, Moses made up a bed in the corner and went to sleep. The volunteer who had escaped the white mob a few hours before by climbing to the roof of a nearby building has remarked of this reticent leader:

This is the only known photograph of both the Reverend Martin Luther King, Jr., and Malcolm X. Toward the end of his life, Malcolm was moderating his views on black separatism, but many of his followers held to his earlier statements. *(Courtesy, AP/Wide World Photos)*

> I just didn't understand what kind of guy this Bob Moses is, that could walk into a place where a lynch mob had just left and make up a bed and prepare to go to sleep, as if the situation was normal. So I guess I was learning.

Another prominent figure in Mississippi SNCC was Fannie Lou Hamer, who with Moses helped to mobilize a challenge to the all-white Mississippi delegation to the 1964 Democratic National Convention. Speaking for her largely black alternate slate of delegates, the MFDP, she told the television camera about her first attempt to register:

> [The policeman] said, 'You bitch, we gon' make you wish you was dead.' I heard the highway patrolman tell the black man [a prisoner], 'If you don't beat her, you *know* what we'll do to you.' The first Negro began to beat, and I was beat until I was exhausted. . . . All this is on account we want to

register, to become first-class citizens, and if the Freedom Democratic Party is not seated now, I question America.

Of the Freedom Summer project of 1964, which brought Kennedy generation northern students to Mississippi to help register blacks, Fannie Lou Hamer wrote: "The big thing about the summer of '64 was that people learned white folks were human."

The Democratic Convention refused to seat the Mississippi Freedom Democratic Party delegation, selecting instead the regular white Mississippi delegates and offering the insurrectionist slate an unacceptable compromise. White and black civil rights volunteers shared a sense of betrayal that had a part in radicalizing both. More particularly, it contributed to the black power movement that became articulate in 1966, especially in the voice of Stokely Carmichael.

The Immigration and Nationality Act of 1965

The growing national concern with race, ethnicity, and civil rights, as well as changing immigration patterns and economic concerns in the United States, also led to extensive reforms in existing immigration laws. Ever since 1924, American immigration laws had established annual quotas by country for new immigrants. But the quotas were biased. Countries in northern and western Europe had relatively large quotas while countries in southern and eastern Europe and Africa had small quotas. Asian immigrants were excluded altogether. The McCarran Act of 1952 eliminated the Asian exclusion but still retained the other quotas. Then in 1965, the Immigration and Nationality Act reversed the forty-year-old policy of imposing ethnic quotas based on national origins.

Under this act the United States permitted a total of 170,000 people from the Eastern Hemisphere to immigrate each year on a first-come, first-served basis, except that no more than twenty thousand people could come from any one country. Preferences went to refugees, people with family members already in the United States, and professional and skilled workers. The act also, for the first time in United States history, limited immigration from the Western Hemisphere to 120,000 people per year, primarily to please the large labor unions that were concerned about immigration from Mexico. Western Hemisphere immigrants were also allowed to enter on the principle first-come, first-served without categorical preference or limits from any given country. A 1976 amendment to the act extended to immigrants from the Western Hemisphere the preference system and the limit of twenty thousand people per country, while exempting Cuban refugees from the limits. Of course, large-scale immigration from Mexico continued, much of it by evasion of the Immigration and Naturalization Service.

The Warren Court

The black revolution of the 1960s inevitably directed judicial attention toward the system of law enforcement, and some of the most controversial decisions of the Warren Court concerned criminal procedure and the rights of the accused. In *Gideon* v. *Wainwright* (1963) the Court guaranteed the right to legal counsel in all felony cases. At a trial in which insolvency forced him to carry on his own defense, Clarence Earl Gideon, a white southerner with a long criminal record, had been convicted of breaking and entering a Florida poolroom. His handwritten appeal to the Supreme Court combined a moving personal history with imperfect legal terminology. The guarantee in *Gideon* of courtroom counsel regardless of capacity to pay expanded to the police station three years later in *Miranda* v. *Arizona*, wherein the Court affirmed a prisoner's right to see an attorney before answering questions, besides requiring the police to inform the prisoner of a range of legal rights.

Other decisions protected rights of speech and privacy. With one notable exception the Court consistently refused to uphold obscenity convictions. More shocking to conventional sensibilities than permissiveness toward pornography was a series of decisions that in 1962 and 1963 outlawed compulsory Bible reading and similar religious activities in public schools. The Court rejected such practices not only for abridging the separation of church and state, but also for imposing, if only symbolically, a particular morality on the individual student.

One of the Warren Court's most notable dicta was the principle "one man, one vote." In a series of legislative apportionment cases beginning with *Baker v. Carr* (1965), the Court required that both houses of the legislature in each state reflect the actual distribution of population in that state. This ruling ended some of the more extreme cases in which rural areas enjoyed a power disproportionate to their population.

The final two years of Johnson's administration were a time of political stalemate. Appropriations for the war on poverty remained fairly constant, but no new programs were initiated. Congress slashed the administration's foreign aid requests. To decrease the deficits caused by Vietnam war spending, the President in 1967 asked for a ten percent tax surcharge, claiming that the surcharge was necessary if the federal government was to provide both "guns and butter," foreign and domestic spending. Congress grudgingly passed the measure in 1968, but also forced budget reductions that began to cut into the butter. Symbolic of the new congressional mood was the defeat of an appropriation for a ghetto rat-control program; the debate centered not on the amount of money, a relatively small $100 million, but on the extent of the federal government's legitimate interest in social welfare. In 1968 Congress enacted the Omnibus Crime Bill, allocating funds to upgrade local police forces, broadening the wire-tapping authority of law enforcement agencies, and attempting to restrict some of the Supreme Court's guarantees of the rights of the accused.

The most important political event in the mid-1960s took place not at home but in Vietnam. For Americans that war began in earnest in 1965.

Points To Think About

1. Between 1929 and 1945 Americans lived in a world of deferred expectations. People delayed getting married; they delayed starting families; they put off purchases even when they had the money because they were afraid to disturb their small savings. People made do with less. Then the war came and prosperity with it, but people still had to put off realizing their dreams. The birthrate remained low because so many men were away in the military. And wartime shortages made unavailable the consumer goods that had suddenly become within their means.

The late forties and fifties were an era given over to catching up. From an economic standpoint, the postwar United States was one of the best places in history to be born. The birthrate zoomed upward, new housing went up at a furious rate, new cars rolled off the assembly lines. People dedicated themselves to realizing their dreams.

For many the dream was of a house of their own in the suburbs where they and their families could live in security and comfort. This idyllic arrangement, which millions achieved, had profound implications for women. The baby boom and the cult of the family reinforced the old idea that a woman's place was in the home. The fifties were the heyday of what Betty Friedan in 1963 assailed as *The Feminine Mystique*. Many women had worked during the war. But as prosperity returned, and the new domesticity with it, women retired from the workplace and devoted themselves to raising babies and keeping house. Feminism had to wait for a new generation, which had not had to struggle through the Depression and the war.

2. The civil rights movement was an object lesson in how to effect change. Or so it seemed to other groups in the 1960s. Many of the leaders of the students' and women's movements had gotten their start in the civil rights crusade. There they learned tactics like the sit-in and the protest march (both used with great effectiveness by the labor movement in the 1930s). And there they learned that American institutions could be altered by direct action. The student radicals adopted, in their struggle against the Vietnam War, the style of confrontation politics they had found in the civil rights crusade.

And just as blacks gained a new sense of themselves through participation in it, so too women, students, gays, ethnic groups, welfare recipients, senior citizens, Spanish-speaking Americans, and others all sought a new self-consciousness in the late 1960s. Ethnics rediscovered their cultural heritage, women engaged in "consciousness raising," and older Americans campaigned for a more favorable image of the elderly.

Among the methods that gained a good deal of visibility during the civil rights struggle itself along with the later antiwar protests was that of nonviolence. Nonviolence does not refer to passivity in the face of power: it involves to the contrary some deliberate breaking of a law or custom—sitting in a segregated restaurant, blocking the entrance to a building, or the like. Perhaps the great majority of its practitioners used it exclusively as a tactic, to be employed as long as it was effective, to be replaced by the force of law and the courts if these could be enlisted on the side of civil rights. But since nonviolence requires that in the face of provocation the protester will resist both the impulse to become violent and the impulse to flee, the practice came to mean for some an exercise in self-control and self-reformation, as demanding in its own way as military training or the routines of a religious order.

3. While the Kennedy and Johnson administrations carried the old New Deal liberalism into the 1960s, the general prosperity of the postwar period meant that their proposals could be far more ambitious than FDR's. Whereas Roosevelt had committed the government to do what it could to relieve distress, Lyndon Johnson promised to abolish it.

People were unemployed. So the government, through proper economic policies, would stimulate the economy and create new jobs. Jobs called for skills the unemployed lacked. So the government would train them. Children from disadvantaged families did poorly in school. So the government, with programs like Upward Bound and Higher Horizons, would provide them with additional cultural opportunities. Hot lunch programs would guarantee that they received the proper nutrition. Minorities discriminated against in hiring, in public facilities, or on the job? The government would enforce the new civil rights legislation.

The Great Society rested upon a simple idea. The United States, the richest nation in the world, could afford to abolish poverty, end discrimination, and guarantee everyone a decent life. The Great Depression, and the limits it had imposed on what the government could do, was over. So what was once only a dream could become reality. So argued LBJ and the American people agreed.

The Great Society was never achieved, but the effort accomplished a great deal. Jobs were created; discrimination, if not ended, was combated; millions benefited from the new programs. Yet within a few years, it was commonplace to assert that the Great Society had been nearly a total failure. What had happened? The question is complex, but elements of the answer seem clear.

One is that the "war on poverty" raised expectations that could not be realized. The disadvantaged, particularly poor blacks, quickly grew impatient with the pace of change. Jobs were not being created quickly enough, they believed. Programs took a long time to implement and then often did not work. Job training programs, for example, admitted only a limited number, had difficulty keeping trainees in the program, and failed to place in permanent jobs a significant percentage of the graduates. Impatience sometimes turned to frustration and then to bitterness and hostility. Riots broke out in many cities. Meanwhile, many other groups in the society took the riots as evidence that it was a waste of time to try to help these people. What was needed, they insisted, was a program to strengthen the police. "Law and Order" became a powerful slogan for use by opponents of the Great Society.

Another problem with the Great Society program was that the bitter social and political divisions over the war in Vietnam destroyed much of its political support. As the war dragged on, with mounting costs and casualties, an antiwar movement emerged. This was largely made up of people who otherwise would have supported the Great Society—liberal politicians, teachers and students, civil rights leaders. The Johnson political coalition collapsed. In 1968 L.B.J. himself withdrew from the presidential race after the New Hampshire primary. And the increasingly dovish Hubert Humphrey, another dedicated advocate of New Deal liberalism, lost the presidential election—partly because many rigidly uncompromising antiwar liberals refused to support him. His Republican opponent, Richard Nixon, would withdraw from Vietnam slowly and at a cost of some 25,000 more American soldiers killed.

4. Between 1948 and 1968 the take-home pay of the average American more than doubled as measured in real dollars (that is, after inflation is accounted for). Like all averages, this one disguised great variations. Some groups, particularly the upper and upper-middle classes, improved their situation even more impressively, while others, such as migrant farm laborers, benefited little from the great postwar prosperity. Even so, most Americans experienced for a full generation a steady improvement in their standard of living. (In contrast, real wages after taxes declined by 7% between 1968 and 1978.) Average Americans found themselves able to purchase a home, a second car, television sets, and other items previously out of their reach. They could even send their children to orthodontists and to college. They could take real vacations. Things were good, and they were getting steadily better.

This broad-based prosperity allowed liberals to

propose sweeping reforms without raising taxes or redistributing wealth. The New Frontier and the Great Society, that is, rested upon the promise of continued growth. During the 1970s, however, growth slackened. The most notable sign of this was the oil price hikes of 1973. As the cost of fuel and other resources soared, so did prices. Wages, though they also rose sharply, lagged behind. Inflation swallowed up growth. People had ever larger sums of money to spend, but found themselves able to buy less. The components of the good life, like ownership of a home, became markedly less attainable.

Suggested Readings

Recent books on the era include Maurice Isserman, *If I Had a Hammer. . . . The Death of the Old Left and the Birth of the New Left* (1987), Robert Divine, *The Johnson Years,* II (1987), Charles Eagles, ed., *The Civil Rights Movement in America* (1986), Richard Powers, *Secrecy and Power: The Life of J. Edgar Hoover* (1983), Paul K. Conkin, *Big Daddy of the Pedernales: Lyndon B. Johnson* (1986), Gerald T. Rice, *The Bold Experiment: JFK's Peace Corps* (1985), C. Eric Lincoln and Lawrence H. Mamiya, *The Black Church in the African American Experience* (1990), and, on the civil rights movement, *Freedom Bound* (1990) by Robert Weisbrot.

Recent studies of Eisenhower emphasize his caution in domestic programs, his restraint in the use of presidential powers, and the absence in his foreign policy of dangerously large involvements. See, for example, the two-volume biography by Stephen Ambrose. On John Kennedy see the two-volume biography by Herbert Parmet, *Jack: The Struggles of John Fitzgerald Kennedy* (1980) and *JFK: The Presidency of John Fitzgerald Kennedy* (1983) and David Burner and Thomas R. West, *The Torch Is Passed: The Kennedy Brothers and American Liberalism* (1984). Arthur Schlesinger, Jr., describes John and Robert Kennedy as expressing the best ideas and possibilities of their times: *A Thousand Days* (1965) and *Robert F. Kennedy and His Times* (1978). Carl Brauer holds that Kennedy supported the civil rights activists strongly and effectively and within the limits imposed by politics and the legal system: *John F. Kennedy and the Second Reconstruction* (1977). Another controversial topic of the Kennedy presidency is covered by Robert A. Divine, ed., *The Cuban Missile Crisis* (1971), and a well-known effort to analyze the crisis is Graham Allison, *Essence of Decision* (1971). A sharply critical book on Kennedy is Garry Wills, *The Kennedy Imprisonment* (1981). On Lyndon Johnson see Doris Kearns, *Lyndon Johnson and the American Dream* (1976), Eric Goldman, *The Tragedy of Lyndon Johnson* (1969), and Merle Miller, *Lyndon: An Oral Biography* (1980). Robert Caro critically details Johnson's early life in his massive *The Path to Power* (1982) and *Means of Ascent* (1989). *Lone Star Rising* (1991), the first volume of Robert Dallek's life of Johnson which can be taken as a refutation of Caro, covers the Texan through 1960.

Richard Kluger's *Simple Justice* (1976) studies the great *Brown v. Board of Education* case and the struggle to implement the Supreme Court's order to desegregate public schools. Taylor Branch has written a magisterial biography of Martin Luther King entitled *Parting the Waters* (1988). William G. McLoughlin studies the moralism of the sixties in *Revivals, Awakenings, and Reform* (1978).

☆ ☆ ☆ POINTS OF VIEW: ☆ ☆ ☆

JFK—A Question of Character?

Thomas Reeves

Good character is an essential framework for the complex mixture of qualities that make an outstanding President and a model leader for a democratic people. Character is a question of values, inclinations, and judgment, all of which are brought to bear in the day-to-day work of leadership.

The real Kennedy—as opposed to the celebrated hero espoused by the Kennedy family, the media, and the Camelot School—lacked greatness in large part because he lacked the qualities inherent in good character. He failed to be a true moral leader of the American people because he lacked the conviction and commitment that create such exemplars of character for all to emulate. . . .

Jack was still incapable of monogamy at the time of his assassination. And it is just as likely that news of the dark side of the president's personal and official activities might have ruined Kennedy's second term and brought the nation another kind of grief and mourning than that which tragically did ensue.

America needs great presidents, which means that this country must find and elect people of high moral character, as well as intelligence and experience. Character and conduct are clearly linked, and the personal weaknesses of a chief executive can often turn out to be public liabilities. It is wise to encourage the careful scrutiny of presidential aspirants that has become the practice in recent years. It is neither priggish nor unrealistic to seek to determine, to the best of our ability, which presidential aspirants live by values that we hope they will uphold in public, values such as honesty, responsibility, fairness, loyalty, and respect for others. Indeed, the pursuit seems simply sensible.

At the same time, the American people must resist the temptation to be won over by a handsome face, expensive campaign efforts, and thrilling rhetoric. In the early 1960s, we became involved in a sort of mindless worship of celebrity; it was a love affair largely with images. . . .

Kennedy died a hero. This has less to do with the facts about Jack than with the image erected during and after his life by romantic, misguided, and sometimes cynical partisans. . . .

A major lesson that emerges from a careful look at Jack Kennedy's life concerns the moral responsibility of our presidents. From the nation's beginnings, in the exemplary George Washington, who thought about such things, there has been an implicit contract between the chief executive and the American people, an understanding that the nation's highest public official should exhibit such virtues as dignity, moderation, disinterestedness, self-mastery, resoluteness, strength of will, and personal integrity. Washington indeed was regarded as an "exemplification of moral values," a president widely perceived to be great because he was good. The public later attributed the same virtues to Abraham Lincoln. . . .

During the Thousand Days, Kennedy arrogantly and irresponsibly violated his covenant with the people. While saying and doing the appropriate things in the public light, he acted covertly in ways that seriously demeaned himself and his office. He got away with it at the time, and the cover-up that followed kept the truth hidden for decades. That this could happen again makes it imperative that we search for presidential candidates who can, by example, elevate and inspire the American people, restoring confidence in their institutions and in themselves. Kennedy's political skills are desirable, to be sure: the charisma, the inspiring oratory, the wit, the intelligence, the courage. But all of these qualities must be connected to an effort to live and lead by those values, known and declared for centuries, that link good character with effective leadership. The United States—and now the world—cannot settle for less.

Thomas R. West

Professor Thomas Reeves misses a distinction between what Kennedy's relationship should have been to his priest-confessor and what were his proper dealings with the public. The President is a symbol of the time, an exemplar of its virtues or a living statement of its vices. And in this capacity a presidency does not merely reflect on the faults or strengths of the era but molds the character of the citizenry. But that means that it is the public character of an administration and its Chief Executive, the image that the President projects out of public acts, that should be at issue.

The image that Kennedy shaped was one of the best that any recent President has had to offer. It recommended by example resoluteness tempered and strengthened by a refusal to act on emotion. It had, moreover, the essential, wholly legitimate value of being an image that the population could respond to. Consider the contrast between Kennedy's tenure and that of President Carter, a man of exemplary character who unlike other Presidents insisted that human rights are human rights, even when our allies violate them. If any President deserved to have the attention and understanding of the country, it was Carter. And this man of conscience got nowhere in the White House as an instructor of the American people.

Foreign policy gave the image of the Kennedy presidency much of its shape. Against the political right, with its frenzied vocabulary, its broodings about the metaphysical evil of Communism, its conviction that the Communist world was monolithic and indivisible, Kennedy was able to present a far more convincing image of strength as a compound of force and restraint. Restraint after the failure at the Bay of Pigs, restraint and measured reaction to the building of the Berlin Wall, restraint when during the blockade of Cuba a harmless Soviet freighter went through the American lines: all this defined Kennedy's foreign policy as much as did its more confrontational elements. The Peace Corps was wholly coherent with the more general temperament of Kennedy's foreign policy. It sent into impoverished regions of the world soldiers of peace armed with advanced academic or technical intelligence and a determination to carry out difficult assignments. The test-ban treaty was a fitting conclusion to an administration that calculated the means to a carefully monitored peace, while phobic conservatives fumed.

Meanwhile there was the civil rights movement, which the administration gave little indication of understanding. The rights movement had its own compound of forcefulness and, in the discipline of nonviolence, self-restraint. It practiced an impassioned liberation, while the administration was more at home with the cooler phenomena of the age: futuristic technology, advanced education, expert knowledge. The one spoke in the prophetic voice of Martin Luther King, Jr., the other in the flat factual radio messages of an astronaut in space. But together the Kennedy image and the rights revolution conquered the hearts and conscience of a young generation.

Whoever the private Kennedy may have been—cheating husband, father of a tight-knit family, or both, passive creature of events or their initiator—it was from the visible and composite figure in the White House that the nation as a whole could receive its moral lessons. That figure, defining itself in policies, exemplified the virtue of a purposeful self-control. For our own time, after a period of self-indulgence and facile patriotism urged on by Republican administrations and a decadence for which neither freemarket conservatives nor lifestyle liberals have any convincing solution, the virtues of the Kennedy era would be a valuable rediscovery.

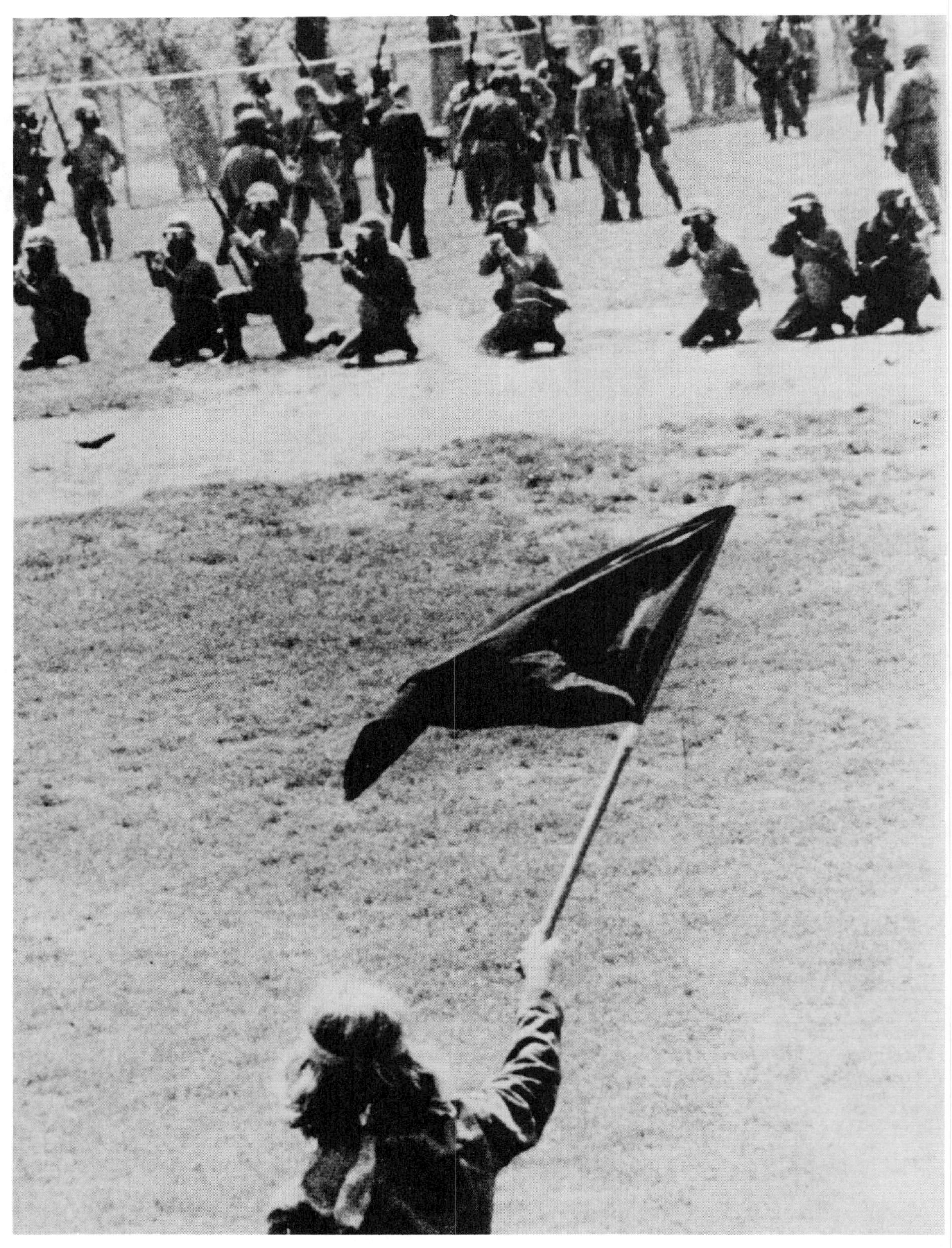

Ohio National Guardsmen advance on demonstrating students. Kent State University, Kent, Ohio.
(Courtesy, AP/Wide World Photos)

CHAPTER 28

American Society and the Vietnam War

THE KENT STATE MASSACRE

Kent State University in northeastern Ohio could have stood as a symbol of the growth of higher education in the 1960s. Although it was common for public universities to expand in this era, few had mushroomed like Kent State. During the 1960s, enrollment tripled to over twenty thousand students. Rapidly constructed new buildings could not keep pace with new enrollment. Students began to complain of alienation from this campus that was so large. The annual mudfight on the first warm spring night was still a tradition; the football team was important. But even Kent State, a middle-American school that had been silent when Harvard and Columbia were erupting in the spring of 1968, became politicized at the end of the decade.

Serious radical activity began at Kent State in November 1968 when the Black United Students and Students for a Democratic Society (SDS) sat in to protest the presence on campus of recruiters from the Oakland, California, police. In April 1969, SDS members attacked the administration building demanding the abolition of the Reserve Officers Training Corps (ROTC). A week later, their suspension hearing turned into a fistfight between fraternity men and members of SDS that brought the Ohio Highway Patrol onto the campus to arrest fifty-eight students. Several SDS leaders went to jail for six months and the organization was banned from the campus.

On the evening of April 30, 1970, President Richard M. Nixon went on national television to announce that as part of our withdrawal from the war in Vietnam we had invaded neighboring Cambodia. "All the kids were around TV sets in the dorm," the Kent State student government president recalls. "They had horrified stares on their faces."

Fearing trouble, local police slapped a curfew on the town and called in the National Guard. Ohio Governor James Rhodes, who had expended more for National Guard service in the past two years than the total of the other forty-nine governors, readily complied. By the time the Guardsmen arrived, already exhausted from six days service at a truckers' strike, radical students had actually given them an occasion to be there: on the night of May 2, a group of students burned the rickety old wooden ROTC building.

The campus mood was surly. Communication among local officials, the Guard, and the university was awkward at best. The Guardsmen were ill-equipped for their duty, which was essentially crowd control. Their weapons were absurdly disproportionate to the job. Well-trained, well-directed guard units in other states were supplied with bird shot and buckshot and were forbidden to carry loaded weapons until directly ordered to do so by their commanders. In Ohio, the Guard troops kept their guns in "locked, loaded, and ready" position. Any tired, nervous young guard could—literally—trigger catastrophe. The weapon was the M-1, with bullets that pass through an eighteen-inch tree trunk at close range or travel for two miles. The odds on killing bystanders in an altercation were high.

On Monday, May 4, Kent State entered the history books. Students had conflicting information about what might happen: all assemblies on campus were forbidden, they heard. Yet classes were still scheduled and so was a rally called for noontime. Or was it? Sometime after 11:00 a.m. someone began tolling a bell and about 1,500 students began to gather for the possible rally. Soon the Guard tried to disperse the crowd, which responded first with obscene chants and then, here and there, with flying stones. Wind and noise drowned out commands. A reporter standing with some Guardsmen heard an officer call: "Fix bayonets, gas masks, load [rifles]." "I could not believe it. What were these guys going to do, mount a charge against a bunch of kids?" With the students about one hundred yards away from this small contingent of troops, the gas canisters began to pop. The wind was blowing back toward the troops and students could easily pick up the canisters and lob them back. No weapons were left except bayonets and the awesome M-1s. Some of the troops dropped to a kneeling position and pointed their rifles at the crowd. Some students ran up the hill behind them, coming closer than before to throw their rocks—perhaps now to somewhat more effect. At the top of the hill the Guardsmen stopped, turned, and in the next thirteen seconds fired sixty-one shots, killing four students and wounding nine.

A veteran of the war in Vietnam seeing the helicopter above and the bloodshed imagined himself back in Vietnam. "I didn't realize the guys were shooting at the kids," one Guardsman has reported, "until I saw this kid's chest break into blood." By 5:00 p.m. the campus was empty. Dangling from a dormitory window near Blanket Hill were several bedsheets tied together to form the backdrop for a large sign with the word WHY? Why indeed? An observer can point to the inappropriateness of using the National Guard; to Nixon's speech on Cambodia (the following day he referred to student dissidents as "bums"); to the hysteria of local officials who called in the Guard; to the governor's overuse of them; to the sour mood of 1970 as the nation unhappily faced the prospect of final defeat in Indochina.

A few days later at Jackson State University in Mississippi, nervous local police riddled the facade of a dormitory with bullets that killed two students. As though in confirmation of what black commentators had been saying about the relative indifference of the white majority to even the grossest incidents involving blacks, an incident very similar to that at Kent State but at a black school received only light press coverage.

The Social Spectrum: From the Fifties to the Seventies

It is customary to present the Eisenhower years that preceded the Kennedy presidency as a time of blissful tranquility. The times had indeed been tranquil, if they are compared to what followed them. But they were in their own way as innovative as any comparable span of years in American history. A technology and economy that demanded literate skills swelled the college population and would swell it still further as the postwar baby boom came to university age. Technical advances were also preparing the way for a cornucopia of new consumer goods that have shaped the behavior of Americans ever since. The beat literature of the 1950s, along with the communal style of life, defined a rebellion that is also remembered today in the shape it took among the communes of the late sixties. The energies of black rhythm and blues, white country music, and jazz were compounding into rock and roll, a prelude to the hard rock of the 1960s. And above all there was the peaceful black uprising at Montgomery and elsewhere, overturning patterns of subordination that whites had taken entirely for granted, and doing so with a method of nonviolent resistance almost unprecedented in the American experience.

The Service Economy Most people associate work with making or growing something. But it is a peculiarity of advanced industrial societies that much of their most skilled and imaginative work goes not into production of visible goods but into services. In the affluent years that followed World War II, the American economy and technology spawned countless jobs of this kind: teaching, radio and television announcing, acting, retailing, the staffing of hotels and motels, restaurants, health spas, movie theaters. Accountants, technicians, clerical workers, and administrators, moreover, are all essential to the making of objects they will never see.

The Consumer Society Away from working hours the participant in the modern economy has become a new creature: the consumer. Consumers in the 1950s and 1960s were barraged with every sales technique Madison Avenue could devise. Advertising costs in 1970 measured eight times those of 1940. Some observers decided that consumerism demonstrated the superiority of American life to that of those societies, especially the Soviet Union, where people still struggled to obtain necessities.

This consumer society was going to be well-stocked with customers. The birth rate for each 1,000 people reached a high 24.1 in 1950 and peaked at 25.0 in 1955 before declining steadily until the 1980s. The bumper crop of children necessitated building new public schools; overcrowded classrooms brought about school financing crises and a national furor over "why Johnny can't read," as the title to a well-known book puts it. These postwar children, in elementary school when the Soviet Union launched its Sputnik satellite in 1957, became the target of elaborate programs of curriculum reform, with particular emphasis on mathematics and the sciences. The baby boom would also furnish an immense audience for television and create an enormous market for rock and roll music, automobiles, surfboards, clothes, skin creams, magazines, movies, and innumerable other commodities. By the mid-1960s enrollment in public higher education had tripled since 1945. The postwar generation created the base for student movements and much of the cultural experimentation of the 1960s.

As these children reached their majority, they entered a world breathtaking in its gadgetry: copiers, credit card billing, cassette tape recorders, computers, direct distance dialing, TV dinners, drive-in banking. Inexpensive, high-fidelity recordings of all kinds of music became available, along with improved phonographic equipment. Paperback books, bringing to mass audiences not only a variety of cheap leisure reading but also ready access to serious and scholarly work, improved high school and college curricula.

Mass Culture Critics reacted to a culture that seemed to express itself in television's trite situation comedies and popular music's banal lyrics. Newton Minow, chairman of the Federal Communications Commission under President Kennedy, called television a "vast wasteland." Some critics suggested that mass culture might be the harbinger of a dangerous social and political stupor. The sociologist David Riesman in

***Painted Bronze* by Jasper Johns, 1964. By the 1960s the consumer culture had spread even to art.**
(Courtesy, Leo Castelli)

The Lonely Crowd described a mass society of "other-directed" individuals dependent on peer approval, and contrasted them with earlier generations of "inner-directed" individuals who were self motivated and independent. While Riesman actually looked with some sympathy on the culture of other-direction, his study suggested that modern conditions threaten independence and individuality.

American Subcultures

The "Beats" Beyond the confines of both traditional high culture and the spreading, popular "mass" culture, a distinctive body of writing originated during the 1950s. It was nurtured among the beats of San Francisco and Greenwich Village. The popular press used "beat," and then "beatnik"; a few beats explained it as short for beatific, indicating a state of ecstacy and understanding. Jack Kerouac spoke for the beats in *On the Road* (1956) and a series of other novels. His unbroken flow of prose chronicled beat culture semi-autobiographically, detailing the simple pleasures and pains of cross-country hitchhiking, evading the police, appreciating cool black jazz, discovering marijuana, dabbling with Zen Buddhism, and generally avoiding the incomprehensible larger society. A revival of Kerouac's novels in the late sixties evidenced a newer generation of alienated youth searching for models and insights. Allen Ginsberg, coming from a radical middle-class family in Paterson, New Jersey, bummed his way around the world several times before composing the central statement of beat culture, a long poem entitled "Howl!" in 1956. Its opening lines read:

> I saw the best minds of my generation
> destroyed
> by madness,
> starving hysterical naked,
> dragging themselves through the negro streets
> at dawn looking for
> an angry fix

Ginsberg and another poet, Gary Snyder, also popularized mystical Asian religion and philosophy among avant-garde groups. Ginsberg, possibly because of his radical background and avowed homosexuality, maintained a more distinctly political position than most beats; he became a fixture at antiwar demonstrations in the sixties, chanting rhythmic Indian mantras in an attempt to immobilize the police.

Rock and Roll The adolescent subculture provided a ready market for the musical explosion of rock and roll.

Early rock and roll relied on two musical strains with long traditions and independent audiences. The primary appropriation, black rhythm and blues, gave the drive, the beat, and the solid, earthy feeling of the music. Rhythm and blues in turn had roots in black jazz, gospel, and blues music, all representing an autonomous market for recorded music until the advent of rock and roll. Some rhythm and blues performers, Little Richard and Fats Domino among them, successfully moved to the newer and larger white audience. But white performers and recording studios simply picked up and bleached much rhythm and blues without payment or acknowledgment. White country music, the other musical source of rock and roll, contributed some vocal patterns, the distinctive lead guitar sound, and many of the most important performers. The Everly Brothers and Buddy Holly came directly from the country tradition, and Elvis Presley, the dominating figure of early rock, worked in the Grand Ole Opry in Nashville. Before his first major recording contract in 1956 and the release of "Heartbreak Hotel"—a hit with country, popular, and rhythm and blues audiences—Presley had been an acclaimed country performer. Rock and roll possessed a vitality with which a new generation readily identified.

***Elvis* by Andy Warhol (1964), a pop tribute to the king of rock and roll.** *(Courtesy, Leo Castelli)*

Popular Diversions

The adolescent devotees of the rock culture and the hot rod consciously circumscribed themselves by their purposeful separation from the adult world. In the movie *Rebel Without a Cause* James Dean dramatized and romanticized the subculture playing the rebellious, drag-racing high school adolescent who defies his middle-class parents and the police in resolving his identity crisis.

Neither knowing nor caring about Allen Ginsberg, and having no wish to enter any culture of the alienated, countless Americans read *Reader's Digest*, with a monthly circulation of about ten million. The most popular books of the fifties were not Kerouac's novels but the *Reader's Digest Condensed Books*, abridgments of milder best sellers, which consistently sold millions of copies. The biggest box-office attractions of the fifties were not James Dean films but romantic comedies starring Rock Hudson and Doris Day, and such spectacular movies as *The Ten Commandments*. Among adult Americans not Elvis but Lawrence Welk held sway, serving waltzlike, romantically light "Champagne Music" over prime-time national television. In a stadium or facing a television set, tens of millions of Americans sat and watched baseball, football, and basketball.

By far the largest commercial culture empire of the fifties was Walt Disney Productions, Inc. In earlier times Disney had achieved success by producing highly innovative animated cartoons and feature movies. By the fifties, he had left the drawing board to oversee a colossal business enterprise, producing cartoons, comic books, a weekly television series, and a host of other projects. In 1955 Disney fulfilled his lifelong dream by opening "Disneyland" in Anaheim, California, which created a fantasy world comprehensive enough to appeal to almost everyone. The pleasures of Disneyland suggest a widely shared mood of the fifties—safe, tranquil, vaguely unreal. But just as thousands of antiwar demonstrators were later to invade Disneyland itself, an angry politics would break through the calm surfaces of mainstream culture.

Religion Many in the 1950s took comfort in the steady rise in church membership, increasing more rapidly than the total population. Between 1950 and 1956, Roman Catholics added five million members, Protestants eight million. Billy Graham, a central figure in evangelical Protestantism, crusaded across the nation and throughout the world. Graham functioned as a popularizer of Christianity rather than as a theologian. While organized religion remained a powerful institution, Protestant membership leveled off in the mid-sixties and declined thereafter. The Roman Catholic Church suffered in 1971, for the first time in its history, a small absolute decline in its American membership and a much larger one over the next decade.

Even in the 1950s that are now remembered as so placid, however, religion was astir. In Protestant theology, neoorthodoxy was applying to human nature some of the hard and skeptical analysis that is to be found in traditional Christianity. In the South, meanwhile, black churches were at the core of a growing resistance to white supremacy, bringing to the rebellion a Christian compound of militancy, patience, and cooperation. During the sixties, the civil-rights movement invaded the consciences of northern white Christians and Jews. Religious opponents of the war in Vietnam or nuclear arms drew not only on general Judeo-Christian concepts of peaceableness but on the specific practice of nonviolent resistance that came out of the civil-rights movement. The celebration of communion within the Roman Catholic Church gives an occasion for innovative liturgies stressing the concepts of reconciliation and community.

The Student Movement

By the time of John Kennedy's presidency, then, much had come about that could quicken the passions of middle-class young white Americans. They had the inspiration of the black civil-rights movement. Rock-and-roll was soon going to join or blend with coffee-house folk songs to produce the varieties of music that would attend the student rebellions like a sound-track. Beat literature offered half-images of cultural rebellion. In 1962 appeared Michael Harrington's *The Other America*, both an agent and a sign of a new stirring within the country. Harrington drew attention to the problem of poverty, a matter almost unnoticed during the fifties, except by the poor.

The first involvement on the part of white college youth in social reform was in interracial civil rights demonstrations. Young northern whites on the freedom rides through the South learned of white southern mob anger. Freedom Summer of 1964 drew college students to Mississippi to work with black activists in the registration campaign. When the Democratic Convention rejected the Mississippi Freedom Democratic Party delegation, the same disillusionment that sent numbers of black activists into black power was an influence in turning white idealists to a radical hostility to the whole political system.

The civil-rights movement was the major initial reason for the engagement of white college youth in liberal or radical politics. But increasingly large numbers of them had found additional reason for protest against their society.

SDS and FSM The early student movement emerged between the 1962 founding convention of the Students for a Democratic Society (SDS) and the 1964 Free Speech Movement (FSM) at the University of California at Berkeley. The SDS convention in Port Huron, Michigan, issued what came to be recognized as the "Port Huron Statement." The document called for social reform, not social revolution; the platform coupled its opposition to the nation's role in the Cold War with explicit opposition to Communism; a demand for educational reform that bespoke a belief in the university as a vehicle for social change; and a systematic critique of American society with an insistence on nonviolence and a loyalty to traditional American ideals. The Free Speech Movement at Berkeley, though ostensibly for specific political rights such as bringing in speakers and distributing political literature on university property, presented in embryo a challenge to the concept Chancellor Clark

THE PORT HURON STATEMENT *by Students for a Democratic Society*

The SDS met in Port Huron, Michigan, in 1962, and wrote an agenda for reform. Tom Hayden was one of its authors.

Introduction: Agenda For a Generation

We are people of this generation, bred in at least modest comfort, housed now in universities, looking uncomfortably to the world we inherit.

When we were kids the United States was the wealthiest and strongest country in the world: the only one with the atom bomb, the least scarred by modern war, an initiator of the United Nations that we thought would distribute Western influence throughout the world. Freedom and equality for each individual, government of, by, and for the people—these American values we found good, principles by which we could live as men. Many of us began maturing in complacency.

As we grew, however, our comfort was penetrated by events too troubling to dismiss. First, the permeating and victimizing fact of human degradation, symbolized by the Southern struggle against racial bigotry, compelled most of us from silence to activism. Second, the enclosing fact of the Cold War, symbolized by the presence of the Bomb, brought awareness that we ourselves, and our friends, and millions of abstract "others" we knew more directly because of our common peril, might die at any time. We might deliberately ignore, or avoid, or fail to feel all other human problems, but not these two, for these were too immediate and crushing in their impact, too challenging in the demand that we as individuals take the responsibility for encounter and resolution.

While these and other problems either directly oppressed us or rankled our consciences and became our own subjective concerns, we began to see complicated and disturbing paradoxes in our surrounding America. The declaration "all men are created equal . . ." rang hollow before the facts of Negro life in the South and the big cities of the North. The proclaimed peaceful intentions of the United States contradicted its economic and military investments in the Cold War status quo.

Kerr called "The Multiversity." While servicing large numbers of students, Kerr's modern university remained closely tied to business and government, performing the research and analysis tasks that supported defense industries, domestic social policies, and corporate technology.

Student movements came at a receptive time. In the early 1960s students were enrolling in colleges and universities in far greater numbers than ever before. Some states advanced an unprecedented one-half of all high school students to some form of college study. California, New York, and Texas led the nation in the expansion of their universities, state colleges, and two-year junior colleges. Their numbers and a degree of common experience gave some college students a sense of collective identity and potential power.

SDS, increasingly radical, came to demand "participatory democracy," a dismantling of centralized bureaucracies and the forming of little democracies throughout American life. Communities should control schools, students should have power in universities, citizens should supervise the police, and workers should have a part in running their plants. SDS helped organize the first major antiwar demonstration. It took place in Washington in April 1965, and surprised everyone by drawing 25,000 people. Campus SDS chapters began campaigns against research sponsored by the Department of Defense, against ROTC, and against recruiting by the Dow Chemical Company, which manufactured napalm—a burning jelly used in Vietnam that fastens on the skin. Campus radicals attacked the military officers as a visible link between the university and American foreign policy. On a few leading campuses, successful campaigns produced a denial of academic credit or university facilities to ROTC, which in effect eliminated these programs altogether.

Confrontation with college administrators and with the world outside the campus sharpened. When small groups resorted to the occupation of buildings and were met with tear gas and police squadrons, broader revolts ensued in 1968 at Columbia, Harvard, and San Francisco State College. The size of antiwar demonstrations in major cities escalated immensely. These levels of protest created divisions within student movements. At a stormy convention in 1969, SDS split into several factions.

Some became intrigued with real violence. The Weathermen, taking their name from Bob Dylan's "You don't need a weatherman to know which way the wind blows," tried in the "days of rage" in 1969 to disrupt the streets of Chicago. Soon Weathermen and others became interested in bombs. Several went off in buildings the bomb-wielders thought were symbolic of American capitalism or the war effort. The attempt was perhaps to bomb only empty buildings, but in 1970 in a New York City townhouse an accidental explosion killed three people who were operating a primitive bomb factory.

The Youth Culture

In the middle years of the 1960s, the student movement had supported the creation of a self-conscious and many-faceted youth culture. The demand for relevant and unprescribed education led to the establishment on some campuses of "free universities"—educational experiments including open registration and courses ranging from traditional academic offerings or political study groups to transcendental meditation and macrobiotic cooking. "Underground" newspapers, made possible by technical progress in inexpensive offset printing, appeared in every major city. The Berkeley *Barb*, the Los Angeles *Free Press*, the East Village *Other*, and the Atlanta *Great Speckled Bird* carried a mixed assortment: political

Confrontations between students and authorities were a hallmark of the late Sixties and early Seventies. *(Courtesy, United Press International Photo)*

analysis and polemics, music reviews, discussions of experimental ways of living, more or less inventive graphic art work, and excursions into mysticism, Asian religion, and the effects of drugs believed to be mind-expanding.

One element of the counterculture specifically merged with political radicalism; some members were quite aloof from politics. But the counterculture was in one sense political to its very core. Its members saw themselves as developing a way of life radically different from a stifling civilization of militarists, capitalists, and the technocratic management: the civilization that, so they argued, had produced the war in Vietnam.

Estimates of the number of college students who had at least tried marijuana reached by the late seventies as high as one-half. Stronger drugs found more limited use—LSD, hashish, mescaline, and amphetamines. Novelist Ken Kesey and his band of Merry Pranksters spiked the punch at rock concerts with the dangerous but not yet illegal LSD.

The beats and the earlier activists who had discovered American folk music provided some of the audience for the urban folk revival of the late fifties and early sixties that popularized authentic performers like Doc Watson, Mississippi John Hurt, and Jean Ritchie. The revival also produced a number of young, topical folksingers—notably Phil Ochs, Joan Baez, and Bob Dylan—who combined their musical talent with political commentary. Then the music hardened as it took in the metallic sounds of rock. Bob Dylan was booed off the stage during the 1965 Newport Rock Festival for using electric instruments in his back-up band, but before long hard rock had won wide acceptance among the young. By the time of the great music festival and gathering at Woodstock, New York, in 1969—still today a part of the folklore of the sixties—a variety of musical styles belonged to the counterculture.

The association of rock with drugs produced innumerable lyrics and a style, softer than the hardest rock and haunting in tone, known as acid or psychedelic rock—the special province of San Francisco-based groups such as the Grateful Dead, the Jefferson Airplane, and Big Brother and the Holding Company. San Francisco's Haight-Ashbury district became the center of 1967's summer of love as thousands of young people swarmed in from across the country. The Grateful Dead gave free concerts in the park; food was distributed by the Diggers, named after a seventeenth-century British sect advocating the abolition of private property. Others pitched in to establish free medical clinics and a host of other services. The summer of love also occasioned a minor business boom as hundreds of small entrepreneurs profited from the provision of drug-culture paraphernalia—black-light posters, water pipes, and chrome-plated roach clips. The head shops merchandising such items merely foreshadowed a systematic commercialization of youth movements, culminating in the advertising campaign to "hear the revolution on Columbia Records." Haight-Ashbury soon became an area of drug addicts and crime.

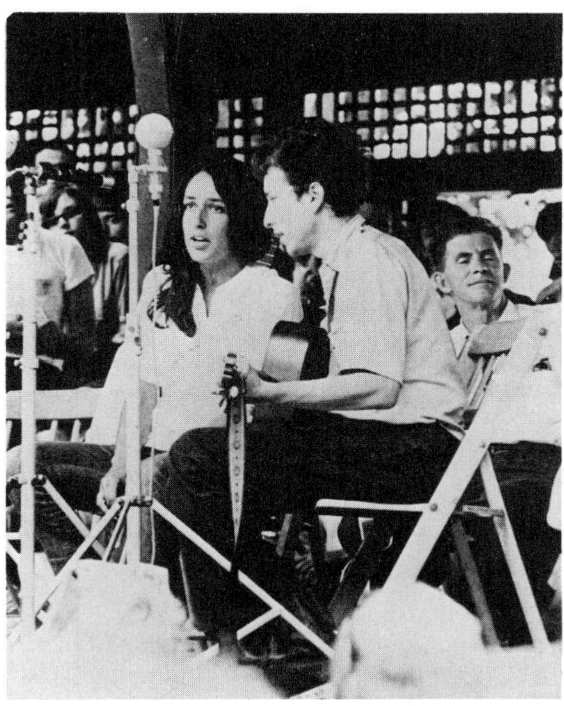

Bob Dylan and Joan Baez, two of the most popular folk singers of the Sixties, in concert. *(Courtesy, AP/Wide World Photos)*

The rest of the country was learning of communes, small groups of people living together. Probably the great majority of communes were not experimental or utopian. Rather, they were practical arrangements, among college students or others, for sharing expenses in an era of sexual tolerance and freedom encouraged by The Pill, the oral birth control breakthrough of the 1960s. Groups of unmarried men and women could now begin to live openly under the same roof. But even in these communes there was the sense that something new was being tried, a free yet family-like association that could be a model for the rest of society.

Theodore Roszak, in *The Making of a Counter-Culture* (1969), wrote about his subject favorably but critically. Charles Reich's *The Greening of America* (1970) exulted that this youthful American generation was beginning to let nature sprout, green and spontaneous, in the metallic and sterile present. And today the ecology movement, having as one of its sources the counterculture, insists that the health of civilization depends on the preserving of nature and a careful integration with it.

Cultural radicalism insisted on toleration and acceptance for varieties of personal behavior, and contributed to a significant modification of one form of bigotry: in recent years many Americans have changed their perception of homosexuality. Gays, a major casualty in Senator Joseph R. McCarthy's Redbaiting crusade against security risks, lived in jeopardy of their employment. Whether in private industry, government, or teaching, thousands of gay people were dismissed upon discovery of their sexual orientation. Worse still was the social stereotype that has stamped homosexuals as emotionally ill. Hollywood films, for example, almost invariably portrayed them as sick, vicious, or insipid. Adolescents in secondary school are particularly savage toward gays, and as a result—so a suppressed Bush administration report concludes—about one third of teenaged suicides are by gays.

Using the civil rights movement as a model, gays have fought these stereotypes and have achieved notable acceptance. In San Francisco, homosexual police and city council members now go about their daily routines like other American citizens. At the 1984 Democratic National Convention in that city, gays were welcomed into that political party and promised substantial funds to fight the sexually transmitted disease of AIDS, which fatally attacks the immune system.

So the current of cultural and political radicalism went in the sixties from the mildness of the Port Huron Statement to the later anger of SDS and the violence of the Weathermen, from the simplicity of folk music to the steel clamor of hard rock, from the sense of liberation and change in the days of the civil rights movement to the more exploratory efforts in the counterculture to liberate consciousness. Yet the movement had another side. Its emphasis on the freeing and cultivation of personal experience could encourage a turning away from community into privacy. And by the 1970s many young Americans were adopting faddish philosophies that advocated one method or another of self-cultivation, to the near exclusion of politics or social concerns.

The Women's Movement

The Nineteenth Amendment to the Constitution, adopted in 1920, provided women with the right to vote. For a time thereafter, women actively participated in politics and social reform movements. After this relatively brief period the women's movement became dormant, not to resurface until the 1960s. Yet during the decades in between the status of women underwent important changes. Some of the most significant occurred in the work force.

Women in the Workplace During the Depression working women were blamed for taking jobs from men, but women were not flooding the labor market and they earned fifty to sixty-five percent less than men. World War II altered the image of the working woman. More than one out of every three worked for a wage, and almost half who did were married. Educated, white middle-class women were entering the wage-earning force in large numbers.

The end of the war provoked a shift in attitudes. Woman was idealized as wife and mother, told to use newly acquired managerial skills to organize the household, arrange the car-pools, and run the PTA. Maintaining their family's mental and physical well-being became a full-time commitment for many women; they adopted the identity of "super-

The women's movement enabled women to increase their role in politics. Included in this photo are Bella Abzug (center) and, on her left, Shirley Chisolm, both elected to Congress in the late Sixties. *(Courtesy, United Press International Photos)*

mom," a concept Betty Friedan termed "the feminine mystique."

Yet the number of female wage earners was higher than before the war, and continued to rise steadily. They were mainly working in occupations defined as female—clerical jobs, domestic service, elementary school teaching; many other occupations, especially the professions, were largely restricted to men. Women were acquiring a smaller proportion of college degrees than they had forty years before. Still, by 1960 the number of working women was almost equal to that of men, and by the end of the decade almost nine out of every ten women, regardless of economic or social background, would be a part of the work force at some time in their lives.

The women's movement in the 1960s was closely related to the other reform movements of that period. The protest that the civil rights activists were raising against inequities in American life brought discrimination against women to public attention. And women, who found themselves relegated to secondary positions in the reform movements of the sixties, recognized that even reformism could reflect the injustices it was supposed to denounce.

The first major recognition of women's rights had come when President Kennedy set up the President's Commission on the Status of Women in 1961. Its purpose was to investigate institutional discrimination against women and to provide concrete recommendations for change. The report confirmed that there was widespread discrimination in both the public and the private sectors, and it urged the passage of new legislative and administrative laws. Title VII of the 1964 Civil Rights Act prohibited job discrimination because of race, color, religion, sex, or national origin; it is still the most powerful legal tool women possess when fighting inequalities in work. A 1991 civil rights law added some additional protection against sexual harassment.

Literature was probing the status of

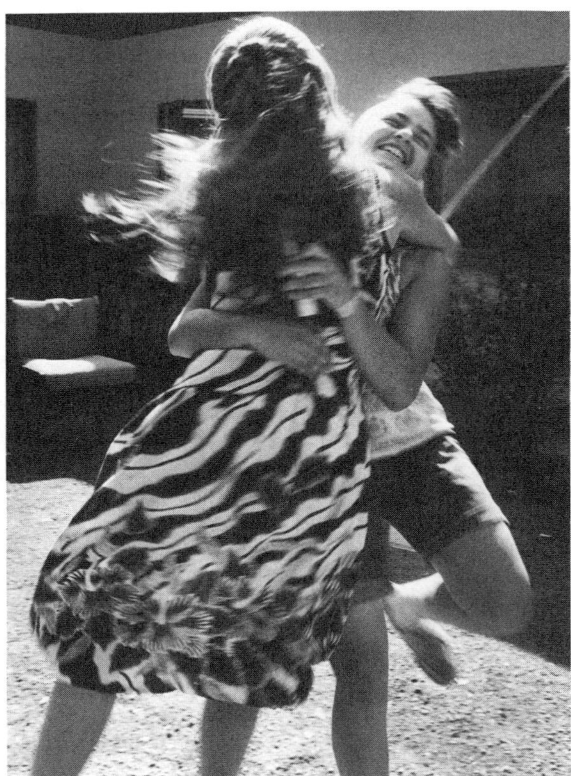

Two young women at Mills College in California learn that their school will remain a woman's institution. *(Courtesy, Jane Cleland, East Setauket, NY)*

women. In 1953 Simone de Beauvoir's *The Second Sex*, tracing the subordination of women throughout history, had been published in the United States. In 1963 Betty Friedan's *The Feminine Mystique* questioned the value and satisfaction middle-class women could derive from being housewives. This book, along with Kate Millett's *Sexual Politics* (1970) and Germaine Greer's *The Female Eunuch* (1971), had enormous impact on women. Also influential was an anthology of shorter writings entitled *Sisterhood is Powerful*, which presented important articles on housework, marriage, minority-group women, the psychology of women and a broad range of other topics.

Organizing Politically Women formed their own groups to press for an end to discrimination. In 1963 the Women's Equity Action League was formed to lobby for legislation concerning women's work and education. The National Organization for Women (NOW) was founded in 1966 with Betty Friedan as its first president; it quickly became the largest and most influential women's group. From the beginning the local chapters were autonomous. NOW concentrated on legal challenges, allowed men to join, and functioned as an umbrella covering many disparate tendencies. NOW committed much of its energies to passage of the Equal Rights Amendment and to abortion rights.

Women also carried the fight into state and federal courts, challenging statutes and practices that used sex as a legal classification. At least three states now provide for prosecution of a husband for raping his wife. Attention to these issues, along with others like the plight of battered wives and the need for child care services, have helped the movement reach women on all levels of society. Many activists avoided permanent organizations, forming groups and caucuses to battle within universities, social welfare agencies, neighborhoods, hospitals, and places of employment. In 1973 both houses of Congress approved the Equal Rights Amendment, but it failed to gain the necessary ratification in three-fourths of the states.

In 1973, in the important decision of *Roe v. Wade*, the Supreme Court handed down two decisions restricting the authority of states to prohibit abortion. The efforts of anti-abortionists to find other means of limiting the practice—federal legislation now allows Medicaid funds only when the woman's life is in danger—made the defense of abortion a central issue for the women's movement.

A Stronger Feminism A less structured movement composed largely of younger, unmarried women developed parallel with the older, more established feminist groups. These feminists stressed the oppression of women by men and argued that childhood socialization results in stereotyped sex roles. The Redstockings issued a manifesto in 1969 declaring male supremacy to be "the oldest, most basic form of domination; we need not to change ourselves, but to change men." From within these unstructured, deliberately leaderless groups came the technique of "consciousness raising"—small, nondirected discussions in which women shared experiences and feelings concerning men, other women, children, jobs, and housework. Many consciousness-raising groups contained activist women, but they generally sought strength and education, not the confrontation of larger political issues.

Women in the movement wanted changes that went far beyond politics and economics. They worked to eliminate the traditional stereotype of feminine behavior, challenging sex role identity that went from the pink blanket in the hospital bassinet to the female senior citizen who received fewer social security benefits than her male counterpart. The work of Masters and Johnson and later researchers contributed to a more accurate understanding of women's sexuality, exploding such ideas inherited from the nineteenth century as the notion that healthy women cannot enjoy sex. Contraception provided security against unwanted pregnancy and so allowed freer sexual expression. But the sexual permissiveness would also injure women: some women found their sex dehumanized, used to entertain men at topless bars, presented half-clad in multimillion dollar advertising campaigns to sell everything from automobiles to shaving cream. Popular music, and especially masculine rock lyrics—witness the Rolling Stones' "Stupid Girl" and "Under My Thumb"—celebrated primarily women's sexuality, not their intelligence, courage, or character. The lyrics of certain rap groups in the early 1990s were infinitely more demeaning to women.

Women questioned assumptions implicit in marriage, the family, the church, and called for open-minded biological and psychological research on the nature of heterosexual relationships. Within consciousness raising groups questions about female sexuality led to discussions about homosexuals, and the fight began against restrictive and discriminatory laws against homosexuality. Feminist lesbians sought legal changes and protection of their civil rights; they also wanted to change attitudes toward lesbianism. Radical lesbians argued that existing heterosexual relationships exploited women and that only homosexuality could free women from this oppression. NOW was at first divided on homosexuality; many members felt the issue too controversial and destructive to the movement. But in 1973 NOW adopted a resolution on sexuality fully supporting "civil rights legislation designed to end discrimination based on sexual orientation."

Minorities of Old American Heritage

It was predictable that the civil-rights movement for black Americans, along with the general political ferment of the 1960s, would attract attention to other ethnic minorities who have suffered discrimination. Mexican and Indian Americans had already engaged in legal and political agitation, and both took further strength from the struggle for black rights. Both needed to come to terms with a dilemma shared among distinctive American ethnicities: how to reconcile their cultures with a common national language and institutions. Like the counterculture, Indian and Mexican American activists acted on the conviction that forms of personal and community expressiveness must be found outside the conformist terms of the larger society. But Indians and Chicanos faced problems of poverty and discrimination that required them to deal with the country's dominant institutions as threatening but perhaps helpful forces.

The Chicano Movement Mexican Americans, like other minorities, joined in the civil rights activism of the 1960s. Much of the movement originated among young Mexican Americans who styled themselves "Chicanos"—a shortened term for Mexicano. Chicanos sought control over their own educational, social, and law enforcement institutions.

In part, the Chicano movement asserted whatever was distinctive to Mexican American society. High school and college students in the Brown Berets staged walkouts for bilingual education. Activists called for Hispanic studies programs. Chicano culture gained recognition in theaters, among artists, and in the media. Alongside the celebration of cultural pluralism appeared separatist persuasions. The youthful urban-based Crusade for Justice, founded in Denver, Colorado, in 1965 by Rodolfo Gonzalez, proposed that

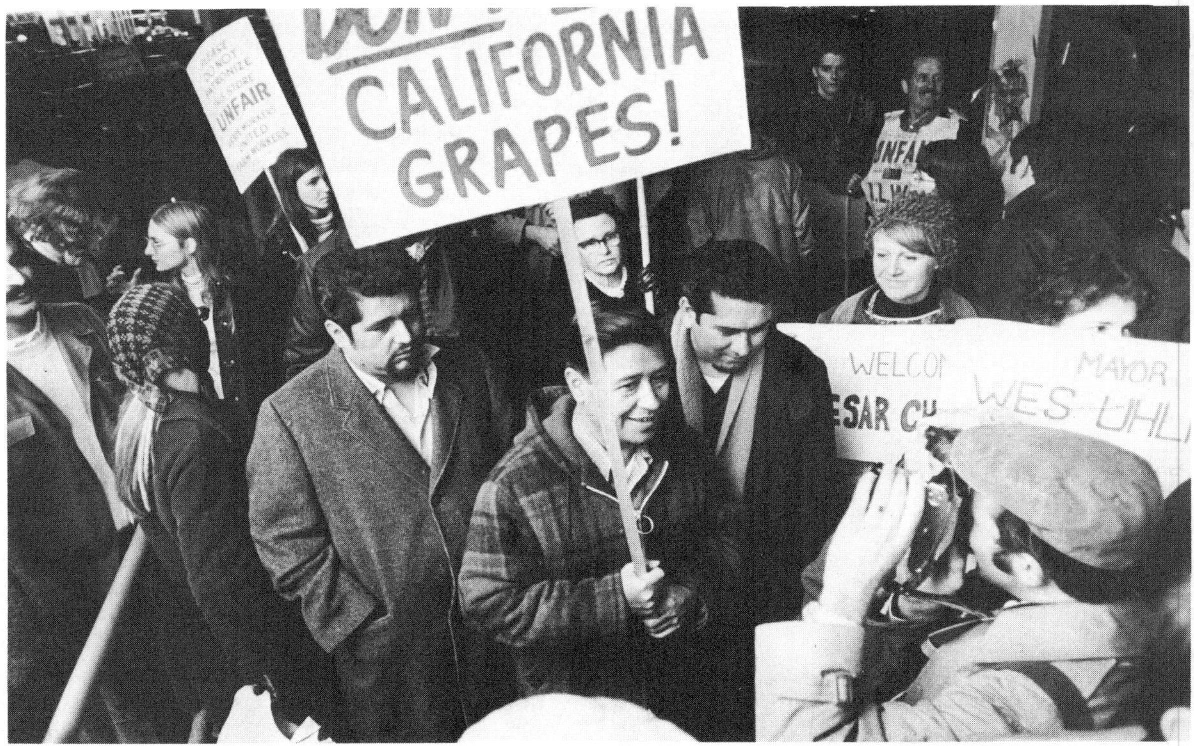

Cesar Chavez, leader of the United Farm Workers, whose nationwide grape boycott in 1965 brought the plight of migrant farm workers to the attention of the nation. *(Courtesy, AP/Wide World Photos)*

Chicanos reacquire the Southwest as their own country. The group also sought jobs and social services for Mexican Americans. The more rural *Alianza,* founded by Reyes Lopez Tijerina in 1963, demanded the return of millions of acres in the Southwest to the descendants of those who had lost them despite guarantees in the Treaty of Guadalupe Hidalgo. The leader hoped to establish a string of city-states. To implement his demands, members of the *Alianza* occupied a court house in Tierra Amarillo, New Mexico, in 1967. After a massive manhunt, Lopez Tijerina was jailed in 1969, after which his movement declined.

More methodical politics also attracted activists. La Raza Unida, founded in Texas under the leadership of José Angel Gutierrez in 1972, aimed to create a separate political party in control of local school boards and rural communities. While the movement gained momentum, it was unable to succeed in the cities. The most far-reaching and successful Chicano effort originated among migrant farm workers. Cesar Chavez, its leader, had also helped establish the Community Service Organization. As a youngster, he had attended more than thirty schools after his family lost its farm during the Depression. Migrant workers lived in camps, complete with drafty shanties and a few outdoor toilets and often a single water faucet for an entire camp. Committed like Martin Luther King to Gandhi's nonviolent tactics, and enlisting the support of the Roman Catholic hierarchy, Chavez has worked to organize the migrants, a portion of the nation's labor force so poor and so transient that unionism had hardly touched it.

Perhaps drawing on a page from the AFL handbook, Chavez concentrated on the most skilled migrant workers, the grape pickers. In 1965 his United Farm Workers struck growers around Delano, California. The union picketed and Chavez sought a nationwide boycott of grapes. In 1966, one company came to terms, including a wage of $1.75 per hour. Within two years, eleven growers had signed, giving a $2.25 wage and some benefits. Civil rights workers, young people, and ministers joined in support of Chavez's efforts. In 1968, Senator Robert Kennedy's active support helped Chavez gain the national prominence the UFW needed, and by 1970, half of the hundred or more growers of table grapes came into line. Chavez then successfully unionized the lettuce growers.

Like other ethnicities, Mexican Americans have struggled with the question of assimilation. Few immigrants came here to cease being what they were and to change their culture. As they accepted the new land and bought into its ways of acquiring and consuming, they little understood what changes they needed in their cultural baggage to attain those ways.

Nothing personifies the dilemma more than the bilingual question. Not only Anglo Americans but Hispanics have divided over the issue. Carter's administration supported it; Reagan's and Bush's have opposed it. Some argue that assimilation is inevitable and should take place sooner rather than later, so that the children of Hispanic parents will not be left indefinitely suspended between two languages and two cultures. By shunning the learning of proficient English, Hispanics are shutting themselves out of economic opportunities. Supporters of bilingual education argue that the maintenance of a Spanish-language alternative in public schools and other institutions, and thereby the sustenance of Mexican American culture, will strengthen the pride of young Chicanos.

This issue will remain a significant one, for the comparative closeness of the United States to Mexico and the openness of the border between the two countries virtually guarantees a reinforcement of old-country values for Mexican American immigrants. Population projections reveal that Hispanic Americans may become the most numerous minority in the United States sometime in the 1990s.

Indian Activism

The Dawes Severalty Act of 1887 that divided tribal lands among individual families had long since failed to assimilate American Indians. By the 1920s, whites had purchased much of the affected land, while other expanses among the original 160-acre tracts had been divided many times among the heirs and would not support Indian families even had they become farmers, as the act intended. Demoralization attended high disease and infant mortality rates, unemployment, illiteracy, malnutrition, and alcoholism.

During the 1920s, reformers in the Indian Defense Association convinced John Collier, a student of Indian life, that the policy embodied in the Dawes Act needed to be reversed. When he became commissioner of Indian affairs under the New Deal, Collier drew up the Wheeler-Howard Indian Reorganization Act (1934). This act sought to have Indians regain lost reservation lands and tribally manage their own affairs, as well as formal relations with local and national government. The act also promoted loans for reservation development and funded the training of Indians for hire by the Bureau of Indian Affairs. In World War II the military used Indian languages and Indian translators, notably Navahȯ, for coded radio communications. During the war, Indian leaders founded the National Congress of American Indians, which at first represented over fifty tribes and eventually doubled in size. It was the first and largest nationwide Indian organization. While promoting educational employment and health services for Indians and lobbying Congress for beneficial laws, the National Congress sought to develop reservation lands and resources and fought for Indian land claims against the government.

In the early 1950s, the relocation services program provided vocational and housing opportunities to Indians leaving their reservations. But most held unskilled city jobs and lived in wretched conditions. Many drifted back and forth between the city and the familiar and more communal reservation. The termination policy ended federal support of some reservations. Indians charged that President Eisenhower was balancing his budget by violating treaty responsibilities and leaving the Indians exposed once again to unfriendly and impoverished state governments. They maintained that termination opened Indian lands to further exploitation by timber companies and land developers. The policy was soon abandoned and the government continued to thrash about in search of a coherent and consistent Indian policy.

In 1961 over 400 Indians from nearly seventy tribes produced a Declaration of Indian Purpose: self-determination, return of reservation lands, improvement of living conditions, and staffing the Bureau of Indian Affairs with Indians. And under Presidents

An Indian encampment in front of the Washington state capitol in 1968 was part of the wider Indian movement calling for return of lands. *(Courtesy, AP/Wide World Photos)*

Kennedy, Johnson, and Nixon the national government again advocated cultural pluralism for Indians. Nixon appointed Louis Bruce the first Indian Commissioner of Indian Affairs, and ordered that the bureau operate directly under presidential supervision to become more responsive to the problems of Indians.

In 1968, Dennis Banks and Clyde Bellecourt founded the American Indian Movement (AIM). That the organization began in Minneapolis reflected how urban the Indian experience was becoming. Of the 800,000 American Indians, approximately one-third now live in cities. While AIM took up the cause of earlier reformers—reorganization of the Bureau, return of lands guaranteed by treaty, and Indian home rule—the tactics were much more militant. In 1969 Indians occupied the abandoned prison island of Alcatraz in San Francisco Bay. Led by a New York Mohawk, Richard Oakes, they demanded return of the island as partial payment for broken treaties. The publicity this event brought to the plight of urban Indians led to a series of Indian occupations of urban government property. In 1972, AIM members took over the main offices of the Indian Bureau in Washington, D.C. The most significant protest occurred at Wounded Knee in South Dakota, the site of the 1890 massacre of over 200 Sioux. Radical members of the Oglala Sioux and leaders of AIM seized and held the town. Led by Dennis Banks and Russell Means, they demanded the restoration of treaty lands. After seventy-one days, two deaths, and several gunfights between the Indians and heavily-armed National Guardsmen and FBI agents, the protesters surrendered. Over 300 were arrested. Most, including Banks and Means, were acquitted on legal technicalities. By the end of the 1970s, Indians all over the country, often with much later success, began lawsuits to recover their treaty rights and lands.

Vietnam To 1960

The French in Vietnam The war that brought together the energies of the sixties was a result of an imperial venture of the previous century. Since the middle of the nineteenth century, Southeast Asia's fertile rice fields, mineral deposits, and strategic position have attracted rival empires and ideologies. In Indochina, which includes Vietnam, Laos, and Cambodia, France established itself. In the southern third of Vietnam, called Cochin-China, the French assumed direct control and began an intensive program of economic development in mines and plantations largely run by Vietnamese labor. Elsewhere, French authorities enlisted the Vietnamese elite—the mandarins. These two groups set up a Grand Council that taxed the Vietnamese, protected monopolies, and turned over to a handful of Frenchmen and Vietnamese land farmed by the peasants.

Almost from the beginning some Vietnamese opposed this economic exploitation and what they feared to be an attempt to replace old Vietnamese ways with French culture. When Paris vetoed moderate reforms during the early 1920s, nationalists adopted more militant tactics. Ho Chi Minh, who had earlier studied Marxism in France, organized the Communist Party in 1930. Ho favored radical reforms and, ultimately, the expulsion of the French from Vietnam. But he was patient. After other nationalist groups led uprisings in the 1930's and were brutally and successfully suppressed by the French, Ho and his fledgling Communist movement moved into the vacuum of nationalist movements. During the Japanese occupation of Indochina from 1940 to 1945, Ho built upon these foundations to create the Vietminh, a united front of anticolonialists. And when Japan's power disintegrated during early 1945, his Vietminh guerrilla forces seized northern border provinces and a popular revolution swept the colony. The Vietminh, the only tightly organized party uncorrupted by collaboration either with the French or with the Japanese, formed a government on September 2, 1945, when Ho Chi Minh declared Vietnam's independence.

President Franklin Roosevelt tended to favor an end to colonial rule. But the new French Republic under General Charles de Gaulle demanded a return of all French possessions. Anglo-French occupation troops forcibly installed a colonial government in Saigon late in 1945. The Vietminh immediately launched a guerrilla counteroffensive against what rapidly became a French war of reconquest.

During the late 1940s, a number of Cold War American policymakers decided that Southeast Asia was critical to United States interests. In their thinking the fall of Southeast Asia would threaten the island chain stretching from Japan to the Philippines, cutting off American air routes to India and South Asia, and eliminating the first line of defense in the Pacific. Australia and New Zealand would be isolated. The region was potentially loaded with important natural and strategic resources, including tin, rubber, rice, copra, iron ore, copper, tungsten, and

Ho Chi Minh, Communist leader of Vietnam from 1945 through the Vietnam War, wrote that the Communists "swam like fishes in the peasant sea." *(Courtesy, AP/Wide World Photos)*

oil, which the United States risked losing along with huge potential markets for American products.

From 1947 to 1950 the French exerted great military pressure throughout Indochina, but still could not break Vietminh dominance in the countryside. President Harry Truman inherited Roosevelt's distaste for France's neocolonialist adventure. Initially, the Americans played no role in Indochinese affairs. But two developments elsewhere in the world combined to focus American attention on Indochina and commit the United States to the side of the French.

Late in 1949 the Communist Mao Zedong defeated Chiang Kai-shek and established the People's Republic of China. Then Communist North Korea invaded South Korea in June 1950. The United States, previously fairly indifferent toward Indochina, became determined to block Communist victories there.

If Indochina were lost to the Communists, so President Truman's National Security Council argued, neighboring Thailand would be next; this would upset the balance of power in Southeast Asia, and Communism might then reach out for either India or the rich islands of Indonesia. The American government was remembering what had happened when Austria, Czechoslovakia, and other European countries fell to Hitler after Britain's giving into Germany at Munich in 1938. In 1950 Truman extended massive military aid to the French. Communist control of the nationalist movement left the United States in a curious dilemma. The best way to defeat the Vietminh would be to replace the French with a non-Communist, nationalist regime, but this awkward realization contradicted another American motive in supporting France in Vietnam. Washington's diplomatic needs in Europe required French support, and the French did not want to surrender to anyone, Communist or nationalist. So we supported the French.

Most Vietnamese nationalists turned to the Communists as the strongest resistance force. The French had superior firepower and were well trained in the mode of conventional European combat, but Ho's native forces knew the land and fought an effective guerrilla war of attrition.

Dien Bien Phu General Vo Nguyen Giap moved the bulk of his Vietminh forces toward Laos in an attempt to win territory and to lure French armies under General Henri Navarre away from their coastal strongholds. Navarre, to prevent future attacks against Laos and to restrict Vietminh movements toward the south, converted an obscure interior outpost at Dien Bien Phu into a major fortress. By March 1954 when the battle began that would bring the first Indochina War to a stalemate, France had concentrated there nearly 16,000 of its best troops, built an airstrip to supply the fort, and set up massive artillery. Navarre was confident that at last he could wipe out the Communists' main force. Yet Giap's forces outnumbered the French nearly three to one, and, with the aid of thousands of Vietnamese who back-packed ammunition into the remote area, he had assembled superior firepower around the hills of Dien Bien Phu. One American observer commented:

> Here you were out in the middle of a jungle, and you have extremely heavy antiaircraft fire coming from positions that we didn't believe the Viet Minh could establish or maintain. We thought no one could put heavy weapons in there except the French, who had flown them in on C-119s and C-54s. But the Viet Minh, who had no air, had somehow put in 105s and 75 millimeters, and heavy mortars and all the rest of it, in what we thought was impenetrable jungle.

Though the French retained control of the air, bombing strikes could not destroy the well-hidden Communist embankments, which soon knocked out the French airstrip. Then Giap encircled the post. The garrison fell to the Vietminh army, and its commander committed suicide. The French military effort to reassert colonial control had collapsed.

While most of the world's diplomats moved toward ending the war, Secretary of State John Foster Dulles took the first steps toward prolonging and Americanizing it. The Eisenhower Administration had already seriously considered active military intervention, not only to save Dien Bien Phu but also to bolster the entire French effort. Washington abandoned ideas of direct interference only after the French government itself refused to continue the war and the military situation in northern Vietnam became hopeless. If the United States were to launch an anti-Communist crusade in Southeast Asia, it would have to find a vehicle other than French colonialism.

Only one day before the fall of Dien Bien Phu, nations involved in Indochina convened in Geneva, Switzerland, to settle the war. After six weeks the representatives reached agreement. The Vietnamese Communists, flush with victory, wanted complete control of all Vietnam. They achieved much less, largely because the Soviet Union and China forced Ho Chi Minh to accept Western terms. Once again, the context of international relations had critically affected the fate of Vietnam. In the aftermath of Stalin's death, the Soviet Union's new leadership wished to explore the possibilities of easing relations with the West. The Chinese, for their part, had no desire to see a swift repeat of the bloody stalemate with America that had been the just-concluded Korean War. The Geneva accords granted independence to the three Indochinese states of Laos, Cambodia, and Vietnam. Vietnam was temporarily divided at the 17th parallel; nationwide elections within two years would determine the country's permanent political future. None of the new states was to permit foreign troops or bases on its soil or to join an outside alliance.

Rather than a compromise, Washington wanted a non-Communist alternative state in Vietnam. Thus the State Department announced that the United States, which had not signed the Geneva accords, intended to adhere to its terms, but would treat North and South Vietnam as separate entities. Then, in September 1954, it negotiated the Southeast Asia Treaty Organization (SEATO), a milder version of the NATO alliance, pledging mutual assistance "in accord with constitutional process." The original signatories—France, Great Britain, the United States, Australia, New Zealand, the Philippines, Pakistan, and Thailand—later extended the pact's protection to include Cambodia, Laos, and South Vietnam. Convinced that his only other option was disengagement and the gradual fall of all Southeast Asia to Communism, Eisenhower pledged vast economic and military aid to the native but increasingly elitist South Vietnamese premier, Ngo Dinh Diem. In 1956 the United States supported Diem's open break with the Geneva settlement. Washington had committed itself to the creation and then to the defense of an anti-Communist government in South Vietnam.

The Diem Regime in South Vietnam Supporting Diem would eventually backfire, for he took American money and built a corrupt personalist regime. At first, however, the new leadership seemed promising. Between 1954 and 1957, generously supported by American financial aid, the country made substantial economic growth and even achieved some land reform. The government suppressed gangsters in Saigon and brought under control the religious sects, many of whose leaders had set up independent fiefdoms in the countryside. But Diem never gained broad popular support, and because the rural areas remained in the hands of opponents, he adopted increasingly repressive tactics.

The northern regime initially hoped that Diem might simply weaken badly. By 1959, though, the Communist movement in South Vietnam was so damaged and demoralized that North Vietnam authorized direct military action against Diem with immediate and significant results.

By the end of the decade the Republican administration had dispatched some 685 American "advisory" personnel to Vietnam—the limit permitted by the Geneva accords; but the nonmilitary alternative, economic growth and thorough land reform, neared collapse because of Diem's noncooperation. While Eisenhower "could conceive of no greater tragedy than for the United States to become involved in an all out land war in Asia," his secretary of state announced that "the free world would intervene in Indochina rather than let the situation deteriorate."

Vietnam: Kennedy and Johnson

Kennedy and Vietnam The Diem government approached chaos in the early sixties. All social and economic reform halted, and even retrogressed, as Diem concentrated on maintaining his power and eliminating all opposition. In response, thousands of southern insurrectionists joined the newly organized Communist National Liberation Front (NLF), and many took the trek north for military training.

Diem dubbed the forces Vietcong, for Vietnamese Communists. Support from the Kennedy Administration, which eventually sent to Vietnam nearly 16,000 American advisers, along with artillery and fighterbombers, kept the Diem regime alive. Kennedy's Secretary of State Dean Rusk confidently asserted: "This great country can do anything when it puts its shoulder to the wheel." Washington also expanded the elaborate clandestine war against North Vietnam that it had begun in 1955. Kennedy now ordered secret agents to sabotage lines of communication throughout the North, and American advisers directed military raids across Hanoi's frontiers and into Laos. At first these tactics appeared successful: during 1962 the NLF lost some of its earlier territorial gains. Although some of Kennedy's partisans have insisted that he—unlike Lyndon Johnson—would have avoided full-scale conflict, his decisions enlarged American goals in Vietnam without assuring their achievement.

In South Vietnam, Diem increasingly reverted to trusting only a small, inner circle of family and friends. These were overwhelmingly Roman Catholic, the religion of choice for Vietnamese families who had wished to rise to high status during the decades of French rule. This initial strength soon turned to weakness, as the South Vietnamese ruling family persuaded the legislature to pass laws requiring Buddhists to obey Catholic moral laws. Also, Diem's Roman Catholic sister-in-law, Madame Nhu, gained notoriety for her cynical dismissal of Buddhist "barbecues"—Vietnamese who set themselves on fire as a form of political protest. Beginning in May 1963, the Buddhists organized strong demonstrations against the Saigon regime; in an attempt to squash this threat, the government attacked Buddhist temples and pagodas throughout South Vietnam in August. When it became clear that the Diem army raids had alienated the urban middle class, most religious sects, and intellectuals, the United States abandoned its support of the premier, while Ambassador Henry Cabot Lodge encouraged a cabal of generals. On November 2, 1963, the group assassinated Diem and set up a new government under Major General Nguyen Khanh. The Vietcong made rapid gains.

The United States might have used the Diem crisis as a convenient reason for withdrawing from the war. Robert Kennedy during a cabinet meeting urged a course of disengagement, and *Time's* editors suggested the possibility of neutralizing all of Southeast Asia as Laos had been neutralized. But Secretary of Defense Robert McNamara and the chairman of the Joint Chiefs of Staff, General Maxwell Taylor, visited Vietnam in September and reported that most American tasks there would be accomplished in fifteen months, with perhaps a thousand troops returning home by the end of 1963. No wonder pursuing the war seemed a course that prudently weighed cost against advantage.

Johnson Escalates the War

By the time President Johnson took office in November 1963 he had few political alternatives. He inherited not only the war itself but also Kennedy's principal advisers on foreign affairs; the United States had many troops in the country, and South Vietnam's new government was completely dependent on American economic and military aid. The new President approached Vietnam on the basis of his knowledge of World War II and Korea. It was, he thought, a matter of halting aggression. Given the militant involvement of Democratic liberals, one member of Students for a Democratic Society (SDS) orated:

> The original commitment in Vietnam was made by President Truman, a mainstream liberal. It was seconded by President Eisenhower, a moderate liberal. It was intensified by President Kennedy, a flaming liberal. Think of the men who now engineer that war—those who study the maps, give the commands, push the buttons and tally the dead. . . .
>
> They are all honorable men.
>
> They are all liberals. . . .

The Gulf of Tonkin Resolution

A pretext to attack North Vietnam—the so-called Gulf of Tonkin crisis—occurred during early August 1964. The navy had helped South Vietnam to conduct extensive operations against shore installations in North Vietnam. A spy ship, the destroyer *Maddox,* loaded with electronic equipment, had supported these raids, often cruising inside the twelve-mile limit prescribed by Hanoi. After one such incursion manned by South Vietnamese but supported by Americans, Hanoi sent several PT boats into the Gulf of Tonkin. The *Maddox,* now over twenty miles from the coast,

A Buddhist priest immolates himself in protest against the Diem regime's religious persecution. Buddhist protests were a leading factor in toppling the Diem regime in 1963. *(Courtesy, United Press International Photos)*

may have fired first upon the approaching North Vietnamese ships, which then launched torpedoes. Johnson remarked privately: "For all I know, our navy was shooting at whales out there." Two days later, on August 4, as the *Maddox* and another destroyer, the *C. Turner Joy,* cruised in the same general area, they reported a second attack by North Vietnamese boats. It is not clear whether the attack actually took place or whether the Americans imagined it in the intense darkness, amid possible malfunctions of sonar and radar equipment.

But in Washington, Johnson publicly denounced "unprovoked aggression" and used the temporary feeling of crisis to extract congressional approval for a project the administration had contemplated for several months. To insure his freedom of action and demonstrate American unity in an election year, Johnson secured a sweeping authorization "to take all necessary measures . . . to prevent further aggression." A nearly unanimous Senate adopted the *de facto* declaration of war, 88–2. Only a few isolated senators, Wayne Morse of Oregon in particular, questioned its ultimate purpose or the advisability of open-ended commitments.

Escalation of American Involvement in the War

By early 1965, the American air offensive named ROLLING THUNDER was under way. Immediately a basic difficulty arose. The South Vietnamese Army was incapable of adequately defending air bases used by American bombers in the South, as a series of aggressive Vietcong attacks made plain. The first actual American combat forces, no longer advisers to the South Vietnamese, came ashore in March 1965 to protect American aircraft. But who would protect the protectors? American field commanders, chafing under the restrictions of passive "base security" tasks, argued for a strategy of actively scouring the countryside for their

Vietcong tormentors. The result eventually led to the "search and destroy" strategy and, inevitably, to the sharp increase of American combat forces in South Vietnam as ROLLING THUNDER proceeded against the North.

Johnson decided to fight the war tactically, somewhere between the extremes of what he thought of as a disgraceful withdrawal and the quick, massive attacks against North Vietnam and the Vietcong advocated by the joint chiefs of staff. He believed that a calculated, steady increase in force would convince his opponents that they could not win.

But Ho Chi Minh, the North Vietnamese, and the Vietcong were willing to make extraordinary sacrifices and sustain huge losses. When it became clear to the Johnson Administration that the Communists were not going to back down, the President switched to attrition—the United States would kill so many Vietcong and North Vietnamese soldiers that their military units would simply be unable to engage in battle. President Johnson and General William Westmoreland intended to kill the Communists faster than the Vietnamese population could replace them. Westmoreland kept talking about this "crossover point." It would take several years of fighting before the United States realized that the arithmetic of attrition did not add up. The American war machine would not be able to kill Vietnamese soldiers faster than Ho Chi Minh could replace them. Washington military planners tripped over another misconception. For strategic and tactical reasons, in any guerrilla war the military defending the established government must be many times the size of the insurgents. Experts in guerrilla warfare estimated that United States and South Vietnamese forces would have to outnumber North Vietnamese and guerrilla troops about ten to one.

Problems in Pursuing the War

Stymied by the inefficiency of Rolling Thunder and by Hanoi's refusal to cave in at an American bargaining table, Johnson massively escalated the ground war in Vietnam during the spring of 1966. For nearly twenty-four months, the world witnessed the nation's military attempt to pursue a will-o'-the-wisp victory and to insure a non-Communist South Vietnam. But obstacles multiplied: the unstable, often arbitrary government in Saigon, a swelling tide of discontent within the United States, and the immunity of the Communist war effort to the tactics of the Saigon and the American forces.

In South Vietnam disagreements over military tactics and economic reforms plagued the junta that had replaced Diem. Even after two generals, Nguyen Van Thieu and Nguyen Cao Ky, emerged on top, Saigon could not heal the split between countryside and city that the insurgency widened. But at a meeting in Honolulu during February 1966 with Thieu and Ky, Johnson extracted promises that the junta would permit an elected government and begin large-scale land redistribution. It was a delicate diplomatic maneuver, for while Johnson to force compliance threatened to cut off American aid, the two Vietnamese leaders knew that they were the President's only option.

American insistence upon the appearance, if not the reality, of democracy, together with the temporary eclipse of Communist progress during the massive United States buildup of 1966, finally brought about nationwide elections for a Constituent Assembly. But this "constitutional convention" was rigged: no Communist delegates attended and the regime blocked neutralist candidates such as the still-restive Buddhists. South Vietnam remained in the control of the military, loosely presided over by Thieu and Ky. Of the two Ky was a particular embarrassment to the United States. A small man neatly attired in air force suit and purple scarf, he carried an ivory-handled pistol on his hip. He told reporters:

> People ask me who my heroes are. I have only one hero—Hitler. . . . We need four or five Hitlers in Vietnam.

While Johnson fashioned events in South Vietnam, his own countrymen proved less malleable. After a brief rather favorable reaction to the latest military crusade against Communism, many Americans increasingly went sour at the inconclusive and frustrating struggle. But one Vietcong soldier wrote in his diary:

> It is the duty of my generation to die for my country.

The more the United States bombed North Vietnam, the more Ho scattered his factories, infiltrated the South, and whipped up war fever in the North. American bombers, moreover, quickly discovered that they lacked advantageous targets. North Vietnam itself was

102°
110°
NORTH VIETNAM
CHINA
Red
Dien Bien Phu
Hanoi
Haiphong
Nam Dinh
Mekong
Luang Prabang
Thanh Hoa
Gulf of Tonkin
HAINAN
LAOS
Vinh
18°
Vientiane
U.S. SEVENTH FLEET
Dong Hoi
Quang Tri
Hue
Khe Sanh
Da Nang
THAILAND
Chu Lai
CHINA SEA
Quang Ngai
Korat
Dak To
Kontum
An Khe
Pleiku
Qui Nhon
Bangkok
CAMBODIA
CENTRAL HIGHLANDS
Sattahip-U-Tapao
Mekong
Nha Trang
Cam Ranh
Loc Ninh
Phan Rang
Phnom Penh
Gulf of Siam
Ben Cat
Bien Hoa
SOUTH VIETNAM
Saigon
Dong Tam
Vung Tau
10°
IV CORPS
Can Tho
Soc Trang
Mekong Delta
17th Parallel
DMZ
Ben Hai
Con Thien
DEMARCATION LINE
Major U.S. Bases
Ho Chi Minh Trail
Sihanouk Trail

Vietnam

an especially poor subject for bombing. The economy was predominantly agrarian, lacking dependency on industries that in modern warfare are the most vulnerable to aerial attack. The country had an elaborate system of dikes to control flooding along the Red River, but the United States decided not to bomb them, since the flooding and starvation that would have resulted are considered international war crimes. Fears about reactions in the Soviet Union and China prevented an assault against the major port of Haiphong, for such an attack would probably have resulted in the deaths of Soviet and Chinese military and civilian personnel. Memories of the Chinese invasion of Korea remained strong.

The only really significant target available for attack was the so-called Ho Chi Minh Trail, which stretched into Laos and from Laos into the northern reaches of South Vietnam, the main thoroughfare for North Vietnam's shipment of troops and supplies to South Vietnam. In the early 1960s, the Trail had been little more than a path, but North Vietnam put a huge investment into developing it. By the early 1970s the Ho Chi Minh Trail was actually an elaborate system of 12,000 miles of paved and unpaved roads and paths over which thousands of trucks, wagons, and people travelled every day. A five-inch pipeline from North Vietnam, through Laos, and into South Vietnam shipped petroleum products.

American aircraft regularly bombed the Ho Chi Minh Trail, but once again the arithmetic of attrition did not compute. On any given day, the United States could keep about 400 aircraft over the trail for a period of one hour. The terrain of the trail consisted of mountainous jungles that made accurate bombing very difficult. The Vietnamese Communists also moved as much of their freight as possible at night. As North Vietnam's air defense systems became more sophisticated, American pilots who had one hour to spend over their target had to take much of that hour dodging surface-to-air missiles (SAMs) or attacking the missile launching sites instead of bombing the supplies moving down the trail.

Meanwhile, the ground war in South Vietnam remained locked in a stalemate despite repeated United States reinforcements. Over half a million American troops guarded major cities and many rural outposts by the end of 1967, but the Communists dominated much of the countryside. When combat units embarked upon search and destroy missions, North Vietnamese regulars shunned combat and Vietcong guerrillas hid among the population. One American soldier related:

> You always had to watch your back, because there was no front line there, and you had women and kids as warriors, too, and you really didn't know who was trustworthy and who wasn't.

Johnson's program to "win the hearts and minds of the Vietnamese people" was similarly indecisive. To "pacify" the countryside, Washington had launched a number of initiatives such as the Combined Action Platoon program. American troops would move into a village, secure it with a series of fortifications, and train the villagers as militia. Although the tactic sometimes protected the village from Vietcong attack, the ill-equipped militia were rarely a match for dedicated North Vietnamese regular units, and the intrusion into their villages and sometimes forced evacuation from them hardly endeared the Americans to the Vietnamese. During the 1960s the United States forced more than two million South Vietnamese civilians to leave their homes. That is another reason why political victory was proving as elusive as military success.

The Antiwar Movement

While inconclusiveness soured public support for Johnson's Vietnam policy, a growing antiwar movement spread across the United States and questioned the morality of the fighting. Students for a Democratic Society called Vietnam

> a civil war . . . a losing war . . . a self-defeating war . . . a dangerous war . . . an undeclared war . . . an immoral war. What kind of America is it whose response to poverty and oppression in South Vietnam is napalm and defoliation, whose response to poverty and oppression in Mississippi is . . . silence?

By 1967 Senator J. William Fulbright, who earlier had guided the Gulf of Tonkin resolution through the Senate, now attacked the administration's "arrogance of power." "Power," observed Fulbright, "tends to confuse itself with virtue." He believed that its history of victory, prosperity, and power gave the United States a sense of omnipotence and righteousness that could distort reality, as it was doing in Vietnam. The nation had been foolish, Fulbright argued, to assume that Western institutions and political methods

An American military adviser on patrol with South Vietnamese troops. By 1968, over half a million U.S. troops were fighting the unconventional war against Vietcong guerrilla forces. *(Courtesy, U.S. Army)*

could establish themselves in an alien culture. While Fulbright and other critics worried about misplaced motives, a mushrooming antiwar coalition directly questioned the war's morality. In October 1967, a rally of 200,000 students, leftists, and other Americans demonstrated in a march through the nation's capital. An important portion of the Democratic Party had rejected Johnson's leadership.

The Tet Offensive Early in the year the Vietnamese customarily observed a month of truce: Tet, the month is called. On the night of January 29, 1968, during Tet, the American embassy and all the major cities of South Vietnam came under attack. Parts of Saigon fell to the enemy and most of the northern city of Hue fell to Vietcong and North Vietnamese control for several days. Carnage spread in this time of truce: in Hue, from a campaign of murder waged by the Communists; in a number of cities, from the massive South Vietnamese and American counteroffensive that eventually restored the urban areas to Allied control. The Vietcong still dominated the rural areas. The Tet offensive ended in a victory for the South Vietnamese and American armies; but Tet's dramatic nature made for a kind of defeat in the United States. When the grandfatherly television anchorman Walter Cronkite heard the news about Tet, he said "What the hell is going on? I thought we were winning the war." Cronkite believed in keeping the news simple, and he and other journalists portrayed Tet as an American defeat.

General Westmoreland immediately flew to the United States and asked for 200,000 more reinforcements, a request that coincided with a major review of war policy in Washington. At this point, Johnson's decision was relatively straightforward. He could not send more men to South Vietnam without endangering the nation's commitments elsewhere and producing severe strains on the inflated American economy. In addition, the President would have had to mobilize the reserves and increase taxes, but both steps required congressional approval, and he doubted whether Congress or the general public would acquiesce. By this time, Johnson also seemed to have realized the futility of escalation. When Westmoreland explained that he could not guarantee victory even with the additional troops, the President replied: "Then where will it all end?" Dismayed and disillusioned, he entrusted the search for an alternative to a study group chaired by a personal friend, Clark Clifford. Since military victory was not in sight, the Clifford committee turned to diplomacy as a solution.

The Pursuit of Peace The simplest solution to the war—withdrawal from it—the administration resisted. Its own conscience caught it in a ruthless logic, the logic of war. The more deeply the South Vietnamese allies committed themselves to the conflict, trusting to the United States to support them, the more terrible it would be to desert them. And so the United States must go on encouraging them to fight. And the more Vietnamese and Americans died, the more terrible it would be to quit the war with nothing gained. And so the killing must go on.

In an anti-guerrilla war among people any one of whom might be a friend, an enemy, or simply a poor peasant who wanted to be left alone, widespread indiscriminate killing of civilians became inevitable. The best known American acts of this kind were at My Lai and Song My. At these places and elsewhere, company commanders and their troops lost self-control and committed atrocities not revealed to the American public until 1970. A rifleman who witnessed the spring 1968 My Lai slaughter of hundreds of civilians later testified:

> Lieutenant Calley and a rifleman pushed the prisoners into the ditch. . .
>
> There was an order to shoot by Lieutenant Calley, I can't remember the exact words—it was something like 'Start firing.'
>
> Meadlo turned to me and said: 'Shoot, why don't you shoot?'
>
> He was crying.
>
> I said, 'I can't, I won't.'
>
> Then Lieutenant Calley and Meadlo pointed their rifles into the ditch and fired.
>
> People were diving on top of each other; mothers were trying to protect their children.

The discipline and restraint of countless other American troops since the beginning of the intervention went thereafter unnoticed.

Meanwhile, domestic events further restricted options. When, in March 1968, Senator Eugene McCarthy received about forty-two percent of the vote in the New Hampshire Democratic primary, voters were rebuking the incumbent President. Students throughout the nation, as well as many journalists, teachers, and groups interested in domestic change, more and more protested the course of the war. A desire to unify his party and the country largely motivated the President in his decision to reverse the course of the war.

In a dramatic television appearance on March 31, 1968, Johnson officially announced the results of the Clifford policy review. The United States would halt bombing north of the 19th parallel in an effort to bring about serious peace negotiations. Westmoreland was to receive only token reinforcements. In addition, South Vietnam would gradually take over active prosecution of the war, an approach President Nixon was later to expand. It became known as "Vietnamization." Johnson believed that the Tet offensive had severely weakened Communist ground forces (which it had) and that a new spirit, a new effectiveness in South Vietnam would enable the Saigon regime ultimately to defeat the Vietcong.

To insure the bombing halt and probably to see what sort of deal the United States contemplated, Hanoi replied favorably to Johnson's offer for talks. On May 10, the peace talks opened in Paris. Xuan Thuy represented Hanoi; Averell Harriman, former ambassador to Moscow, was the chief United States negotiator. Almost immediately, the talks stalled. For five months, the diplomats deadlocked over a question of timing. North Vietnam insisted that effective talks could begin only after the United States pledged to stop bombing. Johnson countered that he must continue raids across the Demilitarized Zone (DMZ) to protect American troops; the question of permanent cessation, he argued, should be included in the peace talks, not decided beforehand. The United States wanted a mutual winding down of the war and the participation of both the Saigon regime and the National Liberation Front in any political settlement. By mid-October 1968 the President had accepted an arrangement worked out between Harriman and Thuy whereby the United States would halt all bombing if Hanoi "by its silence" agreed to negotiate with South Vietnam, not increase its aid to the Vietcong, and permit American reconnaissance flights. But peace would elude the negotiators.

The growing antiwar movement attacked the war's purpose and morality as well as the administration's "arrogance of power." *(Courtesy, AP/Wide World Photos)*

1968: Year of Turmoil

The Democratic Primaries

Senator Eugene McCarthy of Minnesota, a handsome gray-haired man of fifty-three, seemed a study in political detachment and nonchalance. But when Attorney General Nicholas Katzenbach told the Senate Foreign Relations Committee in August 1967 that a President could no longer lose time by consulting the Congress on whether to involve the country in war, McCarthy lost his customary composure. Angrily he told Katzenbach that such extensive executive authority deprived the Senate of any decision-making role in foreign policy. In the thinking of McCarthy, Katzenbach's interpretation was unconstitutional. Late in November McCarthy decided to oppose the President in the coming spring primaries.

The first contest came in New Hampshire on March 21, when snow still covered the ground. An energetic band of young students carried the antiwar message across the state. Gene McCarthy, in his dry and self-contained manner something of a New Englander himself, made sober and highly factual arguments against the war. In the vote, McCarthy's Roman Catholicism must have counted, for about two-thirds of the state's Democrats shared his faith. The senator won 42 percent of the two-party vote, almost as much as Johnson's write-in total of 49 percent. It was unprecedented to come so close to winning against an incumbent President during a war.

Three days later, in what appeared to some as shameless opportunism, Senator Robert Kennedy of New York announced that he, too, would oppose the President in primary contests. The timing of the entry reflected his political practicality: only a Kennedy, so he believed, could unseat Johnson. Kennedy's campaign lost its initial momentum when Lyndon Johnson delivered his television speech of March 31, just two days before the Wisconsin primary. The President declared that he would not only rapidly de-escalate the war and cut back bombing of the North, but also turn down army requests for more troops. In an almost casually presented coda that startled his listeners, he remarked that since he wanted to devote full time to the search for peace, he would not seek reelection in November.

Deprived of their most effective campaign issue—the President himself—Kennedy and McCarthy then had to campaign, to a great extent, against each other. In the process of their bickering the peace movement fragmented. McCarthy, never an admirer of the Kennedy clan, found RFK's fascination with power offensive. Kennedy thought McCarthy lazy, snobbish, and politically ineffectual. The two competed for the support of the young, who could be of assistance in the remaining primaries. McCarthy, after winning decisively against Johnson in Wisconsin, lost to Kennedy in Indiana and Nebraska. Then McCarthy made an unexpected comeback by winning easily in Oregon. One final primary would in large part determine the winner; Kennedy promised to drop out of the race should McCarthy defeat him in California on June 4. Kennedy won by a few percentage points, but on the very night of the election he was murdered by a Jordanian immigrant, Sirhan Bishara Sirhan.

Antiwar protestors outside the Democratic Convention in Chicago, 1968. *(Courtesy, Wide World Photos)*

The Democratic Convention At the Chicago convention that city's mayor Richard Daley encouraged an effort to draft the surviving Kennedy brother, Edward, a Massachusetts senator, and McCarthy offered to withdraw in his favor. It was the last hope of the amorphous peace movement. Edward Kennedy might have denied the nomination to Vice President Humphrey, who was so closely identified with Johnson. Thousands of young people demonstrating outdoors reminded the delegates of their passionate dislike of the administration and of its policy in Vietnam. Several large states would have supported Kennedy, and in the psychology of a national convention enthusiasm for him as a potential winner might have put him across. But Kennedy refused to run.

At the Convention a platform provision calling for a halt to all bombing in Vietnam failed by a 3 to 2 vote. Outside the convention hall in Grant Park, the Chicago police battled the young, engaging in what a government report later termed a "police riot." Inside, Senator Abraham Ribicoff of Connecticut told the delegates about the outside skirmishes and lashed out at the "Gestapo tactics of the police." After the riots, Humphrey's nomination by a 2 to 1 margin over McCarthy seemed anticlimactic. The drama of the Convention was outside in the streets during the confrontation between police and students, which included both harassment of young people by the police and the goading of authorities by the youths.

Hubert Humphrey Vice President Hubert Humphrey was an enigma to liberals. Just two decades before he had forced a split in the Democratic Party when he led the forces demanding that the party make a commitment to civil rights. And he was known as a spokesman for labor and for the most aggressively liberal wing of the party, a fighter for welfare programs. But when asked as Vice President what had happened to the program he once had battled for, he answered simply and correctly: "We passed it." And antiwar liberals were perplexed at his attitude toward the

Richard M. Nixon and Spiro Agnew, the Republican Party ticket chosen at the 1968 convention. *(Courtesy, United Press International Photos)*

conflict. The voluble Humphrey welcomed opportunities to explain the intervention in Vietnam. Before an AFL-CIO convention he associated the critics of the war with appeasers of Hitler. He dismissed the significance of corruption in South Vietnam's government, claiming it merely to be comparable to that in American cities.

Humphrey's position on the war, in fact, accorded with his brand of Democratic liberalism. For one thing, he was a good Democrat, convinced that the fortunes of liberalism depended on the strength of the Democratic Party; and he was loyal to the President. And his anticommunism (he was right about the ruthlessness of Vietnamese Communism) came straight out of years of Cold War liberalism.

Richard Nixon The strongest Republican contestant for the 1968 presidential nomination was former Vice President Richard Nixon. After losing to Kennedy in 1960, Nixon had moved to California and two years later failed in his bid for the governorship. During the 1964 presidential campaign he supported Barry Goldwater and thereby survived the year with political currency among party regulars. In mid-decade he practiced law in New York City, defending the right to privacy in *Time Inc. v. Hill* (1966). In 1968 he hewed to the political center and won victories in the spring primaries. Ronald Reagan of California tried to whittle away Nixon's southern support, and Nelson Rockefeller of New York hoped that preconvention polls would show him as the strongest candidate. But neither strategy succeeded. Nixon won on the first ballot.

George Wallace Alabama's feisty Governor George Wallace got on the ballot in all fifty states and launched the most ambitious third party entry since Robert La Follette's in 1924. Wallace had become the candidate of the South on the strength of a single slogan: "Segregation now—Segregation tomorrow—Segregation forever." But now he reached out for a broader and more general campaign theme and insisted he was no racist. He blasted "bearded bureaucrats," "pointy-headed professors," and "poor-folks haters"—his campaign resembled a class movement, speaking to divisions in taste, style, values, and education. The Wallace campaign employed the slogan "law and order." Above all, Wallace took as his target the Supreme Court under Chief Justice Earl Warren. Wallace denounced court decisions that outlawed school prayers, protected the rights of accused criminals, and strengthened the civil rights of minorities. As late as the second half of September the Gallup poll credited Wallace with about twenty percent of the vote.

Labor unions portrayed Alabama as a low-wage, open-shop state. Wallace's vice-presidential candidate, General Curtis Le May, proved a liability. "We seem to have a phobia about nuclear weapons. . . ," he said. "I don't believe the world would end if we exploded a nuclear weapon." Wallace's presence in the campaign permitted Nixon to portray himself as a middle-of-the-road candidate.

Nixon almost lost the 1968 election. At the end of October peace talks began in Paris and the bombing of North Vietnam ceased; had these signs of the war's diminution come a bit sooner, Humphrey might have won. Wallace's votes, on the other hand, were cast by conservatives who might otherwise have favored Nixon.

Vietnam: Nixon's Policies

Nixon did not want to lose the war. Certain that American troop reductions were necessary, he was nevertheless determined to buy Saigon as much time as possible to build itself up before the last GI left. Part of this strategy led to a massive American and South Vietnamese invasion of Cambodia in late April 1970 designed to destroy enemy supplies and sanctuaries. As in earlier offensive actions, the administration defended this tactic on the grounds that it would speed American withdrawal. Protests and strikes spread throughout the nation, especially on college campuses. During a demonstration at Kent State University in Ohio on May 4, confused and rattled National Guardsmen shot and killed four students. During a disturbance shortly afterward at Mississippi's Jackson State University, students also died, this time from indiscriminate firing by police. Three days after Kent State some eighty colleges had closed down and hundreds of others undertook various forms of protest, while construction workers badly beat up a group of war protesters in New York City. To cool the atmosphere, Nixon promised to end his criticism of students.

The Prisoner of War Issue One of the most sensitive issues in the peace negotiations was the fate of prisoners of war. Many American pilots shot down over North Vietnam had been POWs for four or five years. As their relatives began to insist on concessions to win their release, both supporters and opponents of the war embraced the POW issue for their own ends. On November 23, 1970, the administration authorized massive air strikes on North Vietnam and sent a rescue team to a suspected prisoner of war camp. When the news seeped out that no POWs had been rescued, the antiwar people sharpened their criticism, insisting on full withdrawal to win the POWs' rapid release. In Paris the shrewd Vietcong and North Vietnamese took advantage of this question by making offers to release prisoners in return for a definite date on complete American withdrawal from Indochina.

Nixon's administration would not set a date for a final pullout; indeed, in February 1971 the United States and the South Vietnamese launched an offensive in Laos. Although providing air support for South Vietnamese combat forces, the American command insisted that no United States combat soldiers aid in the operation. Nixon explained the invasion as a means of carrying out Vietnamization and assuring the return home of soldiers. Even though the South Vietnamese soon abandoned the Laos invasion, the administration insisted that it had been a success. On April 7, 1971, President Nixon announced a further withdrawal of 100,000 troops by December 1971. By that time United States troop strength had fallen to 133,000, down from the half million of a few years earlier, but almost half of American soldiers lost in Vietnam and, of course, countless Vietnamese died during the protracted withdrawal under Nixon.

The Long Road Toward Peace

On April 1, 1972, after three days of intense bombardment, North Vietnamese regulars crossed the DMZ to attack South Vietnam with great force. A few days of unsuccessful resistance demonstrated that the South Vietnamese needed help. The United States began the first night attacks on the Hanoi-Haiphong area since March 1968 and the first use of B-52's in this region. On May 8 President Nixon announced that the United States would mine North Vietnamese ports and systematically attack all supply lines.

"Peace Is At Hand." Even as the bombs were dropping, presidential adviser Henry Kissinger was conferring secretly with Soviet Premier Leonid Brezhnev to indicate Washington's decision to permit North Vietnamese troops to remain in the South after a cease-fire had been negotiated. In a later visit to the USSR, Nixon himself conferred with Soviet leaders, exchanged gifts, addressed the Soviet people, and played the tourist. The visit was not irrelevant to Vietnam. Nixon, something of a student of history, hoped that the Soviet Union would value enough the emerging *detente* with the United States to pressure Hanoi to come to terms.

A flurry of pronouncements near the end of October revealed progress in the Paris peace talks. On the twenty-fourth, administration sources stated that bombing north of the 20th parallel had been temporarily halted. The next day North Vietnam announced an agreement that could be signed immediately. Forced by this statement to offer some explanation, Kissinger declared on October 26, 1972, "Peace is at hand," and suggested that one more negotiating session should wrap up the cease-fire. But at least one party to the war had not yet agreed to anything. President Thieu of South Vietnam demanded the withdrawal of all North Vietnamese troops from the South before any cease-fire. It rapidly became clear, moreover, that on several points necessary to the peace, Hanoi's understanding differed from Washington's. More talks produced only a worsening of relations. Kissinger charged the North Vietnamese with reopening questions and with being obstructive; further meetings were suspended.

Renewed Fighting and a Peace Agreement at Last To break the latest deadlock, beginning on December 17 the United States launched against North Vietnam the heaviest bombing campaign yet. For two weeks, with a thirty-six-hour break for Christmas, American planes bombed targets closer to urban populations and to the Chinese border than ever before. Huge B-52s carried on "carpet bombing"—the dropping of bombs by several planes simultaneously in an area over a mile long. This damaged many buildings in Hanoi not themselves targets, including foreign embassies and a major hospital. World opinion recoiled in shock. Yet Hanoi's reaction to the holocaust seemed restrained, as did that of Peking and Moscow. Renewed signs of North Vietnam's desire to negotiate, reinforced by the high costs of the bombing in American men and planes, produced an end to the attacks and a reopening of talks in early January.

A peace agreement, signed on January 23, 1973, was an uneasy compromise. The United States had tacitly consented to allow a substantial North Vietnamese troop presence in the South. Hanoi had been forced to drop its demands for Thieu's resignation and agree to permit substantial American aid to Saigon to continue. Finally, on March 29, with the release of the last prisoners of war and the departure of the last substantial American troop units from Vietnam, the United States apparently ended its direct military role in Vietnam.

Relief but little celebration characterized the American response to the armistice. President Nixon, in his message announcing the peace, did not once use the word "victory." Two years later the war, now chiefly among the Vietnamese themselves, ended with the fall of Saigon to the Communists, and the hasty evacuation of the city by Westerners and those anti-Communist Vietnamese lucky enough to get out. Communists also won in Cambodia and Laos. The conflict had produced, in the words of one journalist, "no famous victories, no national heroes and no stirring patriotic songs"—or rather, it had brought the Americans none of those things.

Points To Think About

1. Truman's presidency very sensibly decided not to intervene in the Chinese civil war. Only massive firepower and an enormous American army would have had any chance of preventing Mao's victory. There was a real possibility that the Soviet Union would also intervene. These harsh realities did not stop Republican critics from blaming Truman for the "loss" of China. Democrats, Republicans were eager to charge, were soft on Communism.

The Democratic chance to pay the Republicans back in kind came in 1960 when John F. Kennedy blamed Eisenhower's administration for the "loss" of Cuba. Kennedy made these charges even after he had been informed of the administration's elaborate plans to invade Cuba (what would become, in his own administration, the Bay of Pigs disaster).

Each political party, then, adopted the practice of blaming the other for events neither could control. Incumbent administrations learned to keep a weather eye on potential Chinas and Cubas. Not only were they opposed to Marxist-inspired revolutions as a matter of policy, but they were also aware of the domestic political consequences.

In the 1960s the American government committed itself to a massive effort to prevent another "loss," that of the South Vietnamese regime. The first escalation in the level of American military activity was designed simply to stave off this disaster. It succeeded. Vietcong activity fell sharply. Actual victory seemed possible. What had happened was that the Vietcong had engaged in a tactical retreat to allow it the time to adopt a new strategy. Once it did, the situation worsened rapidly. A new American escalation followed, again just to prevent immediate defeat. Then there was another lull, new false hopes of victory, a resumed Vietcong offensive, and a new escalation.

2. By the end of the 1960s not only had those opposed to the war grown more numerous, and more radical, but supporters of the war were becoming bitter at the protests against the war and at the government's restraint in the use of force against North Vietnam. Demonstrations and counter demonstrations provoked fighting in the streets. And the ability of local police forces to keep the peace was exhausted.

Yet Nixon's administration felt obliged to withdraw from the war very gradually. Its own supporters would be the citizens and politicians most outraged by an American withdrawal. Even more important were considerations of the nation's place in the world. The Nixon presidency, like the administrations of Kennedy and Johnson, was obsessed with the idea of credibility. If the United States was to be respected as a superpower, its threats to use force had to be believable. Hence Vietnam was, in a sense, an elaborate demonstration both of American might and of the willingness to use it.

The chief threat to that credibility was internal. The longer the war dragged on, the more unpopular it became and the more political pressure built up to end it. The war administrations feared that this dissent from the war would make the United States appear to the world to be ineffective. So successive administrations, to gain support domestically, and thus to preserve American credibility abroad, tried to sell the war to the people. Over the course of several years this seriously undercut the government's credibility at home. And as people ceased to believe the administration, they grew more vocal in their denunciations of the war.

The whole premise that the American will could prove itself only by persistence and victory in Vietnam was flawed. Countless nations with proud military traditions have lost countless wars and suffered no lessening of dignity and standing in the world. Our insistence on winning, lest we be perceived as weak, made us look weak.

3. Critics have written of a mindless consumerism that is the result of the extraordinary productivity of modern technology. The complaint takes many forms, which may for reason of convenience be summed into two: that Americans have learned to equate their worth with their possessions, and that they have become the passive recipients of the services and pleasures that modern consumer goods bring. Each of these indictments needs qualification.

The temptation to place worth and identity in something exterior is an ancient one. Aristocracies have traditionally located their pride in inherited titles. Racial and ethnic groups urge their members to fix their self-satisfaction in their group identity. Preindustrial Americans along with the other agricultural peoples were eager to locate themselves in an impressive stretch of land. Any American who may possibly rush out to buy a car because an advertisement has shown a haughty patrician couple lounging about it is no more a fool than a genuine patrician of the seventeenth century, gazing at the portrait of a splendid ancestor.

The charge that modern consumer goods render

their purchasers passive is more serious. What may be useful here are a few simple distinctions. People watching television merely to pass the time are passive, at least as long as they are watching it: no more passive than a farm boy watching the fireflies blink, but no less so. People using their computers are active. In the final analysis, passivity and activity are a matter of the product and of the way the consumer chooses to relate to it.

Suggested Readings

Recent books on this period include Marilyn Young, *The Vietnam Wars, 1945–1990* (1991), Melanie Billings-Yun, *Decision Against War: Eisenhower and Dien Bien Phu, 1954* (1988), Larry Berman, *Lyndon Johnson's War* (1989), William Braeman, *William Fulbright and the Vietnam War* (1988), Andrew Rotter, *The Path to Vietnam* (1988), Stanley Karnow, *Vietnam: A History* (1983), Gabriel Kolko, *Anatomy of a War* (1986), Kathleen Turner, *Lyndon Johnson's Dual War* (1985), Bruce Palmer, Jr., *The 25-Year War* (1984), Mark Clodfelter, *The Limits of Air Power: The Bombing of North Vietnam* (1989), and the succinct James W. Gipson, *The Perfect War* (1986), which emphasize war technology. Guenther Lewy argues in defense of the Vietnam War in *America in Vietnam* (1978). Neil Sheehan studies the war through the biography of John Paul Vann in *A Bright Shining Lie* (1988).

See also S. Kirkpatrick Sale, *SDS* (1973), Roger Kahn, *The Battle for Morningside Heights* (1970), Robert Wuthnow, *The Restructuring of American Religion* (1988), David Marc, *Demographic Vistas: Television in American Culture* (1984), Alice Kessler-Harris, *Out to Work: A History of Wage-earning Women in the United States* (1982). Alvin M. Josephy, Jr., *Now That the Buffalo's Gone* (1982), is a good introduction to Indian struggles, and Rodoflo Acuna, *Occupied America: A History of Chicanos*, 3rd ed. (1988) is the best account of Chicanos in recent American history.

Two good books on events of the year 1968 are Irwin and Debi Unger, *Turning Point* (1988) and David Farber, *Chicago '68* (1988).

A good short survey of the Vietnam war is George Herring, *America's Longest War* (2nd ed., 1983). Another good introduction to the war is Frances Fitzgerald, *Fire in the Lake: The Vietnamese and the Americans in Vietnam* (1972). She tells of the disruption of traditional Vietnamese society as a result of the war and the American presence. Michael Herr, a journalist in Vietnam, writes of the effect of the war on particular American soldiers: *Dispatches* (1977). David Halberstam, *The Best and the Brightest* (1972), contains a mountain of information based on extensive personal interviews. H. Y. Schandler, *The Unmaking of a President: Lyndon Johnson and Vietnam* (1977), explains why Johnson decided in March 1968 not to press the war harder; Schandler argues that the failure of the war came because of an effort to solve by military means a problem that was fundamentally political. Leslie Gelb and Richard Betts explore *The Irony of Vietnam* (1979).

☆ ☆ ☆ POINTS OF VIEW: ☆ ☆ ☆

Was the Sixties Generation Destructive?

Peter Collier and David Horowitz

From its earliest battle cry—"You can't trust anyone over thirty"—until the end of its brief strut on the stage of national attention, the Sixties generation saw itself as a scouting party for a new world. The "cultural revolution" it was staging would free inmates from the prison of linear thought. It was the social horticulturalist whose "greening of America" would allow the post-industrialist age finally to break through the crust of the Puritan past. It was the avenging angel that would destroy the evil empire of "Amerika" and free the captive peoples of the world.

It is hard to believe in epiphanies now, and it is hard not to wince at these homemade hankerings for Armageddon. Yet while the Sixties, that age of wonders, is over in fact, it is still with us in spirit. Nostalgia artists have made it into a holograph that creates beguiling images of the last good time—a prelapsarian age of good sex, good drugs, and good vibes. For unreconstructed leftists, the Sixties is not just an era of good fun but of good politics too—a time of monumental idealism populated by individuals who wanted nothing more than to give peace a chance; a time of commitment and action when dewy-eyed young people in the throes of a moral passion unknown in our own selfish age sought only to remake the world.

There is truth in the nostalgia. It is the *memory* of the era that is false. The vision we see when we look into the glass of Sixties narcissism is distorted. It may have been the best of times, but it was the worst of times as well. And by this we do not simply mean to add snapshots of the race riots at home and war in Vietnam to the sentimental collage of people being free. It was a time when innocence quickly became cynical, when American mischief fermented into American mayhem. It was a time when a gang of ghetto thugs like the Black Panthers might be anointed as political visionaries, when Merry Pranksters of all stripes could credibly set up shop as social evangelists spreading a chemical gospel.

The Sixties might have been a time of tantalizing glimpses of the New Jerusalem. But it was also a time when the "System"—that collection of values that provide guidelines for societies as well as individuals—was assaulted and mauled. As one center of authority after another was discredited under the New Left offensive, we radicals claimed that we murdered to create. But while we wanted a revolution, we didn't have a plan. The decade ended with a big bang that made society into a collection of splinter groups, special interest organizations and newly minted "minorities," whose only common belief was that America was guilty and untrustworthy. This is perhaps the enduring legacy of the Sixties.

The Sixties are still with us, therefore, as a nostalgic artifact that measures our more somber world and finds it wanting, and also as a goad to radical revival. It has become the decade that would not die, the decade whose long half-life continues to contaminate our own. . . .

Broadly speaking, if there was one event that triggered our reevaluations (and those of others who began to have second thoughts about the Leftism of the Sixties), it was the fate of Vietnam. There was no "new morning" as radicals had predicted, no peasant utopia. Instead, there was a bloodbath greater than the one we set out to oppose and a government worse than the one we had wanted to replace.

Some of the accomplishments were undeniably positive. There *was* an expansion of consciousness, of social space, of tolerance, of prospects for individual fulfillment. But there was a dark side too. In the inchoate attack against authority, we had weakened our culture's immune system, making it vulnerable to opportunistic diseases. The origins of metaphorical epidemics of crime and drugs could be traced to the Sixties, as could literal ones such as AIDS.

Peter Collier and David Horowitz, *Destructive Generation: Second Thoughts About the Sixties* (New York: Summit Books, 1989). Reprinted by permission.

David Burner

During the 60's Mr. Collier and Mr. Horowitz were editors of the radical, high-flying Ramparts magazine. They are candid about the easy way they say Ramparts had with the truth, their willful ignorance of brutalities committed by Communist forces in Vietnam, their obstinate clinging to political orthodoxies. In the political milieu they inhabited, ideas, slogans and fantasies were recited as in the fevered dreams of half-sleep. They see themselves as having changed. Have they?

For Mr. Collier and Mr. Horowitz the matter is quite simple. Their radical politics of the 60's were wrong; their conservative politics of today are correct. This assumes that a correct position could have been found amid the realities of a repressive and brutal Vietnamese Communism, a weak and brutal anti-Communist Saigon and an American war that could only pile up bodies. What the authors might have found—what numbers of Americans on both sides of the Vietnam question had found or had possessed from the first—were skepticism, ironic perception and judgment. But the only concept of discovery offered by the authors of "Destructive Generation" is that of switching sides.

They came to be Reagan supporters, backing the ex-President's Central American policy and attacking liberals and the left. But the large denunciations, the obsession with enemies, the delirium of half-sleep remain. The segment of the left that the authors fix upon is, in effect, their previous selves, which they denounce with the fervor of some party member undergoing public correction. They almost acknowledge that there were leftists who did not think in slogans, but that fact does not instruct them. The antiwar left and the community-action left, the icy liberal empiricists and impassioned Catholic pacifists, the whole brawling movement of the 1960's is shrunk to a strident reductionist polemic in the head of a Peter Collier or a David Horowitz.

Consequently, when the authors talk of the left today, they sound like their previous selves of the 60's: sullen journalists discovering the enemy in his malicious and clever manipulation of events. Back then the enemy would have been capitalism or the White House or the Central Intelligence Agency controlling the nation's collective mind; now the two find agents of Castro or the Sandinistas everywhere and forever at work, starting this or that front, mounting support for the insurgents in El Salvador or against aid to the Nicaraguan contras. . . .

Are the authors of "Destructive Generation" accurate in their appraisal of the present-day supporters of left revolutionary movements or opponents of this country's foreign policy? They are accurate about that portion of the left that they understand, the portion that is like they used to be. Where there are ideologies, there will be Horowitzes and Colliers, and their likenesses exist today in the ranks of the left and in the legions of the right. Mr. Collier and Mr. Horowitz are, of course, utterly sincere. "The clock is running on democracy and freedom," they lament, recalling Whittaker Chambers's remark, "You know, we are leaving the winning world for the losing world."

The Reagan and Bush eras are attributable in part to the public identification of liberalism—the "L" word of the 1988 Presidential campaign—and the responsible left with the travesty that Mr. Collier and Mr. Horowitz contributed to during their residency at Ramparts. Their earlier labors accomplished, they have joined in the exhuming and quartering of the corpse that two decades ago they helped mangle.

Three Mile Island Nuclear Power Plant, Harrisburg, Pennsylvania.

CHAPTER 29

New Boundaries

THREE MILE ISLAND

Nuclear power plants like Three Mile Island, near Harrisburg, Pennsylvania, contain an abundance of protective devices. The uranium fuel pellets are held in steel fuel rods, which trap and hold radioactive materials. The bundles of fuel rods are encased in a steel reactor vessel with walls over eight inches thick. This giant steel tank is, in turn, enshrouded in a set of two steel and concrete shields over nine feet thick. Hugging this entire apparatus is a containment building with four-foot concrete walls. Within this fortress are redundant systems to control the nuclear reaction and to maintain appropriate temperatures. The failure of any one system should automatically shut off the reaction and trigger a back-up system to cool the rods. Unlike breeder reactors, which can become, for all intents, nuclear bombs, these light water fission reactors cannot explode. Their main danger is known as the "China Syndrome." If the hundred tons of uranium in a reactor were somehow to be left without proper cooling, the core would—theoretically at least—become so hot as to melt through the reactor vessel, through the containment building and, perhaps, on down into the ground "to China." It would eventually be quenched by groundwater, and produce a murderous flume of radioactive steam with unknown but presumably formidable capacity to damage human beings and other animals.

In the early morning hours of Wednesday, March 28, 1979, Unit Two at Harrisburg came within an ace of that supposed impossibility: a core meltdown. At thirty-six seconds after 4:00 a.m., a pump supplying water to the reactor's steam turbine stopped functioning and the steam turbine shut down within two seconds, as it was supposed to do. When there was no longer steam to carry away heat from the pressurized water that circulated through the nuclear core, a valve opened to release the pressure, as it was supposed to do. Within eight seconds, the control rods that absorb neutrons and halt the reaction had dropped into place—right on schedule. Heat from ongoing fission reaction ceased. All that remained was for emergency pumps to provide water to absorb the residual heat from the rods. An operator checked: the emergency pumps were running. What he did not know was that the valve system that should have kept water covering the rods was not working properly. One light, which would have indicated this, was covered by a maintenance tag and another, for reasons unknown, was missing. This was the first of several technical problems that made accurate information unavailable to the operators. One problem piled upon another: alarms announced that what the board was registering had no connection with what was happening inside the reactor. "I would have liked to have thrown away the alarm panel," one operator recalls. "It wasn't giving us any useful information." The operators missed several serious signals. One indicator that the reactor temperature had reached 2300 degrees was dismissed as unbelievable. Another pipe temperature that might have revealed the most critical problem, an open valve that prevented the water from staying in the reactor and covering the rods, was ignored because the gauge always read high. "I had been living with a leaky relief valve for quite some time," one operator testified. For over two hours, the operators and other TMI officials notified by the crew labored over their problems. Finally at 6:22 a.m. someone—apparently a shift foreman reporting for work and therefore not yet confused by the surplus of signals—shut the correct valve. A report commissioned by the Nuclear Regulatory Commission calculates that if the valve had stayed open "within 30 to 60 minutes a substantial amount of reactor fuel would have begun to melt down—requiring at least the precautionary evacuation of thousands of people living near the plant, and potentially serious public health and safety consequences for the immediate area." By now, radiation levels within the plant were dangerously high. Supervisors declared a "site emergency" and began notifying various officials.

The biggest danger had ended with the avoidance of a meltdown, but no one was sure of this until much later. By Monday, April 2, the public knew that TMI would not explode. But the nuclear power issue did. An anti-nuclear phobia gripped many people who had no understanding of what had occurred. Environmentalists, who might logically have wanted nuclear power had it been both safe and clean, went on automatic pilot against it in any form.

An unfortunate result of Three Mile Island is that it scared Americans away from the only effective source of clean power available. The burning of fossil fuels kills thousands of human beings each year in an imperceptible way and contributes to global warming. The disposal of nuclear fuel residues presents a long-range problem, but newer kinds of nuclear power plants minimize fuel residue. "Before TMI was built," a worker wrote, "they had a coal-burning plant on the river. They brought the coal in railroad cars, and crushed it, and then burned it to make electricity, and you couldn't breathe without inhaling soot."

Nixon: Years of Triumph

In 1969 Richard M. Nixon came to the presidency after eight years of Democratic rule. In contrast to Lyndon Johnson, Nixon opposed a deeper involvement of the federal government in the solution of social problems, racial discrimination, or poverty. Instead he directed his appeals toward a "silent majority" of middle-class people who had tired of paying taxes to support welfare measures. Capitalizing on their discomfort over student and black protest and the rising crime rate, Nixon, though less stridently than Alabama Governor George Wallace, appealed for "law and order."

In his inaugural address Nixon asserted that the government could not solve all problems and called upon the young to lower their voices. The new President would turn out to be fairly friendly to the basic institutions of the welfare state. But his appointments did not represent the diversity of groups and interests that a leader wanting to bring the country together could have been expected to recognize. The cabinet assembled to heal division and turmoil in the nation contained no blacks, Jews, women, or Democrats. The President stocked the White House with long-time followers whose essential qualification was loyalty to Richard Nixon. William P. Rogers, one of Nixon's closest friends, took office as secretary of state, and Professor Henry Kissinger of Harvard University succeeded Walter Rostow as head of the National Security Council.

The Nixon Doctrine and Salt I

The first elaboration of the President's foreign policy, the Nixon Doctrine of 1969, stated that the United States was reducing its military role in Asia but would continue to respect its world obligations. Concrete applications took the form of troop reductions in Korea and an agreement to return Okinawa to the Japanese.

The question that required immediate attention in 1969 was strategic arms limitation talks with the USSR. After the Soviet invasion of Czechoslovakia in 1968, the United States had postponed these discussions until tensions should ease. Nixon preferred to engage in negotiations from a position of strength, and so proposed in March 1969 a modified antiballistic missile plan. Democratic senators objected to the cost and questioned the effectiveness of the program, but the Senate passed ABM by a single vote. Some who voted in favor believed that Nixon would hold off deployment for fear of jeopardizing talks with the Soviet Union. And the veiled threat of an ABM system seemed to work: in October the Russians did begin SALT talks in Helsinki, Finland. The Soviet Union was chiefly interested in stopping deployment of the ABM. Aware of this, American negotiators pressed for the inclusion of limits on offensive nuclear weapons. They succeeded. The result was a 1972 treaty now called Salt I.

World Conditions

The major powers also reached important agreements on Berlin early in 1971. In part this resulted from the growing strength of the Social Democrats and Chancellor Willy Brandt in West Germany. Brandt himself began talks with the Soviet Union, East Germany, and other eastern European nations; he softened Germany's trade stance toward Communist Poland. An agreement allowed unimpeded access to West Berlin, with provisions for two million West Berliners to visit relatives periodically and to transact business in East Germany.

Latin Americans increasingly demanded economic and political independence from the United States. The government of Peru had seized the International Petroleum Company in 1968, prompting the administration to enforce laws that cut off aid in the event of insufficient compensation. But Peru went on to nationalize other companies, while Ecuador seized fishing vessels of the United States, claiming they had violated their territorial rights, and Chile elected a Marxist President, Salvador Allende (who would later fall to a coup assisted by the CIA.) These events strongly indicated a lessening of United States influence in Latin America. Burdened by commitments in Asia, the Nixon presidency could not provide significant economic assistance, especially when Congress consistently reduced the foreign aid budget. In Africa, Nixon maintained neutrality in the Nigerian civil war, but when it ended he tried to provide aid to both sides to ease the suffering and starvation, particularly severe among the Ibos of rebellious Biafra.

The Arab states of the troublesome Middle East demanded that the Israelis withdraw from territories occupied in the Six-Day War of 1967 before any peace settlement. Israel refused to acquiesce in the absence of any assurance of future security. Many Israelis wanted to hold permanently such areas as Jerusalem and the west bank of the Jordan. In January 1969 sporadic attacks by Israelis and Arabs occurred almost daily despite a cease-fire. And at times both engaged in large-scale operations—assaults on oil refineries, missile sites, pipelines, and troop emplacements.

President Nasser of Egypt offered a plan that called for Israeli withdrawal and a declaration of nonbelligerency, the territorial integrity of all countries in the Mideast including Israel, freedom of navigation on international waterways, and a just solution to the Israeli domination of Palestinian lands and people. Israel, however, rejected Nasser's proposal and resisted American pressures to ease its position on withdrawal. Both sides accepted a cease-fire. This only shifted the focus to Palestinian Arab guerrillas and almost continuous acts of terrorism, including several spectacular airplane hijackings. These led to studied, deadly effective Israeli retaliation. The Israeli-Arab hot and cold war was the most explosive situation in a world otherwise moving slowly toward peace.

Renewed Ties With China In his most surprising reversal of foreign policy, Nixon opened the door to China. In his State of the World message on February 26, 1971, he cited the "People's Republic of China" by name and proposed an increase in trade and the beginning of a "serious dialogue." The People's Republic,

President Nixon's historic trip to China in 1971 and his meeting with Mao Zedong ushered in a new age of détente between the two nations. *(Courtesy, AP/Wide World Photos)*

seeking friends in its confrontation with the Soviet Union, invited an American table tennis team and three newsmen to visit Peking. Shortly afterward, Chou En-lai, the Chinese prime minister, stated that more American newsmen would be admitted; at the same time President Nixon announced an easing of the China trade embargo and the removal of American export restrictions on several nonstrategic items. In Nixon's view this was a significant way to "remove needless obstacles" to more contact between the American and Chinese peoples.

The magnitude of the new thaw became obvious when Nixon announced in a short television address that Henry Kissinger had met with Chou En-lai in Peking from July 9 to 11, 1971. The meeting had been in secret, newsmen having received a bulletin that Kissinger was in bed in Pakistan with a stomach ailment. Then Nixon announced a planned visit to Peking to "seek the normalization of relations between the two countries and also to exchange views on questions of concern to the two sides." He stressed that the visit would not be at the expense of old friends, meaning the Nationalists, the anti-Communist government that had been driven from mainland China to the island of Taiwan but claimed still to be the country's legitimate regime. Yet the nationalist leaders in Taiwan were displeased. When Nixon suggested that the Nationalist Chinese accept a "dual" formula for the China seat in the UN, both Taipei and Peking rejected it. Subsequently, despite half-hearted American opposition, the General Assembly voted to seat the People's Republic of China and to expel the Nationalist Chinese.

Before his trip to Peking in February 1972, Nixon ordered an end to all spy flights over China. After months of preparation, the President finally landed in Peking on February 20, 1972, where Chou En-lai greeted him. During Nixon's five-day visit, Henry Kissinger accompanied him in all meetings with Chou and on an early visit to Mao Zedong. At the end of the week Nixon and Chou En-lai issued a joint communique pledging peaceful coexistence and recognizing Taiwan as an "internal" Chinese problem. In effect, Nixon had granted the fact of a single China; he even promised eventual withdrawal of American forces from Taiwan.

The historic trip to China by a conservative President who was supposed to be a hardline opponent of all Communist regimes jolted right-wing Americans. And the reconciliation with China did represent a softening of the conservative view of the Communist world. But the policy was also hard, balance-of-power politics of the kind that Kissinger favored: American friendship with China gave the Soviet Union more to worry about. Moscow was now thoroughly isolated. That may have spurred the USSR toward the detente with the United States that Nixon was also seeking in the SALT talks, increased cooperation in space, and other diplomatic arrangements. Nixon announced that he would visit Moscow in May 1972 in order to discuss all major issues that divided the two countries. The trip to Moscow took place as planned, and with considerable fanfare. Despite the grave domestic crisis created by the Watergate affair in 1973, Premier Brezhnev made a return visit to the United States.

Nixon: Troubles At Home

Apart from the winding down of the war in Vietnam, Nixon's fresh foreign policy proceeded smoothly. But at home he faced endless frustration. The President's largest problem was an economy threatened by inflation and by increasing deficits in the balance of payments. Congress, however, was not about to accept Nixon's plans for reduced spending. While most Democrats approved of cuts in defense appropriations, they objected to domestic cutbacks, and stalemate ensued.

The President soon asked for a striking program of welfare reform. His welfare proposal would guarantee $1,600 annually for a family of four regardless of state contributions. Families could earn an additional $720 a year with no loss in benefits, but beyond this, assistance would decrease fifty cents on each dollar earned at a job until wages reached $3,920. The more the recipient got paid at a regular job, the less he would get from the government. But the drop in government payments would not be so great as the rise in earned income, and therefore the individual would have reason to seek higher paying work. The administration was attempting to correct what it saw to be one of the worst features of welfare, its discouraging recipients from seeking work. The program, to be administered by the Social Security Administration, would have required recipients to register at the nearest unemployment office and to accept suitable jobs or undergo training; no more food stamps would be issued. The program was not enacted. Many, favoring the establishment of a larger guaranteed annual income, objected to Nixon's assertion that such assistance "would undermine the incentive to work."

More successful was Nixon's plan for revenue sharing, which involved turning tax dollars back to state and local governments, many of which were in serious financial difficulty. The mayors of large cities were particularly interested, for the flight of the middle class and businesses to the suburbs had eroded their tax base.

Like Lyndon Johnson, President Nixon could not easily accept criticism. He was happy to let Vice President Agnew stand in the political foreground and make scathing remarks about the national news media and campus radicals. In a November 1969 speech the Vice President claimed that the three major television networks distorted the news, especially CBS and NBC. While disclaiming any wish for censorship, Agnew complained of the power of a "small and unelected elite" to control public opinion.

The Nixon Court

Agnew was to continue his often colorful attacks during the 1970 campaign, singling out particular senators who had voted against Clement Haynsworth and Harrold G. Carswell—both Nixon nominees who had failed to win confirmation in the Senate to fill vacant Supreme Court seats. Nixon's first appointee to the Court, Chief Justice Warren E. Burger, faced little opposition as the successor to Earl Warren. As for Nixon's nominees that the Senate rejected, Democrats complained the President was putting up candidates merely on the strength of their being southerners and conservative. Denying this, Nixon then nominated Harry Blackmun of Minnesota, who won approval 94 to 0. In 1971 the Senate did approve a southerner, Lewis Powell of Virginia, along with William Rehnquist, an assistant attorney general in the Justice Department and a former Goldwater supporter.

The new Supreme Court refused to back down from strong civil rights decisions issued since 1954. It ruled unanimously that school districts must end segregation "at once" and operate integrated school systems "now and hereafter." In other important decisions, the Court negated residency requirements for welfare recipients, applied a statute of limitations of five years on failure to register for the draft, decided that states had to help the poor pay divorce costs, and held that ethical as well as religious reasons were a sufficient basis for conscientious objection.

On April 20, 1971, the Court ruled 9 to 0 that school busing was a proper means of achieving school integration. Nixon wanted no more busing than the minimum required by law, and the issue was a major one in the 1972 primaries and campaign. Then the Court early that year held in *Roe v. Wade* that for the earlier stages of pregnancy a state could not prohibit a woman from getting an abortion; the vote was a lopsided 7 to 2, with three of Nixon's four appointees in the majority. But a case in 1973, in which the Court gave localities more power to restrict pornography, indicated that it was more conservative than the Warren Court had been, and in future years that conservatism grew.

The Black Panthers and Attica

The 1960s had been an intensely public time when events on the streets and on campuses seemed almost daily to be making as much history as governments. Later in Nixon's administration the crowds would begin to withdraw from the streets. But for the first two or three years visual public events—"street theater," as radicals would perceive it—continued to compete for attention.

The Black Panthers were an African American group professing revolutionary aims and calling for separate black development. There were theatrical courtroom outbursts in the cases of the "Chicago 8," indicted for conspiring to incite riot at the 1968 Democratic Convention in Chicago, and of the "Panther 21," a group charged with conspiracy to blow up buildings in New York City. The trial of the Panthers, postponed for over two months, resumed only when the defen-

Demonstrators protesting the sentencing of Abbie Hoffman, SDS leader. *(Courtesy, United Press International Photo)*

dants promised to restrain themselves. In the Chicago trial the conduct of Bobby Seale, the chairman of the Black Panther party, so infuriated Judge Julius Hoffman that he declared a mistrial and cited Seale for contempt of court. The other seven, although acquitted of the major charge of conspiracy, were convicted along with their lawyers on multiple counts of contempt of court, but secured a reversal of these through appeal.

The Black Panthers, suspected of conspiring to kill policemen, were a particular target of arrest and trial. In some large cities gun battles took place between Panthers and police. In December 1969 Chicago police, acting on information provided by the FBI, broke into an apartment and killed Fred Hampton, chairman of the Illinois Black Panthers. Although an interracial jury declared the killing justifiable, the government eventually dropped felony charges against the surviving Panthers, and in August 1972 a grand jury indicted the Illinois state attorney for blocking the prosecution of police officers responsible for the raid on Hampton's apartment. In almost every trial of Black Panthers from 1969 to January 1972 the juries failed to return convictions.

Among scattered outbreaks of prison violence and related demands for reform, none drew so much attention as that at Attica, New York. On September 9, 1971, 1,000 inmates, most of them members of minorities, revolted and seized thirty-three guards as hostages. New York's Corrections Commissioner Russell Oswald negotiated with the prisoners for four days and acceded to twenty-eight demands for decent treatment but refused the request for amnesty. Then, with the consent of Governor Rockefeller, who had refused to meet with the prisoners, over 1,000 state troopers and deputy sheriffs stormed the prison after helicopters dropped tear gas. Nine hostages and twenty-nine prisoners died. Gunshot wounds by the police had killed the hostages.

Apollo 11 As early as December 1968 the space vehicle Apollo 8 had orbited the moon, and the flights of Apollo 9 and 10 followed soon after, testing the lunar module that was to make the landing. On July 16, 1969, Apollo 11 lifted off for the moon with astronauts Mike Collins, Neil Armstrong, and Edwin Aldrin aboard. Four days later Armstrong and Aldrin landed on the moon, and millions watched on television as Armstrong stepped onto the surface. As John Kennedy had promised, Americans had landed on the moon before the end of the decade. Armstrong and Aldrin set up a seismometer to measure moonquakes, a solar wind screen, and an American flag; they brought home samples of rock showing the moon to be billions of years old. Subsequent flights provided more scientific information.

The moon flights were not greeted with the unquestioning enthusiasm that Lindbergh's solo flight across the Atlantic in 1927 had received. Perhaps television had made the nation more sophisticated, less susceptible to wonder. The matter-of-factness of the first steps on the moon, flashing on the same screens that showed advertisements and local weather reports, made the whole venture reveal itself as a magnificent technological achievement and an act of personal courage and discipline, but not a magical journey.

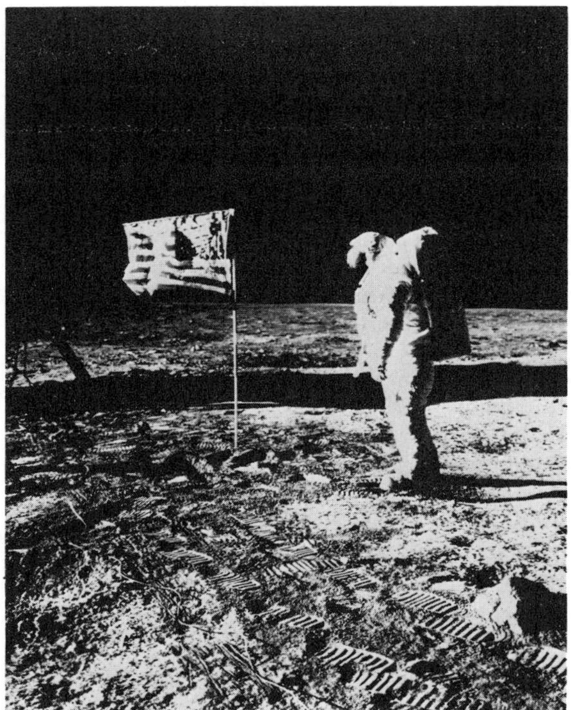

Edwin "Buzz" Aldrin, the second man to walk on the moon, as photographed by Neil Armstrong, the first, during the Apollo 11 mission, July 1969. *(Courtesy, NASA)*

And some Americans asked whether the resources that the country was hurling into space could have better gone to addressing the mundane problems of poverty, pollution, and worldwide overpopulation.

Public pressure mounted for programs against water and air pollution. Oil spills in the Santa Barbara channel in February 1969 offered an immediate opportunity to act against companies responsible for pollution. Environmentalists, at first upset with the appointment of Walter Hickel as interior secretary, were pleased by his call for stiffer laws governing off-shore drilling. In his 1970 State of the Union message Nixon committed himself to improving the "quality of life." He first proposed a $10 billion program to clean up the nation's waterways. The federal government would provide $4 billion and the states the other $6 billion. Nixon also responded to concern over air pollution. Conceding that his proposals were greater than any that had come before, most Democrats argued that they were nonetheless inadequate.

Economic Measures

The President's urban and educational programs, by contrast, looked toward a reduced role for the federal government. Nixon backed away from Johnson's war on poverty, but continued certain popular programs such as Head Start. His education message of March 1970 questioned that federal aid could be as effective as an improvement in social and economic circumstances. Congress overrode his veto, in the summer of 1970, of a $4.4 billion education bill.

On August 15, 1971, Nixon took drastic action against inflation by instituting a freeze for ninety days of wages and prices. At the same time he proposed new tax cuts and called for programs that would add new jobs. The stock market leaped ahead. But labor leaders were not pleased. George Meany called the freeze discriminatory against his AFL-CIO workers, whose wages were frozen while industry received tax benefits. The freeze slowed but did not stop the pace of inflation.

The 1972 Election

In the 1972 election Nixon announced lower draft calls, more federal aid to black colleges, greater purchases of farm surpluses, and new authority for the Civil Rights

George McGovern, Democratic presidential nominee in 1972, appealed to blacks, women, and peace activists by a wide margin. *(Courtesy, United Press International Photo)*

Commission to eliminate discrimination against women.

George McGovern received the Democratic presidential nomination from a convention that, in part as a result of his leadership, gave greater representation to women, minorities, and youth. By directing his appeal to the most cohesive and energetic factions within the Democratic party—youth, peace activists, blacks—McGovern had won key primaries and the nomination, but at the same time the image he gained for being the representative of fringe and dissident groups almost insured his defeat in November. His inept handling of the vice-presidential selection further prejudiced his campaign. Without careful background investigations, McGovern selected Senator Thomas Eagleton of Missouri as his running mate. Ten days later, Eagleton, prodded by newspaper rumors, admitted earlier hospitalization and two sessions of shock therapy for mental depression. Eagleton had come back strongly and courageously from what is a common and treatable illness, but he was now vulnerable to a range of attacks. After first backing Eagleton by "one thousand percent," McGovern, bowing to widespread public doubts, eventually forced his running mate to withdraw as a candidate. After an embarrassing search for a willing replacement, he finally turned to R. Sargent Shriver, a Kennedy kinsman and an energetic speaker.

While Richard Nixon was maintaining a presidential calm, one of the most interesting political incidents in several decades occurred during the 1972 presidential campaign. During the summer of the election year an odd burglary took place that, though McGovern repeatedly brought it up, aroused little interest among the voters. On June 17 five men were captured inside Democratic National Headquarters in Washington while involved in a bugging and spying attempt.

Much as the pollsters predicted, Americans on November 7 gave Richard Nixon 60.8 percent of the popular vote and 521 of 538 electoral votes; only Massachusetts and the District of Columbia went to George McGovern. President Nixon interpreted the overwhelming victory as a great personal mandate, as a prelude to a triumphant second term.

Watergate

During the middle of Nixon's first term, some members of the White House staff had begun to use their power to pursue partisan vendettas. They pointed to the "lawlessness" of their opponents: antiwar demonstrators had pledged to stop the government; radicals had bombed the Capitol building; Daniel Ellsberg had stolen secret documents, the Pentagon Papers. Nixon's assistants, most of them conservative young lawyers and former advertising men lacking political experience, ignored the traditional rules of Washington politics, rationalizing that their predecessors had used sharp practices. By 1972 many of the President's men, claiming that the national interest required Nixon's re-election, justified crimes as necessary for national security.

The Committee to Re-Elect the President (CREEP) had organized the burglary in June of Democratic Party offices at the Watergate Building in Washington. A White House official, G. Gordon Liddy, and a man working for him, E. Howard Hunt, recruited a group of anti-Castro Cubans; and CREEP's director of security, James McCord, led this small band of seven people on two raids. The burglars planted microphones and took pictures of files of the Democratic National Committee. During a second raid, a night watchman discovered their entry and called police. Moments later the burglars were under arrest. Evidence at the scene quickly connected them to Liddy and to CREEP.

CREEP

Some newspaper reporters continued to investigate the Watergate incident. Amid media speculation, Nixon ordered a staff inquiry and told the public that "what really hurts is if you try to cover up" a crime. A federal grand jury indicted McCord and his accomplices, along with Liddy and Hunt. All pleaded guilty, and thus no trial or legal reckoning could be made. But Judge John Sirica, like many others, doubted that these brief judicial proceedings had solved the Watergate case. Then in mid-March 1973 McCord wrote to Sirica, charging that the White House had pressured the defendants into silence with offers of executive clemency and hush money. Government officials had approved the Watergate burglary, McCord claimed, and had conspired also to cover up their own involvement. McCord's letter prompted the Watergate grand jury and the Senate's special Watergate committee, chaired by Sam Ervin of North Carolina, to probe further these mysterious White House activities.

Nixon loyalists could not contain the scandal. One of them, John Dean, thought that the President might blame the whole affair on him, and began to bargain with federal prosecutors from the grand jury. At about the same time, the former deputy chairman of CREEP, Jeb Stuart Magruder, admitted that he had lied in his appearances before the grand jury. He confessed that the bugging of Democratic headquarters was not "a wild scheme concocted by Hunt" but a much-discussed plan, which Attorney General John Mitchell had approved directly. Just at this point, another scandal broke. Two years before, a group of White House operatives authorized to plug security leaks (the "plumbers") had burglarized the office of a Los Angeles psychiatrist treating Daniel Ellsberg. At Ellsberg's trial for theft of government property, the prosecution admitted the illegal entry by the plumbers. The judge found this a violation of Ellsberg's civil rights and declared a mistrial.

Shaken by the sudden reversals, Nixon jettisoned three of his top advisers and tried to seal off the Oval Office from the spreading ooze of Watergate. Before a national television audience on April 30, 1973, he accepted the responsibility—but not the blame—for the actions of "overzealous subordinates." Absorbed in the business of running the country, he explained, he had failed to monitor their campaigning. He also announced the resignations of Ehrlichman and Haldeman, "two of the finest public servants it has been my privilege to know." Dean also left the staff. Under pressure from Congress and even close friends, Nixon appointed a special prosecutor, Harvard law professor Archibald Cox, and promised him "complete independence" to investigate the Watergate affair. These acts provided only temporary surcease for the embattled President.

In the Senate Watergate hearings, Senator Sam Ervin with his shock of white hair and trembling jowls became a national symbol of honor and rectitude. The star witnesses, Magruder and Dean, told their stories. Magruder suggested presidential involvement in the cover-up, and Dean linked Nixon directly with illegal activities. Dean quoted the President as saying that it would be "no problem" to raise a $1 million hush-fund and that payments should be made through E. Howard Hunt. Dean swore that Ehrlichman had instructed him to "deep-six" evidence in the Potomac River.

The White House Tapes Then the committee staff stumbled upon a stunning discovery. A former White House aide, Alexander Butterfield, testified that sophisticated recording equipment had taped most presidential conversations for the last two years. Presumably these reels could determine the extent of Nixon's role in the Watergate affair. The Senate committee, as well as Special Prosecutor Cox and the Watergate grand jury, requested segments of the tapes. The President argued that their disclosure would violate the confidentiality of the presidency and erode the separation of powers. A complicated legal battle ensued. Frus-

President Nixon announcing the release of edited Watergate tapes in April, 1974; four months later he resigned his office.

trated, Cox finally told a televised press conference that he would ask Judge Sirica to declare the President "in violation of a court ruling" for his delay in turning over a set of tapes. When Nixon fired Cox, the top two officials in the Justice Department quit in protest. This "Saturday Night Massacre" produced an outpouring of popular protest, appearing as it did that Nixon was trying to get Cox before Cox got Nixon.

Persistent scandal seemed to envelop Nixon. Just ten days before the Saturday Night Massacre, Spiro Agnew had resigned the vice presidency to escape a jail term for evading income taxes on bribes from Maryland building contractors. His blatant plea-bargaining—Agnew threatened a constitutional crisis unless promised leniency—clashed with his longstanding habit of protesting in grandstanding phrases against lawlessness. The smooth working of the Twenty-Fifth Amendment soon installed Agnew's successor, House Minority Leader Gerald Ford, as Vice President. Popular with his fellow congressmen, Ford had a plainness and lack of public presence that made him seem always at the margin of events. He would serve briefly as Vice President and then as President, with an almost colorless integrity.

Continuing revelations now plagued Nixon. When the White House finally handed over a few tapes, prosecutors discovered that recordings of some conversations "had never existed" and that others contained sizable gaps, erasures that technical experts later judged intentional. During the winter of 1973, newspapers had told of Nixon's having become a millionaire while in the White House, paying only minuscule income taxes. Now Nixon accepted the judgment of a congressional committee and a ruling of the Internal Revenue Service that he owed nearly $450,000 in back taxes. Congressional investigators began probing federal expenditures for extensive remodeling of his estates at Key Biscayne, Florida, and San Clemente, California. The Watergate grand jury, now directed by a new special prosecutor, Texas attorney Leon Jaworski, indicted forty-one people for obstruction of justice and other crimes during the 1972 campaign. Convinced of Nixon's involvement, yet unwilling to confront constitutional issues, the jurors listed Nixon as an "unindicted co-conspirator."

Pressed by public skepticism and a growing pile of subpoenas and court orders for more and more tapes, in late April 1974 Nixon released edited transcripts, not the actual recordings, of meetings concerning Watergate. Even Nixon's version—he had deleted a number of items that damaged his claims of innocence—showed a dubious morality. The new evidence implicated him in the cover-up and openly told of schemes for political revenge against "enemies."

The Final Days Already at work on articles of impeachment was a Judiciary Committee of the House of Representatives, twenty-four Democrats and fourteen Republicans. Nixon made a last, double-edged counterattack. His lawyer fought to prevent release of further tapes. Nixon himself spoke to carefully selected audiences, often in the very conservative deep South, hoping for a show of public support. But his statement, "I am not a crook," shocked more than it soothed. And his lawyer-like argument that only criminal acts would justify impeachment sounded like a tacit admission of serious wrongdoing.

During late July and early August 1974, rapid events finally ended any doubts about the President's fate. The Judiciary Committee heard its Democratic and Republican counsels urge impeachment. On July 24 the Supreme Court ordered the White House to turn over sixty-four additional tapes. That same day the Judiciary Committee began its televised debate on impeachment.

It had been feared that Nixon's impeachment would rip the country apart. But to the contrary, people seemed calm, relieved that a constitutional process would soon end months of uncertainty. Though no irrefutable presidential involvement in Watergate had yet surfaced, most Democrats and a few Republicans argued that a pattern of presidential behavior and a mountain of indirect proof implicated Nixon in obstruction of justice. A Maine Republican compared the President's guilt to snow falling in the night: no one saw it happen, but the next morning it was there.

In compliance with the Supreme Court order, Nixon released additional tapes on Monday, August 5. Though they "might damage my case," he still maintained that he had done nothing to justify his removal from office. But almost no one in Washington believed him any more. Among other things,

Richard Nixon giving the "thumbs up" sign as he prepared to leave the White House following his resignation from the presidency on August 8, 1974. *(Courtesy, AP/Wide World Photos)*

the new transcripts revealed that Nixon had been deceiving his own attorney. After seeing the new evidence, the President's chief of staff, Alexander Haig, began preparations for the accession of Gerald Ford to the presidency. The tape of a conversation on June 23, 1972—Nixon's first day back in Washington after the Watergate break-in—showed the President and Haldeman planning to cloak White House involvement in the crime. Here, after eighteen months of protestations of innocence, was the "smoking pistol." Nixon's defenders on the Judiciary Committee switched their votes, and leading Republican senators visited the White House, telling the President that his removal was a certainty. On August 8 Richard Nixon told the nation that he would resign, but he still confessed only "wrong judgment," not impeachable offenses.

A Quiet Presidency: Gerald Ford

As a presidential jet carried Nixon into seclusion, Ford took the oath of office. The new chief executive found trust, even respect, from a country eager "to put Watergate behind." He and his staff intentionally shed the imperialist trappings of the Nixon years. "I'm a Ford, not a Lincoln," he quipped to White House reporters. Americans watched the President fix his own muffins for breakfast. Ford liked people: the folksy politician sometimes shook hands with surprised tourists waiting in long lines to visit the White House. He experimented with low-key talks on television to explain complicated economic issues and held as many press conferences and delivered as many speeches in eighteen months as Nixon had in five years. The new President smiled a lot, mispronounced a few words, and soon charmed the nation. Within weeks after his inauguration, President Ford had pardoned Nixon for "any and all crimes."

South Vietnam Collapses However much this open affability contrasted with Nixon's moody self-isolation, Ford could not escape his predecessor's legacy. Kissinger, who during Nixon's presidency had moved from chief of the National Security Council to secretary of state, stayed on in that office. Yet even his wizardry did not slow the final collapse of South Vietnam.

The ceasefire there so laboriously worked out had never really functioned. Hanoi increased its troop levels in the South, contrary to the Paris agreements, and stepped up its propaganda campaign. Intermittent war returned again to most of South Vietnam. Nguyen Giap, Hanoi's legendary general, planned a giant assault by both Vietcong and North Vietnamese soldiers for the spring of 1975. Growing chaos in the South facilitated his scheme: Nguyen Thieu arrested opponents indiscriminately, banned political parties, closed down newspapers and television stations.

The end came suddenly. Hard pressed by enemy attacks, Thieu retreated from the three northernmost provinces of South Vietnam. This maneuver consolidated his deteriorating military position and, he calculated, might frighten the Americans into sending more hardware. But Giap's troops turned retreat into rout. They overran the capital on May 1, 1975, renaming it Ho Chi Minh City. The last images of this televised war showed American officials escaping aboard helicopters, while helpless Vietnamese grabbed for a handhold on the departing machines.

Just three weeks after the Communist victory in South Vietnam, the Khmer Rouge triumphed in neighboring Cambodia. During the confusion, overzealous Cambodian local commanders seized an American merchant vessel, the *Mayaguez,* and jailed its crew for smuggling countraband. Ford sent a naval task force and nearly 2,000 marines to rescue the thirty-one Americans involved. Kissinger traveled quietly in western Europe, reassuring NATO allies that the United States would never yield to neo-isolationists. The White House blocked all congressional efforts to cut military spending or reduce the number of American troops stationed overseas. Ford also committed an act notable for a politician: he followed his conscience in defiance of the popular will. Refusing to submit to a public opinion hostile to the admission of refugees, Ford let into the country thousands of Vietnamese, along with Cambodians and Laotians in flight from victorious Communist forces.

President Gerald R. Ford on his first morning in the White House, toasting the English muffins he and his wife Betty enjoyed for breakfast.

The President enthusiastically took up Kissinger's formulas for stability in the Middle East. Leaders in the Arab world, particularly Egypt's Anwar Sadat, resented the relative inactivity of Moscow, once thought to be an ally, during the 1973 war with Israel that Egypt narrowly lost. Kissinger thought peace possible if the Arabs should come to realize that only Washington, not Moscow, could prod Israel into returning occupied Arab lands. He delicately negotiated the wide space of hatreds separating Jew and Arab into a narrow band of agreement. By the fall of 1975, after more rounds of shuttle diplomacy, he secured a cease-fire. Sadat dropped old Egyptian dreams for uniting the Moslem world and rejected demands by Arab militants for Israel's destruction. In return for this long-sought right to exist, the Israeli Knesset promised to restore some of Egypt's lost territories in the Sinai peninsula. The United States underwrote the arrangement, pledging still more military aid to the Israelis and technological aid for the Egyptians. But Israel held most of its occupied lands.

The Carter Years

Stagflation As the American involvement in Vietnam faded and the resignation of President Richard Nixon ended, in the words of Gerald Ford, the "national nightmare," the United States might have expected a moment of calm. But that calm was marred by a curious new kind of economic discontent. The economy of the 1970s was unique in suffering from unemployment and inflation at the same time. Pundits named the problem "stagflation." During the decade the unemployment rate fluctuated between 5.8 and 11 percent, while inflation ranged from 6 to 13 percent.

Back in the late 1960s, when the Vietnam War was at its peak, the inflation spiral began modestly, and President Lyndon B. Johnson could have dealt with it by raising taxes. During World War I, World War II, and the Korean War, other Presidents had done just that to finance the wars and to dampen the purchasing power of consumers. But because the Vietnam War was so unpopular at home, Johnson did not think it politically possible to raise taxes. So although steep increases in federal spending took place during the late 1960s and early 1970s, there were no offsetting tax increases. Consumer purchasing power helped drive up prices.

But the biggest culprit in creating the economic trouble of the 1970s was the energy crisis. During the 1950s and 1960s, American oil consumption had boomed, but an increase in imports of cheaper foreign crude oil drove down American petroleum production. The United States became increasingly dependent on foreign suppliers, especially the Arab countries. Most Arab leaders believed that the United States had sided with the Israelis during the Yom Kippur War of 1973, and in retaliation they launched the Arab oil boycott of 1973–1974. At the same time, the Organization of Petroleum Exporting Countries (OPEC) announced huge increases in oil prices. Before 1973, crude oil prices had averaged only $3 a barrel, but by 1975 they had jumped to more than $12 a barrel.

Early in 1973, at a time that included the traditional Jewish day of atonement Yom Kippur, Israel found herself at war with Egypt and Syria, which wished to retake territory Israel had captured in the Six Days' War of 1967. The war, a sobering reminder of the limits of Israeli security, befittingly took the name of the day of observance. Resenting Western friendship with Israel, the Arabs established oil embargoes. For the first time since World War II, consumers faced fuel shortages and long waiting lines to purchase gasoline. Gasoline prices more than doubled within a year, as did the prices of coal and natural gas. Since energy is a principal ingredient in the manufacture and shipment of all products, producers had to increase their prices. The inflation rate in the United States leapt. At the same time, because consumers were spending so much more of their income on energy, they had less money to spend on other consumer goods, and the economy slowed down. Companies began laying off workers in large numbers. The result was stagflation.

Presidents Gerald Ford and Jimmy Carter faced a dilemma. Traditional Keynesian economic policies offered no way out of the mess. If the government attacked the unemployment problem by raising spending and cutting taxes, large numbers of jobs would be created, but the increased purchasing power in the economy would drive prices even higher. If on the other hand the federal government went after the inflation problem by cutting spending, raising taxes, and increasing interest rates, prices might fall but the economy would slow down and unemployment would get worse.

Carter vs. Ford The presidential election of 1976 was the first in twelve years not dominated by the conflict in Vietnam. An unknown southern governor, Jimmy Carter, blitzed state primaries and captured the Democratic nomination. Ronald Reagan of California challenged his party's incumbent in the White House, Gerald Ford, and almost won.

In the campaign against Ford, Carter argued for full employment, the government if necessary acting as "an employer of last resort" for those unable to find work in the private sector. Carter offered to "avoid future Vietnams." Ford bumbled during a public debate with Carter, telling a stunned American audience that the Soviet Union "does not dominate eastern Europe." Carter won the election by reassembling Franklin Roosevelt's coalition of urban East and upper Midwest with southern Gulf and border states. Democrats swept congressional races, establishing a two-thirds majority in the House and a margin of 62 to 38 in the Senate. The political hassling between White House and Capitol Hill so characteristic of the Nixon-Ford years seemed likely to end.

Jimmy Carter Carter promised an open presidency, a frugal and efficient White House staff, a chief executive in touch with the people. He began his presidency with symbols reminiscent of Andrew Jackson. Dispensing with traditional limousines, he and his family walked down Pennsylvania Avenue after the inauguration. He still called himself "Jimmy." The new chief executive traveled to town meetings across the country, and—in an attempt to manipulate images—occasionally telephoned "ordinary" people. No White House chief of staff funneled reports to an isolated President; instead, all Carter's top aides spoke with him directly. He banished from the administration platoons of expensive lawyers. When he addressed a television audience in February 1977, he wore a cardigan sweater. In this talk, the President promised to reduce government spending, shrink the bureaucracy, and limit regulation. Carter was dismantling what has become known as the "imperial presidency," the resolution on the part of recent administrations to invest the White House with majesty, an aura of secret doings of worldwide importance, and as much power as it can possibly wield, directed especially in foreign policy.

But the former Georgia governor, an outsider, soon ran into trouble with Washington's insider politics. Federal bureaucrats, the butt of his jibes, remained aloof, advising the President correctly but avoiding initiatives. As a result, Carter relied more and more upon his own staff, mostly young people from his home state with little national experience. Relations with Capitol Hill quickly deteriorated.

The President's attempts to deal with the nation's queasy economy and its growing energy crisis speeded his decline. Carter did attempt to close loopholes in income taxes that favored the rich, deriding deductions like "the three martini business lunch." But lobbyists eventually killed most of his reform measures. A spurt in consumer spending boosted the inflation rate to thirteen percent by 1978 and 1979, scaring Carter away from expensive projects. The Federal Reserve Board tightened credit sharply. Interest rates rose to record levels in late 1979; even the most reliable borrowers paid over fifteen percent. Yet the expected slowdown did not materialize. The credit crunch did affect the automobile industry and housing starts, but retail sales and personal income pushed ahead while unemployment dropped under six percent. Carter unsuccessfully tried to talk down inflation with voluntary guidelines.

Energy Problems Energy preoccupied President Carter. In the late 1970s the United States gulped some sixteen million barrels of oil a day, mostly gasoline to fuel private cars and crude oil to run electricity plants. The energy crisis, then, combined depletion of resources with dependence on uncertain sources of supply.

Carter proposed a two-track solution. Selective taxes could discourage gas-guzzling cars and promote home insulation. Lowered thermostats, more carpooling, government aid to mass transit, all could conserve scarce fuel. Federal programs would speed conversion of existing oil-fired electrical plants to coal, a resource in good supply within the United States. An extensive chain of nuclear power stations would further reduce dependence on fossil fuels and cut pollution at the same time. Most of these proposals succumbed to lobbying, the President's own remoteness and—above all—public apathy. The accident at the Three Mile Island nuclear plant in Harrisburg, Pennsylvania, galvanized protests against atomic power, already much delayed by bureaucratic regulation. Environmentalists blocked conversion to coal, a far greater pollutant than oil. Solar power advocates denounced Carter for virtually ignoring the earth's only renewable source, sunlight. For four years interest groups debated, largely canceling one another out. Cosmetic conservation substituted poorly for what Carter once had called "the moral equivalent of war."

The Democratic President embraced détente with the Soviet Union, an American peace for the Middle East, and closer cooperation with old European allies. But Carter added at least one element of his own. From the beginning, he spoke eloquently of "human rights." Breaking with the policy of both liberal and conservative predecessors, he put the United States into moral confrontation with right-wing regimes that employed repression and torture—regimes and tactics that the United States would once have accepted as necessary for the conquest of Communism.

Deregulation For decades businessmen and Republican politicians had complained that excessive government regulation drove up the cost of doing business and contributed to inflation. During the Carter Administration Democrats adopted the idea of deregulation as a way of dealing with stagflation. They wanted to slow inflation without provoking worse unemployment, and it seemed that deregulation would cut business costs, restore price competition in some industries, and, as a result, slow the rise in prices.

Ever since the 1930s the Civil Aeronautics Board had regulated the airline industry. It determined the freight rates and ticket prices the airlines could charge and which routes the airlines could fly. Although regulation created a safe environment for capital investment in the industry, it also lessened any incentives among the carriers for competition and pushed up ticket prices for consumers. During the 1970s, primarily in California and Texas, new airlines appeared that were free of CAB controls because they flew only within one state. They were able to operate at profitable levels while offering extremely cheap fares to customers. In 1978 Congress passed the Airline Deregulation Act, providing for the phase-out of the CAB over a six-year period, free entry of airlines into new routes, and the basing of air fares on competition. The result, over the next several years, was a sharp decrease in ticket prices, an equally sharp increase in ridership, and the bankruptcy of several air carriers.

Congress passed the Motor Carrier Act of 1980 to deregulate the trucking industry. At the time the Interstate Commerce Commission controlled the trucking industry, setting freight rates, determining routes, and limiting access to the business. These controls kept freight rates artificially high. The new legislation gradually withdrew the government from the trucking industry, at least in its ability to control access, rates, and routes. The Rail Act of 1980 brought a measure of deregulation to the railroad industry by allowing railroad executives to negotiate mergers with barge and trucking lines without securing prior approval.

Congress passed the Depository Institutions Deregulation and Monetary Control Act of 1980 to deregulate the banking industry. Existing federal government rules rigidly separated the functions of savings and loans institutions, commercial banks, and securities firms. Savings and loans had the power to write home mortgages, commercial banks to make business loans, and securities firms to underwrite new stock issues. These financial institutions were not allowed to perform other functions in competition with one another. The federal government also put a ceiling on the interest rates they could pay their depositors. The new legislation allowed these institutions to compete with one another by paying whatever interest rates the market would bear and by allowing any of them to write home mortgages, extend commercial loans, and underwrite securities issues.

In time deregulation was to bring disaster to the banking industry, more particularly since it allowed banks and similar institutions to participate in the greedy irresponsibilities of the 1980s. Nor did it solve Jimmy Carter's political problem. Whatever might be the economic effects of deregulation would be years in coming, but the President only had a few months before the election of 1980. Americans in the late 1970s were frustrated at their economic predicament. Carter often appeared on television for his version of Franklin Roosevelt's "fireside chat," but he usually spoke of belt tightening and the hard truth that Americans could not keep living in the future the way they had lived in the past. Carter's problem, of course, was that most Americans wanted to continue doing just that. They wanted to hear the old, traditional messages of progress, prosperity, and power. With the election of 1980, Jimmy Carter would find himself in an impossible position because Republican candidate Ronald Reagan was telling the public just what it wanted to hear.

SALT II Carter and his national security adviser, Zbigniew Brzezinski, were both anxious to control strategic nuclear weapons. The first SALT treaty had not cut into either superpower's

The 1978 meeting of Israeli Prime Minister Menachem Begin (left), Egyptian President Anwar Sadat (right), and President Jimmy Carter at Camp David, Maryland, brought about a historic treaty between Israel and Egypt, but did not bring peace to the volatile Middle East. *(Courtesy, AP/Wide World Photos)*

stockpile; it only limited future production. Its major contribution was to stop proliferation of expensive, potentially destabilizing ABM rockets. The next logical step was balancing existing weaponry into a rough equilibrium. Three years of negotiating followed. Despite footdragging by the military services on both sides, a second SALT treaty was in place by early 1979. It provided caps on the total number of intercontinental ballistic missiles (ICBMs), missiles carrying multiple independent targetable re-entry vehicles (MIRVs)—or missiles that carry more than one nuclear warhead—and other strategic nuclear weapons. Distrust of the Soviet Union slowed SALT II progress in the Senate; then the Soviet leader Leonid Brezhnev's invasion of Afghanistan stalled the ratification procedure altogether early in 1980.

The collapse of further nuclear arms agreements illustrated the fragility of Soviet-American relations. Brezhnev resented Carter's call for human rights, which was directed against the Soviet Union as well as against right-wing regimes. Cuban troops, financed by Moscow, roamed across Angola and Ethiopia. The United States countered with a call for local, black majority rule throughout Africa. Communist rebels in Yemen threatened the rear flanks of Saudi Arabia, now armed more and more heavily with American weapons. Carter's justification to the public for the early return of the Panama Canal to that country was that it would soften hostility to the United States in Latin America. (The United States retained its rights to defend the strategic waterway.) All points of contact between the two great powers resulted in rivalry, not agreement. Nowhere was this growing animosity more worrisome than in the Middle East.

Carter continued Kissinger's plans for an American presence there. He pressured Israel for concessions to convince Arab moderates, like Egypt's Anwar Sadat, that the United States, not the Soviet Union, could best insure return of their occupied lands. Runaway inflation in Israel and a nightmarishly backward economy in Egypt further encouraged the two enemies toward compromise. Sadat and his Israeli counterpart, Menachem Begin, finally signed a peace treaty in 1978 at a ceremony at the White House. Egypt formally recognized Israel's right to exist; in turn, the Israelis restored the Sinai to the Egyptians. Other issues, like the future status of Jerusalem and the Palestinian refugees, remained unresolved. But hopes for stability in the Middle East, a region vital to American security and energy needs, quickly evaporated.

Washington long had supported the Shah of Iran in his efforts to modernize that country; huge amounts of Iranian crude oil were exchanged for sophisticated technological apparatus and also military weapons. But religious fundamentalists among the country's Moslems, together with rebels angry at the Shah's dictatorial rule, combined to overthrow the monarchy early in 1979. Their leader, the Ayatollah Khomeini, turned his back on everything Western, cutting oil exports by one-third, reviving Islamic social customs, halting the drive toward modernization.

Ayatollah Khomeini Then, in a dramatic campaign to consolidate his personal power, Khomeini unleashed a torrent of anti-American propaganda. "Students" stormed the American embassy in Teheran and held hostage Americans still working there. The militants demanded that the United States extradite the Shah, then at a hospital in New York City, to stand trial for crimes against the Iranian people. Until he returned, the Americans would remain hostage. Carter, publicly at least, refused to negotiate with the outlaws and slowly increased pressure against the Iranians, securing United Nations condemnation of the act and squeezing the country with economic sanctions.

In his dealings with the hostage crisis, sharpened by television pictures of mobs in Teheran mocking the United States, Carter exhibited one of his strongest virtues, that of patience. A retaliatory military action against Iran might have gotten the hostages killed. At one moment Carter's patience did slip: in April 1980 he approved a reckless rescue operation that ended in failure with eight American lives lost. But otherwise he outwaited the Iranians and allowed the more sensible elements in that nation to negotiate the release of the hostages. On the inauguration day of Carter's successor, Ronald Reagan, they were released, and the United States had made no significant concession to the mobs.

Brezhnev meanwhile calculated that the Iranian crisis might divert attention from a daring Soviet adventure in the Middle East. In December 1979 the Soviet Union attacked neighboring Afghanistan, invading the country with an army of up to 200,000 soldiers. This poor nation, filled with mountains and barren plateaus, was of strategic value. A Marxist regime had come to power there some years earlier, but the same Islamic backlash that had seized Iran now operated against the pro-Russian rulers in Kabul. When tribal resistance almost toppled the new regime, its leaders appealed to Moscow for help. Just weeks before the invasion, Carter had sought reassurance from Brezhnev, who promised no military action. "He just plain lied to me," the President later admitted. The Red Army overran the backward country but proved unable to deal with a guerrilla resistance movement reminiscent of that in Vietnam. The White House cut grain shipments to the Soviet Union, boycotted the 1980 Moscow Olympics, and finally decided to furnish the Pakistan dictatorship, a staunch American ally, with military weapons. Nothing budged the Soviet Union from the Afghan conquest.

More Stagflation The rise to power of the Ayatollah Khomeini also had important effects on the American economy. During the last year of the Shah's regime, Iran had been one of the world's largest producers of petroleum. The revolution that brought the Ayatollah back to Tehran disrupted the Iranian economy and seriously reduced Iranian oil production. The shrinking world oil supplies pressed oil prices skyward. Between 1979 and 1981, the price of oil went from about \$16 to as high as \$36 a barrel. The effects in the United States were immediate. Gasoline rose from about 60 cents a gallon to \$1.30 a gallon, and the prices of natural gas, kerosene, coal, and home heating fuel went up at similar rates. The inflationary spiral got worse and as Americans pumped more money into their gas tanks and home heaters and therefore less into the rest of the economy, the country began slipping toward recession.

The Reagan "Revolution"

The New Right Ronald Reagan, elected to the presidency in November 1980, represented the portion of Republican conservatism that had its roots in the new-money regions of the South and West, fertilized by funds from Texas and Oklahoma oil tycoons and southern California real estate developers. His Republicanism was of the freewheeling Sunbelt style. He was in the tradition of Arizona's Barry Goldwater, a candidate he had ardently endorsed in 1964. He was also the standard-bearer of the New Right. This was a broad, loose coalition of conservative ideologues, fundamentalist Christians, and neo-populist voters who deplored the liberal social, political, and economic trends of the sixties and hoped to see them reversed.

The New Right was ardent in support of free markets and a determined enemy of government intervention. Some of its adherents were disciples of Milton Friedman, the University of Chicago economist who spoke for a largely unhindered capitalism. In the 1970s many were pulled to the supply-side economic theories of Arthur Laffer, who argued for drastic tax cuts. The money left in private hands, Laffer assumed, would go into investment. The consequent increase in production could ease inflation while providing an increase in revenues for the federal government, which though taxing a smaller percentage of the country's wealth would have created a more productive and therefore wealthier country to tax.

A major component of this New Right was religion. All through the seventies numbers of inhabitants of the nation's Protestant heartland, along with some members of the Jewish and Roman Catholic urban communities, had nursed their anger at social and moral permissiveness. Many pious communicants of the Protestant evangelical denominations that emphasized the literal truth of Scripture feared for Christian civilization, threatened by the irreverence of the young, the rising rate of divorce and illegitimacy, the growing assertiveness of feminists and gays, the spread of pornography, the gulping down of drugs, the increasing availability of abortion, and the breakdown of the family. Evangelical conservatives traced these evils to "secular humanism," a term they applied to the liberal temperament of a heterogeneous, pluralistic society.

In the past, evangelical leaders had been content to combat the forces of Satan by a call to personal salvation, made during revivals and at Sunday sermons. But inspired by the activism of other groups, particularly the similar work of Catholics during the late 1970s, they began to organize politically. The process culminated in the formation of the Moral Majority in 1979, under the leadership of the Reverend Jerry Falwell, a Baptist minister of Roanoke, Virginia. The Moral Majority pledged to fight for federal laws to restrict abortion and check the spread of crime, pornography, and drugs, and to seek the reversal of federal court rulings against prayer in the public schools.

Meanwhile, Richard Viguerie, a right-wing publicist, had marshaled the power of computerized direct-mail advertising to the New Right cause. Soon Viguerie and his imitators were raising large sums from sources hitherto untapped by political fund-raisers.

President Ronald Reagan. *(Courtesy, Michael Evans, The White House)*

One final source of Reaganite inspiration was neoconservatism. The neoconservatives were former liberals repelled by what they perceived as the social and political excesses of the 1960s and early 1970s. They were also unhappy with Nixon's détente with the Soviet Union as continued under Ford and extended under Carter. They charged that the United States was allowing the Soviet Union to become a far more dangerous adversary than ever before. Hiding behind soft words about coexistence and arms limitations agreements like SALT I and SALT II, so argued the neoconservatives, the Soviet Union had surpassed the United States in arms and had been encouraged to engage in reckless adventures like the Afghanistan invasion and to support terrorism and revolutionary movements around the world.

The 1980 Election

The rising right-wing tide contributed powerfully to the 1980 Reagan victory. The Moral Majority worked for the Republican ticket, and conservative PACs (political action committees) targeted for defeat liberal senators and representatives. Reagan promised to work for stricter laws against pornography, drugs, and crime, oppose federal cooperation with abortion on demand, push a major increase in defense spending, and reverse American retreat around the world. During the Republican nomination race, Reagan's chief rival, George Bush, had called the supply-side theory "voodoo economics," but a major tax cut remained part of the Republican agenda.

Energizing the political right, Reagan's candidacy dismayed many in the center and the left. Carter was fighting an uphill battle for reelection. The Iran hostage crisis held him in thrall. At first the seizure of the American embassy personnel in Tehran back in November 1979 had made it necessary to rally 'round the flag. But as the weeks and months passed without a resolution the administration came to look feeble and, after the disastrous attempt at a military rescue, feckless as well. And in the economy Carter had an even greater liability.

Despite the administration's unpopularity, the results on election day were unexpected. Reagan received nearly 44 million popular votes to Carter's 34.7 million and won the electoral votes of all but four states. Going down to defeat along with the President was a contingent of liberal congressmen. In the new Congress the Republicans would control the Senate for the first time since the 1950s and confront a reduced Democratic majority in the House.

Conservatives claimed that the election was a conservative mandate. The Democratic defeat shook the confidence of liberals and seemed likely to reverse the political direction of the previous half century.

Reaganomics

Reagan was inaugurated President with an ostentatious splash. Washington insiders could not remember when the champagne had flowed in such abundance, when the gowns had been so elaborate, the jewels so dazzling, the stretch limousines so numerous. The inaugural parties lasted all week and the dozen balls following the swearing-in ceremony lasted far into the night. Jimmy Carter's deliberately austere introduction to the American people four years before had announced an age of American "limits." His successor's celebration proclaimed a new reign of the unashamed pursuit of wealth.

Reagan's brief inaugural touched most of the standard conservative preoccupations. He attacked both swollen government and swollen federal budgets and blamed them for the country's economic plight. "In this present crisis," he declared, "government is not the solution to our problem; government is the problem." He proposed cutting taxes and unleashing individual enterprise. He pronounced the United States "a beacon of hope throughout the world" and warned "the enemies of freedom" that they should not underestimate the nation's resolve to protect its "national security."

Patco

The attitude on the part of Reagan conservativism toward unions, a longstanding component of the country's liberal coalition, had a demonstration when the members of the Professional Air Traffic Controllers' Organization (PATCO) went on strike for higher wages

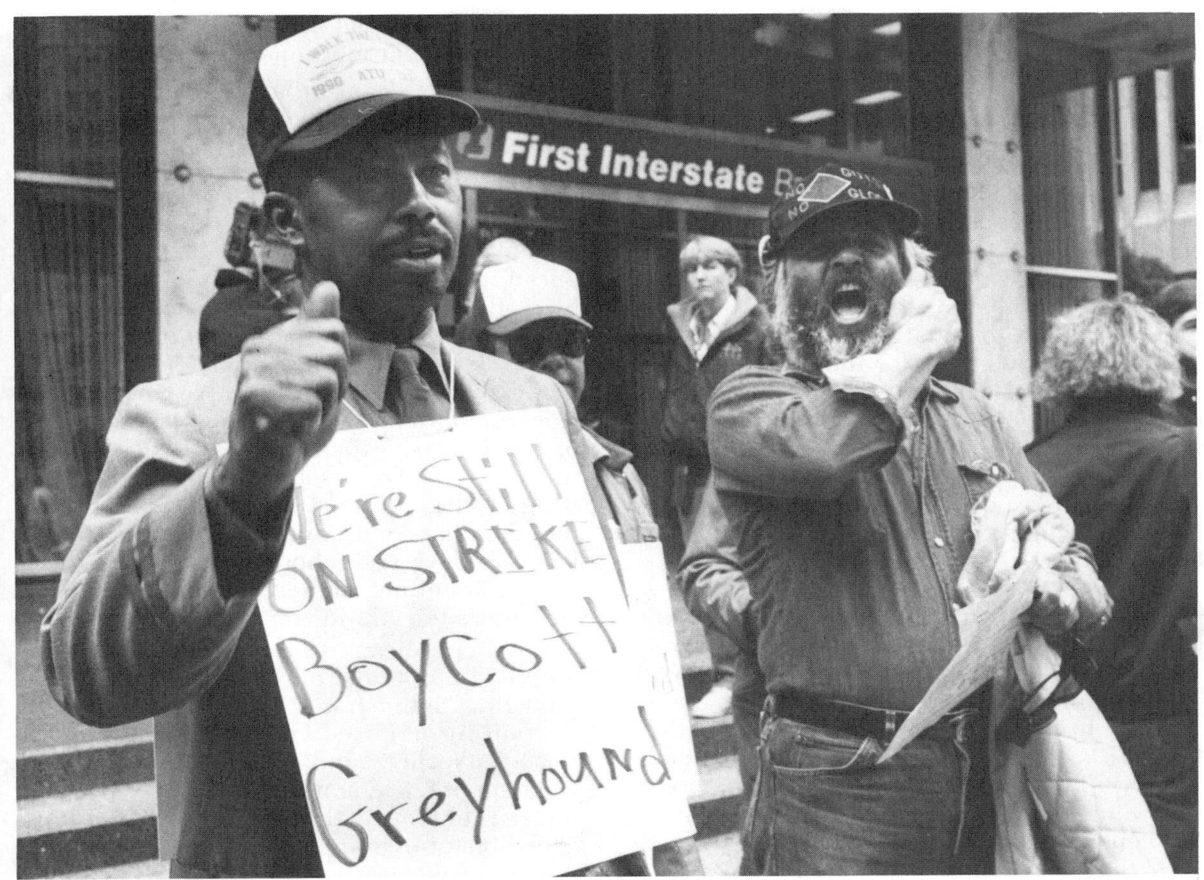

Picketers protest the Greyhound Bus Line's hiring of replacement workers, one of many setbacks for unions in the Reagan Era. *(Courtesy, Jane Cleland, East Setauket, New York)*

and for relief from the stress to which their job subjected them. The President fired them for violating the pledge against strikes that the controllers, like other federal employees, had been required to sign as a condition of working for the government. PATCO was one of the handful of unions that had endorsed Reagan in 1980. Soon unions found that the National Labor Relations Board, in the past a customary supporter of unions, and the Department of Labor as a whole were demonstrating a new sympathy for the self-interest of employers.

Tax Policy The key to the administration's policy, and its first order of business, was a simultaneous tax cut and drastic reduction in the federal budget. David Stockman, director of the Office of Management and Budget, would eliminate "waste and fraud" and cut out expensive domestic programs inherited from the Great Society.

For his program the President needed opposition votes in the House, where the Democrats had a formal party majority. Reagan was widely admired in the South and West and was able, by persuasion, charm, and the judicious use of patronage, to win over a contingent of conservative Democrats, who became known as the Boll Weevils. Near disaster also came to the President's aid. On March 31, as he was leaving a Washington hotel, Reagan was shot and seriously wounded by an unbalanced young man. For a time the President's life was in serious danger, but he made an amazingly rapid recovery. During the crisis and his recuperation, press reports of his bravery, humor, and good spirits sent his popularity ratings soaring. When he appeared before a joint session of Congress in late April to support his economic policies, he received a standing ovation. Thereafter Reagan's tax and budget cut programs had relatively clear going.

The 1982 budget cuts slashed over $35 billion in domestic outlays from the proposed Carter budget while adding over $12.3 billion in defense. The new budget reduced education appropriations by almost fifty percent, canceled the Carter synthetic fuels program, and contracted proposed funding for housing, health, food stamps, school lunches, environmental protection, and the National Endowments for the Arts and Humanities. The Economic Recovery Tax Act enacted a 25 percent cut in personal income taxes spread over three years, reduced the maximum income tax from 70 to 50 percent, sharply increased the individual exemption for inheritance taxes, and reduced the tax on capital gains.

The Recession of 1982 In 1982 the country suffered the most severe recession since the 1930s. The slump was not the administration's fault. In order to check the runaway inflation of the late 1970s, Paul Volcker, head of the Federal Reserve Board of Governors, had imposed heavy interest rates, in effect slamming down hard on the nation's economic brakes. By late 1983 the recession had lifted and unemployment began to fall. By the following year, just in time for the presidential race, the country was enjoying a burst of prosperity combined with a slowing of price increases.

Reagan insisted that despite all the cuts in social programs, the administration would preserve a "safety net" to keep the truly poor and unfortunate from destitution. Economic growth, meanwhile, would benefit everyone.

That is not how it worked out. The economy did rebound and produced countless new jobs. They came just in time to absorb a flood of young adults—"baby-boomers"—coming onto the market. But a large proportion of the new employment slots were at low wages. By 1990 far more Americans proportionately worked in fast food restaurants and supermarkets at a few dollars an hour than in steel mills and auto plants at $20 an hour as many had a decade before. Adult children could not expect on average to exceed their parents' income: a major component of the American Dream, which Reagan was supposed to have restored, was fading.

While those at the lower end of the income scale had lost real income, the rich were gaining it disproportionately. By 1988, the top five percent of income receivers were paying a far smaller proportion of their income as taxes than before 1980. More important than tax breaks was the sheer size of the income explosion among top earners. Even if wealth were calculated without inflation, between the late 1970s and late 1980s the number of millionaires in the United States doubled. By late 1988 *Forbes* magazine put the number of billionaires at fifty-two.

The federal deficit, which Reaganomics had claimed to be able to solve, meanwhile steepened. In part the deficits were the result of the longest expansion in arms in peacetime history. To offset the perceived Soviet danger, the administration poured billions into the military. Between 1980 and 1985 defense outlays rose about forty percent. Domestic spending, moreover, did not fall as sharply as the administration desired.

The Republicans quickly learned that even they could not take on sacred cows. In May 1981 the administration asked for a small reduction in promised cost-of-living increases in social security and a postponement of the full benefit retirement age in order to prevent future problems with social security funding. The firestorm from the seniors' lobby was startling, and a responsive Congress voted 96 to 0 to defeat the proposal. In the end it proved necessary to convene a bipartisan congressional conference to find a formula for soundly funding the social security system. This group established social security tax rates for the poor so high that in many cases they exceeded rates for income taxes.

If federal expenses were not to conform to the wishes of the administration, could it hope for a growth in tax revenue sufficient to control the deficit? Reaganite supply-siders had predicted that a cut in tax rates would so stimulate the economy that the government would in time actually be collecting more taxes: a smaller share of the economy, but an economy more than proportionately expanded and therefore yielding a greater sum of taxation. Federal budget receipts did rise—from $602 billion in 1981 to $909 billion in 1988—but this was not enough to offset the surge of spending for defense and the continuing expenses for domestic programs. Annual federal deficits soared. In 1981 the deficit was $58 billion. By 1986 it was over $220 billion. In 1988, despite attempts under the Gramm-Rudman-Hollings Act that mandated automatic cuts in federal outlays, the total federal debt had risen to more than $2.3 trillion.

Interest payments on the deficit absorbed billions of dollars of savings each year that might have been used for upgrading the nation's schools and highways and its private plant and equipment. The treasury's needs also crowded out private investors by keeping interest rates high.

And Reaganomics did not restore American international competitiveness as promised. Instead, Americans seemed incapable of resisting foreign goods, such as Japanese cars and VCRs, and since foreigners wanted fewer American goods than formerly, United States trade deficits grew. For a century prior to 1980 the country had run surpluses with its foreign trading partners. This changed drastically during the 1970s and 1980s. By 1980 the yearly trade deficit was $40 billion; by 1988 it was $140 billion. These deficits had to be paid for by borrowing abroad. Before the end of the decade the United States was borrowing far more from foreign lenders to satisfy its insatiable appetite for foreign goods than it was lending. It was an international debtor, with billions of dollars going overseas to pay the interest on money owed. This drain further starved American investment.

Reagan Foreign Policy

At the core of Reaganite foreign policy was the conviction that the Soviet Union was behind virtually all the world's disturbances and discords. The USSR, the President told a meeting of evangelical clergymen in 1983, was an "evil empire" with "aggressive impulses." The enormous arms buildup was the most tangible expression of this attitude. But much of foreign policy reflected the same feeling.

When early in Reagan's first term the Polish government, presumably in accordance with Moscow's wishes, suppressed the rebellion of Solidarity, an anti-Communist Polish trade union movement, Reagan imposed sanctions on the Soviet Union. After a Soviet fighter plane shot down a Korean civilian airliner that had strayed off course, Reagan denounced the USSR in terms that increased the ill feelings about an already wretched incident. In the Middle East, the administration tilted more toward Israel than any of its predecessors had done, perceiving that nation as a right-of-center ally against leftist movements. When Israel invaded Lebanon in 1982 to oust the Palestine Liberation Organization (PLO) from its base of anti-Israeli operations, the President muted his criticism.

Central America Reagan blamed Soviet intrusion, much of it through its Cuban surrogate, for fomenting the spirit of revolt in Central America. The United States had traditionally considered Central America its back yard, imposing its will on the region. During Carter's administration, in both El Salvador and Nicaragua left-wing guerrilla movements had risen to challenge the existing conservative regimes. In Nicaragua, the Sandinistas, led by Daniel Ortega, overthrew the dictator Anastasio Somoza in 1979 and imposed an authoritarian regime. Reagan's administration saw the hand of Moscow and Cuba's Fidel Castro behind the Sandinistas and feared the spread of anti-American regimes in the Western Hemisphere. Before long the United States was mining Nicaraguan harbors to keep Cuban and Soviet aid from reaching the Sandinistas, and was supplying guns, food, uniforms, and military advice to the Contras, a band of guerrillas seeking to overthrow the Ortega regime.

Many people in the United States worried about involvement in a long, unwinnable war like that in Vietnam, suspecting that Reagan was seeking merely to replace an authoritarian leftist government with an authoritarian rightist regime. Congress, expressing public opinion, was also skeptical of the administration's Nicaragua policies and over the administration's protest worked to cut off all but humanitarian aid to the Contras.

Behind the particular quarrels between the administration and its critics over Central America lay a broader difference. The Carter presidency had abhorred the Communist systems for the whole range of repressions of

The 1982 World Peace march in New York City brought together some 500,000 demonstrators opposed to the proliferation of nuclear weapons. *(Courtesy, United Press International Photo)*

freedom they carried out. But it had also abhorred the repressive acts of right-wing anticommunist regimes, which had a particular taste for relentless and sophisticated torture. Reaganites, to the contrary, took their instructions from political theorists who made remarkably subtle distinctions between brutality imposed by the left, which they found to be Satanic, and brutality imposed by the right, which they decided to be not so very bad.

The Reagan White House was not insensitive to the evils of the right. It threw its influence behind the presidential candidacy of a moderate, Napoleon Duarte, in El Salvador, and urged a program there of redistribution of land. But in the end it was prepared to support any anti-leftist movement or government. It urged military assistance to Guatemalan regimes distinguished for their viciousness, while Congress balked. When Guatemala acquired later in the decade a barely civilian government thought to be somewhat more sympathetic to human rights, however, Reagan's administration did express its approval.

In October 1983 the administration sent troops to the tiny West Indian island of Grenada, where a leftist coup had overthrown a government also on the left. After a few days of fighting with Grenada and Cuban forces, the United States was in occupation of the island, and national pride, under the Reagan presidency's spread-eagle rhetoric, swelled as large as the undertaking had been small.

World Affairs The administration briefly entangled itself in Lebanon. That small nation north of Israel had become a battleground for many contending groups in the Middle East—Christian against Moslem; Shiite Moslem against Sunni; Jews against Arab; Syrian against Iranian. It was the headquarters of several terrorist bands, some of which had taken American journalists, academics, and businessmen as hostages to force Israel and the United States to meet their demands for release of Arab prisoners and to attract attention to their cause. What especially hurled that nation into turmoil was an Israeli invasion in 1982 with the aim of destroying bases of the Palestine Liberation Organization. Israel was unable to extricate itself from Lebanon, and its Lebanese Christian allies carried out a massacre of hundreds of Palestinian refugees for which world opinion held Israel accountable. Hoping to impose calm on that chaotic nation in 1982, the United States sent marines to Lebanon as part of an international peace-keeping force. But in 1983, 241 marines were killed when a car bomb driven by an Islamic fundamentalist smashed into their barracks. Reagan soon after withdrew the American military forces, leaving Lebanon to descend even further into cataclysmic tribal and religious strife.

The Reagan Administration's main performance was in relations with the Soviet Union itself. The most pressing debate was over the placement of new intermediate range missiles in Europe to offset new, more powerful Soviet missiles aimed at NATO. Out of deference to world opinion, the administration continued the arms limitations talks with the Soviet Union, though choosing hardline negotiators to replace the Carter liberals.

At the Geneva talks, the United States promised to revoke its proposed deployment if the USSR should withdraw its own. Instead, the Soviet representatives mounted a major offensive against the emplacement of the American missiles, claiming they were destabilizing weapons that would bring the world closer to nuclear war. Their most intense attacks were directed against Reagan's plan announced in 1983 to create a Strategic Defense Initiative, a defense system to be launched into space and intended to prevent intercontinental missile attack. Many Americans, including scientists, were skeptical of "Star Wars," a title for SDI taken from a popular science fiction movie of that name. And even if technically feasible, many critics said, SDI would upset the policy of mutually assured destruction (MAD) that for a generation had made each superpower know that launching a first strike of nuclear weapons against the other would bring appalling retaliation. The administration's enemies, Soviet and otherwise, charged that Reagan was pumping up Cold War rivalries and endangering the peace of the world.

But after the West German parliament approved the deployment, new American Pershing missiles were finally rolled onto their launch pads. The Russians had been threatening for months to walk out of the arms talks if the American deployment were completed. Soon after, they did so. For the first time in a decade the superpowers would not be discussing arms limitations.

Society in the Reagan Era

The eighties were a time of revived racism and rising criminality, a time of flamboyance in spending and style. Business became a field of manipulation at the expense of solid productivity, innovation, and services.

Business had as its most visible moneymakers the junk bond and the leveraged buyout. Both brought quick and enormous funds; neither had much to do with making or building or transporting anything good or useful. Junk bonds were corporate securities paying high interest and hitherto shunned by serious investors as too risky. Financiers convinced investors that these bonds were a safe place to put their money, and persuaded corporate executives that they were a superb tool for raising capital. Junk bonds soon caught on and became a favorite device for buying up large flourishing corporations. Sharp-dealing financiers, armed with little cash but mountains of high-yield bonds, would buy out the existing stockholders. Once in possession of a firm they might sell off the profitable individual pieces at higher prices than the total cost of the business. The remaining parts of the firm were then left saddled with heavy debts and dim prospects.

There was also the inside trader who knew in advance about some major financial restructuring and made stock deals to profit from it. The elimination of various government regulations of business gave rise to unscrupulous entrepreneurs. Carter initiated deregulation; Reagan pushed it much farther. In some industries its effects were good. But deregulation also allowed business racketeers to flourish. In the savings and loan industry, for example, greedy financiers gained control of vast pool savings insured by the government. Billions of dollars went into shaky real estate ventures and other dubious business deals. By the end of the decade the federal government found itself legally committed to compensating for the losses of savings and loan depositors that some estimates placed as high as half a trillion dollars.

The new breed of professionals and business executives who rode the wave of prosperity that swept the nation by the mid-1980s were termed "yuppies," an acronym for "young urban professionals." Armed with MBAs or degrees from the major law schools, they rushed to facilitate the corporate seizures and mergers, the savings and loan deals, the new opportunities in high-tech industry. Yuppies displayed all the typical characteristics of young men and women who made large amounts of money quickly: they had a reputation, earned or not, for being self-centered, self-indulgent, and convinced of their own brilliance.

The Underclasses At the other end of society in the Reagan era was the "underclass," the decade's term for the poorest and most discouraged of the ghetto population. The civil rights movement and the subsequent surge of opportunity in business and the professions had helped a substantial group of educated black men and women. But the advances had left behind many black Americans who stagnated in the ghettos and fell prey to all the standard ills—poor health, crime, infant mortality, illegitimacy, family breakup, decrepit housing—and several new ones, most notably the crack plague. The advent of crack, a cheap and highly addictive form of smokeable cocaine, destroyed lives and created a new class of criminals who preyed on their own people and brought a new level of violence to ghetto communities. There was now a two-tier black population: successful middle-class strivers seemed to be a fulfillment of the nation's promise, while urban neighborhoods sagged in poverty and despair.

During the eighties streams of immigrants from Asia, the Caribbean, and Latin America poured into the United States. Many, like the immigrants of the past, were unskilled and found themselves relegated to the lowest levels of the urban poor. But some quickly moved up through higher education and business to achieve middle-class status. Inevitably, perhaps, the relative success of the newcomers encouraged resentment among the black poor.

Other outsiders also suffered setbacks during the eighties. The liberation mood of the 1960s had transformed American gays and lesbians. By the opening of the 1980s many had left the closet and publicly announced their sexual preferences. They had also begun to demand respect, along with equality of economic and legal treatment. Then early in the decade there struck a new, fearful disease, Acquired Immune Deficiency Syndrome (AIDS). Suddenly, more and more gay men began to come down with a mysterious ailment that destroyed their immune system and over many months afflicted them with terrifying infectious diseases that eventually led to death. The health authorities soon learned that the cause was a virus spread by sexual practices and by non-sexual exchange of blood products through drug injection. In the United States AIDS at least initially infected a far larger proportion of gay men than of the rest of society.

For a time, especially among social conservatives who instinctually disliked homosexuality, gays were treated as lepers who endangered straight society. William Buckley of *National Review* recommended tattooing gays to prevent the spread of AIDS. By 1992 even larger numbers of drug addicts, particularly urban blacks, became victims of AIDS through of the use of contaminated syringes.

Womens' Issues

Women made advances in the professions and business during the 1970s and 1980s, yet for whatever reason the highest levels of both eluded them. There were many exceptions. Barbara Walters, Dianne Sawyer, and Connie Chung attained network anchor status on television. Women made remarkable inroads into the academic profession and several became presidents of prestigious universities. In July 1981 Reagan nominated Sandra Day O'Connor of Arizona as the first woman Supreme Court justice. Still, some feminists charged, this was tokenism; the very top echelons of law, medicine, business were still dominated by what had come to be called an old boy network.

Most dismaying to activist women was the failure of the Equal Rights Amendment to win ratification to the Constitution. The 1973 Supreme Court decision *Roe v. Wade*, permitting abortion on demand during the first trimester of pregnancy, had aroused fierce opposition from conservatives, religious and secular, who regarded it as a license for murder. Sympathetic to the "pro-life" movement, the Reagan and succeeding Bush presidencies had promised to use their power to restrict federal funding and support for abortion. They did so by forbidding abortion at military hospitals and restricting the use of federal funds for welfare recipients' abortions.

This federal hostility to abortion made the Supreme Court itself the battleground between "pro-choice" and "pro-life" activists. Perhaps the Court could be induced to change its mind, overturn *Roe*, and leave the issue of abortion to the states to decide. There was little chance that the liberal and centrist members who had approved *Roe* in the first place would change their minds. But many of them were getting on in years, and Reagan and Bush had ample opportunity to choose new, conservative justices who might reverse the 1973 decision. And much more was at stake. Not only had the recent Supreme Court upheld liberal abortion rights; it had also endorsed restrictions on school prayer, restrained the use of tainted evidence in criminal cases, upheld busing for the sake

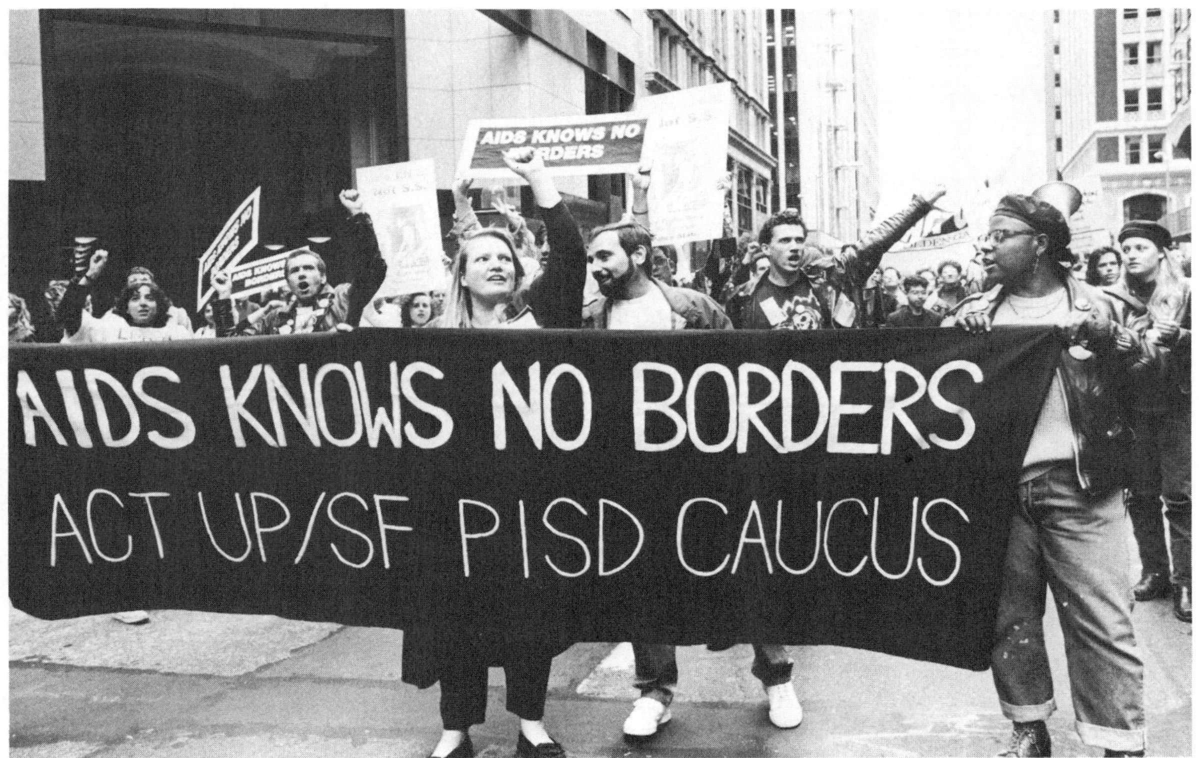

A 1991 San Francisco march for increased funding to combat AIDS. *(Courtesy, Jane Cleland, East Setauket, New York)*

of racial desegregation, and generally displayed a spirit of judicial activism in aid of causes that conservatives hated. New conservative justices might be expected to change the Court's direction. Yet despite the rightward shift of the Supreme Court, the *Roe* ruling remained in effect.

Environmentalism Reagan's and his successor George Bush's records on environmental issues put them at odds with Americans who favored consumer protection, conservation of wildlife and the wilderness, and controls on pollution. By 1980 these citizens had gathered into an environmental lobby determined to exclude as many commercial operations as possible from the public domain and uphold higher standards of purity in the nation's environment. The Reaganites saw the environmentalists as driven by a combination of hysteria and bias against business and growth, and determined to rein them in.

The instruments of their policy were Interior Secretary James Watt and Ann Gorsuch Burford, head of the Environmental Protection Agency (EPA). Watt was a former lawyer for the Sage Brush Rebellion, a movement of western ranchers, timber barons, and mining operators hostile to federal control of western lands. Environmental groups such as the Wilderness Society, the Audubon Society, and the Sierra Club had opposed the appointment of Watt.

Both Watt and Burford soon outraged the environmentalists. As interior secretary, Watt sought to open thousands of acres of wilderness to energy and mineral exploitation. He also sought transfer of federal lands to private interests. Ann Gorsuch proceeded to lessen the environmental monitoring charged to her agency and effectively impeded the operation of the fund established by Congress for the cleaning up of toxic waste.

Neither official lasted long. Ann Gorsuch left in March 1983 following revelations that a subordinate had connived with chemical firms to delay cleaning up toxic dumps. Re-

MALVINA REYNOLDS, *a Californian, wrote more than 500 songs. "Little Boxes," recorded by the folk singer Pete Seeger in 1963, attacked consumerism, conformity, and political indifference. It was greatly liked by college students who had grown up in those "ticky tacky houses" and wanted to show that they had not "come out all the same." The song seems as relevant in the 1980s and 1990s as it was in the 1960s.*

Little boxes on the hillside, little boxes made of ticky tacky
Little boxes on the hillside, little boxes all the same
There's a green one and a pink one and a blue one and a yellow one
And they're all made out of ticky tacky and they all look just the same.

And the people in the houses
All went to the university,
Where they were put in boxes
And they came out all the same,
And there's doctors and there's lawyers,
And business executives,
And they're all made out of ticky tacky
And they all look just the same.

And they all play on the golf course
And drink their martinis dry,
And they all have pretty children
And the children go to school,
And the children go to summer camp
And then to the university,
Where they are put in boxes and they come out all the same.

And the boys go into business
and marry and raise a family
In boxes made of ticky tacky
And they all look just the same.

placing her as head of EPA was its first chief, appointed originally by Nixon, the respected William Ruckelshaus. In October 1983 the President removed Watt after the secretary made a crude remark that succeeded in insulting Jews, blacks, and the handicapped, all at the same time.

As the 1992 election approached the Bush-Quayle Administration made a series of decisions affecting the environment. In an attempt to cater to large lumber corporations that sold timber from ancient western forests to the Japanese, Vice President Quayle, in charge of some major decisions, ordered the opening for clearcutting of tens of thousands of acres of giant trees. And President Bush chose to enforce pollution laws laxly throughout the nation.

Reagan's Second Term

The growing gap between rich and poor, the savings and loan frauds, the corruption in Housing and Urban Development would not become common knowledge until Reagan's administration had ended. Meanwhile, the American public prepared to give the President a vote of confidence. By the summer of 1984 the country was prosperous. Inflation and unemployment were down and Americans, so they thought, were paying fewer taxes than they had paid in years. The Republican campaign slogan—"It's Morning in America"—caught the optimistic mood.

The End of Stagflation The recession of 1982, although a severe setback for the American economy, did not hurt President Ronald Reagan politically, for he could still blame Jimmy Carter and the Democrats for the problem. As the election of 1984 approached, Reagan also found himself in the enviable position of riding the crest of an economic surge. By late 1983 and early 1984, the inflation rate slowed considerably, interest rates fell rapidly, and unemployment declined. The reasons for the economic gains, however, had little to do with Reagan policies. Once again, American economic fortunes were closely tied to international oil prices. By 1984 the world was awash in a sea of oil.

In the years since the Arab oil boycott of 1973 and 1974, the industrialized countries had implemented a series of energy-saving measures that pushed down the demand for oil. The 1981 price, moreover, enticed new producers into the oil fields, raising global production. A bloody war between Iran and Iraq, which erupted in 1981, increased world oil supplies, for both countries intensified their oil production to finance their battles. By 1984 oil prices were beginning a free fall. When Ronald Reagan entered the White House in 1981, international oil prices had stood at $36 a barrel. By 1984 they had fallen to $21, and within a year they would drop again, reaching $8 in late 1985. The prices of gasoline, heating fuel, natural gas, and coal dropped as well. The inflation rate in the United States fell with the decline of energy prices. As consumers were not putting so much of their disposable income into their gasoline and heating oil tanks, they enjoyed more purchasing power, and their demand for consumer products stimulated the economy and created millions of new jobs.

The Election of 1984 After winning the Democratic nomination at San Francisco over a field of candidates that included the first serious black contender, the Reverend Jesse Jackson, former Vice President Walter Mondale chose Congresswoman Geraldine Ferraro of New York as his running mate, the first woman ever to be on a national presidential ticket. In his acceptance speech Mondale chided the Republicans on their debt-swelling fiscal policies and vowed to raise taxes to stem the deficit.

Neither tack worked. Some Americans ad-

Walter Mondale, Democratic presidential nominee, and President Reagan following their October 1984 debate. The choice for voters was a clear one: a traditional Democratic platform vs. Reagan's new conservatism. *(Courtesy, AP/Wide World Photos)*

History makers in the 1984 election: The Reverend Jesse Jackson, the first black to be a serious contender for the presidential nomination, and Geraldine Ferraro, the first woman to be nominated for the office of Vice President by a major party. *(Courtesy, AP/Wide World Photos)*

mired Mondale's honest prescription for fiscal health; many women cheered the selection of Geraldine Ferraro. But the public as a whole was in no mood to be taxed further. Probably no Democratic candidacy or platform could have captured the public. The Republican ticket won by a landslide, carrying every state in the Union except Mondale's own Minnesota.

Tax Reform After the election victory of 1984 and his inauguration to a second term early in 1985, President Ronald Reagan pushed for tax reform. Conservative economists had long argued that tax rates on the rich and well-to-do were so high as to discourage investment in the economy. No one, they argued, would be eager to risk money on an investment when the government stood to take most of the profits away in the form of capital gains, personal, or corporate income taxes. The President's supply-side economic theories accepted that argument. Reagan and his advisors were convinced that if tax rates were reduced at the higher income levels, the money saved would find its way into productive investment and stimulate economic growth. The administration also told the public that the existing Internal Revenue Tax Code was too complicated; most Americans would have agreed wholeheartedly.

The Tax Reform Act of 1986 emerged as a bipartisan effort to simplify the tax codes and to reduce the highest tax brackets in order to encourage saving and investment, as well as to eliminate the most notorious of the so-called tax shelters. Congress intended the legislation to be "revenue neutral"—raising no additional revenues for the government. The Tax Reform Act of 1986 did reduce tax rates. The law lowered the highest tax bracket from 50 to about 33 percent. The lowest rate paid was reduced from 19 to 15 percent. The average rate paid by middle-class families went from 37 to 27 percent. The legislation also eliminated deductions for consumer interest, investment tax credits to businesses, and real estate tax shelters.

The plan had assumed an almost automatic ratio between private wealth and private investment. The implicit assumption is that people will be frugal and energetic capitalists, putting their money into long-range productive investment. But the money freed up by the tax cut failed to show up in the economy in this way. Whether it was going into personal luxury spending, unwise investment or flash ventures promising quick return, it was not nourishing fundamental production or research.

Iran-Contra Reagan's second term brought the administration a major humiliation. It was in foreign policy, a field in which the Reagan presidency, while having done very little that was strenuous, had managed to appear to the public to be standing tall.

The humiliation came of a complex scheme to achieve several foreign policy goals simultaneously: free the hostages taken and held by Moslem terrorist groups in Lebanon; help pay the continuing costs of supporting the Nicaraguan Contras in the face of congressional refusal to vote funds; open channels with the Iranians with whom, ever since the embassy hostage crisis of 1979 and 1980, the nation had been on bad terms. None of this could be undertaken publicly. The United States was on record never to deal with terrorists and to punish those implicated in terrorism. In 1986 the United States launched an air attack against Libya, one of the Moslem states that, under Muammar Qaddafi, supported terrorist attacks against Americans in Europe and the Middle East. The government was also bound by congressional action in its relations with the Contras, and Congress had balked at an open ended military commitment in Central America. As for Iran, few Americans could see any grounds for serious dialogue. The Moslem fundamentalists under the Ayatollah Khomeini remained in power and still considered the United States "the Great Satan." In all this, Washington had to act secretly.

The administration's foreign policy insiders, among them CIA director William Casey, national security adviser Admiral John Poindexter, and his aide, Colonel Oliver North, believed that secrecy was possible. The plan they concocted involved selling American weapons to Iran, at the time engaged in a desperate war with Iraq. In exchange, they thought, the Iranians would order their allies among the hostage-takers in Lebanon to release the American captives. Meanwhile, the profits from the arms sales could be used to finance covertly the money-starved Contras. In a series of secret trips by North, former national security adviser Robert McFarlane, and others to Iran, the deal was struck. But it was botched. Iran bought American weapons, but only one or two American captives in Lebanon were released. Some of the money from the deal probably got to the Contras, but apparently various wily middlemen siphoned off a lot of it. News of the scheme got out when a Lebanese paper disclosed its details in November 1986. The administration now seemed engaged in hypocrisy, folly, and law-breaking all at once.

Critics quickly besieged the President with questions. Had he concocted this nefarious scheme? Reagan denied knowledge of the plan to get around Congress. He had known about the arms sales, he said, but it was merely an attempt to open a dialogue with the Iranians; it was not ransom for hostages. Under growing pressure from critics, at the end of November he fired North and announced Poindexter's resignation. The next day he agreed to appoint a special committee headed by former Senator John Tower to investigate the Iran-Contra affair, and followed this by the choice of a special prosecutor to seek out culprits and bring them to justice. Congress soon announced hearings to investigate the labyrinthine events.

The Iran-Contra affair damaged Reagan's reputation. The President, who had long basked in his Hollywood image of a tough frontier lawman, stood revealed as unable to form an open and convincing foreign policy. His testimony before the Tower commission reinforced this impression. Reagan remembered little of the arms deal discussions and admitted in effect that he delegated foreign policy making to others. Until this point Reagan's critics had called him a Teflon President: his mistakes simply did not stick to his glossy image. Now, with the Iran-Contra revelations, the Teflon began to peel. Reagan's approval ratings soon declined.

And yet Reagan loyalists did not desert him. Many American conservatives approved the deal, especially the covert support of the Contras. When Oliver North appeared before the televised congressional hearings, many people cheered his flag-waving defense of the administration's hidden initiatives. (Later he would contradict Reagan's claims about his knowledge of Iran Contra.) Eventually, North, Poindexter, McFarlane, and others were indicted by the special prosecutor for violating various federal laws. But the cases dragged on past Reagan's second term and past the public's patience. And the results proved inconclusive: no defendant received a heavy sentence.

Wall Street At the end of 1987 events on Wall Street further damaged the administration. On October 19, 1987, Wall Street crashed with a thunderous roar. That "Black Monday" stocks dropped 500 points in a few hours, the most disastrous one-day decline in the history of Wall Street. The market's collapse did not bring the cataclysm that many pundits, remembering 1929, were predicting. Yet Black Monday marked a significant boundary. It pricked the overblown confidence in Reagan era prosperity. Before many months the real estate swell, inflated largely by expectations, began to flatten. Leveraged buyouts dwindled amid an orgy of Wall Street prosecutions for insider trading. Among the yuppie rich, some of them employed in law firms and brokerage houses that had done deals and sold junk bonds, prospects faded. The public was soon watching TV clips of the young brokers and traders at Drexel, Burnham, Lambert, Michael Milken's junk bond marketing business, moving out with their attaché cases and computers as the firm closed its doors. In the wake of Black Monday popular journalists began to proclaim the "end of the eighties."

Another sign of change was the retreat of the New Right. Social, religious, and ideological conservatism continued of course, much of it in opposition to abortion. But in the organized forms that it had enjoyed during the Reagan upsurge, it retreated. In the last years of Reagan's second term TV evangelism suffered severely when major figures were accused of sexual adventures out of wedlock. In 1987 Jerry Falwell, untouched by scandal, announced that he was getting out of politics. In 1989 he disbanded the Moral Majority.

Détente Whatever the fate of the revolution Reagan's adherents claimed that he had achieved, his personal popularity rose with swift and dramatic changes in the relations between the United States and its chief adversary, the Soviet Union. These were in part the product of circumstances beyond American control. Between 1982 and 1985 the Soviet Union underwent a remarkable progression of leadership from the rigid, old-line Communist, Leonid Brezhnev, to the undogmatic reformer Mikhail Gorbachev. A Marxist and a Soviet patriot, Gorbachev sought within those tight limits to promote *glasnost*, or openness, an end to the intellectual and political repression in Soviet society. He also aimed to replace the faltering Soviet command economy with a more efficient and productive system drawing on individual incentives and private initiative. This was called *perestroika*.

From 1985 onward relations between the Soviet Union and the West improved remarkably. Reagan, his saber-rattling and talk of an evil empire notwithstanding, proved a flexible and moderate negotiator. Right-wing admirers of Reagan have liked to claim that his toughness toward the Soviety Union had something to do with the crumbling of Communism there. But Western toughness in the past had merely largely confined the spread of the Soviet empire. It is not Reagan's posturing toughness but his openness toward Gorbachev that is more likely to have aided in destroying the repressive Soviet system, for Reagan's civility to him gave Gorbachev international credibility. In the course of a series of summit meetings the two leaders resumed the arms control process terminated after the American Pershing missile deployment at the end of 1983. In December 1987 Gorbachev arrived in the United States prepared to sign an agreement eliminating all Soviet and American intermediate range missiles on the same terms that the United States had offered five years before at Geneva. His visit was a triumph of public relations. Gorbachev was a friendly man with a winning smile. He stopped his limousine on the streets of Washington and got out to shake hands with passersby. The INF (intermediate nuclear forces) treaty finally signed by the Senate in June 1988 eliminated entirely a whole class of nuclear weapons, an unprecedented achievement.

The process of improving relations continued. The United States and the Soviet Union were soon promising to reduce conventional arms in Europe and to take major strides toward scaling down their strategic nuclear arsenals. Moscow also agreed to leave Afghanistan and, by the spring of 1988, had withdrawn all its troops. The waning of the Cold War was even felt in Central America. Accepting the initiative of the President of Costa Rica, Sandinista leader Daniel Ortega agreed to hold free elections that would include his Contra opponents. The receding of the Iran-Contra fiasco and the remarkable advances in relations with the Soviet Union revived Reagan's reputation. By the time he was ready to leave office and retire to his home in Los Angeles, most Americans once more admired him.

The Bush Years

In 1988 Vice President George Bush had little serious opposition in winning his party's nomination for the presidency. As his running mate he chose Dan Quayle, a young senator from Indiana. The Republican platform defended Reagan's administration and confirmed its resistance to abortion rights.

The 1988 Election The campaign was one of the dirtiest on record. In the Willie Horton television clip, Republicans appealed to the public's worst fears and hatreds. Horton was a criminal who, while on release from a Massachusetts prison, had raped a white woman. The Republican TV spot suggested that the Democratic presidential candidate, Massachusetts governor Michael Dukakis, was responsible. Republicans also showed pictures suggestive of a polluted Boston Harbor, implying that Dukakis as governor of the state was to blame. The Democrats attacked Quayle as an intellectual lightweight with a poor academic record and a privileged rich boy whose parents had got him into the National Guard to evade the Vietnam War. In principle negative campaigning, as it was called, met with universal disapproval, but expressions of disapproval apparently had not the slightest ability to lessen the practice. At the moment of composing a campaign advertisement in a time of quick fixes, the temptation of one more quick fix was irresistible.

The candidates also appealed to more legitimate feelings. Bush distanced himself a little from his predecessor by talk of "a kinder, gentler" nation that would succor the downtrodden. But this need not cost money. Instead, it would be accomplished by a multitude of private service and charity initiatives—"a thousand points of light." The Republican candidate supported policies to end abortion on demand. He also appealed to the tax aversion of the American people. His most telling phrase was "Read my lips; no new taxes."

Dukakis proved an inept campaigner. He did not respond promptly to devastating Republican attacks, and he refused until too late to emphasize the class issues that had traditionally aroused Democrats and focused instead on "competence." Bush won decisively.

The Bush Presidency In his first months in office Bush impressed many Americans with his amiability. But he also seemed unable to get much accomplished. He proposed measures to improve the quality of American education and raise environmental standards, but then refused to seek additional funding for his programs. His one environmental accomplishment, the Clean Air Act of 1990, had been largely thrust upon him by Congress. The federal budget deficits worsened, and since he had promised not to raise taxes, any reforms would have to be done on the cheap.

At times the President seemed to hide behind superpatriotism to obscure his inability to act on domestic programs. When the Supreme Court declared that the free speech clause of the Constitution protected the right to burn the American flag, he sought to ride the wave of popular indignation by sponsoring an amendment to the Constitution that would ban flag burning.

A more substantive question was that of abortion, presenting fundamental problems of defining both human life and the scope of freedom and privacy. Bush placed the administration squarely behind initiatives to strike down the *Roe v. Wade* decision. That landmark decision came under renewed attack in 1989 when the Court in *Webster v. Reproductive Health Services* allowed the state of Missouri to place conditions on abortion that modified *Roe*. In the summer of 1990 liberal Supreme Court Justice William Brennan resigned, freeing another slot for a conservative appointment. Bush promptly nominated David H. Souter of New Hampshire, a jurist who, it was hoped, would further weaken federally protected abortion rights. Before long, the whole abortion issue might be thrown back to the states with each state legislature converted into a battleground between the opposing forces. But it did not seem likely that Republicans would be the gainers. In several states where the abortion issue was tested at the polls between 1988 and 1990 pro-choice Democrats had won. By 1991 officials of the Republican National Committee were claiming that the Republican roof was broad enough to include pro-choice as well as pro-life members, the party national platform notwithstanding.

Still another disquieting problem of the new President's early months was the unraveling savings and loan scandal. It was only in the early months of the new administration that the media and public realized the full extent of the fraud, waste, and incompetence that had saddled the nation with hundreds of billions of dollars of obligations to repay cheated S&L depositors. Congress created an agency to take over the S&Ls, manage the sell-off of remaining assets, and rescue depositors. By 1990 it looked as if the whole savings and loan system was on the verge of bankruptcy with the middle class paying the price. The President alone could not be blamed for the debacle. And many observers noted that some Democrats in Congress, as well as Republicans, had accepted favors from S&L lobbies to support an easing of federal restrictions. Yet the slack regulation had occurred during the big-money Reagan years and seemed a part of that time of quick wealth.

Bush got into further trouble when he finally reneged on his promise in 1990 to resist any new taxation. Faced with the worsening budget deficit and the galling restraints it imposed on all new initiatives, he finally relented. In a budget conference of congressional leaders planned to avoid partisan use of the budget issue by either party, he called for additional revenues. Students of government finance saw the action as realistic and statesmanlike, but to conservative Republicans it seemed a betrayal of the party's most sacred pledge. Many conservative Republican politicians soon began to distance themselves from their party's leader.

Bush's Foreign Policy In foreign policy the news for Bush was far better. Remarkable changes were coming with a rush in eastern Europe. In 1989 Soviet dominance in the East Bloc simply collapsed. By the end of the year popular uprisings had overthrown all the puppet Communist regimes and led to new, non-Communist governments in the former satellites. In Poland, Hungary, and Czechoslovakia, particularly, these seemed to be moving fast toward democracy. The most significant change of all took place in East Germany, the German Democratic Republic. In 1989 angry demonstrators overthrew the East German Communist regime, tore down the notorious Berlin Wall—the most vivid symbol of the Cold War—opened the long-closed border between the two Germanies to free move-

U.S. President George Bush and Soviet President Mikhail Gorbachev. *(Courtesy, AP/Wide World Photos)*

The Berlin Wall, erected by East German Communists in 1961, was torn down by anticommunist demonstrators in 1989. *(Courtesy, AP/Wide World Photos)*

ment, and began to demand the reunification of the German nation.

Some Europeans and Americans who remembered the role of Germany in the period between 1933 and 1945 were not entirely happy at the prospect of a reunited German *Reich*. The Soviet Union too considered it dangerous. Yet the reunion was unstoppable. After giving assurances on borders to the Poles and promising to provide major economic aid to the Soviet Union, German Chancellor Helmut Kohl, in the summer of 1990, was able to merge the two Germanies economically. In October 1990 the political union was achieved. A new nation of some sixty million now existed, the richest and most populous in all of western Europe.

The larger truth was that the Cold War is finally over. With the uprisings in the East Bloc the Warsaw Pact was defunct. The chances of an attack on NATO from the East was virtually nonexistent. There still remained the Soviet superpower with its nuclear arsenal, but by the early 1990s the Soviet Union was beset with enormous distracting internal problems. Some of the constituent Soviet republics were seceding from the USSR. The Soviet economy was producing fewer goods than ever, and the Soviet people were becoming increasingly restless. Meanwhile, the Soviet military was being cut drastically in size to ease the burden on the economy. And with a few exceptions the Soviet leadership, even that portion of it that professed some commitment to Communism, had lost any interest in the ideological and military warfare against the non-Communist world. Clearly, the USSR, for the first time in almost half a century, was not a threat to world peace. By the summer of 1990 Americans were gleefully contemplating the size of the "peace dividend" that could be squeezed out of the bloated defense budget and used for peaceful domestic purposes.

Early in 1990 a success in Central America had come both for the administration and for its liberal opponents. Liberals in Congress, after halting Reagan's policy of military assistance to the Nicaraguan Contras, had insisted, and conservatives denied, that in the absence of military pressure from the outside Nicaragua could be prompted to hold elections in which anti-Sandinista candidates might stand a chance. In time, regional opinion and enormous confidence on the part of the Sandinistas in their own popularity did bring them to put their government to the electoral test. Just before the Nicaraguan elections, Bush indicated his willingness to make his peace even with the Sandinistas if they should win, as they were expected to do. But they lost, thereupon accepting their defeat; and liberals joined the astonished White House in celebrating the success of a peaceful outcome.

Crisis in the Gulf

In August 1990 Iraq, led by its reckless strong man, Saddam Hussein, invaded and occupied the oil-rich kingdom of Kuwait on its southern border. In 1980 Saddam had launched a disastrous war against Iran that lasted eight years, cost countless lives, and squandered billions of dollars. The war ended in a victory for Iraq but left that nation depleted and deeply in debt. The Iraqi invasion of Kuwait may have been motivated primarily by Saddam Hussein's need to replenish his country's empty coffers from Kuwaiti treasure and oil, but many of his neighbors, the United States, and other industrial country's dependent on Mideast oil feared that his next act would be to invade Saudi Arabia, the richest in oil of all the Mideast countries. Success would give Iraq enormous arbitrary power over the economic fate of much of the world. For a man of such brutal and heedless temperament, a ruler who had murdered with poison gas thousands of his own dissident Iraqi Kurds, such power seemed intolerable.

Prompted by Saudi and Kuwaiti pleas, economic self-interest, and his sense that Saddam Hussein, whom he compared to Hitler, must be stopped, President Bush persuaded the United Nations to call for a blockade of Iraq. The UN also approved the sending of massive military forces to Saudi Arabia to repel any Iraqi invasion. These troops, so Bush hoped, would ultimately persuade Iraq to leave conquered Kuwait. For the first time the full UN Security Council, including the People's Republic of China and the USSR, had voted with the West to endorse condemnation of an aggressor. Dozens of nations, including several important Arab states, sent supplies, ships, and troops to reinforce the predominantly American forces soon landing in the thousands in Saudi Arabia as part of Operation Desert Shield.

Secretary of Defense Richard Cheney consults with military figures in Saudi Arabia, December 1990. *(Courtesy, AP/Wide World Photos)*

Saddam Hussein soon took prisoner thousands of civilians in Kuwait and Iraq, including many Americans, but released them late in 1990. When Iraq refused to leave Kuwait by a deadline of January 15 endorsed by the United Nations and the United States Congress, the President began Operation Desert Storm attacking the enemy on all fronts in open war. The majority of Americans, and a slight majority in the predominantly Democratic Senate, supported the President.

1991–92: The Years That Turned Sour

Desert Storm The new year opened with the Middle East crisis unresolved. On January 3 President Bush announced that the United States was willing to "go the extra mile for peace" and proposed a meeting at Geneva between Secretary of State James Baker and the Iraqi foreign minister, Tariq Aziz. The meeting accomplished almost nothing. Congress began to debate whether, in effect, to go to war.

The administration had at first opposed such a debate, claiming that the President's authority to use force did not require congressional approval. Bush feared, in fact, that Congress might refuse to support his policies. In the debate that ensued, a sizable majority of the Democrats urged a delay in taking military action to allow the UN blockade and economic sanctions to work. But on January 12 Congress adopted a joint resolution to use American armed forces "pursuant to U.N. Security Council Resolution 678." The vote was three to two in favor.

The UN attack led by the United States finally began on the night of January 16 with a ferocious assault by planes and missiles. Prime targets were Iraqi command and control centers, air fields, power stations, chemical and nuclear warfare facilities, and Scud missile sites. The Scuds were especially feared as terror weapons that, if directed at Israel, might bring that nation to intervene. An Israeli counterattack against Iraq, however justified, seemed certain to offend the Arab world and might weaken the fragile anti-Iraqi coalition that Bush and Baker had so painfully constructed. Saddam launched the Scuds against both Saudi Arabia and major Israeli cities. Fortunately for the coalition, Bush was able to induce the Israelis to hold their fire and accept some civilian losses while UN forces sought desperately to eliminate the Scuds.

The effect of the initial air attack was astonishing. High-tech American weapons devastated Iraqi targets while risking few American lives. Some 3,000 civilians were killed, though the enormous destruction of bridges, power stations, and other facilities produced civilian hardships and deaths long after the war ended. In a matter of days the Iraqi air force was immobilized, and in late January most of its planes were despatched to Iran. Still, the Iraqis refused to evacuate Kuwait, and many Americans thought that a ground attack, risking thousands of UN lives, would be unavoidable. Especially feared was the elite Iraqi Republican Guard, the special troops who had so effectively resisted the mass wave attacks by the Iranians in the recent war between Iraq and Iran. Day after day, high-flying B-52 bombers pounded the dug-in Republican Guards in the hope that remorseless air attack might destroy their morale and reduce their fighting effectiveness.

At home, once the actual fighting broke out, public opinion shifted massively in support of the war. A great surge of patriotism marked by soaring flag and bunting sales and wide display of yellow ribbons tied to trees, doorknobs, and street lamps signified overwhelming support for the fighting men and women in the Middle East. Americans felt a rush of pride for their military. The public was pleased by the effectiveness of high-priced arms technology. It also came to admire the role of blacks and Hispanics who formed such a large part of the armed forces, and of women, tested for the first time as part of the military. Two heroes emerged from the war, General Norman Schwarzkopf, commander of all the UN forces in the Middle East, and General Colin Powell, chairman of the American Joint Chiefs of Staff, the first black soldier to occupy so high a position. The underside of this tide of patriotism was that the war became something of a Roman circus. While Iraqi troops endured massive daily bombings and coalition troops readied themselves for possibly massive casualties,

Saddam Hussein of Iraq. *(Courtesy, AP/Wide World Photos)*

American television presented the whole business as nightly entertainment, complete with breaks for commercials.

Despite a last minute Soviet peace initiative that threatened to derail UN military plans, early in the morning of February 24 the coalition forces launched a ground attack against the Iraqis. While United States marines and coalition Arab troops attacked frontally across the Saudi-Kuwaiti border, American, British, and French armored and infantry forces swung far to the west to outflank the main Iraqi army. The attack was a pushover. Thousands of enemy troops surrendered without firing a shot. Many others fled northward toward Baghdad and were pounded mercilessly by coalition planes as they sought escape. In a hundred hours almost 4,000 Iraqi tanks were destroyed along with thousands of enemy vehicles and guns. A feared Iraqi chemical weapons attack never materialized. Coalition casualties were astonishingly low: only about one hundred Americans were killed in action. The horror of modern hi-tech warfare was highlighted by one American's bizarre account of how plows mounted on tanks and combat earthmovers buried thousands of dug-in Iraqi soldiers, some still alive and firing their weapons:

> What you saw was a bunch of buried trenches with peoples' arms and things sticking out of them.

A cease-fire ended the fighting on February 28. Iraq had been ejected from Kuwait after devastating that country. Enemy troops had carried away almost everything portable, destroying much of Kuwait City and leaving behind hundreds of burning oil wells that continued to spew Stygian clouds of smoke into the atmosphere for almost nine months. The administration had not driven on to Baghdad to oust Saddam's Baath regime. The dictator remained in power. In the wake of the Iraqi defeat, moreover, the country's Kurds in the north and its Shiite population around Basra had risen in revolt against the tyrant Saddam. Despite criticisms, Bush and his advisers refused to support the rebels and before long thousands of Kurdish refugees had fled to the mountains and to Iraq's neighbors. A major international relief effort prevented mass starvation among them, but the Kurdish incident in particular raised at least some questions about how much had really been accomplished by the Gulf War. This sense was reinforced when, toward the end of 1991, UN inspection teams encountered resistance to their efforts to uncover and stamp out Saddam's still-intact nuclear and chemical-biological weapons programs. Repeated threats of further American military action sufficed to force Iraqi compliance. Throughout the first half of 1992, United Nations teams destroyed Scud missiles along with thousands of chemical weapons and demolished facilities involved in Iraq's nuclear weapons program. But in spite of all the efforts of the United States and the UN, Iraqi action against Kurdish rebels continued, and Saddam Hussein remained firmly in power.

Soviet Decline The Soviet economy, already in a shambles, was further deteriorating all through 1991 despite efforts by Mikhail Gorbachev to free it from some of the handicaps imposed by seventy years of centralized, totalitarian control. There was talk of famine when winter came, and the Bush Administration provided massive aid to keep the Soviet people from starvation.

As its economy sank, the Soviet Union as a political entity began to weaken. The Baltic republics—Lithuania, Latvia, and Estonia, all annexed forcibly by the USSR in the 1940s—declared their independence. Soon Ukrainians, Moldavians, Georgians, Kazakhs, and other peoples of the Union began to insist on self-rule. Meanwhile, Boris Yeltsin, a high Soviet official who had repudiated the Communist Party, was in June 1991 elected president of the Russian Republic in a landslide popular vote hailed in the West as the first free election ever held in Russia. Yeltsin was soon moving to assert the power of Russia in the Union, to disband the Communist Party, and to reduce the power of Union officials, including Gorbachev.

Then on August 19 a group of hardliners, seeking to reverse the changes ushered in by Gorbachev and to prop up the rule of the Communist Party, staged a coup. Imprisoning Gorbachev at his dacha in the Crimea, they announced their intention to stop the wave of disorder and immorality that they believed had swept over the Soviet Union, restore national pride, and replace economic decline by new growth. The coup organizers obviously hoped for wide support, but even though the Gorbachev regime had slim popularity among the Soviet people it was preferred to the coup leaders. Led by Yeltsin, the leaders of the Russian Republic rallied to Gorbachev and refused to yield control to the plotters. Backed by thousands of supporters in the streets of Moscow, the democratic forces faced down the tanks and soldiers of hardliners, who soon surrendered and were placed under arrest. The coup's collapse restored Gorbachev as president of the Soviet Union. But he was now beholden to Yeltsin and no longer able to act alone.

In the wake of the failed coup, the movement for drastic economic reform gained momentum, as did the forces tearing the Soviet Union apart. Communist rule had been the only effective force holding together the many nations of the Soviet Union; with its demise, the splintering of the empire became inevitable. Gorbachev had sought to preserve the Union. Exhausted by his long struggle, blamed by the population for economic turmoil and the seeming collapse of the public order, and finally eclipsed by Boris Yeltsin, Gorbachev resigned in frustration. In December 1991 the citizens of Leningrad voted to return to the city's traditional name Petrograd (St. Petersburg), expressing their revulsion toward every vestige of the Communist past. Shortly before Christmas, 1991, the Congress of People's Deputies formally announced the dissolution of the Soviet Union, creating in its stead the Commonwealth of Independent States. This was intended to be a loose economic and military confederation of cooperative equals, but members feared domination by the populous and well-armed Russian Republic. Wrangling among the member states soon raised serious questions about the Commonwealth's chances for survival.

The passing of the Soviet Union was a postscript to the ending of the Cold War. Arguments were sure to continue over just why the Communist empire had fallen. Conservatives claimed that the credit should go to the hard-line policies of the Reagan Administration, more especially to the American arms buildup that the Soviet economy was too fragile to match. Liberals believed the fall of Communism to vindicate the containment policies of President Truman and subsequent Democratic cold warriors, balancing confrontation and restraint. Liberals also observed that the swiftness with which Communism in the Gorbachev era went out of business mocked the earlier pronouncements among American conservatives about the unchangeability of the Communist evil. But with the crumbling of Communism, perhaps one of the most startlingly sudden and unpredictable events in history, the subject of why it had crumbled became another matter for historians to decide.

The collapse of Soviet power changed the political equations in the Middle East and offered a chance for a final settlement of the decades-long conflict between Israel and the Arabs. At the end of the Gulf War the most anti-Israel Arab states no longer had the support of their protector, the Soviet Union. In effect, the USSR had ceased competing with the United States in the region. And the Palestine Liberation Organization, chief agent of Palestinian national aspirations, had been profoundly weakened by its support of Iraq in the Gulf War. In addition, the major Gulf oil producers were obliged to the United States for protection and ready to accept its leadership.

All of these factors made it possible for Secretary of State Baker to bring together Israel, Syria, Jordan, the Palestinians, and Lebanon in a face-to-face conference held in Madrid in November 1991. The participants spent much of their time hurling insults and recriminations against each other. The Israelis, concerned with their national security, resisted any exchange of occupied land for peace and rejected major concessions to Palestinian national aspirations. The Palestinians, in turn, demanded the right to their own nationhood. Syria refused to consider any other arrangement than complete surrender of the strategic Golan Heights, lost to the Israelis during an earlier Arab-Israeli war. And yet as the initial meeting at Madrid adjourned, the world stood amazed that all these antagonists after all these years had come as far as that.

The Peace Dividend The United States had already achieved breakthrough agreements with the Soviet Union to reduce conventional arms and shrink the number of troops. The Bush Administration also took important unilateral steps to reduce the threat of nuclear war. With the USSR barely alive, was there any need for an enormous American military establishment? Could not billions be cut from the defense budget and used for vital purposes at home? Toward the end of 1991 major weapons programs, including the Stealth Bomber, seemed likely to be canceled despite opposition by the administration. More than half of the 300,000 troops stationed in Europe were called home, and all the presidential contenders in the 1992 race promised greater reductions still in the nation's contribution to the North Atlantic Treaty Organization (NATO). The exact nature of the role of the United States in the world from which the Cold War had passed was difficult to determine. President Bush defined as a vital national interest the transition of the former Soviet empire to a democracy. In the spring of 1992, the United States joined in a multinational aid program for the Russian Republic.

Among unmet domestic needs was education. A federal commission issued a "report card" showing that American students had barely held their own during the 1980s in math and language skills despite a succession of programs designed to check a long decline. Bush endorsed programs that emphasized parental choice of schools and national testing rather than new outlays. Such cheap programs, the critics insisted, could never be expected to mend a sick system. Bush also wished to be known as the environmental President. Yet his interior secretary authorized enormous crosscutting of ancient forests on public lands in the West, and his administration did little to cooperate with international efforts to save the ozone layer in the outer atmosphere.

Many other needs demanded attention. The nation's roads, bridges, hospitals, and public buildings were becoming decrepit and would have to be restored. Health care needed a major overhaul. The United States was spending a greater proportion of its gross national product on health care than any other industrial nation and the amount was rising rapidly each year. At the same time the system of private health insurance, even when joined with Medicaid for the indigent and Medicare for the retired, left millions of Americans without the means to pay the bills when they became ill.

Worrisome for the Republicans was the general state of the economy. A moderate recession had begun in the fall of 1990. Observers predicted that once the Gulf War ended consumer and business confidence would return and the economy would quickly recover. And there was indeed a mild rebound during the summer of 1991 following the defeat of Iraq. But despite sharp Federal Reserve cuts in interest rates to encourage borrowing and investment, in April 1992 the unemployment rate had climbed to over 7 percent, the highest since the deep recession of 1982. A recovery was underway by mid-1992, but its pace seemed excruciatingly slow to the party in power.

Racial Issues Racial issues also bedeviled the country. Statistics and other analyses continued to show a black population divided in two, a modestly affluent community that was the beneficiary of the civil rights movement of the 1960s, and another, impoverished, crime-ridden, demoralized, unable to lift itself out of dependency.

One issue that became politically hot was affirmative action, government policies to give preference to blacks and other minority members in college and professional school admissions, training programs, and jobs. These policies had enabled many blacks as well as women and some ethnic minorities to break into professional and occupational fields from which they had been generally excluded before. But for some whites it seemed reverse racism, a system that injured white males.

During the Reagan years the conservative federal courts had whittled away at affirmative action programs. A central argument was that a governmental policy forcing preferential treatment violates the constitutional prohibition of racial discrimination by the federal and state government. Congressional liberals had introduced a new civil rights bill that passed the House in June 1991. President Bush charged that the bill imposed quotas and threatened to veto it. Abruptly, in early November, Bush accepted much of the Democratic bill.

Another administration strategy to change the course of the country's social policy was the nomination of Clarence Thomas to a seat on the Supreme Court. Thomas is a conservative black attorney from a poor rural southern background who attended Yale Law School. Reagan appointed him head of the Equal Employment Opportunity Commission, the agency that administered affirmative action programs, and Bush then elevated him to a position of federal appeals judge. In July 1991 Bush nominated Thomas to replace the retiring liberal Thurgood Marshall as associate justice of the Supreme Court. The President claimed that Thomas was the best qualified candidate for the post, but critics immediately charged that the selection was an unusually cynical political maneuver. By nominating a black conservative, the President was putting liberal senators on the spot. If they rejected Thomas they exposed themselves to the charge of denying a black man a place on the Supreme Court. Here was a way, then, to put on the court another social and philosophical conservative without the bruising fight that had scuttled the Supreme Court nomination of Judge Robert Bork two years before.

At the hearings during September, the carefully coached nominee successfully ducked questions over social philosophy and even denied that he had ever discussed *Roe v. Wade,* the critical abortion decision. Thomas depicted himself as a rags-to-riches success, a self-made man who could serve as an extraordinary role model for young blacks. Though several black civil rights groups and women's organizations attacked his conservative record, liberals on the Senate Judiciary Committee seemed afraid to tackle him. It looked as though his confirmation would sail through. Then in mid-October, charges abruptly surfaced that while at the Department of Education and at the Equal Employment Opportunity Commission, Thomas had sexually harassed a woman subordinate, Anita Hill, now a law professor at the University of Oklahoma and another black graduate of Yale Law School. The charges were aired publicly at a series of hearings before the Senate Judiciary Committee. As millions of thunderstruck viewers watched the fascinating proceedings, the dignified, well-spoken Hill accused Thomas of using awesomely suggestive sexual language toward her and, at least by indirection, seeking sexual favors. Thomas angrily and bombastically denied the charges and claimed that the hearing had become a "high-tech lynching."

The Senate confirmed the nomination by a vote of 52 to 48. The closest confirmation vote for a Supreme Court nominee on record, it added another conservative vote to an already conservative Court. Observers expected that the impact would soon be felt as cases challenging liberal judicial interpretations, and especially the 1973 abortion rights decision of *Roe v. Wade,* came before the Court.

A Sullen Politics

The autumn off-year elections in 1991 were angrier than most but revealed no one public attitude save for a diffusive dislike of things as they were. Economic recession continued to embitter the public mood. Statewide contests in New Jersey brought victory to the Republicans, registering a dislike of Democratic taxes. A race for a Senate seat from Pennsylvania brought victory to the Democrat, registering a dislike of Republican resistance to national health care and extended unemployment benefits. In an early November runoff election for governor of Louisiana, the Democratic candidate handily defeated the Republican, David Duke. The loser, a former Grand Wizard of the Ku Klux Klan, had shed his overt expressions of racism. But his attacks on civil rights and welfare policies were so phrased as to raise doubts about his conversion to civility. He

(From left to right) 1992 Democratic vice-presidential nominee Senator Al Gore of Tennessee, his wife Tipper, presidential nominee Bill Clinton, and his wife Hilary. *(Courtesy, AP/Wide World Photos)*

won a modest majority of the white vote, and the black vote buried him.

In the presidential campaigning that began early in 1992, the Democratic field quickly narrowed to two contenders. Jerry Brown, a former California governor, described American politics as perverted by short-sighted policymaking and political campaign financing that played to special interest groups. Governor Bill Clinton offered a more conventional, less confrontational party politics designed to address a variety of popular and special interests. Despite charges that he was a philanderer, he easily defeated Brown in the primaries. At the July convention Clinton chose as his running mate Tennessee Senator Al Gore, a strong environmentalist whose record in that area contrasted with the weak ones of both President Bush and Vice President Quayle.

In the Republican primaries President Bush avoided direct involvement in his own nomination. This helped insulate him from the press, which concentrated on the bruising fight among the Democrats. Bush was briefly challenged by Patrick Buchanan, a conservative columnist who urged an isolationist foreign policy and attacked the President for succumbing to liberalism at home. Buchanan did surprisingly well at first, notably in the opening primary in New Hampshire. There the vote for him, while less than that for Bush, was large enough to be embarrassing to the renomination candidacy of an incumbent President.

A banking scandal in the House of Representatives further eroded public confidence in elected officials. Members had the special privilege of having checks paid on unavailable funds at the private Capitol bank. The revelation became a focus for discontent over congressional inability to make progress against the continuing recession and the rest of the country's ills. The perception of the nation's leaders as unprincipled and ineffectual was soon registered in the Democratic congressional primaries, where a number of long-term incumbents were ousted from the party's fall ticket. More than fifty congressmen, among them hard-working and dedicated public servants, so dreaded facing an angered electorate or became so disgusted with the temper of politics that they announced their retirement.

Americans of each party, meanwhile, were showing a startling interest in the presidential candidacy of the Texas billionaire H. Ross Perot. He had no direct experience in government, and this was a reason for his popularity. He displayed, however, the same mastery of sound-bite politicking and avoidance of specific proposals that many believed had accompanied the breakdown of the political system in the first place. Yet this was much the same technique employed by Franklin Roosevelt in the 1932 presidential campaign. Perot's candidacy raised the possibility that no candidate would receive a majority in the electoral college and the election would be decided in the House of Representatives. Perot promised an activist government with specific proposals to be released for his fall campaign.

It seemed, at any rate, to be a year of politics directed to the troubles of the middle classes. The recession was a major issue, but much was made of its effect on middle-class jobs and incomes. The concerns of suburbanites and others among the nation's better-off whites and luckier minorities were the stock subjects of politicians. That put the Republicans in their familiar territory, but Democrats sought to occupy it too, talking of a middle-class tax break. Then, on April 29, occurred an event that might have shifted the focus of the campaign.

For a long time, the Los Angeles police had held a reputation for casually harassing black youths, stopping them at will and questioning them as potential suspects. Los Angeles was also a prey to violent and lethal gangs engaged in the drug trade. On March 3, 1991, after a high-speed car chase, a group of police repeatedly clubbed Rodney King while an onlooker unnoticed by the assailants videotaped the beating. Recorded messages between the officers and their headquarters contained gloating racist remarks. Four policemen were put on trial, which the defense succeeded in getting removed to the comfortable white suburb of Simi Valley on the grounds that in the city a fair verdict would be difficult to obtain. Conviction seemed nevertheless certain: the crime was captured visually and in sound. On April 29, 1992, came the astonishing verdict: after some dissension among its members, the jury in effect acquitted the four.

Ghettoes in Los Angeles exploded. Whites were beaten, including a truck driver whose near-fatal assault was recorded by video from a helicopter: in a heroic act, some black pass-

H. Ross Perot, independent presidential candidate in 1992 who in November received nineteen percent of the popular vote.

ersby rescued him. "That's how Rodney King felt," said one rioter to a victim, doubtless unaware that in identifying the hapless white with King he was identifying himself with the white police thugs of the original incident. There was the usual looting and burning, which wrecked the neighborhood economy and the hopes of the innocent who live in the riot sections of the city. Fifty-eight deaths were reported. The several days of violence, which ended with the help of federal troops and the National Guard, had its dramatic moment: a simple, halting, and moving public appeal from Rodney King himself for an end to it.

Suddenly politicians found themselves having to think, at least briefly, about the rebuilding of Los Angeles and other cities. That meant going contrary to a recent acceleration of the withdrawal of classes and ethnicities into separate protective enclaves. Tribalism is a worldwide happening, setting Azeris against Armenians, Serbs against Croats and Moslems, Israelis against Arabs, Germans and French against immigrants. Notable in this country has been a shift of the middle classes from the cities to surrounding belts, and therein the shrinking of the tax base for urban schools and renewal. Politicians wishing to expand that aid were going to have to find in the affluent white communities civil leaders prepared to argue with their neighbors the case for sharing some of their revenues with the cities. Politicians meanwhile would have to deal with the tribalism of the suburbs as well as the tribalism of the inner cities.

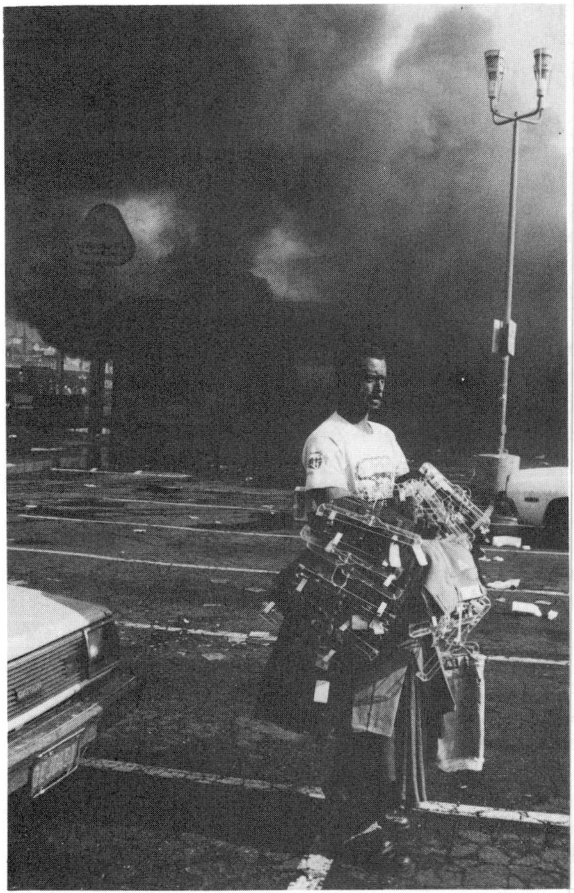

A looter walks away from a South Central Los Angeles mall with an arm full of goods as a fire burns in the background during the second day of rioting in the area. *(Courtesy, AP/Wide World Photos)*

Politics 1992 and 1993 The Republican convention at Houston, Texas, selected the incumbents Bush and Quayle to run for office for the second time. The convention also tried what the party's right wing had expected to make a winning issue: speakers denounced Democrats and liberals as being alien to American family and moral values. It could have been a popular theme, but tests of public opinion after the convention indicated that the Republicans were perceived as having overdone it, sounding harsh and divisive.

Clinton as a campaigner offered a number of general ideas for economic revival, among them a carefully targeted injection of federal funds into efforts to renew and advance American technology and into training workers for the sophisticated skills of the future. He also pledged to undertake a task that politicians had been ducking for decades: to devise a scheme that would make basic health care available to the millions of Americans who could not afford to get sick.

There was a third presidential candidate. H. Ross Perot, having temporarily dropped out, reentered the race, stressing the importance of putting debt reduction above all other considerations.

The national debt was widely understood to be a major problem. Republicans had disliked paying for military and other programs with heightened taxes, and under them the public debt, already huge, had grown enormously. When the unpaid debt, public and private, is large, lending agencies will raise their interest rates on further loans. This discourages the borrowing by industry that would have been invested in increased productivity and the borrowing by private citizens that would have gone into the consumption that quickens an economy. Republicans had for a long time contended that not raising but lowering taxes would ultimately cut the debt. Tax reductions, they insisted, would make for a more productive economy yielding tax revenues far more than adequate to compensate for the taxes temporarily lost through lowered rates. President Bush in his campaign was still claiming that a cut in the capital gains tax would be just what the economy needed. But by 1992, after years of Republican refusal significantly to raise the tax rates, the economy had slackened rather than sped up, and a bulging public debt demanded immediate attention.

Perot's solution was direct and blunt. The country needed an increase in taxation, the revenue to go into reducing the debt. Perot was the only one of the three candidates to say frankly that Americans were going to have to pay higher taxes (Clinton spoke of giving a tax break to the middle classes). He also insisted that cuts in government spending were necessary for lowering the debt. Perot further campaigned as an outsider to the political process, a practical businessman who not being part of a degenerate political establishment could remake politics.

The issue of family values having done them at most only a little good, Republicans turned to attacking Clinton's character, particularly his opposition to the Vietnam war during the conflict. They made an issue of his having looked for ways to keep out of the draft. As a student at Oxford, Clinton had also engaged in antiwar activity. In addition, so the Republicans discovered, Clinton during the war had gone to Moscow as part of a European tour. With an almost embarrassed hesitancy, Bush on a talk show hinted that something disloyal to the United States might have been connected with the Moscow trip. It did not work. The Cold War and the emotions associated with it were gone. On election day, the Democrat won a handsome majority of the presidential electors and forty-three percent of the popular vote to Bush's thirty-eight and Perot's nineteen percent.

During the period of transition from the November elections to the inauguration of the new President, Clinton backed President Bush on a decision to order troops to Somalia, where warring factions were seizing food for themselves and causing starvation among civilians. Bush was acting in cooperation with the United Nations, which had determined to send in military units from several countries to protect food supplies and open up routes to starving regions.

The Clinton administration, which for months was going to suffer an astonishing number of stresses and political difficulties, had its first major trouble in the President's attempt to find a nominee for attorney general. His opening choice turned out not to have paid social security on an undocumented immigrant couple she had hired for housework. Pressing through the Senate for the office of chief law enforcer a candidate who had broken the law, however innocently, would make for both her and the President more problems than either could afford. A second choice had also been lax in social security payments. Clinton finally chose Janet Reno, and the Miami prosecutor won the confirmation vote in the Senate. But the difficulty of finding an acceptable nominee had contributed to an appearance of disorganization and incompetence on the part of the White House.

State of the Union: 1993 Then, for a moment, the fortunes of the President brightened. Clinton in a State of the Union address in mid-February captured the country's imagination and support.

Insisting that new figures revealed an even larger national debt than he had previously thought to exist, Clinton explained that lowering taxes would now be impossible. He proposed to the contrary a rise in taxation so designed as to draw most heavily on the wealthier classes. Clinton also urged cuts in government spending. Another part of his program was for spending in ways that would in the short run stimulate the nation's weak economy. For a long time it had been assumed that any national figure who suggested raising taxes was inviting political death. The administrations of Reagan and Bush had made hostility to higher taxation a tenet of Republican orthodoxy and, so it seemed, convinced the public that increases in taxes are un-American. When Bush as

President went back on his famous campaign pledge "no more taxes," his popularity had fallen. But Clinton's address, in its call to sacrifice and its argument for the economic necessity of taxation, won soaring figures in public opinion polling. Beyond the specific measures of his program as presented in the State of the Union address was the President's vision, presented in the days of the campaign, of making the government a partner in the country's technological and economic renovation.

Before long, however, Clinton's grip on political events suffered from what was widely thought to be a political mishandling of the stimulus component of his proposed program. The idea was consistent with the wider aim of reviving the economy but clashed with the goal of cutting the debt. The Democrats attempted to press their unmodified stimulus package through the Senate. Republicans filibustered, determined to keep talking and stave off a vote on the bill. The stimulus bill was finished.

During his campaign Clinton had criticized President Bush for turning back from the United States immigrants from Haiti fleeing that country's military regime and wretched economic conditions. But early in his administration he reversed himself and continued Bush's policy. He announced instead a determination to put pressure on the Haitian military to take back the expelled President Jean-Bertrand Aristide and restore human rights.

Events in the former Yugoslav republic of Bosnia, where ethnic Serbs were waging a brutal war of conquest and expulsion against Croats and Muslims (both groups have responded in kind toward the Serbs and each other), would force Clinton once more to retreat from an apparently firm policy. Again, Clinton as a candidate had criticized President Bush, in this case for not providing material aid to the besieged Muslims, whom public opinion worldwide along with the United Nations perceived as the victims. Now in the presidency himself, Clinton ordered American planes to airdrop humanitarian but not military supplies to Muslim civilians under Serb assault. He also sent his secretary of state Warren Christopher on an attempt to rally European governments to a policy involving some military intervention. But Christopher's effort was fruitless.

On one of the politically riskiest of his policies, Clinton was showing consistency, suffering the consequences as his inconsistencies were also punishing him. He had pledged to open the military service to homosexuals, and this increased the distance between him and the military and got little sympathy from the public. By the summer of 1993 Clinton, the Congress, and the military were still searching for a satisfactory formula.

As week after dreary week of Clinton's early presidency slogged on, his standing in public-opinion polls plummeted from the impressive numbers that he had enjoyed just after his State of the Union address. By the time his debt-reduction plan, combining taxation and cutting governmental programs, reached the House of Representatives, his ability to make a political difference was so weakened that he was able barely to muster a passing vote. Worse trouble threatened in the Senate. In addition to projecting a rise in income taxes for Americans most able to pay it, Clinton's plan had called for an energy tax. This was supposed to yield several advantages: a gain in revenue for the government and a curtailment in the use of energy, which would lessen the nation's dependence on foreign oil and ease the damage that energy use was doing to the environment. The energy tax encountered much hostility, especially from the oil industry, and in the Senate some members of his own party indicated that they could not support it.

During the months of Clinton's own tribulations, his wife Hillary Rodham Clinton had been winning considerable popular respect. At the President's request, she headed a task force devising a scheme for national health care aiming to satisfy at once the politically powerful medical profession, the insurance companies, and the people who both needed assured health care and would have to pay for it. Her discussions with concerned parties and announcements to the public gave her work the clarity and direction that the White House was still struggling to achieve in its other activities.

In the middle of June, Clinton's political position began to solidify. After a painful episode over a failed nomination for assistant attorney general for civil rights, he selected for a seat on the Supreme Court a judge, Ruth Bader Ginsburg, who drew praise from Republicans as well as Democrats. During the same week he started to get through Congress a foreign aid bill to nourish Russia's economic and political turn to democracy. In the Senate, Democrats moved toward settling on a compromise, and later Clinton would get a version of his budget plan through Congress.

Seldom before had a President confronted so politically trouble-ridden a first few months in office. The country over which Clinton was precariously presiding had for years been losing any clear sense of where it was going privately or publicly, any notion of what kind of common enterprise its people and government were supposed to be pursuing. That was, in a way, what Clinton was in office to identify. In his State of the Union address, he came close to doing it, especially in his cautious presentation of the heartening though politically dangerous idea of sacrifice. Then for a time the confusion returned: in the public's wishes, in the aims of the Democratic party, in the President's own explanations of his policies. It could be predicted that for the rest of his presidency the search for a common language and purpose was going to define national politics. The nation, which nearly from its beginnings has been a continental workshop and an ongoing act of self-construction, was going to have to learn once more how to work with confidence and cooperation.

SENATOR BOB KERREY, *Democrat from Nebraska, on voting for the 1993 Clinton Tax Bill*

Mr. President, I've taken too long, I'm afraid, to reach this decision. My head, I confess, aches with all the thinking. But my heart aches with the conclusion that I will vote yes for a bill which challenges Americans too little, because I do not trust what my colleagues on the other side of the aisle will do if I say no. . . .

[T]he truth, Mr. President, is that in fact the price of this proposal is too low. It's too little to match the greatness needed from Americans now at this critical moment in this world's history.

This is not to say we are free from blame on this side of the aisle. When the challenge came from someone who didn't want to pay or didn't want to accept less from their government, we unfortunately all too often ran too. We ran when opposition arose to the "Btu" tax. . . .

America cannot afford, Mr. President, to have you take the low road of the too-easy compromise or the too-early collapse. You have gotten where you are today because you are strong, not because you are weak. Get back on the high road, Mr. President, where you are at your best.

On February 17, you told America that deficit reduction was a moral issue and that "shared sacrifice" was needed to put it behind us. And, Mr. President, you were right. But it is not shared sacrifice for us to brag that we are only raising taxes on those who earn over $180,000 a year. It is political revenge, Mr. President. Our fiscal problems do not exist because wealthy Americans aren't paying enough taxes. Our fiscal problems exist because of rapid, uncontrolled growth in programs that primarily benefit the middle class.

So, what do we achieve by our actions, Mr. President? Unfortunately, it is disdain, distrust and disillusionment. Shared sacrifice, Mr. President: It is our highest ideal and the only way we will build the moral consensus needed to end this nightmare of borrowing from our children.

Get back on the high road, Mr. President. On February 17, you told America that our tax system must encourage us to save rather than consume. Savings, Mr. President, is just as difficult as shared sacrifice. To save, I must say "no" to something that I want now, because I believe deeply that the dollar I save today will be worth considerably more tomorrow.

You had the right idea, Mr. President, with the Btu tax. And we, when we came after you with both barrels blazing, threatening to walk if you did not yield, you should have let us walk. You should have said to us that at least we'd be exercising something other than our mouths. Instead, we find ourselves with a bill that asks Americans to pay 4.3 cents a gallon more [for gasoline]. If they notice, I'll be surprised. And if they complain, I will be ashamed.

This legislation will now become law. And, as such, it represents a first step. But, if it's to be a first step towards regaining the confidence of the American people in their Congress and their federal government . . .

I began by saying that I did not trust 44 Republicans enough to say "no" to this bill. And I close by saying I suspect the feeling is mutual. But the challenge for us—and too much is at stake for us to even consider the possibility of failure—is for us to end this distrust and to put this too partisan debate behind us, and, for the sake of our place in history, rise to the high road the occasion requires.

Points To Think About

1. To the members of Nixon's administration—a group given to delusions of persecution even when things were going their way—the worst feature of the Watergate investigation was that they were being blamed for doing nothing worse than what earlier administrations had done. As a legal defense, this argument did not amount to much. As a historical claim, however, it deserves serious consideration. The imperial presidency, as Arthur Schlesinger, Jr., names this phenomenon, was not built in a day.

The preceding forty years encompassed an enormous growth in the power of the executive branch, which became the first among the three supposedly co-equal parts of the government. Initiative for legislation passed to the Executive; Congress further weakened itself by adopting a style of lawmaking that Theodore Lowi has called "discretionary liberalism." More and more typically, laws established goals such as a cleaner environment or lower unemployment but left to executive agencies the formulation of policies to realize the goals. The Cold War also strengthened the Executive Branch relative to the other two. Foreign policy came to be shrouded ever more deeply in secrecy. The phrase "national security" effectively blocked free debate. And secret agencies like the Central Intelligence Agency further extended the Executive policy of acting without congressional knowledge or consent.

Such great power invited abuse. And Nixon was not the first President to succumb to temptation. Virtually every abuse had precedents in other administrations. The FBI, for instance, had for thirty years been giving Presidents illegally obtained information about their political opponents. And the Internal Revenue Service had cooperated in harassing those same opponents. In fact, one of the reasons why Nixon's administration created its own in-house dirty tricksters was that the FBI and IRS proved unexpectedly reluctant to play ball with the administration.

What was new, if anything, in the Nixon presidency was that the pattern of abuse of power ceased to be that of occasional excess. Abuses of power became central to the whole approach to government, for Nixon apparently determined that the executive could become the entire government.

2. The present problem of the cities touches on a dilemma that has shaped much of the nation's political existence from the beginning of the republic, or before. From the moment that easterners set out to get some plot of empty land on the frontier, Americans have craved privacy and self-sufficiency. They have also lived by ideologies, both religious and secular, that instruct them that mature inwardness of character will express itself by service to a greater good. The simplest resolution to the problem of compounding the personal and the social is the tribal one, a commitment to a larger group that is merely a comfortable extension of the individual who belongs to it: the way of the suburbs and the street gangs (or perhaps of the whole nation at war with other nation-tribes). The difficult achievement of an ethic that is at once centered in individuality and directed to the good of others has been the elusive quest of much of the nation's history.

The Puritans set the terms of the dilemma. They conceived of faith as an intensely private and experiential matter; yet they expected faith to fulfill itself in useful work. The democratic vision has represented throughout the nation's history a secular form of the paradox, but it has done so precariously, at times celebrating individualism as a private good and at others calling on the individual to participate in a larger or even a global project. Twentieth-century American liberals, eager as they have been to have Americans enter into wider communities under government planning, are equally suspicious of the surrender of the individual to group conformities and prejudices. The civil rights movement therefore suited the liberal ideal precisely: individuals strong-minded and self-possessed enough to face down tradition-bound prejudice were to do so for the sake of a general good. Liberalism, at any rate, has continued to speak the paradoxical language of individuality and social responsibility.

A nation fractured into gangs and suburbs would appear to reflect exactly the worst elements of individuality gone to privacy and community gone to neighborhood patriotism. Addressing the national mood in its present form should put a burden on even the most carefully phrased political speech.

Suggested Readings

Recent books include, on the Gulf War, Jean Edward Smith, *George Bush's War* (1992) and Stephen R. Graubard, *Mr. Bush's War* (1992), Michael Paul Rogin, *Ronald Reagan* (1987), Samuel P. Hays, *Beauty, Health, and Permanence: Environmental Politics in the United States, 1955–1985* (1987), Barbara Anderson, *"Daughters of Jefferson, Daughters of Bootblacks": Racism and American Feminism* (1980), Erwin Hargrove, *Jimmy Carter as President* (1988), Fred Block *et al., The Mean Season: The Attack on the Welfare State* (1987), Linda Killen, *The Soviet Union and the United States* (1989), Morris Morley, *Imperial State and Revolution: The United States and Cuba* (1987), and Dino A. Brugioni, *Eyeball to Eyeball: The Inside Story of the Cuban Missile Crisis* (1992).

Garry Wills has revised his perceptive *Nixon Agonistes: The Crisis of the Self-Made Man* (1979); see also Richard M. Nixon, *RN: The Memoirs of Richard Nixon* (1978). Carl Bernstein and Bob Woodward's *All the President's Men* (1974), Philip B. Kurland, *Watergate and the Constitution* (1978), and John R. Labovitz, *Presidential Impeachment* (1978), are important works. Henry Kissinger's own memoirs, *The White House Years* (1979), should be supplemented by *Uncertain Greatness: Henry Kissinger and American Foreign Policy* (1977). Another important book on foreign affairs is William B. Quandt, *Decade of Decisions: American Policy Toward the Arab-Israeli Conflict, 1967–1976* (1977). On Jimmy Carter, see also the President's own *Keeping Faith* (1982) and James Wooten, *Dasher* (1978). For a critical view there is Haynes Johnson, *In the Absence of Power* (1980). Lawrence Barrett, *Gambling with History* (1984) and Robert Dallek, *Ronald Reagan* (1984) attempt to fathom that President. Thomas R. West and David Burner study conservative journalists of the Reagan Era in *Column Right* (1988).

Christopher Lasch, *The Culture of Narcissism: American Life in an Age of Diminishing Expectations* (1978), freely employs Freudian terms to comment on the condition of American civilization, or that part of it that can be evoked as "narcissistic." Lasch distinguishes narcissism from simple selfishness: the narcissist, not having been provided with the interior restraints that would make it possible to direct the passions and desires, lacks an identity and searches self-indulgently for images of himself. Norman O. Brown, in *Love Against Death* (1958), celebrates a "polymorphous perversity" that is more in agreement with the styles of the late 1960s. Another important book is Robert Heilbroner, *An Inquiry into the Human Prospect* (1974).

An early study of energy questions is Anthony Sampson, *The Seven Sisters: The Great Oil Companies and the World They Made* (1975). Tad Szulc studies *The Energy Crisis* (revised edition, 1978) while Daniel Ford is thorough on *Three Mile Island* (1982). Lester C. Thurow gives a broad view of the age of scarcity in the *Zero-Sum Society: Distribution and the Possibilities for Economic Change* (1981).

☆ ☆ ☆ POINTS OF VIEW: ☆ ☆ ☆

Why Did the Soviet Union Crumble?

Patricia Guerrin

Ronald Reagan's conservative Republican administration resolved to reverse a foreign policy that had attempted to accommodate the international Communist menace. The inauguration of Reagan's presidency in January 1981 was not a second too soon.

The foreign policy of previous years, and especially under Jimmy Carter, had suffered from a number of interrelated mistakes. One of them was an underestimation of the military capacity of the Soviet bloc, and therefore a neglect of needed weaponry. Another was a failure to see just how closely connected were the various Communist movements throughout the world: an ignorance, for example, of how closely the Sandinista regime in Nicaragua suited the geopolitical ambitions of Moscow. The indifference on the part of previous administrations to the threat that Cuba's Fidel Castro posed to Latin America measured their neglect of reality. Another failing was a refusal to see how different was Communism from any other form of government or political movement. This last had led in Carter's administration to a flawed human-rights policy based on a notion that the acts of repression under military or oligarchical regimes friendly to the United States were no different from the repression that people daily suffered under Communism.

Under Ronald Reagan the change of policy was swift and decisive. Crash expenditures on American armaments, most notably on the Strategic Defense Initiative, forced the Soviet economy into a competition that it could not endure. The invasion of Grenada in 1982, the aerial punishment of Libya in 1986 for its aid to terrorism, the support of the anti-Sandinista Contras, the denunciations of the Soviet Union: all this put the world on notice that the struggle with Communism was to be total, and threw Moscow on the psychological defensive. The degree of assistance that Reagan was able to give to the Contras lessened the hold of the Marxist Sandinistas on Nicaragua.

The results are history. Mikhail Gorbachev, the last Communist chief of the Soviet Union, inherited a broken economy, and his mild set of reforms grew beyond the control of the party, leading in time to the crumbling of Communism in eastern Europe and the USSR. On this continent, the Sandinistas in the time of George Bush fell in an election that had been forced upon them. In less than a decade, a world had been liberated.

James Mooney

The political right today must be in psychological shock, or at the least in a state of terminal embarrassment. It came to the presidency in 1981 insisting, as it had for decades, that liberalism had never understood the true depth of the Communist evil, that only conservatives fully realized the spiritual crisis of the West in the face of an indivisible, unchangeable Communist peril. And within a few years, that unchangeable and indivisible peril had changed itself out of existence, disintegrated in the course of reforming itself. All the verbal profundity of American anti-Communist conservatism proved to have been vapid posturing in the face of an enemy that had ceased long ago to be a serious danger to anyone outside its borders.

So closed the last chapter in a continuing quarrel between liberalism and the right over the nature of international politics. For decades, liberal administrations had stubbornly and patiently withstood Communism. They built alliances. When they could, they bargained with the enemy for enough peace to keep the world a little safer. When they thought it was necessary, they went to war. At all times, they demanded of the nation enough of its treasure to sustain the necessary military and foreign aid. They passed the Marshall Plan and created NATO; they sent forth the Peace Corps; they fought in Korea and Vietnam. It was an unbearable strain on the nerves of right-wingers. They hated the taxation; they hated the entanglements in diplomatic alliances; above all, they hated the grim, persistent patience of liberal foreign policy. Rightists wanted a more gratifying kind of anti-Communism, stronger in its anti-Communist posturings, its relentless denunciations of the Communist evil. What they did not want is real difficulty.

Here Reagan's administration was quick to satisfy them. The Republicans had no intention of putting its affluent American constituency through the slightest effort and pain. Their actions were dramatic, but essentially safe. The invasion of Grenada was minor; the spread-eagle rhetoric that attended it was immense. The same is true of the bombing of Libya. Reaganites would not tax the public for the Cold War: their strategy was to cut down on domestic programs, build up the military, and borrow the money. That way the prosperous classes could play for a moment at getting wealthier, and at no expense, while the administration played at being confrontational. Today the public, faced with the monumental public debt the Republicans incurred, is not playing. And the human-rights policy of the Carter years, which required condemnation of repression in rightist and leftist regimes alike, was far too complicated and demanding for the Republican administration's taste.

Communism, meanwhile, was doing visibly what it must have been doing invisibly for a long time: it was crumbling from inefficiency, expiring as it continued mechanically to speak the dead formulas of its ideology—until finally, in relief, its spokesmen gave up the formulas and the ideology. The sober resistance of the West for four decades, the struggles by dissidents within the Communist bloc, and finally the internal absurdity of Communism itself had defeated it.

Appendixes

Succeeding in History Courses

by John McClymer

STUDYING HISTORY AND STUDYING FOR EXAMS

The instructor who designed this course hopes you will take advantage of the opportunity to learn about the American past. Your own objectives in taking the course may be somewhat different. You may be taking it because it fulfills some requirement for graduation or because it fits into your schedule or, perish the thought, because it seems less objectionable than the alternative you could be taking.

In a better world, these differences between your objectives and those of the course would not matter. The studying you do to perform well on exams and papers would involve your learning a fair amount of history. And so your grade would certify that you had indeed left the course with a more informed and thoughtful understanding of the American past than you had when you entered it. Unhappily, in the world we must actually live in, the connection between studying history and studying for exams in history is not necessarily so clear or straightforward.

The hard fact is that many students manage to prepare themselves for mid-terms and finals without permanently adding to their understanding. There they sit, yellow hi-liting pens in hand, plodding through the assigned chapters. Grim-faced, they underline every declarative sentence in sight. Then they trace and retrace their tracks trying to commit every yellowed fact to memory. As the time of the test draws near, they choke back that first faint feeling of panic by trying to guess the likeliest question. The instructor is never, they say to themselves, going to ask us to identify George Washington. But what about Silas Deane? And Pinckney? No, wait. There were TWO Pinckneys! That means there is almost certainly going to be a question about ONE of them. So it is that some students devote more energy to Thomas and Charles Cotesworth Pinckney than they do to George Washington. By such tactics they may get ready for the exam, but sabotage their chance of gaining any insight into American history.

Life does afford worse tragedies. This one, however, is remediable. And this appendix can help. It is designed to help you do well in the course, and to help you learn some history. It is, in fact, dedicated to the proposition that the easiest and most satisfying way to succeed in a history course is to learn some history. It makes very little sense, after all is said and done, to spend your time trying to keep the Pinckneys straight or running down a fact or two about Silas Deane. What will it profit you? You may pick up a few points on the short answer section of the exam, but those few points are a small reward for hours of studying. And, in the meantime, your essay on Washington as a political leader was distinctly mediocre. Clearly something is wrong.

That something is that studying for exams is a poor way of learning history. On the other hand, studying history is an excellent way of preparing for exams. If you had, for example, thought about American relations with France during John Adams' presidency, you would very probably remember who Charles C. Pinckney was. And you would scarcely have had to memorize anything.

The object of this essay is to persuade you to make some changes in the way you study. The first is to conserve your yellow pens. All that hi-liting simply lowers the resale value of the book. If you underline everything you read, you will wind up with a book of underlinings. There may be some psychological comfort in that. All of that yellow does provide visible evidence that you read the material. Unfortunately, it will not leave you with a useful guide to what to review. You have hi-lited too much.

A second drawback follows from the first. You have created a democracy of facts. All names, dates, and events are equally yellow. The Pinckneys and Silas Deane, in other words, have just become as noteworthy as George Washington or John Adams. You need, more than anything else, some way of determining what is important.

The next step may prove harder. You will have to give up trying to learn history by rote. A certain amount of memorizing may be unavoidable in a survey course, but ultimately it is the enemy of understanding. That is because many people use it as an alternative to thinking. Have you ever wished there were a better way? Well, there is. If you understand what Lincoln had hoped to accomplish with the Emancipation Proclamation, for example, you will not need to memorize its provisions. You will know why it did not promise freedom to any of the slaves in states (like Maryland or Missouri) which remained loyal to the Union. You will know why the Proclamation did not go into effect until one hundred days after it was issued. You will not, in short, stumble over a question like: "Whom did the Emancipation Proclamation emancipate?"

Facts are by no means unimportant. It is essential to have something to think about. But it is generally more fun to pay attention to ideas. Lincoln, to pursue this example, was interested above all else in restoring the Union. He was perfectly willing, he said, to keep slavery if that would accomplish his purpose; he was equally willing to abolish slavery if that would do the trick. So there is no mystery that in the Emancipation Proclamation he gave the states of the Confederacy one hundred days to return to the Union on pain of losing their slaves if they did not. The same reason explains why the Proclamation did not apply to slave states still in the Union.

If you take care of the ideas, the facts will assemble themselves. There are two reasons for this happy state of affairs. One has to do with the way in which textbooks are written and courses taught. The other has to do with the way people learn.

No historian, including the authors of the text and your instructor, pretends that history is the story of everything that ever happened. Obviously, many things happened for which there are no surviving records. More importantly, scholars use the records that have survived in a highly selective way. Even though they are always interested in finding new information, and in finding new ways of using information already known, each individual work of history—be it an article, a doctoral dissertation, a monograph, a textbook, a course of lectures—represents hundreds and thousands of choices about what to include and what to omit. Much more is known, for example, about the signers of the Declaration of Independence than you will read in any textbook. What you actually encounter in this course, as a result, is here because the text authors or your teacher decided for some reason to include it. Usually the reason is that this particular bit of information helps explain or illustrate some pattern of behavior or thought. The moral for you should be clear. Focus on these patterns. They are what you should be thinking about.

If you do, learning theorists have some good news for you. They have found that while it is difficult for the average person to recall disconnected bits of data (for example, which Pinckney was an emissary to France during the XYZ affair), it is comparatively easy to remember details of coherent stories. This is not a very startling finding. Details make sense once you see how they fit together. Let us return to the example of the Emancipation Proclamation. Lincoln's actions followed from: 1) his political priorities in which the integrity of the Union outranked achieving peace or ending slavery, 2) his analysis of the course of the war, and, 3) his perception of the choices open to him. Had Lincoln valued peace or ending slavery more highly than the Union, had easy victory or actual defeat seemed near at hand, had other inducements to the states of Confederacy to return to the Union seemed more promising, he would have acted differently. Once Lincoln's perception of the situation becomes clear to you, you will have little, if any, difficulty remembering what he did.

Neither compulsive underlining nor prodigious memorization will help you to understand these patterns. What will? We can rephrase the question: What does it mean to read and listen intelligently? For most of us, reading and listening are passive forms of behavior. We sit and wait to be told. Someone else, we expect, will provide the answers. Worse, we expect someone else will provide the questions. And, of course, they do. For our part, we limit ourselves to hi-liting and jotting notes. At best, this situation leaves us with a more or less adequate record of what someone else thinks we should know.

Most of what passes for studying involves not a conscientious effort to wrestle with the subject, but a determined effort to be prepared to answer likely questions. That is why we pay more heed to Silas Deane than to George Washington. It is why studying for exams is such a poor way to learn history. And, its chief drawback perhaps from your point of view, it is usually a recipe for earning a mediocre grade.

Letting your teacher or the authors of the text do your thinking for you also leads to tedium. The simple truth is that passivity is boring. Yet we rarely blame ourselves for being bored. It can not be our own fault. We are only "taking" the course. Someone else is "giving" it, and so we look to the instructor to liven things up a bit. Maybe some audio-visuals or a bit of humor, we think, would make the course less dreary. These hopes are misplaced for, while humor is a blessed thing and audio-visuals have their place, it is the nitty-gritty of the course that should interest us.

Boredom is almost always a self-inflicted wound. Students are bored because they expect the instructor to be interesting when it is they who must themselves take an interest. Teacher and students are equally responsible for the success of a course. Most of the students in American history courses will live out the rest of their lives in the United States. Their lives will be affected for both good and ill by what has happened in the American past. It follows that the simple desire to make sense of their own lives should lead them to take an interest in this course.

Taking an interest involves learning to read and listen actively. Intellectual activity begins with questions—Your own questions directed, in the first instance, to yourself and then to your teacher. Why is it, you might wonder, that the United States is the only industrialized country without a comprehensive national system of health care? Why did slavery last so long in the American South? Why did the Founding Fathers establish a republic? And why did a party system develop even though the founders were bitterly opposed to political parties? Why, for that matter, were they so set against parties in the first place?

You will not always find satisfactory answers. But you will have started to think about the meaning of the American past. And when you do, something quite desirable happens to all of those facts. They will take on life and become evidence, clues to the answers you are seeking. The questions, that is, will give you a rational basis for deciding which facts are important. And George Washington will finally receive his well-deserved priority over the Pinckneys.

All of this leads directly to the question of how you should study for this course. It is a truism that students do poorly when they are ill-prepared. But we too easily assume that the sole reason why we are sometimes ill-prepared is because we did not spend enough time getting ready. This is a half-truth, and a dangerous one. It ignores the critical fact that we often use the time we spend reviewing very inefficiently. And, since there is often no practical way of increasing the time we have to review (there being, after all, only so many working hours in the day), it makes far more sense to use the time we do have effectively instead of moaning about how we should have studied more.

How do you get ready for an exam? Do you get out your textbook and notes and pour over them again and again until the time runs out or the sheer boredom of it all crushes your good intentions? If so, then you have lots of company—a consolation of sorts. There is, on the other hand, a better way.

Find a quiet and comfortable spot (something not always easy to do in a dormitory). Bring along a blank pad and something to write with. Then jot down, just as they occur to you, whatever items you can remember about the course. Do not rush yourself. And do not try, at this stage, to put things in order. Just sit there and scribble down whatever pops into your mind. After a while you will have quite a large and varied mix of names, ideas, dates and events. Then see how much of this you can put together. There is no need to write out whole sentences or paragraphs. An arrow or a word or two will frequently be enough. You are not, after all, going to hand these scribbles in. You are just collecting your thoughts. Do not be concerned if this process seems to be taking up some of the limited time you have to study. It will prove to be time well spent.

Now look over what you have written. Where are the gaps? You will find that you know a fair bit about the material just from your previous reading of the text and from listening in class. But some topics will still be obscure. You may, for example, pretty well understand why Polk declared war on Mexico, but you may feel less sure about his negotiations with Great Britain over Oregon. All right. Now you know what you should be studying. There is no reason for you to go over the war with Mexico. Why study what you already know. And here is the nub of the matter, for an intelligent review is one that focuses on what you need to refresh your mind about.

You will doubtless have noticed that this strategy presupposes that you have read the textbook and taken good notes in class. Just what, you might wonder, are good notes? Many students think that the closer they come to transcribing the instructor's every word the better their notes are. They are mistaken. There are several reasons why. Unless your shorthand is topnotch, you will not succeed. Instead you will be frantically scrambling to catch up. In the process you will not only miss some of what is said, but you will pay attention to scarcely any of the lecture. At the end of class you will have: 1) a sore hand; 2) a great deal of barely legible notes; and 3) little if any idea of what the class was about.

Another reason not to attempt to transcribe lectures (taping them, by the way, is usually a poor idea) is that you will spend much of your time taking down information you either already know or can easily find in the textbook. How often do you need to see the fact that Jefferson Davis was the president of the Confederacy? A sensible person will decide once is enough.

The most important reason not to take down everything is that it prevents you from doing what you ought to be doing during class, listening intelligently. Your instructor is not simply transmitting information during a lecture but is also seeking to explain the hows and whys of the American past. It is these explanations you should be listening for, and your notes should focus on them. It is much easier to do this if you have read the relevant textbook chapters first. That way you will already know much of the factual information. And you will have, one hopes, some questions already in your mind. You will have, that is, something to listen for. And you can take notes sensibly. You can fill in explanations of points that had puzzled you, jot down unfamiliar facts, and devote most of your time to listening instead of writing. Your hand will not be sore; you will know what the class was about; and your notes will complement rather than duplicate what you already knew.

So far we have dealt mainly with the mechanics of studying—taking notes, reviewing for exams, and the like. Valuable as knowing the mechanics can be, and in terms of your grade they can be very valuable indeed, the real secret to studying history is learning how to think historically. History is both a body of knowledge about the past and a way of thinking about the human condition. You are probably familiar with the first of these two aspects of the subject. History is knowing about the Revolution, the Civil War, and so on. It is knowing, that is, that they happened, when they happened, and how they happened. It is also having some explanation of why they happened as they did, and of the differences their happening made. All of that is undoubtedly perfectly obvious to you. It may, in fact, seem to include the sum and substance of history. It does not.

History is also a way of thinking. It rests on the assumption that you understand what something is by finding out how it came to be that way. This is an assumption which, consciously or not, you share. When you ask friends how they are doing, for example, you are really asking what has happened to them since you last met. You are asking about the past—the recent past to be sure—but the past nonetheless. You accept, that is, the axiom that the past has consequences for the present and the future. If your roommate has just failed an organic chemistry final, to use a sad but not uncommon occurrence, you both know what that will mean for her chances of getting into medical school.

You also know, if you think about it for a minute, that the political beliefs of the Founding Fathers still matter. They matter not only because their beliefs continue to influence our own but also because we continue to use them as the standard against which we measure present-day political figures. You can even appreciate that the child-rearing practices of the Puritans are worth knowing about—not of course because they have been passed down unchanged from the seventeenth century nor because they provide a model for you in raising your own family, but because we can not understand changing cultural realities or social practices unless we first have a clear idea of what they were once like. Change, in short, is incomprehensible if we do not have a point of reference from which to measure it. And history alone can provide us with such a fixed point.

Learning to think historically is a simple necessity if we hope to make sense of the world around us. Fortunately, it involves nothing more than learning to employ in a disciplined way the same patterns of thought we already use on a daily basis. That your roommate failed organic chemistry is a historical fact just as Lincoln's victory in the presidential election of 1860 is. How your roommate failed, and how Lincoln won, can also be determined factually, to some degree. You can, that is, discover which questions your roommate got wrong, just as you can find out which states Lincoln carried. You can even begin to assemble facts which will help explain why your roommate missed those particular questions and why Lincoln won those particular states. With regard to your roommate, you might recall that she cut a number of classes. You could hypothesize that some of the material covered in those classes was on the exam. You might recall that your roommate had a political science paper to finish the week before the exam. Perhaps that kept her from studying chemistry thoroughly.

Similarly you could determine with some accuracy which voting blocs went for Lincoln. You could then analyze the campaign issues and speculate about how those constituencies lined up on those issues. In both cases you would be trying to marshall the facts so that they would support some interpretation. Clearly, if you could know all of the facts, and if there were only one possible explanation for them, your interpretation would be true in the same way that the facts themselves are true. You could say: it happened this way and no other.

Unfortunately, life is not so amenable to explanation. You will never have all the facts, and no explanation will ever be the only one possible. Consider your roommate's "F" in organic. You know which questions were missed. But the questions on the exam could have been different. Then your roommate's grade would, possibly, have also been different. So knowing which questions your roommate lost points on is not enough. You would also have to know why these particular questions, and not others, were on the test in the first place. Consider too that the test scores were probably "curved." A more forgiving curve might have allowed your roommate to pass. But to know why the curve was the way it was you would have to know why the other raw scores were the way they were. Your roommate's raw score, the actual points lost on particular questions, in other words, is only half the story. That score could, presumably, have become an "A" if other students in the course had done even worse than your roommate. There is no need to pursue the point any farther. It is clear that you could never be sure you knew all of the relevant facts. And if this be true for your roommate's "F", how much more obviously true it must be for Lincoln's election. There were millions of voters. Who could know why they all voted as they did?

Despite all of this you may feel—and quite sensibly—that your roommate's "F" is hardly an impenetrable enigma. You may not know everything about it, but you know enough. You can offer an explanation that fits the facts you do know and is congruent with what you know of your roommate's study habits, general intelligence, and so forth. What you have is an interpretation. So too with Lincoln's election. People may have had reasons for voting as they did that you will never know, but you can supply enough reasons to explain why he won. You can explain, that is, what is known, and your view is compatible with what is known about American elections during that period.

You can perhaps already see how to define a convincing interpretation. It is one that provides that simplest sensible account of why something happened. The goal of historical inquiry is interpretation. And while, as we have seen, interpretation is not synonymous with truth, it is something more than mere opinion.

Anyone can have an opinion. People claim that have a right to have opinions about anything and everything (some even seem to feel it is their duty to have an opinion about everything). But you have to earn the right to offer an interpretation because an interpretation is a thoughtful explanation based on a careful assessment of evidence. It follows that when you find scholars disagreeing over how to interpret the American Revolution, say, as Professors McDonald and Genovese do in one of their debates, you ought not to conclude that their dispute is "just a matter of opinion" or that the truth probably lies somewhere in the middle (an old saw that should be permanently retired) or that one opinion (yours included) is just as good as another. Rather you need to ask: how well do these interpretations accord with what I know about the Revolution? How much sense can I make of what happened before and after it by using one or another of these explanations? The debates, in short, are an invitation to you to think about the meaning of American history. They should prompt you to struggle with the issues in your own mind and to come up with your own interpretation.

You may feel somewhat hesitant about putting your own interpretation forward, particularly if it differs markedly from those offered by your instructor or the authors of the text. And, within limits, you should be hesitant. A certain intellectual modesty is becoming in a beginning student. But you have read the material; you have listened intelligently in class; and you have thought about the issues. So you have the right to a view of your own. Teaching is not indoctrination. The object of the course is not to tell you what to think. The goal is to help you learn to think for yourself. You are therefore entitled to disagree.

When presenting your own interpretation, whether or not it agrees with one you have already encountered, you should always explain clearly how you reached that particular conclusion. This means explaining what evidence you found most important; it means explaining why that evidence struck you as important; and it means explaining the logic of your position. If you can do these three things, then you need not fear presenting your own ideas.

This appendix has an additional feature designed to help you think about how historical interpretations are developed and tested. This is a section on how to read the McDonald-Genovese debates. You will quickly realize, as you read the debates, that McDonald and Genovese rarely disagree over the facts of American history. They disagree over which facts are important and over how they should be interpreted. This section contains suggested exercises you can do on your own, or which your instructor can assign, that will enable you to read the debates more critically.

It is now time to see how these general considerations about studying history apply to specific tasks you will have to undertake in this course. We will start with how to take midterm and final examinations.

HOW TO TAKE EXAMS

In the best of all possible worlds examinations would hold no terrors. You would be so well prepared that no question, no matter how tricky or obscure, could shake your serene confidence. Unfortunately, the real world normally finds the average student in a different situation. Somehow it seems one's preparation is always less than complete. And so one approaches exams with some anxiety. "Of course," one says to oneself, "I should have studied more. But I did not. Now what?" This section can not tell you how to get A's without studying, but it can suggest some practical steps which can help you earn the highest grade compatible with what you do know.

The first step is to look over the entire exam before you start answering any of it. It is impossible to budget your time sensibly until you know what the whole exam looks like. And if you fail to allow enough time for each question, two things—both bad—are likely to happen. The first is that you may have to leave some questions out, including perhaps some you might have answered very effectively. How often have you muttered: "I really knew that one!"? The other unhappy consequence is that you may have to rush through the last part of the exam. Again, there may be questions you could have answered very well if you had had more time.

How do you budget your time effectively? The idea, after all, is to make sure that you have enough time to answer fully all the questions you do know. So the best plan is also the simplest. Answer those questions first. It may feel a bit odd at first answering question #7 before #4, but you will soon enough get used to it. And you will find that, if you still run out of time, you at least have the satisfaction of knowing you are rushing through or leaving out questions you could not have answered very well anyway. You will, in other words, have guaranteed that you will receive the maximum credit for what you do know.

There is another advantage to answering questions in the order of your knowledge instead of in the order asked. Most students are at least a little tense before an exam. If you answer the first several questions well, that tension will likely go away. As you relax, you will find it easier to remember names, dates, and other bits of information. Contrariwise, if you get off to a shaky start, that simple case of pre-exam jitters can become full-scale panic. Should that happen, you may have trouble remembering your own phone number, and your chances of recalling those facts which are just on the tip of your tongue will shrink to the vanishing point. Obviously, it is very important to get off to a good start. So do not trust to luck. Do not just hope the first couple of questions are easy. You can make sure you get off on the right foot by answering first whatever questions you are sure of.

Let us suppose you have gotten through everything you think you know on the exam and you still have some time left. What should you do? You can now try to pick up a few extra points with some judicious guessing. There is not much point to trying to guess with essay questions. In all probability you will write something so vague that you will not get any credit for it anyway. Rather you should try to score on the short-answer section. Some types of questions were made for shrewd guesswork. Matching columns are ideal. A process of elimination will often tell you what the answer has to be. Multiple choice questions are almost as good. Here too you can eliminate some of the possibilities. Most teachers feel obligated to give you a choice of four or five possible answers, but find it hard to come up with more than three that are plausible. So you can normally count on being able to recognize the one or two that are just there as padding.

Once you have narrowed the choices down to two or three, you are ready to make your educated guess. There are three rules. 1) Always play your hunches, however vague. Your hunch is based on something you heard or read even if you can not remember what it is. So go with it. 2) Do not take your time. If you can not think of the answer, just pick one and have done with it. 3) Try to avoid changing answers. There are a number of studies showing that you are more likely to change a right answer than to correct a wrong one.

Identifications are the type of short-answer question most resistant to guesswork. Unless you have a fairly strong hunch about the answer, you should leave this sort of question blank. The reason is that while it is true that an incorrect answer will cost you no more points than leaving the question out altogether, it is also true that an incorrect answer says something about the depths of your ignorance which a blank space does not. You want the exam as a whole to convey what you do know. Supplying a mass of misinformation usually creates a presumption that you do not know what you are talking about even on those sections of the exam when you really do. So be careful about wild guesses. They are almost sure to do more harm than good.

These suggestions are not substitutes for studying. They may, however, help you get the most out of what you know. They may, that is, spell the difference between a mediocre grade and a good one.

HOW TO WRITE BOOK REVIEWS

One goal of book reviews is to set forth clearly and succinctly who (if anyone) would benefit from reading the work in question. It follows that a good review indicates the scope of the book, identifies its point of view, summarizes its main conclusions, evaluates its use of evidence, and—where possible—compares the book with others on the subject.

It is highly likely that you have written book reviews in high school or in other college courses so it is important that you do not approach this kind of assignment with a false sense of security. It sounds easy, after all, to write a five-hundred-or-so word essay. And you have written lots of other reviews. But did those other reviews focus clearly on the questions a good review must address? If they did not, your previous experience is not going to prove especially helpful. It may even prove something of a handicap. You may have developed some bad habits.

Easily the worst habit is that of summarizing not the book's argument but its contents. Let us suppose you are reviewing a biography of George Washington. The temptation is to write about Washington rather than about the book. This is a sure path to disaster. Washington had, to put it mildly, an eventful career. You are certainly not going to do it justice in a few paragraphs. And you are not, in all probability, going to find that much that is fresh or interesting to say about him. Meanwhile you have ignored your primary responsibility which is to tell the reader whether this biography has anything fresh or interesting to say.

So you need to remind yourself as forcefully as possible that your job is to review the book and not the subject of the book. Does the book focus narrowly on Washington or does it also go into the general history of America during those years? Is the author sympathetic to Washington, tending to see things Washington's way? Does the writer attempt to psychoanalyze Washington or stick to political and military questions? Is there a firm command of the available evidence (this requires you, alas, to read the footnotes)? And, last but not least, does the author have something new to say about Washington and his times? If so, how well documented is this new interpretation?

It is less important to evaluate how well the author writes. While it is hard to imagine a poorly written novel that is still worth reading, it is common enough (unhappily) for important historical works to be written in a plodding fashion. So you should comment on the quality of the author's prose, but you should generally not make that an important part of your overall evaluation unless it is so good or so awful that it makes reading the work sheer bliss or unrelieved torture.

You should generally not comment on whether or not you enjoyed the book. That is undoubtedly an important consideration for you, but it is of little interest to anyone else. There are some occasions when you need to suffer in silence. This is one of them.

HOW TO SELECT A TERM PAPER TOPIC

Doing research, as you may already have had occasion to learn, is hard work. Worse yet, it is often boring. Typically it involves long periods of going through material that is not what you were looking for and is not particularly interesting. It also involves taking detailed and careful notes, many of which you will never use. These are the dues you must pay if you are ever to earn the excitement which comes when you finally find that missing piece of evidence and make sense of things.

Not everything about doing research is boring. Aside from the indescribable sensation of actually finding out what you wanted to know, there are also occasional happy accidents where you stumble across something which, while not relevant to your research, nonetheless pricks your imagination. Many a historian studying an old political campaign has read up on the pennant races or fashions or radio listings for that year. These are, as one scholar put it, oases in the desert of historical evidence. But, as he quickly added, no one crosses the desert just to get to the oasis. The truth of the matter is that you have to have a good reason for getting to the other side. This means a topic you are genuinely interested in.

The point cannot be overemphasized. If you have a question you really want to answer, you will find it much easier to endure the tedium of turning all those pages. You will have a motive for taking good notes and for keeping your facts straight. If you are not truly interested in your topic, on the other hand, you may be in trouble. You are going to be constantly tempted to take short-cuts. And even if you resist temptation, you are going to find it hard to think seriously about what you do find.

So the topic has to interest you. That, you may be thinking, is easy to say. But what if your interest in American history is less than compelling? What if, perish the thought, you do not give two figs about the whole American past? Are you then going to be stuck with some topic you could care little about? The answer is "No". "No," that is, unless it turns out that you have no curiosity about anything at all; and, if that is the case, you are probably dead already or nearly so. Anything that can be examined chronologically is fair game for the historian. There are histories of sports and of sciences, of sexual practices and jokes about them, of work and of recreation. It is odd, to say the least, that students so often choose to write of war, politics, and diplomacy even when their real interests lie elsewhere. If you use your imagination, you should be able to find a topic which you are genuinely interested in and which your teacher agrees merits serious study. This being true, you have no one to blame but yourself if you wind up writing on some question you are not passionately concerned with answering.

Once you have such a topic you need to find ways of defining it so that you can write an intelligent essay. "The Automobile in American Life" could well serve as the subject for a very long book. It is not going to work as a subject for a term paper, and for two compelling reasons. First, you could not possibly research so vast a topic in the time you have to work with. Second, your paper, however long, is not going to be of book length—in fact it is not likely to exceed 5,000 words. So you would be stuck with trying to compress an immense amount of information into a brief essay. The final product will be a disaster.

You need to focus on some aspect of the general topic which can be intelligently treated in the space and time you have to work with. Students usually look at this problem backwards. They complain about how long their papers have to be. They should complain about how short they have to be. Space is a luxury you normally can not afford. If you have done a fair amount of research on an interesting topic, your problem is going to be one of finding a way of getting all you have to say into your paper. Writing consists of choices about what you want to say. And if you have done your work properly, the hard choices involve deciding what to leave out.

"Fair enough," you may be thinking, "but I do not want to get stuck researching some minute bit of trivia, the 'gear shift level from 1940 to 1953,' for example. I want to study the automobile in American life." Here we come to the heart of the matter. Your topic must be narrowly defined so that you can do it justice, but it must also throw some light on the broad question that interested you in the first place. This is easier said than done, but it can be done. The trick is to decide just what it is about your topic—cars in this instance—that really interests you. Cars are means of transportation, of course, but they are also examples of technology, status symbols, and much else besides. Because of the automobile, cities and suburbs are designed in ways very different from how they were when people traveled by trolley or train. Because of the automobile, even teenage dating patterns are what they are. Having a driver's license, and regular access to a car, has become a crucial part of growing up.

The point is that you have to think about your topic and then decide what aspect of it to examine. If you wind up doing a treatise on changing methods of changing tires, you have only yourself to blame. You could have been studying sex and sexism in automobile advertising.

HOW TO LOCATE MATERIAL

Once you have worked up an interesting and practical topic for your term paper, you are ready to begin your research. For many students this means ambling over to the library and poking around in the card catalog. This may not be the best way to begin because the librarians who catalog the library's holdings, while skilled professionals, cannot possibly anticipate the needs of every individual researcher. So they catalog books by their main subject headings and then include obvious cross-references. Much of what you need, on the other hand, may not be obvious. So, for example, if you are interested in the causes of the Civil War, you will have no trouble finding a title like Kenneth Stampp's *And The War Came* listed under "U.S. History, Civil War." But will you find Roy Nichol's *Disruption of the American Democracy?* You may not.

The point is that there may be a number of important works in your library you will not be able to find if you start by checking the card catalog. What should you do instead? The first thing is to locate the *Harvard Guide To American History.* This is an invaluable tool. It will tell you the best (in the editors' opinion) books and articles on your subject. For each title prepare a separate card listing full bibliographic specifics (i.e., the author's full name, the complete title including subtitle, the place of publication, the edition, and if a journal article the volume and issue numbers). You will need all of this information.

Now you have the beginnings of a decent bibliography. Your next step should be to introduce yourself to the research librarian. This person's specialty is helping people look for information. Yet many students never consult with a librarian. Do not pass up an opportunity to make your work easier! Ask your research librarian to help. Often he can point you to more specialized bibliographical guides, can show you where to learn of the most recent books and articles, and can help you refine your topic by indicating what aspects are easiest to get information on.

You now have a reasonably extensive set of cards. And you can now safely consult the card catalog to see which of these titles your library has. Prepare yourself for some disappointments. Even good undergraduate libraries will not have everything you need. They will have some (unless your library is very weak or your topic very esoteric). Virtually all college libraries participate in the inter-library loan system. This system, which the library staff will gladly explain to you, will permit you to get virtually any title you could wish for. The only catch is that you must give the library enough lead time. For books and articles which are not especially rare this normally means one to three weeks.

HOW TO TAKE NOTES

As you sift through the material you have found you will need to take careful notes. As you do, you should write down each piece of information which you believe might prove relevant on a notecard. You also will need to specify the full source for each piece of information.

If you follow these two bits of advice, you will save yourself much time and trouble. Finding information the first time, in your sources, is trouble enough. You do not want to have to find it all over again when you sit down to write your paper. But this is often just what students have to do because they discover that they did not bother to write down some bit of data (which, perhaps, seemed only marginally important at the time) or because they took all of their notes on loose leaf paper and now must search through every page to find this one fact. It is far easier, over the long run, to have a separate card for each piece, or closely related pieces, of information. Tell yourself that you are the last of the big time spenders and can afford to use up index cards as though they were blank pieces of paper. After all, that is what they are.

The general rule is that you should take extra pains when compiling your research notes so that the actual writing will be as trouble-free as possible. It follows from this that you should take lots of notes. Do not try to determine in advance whether or not you are going to use a particular bit of data. Always give yourself the benefit of the doubt. Similarly, do not try to decide in advance whether you will quote the source exactly or simply paraphrase it. If you take down the exact words, you can always decide to make the idea your own by qualifying it in various ways and putting it in your own words. When taking notes, in brief, your motto should be: the more the merrier.

WRITING TERM PAPERS AND OTHER ESSAYS

You have no doubt already learned that next to mastery of the subject matter nothing is more important for earning good grades than effective writing. You surely know people whose study habits are not all that they should be but whose grades are high. Nine times out of ten the secret of their success is their ability to write well. What they have to say may not always be all that impressive, but the way they say it is.

Students who are not among that relatively small group who write well sometimes think it unfair that writing skills should count so heavily. The course, some complain, is American History, not Creative Writing, and so their grade should not be influenced by their prose. Only what they know about history should count. But most teachers continue to believe that the ability to express what you know clearly and forcefully is an indispensable measure of how well you have learned the subject matter. So, like it or not, your writing is going to count. Writing well is an invaluable skill, and not only in college. Most good jobs (and most not-so-good ones) involve writing. There is correspondence, there are reports, there are memoranda. The writing will never stop.

No matter how poorly you write, you can learn to write effectively. This is not to say that anyone who desires it can become a brilliant prose stylist. Great talent is rare in every field. But anyone who can speak English effectively can learn to write it effectively. It is simply a matter of expressing your ideas clearly. This you can learn to do. It does not require genius, merely patience and practice.

Charity, St. Paul said, was the chief of all the virtues. In expository prose, however, the chief virtue is clarity. And like charity, it covers a multitude of sins. Be they ever so humble, or homely, your sentences will receive a sympathetic reading if they are clear. Why? There are a number of reasons. The first is that your papers, reviews, and essays—while they may seem very long to you when writing them—are in reality quite brief. A twenty-page paper, for example, only contains 5,000 words. This means that you do not have very much space to get your ideas across. The less space you have, the more carefully you have to choose your words. If it takes you four or five pages to get to the point, you have wasted a substantial portion of your essay. (If, on the other hand, you were writing a 500 page book, those four or five pages would not matter so much.)

It has perhaps crossed your mind that there are occasions when you are not very eager to get to the point. Sometimes you may not be sure just what the point is. Sometimes you do know, but are not convinced that your point is a very good one. At such times, a little obfuscation may seem a better idea than clarity. It is not. I can assure you, based on my experience as a college teacher (which has involved reading thousands of student papers), there is nothing more troubling than reading a paper where the author tried to hedge bets or fudge ideas. The very worst thing you can do is leave it up to your reader (also known as your instructor) to decide what you are trying to say. Teachers, as a group, have not heeded St. Paul. They conspicuously lack charity when reading student papers. They will not give you the benefit of the doubt. They will, more often than not, decide that you did not get to the point because you do not know the material. We teachers can be a heartless breed. So, no matter how weak your ideas seem to you, set them forth clearly. Something is always better than nothing.

Clarity is a virtue in part because so many papers from other students will not exemplify it. As a result, your teacher will be inclined to read yours more sympathetically. What you said may not have been brilliant, but it did make sense. And, contrary to popular reports, most teachers really are interested in helping students. It is much easier to help you if your instructor can figure out what you were trying to say.

My mistakes will stand out, you are thinking. That sounds very dangerous. We have all been conditioned to avoid detection. The last thing we want is for the teacher to find out that we do not know something. But teachers delight in watching students improve. The reason is obvious: they see it as proof that they are doing a good job. They take special pleasure in the progress of students who start off poorly but steadily get better over the course of the semester. You can do a lot worse than be one of those students.

Let us assume that you are willing to give clarify a try. How do you go about writing clearly? The first rule of thumb is to avoid complexity. You should strive to write simply and directly. This does not mean that you are limited to a basic 1500-word vocabulary. There are hundreds of thousands of words in the language and you are entitled to use any of them, provided only that you use them correctly. You should not, on the other hand, go out of your way to find esoteric words or expressions. Use words that accurately express your meaning. Wherever possible use words that are part of your ordinary vocabulary. Above all, do not try to impress your instructor by using synonyms you located in a dictionary or, worse yet, a thesaurus. You run a high risk of using these words incorrectly because they may have connotations you are unaware of.

You should also avoid complicated grammatical structures. Do you know when to use the subjunctive mood? Do you know the rules about using semi-colons? Do you know which types of subordinate clauses require commas? If you have answered any or all of these questions negatively, then you should bone up on your grammar. And, in the meantime, you should avoid writing sentences where these kinds of questions arise. There is no reason to increase the probability of making an error. Grammatical errors can often be avoided simply by keeping your sentences fairly short. Qualifications of your main idea can go into separate sentences. You do not have to fit everything into a single sentence. Furthermore, your sentences will have more pace and rhythm if you keep them relatively short.

Grammatical difficulties—be they outright errors or merely negligent constructions—are a writer's nightmare. Each time you make an error or use an awkward phrase you distract the reader. He or she stops paying attention to what you are saying and instead focuses on how you are saying it. If you distract the reader often enough (four or five times a page will do it in most cases), you will have reduced your chances of getting your ideas across virtually to zero.

So it is vitally important to eliminate grammatical problems. This is, of course, easier said than done. But there are ways to do it. Many schools have writing centers where you can get help with your papers. If your school has such a center, use it. The improvement in both your prose and your G.P.A. can be dramatic. If your school lacks a writing workshop, ask your teacher to read over an early draft of your paper. This is the reader you have to please after all. So why not go straight to the source?

You may have observed that both of these suggestions presume that you will have completed an early draft. And so you should. But let us suppose that, like most college students, you write your papers by the dawn's early light just before they are due. You do not have an early draft. If you find yourself in this all-too-common situation, you may still be able to find someone who will, as a favor, read over your paper before you type the final version. There are college students who have a good working knowledge of grammar. You need to find one and get him or her to edit your work, that is, help you get rid of the most blatant errors. This person can also tell you if your paper is easy to follow. You should write so that someone unfamiliar with the subject but reasonably well informed in other respects can understand what you are saying. Such a person makes an excellent reader and can help you pinpoint the ideas you need to explain more fully.

Once you have worked out a scheme for eliminating grammatical shortcomings, you can turn to the equally crucial chore of articulating your ideas. This means deciding the most cogent sequence in which to present them, on the one hand, and explicating the connections between them on the other. The first order of business is making sure that your opening paragraphs clearly set out what your paper is about and how you are going to approach this topic. Your opening sentences should explain: what your topic involves; why it is worth investigating; and how you are going to look into it. If your topic were, for example, "Sex and Sexism in Automobile Advertising," you might write something like the following:

> The automobile is more than a means of transportation. It is also a powerful engine of change. Highways and suburbs have altered the human and physical geography of the nation. Shopping malls and drive-ins have transformed the retail economy. Social practices—from dating customs to recreational patterns—bear the imprint of the car. Cars have also come to symbolize status and prestige. Expensive models are perceived, and marketed, as visible signs of success. As a result, changing automotive advertising campaigns provide a wealth of data about how Americans have conceptualized the "good life" in this century.
>
> Success means different things to different people, but—if the car ads are to be believed—Americans tend to think of success in terms of power and sex.

You will note that this example sets the topic in a larger context, explains what the paper will examine (power and sex as components of the American idea of success), and how it will examine them (by analyzing changing patterns of automotive advertising). Further it explains why these ads are an important source of material for this topic.

"Well begun," the adage runs, "is half done." This is especially true in writing papers and essays. A good opening tells the reader what to expect. It piques curiosity and makes one eager to read on. A poor opening (one, that is, which leaves the reader still wondering what the paper is about or why a certain topic is important) does the opposite. So work on your openings! You may not have the time to write several drafts of your paper (although you should make the time), but you must take the time to rewrite your introduction as many times as necessary for it to sparkle.

You, as the author, have the responsibility of directing your reader's attention. You do this by explaining the logical connection(s) between the points you raise. You can not assume that your reader will figure out the logic of your paper. Your reader, you should recall, is a professional skeptic who starts from the assumption that you do not know what you are talking about. So it is the height of folly to assume that your instructor will supply logical connections for you. You have to supply them, and you do this—principally—by means of topic and transitional sentences.

Topic sentences introduce ideas. They belong at the beginning of paragraphs. All too often students bury their central ideas in the middle of paragraphs. Only the most attentive reader is likely to ferret them out. And while every teacher strives to be most attentive, the unvarnished truth of the matter is that there is usually a stack of papers to go through—a prospect that inspires a certain dread and tends to make one somewhat eager to get the whole business over with. So, despite our best intentions, we teachers are often less attentive than we should be. The lesson for you is clear. Do not risk having your best notions go unnoticed.

Transitional sentences explain connections. You can put them at the end of paragraphs if you wish. Wherever you put them, be sure you write them as carefully as you do your introduction and your topic sentences. A good topic sentence may also be a transitional device and improve the flow of your writing.

These few hints will not suffice to turn you into a good writer, but they can help you avoid fatal errors. If your writing is a problem, then you owe it to yourself to seek sustained professional help either in writing courses or at your school's writing center. Remember, a serviceable prose style will not only measurably improve your grade in this course (and many others), it will also improve your chances for success in whatever career you enter.

WHEN AND HOW TO USE FOOTNOTES

Many students apparently believe that the only thing worse than having to read footnotes is having to write them. It is easy to understand why they feel that way, but they are making much ado about very little. Footnotes are used to inform the reader (including your reader) where the information being used in the body of the paper can be found. That is the sum and substance of the matter.

So, when should you use a footnote? These are two occasions when you must. The first is when you are referring to someone's exact words whether by direct quotation or by paraphrase. The second is when you are referring to some bit of information that is not already well known or is someone's interpretation of the facts. How, you might wonder, can you tell whether or not something is already well-known? There is, fortunately, a simple rule. Any thing you can find in a standard textbook (like *Firsthand America*) does not need to be footnoted. Hence, for example, you do not need to footnote that George Washington was the first president of the United States. You do need to footnote an exact quotation from his "Farewell Address." You do not need to footnote that Henry Ford introduced the assembly line to the manufacture of automobiles. You do need to footnote your source for his political opinions.

As you can see from these examples, there is no mystery about using footnotes. If you are in doubt about a particular case, you still have two steps open to you. One is to ask your instructor, the reader you are seeking to inform in the first place. The other, if you find it impracticable to contact your teacher, is to use the footnote. Having an unnecessary footnote is a minor flaw. Not having a necessary one is a serious omission. So you can simply err on the safe side.

Now that you know when to use footnotes, you can consider the matter of how to use them. There are several commonly used formats. Simply ask your instructor which one is preferred. If your teacher has no preference, amble over to your campus bookstore and invest in the University of Chicago's *Manual of Style*. It is brief, clearly written, reliable, and cheap. It is very unlikely you will encounter a question the *Manual of Style* will not answer.

WHAT TO INCLUDE IN YOUR BIBLIOGRAPHY

Early in your research you compiled a list of possible sources. The temptation is to type out a bibliography from those cards. This is fine provided that you actually used all of those sources. Your bibliography should include all the sources you consulted and only the sources you consulted. So even though you have all sorts of cards, and even though your bibliography would look far more impressive if you included sources you looked up but did not use, do not. The game is not worth the candle. Your instructor will have a quite accurate sense of what sources you used just from reading your paper. So it is most unlikely that padding your bibliography will impress. In fact, your teacher is more than likely to challenge your reliability if any part of your paper seems padded. In scholarship, honesty really is the best policy.

A WORD ABOUT PLAGIARISM AND ABOUT ORIGINALITY

Plagiarism is the act of claiming another's work as your own. It is about as serious an offense as you can commit. Many colleges require teachers to report all instances of plagiarism and, while the punishment can vary, it is always stiff. Moreover, of all the various ways of cheating teachers find plagiarism the easiest to detect.

Some students even manage to plagiarize without realizing that this is what they are doing. They either quote or paraphrase a book or article without indicating that. (They omit the quotation marks or they omit the footnote.) They have, without necessarily intending to, passed off someone else's work as their own. Sometimes this results in nothing worse than a private lecture from the instructor on the necessity of correctly attributing all information. Even so it is embarrassing, and it creates the impression that you do not know what you are doing. So, be sure you indicate the sources not only of your information but also of the interpretations or ideas you include in your papers.

Teachers will often tell their students that their papers should be original. Since scholars use this word in a somewhat different sense than you might expect, a word of explanation may prove helpful. In ordinary speech something is original if it is the first of its kind or if it is the only one of its kind. Historians and other scholars mean something less dramatic than that. We refer to research as "original" if the researcher did the work himself. We do not mean that his conclusions have never been reached before or that no one else has ever used his source materials. The way you put familiar information and ideas together may be original.

Do not hesitate to make use of ideas from other historians. No one with any sense expects beginning students to make startling discoveries or to develop radically new perspectives on the past. Of course it would be wonderful if you did, but no one anticipates that you will. It is, accordingly, perfectly legitimate for you to use other people's insights. The only hitch is that you must always acknowledge where they came from.

The Declaration of Independence

When in the Course of human events, it becomes necessary for one people to dissolve the political bands which have connected them with another, and to assume among the Powers of the earth, the separate and equal station to which the Laws of Nature and of Nature's God entitle them, a decent respect to the opinions of mankind requires that they should declare the causes which impel them to the separation.

We hold these truths to be self-evident, that all men are created equal, that they are endowed by their Creator with certain unalienable Rights, that among these are Life, Liberty and the pursuit of Happiness. That to secure these rights, Governments are instituted among Men, deriving their just powers from the consent of the governed, That whenever any Form of Government becomes destructive of these ends, it is the Right of the People to alter or to abolish it, and to institute new Government, laying its foundation on such principles and organizing its powers in such form, as to them shall seem most likely to effect their Safety and Happiness. Prudence, indeed, will dictate that Governments long established should not be changed for light and transient causes; and accordingly all experience hath shown, that mankind are more disposed to suffer, while evils are sufferable, than to right themselves by abolishing the forms to which they are accustomed. When a long train of abuses and usurpations, pursuing invariably the same Object evinces a design to reduce them under absolute Despotism, it is their right, it is their duty, to throw off such Government, and to provide new Guards for their future security.—Such has been the patient sufferance of these Colonies; and such is now the necessity which constrains them to alter their former Systems of Government. The history of the present King of Great Britain is a history of repeated injuries and usurpations, all having in direct object the establishment of an absolute Tyranny over these States. To prove this, let Facts be submitted to a candid world.

He has refused his Assent to Laws, the most wholesome and necessary for the public good.

He has forbidden his Governors to pass Laws of immediate and pressing importance, unless suspended in their operation till his Assent should be obtained; and when so suspended, he has utterly neglected to attend to them.

He has refused to pass other Laws for the accommodation of large districts of people, unless those people would relinquish the right of Representation in the Legislature, a right inestimable to them and formidable to tyrants only.

He has dissolved Representative Houses repeatedly, for opposing with manly firmness his invasions on the rights of the people.

He has refused for a long time, after such dissolutions, to cause others to be elected; whereby the Legislative Powers, incapable of Annihilation, have returned to the People at large for their exercise; the State remaining in the mean time exposed to all the dangers of invasion from without, and convulsions within.

He has endeavoured to prevent the population of these States; for that purpose obstructing the Laws of Naturalization of Foreigners; refusing to pass others to encourage their migration hither, and raising the conditions of new Appropriations of Lands.

He has obstructed the Administration of Justice, by refusing his Assent to Laws for establishing Judiciary Powers.

He has made Judges dependent on his Will alone, for the tenure of their offices, and the amount and payment of their salaries.

He has erected a multitude of New Offices, and sent hither swarms of Officers to harass our People, and eat out their substance.

He has kept among us, in times of peace, Standing Armies without the Consent of our legislature.

He has affected to render the Military independent of and superior to the Civil Power.

He has combined with others to subject us to a jurisdiction foreign to our constitution, and unacknowledged by our laws; giving his Assent to their acts of pretended legislation:

For quartering large bodies of armed troops among us:

For protecting them, by a mock Trial, from Punishment for any Murders which they should commit on the Inhabitants of these States:

For cutting off our Trade with all parts of the world:

For imposing taxes on us without our Consent:

For depriving us in many cases, of the benefits of Trial by Jury:

For transporting us beyond Seas to be tried for pretended offences:

For abolishing the free System of English Laws in a neighbouring Province, establishing therein an Arbitrary government, and enlarging its Boundaries so as to render it at once an example and fit instrument for introducing the same absolute rule into these Colonies:

For taking away our Charters, abolishing our most valuable Laws, and altering fundamentally the Forms of our Governments:

For suspending our own Legislature, and declaring themselves invested with Power to legislate for us in all cases whatsoever.

He has abdicated Government here, by declaring us out of his Protection and waging War against us.

He has plundered our seas, ravaged our Coasts, burnt our towns, and destroyed the lives of our people.

He is at this time transporting large armies of foreign mercenaries to compleat the works of death, desolation and tyranny, already begun with circumstances of Cruelty & perfidy scarcely paralleled in the most barbarous ages, and totally unworthy the Head of a civilized nation.

He has constrained our fellow Citizens taken Captive on the high Seas to bear Arms against their Country, to become the executioners of their friends and Brethren, or to fall themselves by their Hands.

He has excited domestic insurrections amongst us, and has endeavoured to bring on the inhabitants of our frontiers, the merciless Indian Savages, whose known rule of warfare, is an undistinguished destruction of all ages, sexes and conditions.

In every stage of these Oppressions We have Petitioned for Redress in the most humble terms: Our repeated Petitions have been answered only by repeated injury. A Prince, whose character is thus marked by every act which may define a Tyrant, is unfit to be the ruler of a free People.

Nor have We been wanting in attention to our British brethren. We have warned them from time to time of attempts by their legislature to extend an unwarrantable jurisdiction over us. We have reminded them of the circumstances of our emigration and settlement here. We have appealed to their native justice and magnanimity, and we have conjured them by the ties of our common kindred to disavow these usurpations, which, would inevitably interrupt our connections and correspondence. They too have been deaf to the voice of justice and of consanguinity. We must, therefore, acquiesce in the necessity, which denounces our Separation, and hold them, as we hold the rest of mankind, Enemies in War, in Peace Friends.

We, therefore, the Representatives of the United States of America, in General Congress, Assembled, appealing to the Supreme Judge of the world for the rectitude of our intentions, do, in the Name, and by Authority of the good People of these Colonies, solemnly publish and declare, That these United Colonies are, and of Right ought to be Free and Independent States; that they are Absolved from all Allegiance to the British Crown, and that all political connection between them and the State of Great Britain, is and ought to be totally dissolved; and that as Free and Independent States, they have full Power to levy War, conclude Peace, contract Alliances, establish Commerce, and to do all other Acts and Things which Independent States may of right do. And for the support of this Declaration, with a firm reliance on the Protection of Divine Providence, we mutually pledge to each other our Lives, our Fortunes and our sacred Honor.

The Constitution of the United States

We the people of the United States, in Order to form a more perfect Union, establish Justice, insure domestic Tranquility, provide for the common defense, promote the general Welfare, and secure the Blessings of Liberty to ourselves and our Posterity, do ordain and establish this CONSTITUTION for the United States of America.

ARTICLE 1

Section 1. All legislative Powers herein granted shall be vested in a Congress of the United States which shall consist of a Senate and House of Representatives.

Section 2. The House of Representatives shall be composed of Members chosen every second Year by the People of the several States, and the Electors in each State shall have the Qualifications requisite for Electors of the most numerous Branch of the State Legislature.

No Person shall be a Representative who shall not have attained to the Age of twenty-five Years, and been seven Years a Citizen of the United States, and who shall not, when elected, be an inhabitant of that State in which he shall be chosen.

Representatives and direct Taxes shall be apportioned among the several States which may be included within this Union, according to their respective Numbers, which shall be determined by adding to the whole Number of free Persons, including those bound to Service for a Term of Years and excluding Indians not taxed, three fifths of all other Persons. The actual Enumeration shall be made within three Years after the first Meeting of the Congress of the United States, and within every subsequent Term of ten Years, in such Manner as they shall by Law direct. The Number of Representatives shall not exceed one for every thirty Thousand, but each State shall have at Least one Representative; and until such enumeration shall be made, the State of New Hampshire shall be entitled to chuse three, Massachusetts eight, Rhode-Island and Providence Plantations one, Connecticut five, New-York six, New Jersey four, Pennsylvania eight, Delaware one, Maryland six, Virginia ten, North Carolina five, South Carolina five, and Georgia three.

When vacancies happen in the Representation from any State, the Executive Authority thereof shall issue Writs of Election to fill such Vacancies.

The House of Representatives shall chuse their Speaker and other Officers; and shall have the sole Power of Impeachment.

Section 3. The Senate of the United States shall be composed of two Senators from each State, chosen by the Legislature thereof, for six Years; and each Senator shall have one Vote.

Immediately after they shall be assembled in Consequence of the first Election, they shall be divided as equally as may be into three Classes. The Seats of the Senators of the first Class shall be vacated at the Expiration of the second Year, of the second Class at the Expiration of the fourth Year, and of the third Class at the Expiration of the sixth Year, so that one-third may be chosen every second Year; and if Vacancies happen by Resignation, or otherwise, during the Recess of the Legislature of any State, the Executive thereof may make temporary Appointments until the next Meeting of the Legislature, which shall then fill such Vacancies.

No Person shall be a Senator who shall not have attained to the Age of thirty Years, and been nine Years a Citizen of the United States, and who shall not, when elected, be an Inhabitant of that State in which he shall be chosen.

The Vice President of the United States shall be President of the Senate, but shall have no vote, unless they be equally divided.

The Senate shall chuse their other Officers, and also a President pro tempore, in the absence of the Vice President, or when he shall exercise the Office of the President of the United States.

The Senate shall have the sole Power to try all Impeachments. When sitting for that purpose, they shall be on Oath or Affirmation. When the President of the United States is tried, the Chief Justice shall preside: And no person shall be convicted without the Concurrence of two thirds of the Members present.

Judgment in Cases of Impeachment shall not extend further than to removal from Office, and disqualification to hold and enjoy an Office of honor, Trust, or Profit under the United States: but the Party convicted shall nevertheless be liable and subject to Indictment, Trial, Judgment, and Punishment, according to Law.

Section 4. The Times, Places and Manner of holding Elections for Senators and Representatives, shall be prescribed in each state by the Legislature thereof; but the Congress may at any time by Law make or alter such Regulations, except as to the Places of Chusing Senators.

The Congress shall assemble at least once in every Year, and such Meeting shall be on the first Monday in December, unless they shall by Law appoint a different Day.

Section 5. Each House shall be the Judge of the Elections, Returns and Qualifications of its own Members, and a Majority of each shall constitute a Quorum to do Business from day to day, and may be authorized to compel the Attendance of absent Members, in such Manner, and under such Penalties, as each House may provide.

Each House may determine the Rules of its Proceedings, punish its Members for disorderly Behavior, and, with the Concurrence of two thirds, expel a Member.

Each House shall keep a Journal of its Proceedings, and from time to time publish the same, excepting such Parts as may in their Judgment require Secrecy; and the Yeas and Nays of the Members of either House on any question shall, at the Desire of one fifth of those Present, be entered on the Journal.

Neither House, during the Session of Congress, shall, without the Consent of the other, adjourn for more than three days, nor to any other Place than that in which the two Houses shall be sitting.

Section 6. The Senators and Representatives shall receive a Compensation for their Services, to be ascertained by Law, and paid out of the Treasury of the United States. They shall in all Cases, except Treason, Felony, and Breach of the Peace, be privileged from Arrest during their Attendance at the Session of their respective Houses, and in going to and returning from the same; and for any Speech or Debate in either House, they shall not be questioned in any other Place.

No Senator or Representative shall, during the Time for which he was elected, be appointed to any civil Office under the Authority of the United States, which shall have been created, or the Emoluments whereof shall have been encreased during such time; and no Person holding any Office under the United States shall be a Member of either House during his continuance in Office.

Section 7. All Bills for raising Revenue shall originate in the House of Representatives; but the Senate may propose or concur with Amendments as on other bills.

Every Bill which shall have passed the House of Representatives and the Senate, shall, before it become a Law, be presented to the President of the United States. If he approve he shall sign it, but if not he shall return it, with his Objections, to that House in which it shall have originated, who shall enter the Objections at large on their Journal, and proceed to reconsider it. If after such Reconsideration two thirds of that House shall agree to pass the bill, it shall be sent, together with the objections, to the other House, by which it shall likewise be reconsidered, and if approved by two thirds of that House, it shall become a Law. But in all such Cases the Votes of both Houses shall be determined by Yeas and Nays, and the Names of the Persons voting for and against the Bill shall be entered on the Journal of each House respectively. If any Bill shall not be returned by the President within ten Days (Sundays excepted) after it shall have been presented to him, the Same shall be a Law, in like Manner as if he had signed it, unless the Congress by their Adjournment prevent its Return, in which Case it shall not be a Law.

Every Order, Resolution, or Vote to which the Concurrence of the Senate and House of Representatives may be necessary (except on a question of Adjournment) shall be presented to the President of the United States; and before the Same shall take Effect, shall be approved by him, or being disapproved by him, shall be repassed by two thirds of the Senate and House of Representatives, according to the Rules and Limitations prescribed in the Case of a Bill.

Section 8. The Congress shall have Power To lay and collect Taxes, Duties, Imposts and Excises, to pay the Debts and provide for the common Defence and general Welfare of the United States; but all Duties, Imposts and Excises shall be uniform throughout the United States;

To borrow money on the credit of the United States;

To regulate Commerce with foreign Nations, and among the several States, and with the Indian Tribes;

To establish an uniform Rule of Naturalization, and uniform Laws on the subject of Bankruptcies throughout the United States;

To coin Money, regulate the Value thereof, and of foreign Coin, and fix the Standard of Weights and Measures;

To provide for the Punishment of counterfeiting the Securities and current Coin of the United States;

To establish Post Offices and Post Roads;

To promote the Progress of Science and useful Arts, by securing for limited Times to Authors and Inventors the exclusive Right to their respective Writings and Discoveries;

To constitute Tribunals inferior to the Supreme Court;

To define and punish Piracies and Felonies committed on the high Seas, and Offences against the Law of Nations;

To declare War, grant Letters of Marque and Reprisal, and make Rules concerning Captures on Land and Water;

To raise and support Armies, but no Appropriation of Money to that Use shall be for a longer Term than two Years;

To provide and maintain a Navy;

To make Rules for the Government and Regulation of the land and naval forces;

To provide for calling forth the Militia to execute the Laws of the Union, suppress Insurrections and repel Invasions;

To provide for organizing, arming, and disciplining the Militia, and for governing such Part of them as may be employed in the Service of the United States, reserving to the States respectively, the Appointment of the Officers, and the Authority of training the Militia according to the discipline prescribed by Congress;

To exercise exclusive Legislation in all Cases whatsoever, over such District (not exceeding ten Miles square) as may, by Cession of particular States, and the acceptance of Congress, become the Seat of Government of the United States, and to exercise like Authority over all Places purchased by the Consent of the Legislature of the States in which the Same shall be, for the Erection of Forts, Magazines, Arsenals, dock-Yards, and other needful Buildings—And

To make all Laws which shall be necessary and proper for carrying into Execution the foregoing Powers, and all other Powers vested by this Constitution in the Government of the United States, or in any Department or Officer thereof.

Section 9. The Migration or Importation of such Persons as any of the States now existing shall think proper to admit, shall not be prohibited by the Congress prior to the Year one thousand eight hundred and eight, but a tax or duty may be imposed on such Importation, not exceeding ten dollars for each Person.

The privilege of the Writ of Habeas Corpus shall not be suspended, unless when in Cases of Rebellion or Invasion the public Safety may require it.

No Bill of Attainder or ex post facto Law shall be passed.

No Capitation, or other direct, Tax shall be laid unless in Proportion to the Census or Enumeration herein before directed to be taken.

No Tax or Duty shall be laid on Articles exported from any State.

No Preference shall be given by any Regulation of Revenue to the Ports of one State over those of another: nor shall Vessels bound to, or from, one State, be obliged to enter, clear, or pay Duties in another.

No Money shall be drawn from the Treasury, but in Consequence of Appropriations made by Law; and a regular Statement and Account of the Receipts and Expenditures of all public Money shall be published from time to time.

No Title of Nobility shall be granted by the United States: And no Person holding any Office of Profit or Trust under them, shall, without the Consent of the Congress, accept of any present, Emolument, Office, or Title, of any kind whatever, from any King, Prince, or foreign State.

Section 10. No State shall enter any Treaty, Alliance, or Confederation; grant Letters of Marque and Reprisal; coin Money; emit Bills of Credit; make any Thing but gold and silver Coin a Tender in Payment of Debts; pass any Bill of Attainder, ex post facto Law, or Law impairing the Obligation of Contracts, or grant any Title of Nobility.

No State shall, without the Consent of the Congress, lay any Imposts or Duties on Imports or Exports, except what may be absolutely necessary for executing its inspection Laws: and the net Produce of all Duties and Imposts, laid by any State on Imports or Exports, shall be for the Use of the Treasury of the United States; and all such Laws shall be subject to the Revision and Control of the Congress.

No State shall, without the Consent of Congress, lay any duty of Tonnage, keep Troops, or Ships of War in time of Peace, enter into any Agreement or Compact with another State, or with a foreign Power, or engage in War, unless actually invaded, or in such imminent Danger as will not admit of delay.

ARTICLE II

Section 1. The executive Power shall be vested in a President of the United States of America. He shall hold his Office during the Term of four years, and, together with the Vice-President, chosen for the same Term, be elected, as follows:

Each State shall appoint, in such Manner as the Legislature thereof may direct, a Number of Electors, equal to the whole Number of Senators and Representatives to which the State may be entitled in the Congress; but no Senator or Representative, or Person holding an Office of Trust or Profit under the United States, shall be appointed an Elector.

The Electors shall meet in their respective States, and vote by Ballot for two persons, of whom one at least shall not be an Inhabitant of the same State with themselves. And they shall make a List of all the Persons voted for, and of the Number of Votes for each; which List they shall sign and certify, and transmit sealed to the Seat of the Government of the United States, directed to the President of the Senate. The President of the Senate shall, in the Presence of the Senate and House of Representatives, open all the Certificates, and the Votes shall then be counted. The Person having the greatest Number of Votes shall be the President, if such Number be a Majority of the whole Number of Electors appointed; and if there be more than one who have such Majority, and have an equal Number of Votes, then the House of Representatives shall immediately chuse by Ballot one of them for President; and if no Person have a Majority, then from the five highest on the List the said House shall in like Manner chuse the President. But in chusing the President, the Votes shall be taken by States, the Representation from each State having one Vote; a quorum for this Purpose shall consist of a Member or Members from two-thirds of the States, and a Majority of all the States shall be necessary to a Choice. In every Case, after the Choice of the President, the Person having the greatest Number of Votes of the Electors shall be the Vice President. But if there should remain two or more who have equal votes, the Senate shall chuse from them by Ballot the Vice-President.

The Congress may determine the Time of chusing the Electors, and the Day on which they shall give their Votes; which Day shall be the same throughout the United States.

No person except a natural-born Citizen, or a Citizen of the United States, at the time of the Adoption of this Constitution, shall be eligible to the Office of President; neither shall any Person be eligible to that Office who shall not have attained to the Age of thirty-five years, and been fourteen Years a Resident within the United States.

In Case of the Removal of the President from Office, or of his Death, Resignation, or Inability to discharge the Powers and Duties of the said Office, the same shall devolve on the Vice-President, and the Congress may by Law provide for the Case of Removal, Death, Resignation, or Inability, both of the President and Vice-President, declaring what Officer shall then act as President, and such Officer shall act accordingly, until the disability be removed, or a President shall be elected.

The President shall, at stated Times, receive for his Services a Compensation, which shall neither be increased nor diminished during the Period for which he shall have been elected, and he shall not receive within that Period any other Emolument from the United States, or any of them.

Before he enters on the execution of his Office, he shall take the following Oath or Affirmation:—"I do solemnly swear (or affirm) that I will faithfully execute the Office of President of the United States, and will, to the best of my Ability, preserve, protect, and defend the Constitution of the United States."

Section 2. The President shall be Commander in Chief of the Army and Navy of the United States, and of the Militia of the several States, when called into the actual Service of the United States; he may require the Opinion, in writing, of the principal Officer in each of the executive Departments, upon any subject relating to the Duties of their respective Offices, and he shall have Power to Grant Reprieves and Pardons for Offences against the United States, except in Cases of Impeachment.

He shall have Power, by and with the Advice and Consent of the Senate, to make Treaties, provided two thirds of the Senators present concur; and he shall nominate, and by and with the Advice and Consent of the Senate, shall appoint Ambassadors, other public Ministers and Counsuls, Judges of the Supreme Court, and all other Officers of the United States, whose Appointments are herein otherwise provided for, and which shall be established by Law: but the Congress may by Law vest the Appointments of such inferior Officers, as they think proper, in the President alone, in the Courts of Law, or in the Heads of Departments.

The President shall have Power to fill up all Vacancies that may happen during the Recess of the Senate, by granting Commissions which shall expire at the End of their next Session.

Section 3. He shall from time to time give to the Congress Information of the State of the Union, and recommend to their Consideration such Measures as he shall judge necessary and expedient; he may, on extraordinary occasions, convene both Houses, or either of them, and in Case of Disagreement between them, with respect to the Time of Adjournment, he may adjourn them to such Time as he shall think proper; he shall receive Ambassadors and other public Ministers; he shall take Care that the Laws be faithfully executed, and shall Commission all the Officers of the United States

Section 4. The President, Vice President and all civil Officers of the United States, shall be removed from Office on Impeachment for, and Conviction of, Treason, Bribery, or other high Crimes and Misdemeanors.

ARTICLE III

Section 1. The judicial Power of the United States, shall be vested in one supreme Court, and in such inferior Courts as the Congress may from time to time ordain and establish. The Judges, both of the supreme and inferior Courts, shall hold their Offices during good Behavior, and shall, at stated Times, receive for their Services, a compensation, which shall not be diminished during their Continuance in Office.

Section 2. The judicial Power shall extend to all Cases, in Law and Equity, arising under this constitution, the Laws of the United States, and treaties made, or which shall be made, under their Authority;—to all Cases affecting ambassadors, other public ministers and consuls;—to all cases of admiralty and maritime Jurisdiction;—to Controversies to which the United States shall be a Party;—to Controversies between two or more States;—between a State and Citizens of another State;—between Citizens of different States,—between Citizens of the same State claiming Lands under Grants of different States, and between a State, or the Citizens thereof, and foreign States, Citizens or Subjects.

In all Cases affecting Ambassadors, other public Ministers and Consuls, and those in which a State shall be Party, the supreme Court shall have original Jurisdiction. In all the other Cases before mentioned, the supreme Court shall have appellate Jurisdiction, both as to Law and Fact, with such Exception, and under such Regulations as the Congress shall make.

The trial of all Crimes, except in Cases of Impeachment, shall be by Jury; and such Trial shall be held in the State where the said Crimes shall have been committed; but when not committed within any State, the Trial shall be at such Place or Places as the Congress may by Law have directed.

Section 3. Treason against the United States, shall consist only in levying War against them, or in adhering to their Enemies, giving them Aid and Comfort. No Person shall be convicted of Treason unless on the Testimony of two Witnesses to the same overt Act, or on Confession in open Court.

The Congress shall have power to declare the Punishment of Treason, but no Attainder of Treason shall work Corruption of Blood, or Forfeiture except during the Life of the Person attainted.

ARTICLE IV

Section 1. Full Faith and Credit shall be given in each State to the public Acts, Records, and judicial Proceedings of every other State. And the Congress may by general laws prescribe the Manner in which such Acts, Records and Proceedings shall be proved, and the Effect thereof.

Section 2. The Citizens of each State shall be entitled to all Privileges and Immunities of Citizens in the several States.

A Person charged in any State with Treason, Felony, or other Crime, who shall flee from Justice, and be found in another State, shall on demand of the executive Authority of the State from which he fled, be delivered up, to be removed to the State having Jurisdiction of the crime.

No Person held to Service or Labour in one State, under the Laws thereof, escaping into another, shall, in Consequence of any Law or Regulation therein, be discharged from such Service or Labour, but shall be delivered up on Claim of the Party to whom such Service or Labour may be due.

Section 3. New States may be admitted by the Congress into this Union; but no new State shall be formed or erected within the Jurisdiction of any other State; nor any State be formed by the Junction of two or more States, or parts of States, without the Consent of the Legislatures of the States concerned as well as of the Congress.

The Congress shall have Power to dispose of and make all needful Rules and Regulations respecting the Territory or other Property belonging to the United States; and nothing in this constitution shall be so construed as to Prejudice any Claims of the United States, or of any particular State.

Section 4. The United States shall guarantee to every State in this Union a Republican Form of Government, and shall protect each of them against Invasion; and on Application of the Legislature, or the Executive (when the Legislature cannot be convened) against domestic Violence.

ARTICLE V

The Congress, whenever two-thirds of both Houses shall deem it necessary, shall propose Amendments to this Constitution, or, on the Application of the Legislatures of two-thirds of the several States, shall call a Convention for proposing Amendments, which, in either Case, shall be valid to all Intents and Purposes, as part of this Constitution, when ratified by the Legislatures of three-fourths of the several States, or by Conventions in three-fourths thereof, as the one or the other Mode of Ratification may be proposed by the Congress; Provided that no Amendment which may be made prior to the Year One thousand eight hundred and eight shall in any Manner affect the first and fourth Clauses in the Ninth Section of the first Article; and that no State, without its Consent, shall be deprived of its equal Suffrage in the Senate.

ARTICLE VI

Debts contracted and Engagements entered into, before the Adoption of this Constitution, shall be as valid against the United States under this Constitution, as under the Confederation.

This Constitution, and the Laws of the United States which shall be made in Pursuance thereof; and the Treaties made, or which shall be made, under the Authority of the United States, shall be the supreme Law of the Land; and the Judges in every State shall be bound thereby, any Thing in the Constitution of Laws of any State to the Contrary notwithstanding.

The Senators and Representatives before mentioned, and the Members of the several State Legislatures, and all executive and judicial Officers, both of the United States and of the several States, shall be bound by Oath or Affirmation to support this Constitution; but no religious Test shall ever be required as a qualification to any Office or public Trust under the United States.

ARTICLE VII

The Ratification of the Conventions of nine States shall be sufficient for the Establishment of this Constitution between the States so ratifying the same.

Done in Convention by the Unanimous Consent of the States present the Seventeenth Day of September in the Year of our Lord one thousand seven hundred and Eighty seven, and of the Independence of the United States of America the Twelfth. In Witness whereof We have hereunto subscribed our names.

Signed by
George Washington
Presidt and Deputy from Virginia
(and thirty-eight others)

Articles in Addition to, and Amendment of, the Constitution of the United States of America. Proposed by Congress, and Ratified by the Legislatures of the Several States, Pursuant to the Fifth Article of the Original Constitution.

AMENDMENT I [1791]

Congress shall make no law respecting an establishment of religion, or prohibiting the free exercise thereof; or abridging the freedom of speech, or of the press; or the right of the people peaceably to assemble, and to petition the Government for a redress of grievances.

AMENDMENT II [1791]

A well regulated Militia, being necessary to the security of a free State, the right of the people to keep and bear Arms, shall not be infringed.

AMENDMENT III [1791]

No Soldier shall, in time of peace be quartered in any house, without the consent of the Owner, nor in time of war, but in a manner to be prescribed by law.

AMENDMENT IV [1791]

The right of the people to be secure in their persons, houses, papers, and effects, against unreasonable searches and seizures, shall not be violated, and no Warrants shall issue, but upon probable cause, supported by Oath or affirmation, and particularly describing the place to be searched, and the persons or things to be seized.

AMENDMENT V [1791]

No person shall be held to answer for a capital or otherwise infamous crime, unless on a presentment or indictment of a Grand Jury, except in cases arising in the land or naval forces, or in the Militia, when in actual service in time of war or public danger; nor shall any person be subject for the same offence to be twice put in jeopardy of life or limb; nor shall be compelled in any criminal case to be a witness against himself, nor be deprived of life, liberty, or property, without due process of law; nor shall private property be taken for public use, without just compensation.

AMENDMENT VI [1791]

In all criminal prosecutions, the accused shall enjoy the right to a speedy and public trial, by an impartial jury of the State and district wherein the crime shall have been committed, which district shall have been previously ascertained by law, and to be informed of the nature and cause of the accusation; to be confronted with the witnesses against him; to have compulsory process for obtaining witnesses in his favor, and to have the Assistance of Counsel for his defence.

AMENDMENT VII [1791]

In suits at common law, where the value in controversy shall exceed twenty dollars, the right of trial by jury shall be preserved, and no fact tried by a jury, shall be otherwise reexamined in any Court of the United States, than according to the rules of the common law.

AMENDMENT VIII [1791]

Excessive bail shall not be required, nor excessive fines imposed, nor cruel and unusual punishments inflicted.

AMENDMENT IX [1791]

The enumeration in the Constitution, of certain rights, shall not be construed to deny or disparage others retained by the people.

AMENDMENT X [1791]

The powers not delegated to the United States by the Constitution, nor prohibited by it to the States, are reserved to the States respectively, or to the people.

AMENDMENT XI [1798]

The Judicial power of the United States shall not be construed to extend to any suit in law or equity, commenced or prosecuted against one of the United States by Citizens of another State, or by Citizens or Subjects of any Foreign State.

AMENDMENT XII [1804]

The Electors shall meet in their respective States and vote by ballot for President and Vice-President, one of whom, at least, shall not be an inhabitant of the same State with themselves; they shall name in their ballots the person voted for as President, and in distinct ballots the person voted for as Vice-President, and they shall make distinct lists of all persons voted for as President, and of all persons voted for as Vice-President, and of the number of votes for each, which lists they shall sign and certify, and transmit sealed to the seat of the government of the United States, directed to the President of the Senate;—The President of the Senate shall, in the presence of the Senate and House of Representatives, open all the certificates and the votes shall then be counted;—The person having the greatest number of votes for President, shall be the President, if such number by a majority of the whole number of Electors appointed; and if no person have such majority, then from the persons having the highest numbers not exceeding three on the list of those voted for as President, the House of Representatives shall choose immediately, by ballot, the President. But in choosing the President, the votes shall be taken by states, the representation from each state having one vote; a quorum for this purpose shall consist of a member or members from two-thirds of the states, and a majority of all the states shall be necessary to a choice. And if the House of Representatives shall not choose a President whenever the right of choice shall devolve upon them, before the fourth day of March next following, then the Vice-President shall act as President, as in the case of the death or other constitutional disability of the President.—The person having the greatest number of votes as Vice-President, shall be the Vice-President, if such number be a majority of the whole number of Electors appointed, and if no person have a majority, then from the two highest numbers on the list, the Senate shall choose the Vice-President; a quorum for the purpose shall consist of two-thirds of the whole number of Senators, and a majority of the whole number shall be necessary to a choice. But no person constitutionally ineligible to the office of President shall be eligible to that of Vice-President of the United States.

AMENDMENT XIII [1865]

Section 1. Neither slavery nor involuntary servitude, except as a punishment for crime whereof the party shall have been duly convicted, shall exist within the United States, or any place subject to their jurisdiction.

Section 2. Congress shall have power to enforce this article by appropriate legislation.

AMENDMENT XIV [1868]

Section 1. All persons born or naturalized in the United States, and subject to the jurisdiction thereof, are citizens of the United States and of the State wherein they reside. No State shall make or enforce any law which shall abridge the privileges or immunities of citizens of the United States; nor shall any State deprive any person of life, liberty, or property, without due process of law; nor deny to any person within its jurisdiction the equal protection of the laws.

Section 2. Representatives shall be apportioned among the several States according to their respective numbers, counting the whole number of persons in each State, excluding Indians not taxed. But when the right to vote at any election for the choice of electors for President and Vice-President of the United States, Representatives in Congress, the Executive and Judicial officers of a State, or the members of the Legislature thereof, is denied to any of the male inhabitants of such State, being twenty-one years of age, and citizens of the United States, or in any way abridged, except for participation in rebellion, or other crime, the basis of representation therein shall be reduced in the proportion which the number of such male citizens shall bear to the whole number of male citizens twenty-one years of age in such State.

Section 3. No person shall be a Senator or Representative in Congress, or elector of President and Vice-President, or hold any office, civil or military, under the United States, or under any State, who, having previously taken an oath, as a member of Congress, or as an officer of the United States, or as a member of any State legislature, or as an executive or judicial officer of any State, to support the Constitution of the United States, shall have engaged in insurrection or rebellion against the same, or given aid or comfort to the enemies thereof. But Congress may by a vote of two-thirds of each House, remove such disability.

Section 4. The validity of the public debt of the United States, authorized by law, including debts incurred for payment of pensions and bounties for services in suppressing insurrection or rebellion, shall not be questioned. But neither the United States nor any State shall assume or pay any debt or obligation incurred in aid of insurrection or rebellion against the United States or any claim for the loss or emancipation of any slave; but all such debts, obligations, and claims shall be held illegal and void.

Section 5. The Congress shall have the power to enforce, by appropriate legislation, the provisions of this article.

AMENDMENT XV [1870]

Section 1. The right of citizens of the United States to vote shall not be denied or abridged by the United States or by any State on account of race, color, or previous condition of servitude—

Section 2. The Congress shall have power to enforce this article by appropriate legislation.

AMENDMENT XVI [1913]

The Congress shall have power to lay and collect taxes on incomes, from whatever source derived, without apportionment among the several States, and without regard to any census or enumeration.

AMENDMENT XVII [1913]

The Senate of the United States shall be composed of two Senators from each State, elected by the people thereof, for six years; and each Senator shall have one vote. The electors in each State shall have the qualifications requisite for electors of the most numerous branch of the State legislature.

When vacancies happen in the representation of any State in the Senate, the executive authority of such State shall issue writs of election to fill such vacancies: *Provided,* That the legislature of any State may empower the executive thereof to make temporary appointments until the people fill the vacancies by election as the legislature may direct.

This amendment shall not be so construed as to affect the election or term of any Senator chosen before it becomes valid as part of the Constitution.

AMENDMENT XVIII [1919]

Section 1. After one year from the ratification of this article the manufacture, sale, or transportation of intoxicating liquors within, the importation thereof into, or the exportation thereof from the United States and all territory subject to the jurisdiction thereof for beverage purposes is hereby prohibited.

Section 2. The Congress and the several States shall have concurrent power to enforce this article by appropriate legislation.

Section 3. This article shall be inoperative unless it shall have been ratified as an amendment to the Constitution by the legislatures of the several States, as provided in the Constitution, within seven years from the date of the submission hereof to the States by the Congress.

AMENDMENT XIX [1920]

The right of citizens of the United States to vote shall not be denied or abridged by the United States or by any State on account of sex.

Congress shall have power to enforce this article by appropriate legislation.

AMENDMENT XX [1933]

Section 1. The terms of the President and Vice-President shall end at noon on the 20th day of January, and the terms of Senators and Representatives at noon on the 3d day of January, of the years in which such terms would have ended if this article had not been ratified; and the terms of their successors shall then begin.

Section 2. The Congress shall assemble at least once in every year, and such meeting shall begin at noon on the 3d day of January, unless they shall by law appoint a different day.

Section 3. If, at the time fixed for the beginning of the term of the President, the President elect shall have died, the Vice-President elect shall become President. If a President shall not have been chosen before the time fixed for the beginning of his term, or if the President elect shall have failed to qualify, then the Vice-President until a President shall have qualified; and the Congress may by law provide for the case wherein neither a President elect nor a Vice-President elect shall have qualified, declaring who shall then act as President, or the manner in which one who is to act shall be selected, and such person shall act accordingly until a President or Vice-President shall have qualified.

Section 4. The Congress may by law provide for the case of the death of any of the persons from whom the House of Representatives may choose a President whenever the right of choice shall have devolved upon them, and for the case of the death of any of the persons from whom the Senate may choose a Vice-President whenever the right of choice shall have devolved upon them.

Section 5. Sections 1 and 2 shall take effect on the 15th day of October following the ratification of this article.

Section 6. This article shall be inoperative unless it shall have been ratified as an amendment to the Constitution by the legislatures of three-fourths of the several States within seven years from the date of its submission.

AMENDMENT XXI [1933]

Section 1. The eighteenth article of amendment to the Constitution of the United States is hereby repealed.

Section 2. The transportation or importation into any State, Territory, or possession of the United States for delivery or use therein of intoxicating liquors, in violation of the laws thereof, is hereby prohibited.

Section 3. This article shall be inoperative unless it shall have been ratified as an amendment to the Constitution by conventions in the several States, as provided in the Constitution, within seven years from the date of the submission hereof to the States by the Congress.

AMENDMENT XXII [1951]

No person shall be elected to the office of the President more than twice, and no person who has held the office of President, or acted as President, for more than two years of a term to which some other person was elected President shall be elected to the office of the President more than once.

But this Article shall not apply to any person holding the office of President when this Article was proposed by the Congress, and shall not prevent any person who may be holding the office of President, or acting as President, during the term within which this Article becomes operative from holding the office of President or acting as President during the remainder of such term.

AMENDMENT XXIII [1961]

Section 1. The District constituting the seat of Government of the United States shall appoint in such manner as the Congress may direct:

A number of electors of President and Vice President equal to the whole number of Senators and Representatives in Congress to which the District would be entitled if it were a State, but in no event more than the least populous State; they shall be in addition to those appointed by the States, but they shall be considered, for the purposes of the election of President and Vice President, to be electors appointed by a State; and they shall meet in the District and perform such duties as provided by the twelfth article of amendment.

Section 2. The Congress shall have power to enforce this article by appropriate legislation.

AMENDMENT XXIV [1964]

Section 1. The right of citizens of the United States to vote in any primary or other election for President or Vice President, for electors for President or Vice President, or for Senator or Representative in Congress, shall not be denied or abridged by the United States or any State by reason of failure to pay any poll tax or other tax.

Section 2. The Congress shall have the power to enforce this article by appropriate legislation.

AMENDMENT XXV [1967]

Section 1. In case of the removal of the President from office or his death or resignation, the Vice President shall become President.

Section 2. Whenever there is a vacancy in the office of the Vice President, the President shall nominate a Vice President who shall take the office upon confirmation by a majority vote of both houses of Congress.

Section 3. Whenever the President transmits to the President pro tempore of the Senate and the Speaker of the House of Representatives his written declaration that he is unable to discharge the powers and duties of his office, and until he transmits to them a written declaration to the contrary, such powers and duties shall be discharged by the Vice President as Acting President.

Section 4. Whenever the Vice President and a majority of either the principal officers of the executive departments, or of such other body as Congress may by law provide, transmit to the President pro tempore of the Senate and the Speaker of the House of Representatives their written declaration that the President is unable to discharge the powers and duties of his office, the Vice President shall immediately assume the powers and duties of the office as Acting President.

Thereafter, when the President transmits to the President pro tempore of the Senate and the Speaker of the House of Representatives his written declaration that no inability exists, he shall resume the powers and duties of his office unless the Vice President and a majority of either the principal officers of the executive departments, or of such other body as Congress may by law provide, transmit within four days to the President pro tempore of the Senate and the Speaker of the House of Representatives their written declaration that the President is unable to discharge the powers and duties of his office. Thereupon Congress shall decide the issue, assembling within 48 hours for that purpose if not in session. If the Congress, within 21 days after receipt of the latter written declaration, or, if Congress is not in session, within 21 days after Congress is required to assemble, determines by two-thirds vote of both houses that the President is unable to discharge the powers and duties of his office, the Vice President shall continue to discharge the same as Acting President; otherwise, the President shall resume the powers and duties of his office.

AMENDMENT XXVI [1971]

Section 1. The right of citizens of the United States, who are eighteen years of age or older, to vote shall not be denied or abridged by the United States or by any State on account of age.

Section 2. The Congress shall have power to enforce this article by appropriate legislation.

Admission of States to the Union

No.	State	Date	No.	State	Date
1	Delaware	Dec. 7, 1787	26	Michigan	Jan. 26, 1837
2	Pennsylvania	Dec. 12, 1787	27	Florida	Mar. 3, 1845
3	New Jersey	Dec. 18, 1787	28	Texas	Dec. 29, 1845
4	Georgia	Jan. 2, 1788	29	Iowa	Dec. 28, 1846
5	Connecticut	Jan. 9, 1788	30	Wisconsin	May 29, 1848
6	Massachusetts	Feb. 6, 1788	31	California	Sept. 9, 1850
7	Maryland	Apr. 28, 1788	32	Minnesota	May 11, 1858
8	South Carolina	May 23, 1788	33	Oregon	Feb. 14, 1859
9	New Hampshire	June 21, 1788	34	Kansas	Jan. 29, 1861
10	Virginia	June 25, 1788	35	West Virginia	June 19, 1863
11	New York	July 26, 1788	36	Nevada	Oct. 31, 1864
12	North Carolina	Nov. 21, 1789	37	Nebraska	Mar. 1, 1867
13	Rhode Island	May 29, 1790	38	Colorado	Aug. 1, 1876
14	Vermont	Mar. 4, 1791	39	North Dakota	Nov. 2, 1889
15	Kentucky	June 1, 1792	40	South Dakota	Nov. 2, 1889
16	Tennessee	June 1, 1796	41	Montana	Nov. 8, 1889
17	Ohio	Mar. 1, 1803	42	Washington	Nov. 11, 1889
18	Louisiana	Apr. 30, 1812	43	Idaho	July 3, 1890
19	Indiana	Dec. 11, 1816	44	Wyoming	July 10, 1890
20	Mississippi	Dec. 10, 1817	45	Utah	Jan. 4, 1896
21	Illinois	Dec. 3, 1818	46	Oklahoma	Nov. 16, 1907
22	Alabama	Dec. 14, 1819	47	New Mexico	Jan. 6, 1912
23	Maine	Mar. 15, 1820	48	Arizona	Feb. 14, 1912
24	Missouri	Aug. 10, 1821	49	Alaska	Jan. 3, 1959
25	Arkansas	June 15, 1836	50	Hawaii	Aug. 21, 1959

Population of the United States, 1790–1990

YEAR	NUMBER OF STATES	POPULATION	PERCENT INCREASE
1790	13	3,929,214	
1800	16	5,308,483	35.1
1810	17	7,239,881	36.4
1820	23	9,638,453	33.1
1830	24	12,866,020	33.5
1840	26	17,069,453	32.7
1850	31	23,191,876	35.9
1860	33	31,443,321	35.6
1870	37	39,818,449	26.6
1880	38	50,155,783	26.0
1890	44	62,947,714	25.5
1900	45	75,994,575	20.7
1910	46	91,972,266	21.0
1920	48	105,710,620	14.9
1930	48	122,775,046	16.1
1940	48	131,669,275	7.2
1950	48	150,697,361	14.5
1960	50	179,323,175	19.0
1970	50	203,235,298	13.3
1980	50	226,504,825	11.4
1990	50	249,632,692	10.2

The Vice Presidents and the Cabinet

SECRETARY OF STATE
(1789–)

Thomas Jefferson	1789
Edmund Randolph	1794
Timothy Pickering	1795
John Marshall	1800
James Madison	1801
Robert Smith	1809
James Monroe	1811
John Q. Adams	1817
Henry Clay	1825
Martin Van Buren	1829
Edward Livingston	1831
Louis McLane	1833
John Forsyth	1834
Daniel Webster	1841
Hugh S. Legaré	1843
Abel P. Upshur	1843
John C. Calhoun	1844
James Buchanan	1845
John M. Clayton	1849
Daniel Webster	1850
Edward Everett	1852
William L. Marcy	1853
Lewis Cass	1857
Jeremiah S. Black	1860
William H. Seward	1861
E. B. Washburne	1869
Hamilton Fish	1869
William M. Evarts	1877
James G. Blaine	1881
F. T. Frelinghuysen	1881
Thomas F. Bayard	1885
James G. Blaine	1889
John W. Foster	1892
Walter Q. Gresham	1893
Richard Olney	1895
John Sherman	1897
William R. Day	1897
John Hay	1898
Elihu Root	1905
Robert Bacon	1909
Philander C. Knox	1909
William J. Bryan	1913
Robert Lansing	1915
Bainbridge Colby	1920
Charles E. Hughes	1921
Frank B. Kellogg	1925
Henry L. Stimson	1929
Cordell Hull	1933
E. R. Stettinius, Jr.	1944
James F. Byrnes	1945
George C. Marshall	1947
Dean Acheson	1949
John Foster Dulles	1953
Christian A. Herter	1959
Dean Rusk	1961
William P. Rogers	1969
Henry A. Kissinger	1973

Cyrus Vance	1977
Edmund Muskie	1979
Alexander M. Haig, Jr.	1981
George Shultz	1982
James A. Baker III	1989
Warren Christopher	1993

SECRETARY OF THE TREASURY (1789–)

Alexander Hamilton	1789
Oliver Wolcott	1795
Samuel Dexter	1801
Albert Gallatin	1801
G. W. Campbell	1814
A. J. Dallas	1814
William H. Crawford	1816
Richard Rush	1825
Samuel D. Ingham	1829
Louis McLane	1831
William J. Duane	1833
Roger B. Taney	1833
Levi Woodbury	1834
Thomas Ewing	1841
Walter Forward	1841
John C. Spencer	1843
George M. Bibb	1844
Robert J. Walker	1845
William M. Meredith	1849
Thomas Corwin	1850
James Guthrie	1853
Howell Cobb	1857
Philip F. Thomas	1860
John A. Dix	1861
Salmon P. Chase	1861
Wm. P. Fessenden	1864
Hugh McCulloch	1865
George S. Boutwell	1869
William A. Richardson	1873
Benjamin H. Bristow	1874
Lot M. Morrill	1876
John Sherman	1877
William Windom	1881
Charles J. Folger	1881
Walter Q. Gresham	1884
Hugh McCulloch	1884
Daniel Manning	1885
Charles S. Fairchild	1887
William Windom	1889
Charles Foster	1891
John G. Carlisle	1893
Lyman J. Gage	1897
Leslie M. Shaw	1902
George B. Cortelyou	1907
Franklin MacVeagh	1909
William G. McAdoo	1913
Carter Glass	1919
David F. Houston	1919
Andrew W. Mellon	1921
Ogden L. Mills	1932
William H. Woodin	1933
Henry Morgenthau, Jr.	1934
Fred M. Vinson	1945
John W. Snyder	1946
George M. Humphrey	1953
Robert B. Anderson	1957
C. Douglas Dillon	1961
Henry H. Fowler	1965
David M. Kennedy	1969
John B. Connally	1970
George P. Shultz	1972
William E. Simon	1974
Michael W. Blumenthal	1977
G. William Miller	1979
Donald T. Regan	1981
James A. Baker III	1985
Nicholas Brady	1988
Lloyd Bentsen	1993

SECRETARY OF WAR (1789–1947)

Henry Knox	1789
Timothy Pickering	1795
James McHenry	1796
John Marshall	1800
Samuel Dexter	1800
Roger Griswold	1801
Henry Dearborn	1801
William Eustis	1809
John Armstrong	1813
James Monroe	1814
William H. Crawford	1815
Isaac Shelby	1817
George Graham	1817
John C. Calhoun	1817
James Barbour	1825
Peter B. Porter	1828
John H. Eaton	1829
Lewis Cass	1831
Benjamin F. Butler	1837
Joel R. Poinsett	1837
John Bell	1841
John McLean	1841
John C. Spencer	1841
James M. Porter	1843
William Wilkins	1844
William L. Marcy	1845
George W. Crawford	1849
Charles M. Conrad	1850
Jefferson Davis	1853
John B. Floyd	1857
Joseph Holt	1861
Simon Cameron	1861
Edwin M. Stanton	1862
Ulysses S. Grant	1867
Lorenzo Thomas	1868
John M. Schofield	1868
John A. Rawlins	1869
William T. Sherman	1869
William W. Belknap	1869
Alphonso Taft	1876
James D. Cameron	1876
George W. McCrary	1877
Alexander Ramsey	1879
Robert T. Lincoln	1881
William C. Endicott	1885
Redfield Proctor	1889
Stephen B. Elkins	1891
Daniel S. Lamont	1893
Russell A. Alger	1897
Elihu Root	1899
William H. Taft	1904
Luke E. Wright	1908
J. M. Dickinson	1909
Henry L. Stimson	1911
L. M. Garrison	1913
Newton D. Baker	1916
John W. Weeks	1921
Dwight F. Davis	1925
James W. Good	1929
Patrick J. Hurley	1929
George H. Dern	1933
H. A. Woodring	1936
Henry L. Stimson	1940
Robert P. Patterson	1945
Kenneth C. Royall	1947

SECRETARY OF THE NAVY (1798–1947)

Benjamin Stoddert	1798
Robert Smith	1801
Paul Hamilton	1809
William Jones	1813
B. W. Crowninshield	1814
Smith Thompson	1818
S. L. Southard	1823
John Branch	1829
Levi Woodbury	1831
Mahlon Dickerson	1834
James K. Paulding	1838
George E. Badger	1841
Abel P. Upshur	1841
David Henshaw	1843

Thomas W. Gilmer	1844
John Y. Mason	1844
George Bancroft	1845
John Y. Mason	1846
William B. Preston	1849
William A. Graham	1850
John P. Kennedy	1852
James C. Dobbin	1853
Isaac Toucey	1857
Gideon Welles	1861
Adolph E. Borie	1869
George M. Robeson	1869
R. W. Thompson	1877
Nathan Goff, Jr.	1881
William H. Hunt	1881
William E. Chandler	1881
William C. Whitney	1885
Benjamin F. Tracy	1889
Hilary A. Herbert	1893
John D. Long	1897
William H. Moody	1902
Paul Morton	1904
Charles J. Bonaparte	1905
Victor H. Metcalf	1907
T. H. Newberry	1908
George von L. Meyer	1909
Josephus Daniels	1913
Edwin Denby	1921
Curtis D. Wilbur	1924
Charles F. Adams	1929
Claude A. Swanson	1933
Charles Edison	1940
Frank Knox	1940
James V. Forrestal	1945

SECRETARY OF DEFENSE (1947–)

James V. Forrestal	1947
Louis A. Johnson	1949
George C. Marshall	1950
Robert A. Lovett	1951
Charles E. Wilson	1953
Neil H. McElroy	1957
Thomas S. Gates, Jr.	1959
Robert S. McNamara	1961
Clark M. Clifford	1968
Melvin R. Laird	1969
Elliot L. Richardson	1973
James R. Schlesinger	1973
Donald Rumsfield	1974
Harold Brown	1977
Caspar Weinberger	1981
Frank Carlucci	1988
Richard Cheney	1989
Leslie Aspin, Jr.	1993

POSTMASTER GENERAL (1789–1970)

Samuel Osgood	1789
Timothy Pickering	1791
Joseph Habersham	1795
Gideon Granger	1801
Return J. Meigs, Jr.	1814
John McLean	1823
William T. Barry	1829
Amos Kendall	1835
John M. Niles	1840
Francis Granger	1841
Charles A. Wickliffe	1841
Cave Johnson	1845
Jacob Collamer	1849
Nathan K. Hall	1850
Samuel D. Hubbard	1852
James Campbell	1853
Aaron V. Brown	1857
Joseph Holt	1859
Horatio King	1861
Montgomery Blair	1861
William Dennison	1864
Alexander W. Randall	1866
John A. J. Creswell	1869
James W. Marshall	1874
Marshall Jewell	1874
James N. Tyner	1876
David M. Key	1877
Horace Maynard	1880
Thomas L. James	1881
Timothy O. Howe	1881
Walter Q. Gresham	1883
Frank Hatton	1884
William F. Vilas	1885
Don M. Dickinson	1888
John Wanamaker	1889
Wilson S. Bissel	1893
William L. Wilson	1895
James A. Gary	1897
Charles E. Smith	1898
Henry C. Payne	1902
Robert J. Wynne	1904
George B. Cortelyou	1905
George von L. Meyer	1907
F. H. Hitchcock	1909
Albert S. Burleson	1913
Will H. Hays	1921
Hubert Work	1922
Harry S. New	1923
Walter F. Brown	1929
James A. Farley	1933
Frank C. Walker	1940
Robert E. Hannegan	1945
J. M. Donaldson	1947
A. E. Summerfield	1953
J. Edward Day	1961
John A. Gronouski	1963
Lawrence F. O'Brien	1965
W. Marvin Watson	1968
Winton M. Blount	1969

ATTORNEY GENERAL (1789–)

Edmund Randolph	1789
William Bradford	1794
Charles Lee	1795
Theophilus Parsons	1801
Levi Lincoln	1801
Robert Smith	1805
John Breckinridge	1805
Caesar A. Rodney	1807
William Pinkney	1811
Richard Rush	1814
William Wirt	1817
John M. Berrien	1829
Roger B. Taney	1831
Benjamin F. Butler	1833
Felix Grundy	1838
Henry D. Gilpin	1840
John J. Crittenden	1841
Hugh S. Legare	1841
John Nelson	1843
John Y. Mason	1845
Nathan Clifford	1846
Isaac Toucey	1848
Reverdy Johnson	1849
John J. Crittenden	1850
Caleb Cushing	1853
Jeremiah S. Black	1857
Edwin M. Stanton	1860
Edward Bates	1861
Titian J. Coffey	1863
James Speed	1864
Henry Stanbery	1866
William M. Evarts	1868
Ebenezer R. Hoar	1869
Amos T. Ackerman	1870
George H. Williams	1871
Edward Pierrepont	1875
Alphonso Taft	1876
Charles Devens	1877
Wayne MacVeagh	1881
Benjamin H. Brewster	1881
A. H. Garland	1885
William H. H. Miller	1889
Richard Olney	1893
Judson Harmon	1895
Joseph McKenna	1897
John W. Griggs	1897
Philander C. Knox	1901

William H. Moody	1904
Charles J. Bonaparte	1907
G. W. Wickersham	1909
J. C. McReynolds	1913
Thomas W. Gregory	1914
A. Mitchell Palmer	1919
H. M. Daugherty	1921
Harlan F. Stone	1924
John G. Sargent	1925
William D. Mitchell	1929
H. S. Cummings	1933
Frank Murphy	1939
Robert H. Jackson	1940
Francis Biddle	1941
Tom C. Clark	1945
J. H. McGrath	1949
J. P. McGranery	1952
H. Brownell, Jr.	1953
William P. Rogers	1957
Robert F. Kennedy	1961
Nicholas Katzenback	1964
Ramsey Clark	1967
John N. Mitchell	1969
Richard G. Kleindienst	1972
Elliot L. Richardson	1973
William Saxbe	1974
Edward H. Levi	1974
Griffin B. Bell	1977
Benjamin R. Civiletti	1979
William French Smith	1981
Edwin A. Meese III	1985
Richard Thornburgh	1988
William P. Barr	1992
Janet Reno	1993

SECRETARY OF THE INTERIOR (1849–)

Thomas Ewing	1849
T. M. T. McKennan	1850
Alexander H. H. Stuart	1850
Robert McClelland	1853
Jacob Thompson	1857
Caleb B. Smith	1861
John P. Usher	1863
James Harlan	1865
O. H. Browning	1866
Jacob D. Cox	1869
Columbus Delano	1870
Zachariah Chandler	1875
Carl Schurz	1877
Samuel J. Kirkwood	1881
Henry M. Teller	1881
L. Q. C. Lamar	1885
William F. Vilas	1888
John W. Noble	1889
Hoke Smith	1893
David R. Francis	1896
Cornelius N. Bliss	1897
E. A. Hitchcock	1899
James R. Garfield	1907
R. A. Ballinger	1909
Walter L. Fisher	1911
Franklin K. Lane	1913
John B. Payne	1920
Albert B. Fall	1921
Hubert Work	1923
Roy O. West	1928
Ray L. Wilbur	1929
Harold L. Ickes	1933
Julius A. Krug	1946
Oscar L. Chapman	1949
Douglas McKay	1953
Fred A. Seaton	1956
Steward L. Udall	1961
Walter J. Hickel	1969
Rogers C. B. Morton	1971
Thomas S. Kleppe	1975
Cecil D. Andrus	1977
James G. Watt	1981
William P. Clark, Jr.	1983
Donald P. Hodel	1985
Manuel Lujan	1989
Bruce Babbitt	1993

SECRETARY OF AGRICULTURE (1889–)

Norman J. Colman	1889
Jeremiah M. Rusk	1889
J. Sterling Morton	1893
James Wilson	1897
David F. Houston	1913
Edward T. Meredith	1920
Henry C. Wallace	1921
Howard M. Gore	1924
William M. Jardine	1925
Arthur M. Hyde	1929
Henry A. Wallace	1933
Claude R. Wickard	1940
Clinton P. Anderson	1945
Charles F. Brannan	1948
Ezra Taft Benson	1953
Orville L. Freeman	1961
Clifford M. Hardin	1969
Earl L. Butz	1971
John A. Knebel	1976
Bob Bergland	1977
John R. Block	1981
Richard E. Lyng	1986
Clayton Yeutter	1989
Edward Madigan	1991
Mike Espy	1993

SECRETARY OF COMMERCE AND LABOR (1903–1913)

George B. Cortelyou	1903
Victor H. Metcalf	1904
Oscar S. Straus	1906
Charles Nagel	1909

SECRETARY OF COMMERCE (1913–)

William C. Redfield	1913
Joshua W. Alexander	1919
Herbert Hoover	1921
William F. Whiting	1928
Robert P. Lamont	1929
Roy D. Chapin	1932
Daniel C. Roper	1933
Henry L. Hopkins	1939
Jesse Jones	1940
Henry A. Wallace	1945
W. A. Harriman	1946
Charles Sawyer	1948
Sinclair Weeks	1953
Lewis L. Strauss	1958
F. H. Mueller	1959
Luther Hodges	1961
John T. Connor	1965
A. B. Trowbridge	1967
C. R. Smith	1968
Maurice H. Stans	1969
Peter G. Peterson	1972
Frederick B. Dent	1973
Elliot L. Richardson	1974
Juanita M. Kreps	1977
Philip M. Klutznick	1979
Malcolm Baldridge	1981
C. William Verity, Jr.	1987
Robert Mosbacher	1989
Ronald H. Brown	1993

SECRETARY OF LABOR (1913–)

William B. Wilson	1913
James J. Davis	1921
William N. Doak	1930
Frances Perkins	1933
L. B. Schwellenbach	1945
Maurice J. Tobin	1948
Martin P. Durkin	1953
James P. Mitchell	1953
Arthur J. Goldberg	1961
W. Willard Wirtz	1962
George P. Shultz	1969
James D. Hodgson	1970
Peter J. Brennan	1973
W. J. Usery, Jr.	1974
Ray Marshall	1977

Raymond J. Donovan	1981
Elizabeth Dole	1990
Lynn Martin	1991
Robert B. Reich	1993

SECRETARY OF HEALTH, EDUCATION, AND WELFARE (1953–1979)

Oveta Culp Hobby	1953
Marion B. Folsom	1955
Arthur S. Flemming	1958
Abraham A. Ribicoff	1961
Anthony J. Celebrezze	1962
John W. Gardner	1965
Wilbur J. Cohen	1968
Robert H. Finch	1969
Elliot L. Richardson	1970
Caspar W. Weinberger	1973
David Matthews	1974
Joseph A. Califano, Jr.	1977

SECRETARY OF HEALTH AND HUMAN SERVICES (1979–)

Patricia R. Harris	1979
Richard S. Schweiker	1981
Margaret Heckler	1983
Otis R. Bowen	1985
Louis W. Sullivan	1989
Donna E. Shalala	1993

SECRETARY OF HOUSING AND URBAN DEVELOPMENT (1966–)

Robert C. Weaver	1966
George W. Romney	1969
James T. Lynn	1973
Carla Anderson Hills	1974
Patricia Harris	1977
Moon Landrieu	1979
Samuel R. Pierce, Jr.	1981
Jack Kemp	1989
Henry G. Cisneros	1993

SECRETARY OF ENERGY (1977–)

James R. Schlesinger	1977
Charles W. Duncan, Jr.	1979
James B. Edwards	1981
Donald Hodel	1982
John S. Herrington	1985
James Watkins	1989
Hazel R. O'Leary	1993

SECRETARY OF TRANSPORTATION (1967–)

Alan S. Boyd	1967
John A. Volpe	1969
Claude S. Brinegar	1973
William T. Coleman	1975
Brock Adams	1977
Neil E. Goldschmidt	1979
Andrew L. Lewis, Jr.	1981
Elizabeth Dole	1983
James L. Burnley IV	1987
Samuel Skinner	1989
Frederico Pena	1993

SECRETARY OF EDUCATION (1979–)

Shirley M. Hufstedter	1979
Terrel Bell	1981
William J. Bennett	1985
Laura F. Cavozos	1988
Lamar Alexander	1991
Richard W. Riley	1993

SECRETARY OF VETERANS AFFAIRS (1989–)

Edward Derwinski	1989
Jesse Brown	1993

VICE PRESIDENT

John Adams	1789–97
Thomas Jefferson	1797–1801
Aaron Burr	1801–05
George Clinton	1805–13
Elbridge Gerry	1813–17
Daniel D. Tompkins	1817–25
John C. Calhoun	1825–33
Martin Van Buren	1833–37
Richard M. Johnson	1837–41
John Tyler	1841
George M. Dallas	1845–49
Millard Fillmore	1849–50
William R. King	1853–57
John C. Breckinridge	1857–61
Hannibal Hamlin	1861–65
Andrew Johnson	1865
Schuyler Colfax	1869–73
Henry Wilson	1873–77
William A. Wheeler	1877–81
Chester A. Arthur	1881
Thomas A. Hendricks	1885–89
Levi P. Morton	1889–93
Adlai E. Stevenson	1893–97
Garret A. Hobart	1897–1901
Theodore Roosevelt	1901
Charles W. Fairbanks	1905–09
James S. Sherman	1909–13
Thomas R. Marshall	1913–21
Calvin Coolidge	1921–23
Charles G. Dawes	1925–29
Charles Curtis	1929–33
John Nance Garner	1933–41
Henry A. Wallace	1941–45
Harry S Truman	1945
Alben W. Barkley	1949–53
Richard M. Nixon	1953–61
Lyndon B. Johnson	1961–63
Hubert H. Humphrey	1965–69
Spiro T. Agnew	1969–73
Gerald R. Ford	1973–74
Nelson W. Rockefeller	1974–77
Walter F. Mondale	1977–81
George Bush	1981–88
J. Danforth Quayle III	1989–93
Al Gore	1993–

Presidential Elections, 1789–1992

Year	Candidates	Party	Popular Vote	Electoral Vote
1789	**George Washington**			69
	John Adams			34
	Others			35
1792	**George Washington**			132
	John Adams			77
	George Clinton			50
	Others			5
1796	**John Adams**	Federalist		71
	Thomas Jefferson	Democratic-Republican		68
	Thomas Pinckney	Federalist		59
	Aaron Burr	Democratic-Republican		30
	Others			48
1800	**Thomas Jefferson**	Democratic-Republican		73
	Aaron Burr	Democratic-Republican		73
	John Adams	Federalist		65
	Charles C. Pinckney	Federalist		64
1804	**Thomas Jefferson**	Democratic-Republican		162
	Charles C. Pinckney	Federalist		14
1808	**James Madison**	Democratic-Republican		122
	Charles C. Pinckney	Federalist		47
	George Clinton	Independent-Republican		6
1812	**James Madison**	Democratic-Republican		128
	DeWitt Clinton	Federalist		89
1816	**James Monroe**	Democratic-Republican		183
	Rufus King	Federalist		34
1820	**James Monroe**	Democratic-Republican		231
	John Quincy Adams	Independent-Republican		1
1824	**John Quincy Adams**	Democratic-Republican	113,122 (30.9%)	84
	Andrew Jackson	Democratic-Republican	151,271 (41.3%)	99
	Henry Clay	Democratic-Republican	47,531 (12.9%)	37
	William H. Crawford	Democratic Republican	40,856 (11.1%)	41
1828	**Andrew Jackson**	Democratic	642,553 (55.9%)	178
	John Quincy Adams	National Republican	500,897 (43.6%)	83
1832	**Andrew Jackson**	Democratic	701,780 (54.2%)	219
	Henry Clay	National Republican	484,205 (37.4%)	49
	William Wirt	Anti-Masonic	100,715 (7.7%)	7
1836	**Martin Van Buren**	Democratic	763,176 (50.8%)	170
	William H. Harrison	Whig	550,816 (36.6%)	73
	Hugh L. White	Whig	146,107 (9.7%)	26
	Daniel Webster	Whig	41,201 (2.7%)	14
1840	**William H. Harrison** **(John Tyler,** 1841)	Whig	1,275,390 (52.8%)	234
	Martin Van Buren	Democratic	1,128,854 (46.8%)	60

Year	Candidates	Party	Popular Vote	Electoral Vote
1844	**James K. Polk**	Democratic	1,339,494 (49.5%)	170
	Henry Clay	Whig	1,300,004 (48.0%)	105
	James G. Birney	Liberty	62,103 (2.3%)	
1848	**Zachary Taylor**	Whig	1,361,393 (47.2%)	163
	(Millard Fillmore, 1850)			
	Lewis Cass	Democratic	1,223,460 (42.4%)	127
	Martin Van Buren	Free Soil	291,501 (10.1%)	
1852	**Franklin Pierce**	Democratic	1,607,510 (50.8%)	254
	Winfield Scott	Whig	1,386,942 (43.8%)	42
1856	**James Buchanan**	Democratic	1,836,072 (45.2%)	174
	John C. Frémont	Republican	1,342,345 (33.1%)	114
	Millard Fillmore	American	873,053 (21.5%)	8
1860	**Abraham Lincoln**	Republican	1,865,908 (39.8%)	180
	Stephen A. Douglas	Democratic	1,382,202 (29.4%)	12
	John C. Breckinridge	Democratic	848,019 (18.0%)	72
	John Bell	Constitutional Union	591,901 (12.6%)	39
1864	**Abraham Lincoln**	Republican	2,218,388 (55.0%)	212
	(Andrew Johnson, 1865)			
	George B. McClellan	Democratic	1,812,807 (44.9%)	21
1868	**Ulysses S. Grant**	Republican	3,013,650 (52.6%)	214
	Horatio Seymour	Democratic	2,708,744 (47.3%)	80
1872	**Ulysses S. Grant**	Republican	3,598,235 (55.6%)	286
	Horace Greeley	Democratic	2,834,761 (43.8%)	66
1876	**Rutherford B. Hayes**	Republican	4,034,311 (47.9%)	185
	Samuel J. Tilden	Democratic	4,288,546 (50.0%)	184
1880	**James A. Garfield**	Republican	4,446,158 (48.2%)	214
	(Chester A. Arthur, 1881)			
	Winfield S. Hancock	Democratic	4,444,260 (48.2%)	155
	James B. Weaver	Greenback-Labor	305,997 (3.3%)	
1884	**Grover Cleveland**	Democratic	4,874,621 (48.5%)	219
	James G. Blaine	Republican	4,848,936 (48.2%)	182
	Benjamin F. Butler	Greenback-Labor	175,096 (1.7%)	
1888	**Benjamin Harrison**	Republican	5,443,892 (47.8%)	233
	Grover Cleveland	Democratic	5,534,488 (48.6%)	168
1892	**Grover Cleveland**	Democratic	5,551,883 (46.0%)	277
	Benjamin Harrison	Republican	5,179,244 (42.9%)	145
	James B. Weaver	People's	1,024,280 (8.5%)	22
1896	**William McKinley**	Republican	7,108,480 (51.0%)	271
	William J. Bryan	Democratic; Populist	6,511,495 (46.7%)	176
1900	**William McKinley**	Republican	7,218,039 (51.6%)	292
	(Theodore Roosevelt, 1901)			
	William J. Bryan	Democratic; Populist	6,358,345 (45.5%)	155

Year	Candidates	Party	Popular Vote	Electoral Vote
1904	**Theodore Roosevelt**	Republican	7,626,593 (56.4%)	336
	Alton B. Parker	Democratic	5,082,898 (37.6%)	140
	Eugene V. Debs	Socialist	402,489 (2.9%)	
1908	**William H. Taft**	Republican	7,676,258 (51.5%)	321
	William J. Bryan	Democratic	6,406,801 (43.0%)	162
	Eugene V. Debs	Socialist	420,380 (2.8%)	
1912	**Woodrow Wilson**	Democratic	6,293,152 (41.8%)	435
	Theodore Roosevelt	Progressive	4,119,207 (27.3%)	88
	William H. Taft	Republican	3,486,383 (23.1%)	8
	Eugene V. Debs	Socialist	900,369 (5.9%)	
1916	**Woodrow Wilson**	Democratic	9,126,300 (49.2%)	277
	Charles E. Hughes	Republican	8,546,789 (46.1%)	254
1920	**Warren G. Harding** (**Calvin Coolidge**, 1923)	Republican	16,133,314 (60.3%)	404
	James M. Cox	Democratic	9,140,884 (34.1%)	127
	Eugene V. Debs	Socialist	913,664 (3.4%)	
1924	**Calvin Coolidge**	Republican	15,717,553 (54.0%)	382
	John W. Davis	Democratic	8,386,169 (28.8%)	136
	Robert M. La Follette	Progressive	4,814,050 (16.5%)	13
1928	**Herbert C. Hoover**	Republican	21,411,991 (58.2%)	444
	Alfred E. Smith	Democratic	15,000,185 (40.7%)	87
1932	**Franklin D. Roosevelt**	Democratic	22,825,016 (57.4%)	472
	Herbert C. Hoover	Republican	15,758,397 (39.6%)	59
	Norman Thomas	Socialist	883,990 (2.2%)	
1936	**Franklin D. Roosevelt**	Democratic	27,747,636 (60.7%)	523
	Alfred M. Landon	Republican	16,679,543 (36.5%)	8
	William Lemke	Union	892,492 (1.9%)	
1940	**Franklin D. Roosevelt**	Democratic	27,263,448 (54.7%)	449
	Wendell L. Wilkie	Republican	22,336,260 (44.8%)	82
1944	**Franklin D. Roosevelt** (**Harry S Truman**, 1945)	Democratic	25,611,936 (53.3%)	432
	Thomas E. Dewey	Republican	22,013,372 (45.8%)	99
1948	**Harry S Truman**	Democratic	24,105,587 (49.5%)	303
	Thomas E. Dewey	Republican	21,970,017 (45.1%)	189
	J. Strom Thurmond	States' Rights	1,169,134 (2.4%)	39
	Henry A. Wallace	Progressive	1,157,057 (2.3%)	
1952	**Dwight D. Eisenhower**	Republican	33,936,137 (55.1%)	442
	Adlai E. Stevenson	Democratic	27,314,649 (44.3%)	89
1956	**Dwight D. Eisenhower**	Republican	35,585,245 (57.3%)	457
	Adlai E. Stevenson	Democratic	26,030,172 (41.9%)	73
1960	**John F. Kennedy** (**Lyndon B. Johnson**, 1963)	Democratic	34,221,344 (49.7%)	303
	Richard M. Nixon	Republican	34,106,671 (49.5%)	219

Year	Candidates	Party	Popular Vote	Electoral Vote
1964	**Lyndon B. Johnson**	Democratic	43,126,584 (61.0%)	486
	Barry M. Goldwater	Republican	27,177,838 (38.4%)	52
1968	**Richard M. Nixon**	Republican	31,783,148 (43.4%)	301
	Hubert H. Humphrey	Democratic	31,274,503 (42.7%)	191
	George C. Wallace	Amer. Independent	9,901,151 (13.5%)	46
1972	**Richard M. Nixon**	Republican	47,170,179 (60.6%)	520
	George S. McGovern	Democratic	29,171,791 (37.5%)	17
1974	**Gerald R. Ford**	Republican	Appointed on August 9, 1974, as President after the resignation of Richard M. Nixon.	
1976	**Jimmy Carter**	Democratic	40,828,587 (50.1%)	297
	Gerald R. Ford	Republican	39,147,613 (48.0%)	240
1980	**Ronald Reagan**	Republican	43,899,248 (50.7%)	489
	Jimmy Carter	Democratic	35,481,435 (41.0%)	49
	John Anderson	Independent	5,719,437 (6.6%)	
	Ed Clark	Libertarian	920,859 (1.0%)	
1984	**Ronald Reagan**	Republican	54,451,521 (58.8%)	525
	Walter F. Mondale	Democratic	37,565,334 (40.5%)	13
1988	**George H. Bush**	Republican	47,946,422 (54.0%)	426
	Michael S. Dukakis	Democratic	41,016,429 (46.0%)	112
1992	**Bill Clinton**	Democrat	43,682,624 (43.2%)	378
	George H. Bush	Republican	38,117,331 (37.7%)	168
	H. Ross Perot	Independent	19,217,212 (19.0%)	0

Index